# The Crisis of Argentine Capitalism

PAUL H. LEWIS

# The Crisis of Argentine Capitalism

The University of North Carolina Press

Chapel Hill and London

The paper in this book meets the guidelines for permanence and
durability of the Committee on Production Guidelines for Book
Longevity of the Council on Library Resources.

94  93  92     5  4  3  2

Library of Congress Cataloging-in-Publication Data

Lewis, Paul H.
   The crisis of Argentine capitalism / by Paul H. Lewis.
      p.   cm.
   Bibliography: p.
   Includes index.
   ISBN 0-8078-1862-3
   ISBN 0-8078-4356-3 (pbk.)
   1. Argentina—Economic conditions—1919–  . 2. Capitalism—
Argentina—History—20th century.  3. Corporate state—
Argentina—History—20th century.  4. Peronism—History.
5. Argentina—Politics and government—1910–1943.
6. Argentina—Politics and government—1943–1955.  I. Title.
HC172.L48  1990
338.982—dc19                                      89-31350
                                                        CIP

*For my mother,*
*Kathryn Derenthal Lewis*

# CONTENTS

# Contents

# TABLES

Since the appearance of *The Crisis of Argentine Capitalism* in the spring of 1990, people have asked me whether I would revise my pessimistic conclusions in light of President Carlos Menem's progress in attacking many of Argentina's deep-rooted economic problems. Like most other Argentina-watchers, I am impressed by President Menem's boldness in breaking with the past and his courage in supporting his economics ministers as they struggle for reform in the face of relentless political pressure. If ever a governing team deserved success, it is this one; and at this writing Menem's Justicialist party has just won a resounding victory in the September 1991 congressional and gubernatorial elections. The triumph coincided with a tremendous boom on the Buenos Aires stock exchange, which many believe to be an expression of public confidence in Domingo Cavallo, the economics minister. Political commentators are calling Cavallo a genius, although Menem also comes in for his share of the praise for allowing the economic program to proceed despite the approaching elections and the hysterical calls from Justicialist politicians and labor leaders for a respite. Though behind in the polls as late as July, Menem gambled, and the public repaid him with their confidence.

Elected in May 1989, Menem took office under very inauspicious circumstances. His inauguration was moved forward from December to July after rioting, looting, and bombing in Argentina's main cities convinced lame-duck president Raúl Alfonsín to surrender power early. Runaway inflation, falling production, and high unemployment combined to make Alfonsín so unpopular that when he announced a set of emergency measures at the end of May he found the country to be ungovernable. A brief postmortem on Alfonsín's administration may illustrate the lessons Menem had to learn if he was to avoid a similar fate.

When Alfonsín became president in late 1983 he faced two fundamental tasks. The first was to institutionalize democracy by making the military subordinate itself to civilian rule. Humiliated by the Falklands War and knowing itself to be unpopular because of the human rights abuses committed under its rule from 1976 to 1983, the military was sullenly quiescent. The second task was to revitalize the economy by attracting capital.

Throughout his administration Alfonsín rated high in the opinion polls for respecting human rights, nurturing democracy, and improving Argentina's international image. Realpolitik might have questioned his decision to place on trial military officers accused of human rights violations, but the public supported this move. He received much criticism later when, under military pressure, he decreed the Full Stop Law in December 1986, which fixed a deadline for further trials. More criticism followed when, after the 1987 Easter Week Rebellion led by Lt. Col. Aldo Rico, all but the most senior officers were exempted from prosecution under the Law of Due Obedience. Still, when Alfonsín successfully rode out Rico's second revolt, in January 1988, and a more serious attempt by Col. Mohammed Ali Seineldín, in December 1988, one could claim that by giving in a little to the military Alfonsín had preserved democracy. The military even gained slightly in moderate opinion when, on 23 January 1989, the La Tablada infantry base outside Buenos Aires was attacked by leftist guerrillas. The thirty-hour gunbattle revived the worst memories of the early 1970s.

Although around 60 percent of the public approved of Alfonsín's democratic record, a much smaller number liked the way he handled inflation, unemployment, and scarcity. By the midpoint of his administration these had become the salient issues. Alfonsín's first economics minister, Bernardo Grinspun, courted popularity by refusing to pay the foreign debt, pump-priming the economy, and redistributing income. But after a year inflation soared to over 1,000 percent, and support for the government plunged from a high of 64 percent in May 1984 to only 37 percent the following April. Grinspun was replaced in February 1985 by Juan Sourrouille. Having studied Hjalmar Schacht's successful antiinflationary strategy under the Weimar Republic, Sourrouille promised to stop Central Bank financing of the government's deficits and to balance the budget. Like Schacht, he focused public attention on his program by introducing a new currency, the *austral*.

To almost everyone's surprise, every major Argentine pressure group supported the Austral Plan. By August 1985 Alfonsín's popularity rating was back up to 63 percent, and it stayed there until the following March. Then, in response to pressure from the labor unions and from politicians in his own Radical party, he ordered

Sourrouille to lift wage and price controls and to expand the money supply. Inflation moved up quickly again, and subsequent attempts to rein it in were unsuccessful. The government had lost its credibility. By May 1988 Alfonsín's approval rating had sunk to around 20 percent. It never rose again beyond 30 percent, and the Radicals went down to a crushing defeat in the May 1989 elections.

Such was the example Menem had to ponder. Many political analysts, including me, doubted whether he could learn from his predecessor's mistakes. With his shiny suits, muttonchop whiskers, and populist rhetoric, he was the city dweller's nightmare of a provincial *caudillo*. He had made deals with corrupt, right-wing Peronists in order to defeat Antonio Cafiero, a "civilized" Peronist from Buenos Aires Province, for the party's nomination. Then he trounced the Radicals' Eduardo Angeloz, the competent but colorless governor of Córdoba. Menem's campaign was utterly unprogrammatic; its slogan was simply "Follow me, I won't deceive you."

Menem's first cabinet contained several big surprises. The Economics Ministry went to an economist from the Bunge & Born food conglomerate, and the Foreign Ministry went to a man who had served as Central Bank president under the Proceso. The economics minister, Miguel Roig, died after a week in office, and Menem appointed another Bunge & Born man, Néstor Rapanelli, to take his place. An even greater shock was that Álvaro Alsogaray, a noted anti-Peronist, was made a presidential economic advisor, and his daughter, Maria Julia, was appointed head of the state telephone company (ENTEL), with orders to prepare a privatization plan.

Such an alliance between provincial Peronism and big business showed that Menem intended to be an innovative president, to say the least. Nor did it cost him in terms of popularity. His apparent determination to confront the all-important economic issues earned him an 85 percent approval rating in September 1989. Cynics who may have suspected Menem of being merely a Bunge & Born puppet were confounded when Rapanelli was dismissed in December after failing to bring inflation under control. Rapanelli's approach had been similar to Sourrouille's in his efforts to control inflation through direct price controls and his failure to restrict government spending. He was replaced by Antonio Erman González, who once had been economics minister of La Rioja Province when Menem was governor.

González's appointment looked like a turn toward cronyism and populist economics. Though he promised to liberalize the economy, there was a run on bank deposits. "With good reason, as it turned out," noted the *International Currency Review* in its February–March 1990 edition:

> For with malicious folly, the Government invented a new method of trying to cure inflation without stopping its own spending orgy—a method which is unprecedented, even in Argentina, for its total disregard of moral values and respect for the individual. The Government's "reasoning" went more or less as follows: "Inflation is, after all, the product of too much money chasing too few goods. So let us simply therefore reduce the amount of money. And since we can't do that by stopping government waste, or by issuing any more bonds (since no-one will buy them), or by raising taxes (since no-one will pay them), let's do it by robbing people of their bank accounts." On 8 January, without any warning or prior announcement, all term deposits at commercial banks, of one million australes or more (about $500 at the free rate), were frozen and converted into *"bonex"* or dollar-denominated bonds maturing in ten years. (p. 165)

The *Plan Bonex* worked in the short run, stopping a truly vicious rate of inflation that might otherwise have exceeded 20,000 percent by the end of the year. It was bought at the cost of a midyear economic recession that closed about a third of the shops in downtown Buenos Aires. Bonex bonds fell on the market to about 30 percent of their face value.

On the positive side, real progress was made toward privatization. ENTEL was sold, as were Aerolineas Argentinas, several railroad branch lines, petrochemical plants, and radio and television stations. Major highways were turned into private toll roads. The National Mortgage Bank and the National Development Bank were simply shut down.

All in all, Menem ended 1990 with a 70 percent approval rating, despite presidential pardons issued in October to many military officers convicted of human rights crimes and also to some convicted leftist guerrillas. He had even pardoned Gen. Leopoldo Galtieri and his collaborators in the junta for their misconduct during the Falklands War. At the end of December he pardoned the remaining military officers in jail, including Generals Videla, Viola, and Suárez Masón, and Admiral Massera. Mario Firmenich, the Montonero leader, was released as well. Though certainly not popular, such pardons were accepted as part of a national reconciliation, especially after a second attempt by Colonel Seineldín to overthrow the government.

Menem's popularity plunged suddenly in February 1991, however, following a disastrous month in which the U.S. ambassador revealed that American firms were being asked to pay bribes to cabinet ministers and presidential advisors. Argentines used to shrug their shoulders at corruption, but that was when the country had thought itself rich. Now, with so many businesses closing and so much open and disguised unemployment, the old tolerance was gone. Although Menem himself was not personally accused, members of his family were. Indeed, in the months to come, worse scandals would emerge that linked his in-laws to drug-money laundering schemes. Again, Menem was evidently not involved, but the publicity highlighted his playboy life-style, including a red Ferrari bought for him by the Fiat Motor Company. Argentines resented the gap between the many who were tightening their belts and the governing few who were living lavishly. Then, too, in January 1991 the crisis coincided with another sickening plunge in the value of the *austral* relative to the dollar. González still had not brought the money supply under control. Furthermore, he had raised charges for public services and increased bank interest rates to lure back depositors. These costs were passed on to consumers. Inflation was now running at just above 1,300 percent. Discouraged and exhausted, González resigned, and Domingo Cavallo, the erstwhile foreign minister, took his place.

Upon taking office Cavallo announced that the Central Bank and other state-owned banks would no longer cover public sector deficits or grant loans to big private debtors. The *austral* would be freely convertible to dollars, which meant that no currency could be printed unless it were backed by dollars or gold. Industrial subsidies and wage indexation would be ended, defunct provincial banks would be closed, and the federal government would cut back on revenue-sharing with the provinces. Large cuts were to be made in the defense budget by selling most Fabricaciones Militares enterprises, cutting both civilian and military staff by 40 percent, scrapping the Condor missile project, and eliminating many overseas military attaché posts. Import duties were greatly lowered, and the hated export "retentions" on agricultural goods were eliminated in return for the farmers' promise to start paying their taxes. Fiscal discipline and balanced budgets were the order of the day.

Cynics could say they had heard it all many times before, but as 1991 wore on Cavallo lived up to his promises. The economy was indeed dollarized and no money was printed without proper backing. There was a freeze on public sector wages. Some 21,000 civil servants and 50,000 state enterprise employees were dismissed, including half of the workers at the SOMISA steelworks. Parts of Fabricaciones Militares's economic empire were closed, including the Patagonian iron mines, the Rio Túrbio coal mine, and the Altos Hornos de Zapla steel mill. So were the merchant fleet (ELMA), the railroads, and many of the YPF oil fields, pending their privatization. All of these actions provoked protest. Violent strikes broke out in the steel and railway sectors. May elections in the Unión Industrial Argentina, the industrialists' peak association, were won by a slate, representing the smaller companies, that called for more state protection.

As the 8 September midterm elections approached and pollsters began predicting big losses for the Justicialist party, Menem's political advisors urged him to rein in his economics minister. If the polls were right, they argued, the government would lose many congressional seats and be hamstrung. Naturally, they did not advocate *abandoning* the current economic program—just *relaxing* it until after the elections were safely past. Had this course been adopted, the Cavallo Plan would have gone the same way as the Austral Plan, and Menem would have ended like Alfonsín. But on 31 July Menem took his big gamble and, after a stormy cabinet meeting, gave Cavallo the green light.

The gamble paid off. Facing a 27 percent monthly inflation rate upon taking office, Cavallo had brought that rate down to 1.3 percent in August while simultaneously raising production. Suddenly business confidence was reflected in a surge of investment. The Buenos Aires stock market, which had registered a daily turnover of just under $8 million at the beginning of August, was doing about $65 million a day by the end of the month. Optimism spread, fueling an impressive electoral victory for the Justicialists.

Will the momentum continue? Argentines have seen many brilliant economics ministers and many brave starts at reform in the past. Up to now, all have succumbed to political inertia. On the other hand, the current program passed its first big political test, and there are many factors favoring its continuation. First, Cavallo has two years of breathing room before the next big midterm elections. Second, Menem has no political challengers on the horizon. Third, the Argentine public, and Menem himself, seem aware that this experiment is perhaps the last chance for Argentina—certainly for Argentine democracy. The political costs of failure would very likely entail a return to military rule, a consequence that is deeply dreaded. The economic costs might well be a free-fall into a black hole. Those considerations may help the public tolerate Cavallo's surgery.

But nothing is certain and there are many possible pitfalls ahead. Suppose, for all his efforts, Cavallo fails to attract enough long-term investment capital to really revitalize the Argentine economy? What if the stock market boom is based on speculation and only proves ephemeral? What if Argentina's trade deficit persists? Suppose Menem decides to reward his patient followers once there is an economic turnaround? Suppose he is directly implicated in one of the corruption scandals? What if either he or Cavallo gets sick or falls to an assassin's bullet? Both the political system and the economic system are still too feebly institutionalized to withstand a major shock; too much of the public's confidence rests upon particular personalities. There must be at least one more transition from one party's administration to another's before we can say that democracy has taken root, and there must be a real display of entrepreneurial spirit before we can say that Argentina has returned to the development path it strayed from in the 1940s.

New Orleans, Louisiana
October 1991

This study is the product of a long-established interest I have in the political behavior of business groups in Latin America. In my opinion, it is a subject that Latin American specialists have overlooked in favor of studying more obvious political actors such as the military, labor, students, peasants, the Church, or the landlords. To the extent that industrialists or merchants are considered at all, they tend to be dismissed as marginal groups dependent upon more powerful economic actors in the world economy or on the traditional sectors of the domestic economy. That is a superficial view, especially of the larger, more developed nations of Latin America where industrialization and domestic trade have reached levels capable of supporting a sizable and influential urban bourgeoisie. In Argentina, a country that I am especially familiar with, and for which I have a strong affection, these bourgeois capitalists are taken very seriously by the state. They may not always get their interests written into law, but they do so frequently, and they are at all times a powerful veto group. The industrialists among them are, as a class, the oldest in Latin America. Because of this, and because of my interest in Argentina, I have chosen to focus my attention on them.

A study of the Argentine industrialist bourgeoisie requires a historical approach, I believe, because at one time the country boasted of a very promising rate of industrial growth based on private enterprise, whereas today it is economically stagnant. As the title of this work acknowledges, Argentina's capitalist economy is now in crisis, which implies a previously satisfactory state of affairs. To understand the causes and the character of that crisis it is necessary to understand the industrial bourgeoisie. Such an understanding requires an examination of the world in which those Argentine industrialists operate: their relations with the state, the unions, foreign capital, politicians, and all other organized interests that affect their decisions. That is what this study attempts to do: to describe Argentine capitalists, their development, and their relationships with other groups that impinge upon them. The period of time covered is roughly from the turn of the century through the first half of President Raúl Alfonsín's administration.

In treating this subject I have tried to make it come alive for the reader by quoting frequently from the principal participants. Except where the *Review of the River Plate* or some other English language source is cited, in almost every case the translation from Spanish to English is my own. When translating, I have tried to be as faithful as possible to the meaning and style of the writer or speaker, while at the same time aiming for clear, comprehensible English. Occasionally it was necessary to change the sentence structure, or use different idioms, or substitute a slang phrase more comprehensible to an American reader. These changes were frequently required when quoting Perón, who often used popular expressions and slang.

In carrying out my research I had the crucial support of my own institution, Tulane University, which helped to finance my work through the Center for Latin American Studies, the Murphy Institute for Political Economy, and the Graduate School. Tulane also granted me a year's sabbatical leave when the University of Texas was kind enough to make me a visiting scholar at its own Latin American Center. Finally, in the last stages of my research I had the help of a summer's grant from the Organization of American States. Most of this study is based on library research, and I am grateful for the kindly assistance I received not just from Tulane's library but also from the staffs in the Latin American section of the Library of Congress, the Nettie Lee Benson Library at the University of Texas, the Instituto Torcuato Di Tella and the Centro de Estudios del Estado y la Sociedad (CEDES) in Buenos Aires, and the newspaper reading room at *La Prensa*. I also owe special thanks to Professor Donna Guy of the University of Arizona for providing me with some hard-to-get materials on Argentina's economic history. I hope that what follows will justify their efforts to facilitate my work.

Paul H. Lewis
New Orleans

# ABBREVIATIONS

| | |
|---|---|
| AAA | Argentine Anticommunist Alliance |
| AAPIC | Association of Production, Industry, and Commerce |
| ACIEL | Coordinated Action of Free Entrepreneurial Associations |
| AOT | textile workers' union |
| APEGE | Permanent Assembly of Employers' Trade Associations |
| BIR | Banco de Intercambio Regional |
| CAC | Chamber of Commerce (Cámara Argentina de Comércio) |
| CACIP | Argentine Confederation of Commerce, Industry, and Production |
| CAI | Argentine Industrial Council |
| CAP | Argentine Meat-Producers' Corporation |
| CARBAP | Confederation of Rural Associations of Buenos Aires and La Pampa |
| CC | Confederación de Comércio |
| CEA | Argentine Economic Confederation |
| CGC | General Confederation of Commerce |
| CGE | General Economic Confederation (Confederación General Económica) |
| CGP | General Confederation of Professionals |
| CGT | General Confederation of Workers (Confederación General de Trabajadores) |

| | |
|---|---|
| CGU | General University Confederation |
| CI | Confederation of Industry |
| CINA | Argentine Industrial Confederation |
| CNT | National Labor Commission |
| CONADE | National Development Council (Consejo Nacional de Desarrollo) |
| CONES | National Social and Economic Council |
| CONINAGRO | Agricultural Cooperative Confederation |
| CP | Confederation of Production |
| CRA | Argentine Rural Confederation |
| CTERA | non-Peronist teachers' federation |
| CUCO | University Commandos for Organized Combat |
| CUTA | United Leadership of Argentine Workers |
| DEP | Directorate of Public Enterprises |
| DGI | Office of Internal Revenue (Dirección General de Impuestos) |
| DNT | National Labor Department (Departamento Nacional de Trabajo) |
| ECA | Economic Cooperative Commission |
| ECLA | United Nations Economic Commission for Latin America |
| ERP | People's Revolutionary Army |
| FAA | Argentine Agrarian Federation (Federación Agraria Argentina) |
| FAL | Armed Forces of Liberation |
| FAP | Peronist Armed Forces |
| FAR | Revolutionary Armed Forces |
| FIEL | Fundación de Investigaciones Económicas Latinoamericanas |
| FOA | Argentine Workers' Federation |

| FOF | Federation of Railway Workers |
| FORA | Workers' Federation of the Argentine Region |
| FREJULI | Justicialist Liberation Front |
| FTRA | Federation of Workers of the Argentine Region |
| FUA | Argentine University Federation |
| GDP | gross domestic production |
| GNP | gross national product |
| GOU | Group of United Officers |
| *HAR* | *Hispanic American Report* |
| IAPI | Argentine Industry for Production and Trade |
| IKA | Industrias Kaiser Argentina |
| IME | Industrias Mecánicas del Estado |
| IMF | International Monetary Fund |
| IMIM | Mixed Commission on Liquid Investments |
| INDEC | National Institute for Statistics and Census (Instituto Nacional de Estadística y Censos) |
| IRI | Industrial Reconstruction Institute |
| JSP | Peronist Syndical Youth |
| LAFTA | Latin American Free Trade Area |
| MEDI | Movimiento Empresario del Interior |
| MIA | Movimiento Industrial Argentina |
| MIN | Movimiento Industrial Nacional |
| MNRP | National Revolutionary Peronist Movement |
| MUI | Movimiento Unido del Interior |
| PAN | National Autonomy Party (Partido Autonomista Nacional) |
| PJ | Partido Justicialista |
| *PP* | *Primera Plana* |
| *RRP* | *Review of the River Plate* |

| SITRAC | Sindicato de Trabajadores de Concord (union at Fiat-Concord plant) |
| SITRAM | Sindicato de Trabajadores de Matafer (union at Fiat's Matafer plant) |
| SMATA | Automotive Mechanics' Union |
| SRA | Argentine Rural Society (Sociedad Rural Argentina) |
| SUPA | Sindicato Unido de Portuarios Argentinos (longshoremen's union) |
| UCR | Unión Cívica Radical |
| UCRI | Unión Cívica Radical Intransigente |
| UCRP | Unión Cívica Radical del Pueblo |
| UES | Union of Secondary School Students |
| UF | Unión Ferroviaria (railway workers' union) |
| UGT | General Union of Workers |
| UIA | Argentine Industrial Union (Unión Industrial Argentina) |
| UOM | Metalworkers' Union |
| USA | Unión Sindical Argentina |
| YCF | Yacimientos Carboníferos Fiscales |
| YPF | Yacimientos Petrolíferos Fiscales |

*The Crisis of Argentine Capitalism*

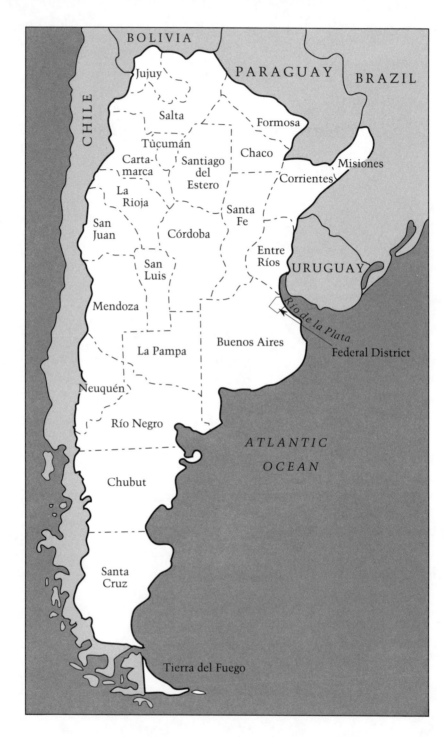

Argentina and Its Provinces

## CHAPTER ONE

# Introduction

## Answers to a Riddle

Argentina holds a morbid fascination for students of political economy because it has a system in which power is so thoroughly spread out among well-organized and entrenched interests that it is an almost perfect example of entropy. Also, Argentina fascinates students of development because, in many respects, it seems to be going backward. Although it possesses many modern institutions, they are decaying rapidly. Argentines are sensitive to this and spend much time analyzing their society's shortcomings and prescribing remedies, like patients suffering from a rare, wasting disease. They once aspired to becoming one of the world's advanced nations, but they failed. That failure is all the more puzzling because Argentina possesses a temperate climate, an integrated national territory, vast stretches of fertile soil, large deposits of petroleum, easy access to the sea, and a literate and fairly homogeneous population. There have been many attempts in both the scholarly and popular literature to explain Argentina's stagnation. Broadly speaking, the following are the most frequently cited causes: (1) the traditional cattle-raising and export merchant oligarchy's refusal to accept modern social and political change; (2) the military's increasing interference in politics, which exacerbates instability rather than avoids it; (3) the exploitation of Argentina by foreign capital; (4) the lack of a native industrial class with a true entrepreneurial spirit; (5) the personal machinations of one man, Juan Domingo Perón, who was Argentina's president from 1946 to 1955 and continued to influence its politics for two decades after that; and, finally, (6) the Argentine national character in general, which is held to be egotistical, inflexible, and conflictive, thus making impossible all cooperative effort, including that required for development. Let us describe each of these causes in a little more detail and establish working hypotheses or tools with which to explore the complexities of Argentina's recent history.

First, the idea that the agro-exporter class is to blame is widespread among nationalistic Argentine intellectuals, especially those on the Left.[1] For them, Argentine history since independence has been a struggle between "the people" and "the oligarchy," or between those who defend Argentina's economic independence and native culture as opposed to those cosmopolitans whose economic interests are entwined with foreigners and who admire foreign ways more than their own. From the earliest times to the present, according to this theory, the oligarchy has conspired to monopolize Argentina's fertile pampa in order to gain political power and social prestige rather than to tap to the fullest extent its great potential wealth. But even though the oligarchs have become rich, they do not use their land or their capital efficiently to increase production, for investment, or to create jobs. Instead, they evade taxes whenever possible and send their profits out of the country. Though a distinct minority, the oligarchs are perceived by populist writers to be politically astute. In league with the military, they are said to have conspired successfully to bring down the two great popular leaders of this century: Hipólito Yrigoyen in 1930, and Juan Perón in 1955. In recent years they have concluded tactical alliances with the industrialists to combat the power of Peronist labor unions. To the extent that they succeed, so this theory goes, they retard Argentina's development by preventing the growth of a domestic market.

A second variation on this theme of internal stagnation puts the blame more squarely upon the military, which is seen as a separate class with its own special interests.[2] In 1943 the Argentine army abandoned its traditional support of the oligarchy and subsequently allied with labor to form a developmentalist coalition under Perón's leadership. But although the oligarchy can no longer count on the military automatically, there is a long-range tendency for the two groups' interests to overlap. After turning against Perón in 1955, the armed forces have frequently intervened to put down unruly Peronist unions and the revolutionary Left. Thus, for some writers, the military and the oligarchy have become the senior partners on the Right: defenders of order and privilege in an age of mass politics.

"Dependency theory" may be seen as a third variation, in which the oligarchy and the military are junior partners in league with foreign interests to exploit the Argentine middle and lower classes. Essentially Marxist-Leninist in inspiration, dependency theory holds that there is a single "world capitalist economy" made up of a complex web of exploitative relationships. Each country, and each region within a country, has a hierarchy of political and economic elites that wring wealth out of the classes below them. National elites, in turn, are connected to the world capitalist economy in a hierarchical fashion, with the leaders of the world's industrial center at the top and the leaders of the peripheral and semiperipheral nations clinging to them from below as subordinates and allies.[3]

Argentina, according to this theory, is an example of a middle-level country in the world system. It may lord it over its smaller neighbors, but it in turn is exploited by British and American capital. Investments, technology, and economic aid imported into the country do not lead to economic independence but rather to debts, deficits, dependency, and impoverishment. Foreign investors take more wealth out of the country in profits than they put in with their investments, and the technology they bring with them is obsolete in comparison with that being used in the center. The industries they create are capital-intensive enclaves that provide no jobs and undermine, with their competition, the development of a native entrepreneurial class.

Most sinister of all, foreign investors tend to march in step with the military-strategic interests of the advanced capitalist industrial powers, among whom the United States is paramount. Close connections between the American and Argentine military establishments help to cement the political alliance between the latter and the Argentine oligarchy. All of this is based on a logical division of labor: the agro-exporter elites furnish raw materials to the foreign industrialists; the native military keeps order; and the balance of payments deficits that result from the economic superiority of the industrial center provide international bankers with opportunities to get rich.[4]

Writers who adopt the view that the oligarchy, the military, or foreign imperialists are—singly or in combination—responsible for Argentina's stagnation are concerned with exposing the fallacies of the ideology that justifies the actions of these groups: liberalism. For an American audience accustomed to thinking of liberals as people who advocate active government, it is important to emphasize that in this study "liberalism" is used in its original sense (which is how Argentines and Europeans use it) as standing for free enterprise and a limited role for government. In the opinion of Argentine nationalists of the Left, such an ideology is an excuse for free-trade policies that open the country to foreign economic exploitation and for laissez-faire domestic policies that prevent the government from correcting social injustices.

A fourth hypothesis locates the cause of Argentina's failure in the absence of a dynamic class of native industrialists. This is an argument that finds proponents on both the Left and the Right, although obviously for different reasons. Leftists accuse Argentine industrialists of lacking a true entrepreneurial spirit, or "calling." Arising, in the vast majority, from immigrant families, they are accused of using their profits to advance up the social ladder by imitating the consumption patterns of the oligarchy rather than to build up their industrial enterprises. Economically conservative and socially reactionary in outlook, they conspire with the oligarchy and the military to shut out foreign competition and hold down wages and welfare spending.[5]

For Argentine traditionalists, on the other hand, much of the country's industry is artificial and useless. It represents the hubris of economic nationalists in their pursuit of self-sufficiency. Citing the "law of comparative advantage," the traditionalists deny that Argentina possesses the requirements for being an industrial nation. The country's wealth lies in its land, they argue, whereas most native industry is incapable of ever becoming competitive and can be kept going only with high levels of government protection and subsidization. Consequently, the industrialization policies of the last forty years have been mistaken. All these policies have accomplished is the fostering of a parasitical class of businessmen who exploit a captive domestic market with high prices and shoddy goods while simultaneously draining capital from potentially more productive sectors. The traditionalists' remedy is an icy blast of free-trade, free-enterprise liberalism that will eliminate artificial industries and leave only the truly competitive.[6]

A fifth body of thought focuses on Perón's impact on Argentina. Although the "Great Man Theory" is unfashionable among social scientists, who prefer to view the march of events as the product of impersonal "social forces," it is undeniable (to all but the most hardened determinists) that certain men have the power, at given moments, to make decisions with far-reaching effects for the future. Thus, while it may be an oversimplification to assign all the blame for Argentina's troubles to Juan D. Perón, there can be little doubt that his career influenced the course of Argentina's development. According to writers on both the Left and the Right, Perón's years in power, 1946–55, were a lost opportunity.

Conservatives point to the fact that Perón wasted vast sums of money in nationalizing dilapidated foreign enterprises, in graft, and in ill-planned social welfare schemes. It is claimed that, after nine years in office, his legacy to the nation was a prehensile trade union movement, a parasitical bureaucracy, an empty treasury, and a distorted economy saddled with loss-producing state companies. Conversely, leftist critics fault Perón for failing to use his powers to carry out a true social revolution. In the words of one writer, Perón's program of "state-controlled class harmony" was an inadequate response to a "dynamic situation of intensifying class conflict." Rather than create a proletarian state, he attempted to "regenerate Argentina's capitalist structure by providing political consensus."[7]

Whatever one might think of Perón, he was thoroughly Argentine—a true product of his society—which brings us to the last hypothesis we shall consider: that Argentina's failure reflects a fatal defect in the national character, or, if one prefers, in the political culture. This idea underlies the thesis of James Scobie, for whom the fatal characteristics of contemporary Argentine society are its extreme nationalism and its militarism. Nationalism is a destructive force welling up from the lower ranks that intimidates politicians and frightens off the foreign capital Argentina so badly needs. It is all the more effective for having the power of the trade union movement behind it. Militarism, in his view, also stems from flaws in the national character in that it is encouraged by "the apparent unwillingness or inability of political parties to compromise or work together."[8]

Robert D. Crassweller's *Perón and the Enigmas of Argentina* explores the problem of national character even further as it relates particularly to the phenomenon of Perón.[9] For Crassweller, Perón was the "personification of Argentina's Hispanic and Creole civilization" in which qualities like authoritarianism, intolerance, hierarchy, corporatism, personalism, machismo, honor, and individualism are inherited from Spain. Taken together, these qualities help to fashion a Hispanic civilization that rejects the liberal, democratic, and scientific outlook of Northern Europe. Over these Hispanic characteristics are laid the specific Argentine social rifts: "the brooding ill-will that set the interior apart from Buenos Aires," the mutual incomprehension of the immigrant and the Creole, the resentment of the workers toward their bosses, and the sense of betrayal that modern nationalist intellectuals feel toward the cosmopolitan upper classes.

A variation on this theme of national character suggests that Argentina and its political culture are the victims of a peculiarly spasmodic history. In Juan Corradi's words, the country "has been built like a palimpsest of half-concluded projects" marked by "inconclusive revolutions of all sorts." As a result, "change has not taken place through the progressive incorporation of new actors and practices within an ongoing socioeconomic order." Instead, anachronistic interests retained their privileges while new interests were half incorporated into the system. "As with the accretion of strata in the history of a geological formation, none of these societal forms managed to displace the others entirely." But each group became more efficient at mobilizing its members to defend its interests, and the nastiness of the political standoff has increased as the economy has deteriorated. Argentine society today is in decay, with no firm foundation for any sort of political order: "No democracy ever appears, only disorder; no solid authoritarian state, but merely military regimes haunted by their lack of legitimacy and fearing retribution for their crimes; no revolutionary situation, but terrorism."

A society that was once full of promise and is still young in age has entered a fateful spiral of decay that sometimes seizes much older nations. But in the latter, the strength of traditions, the respect for weathered and tested institutions, and the commonality of beliefs makes decadence supportable and even sometimes genteel. For Argentina, decadence is hell. Without the appropriate moral, if not natural, resources to muddle through in an unsteady world, lacking the habits of conviviality on which to fall back and repose, the country declines frenetically, in ugly ways, tormented by the image of a past for whose disappearance no consolation seems possible.[10]

## The Approach to Be Taken

Each of the hypotheses discussed above will be tested in this study by describing how politics and economics interacted in Argentina from approximately 1910 to 1987. We will begin at the time of Argentina's centennial, when the nation seemed perched on the verge of a takeoff that would soon allow it to take its place among the world's leading countries; and we will end with a brief summary of the first four years of Raúl Alfonsín's democratic regime, which followed a time of military dictatorship, economic exhaustion, institutional decay, and terror. In between those two boundary markers is the history of Argentina's sudden rise and slow decline. Those seventy-seven years were filled with attempts to apply a wide variety of economic plans and political formulas aimed at reversing the country's decline. These plans and formulas and the debates surrounding them will be discussed during this study, along with the politics of policymaking and the impact of economic conditions upon the political system. Argentina's experience seems to show that what may be rational and correct in economic terms is usually incompatible with the chief imperative of political leadership— survival.

In dealing with Argentine politics, this study focuses on pressure groups: the military, labor unions, industrialists, farmers, ranchers, merchants, and foreign capitalists. These seem to be the most important factors operating on a continuing basis in the political system. Governmental institutions and political parties frequently have been disrupted in their functioning by Argentina's many military coups; consequently, their development has been hindered. Rather than being leading actors in the political process, they tend to be the targets of political action. By contrast, Argentine pressure groups are well organized and experienced at promoting or defending their interests, so it is they who determine, through their struggles, the outcome of policy.

This study is divided into four parts. Part I, "Argentine Industrial Capitalism before Perón," describes the emergence of industry from being a marginal activity largely ignored by the government to its superseding of agriculture as the main concern of policymakers and investors. Part I begins with the processes of political integration and capital formation that were the prerequisites of economic growth, then discusses the appearance of local entrepreneurs and the debates that arose over whether and how Argentina should become industrialized, and finally describes the labor conditions and living standards of the working classes that attended the industrialization process.

This section does not support those who hold that Argentina's problems stem from its landowning or industrial elites. The image of the agro-exporter class as being unprogressive needs revision in light of how Argentina was so greatly transformed, economically and socially, during the late nineteenth century under the leadership of its liberal oligarchy. By the same token, Part I demonstrates that Argentina did, at one time, possess a dynamic industrial class. Industry came a long way in Argentina until World War II largely because of the efforts of a number of true entrepreneurs. With little or no help from the government or from private banks, they nonetheless laid down the foundations of Argentina's industrial transformation. Finally, the crucial role played by foreign capital, especially in the pre–World War I years, is emphasized. That Argentina's industrial progress was not more rapid after World War I is due to the contraction of the world economy and the decrease in available risk capital during the depression of the 1930s and both world wars.

Also in Part I, however, we will see the origins of Argentina's future crisis stemming from the import substitution policies adopted in the 1930s. Originating as a series of more or less unplanned emergency measures in the face of a disastrous fall in Argentina's export earnings, they extended government economic regulation to an unprecedented degree, began the shift in emphasis from agriculture to industry, and helped to foment a sizable class of small factory owners. A whole new complex of political and economic interests was created.

Part II, "The Peronist Watershed," deals with the charismatic leadership of Juan Domingo Perón, the political and economic policies of his government, and their influence on the country's development. In essence, Peronism accentuated the transition from an essentially laissez-faire system to state regulation; for the Perón regime, unlike preceding governments, state authority and military power were the legitimating ends. Perón's model system bore an extremely close resemblance to European fascism, even though, in contrast to fascist regimes, it based its political support chiefly upon the trade unions. Its main intention was to force all occupational groups into government-controlled syndicates for the purpose of mobilizing national power to the maximum. The period from 1943 to 1955 is pivotal because it explains the subsequent polarization of Argentina's politics, which in turn has economic ramifications.

Part III, "Political Stalemate and Economic Decline," deals with the period between Perón's overthrow by a coup in 1955 to his triumphal return to power in 1973. It shows how attempts by both civilian and military governments to "de-Peronize" Argentina failed largely because of a fundamental inability to reconcile orthodox economic cures for inflation and stagnant productivity with political popularity. It examines the various attempts to impose orthodox liberal, neoliberal, and populist policies upon the country and how powerful pressure groups were able to undermine these policies whenever they threatened the groups' special interests. The fundamental inability of the Argentine state, whether under democratic or authoritarian rule, to carry out its functions is analyzed, as are the political tactics of each of Argentina's major pressure groups. This is the most complex and lengthy part of the study.

Part IV, "Descent into Chaos," covers the return of the Peronists to power from 1973 to 1976, the military "Process of National Reorganization" which followed that, and the return to democracy under Alfonsín. The Peronist administration was an attempt to restore the corporate state, while Videla's regime permitted a partial return to a free market. Both failed, and both were characterized by terrorism and widespread official violations of human rights. A nation which once prided itself on being the most European and civilized of the American nations had descended into unrestrained savagery. For this reason, the current Alfonsín administration is discussed for the purpose of assessing whether Argentina's return to democracy in 1983 signals a new departure. Part IV concludes that, while one might hope for the best, there are few signs that Alfonsín and his Radical party are willing to undertake the basic reforms needed to restore dynamism to the economy. Should they fail to do so, the prospects seem dim for democracy's survival because successful economic performance is the sine qua non for achieving stability and legitimacy in today's Argentina.

# PART ONE

# Argentine Industrial Capitalism before Perón

## CHAPTER TWO

# The Preconditions for Growth

**A**rgentina celebrated its centennial in 1910. Great changes had taken place since the country won its independence from Spain, and its citizens were justly proud of the progress made. In the last few decades Argentina had become one of the world's leading exporters of beef, wheat, corn, and linseed, and as a result it was one of the wealthiest of nations. In terms of per capita gold reserves, it ranked ahead of the United States and Great Britain and only slightly behind France.[1]

Visitors who came to Argentina about this time were impressed by the prosperity, modernity, and optimism they encountered. One of them, the English writer James Bryce, noted, "Every visitor is struck by the dominance of material interests and a material view of things. Compared with the raking in of money and the spending of it in betting or in ostentatious luxury, a passion for the development of the country's resources and the adornment of its capital stand out as aims that widen the vision and elevate the soul." As for the capital, "Buenos Aires is something between Paris and New York. It has the business rush and luxury of the one, the gaiety and pleasure-loving aspect of the other. Everybody seems to have money, and to like spending it, and to like letting everybody else know that it is being spent." It was a city of imposing buildings, narrow streets jammed with handsome horsedrawn carriages and even costlier motorcars, spacious parks, and many shady little plazas adorned with equestrian statues. Bryce noted especially the gleaming new Congress building with its "tall and handsome dome"; the stately Colón Opera House, "the interior of which equals any in Europe"; and the Jockey Club, social center for the country's proud elite, "whose scale and elaborate appointments surpass even the club-houses of New York." The city's one great thoroughfare, the Avenida de Mayo, was "wide, and being well planted with trees," was "altogether a noble street, statelier than Picadilly in London, or Unter den Linden in Berlin, or Pennsylvania Avenue in Washington." It connected the Plaza del Congreso with the Plaza de Mayo, around which were grouped the Presidential Palace (the Casa Rosada, or "Pink House"), the National Cathedral, Buenos Aires City Hall (the Cabildo), and other government buildings. "Loitering in the great Avenida de Mayo," Bryce recalled, "and watching the hurrying crowd and the whirl of motor-cars, and the gay shop-windows, and the open-air cafes on the sidewalks, and the Parisian glitter of the women's dresses, one feels nearer to Europe than anywhere else in South America."[2]

Buenos Aires, which only half a century before was known as the "overgrown village" (la gran aldea), now had one of the busiest harbors in the world, for Argentina ranked eighth among nations in the value of its exports, tenth in the value of its imports, and ninth in overall trade. It was a cosmopolitan city, since the porteños, as the residents of this port are called, were mostly immigrants or their first-generation offspring. Immigrants had come mainly from Italy and Spain, but there were significant numbers of Germans, Frenchmen, Englishmen, Jews, Irishmen, and Slavs. Collectively, they were a bustling, commercial people, eager to make their mark in the New World and were often considered too materialistic and aggressive by their Creole neighbors.

The influence of modernity was not confined to Buenos Aires, however. From the city there fanned out into the countryside a far-flung web of railroad lines which carried a great variety of goods to the port: cattle from the vast ranches (estancias) of the pampa, wheat and corn from the granaries of Santa Fé, sugar from Tucumán, wine and olives from the desert oases of Mendoza, wool and lamb from the sub-Antarctic plateau of Patagonia, and cotton and yerba mate (a bitter green tea) from the tropical lowlands of the northern border. The railroads, built within the preceding thirty years, had transformed the Argentine interior by facilitating settlement and trade. The lure of larger profits led to investment in agricultural improvements. Given the country's abundance of flat, fertile land, production quickly boomed, and Argentina rose to the forefront of the world's suppliers of meat and grain.

In the countryside, economic growth did not necessarily lead directly to social change. Bryce divided the rural population into two broad classes: the rich cattle ranchers (estancieros), "who are becoming opulent, not only by the sale of their crops and their live stock, but simply by the rapid rise in the value of land," and "the laboring class, who gather like feudal dependents round the estancia." This latter class he further subdivided into the native offspring of the old gauchos who used to roam the pampa and immigrant Italian wage laborers who tended to come and go with the seasons.[3] This picture, though roughly accurate as applied to the pampa, was oversimplified. For one thing, it neglected the recent appearance of many wealthy Englishmen, Scots, and Irishmen among the *estancia* owners. More importantly, it failed to mention the rise of a significant class of medium-sized farmers, drawn largely from the Italian immigrants, especially in the secondary agricultural regions: grain growers in Santa Fé, wine growers in Mendoza, and fruit growers in northern Patagonia. On the other hand, in the mountain regions of the northwest, in the sugar areas of Tucumán and Salta, and in the yerba mate belt agricultural techniques and rural life were still practically feudal.

The opulence of the newly rich *estancieros* and their merchant allies was reflected in their ornate Buenos Aires town homes and apartments that began downtown near the edge of San Martín Park and continued, block after block, past Palermo Park, with its gardens and fancy racetrack, to the proud Victorian mansions of Belgrano and out to the country estates of Olivos and Vicente López. This zone running along the northern edge of the city was called the Barrio Norte, and within its precincts the Argentine upper classes lived in conscious imitation of European aristocracy. As Bryce noted: "Nowhere in the world does one get a stronger impression of wealth and extravagance." Life was a round of fashionable restaurants, boutiques, art shows, opera, and socializing at lavish private clubs. Business interests were pursued at the headquarters of the powerful Argentine Rural Society (Sociedad Rural Argentina, or SRA), the lobbying organization for the largest *estancieros*; at the Chamber of Commerce (Cámara Argentina de Comércio, or CAC); or at the Stock Exchange (Bolsa de Comércio). It was often inside those offices, and not in the Congress or at the Casa Rosada, that the country's really important decisions were made.

In such a society there were naturally great differences in wealth and living standards. On the opposite side of town from the Barrio Norte, the stockyards were surrounded by sprawling, dirty slums where streets were dirt ruts, and where filth collected in open ditches. Bryce commented: "If the best parts of Buenos Aires are as tasteful as those of Paris, there is plenty of ugliness in the worst suburbs. On its land side, the city dies out in a waste of scattered shanties, or 'shacks' (as they are called in the United States), dirty and squalid, with corrugated iron roofs, their boards gaping like rents in tattered clothes. These are inhabited by the newest and poorest of the immigrants from southern Italy and southern Spain, a large and not very desireable element among whom anarchism is rife."[4]

Again, the picture is too simple. The slums were bad indeed, and anarchists were always busy trying to recruit followers, but for every political radical there were many other immigrants who had made the trip across the ocean to get a fresh start in the New World. They were optimistic about their chances to rise in Argentina, and their poverty was blunted by an adequate supply of cheap food. In a big meat- and grain-producing country like this, even a proletarian could afford his *churrasco* (strip steak), accompanied by bread and wine. Moreover, in an age of urban expansion there were plenty of workers who had risen to the lower middle class as foremen, managers, or shop owners. Unlike southern Europe, Argentina was no backward-looking, caste-ridden society—at least not in the cities. As Bryce himself observed:

> In the cities there exists, between the wealthy and the workingmen, a considerable body of professional men, shopkeepers, and clerks, who are rather less of a defined middle class than they would be in European countries. Society is something like that of North American cities, for the lines between classes are not sharply drawn, and the spirit of equality has gone further than in France, and, of course, far further than in Germany or Spain. One cannot speak of an aristocracy, . . . for although a few old colonial families have the Spanish pride of lineage, it is, as a rule, wealth and only wealth that gives station and social eminence.[5]

In 1913 the country's Third National Census showed that over three-fourths of the owners of industrial and commercial establishments were foreign-born; and of those, not a few arose from the ranks of the working class.

## The Achievements of the Liberal Oligarchy

Although Argentina's progress was undeniable, the country was still about a century behind Great Britain or the United States in developing its industries. This is somewhat puzzling because Argentina has a temperate climate, abundant fertile soil, a long coastline, and no internal geographical barriers to inhibit the flow of trade: factors that should have encouraged the early development of agriculture and commerce, which in turn are the bases of capital formation for industry. Although it had been independent for a hundred years, it was not until the previous decade that agriculture was modernized and foreign trade reached impressive levels. Industry began to appear about that time too; but not until after World War I did it approach what W. W. Rostow calls the "takeoff" stage. Why, then, was Argentina so late in realizing its economic potential?

The influence of history was an important factor in Argentina's slow development. Spanish colonial rule, with its mercantilist economics, had a dampening effect on trade and production. The colony was a captive market for finished goods sent from Spain and was forbidden to produce anything for itself that might compete with Spanish imports. More importantly, Spanish rule prevented the colonists from acquiring experience in self-government. Unlike the English colonies of North America, Spanish colonies were not permitted to have their own legislatures. All decisions flowed from Spain and were applied by Spanish officials. Consequently, when Argentina won its independence in 1810, its patriot leaders had almost no experience in running a government. For the next forty-two years the country was torn by factions struggling over whether it should be ruled as a centralized system from Buenos Aires or as a decentralized federal republic; then Juan Manuel Rosas seized power at the head of a gaucho army and established a dictatorship. During his rule trade, finance, and investment suffered. Government, instead of becoming institutionalized, reflected one man's personal whims. Education was neglected. The Catholic church, eager to support Rosas against urban liberals, was hostile to any sign of progressive thought. Immigration was discouraged, and many of the best-educated and most-talented people left the country to escape persecution. Argentina's economic modernization really began only after Rosas's fall. It was left to Rosas's successors to create an orderly government, encourage immigration, attract capital, build schools, improve transportation and communications, and link Argentina to the rest of the world: in short, to establish what Rostow calls the "preconditions for take-off."

## The Achievement of Political Stability

The new leaders' first task, as they saw it, was to overcome the political divisions of the past and create a constitutional order that would win the allegiance of all the provincial leaders. The men who headed the new government looked to the United States as the best model of a large, successful republic. Inspired by *The Federalist Papers*, they drew up a constitution in 1853 that provided for a similar type of government; however, the Argentine president and vice-president were elected for six years instead of four and could not stand for immediate reelection. Acceptance of the new constitution came only after two wars between Buenos Aires and the provinces, when a compromise got the former to accept a federal system in return for the provinces' acceptance of the city of Buenos Aires as the capital.

Provincial leaders proved to be better politicians than their *porteño* rivals. Within a few years they formed a loose political association known as the National Autonomy Party (Partido Autonomista Nacional, or PAN). The military's political control was considerably bolstered when General Julio A. Roca, head of the army, became PAN's leader.

Although crude and corrupt, PAN provided for more orderly government. Despite their cynical manipulation of the constitution, PAN's leaders accepted the doctrine of liberalism, with its emphasis on limited government. Although Argentina was still far from being a model republic, at least the brutality and terror of a dictatorship like Rosas's were missing. There was a great deal of economic liberty and even a certain amount of political liberty. Opposition parties were tolerated, and in the urban areas, where the machine had less control, they frequently won. Moreover, the oligarchy itself was not united, and its more enlightened members were sincerely interested in reforming political practices.

One group of reformers, drawn from the same *estanciero* upper class as the PAN leaders, formed the Unión Cívica Radical (UCR) in 1889. Although the Radicals advocated expanding the suffrage, they had little faith that PAN would peacefully surrender power; so, having won over part of the army, they attempted a revolution in 1890. They failed, but tried again in 1893 and 1905, after losing fraudulent elections. Repeated failure, both at the ballot box and the barricades, convinced the Radicals to go underground and prepare more carefully. Their leader, Hipólito Yrigoyen, announced a policy of "intransigence" against the ruling regime—a policy that promised a future Armageddon.

Fortunately, a battle never became necessary. Within the ranks of the ruling political machine, now rebaptized the Conservative party, a progressive faction was pushing for reform. These Argentine "Whigs" were led by Roque Sáenz Peña, a man of impeccable conservative credentials. Son of a former president, scion of one of Argentina's oldest and richest families, educated in Paris, and member of the snobbish Jockey Club, Sáenz Peña nevertheless believed in free and honest elections. Taking advantage of a split in the Conservative party and the Radicals' abstentionism, he won the presidency in 1910 and two years later produced an electoral law that instituted the secret ballot and gave the vote to every male citizen who completed his military service. He also sent federal observers to police the balloting in the 1914 congressional elections. Assured of a fair count, the Radicals agreed to participate in the 1916 general elections, with Yrigoyen at the head of the ticket. Their victory brought an end to the liberal oligarchy's political monopoly and ushered in a new era of mass politics.

## The Spread of Modern Values

Development requires social attitudes that will allow people to be valued for their abilities rather than for their inherited status. In late nineteenth-century Argentina these attitudes were fostered by the doctrine of classical liberalism, which encouraged individualism, free enterprise, and free trade. The 1853 constitution expressed those principles in several places. Articles 10, 11, and 12 encouraged free trade among the provinces by suppressing internal tariffs and other restrictions on the free passage of goods across provincial boundaries. Article 14 guaranteed to every inhabitant the right "to work and exercise any legitimate trade; to travel and engage in commerce; to petition the authorities; to enter, remain in, cross, or leave Argentine territory; to publish his ideas in the press without prior censorship; to use and dispose of his property; to associate with others for useful purposes; to profess his faith freely; and to teach and learn." Article 17 declared private property to be inviolable. Its expropriation could be justified only by public need, and owners had to be previously indemnified. Article 18 guaranteed inhabitants against arbitrary arrest and unfair judicial procedures. Article 20 extended all civil liberties to foreign residents. Finally, Article 19 stated broadly that "the private actions of men which in no way offend public order and morals, nor prejudice others, are the affairs of God only, and are beyond the authority of the Magistrates. No inhabitant of the Nation shall be obliged to do what the law does not demand, nor prevented from doing what it does not prohibit."

A secondary, and perhaps contradictory, theme in the thinking of the liberal oligarchy was the positivist doctrine of progress. Whereas classical liberalism was concerned chiefly with removing obstacles to individual effort, positivism was more "activist" in emphasizing the state's responsibility for creating conditions favorable to progress, such as building public schools or encouraging European immigration. Thus, by the end of the century Argentina had probably the most advanced public school system in Latin America, a handsome investment in "social overhead capital." Also, between 1857 and World War I the population increased by more than 6 million people, of whom about half were settlers from abroad. By 1914 just less than half of Argentina's 7.8 million inhabitants were either immigrants or their children. In Buenos Aires, Santa Fé, and Entre Ríos the foreign-born constituted a majority; and since most immigrants were adult males, they were a very large majority of the economically active population.[6]

The more successful immigrants and their offspring found the Argentine oligarchy to be quite permeable. Among the hundred charter members of the ultraprestigious Jockey Club there figured many foreign names: Anderson, Bosch, Brown, Casey, Church, Davis, Diehl, Dowling, Duggan, Eastman, Gaban, Ham, Kemmis, Lawry, Löwe, Malcolm, Murphy, Nash, Rouaix, Schang, Shaw, and Taylor. One of the original founders was a Jew (Bemberg), and the man who initiated the idea, Carlos Pellegrini, was the son of an Italian immigrant.[7] As Bryce had noted, it was wealth, and wealth alone, that gave status.

## The Agricultural Revolution

Immigration produced far-reaching changes on the pampa. Largely because of ideas brought by the new settlers, great improvements were made in the breeding of cattle; sheep raising was introduced; and grain crops like wheat, corn, and linseed began to provide a source of income that would eventually outstrip the livestock industry in importance.

All of this was in response to a growing demand for raw materials and foodstuffs in western Europe that was created by the spread of industry and a rapidly rising population. Argentina was in a peculiarly favorable position to supply that demand because of the temperate climate and fertile soil that made it one of the few places in the world capable of large-scale cereal agriculture and stock raising. Argentina's exports soared in value from about 26 million gold pesos in 1870 to 373 million by 1910, while the amount of land under cultivation rose from about 1.5 million to almost 51 million acres.[8]

Large holdings dominated production. If we define a large holding as any farm or ranch with 5,000 or more hectares (12,500 acres plus), then some 5,233 properties fell into that category in 1913. They constituted only 2.4 percent of all rural holdings, yet they controlled 55 percent of the land. At the other extreme, small holdings of 25 hectares (63 acres) or less constituted 46 percent of the rural properties in Argentina but occupied only 1 percent of the land. Define middle-sized farms as ranging from 26 to 1,000 hectares and you take in slightly fewer than 43 percent of all holdings but only 10 percent of the land.[9]

The importance of large, medium, and small landholdings varied with the region and predominating type of agricultural activity. In Buenos Aires Province, which occupied most of the pampa, large estates were only 1 percent of the holdings but claimed 35 percent of the land. They were concentrated especially in the cattle-raising zones of the southern and western parts of the province. In the northern part, where grain farming was more important, medium-sized holdings were common; but it was only in Santa Fé and Entre Ríos, situated to the north of Buenos Aires, where the yeoman farmer prevailed as a type. Those were areas where colonization was planned, and the family farm had been a deliberate policy goal. At the other extreme, Patagonia was carved up into enormous sheep ranches that spread for miles in every direction. The dryness of the land, which supported only poor forage for grazing, made extensive holdings there an economic necessity. In the sugar and yerba mate belts along the northern border, the traditional *latifundio*, with its feudalistic social patterns still dominated. Those areas were scarcely touched by modernization, had received little immigration, and produced mainly for the domestic market.

Even where the large holdings prevailed, however, there were no laws of primogeniture or entail, and although there was great social prestige in being a large landowner, it was increasingly important to be progressive in the management of one's property. Ranchers boasted of their improved pasturage, their imported shorthorn cattle, and their scientific breeding methods. The SRA, founded in 1866 by a group of forward-looking *estancieros*, promoted modernization. Every year in late July it held a gala livestock fair where stockbreeders displayed their finest specimens of cattle, sheep, horses, and pigs in Buenos Aires's fashionable Palermo Park. It was a social event of the first magnitude, bringing together the nation's rural elite and stimulating the *estancieros'* sense of pride as they competed in showing off their achievements. The fair also provided a forum for the *estancieros* to voice their opinions about public affairs. The annual address of the SRA's president was an eagerly awaited event because it was a barometer of how the incumbent politicians stood vis-à-vis the country's most powerful interests.[10] It should be emphasized, however, that the SRA, like the Jockey Club, was open to immigrants. To join, one need have only a certain number of cattle.

Below the *estancieros* in status were the medium-sized and small landholders. They were most common in the grain belt, in the fruit- and garden-crops region of northwestern Patagonia along the Río Negro, and in the vineyard zone of Mendoza. Small farmers constituted a majority in the sugar-producing areas of Tucumán and Salta, although large plantations accounted for most of the production, and most of Argentina's cotton was raised by small immigrant landowners or squatters in the Chaco Territory along the Paraguayan border. Thirty-five percent of all landholders owned properties of ten hectares or less. Many were subsistence farmers, although a few were able to contribute something to the market. Neither they nor the middling landowners were members of the SRA, which admitted only the largest cattlemen. In fact, they had no organization to represent their interests until the Great Depression of the 1930s forced them to battle with the *estancieros* for an adequate share of a shrinking market. Then they, along with other modest landholders in the region, established the Confederation of Rural Associations of Buenos Aires and La Pampa (CARBAP). Small ranchers and farmers in other regions followed suit, and in 1943 these regional associations linked up to form the Argentine Rural Confederation (CRA). Until then, however, the SRA had the political field to itself, and the *estancieros'* prestige gave it tremendous influence. In general, small landowners, especially those in the grain and fruit areas, were optimistic and proud of their status as landowners.

Of lower status than the small landowners were the tenant farmers, who comprised perhaps 40 percent of all those engaged in agriculture and were especially common in the corn and wheat regions. Tenants worked on contracts that usually ran for five years and stipulated which crops were to be grown. The *estancieros* would often lease their land to insure themselves of a steady income, especially if meat prices were low. In that case, the contract would require the tenants to concentrate on grain production and forbid them to put more than 5 percent of the land into pasture. If meat prices stayed down and grain prices went up, the contract probably would be renewed; otherwise the tenants had to move on. All improvements in buildings, land, or fences reverted to the owner at no cost. Rent was paid in kind and was usually about a third of the crop.[11]

The dream of every tenant, of course, was to save up and buy a farm, but rising land values made that goal a mirage for most of them. Nevertheless, "in strictly economic terms the system worked relatively well; tenant farms were generally efficiently operated, and tenants could earn good incomes."[12] The chief drawback of the system was its uncertainty. Tenants were condemned to a nomadic way of life. Since they could never settle down, they lived in makeshift shacks, preferring to invest all their money in equipment which they took with them when they left. Despite the frustrations of this kind of life, many tenants were prosperous—more so, on the average, than the small farmers. Besides spending their money on machinery, tenants could also rent more land, even if they couldn't buy it, and many of them became large-scale operators. They pyramided their efforts like gamblers, hoping that someday a really big year would allow them to earn the cash to buy a farm. It was precisely that dream that made the tenant farmers so middle class in outlook. Essentially, they identified with the owners because they hoped to become owners themselves.[13] Nevertheless, tensions did exist between owners and tenants. In 1912 a tenants' strike broke out which led to the founding of the Argentine Agrarian Federation (FAA) to defend the tenants' interests. The FAA quickly became an active and well-organized lobbying group with plenty of influence in Congress. With 27,000 dues-paying members, it was able to set up a legal defense fund and a strike fund. A successful rent strike in 1919 showed that the group had muscle. Besides fighting landlords, the FAA organized buyers' and sellers' cooperatives to combat gouging merchants and middlemen. In 1921 it got Congress to pass legislation forbidding clauses in tenant contracts restricting what could be planted and to whom it could be sold. The law also required owners to indemnify tenants for all improvements and forbade the seizure of tenants' tools and animals to pay off a debt. These rules were tightened further in 1932, and in 1940 Congress aided tenants suffering from the Great Depression by making it extremely difficult for owners to evict them.[14]

Managers and estate administrators were a small but important segment of the rural population. They were common especially in the cattle areas of the pampa and the sheep ranches of Patagonia where many *estancias* had absentee landlords. Many managers were Englishmen or Scotsmen. Successful managers were well paid and sometimes were given a share of the *estancia's* profits. A few earned enough to become *estancieros* in their own right, but many preferred to remain as managers, drawing a good salary without risking any capital.[15]

At the bottom of rural society were the laborers, who were drawn from various sources. Some were small proprietors who supplemented their meager income by hiring out as part-time laborers. Others were newly arrived immigrants who were starting on the bottom rung of the ladder with hopes of saving enough of their wages to buy a tractor and move up to the status of tenants. Others were the offspring of immigrants who had failed to move up or of old lower-class Creole stock, the gauchos. Still others were former tenants who had hit a run of bad luck and lost their capital. Then there were the Indians and the seasonal migrants from poor neighboring countries like Bolivia or Paraguay. These were the lowest-paid and most ill-treated farmworkers.

Taking all classes into consideration, rural living standards were not bad. Food, including meat, was plentiful. The average Argentine in the countryside had an adequate, if somewhat starchy, diet. Housing for workers and tenants, while simple, was acceptable. The typical hut was a small adobe structure with cement-coated walls, a thatched roof, and wooden floors. Medium-sized landowners usually graduated to a frame or brick house. Schools, the key to mobility, were usually present and were of good quality, especially on the pampa. Health facilities varied by region, with communities on the pampa again providing the best services. Except in the remote border regions, living standards were far from desperate, even for the lowly *peóns*. Throughout the hierarchy there was a pervasive optimism, a dogged belief that hard work could carry a person up the ladder, "even if only slowly." Four decades of phenomenal growth had made the average Argentine a believer in progress.

### The Formation of Social Overhead Capital

Railroads were the key to Argentina's agricultural revolution. At the time of political unification in 1862 there were only 83 miles of track; that figure rose to 1,388 in 1880. Between 1880 and 1900, at the height of PAN's political dominance, the bulk of Argentina's 13,690-mile railroad network was laid down. It spanned the country's midsection from the Atlantic to the Andes, drove deep into the remote northwestern region as far as the provinces of Catamarca and Santiago del Estero, crossed the northern pampa to Santa Fé and then swept westward to Tucumán and Salta, and pushed down into the southern pampa and Patagonia. Apart from these main lines, various capillary lines spread out to the far corners of the republic. The centennial year was capped by a masterful feat of railroad engineering when a tunnel was dug through the Andes, linking the Argentine and Chilean systems and allowing goods to flow all the way across the continent.[16]

The first railroad lines were built with private Argentine capital in conjunction with the national or provincial governments, but the big boom in railroad building was financed by foreign—chiefly British—capital. By the centennial, all of the original Argentine-owned lines had been sold to foreigners. Although the foreign-owned railroads played an important part in developing the country, they were very unpopular because of their allegedly high rates, poor service, and political influence. Their detractors accused them of watering their stock and evading taxes by doctoring their account books. To keep the government from interfering, they placed relatives and friends of influential politicians on their boards of directors or hired them as company lawyers or consultants. If any government tried to regulate them or collect taxes owed, they did not hesitate to stop the flow of freight until the government capitulated.[17]

As with railroads, so with other areas of heavy capital formation: an estimated $10 billion, in today's currency, was invested by foreigners between the fall of Rosas and World War I to build extensive trolley and subway systems for the capital, telegraph lines across the country, an overseas cable, electric power plants, gas and water works, and a modern telephone system.[18]

Banking was a crucial aspect of capital formation, of course. Here again foreign capital, especially British, played a predominant part—although the Italians, French, Germans, Dutch, Belgians, and Americans were well represented. Argentines were active in finance too. One of the most successful banks was the Banco Popular Argentino, founded in 1887 by a group of *estancieros*. Another thriving bank, oriented toward smaller depositors and borrowers, was the Banco El Hogar Argentino, founded in 1889 and specializing in easy loans to buyers of family-sized farms. The biggest bank was the Banco de la

Província de Buenos Aires. Despite its name, it was funded by private capital. In the absence of any public banks between 1852 and 1872, it was authorized to emit gold-backed currency, in addition to its normal banking activities.

In 1872 a financial crisis shook the national economy and forced a change in the banking system. A Banco Nacional, composed of government and private capital, took over the printing of currency. There were also several smaller banks of both public and private capital located in the interior provinces as well as municipal banks in Buenos Aires, Rosario, Paraná, and Tucumán.

Private banking practice was very conservative. For example, between 1900 and 1922 the Banco de Italia y Río de La Plata made most of its loans to the national government and the provinces. Its private borrowers were a select group of railroads, streetcar companies, ship suppliers, and construction firms with public works contracts.[19] On the other hand, the bank took little interest in lending to manufacturers.

Although foreign capital was helpful in developing the Argentine economy, it also created problems. Large sums of money were being sent abroad as profits, royalties, and loan repayments. Argentina's balance of payments was usually in deficit, and it was forced to set aside as much as half of its income earned from exports to pay its external debts. Unfortunately, much of the money borrowed by its national, provincial, and municipal governments was used for graft, padded payrolls, and unproductive showcase projects. Between 1880 and 1911 administrative salaries, overhead expenses, and pork-barrel outlays rose from less than 10 percent of all government expenditures to over 45 percent. The orgy of corruption and featherbedding reached its climax in the last years of the liberal oligarchy's rule as the Conservative party realized that its hold on power was beginning to slip. As it became more difficult to float new loans, governments began the shameful practice of cutting their appropriations for education and health services in order to pay for unnecessary staff and expenses.[20]

The government might have balanced its budget by raising taxes, of course, but that was considered politically infeasible. The income received from indirect sources like sales taxes and tariffs was never adequate to cover expenses, however, so the government had frequent recourse to foreign borrowing—or, when loans were difficult to get, to printing cheap paper money.

Borrowing was easy when the world economy was expanding and

Argentina's exports were in demand; but when times were bad and loan money dried up, the government faced a crisis. The first years after unification in 1862 were a boom period; but by the early 1870s there were signs of trouble. Exports had risen, but imports had risen still faster, and the resultant trade deficit was covered by foreign borrowing. As borrowing became chronic, the debt mounted. In 1874 the country's finances were thrown into a crisis by a political revolt. Alarmed by this display of political instability, European bankers demanded the repayment of all outstanding loans before they would furnish any new credit. The demand set off a panic, leading to a rash of loan defaults and company bankruptcies. Imports were cut drastically, and to make up for the loss of revenue the government raised tariffs. Even so, there was a huge budget deficit, forcing a drastic reduction in the public payroll and the cancellation of most public works projects. Not until 1880, when the federalization of the city of Buenos Aires provided the national government with a new source of revenue, did public spending pick up again, stimulating an economic recovery. Along with this recovery, the opening of new lands in the west as a result of the Indian wars provided new opportunities for investment and speculation, leading to another boom decade.

An even worse collapse came in 1890. As in the previous financial crisis, chronic trade deficits and excessive borrowing were to blame. The government had again become swollen with political appointees and had undertaken even more ambitious public works that provided lucrative contracts for people with good party connections. Also, since foreign loans had not furnished enough liquid capital to satisfy the land-speculation fever that gripped Argentina in the 1880s, the government had printed large batches of paper money. As early as 1884 European bankers were getting worried and threatening to hold back on additional loans, but they were pacified temporarily by Argentina's finance minister, Carlos Pellegrini, who assured them that the economy was fundamentally sound. Argentina's chief creditor, the House of Baring Brothers, agreed to another big loan, but only on the condition that the bank hold a mortgage on the national customs receipts. Having squirmed out of its narrow corner, Argentina resumed its profligate ways: more speculation, more paper money, more public spending, more patronage, more deficits, and more debt—at all levels, national and local, public and private. By 1890 the nation's creditors were convinced that things had gone far enough. No more loans would be made until all current debts were paid. In June 1890 the creditors got their reply: the Argentine government was unable to make payment on its quarterly dividend.[21]

The repercussions were tremendous. Without new loans, exporters were unable to ship their goods, and merchants could not order imports. Customs receipts plummeted, and once again the government was forced to slash its payroll and cancel spending on public works. People were thrown out of their jobs, debtors were forced into bankruptcy, and banks—unable to collect on loans—had to suspend their operations. The financial crisis precipitated a political crisis. The Unión Cívica Radical pointed to the whole sorry mess as proof of the government's complete corruption and incompetence. Backed by part of the army, the UCR rose up against President Juárez Celman in July. The revolt was put down, thanks to the influence General Roca still had over most of the military establishment, but Juárez Celman and his ministers were forced to resign. Power was turned over to Vice-President Carlos Pellegrini, who was given a free hand to clean up the financial mess.

Pellegrini started by negotiating with Argentina's creditors for a three-year moratorium. It was expected that exports would recover their former levels within the three-year period, and the proceeds would be applied toward paying the debt. Next, Pellegrini reorganized the national banking system by creating a new bank, the Banco de la Nación Argentina, whose capital was raised by issuing stock. This bank had a monopoly over the issuing of money but could print only as much as there was gold to back it. Loans could be made only to encourage sound, private, commercial, and industrial activities; on no account was the bank ever to lend to the state. These orthodox measures worked: by 1896 prosperity had returned, though not before some of Argentina's creditors, including Baring Brothers, came very near collapse.[22]

From the time of Pellegrini's reforms until World War I, Argentina enjoyed a period of high, sustained growth. Gross fixed investment rose from 2.4 billion (1950) pesos in 1900 to 10.2 billion by the centennial; and since the total amount of capital invested grew at a rate of 8.6 percent annually between 1900 and 1914, and the population grew by only 4.2 percent a year, there was a large net increase in per capita wealth. As we saw at the beginning of this chapter, in terms of trade, the country was among the top ten of the world's nations and the leading exporter of meat, wheat, and linseed. Politically unified under a modernizing oligarchy, with a productive agricultural system, good transportation and communications networks, a literate and growing population, expanding commerce, and a cosmopolitan leadership, Argentina seemed perched on the verge of what Rostow calls the "takeoff." The next chapter will describe the evolution of industry in Argentina and will explore the question of whether this promise of a takeoff was ever really fulfilled.

## CHAPTER THREE

# The Emergence of Industry

**T**he Third National Census, published in 1913, was the most complete survey ever taken of Argentina's population, agriculture, commerce, and industry. Its results only confirmed with statistics the enormous changes that everyone could see. Since 1895, when the previous census was taken, the population had doubled from 3.9 million to over 7.8 million. The amount of land under cultivation had quadrupled. Better methods of farming and stock raising had increased the principal exports, both in volume and in value, by seven or eight times what they had been a quarter of a century before.[1] Since Argentine prosperity was based on the production of meat and grain, these gains were widely celebrated. On the other hand, industry had made much progress too, but that was less well known. "The enormous development and growth in value of cattle-raising and farming—our 'mother industries,' as we say— are well-known because after satisfying the domestic market they are able, by meeting foreign demand for their products, to publicize their worth by way of export figures published in the annual statistical reports on our foreign trade."

So wrote engineer Eusebio E. García in an introductory essay to the volume containing the industrial census. By contrast, he complained, few people were aware of the great strides made by domestic manufacturing. "Orphans of every national tradition," the country's industries "were born and have grown up, spontaneously but timidly, in a hostile environment that favors European finished goods. They have had neither capital, credit, nor any field of action greater than our own country's needs. They have had to confront constantly the implacable competition of foreign imports which, since 1777, when the La Plata River was opened to free trade, have supplied our people's needs, right down to the flour for their bread."[2]

Industrial activities had been considered so marginal in the past that it was not until 1895 that any attempt was made to get a nationwide account of the number of factories or the number of people employed in them. Prior to that, many activities later classified as industrial, such as flour milling, lumbering, sugar refining, the curing and roasting of yerba mate, the making of tannin from *quebracho* trees, and the tanning of hides, had been carried out as part of farmwork. Other industrial products such as furniture, cloth, candles, preserved foods, and leather goods were turned out in rural cottages. Metallurgy was limited to blacksmith shops, located mostly in villages or small towns or on the big *estancias*. Thus, it was no great exaggeration for García to conclude that "the progress which our industries have made is truly extraordinary, considering that hardly forty years ago this country had no industry."

Although the First National Census of 1869 had not recorded any industry, by the time of the second national census twenty-six years later the picture had changed dramatically. Some 24,114 industrial shops employing a total of 174,782 people and involving an investment of 327.4 million pesos were counted. The next eighteen years were just as impressive. Between 1895 and 1913 the number of industrial establishments doubled to 48,779; the work force grew by 135 percent to 410,201; and the total amount of fixed capital investment quintupled to almost 1.8 billion pesos. Much of that investment went into machinery, as shown by the tenfold jump in the amount of horsepower installed in factories. The average factory was larger, as measured by the number of workers employed (7.7 in 1913, compared with 7.2 in 1895), better capitalized, and more modern—in terms of the ratio of horsepower to hand labor.

Nevertheless, García was right about industry being treated like an orphan, and like an orphan its growth was both unplanned and unencouraged. Industrial growth was a by-product of the agricultural boom, railroad building, and rapid population growth. The buzz and bustle of a burgeoning country created its own demand for industrial goods, which often were needed on the spot. Railroad building required tools and construction materials. Equipment had to be repaired, sometimes with locally-made parts and by local mechanics. The growth of commerce meant warehouses had to be built, ports expanded and modernized, and ships repaired and supplied. All of that encouraged the growth of the construction business and repair shops which in turn increased the demand for lumber, cement, bricks, tools, and sheet metal. The rapid growth of population, especially in the cities, meant more buildings were built, streets paved, and services such as gas, water, electricity, and sewers installed. That, in turn, encouraged the introduction and expansion of a great variety of industries: tile and brickmaking, ceramics, glass, metalworking, cement, simple toolmaking, sawmilling, wire making, the construction of crates, and the manufacture of burlap bags. Commercial establishments needed paper, furniture, and printing services. A growing population meant more demand for soap, cosmetics, pharmaceuticals, cloth, and foodstuffs. Impressive growth was recorded in the beverage, sugar, yerba mate, and bakery goods industries. The impact of immigration was reflected in the great increase in Argentina's output of wine and olive oil and by the appearance and spread of the beer, dairy, and pasta industries.

The period from about 1880 to World War I was one of feverish industrial activity on a modest scale but throbbing with entrepreneurial optimism and energy. Paradoxically, the financial crisis of 1890 gave this emergent industrial sector a great push forward because of Argentina's inability to import coupled with a continuing high demand for certain finished products. Most industry was located either in the city of Buenos Aires or in the *partidos* (counties) in Buenos Aires Province just outside the federal district. Food and beverage processing led the way, and within that branch of industry meatpacking was undoubtedly the most important activity. Between 1895 and 1913 the number of food-processing establishments grew by over 20 percent a year, their work force by over 221 percent a year, and the amount of capital invested by over 8 percent. By the time of the third national census, this sector accounted for almost 40 percent of Argentina's industrial shops, a third of its industrial labor force, and 43 percent of all industrial investment.

The utilities industries constituted another dynamic field. From about 1890 to the centennial, Argentina acquired its basic electric, gas, and water systems. Like the railroads and the meatpacking plants, the utilities were largely in the hands of foreign investors. Big in scale by local standards, they employed only 2 percent of the industrial work force but represented nearly one-fourth of all industrial investment.

Regarding local investment, there was considerable activity in the construction industry in response to the government's large outlays for internal improvements and because of the rapid growth of the cities. There was also a notable increase in capital investment in the metallurgical and chemicals sectors. In the latter case, this was directed mainly into the soap, cosmetic, medicine, and paint and varnish industries.

## In Search of the Takeoff

By the eve of World War I, Argentina had satisfied at least two of W. W. Rostow's criteria for achieving an industrial takeoff or self-sustained growth. Since capital investment had tripled in the previous eighteen years while the population only doubled, the country had surmounted the first Rostovian hurdle of "a rise in the rate of investment to a level which regularly, substantially outstrips population growth." Meanwhile, the meatpacking industry, which had grown to international significance, allowed Argentina to clear a second hurdle: "the development of one or more substantial manufacturing sectors with a high rate of growth."[3] As for Rostow's third criterion, "the existence . . . of a political, social, and institutional framework which exploits the impulses to expand in the modern sector," implying "a considerable capacity to mobilize capital from domestic sources," this subject will be explored in the next chapter. For the present, it is enough to question whether or not Argentina's achievement of most of the preconditions actually led to a takeoff. And if so, when did it occur?

Clearly, Argentina today is an industrialized country capable not only of producing a complete range of consumer goods but also possessing many heavy industries such as steel, oil, automobiles, aluminum, and petrochemicals. Some sort of transition took place, but in studying it both Argentine and foreign writers disagree over just what happened. Guido Di Tella and Manuel Zymelman have located Argentina's takeoff in the 1930s, but rather than describing it as a sudden surge forward, as the term "takeoff" implies, they view it as a somewhat drawn-out process. The first phase, from 1932 to 1938, occurred when the Great Depression disrupted traditional international trade patterns and forced Argentina to become more self-reliant in the production of industrial goods. World War II, which also cut off traditional imports and spurred more efforts at creating national industry, was the second phase. The third phase coincided with Perón's first presidency, from 1946 to 1951, when the government adopted a deliberate policy of fostering industrial self-reliance. This analysis, which assumes that the preconditioning stage of development ended with World War I, raises the question of how to characterize the 1920s. Rostow offers no intermediate stage between preconditioning and takeoff, except to say that "quite substantial economic progress . . . can occur in an economy before a truly self-reinforcing growth process gets under way." However, Di Tella and Zymelman argue that Argentina experienced a "great pause" (*gran demora*) during the 1920s—a kind of Indian summer for traditional society when industry consolidated its energies for the coming takeoff. To continue the metaphor, the Great Depression was the bracing blast of wintry air that finally forced the country to shake off its daydreams and face the need to complete its industrialization.[4]

Javier Villanueva, on the other hand, places the takeoff in the 1920s. Basing his argument on investment figures collected by the United Nations Economic Commission for Latin America (ECLA), he divides the great pause into two phases: World War I and the postwar decade. He concedes that the war disrupted the steady march toward industrialization by cutting off foreign investment and capital goods imports. But the postwar years saw a resurgence of investment in industry that reached a peak in 1929 and was unequaled until Perón came to power. Therefore, Villanueva argues, while the 1930s were surely a time of industrial growth the real takeoff actually began a decade earlier.[5]

Rostow himself dates Argentina's takeoff at around 1935: "In one sense the Argentine economy began its take-off during the First World War. But by and large, down to the post-1929 depression, the growth of its modern sector, stimulated by the war, tended to slacken; and, like a good part of the Western world, the Argentines sought during the 1920s to return to a pre-1914 normalcy. It was not until the mid-1930s that a sustained take-off was inaugurated, which by and large can now be judged to have been successful despite the structural vicissitudes of that economy."[6]

This statement that supports Di Tella and Zymelman in locating the takeoff, contradicts both them and Villanueva by viewing World War I as a stimulus to industry rather than as slowing it down. Thus, in searching for this elusive takeoff it might be well to begin by examining the impact of the First World War.

## Industry during World War I

A serious problem arises at the outset when trying to assess the effect of World War I on Argentine industry. No industrial census was taken between 1913 and 1935, so there is no way of directly comparing the level of manufacturing in the immediate prewar and postwar periods nor at the beginning and end of the 1920s. We know that the number of industrial establishments dropped between 1913 and 1935 from 48,779 to only 38,456. That decrease occurred partly because census takers in 1935 eliminated certain activities that previously had been counted as industrial: shoe repair shops, photography studios, seamstresses' shops, hairdressing parlors, etc. Those businesses accounted for about 4,000 establishments, so the remaining 60 percent of the decline was still due to contraction. The knotty question is: Did that contraction take place mainly during the war, during the 1920s, or between the onset of the depression and 1935?

Other intriguing and equally difficult questions arise in comparing these two censuses. For example, in contrast to the decline in establishments there was a slight increase in the number of industrial workers and a very great increase in the amount of horsepower used in industry. The number of workers rose from 410,201 in 1913 to 467,315: an increase of 14 percent, or less than 1 percent a year. (The increase would have been only slightly higher if the establishments not counted in 1935 had been left out of the 1913 census as well.) But if the average factory gained somewhat in scale, the real leap forward was in installed horsepower, which quadrupled. That indicates a determined drive toward modernization, but again the question confronts us: At what point did this drive begin?

Some contemporary observers, as well as subsequent scholars, argued that Germany's submarine blockade of Britain that cut off Argentina's supply of industrial imports forced many local producers into existence to fill the vacuum. Alejandro Bunge, head of the National Statistical Office, estimated that between 1913 and 1923 the number of factories increased from 48,779 to around 61,000; the number of workers from 410,201 to 600,000; the amount of capital invested from 1.8 billion to 2.5 billion pesos; installed horsepower from 679,000 to over 1 million; and the value of production from 1.9 billion to 2.9 billion pesos.[7]

On the other hand, an equally impressive body of scholarship emphasizes the war's negative impact. While certain industries may have expanded, others, like metallurgy and machine building, were hurt for want of capital goods, fuel, replacement parts, and raw materials. There was a sharp increase in business failures, with liabilities involved in bankruptcy proceedings rising from 198.4 million pesos in 1913 to 440.1 million the following year. Urban unemployment tripled between 1913 and 1917 from 6.7 to 19.4 percent. Overall investment dropped considerably between 1915 and 1919 as compared with its rapid increase in the years just before the war.[8]

It is true, nevertheless, that conditions improved as the war went on. Toward the end of 1916 the Public Works Bureau of the city of Buenos Aires began to issue more licenses to open factories. Indus-

Table 3.1 Patterns of Industrial Growth, 1895–1946

| Year | Number of Establishments | Annual Increase (%) | Number of Workers | Annual Increase (%) |
|------|------|------|------|------|
| 1895 | 24,114 |  | 174,782 |  |
| 1913 | 47,343 | 5.4 | 363,771 | 6.0 |
| 1923[a] | 61,000[a] | 2.9[b] | 600,000[a] | 6.5[b] |
| 1935 | 37,362 | −3.2[b] | 437,816 | −2.3[b] |
|  |  | −1.0[c] |  | 0.9[c] |
| 1937 | 45,263 | 10.6 | 539,525 | 11.6 |
| 1939 | 49,100 | 4.2 | 581,599 | 3.9 |
| 1941 | 52,445 | 3.4 | 684,497 | 8.8 |
| 1943 | 59,765 | 7.0 | 820,470 | 9.9 |
| 1946 | 84,905 | 14.0 | 1,058,673 | 9.7 |

Source: All except 1923 are from official Argentine industrial censuses.
[a] Bunge's estimates.
[b] Relative to Bunge's estimates.
[c] Relative to the 1913 census.

trial output began to swing upward to prewar levels during 1918–19, and more jobs were available. However, all things considered, the period from 1913 to 1917 was one of the worst recessions that Argentina had ever faced.

## The Postwar Shakeout

If Bunge's estimates are even approximately right, the war years saw the emergence of domestic industrial capital in a leadership role. Using horsepower as a proxy for capital investment, which we must do since the 1935 census did not publish figures on the latter, it seems as if the period from 1913 to 1923 was a time of unprecedented industrial growth. That spurt forward was followed by retrenchment, however. The 1920s were a time of painful readjustments for industry because the number of firms dropped by 37 percent between 1923 and 1935 while the work force decreased by about one-fifth. Companies launched to meet the wartime demand with little capital could not survive once peacetime brought competing foreign manufactures back to the marketplace. Knowing that the good times would not last, many wartime entrepreneurs did

| Workers per Establishment | Installed Horsepower | Annual Increase (%) | Horsepower per Establishment | Horsepower per Worker |
|---|---|---|---|---|
| 7.2 | 60,033 | | 2.49 | 0.34 |
| 7.7 | 237,817 | 16.5 | 5.02 | 0.65 |
| 9.8[b] | 1,000,000 | 32.0[b] | 16.39[b] | 1.67[b] |
| 11.7 | 1,026,086 | 0.2[b] | 27.46 | 2.34 |
| | | 15.1[c] | | |
| 11.9 | 1,190,493 | 8.0 | 26.30 | 2.21 |
| 11.8 | 1,423,872 | 9.8 | 29.00 | 2.45 |
| 13.1 | 1,645,041 | 7.8 | 31.37 | 2.40 |
| 13.7 | 1,836,453 | 5.8 | 30.73 | 2.24 |
| 12.5 | 2,076,531 | 4.4 | 24.46 | 1.96 |

not reinvest their profits in better equipment or larger plants, preferring instead to put their money into government bonds and treasury notes. By contrast, those companies that survived the postwar shakeout were larger and better capitalized than before. This suggests that the takeoff occurred sometime between 1919 and 1929, since the early war years and the early depression years were periods of disruption.

If, on the other hand, we dismiss Bunge's estimates as being too uncertain, then it is impossible to fix the approximate date of the takeoff except to say that it must have occurred sometime between 1913 and 1935. After 1935 there was a slackening in the rate of increase in installed horsepower, in the ratio of horsepower to establishments, and in the ratio of horsepower to hand labor. In fact, the takeoff probably took place before 1935 or 1929, since it is generally conceded that the economy was at first thrown into confusion by the depression and did not begin to recover until after 1932. Bankruptcy statistics support this idea: in terms of peso liabilities involved, bankruptcies rose from 1929 to a peak in 1931 and did not drop below the 1929 level again until 1934.[9]

Of course this is only from the point of view of the magnitude of investment, which is central to Rostow's definition of takeoff. In other respects, industrialization proceeded more rapidly after 1935. There were constant increases in the number of factories, workers employed, and the ratio of workers to establishments. All of these increases occurred as the rate of adding horsepower slowed down, which suggests that while Argentine industry had been getting more capital intensive during the 1920s it turned to more labor-intensive methods in the 1930s. That was not the sort of industrialization that would turn Argentina into a world economic power.

## The Era of Import Substitution

Was there a takeoff in the 1920s? In terms of the magnitude of investment, yes. But if takeoff means a great upward and onward thrust leading to self-sustaining growth, then the 1920s produced a false start, for they were followed by a period of makeshift industrialization during which industry expanded in terms of entrepreneurs, factories, and workers, but not in capital intensity. Thus, the Rostovian theory of how growth proceeds in stages seems less applicable to the Argentine case than the theory of W. A. Lewis who prefers to see growth as happening in occasional surges that have no predictable pattern. For Lewis, those bursts of economic energy result from various stimuli—a technological breakthrough, the discovery of new resources, the opening of new markets—that eventually run their course. After they do, the dynamic period is followed by one of relative inactivity.[10]

Capital investment in industry slowed down, first, because during the depression Argentina could not afford imports of machinery, fuel, and equipment. Falling exports deprived the country of the necessary foreign exchange, and it was only by signing the unpopular Roca-Runciman Treaty with Great Britain in 1932 that the government was able to prevent the loss of the country's most important market for its beef. By that agreement, Argentina promised to give preferential treatment to British manufactures and to be especially accommodating to British businesses already located in Argentina, in return for a British promise to keep meat purchases at their 1931 levels. At first this looked like the sacrifice of Argentine industry in order to save agriculture, but things did not work out that way. Although the volume of meat exports was maintained, falling world prices kept farmers on the edge of bankruptcy and lowered Argentina's capacity to import. Unfavorable trade balances drained the country's exchange reserves, forcing it off the gold standard in 1933 and making it necessary to restrict imports through a licensing system. The peso was deliberately undervalued so as to increase exports; but this devaluation also had the effect of making imports more expensive.[11] While those measures limited the inflow of foreign industrial goods, the demand for textiles, clothing, hardware, cosmetics, drugs, finished metal products, cigarettes, appliances, and alcoholic beverages remained high. Local industry quickly expanded to fill the gap, but at the same time Argentina's reduced import capacity meant that there would be shortages of machinery, motors, fuels, lubricants, and electrical parts. Thus, industry could expand to meet demand only by hiring more workers and becoming more labor intensive rather than capital intensive. At the time, that was a welcome solution because of the need to reduce unemployment, but it was to have serious consequences for future development.

The period from the beginning of the Great Depression to Perón's first presidency can be divided into four phases. The first, from 1929 to 1932, was one of disorientation characterized by the 1930 military coup that replaced Yrigoyen with General Uriburu, the sudden plunge in export sales, and a rising number of bankruptcies—including many *estancieros*. The second phase, from 1932 to 1937, showed a revival of industry. Note, in table 3.1, the big jump in industrial establishments and industrial workers between 1935 and 1937. (Note too, however, the sharp slowdown in the addition of horsepower.) The third phase, from 1937 to about 1941, marked another recession, as indicated by a slowdown in new establishments, new workers, and horsepower. The number of bankruptcies, which had been declining steadily from 1931 through 1936, suddenly rose again and continued to rise through 1940. The fourth phase, from 1941 to 1946, saw another industrial recovery due to the stimulus of war. Again, however, this recovery was based on labor-intensive, not capital-intensive, industry. The ratio of horsepower to hand labor was lower during World War II than it had been in 1935. Although many new establishments appeared and large numbers of workers were hired, the average factory was actually smaller in 1946 than in 1941. In brief, the war mainly encouraged the proliferation of many small-scale, poorly capitalized, and technologically backward firms.

Unlike older, well-established businesses, these newer firms could exist only with government protection. Spared from competition during the depression, they were coddled even more after a very nationalistic military regime took power via a coup in June 1943. Determined to make Argentina self-sufficient, the military rulers gave official encouragement, through tariffs and subsidies, to any import-substituting activity. Consequently, Argentine industry acquired a dualistic character. As table 3.2 shows, those enterprises

Table 3.2 Employment and Productivity
in Argentine Industrial Firms

| Period of Founding | Percentage of Establishments | Percentage of Workers | Percentage of Value of Production |
|---|---|---|---|
| *Liberal era* | | | |
| Before 1870 | 0.3 | 1.7 | 2.0 |
| 1871–90 | 1.4 | 6.4 | 6.8 |
| 1891–1900 | 2.1 | 6.8 | 7.8 |
| 1901–10 | 4.6 | 10.5 | 10.1 |
| 1911–20 | 8.9 | 12.5 | 14.2 |
| 1921–30 | 19.7 | 18.7 | 20.5 |
| Subtotal | 37.0 | 56.6 | 61.4 |
| | | | |
| *Import-substitution era* | | | |
| 1931–41 | 32.5 | 25.6 | 25.2 |
| 1941–46 | 29.1 | 15.2 | 11.4 |
| Subtotal | 61.6 | 40.8 | 36.6 |
| | | | |
| *Unknown* | 1.4 | 2.5 | 2.0 |
| | | | |
| Total | 100.0 | 100.0 | 100.0 |

Source: *Cuarto censo nacional* (Buenos Aires: Dirección General del Servício Estadístico Nacional, 1952).

founded before the age of protectionism, when industry was still "the orphan of every national tradition," were larger and more productive. Although they were only 37 percent of all establishments, they employed 56.6 percent of the workers and accounted for 61.4 percent of the value of all industrial goods produced in 1946. By contrast, establishments founded after 1930 during the era of officially encouraged import substitution constituted 61.6 percent of all firms but employed only 40 percent of the workers and contributed only 36.6 percent of the total value of production.

Though relatively inefficient, these newer industries were more likely to receive official encouragement because they were in dynamic fields like metallurgy, chemicals, rubber, petroleum derivatives, and electrical machinery that were deemed essential to industrial self-sufficiency. A symbiotic relationship grew up in which these infant industries gladly accepted state regulation in return for protection and nurturing. Older sectors of industry were by no means loathe to accept loans and tariff protection, but, having sprung from a more laissez-faire tradition, they were more likely to resist the controls that came with government aid.

## The Location of Industry

Between 1913 and 1935, industry was concentrated in Greater Buenos Aires. Whereas the federal district and Buenos Aires Province had 51.6 percent of the factories, 60.5 percent of the workers, and 66 percent of the horsepower in the former year, by the latter these areas contained 58.2 percent, 72.2 percent, and 68 percent, respectively. After 1935 the interior began to recover some lost ground. As of 1946, the Buenos Aires hub had declined slightly to only 56.6 percent of the factories, 69.7 percent of the work force, and 61.8 percent of the horsepower. Still, the average factory there was much larger, employing 17.7 workers in the federal district and 13.8 in Buenos Aires Province as compared with 8.8 for the rest of the country. On the other hand, the most capital-intensive industry was to be found in the interior. In 1946 the ratio of horsepower to hand labor was 4.73 in the interior, 4.38 in Buenos Aires Province, and 2.56 in the federal district. This was not just a statistical fluke caused by a decline in the number of factories or workers. There were many more of both in 1946 than in 1935, so the gains must be interpreted as reflecting an effort on the part of provincial entrepreneurs to modernize. The popular image that *porteños* are progressive while the interior is hidebound needs to be modified.

## The Branches of Industry

Food processing was the most important branch of industry in terms of the number of entrepreneurs it attracted, the number of workers employed, and the volume and value of production. Although most establishments were small in scale, some lines of production, such as meatpacking, sugar refining, and beer brewing, were dominated by a few big companies. American firms like Swift, Wilson, and Armour and the British firms of Smithfield and Vesty dominated meatpacking, with only Sansenina representing local capital. Sugar refining was under the control of two giant local companies: San Martín de Tabacal, owned by Robustiano Patrón Costas, the boss of Salta Province; and Ledesma Estates and Refining Company, owned by Hermínio Arrieta, the boss of Jujuy Province. Despite their political conservatism, both Arrieta and Patrón Costas were progressive businessmen who were willing to spend a lot of money mechanizing their refineries. In fact, they produced more sugar than the market would bear, forcing the state to buy up the surplus to avoid a collapse that would have thrown hundreds of growers into bankruptcy. As for the beer industry, the largest company, Quilmes, was one of the world's leading producers. Owned by Otto Bemberg, the head of one of Argentina's richest families, its operations were completely modern.

At the other end of the spectrum, the bakery, dairy, wine, and nonalcoholic beverage industries were typified by small, poorly equipped shops that competed ferociously for limited markets. Medium-sized and slightly mechanized plants were the rule in the flour-milling, edible oil, candy, and alcoholic beverage sectors. These assessments are generalizations based on statistical averages. One important exception was the huge Molinos Río de La Plata, Argentina's leading producer of flour, vegetable oil, margarine, rice, yerba mate, and mayonnaise. Indeed, Molinos was multinational in scope, with branch factories in Paraguay and Uruguay.

More dynamic than food processing, however, was the textile industry, which underwent a real revolution in the 1920s. In 1913 there were 1,530 spinning and weaving shops in Argentina, most of them cottage-type establishments located in the northwestern provinces of Catamarca and Salta. The vast majority of these consisted of women spinning yarn by hand or weaving cloth on hand looms. By 1935 that type of textile operation had all but disappeared. The number of establishments dropped drastically to only 148; by contrast, the amount of installed horsepower increased from 1,832 to 37,268, the number of workers employed from 5,690 to 25,055, and the average size of an establishment from 3.7 workers to 169.3. Production was centered in Greater Buenos Aires. Cotton yarn and cloth were the leading goods followed by wool. Silk lagged far behind these, and synthetics did not begin to assume importance until the 1940s.

After 1935 the textile industry lost some of its dynamism. Although more factories were started and more workers employed, the combination of protectionism and the scarcity of capital goods imports meant that most new enterprises were poorly capitalized and inefficient. The average factory was smaller and had a poorer ratio of horsepower to hand labor. Still, the average textile mill was larger than the average food-processing plant or tobacco factory.

Argentina took its first steps toward creating heavy industry with the help of some foreign capital, but efforts by local entrepreneurs were also involved. Until the 1930s, Argentina's chemical industry consisted almost entirely of small shops that turned out soap, perfumes, simple medicines, and paint. This began to change with the arrival of Duperial, a British firm, and Ducilo, a subsidiary of Dupont. Also during the 1930s, the Bunge & Born food-processing conglomerate started Compañía Química to produce tartaric acid and cream of tartar, which are by-products of wine making, and soon branched into producing synthetic resins. Another local conglomerate, Fabril Financiera, started Electroclor, a producer of caustic soda, chlorine, and synthetic fibers, as a spin-off of its paper and pulp mills. In 1938 a consortium of *porteño* investors created Atanor to produce oxygenized water, alcohol from cane sugar, and various acetates needed for the booming textile industry.

The petroleum industry, which began in 1907 with the discovery of oil in Patagonia, was divided into concessions granted to foreign companies such as Standard Oil and Shell and those reserved for the state oil company, Yacimientos Petrolíferos Fiscales (YPF). The state reserves were inefficiently exploited, thanks to neglect by the Radical governments during the 1920s. Short of trained workers and administrators, YPF was forced to finance its own growth with its profits. To its credit, it increased production sevenfold during the 1920s. Private output also rose, but Argentina did not become a main target for oil investment. With the growth of nationalist sentiment in the 1930s, foreign capital began to withdraw, and there was not enough local investment to make up the difference. This situation created a bottleneck that hindered industrial growth.

The metallurgical sector was quite modest by American or European standards. There was nothing that could really be called a steel mill. The lack of iron ore and coking coal held back the development of this industry, although after 1943 the military began a push to develop domestic steel production at any cost for defense purposes. As of the 1946 census, steel was still being produced mainly by small foundries, of which only four were significant. Three, TAMET, La Cantábrica, and Gurmendi, were locally owned. The fourth, a factory called Santa Rosa, was founded in 1943 by French capital fleeing the war in Europe.

More progress was evident in the machine-building industry, which, unlike most other sectors during the depression, added more factories, workers, and horsepower. Even so, it was still small-scale, and very little capital was needed to get a start. Many factory own-

ers had a more artisan than capitalist outlook. Grandes Estableci-
mientos, the leading manufacturer of lathes, produced only 800 a
year on the eve of World War II. Its owner, Adam Goscilo, a Polish
immigrant mechanic, preferred to concentrate on improving the
style and quantity of his lathes rather than produce in quantity. His
concentration on craftsmanship paid off by earning him a reputation that allowed him to beat even foreign competition in certain
lines. Very similar in its approach was La Lombarda, the country's
foremost producer of valves. This company was started during the
depression by Carlos Maria Frigeri, an Italian immigrant whose
original capital of 500 pesos was spent in buying a used lathe, a five-
horsepower motor, a used furnace and boiler, and enough tin to
build a shed on a vacant lot. His first contract was to cast parts for
ship repairs. Like Goscilo, Frigeri quickly won a reputation for high-
quality work, and soon many firms were sending him orders. One
customer, a company owned by the Austrian magnate Thyssen,
gave him a permanent contract to do all its work. Within ten years,
Frigeri was able to build a whole new plant equipped with the latest
machinery and to diversify his operations.[12]

Another dynamic industrial sector produced electrical machinery
and appliances, including a wide range of goods from lamps and
radios to refrigerators and electrical motors for industry. The largest company was a giant called SIAM Di Tella, the creation of an
amazing individual, Torcuato S. Di Tella. A young Italian immigrant
who started his first plant in 1910 on borrowed money, Di Tella
made electric bread-kneading machines. By 1920 he was producing
his own replacement parts from a foundry he had purchased. The
foundry, in turn, enabled him to explore other production lines such
as gasoline pumps. Through his close association with another
Italo-Argentine, General Enrique Mosconi, the director of YPF, Di
Tella landed a contract to supply pumps to all the state-owned gas
stations. Other service station equipment soon followed. Meanwhile, Di Tella also developed an electric oven for the bakery industry. In the following decade SIAM branched out into electric motors,
hydraulic pumps, freezers, heaters, and refrigerators. By World War
II, SIAM's original capital of 10,000 pesos had grown to assets total-
ing 128 million. It was the largest company of its kind in South
America and had become a multinational with branches in Brazil,
Chile, and Uruguay.[13]

The rise of great industrial establishments like SIAM would have
been impossible, of course, without the parallel development of the
electrical and gas sectors. Between 1913 and 1946 the number of

such utilities tripled from 305 to 991; the number of workers employed in them increased by 138 percent from 9,916 to 23,627; and installed horsepower rose by 374 percent from 391,959 to 1,858,856. Most of this growth occurred before 1935. Foreign capital played an essential role in the initiation, expansion, and modernization of these services.

At the other extreme, traditional industries like the production of clothing and leather goods, woodworking, brickmaking, and glassmaking continued to be typified by very small, poorly capitalized, and technologically backward firms. For example, as late as the 1946 census almost a third of the enterprises in the clothing industry were merely tailors or seamstresses working on their own— most of them without even an electric sewing machine.

## Summary

At the time of Argentina's centennial, in 1910, industry had emerged as a dynamic and diverse part of the economy. No manufacturing activity had been recorded in 1869. By 1895, however, agricultural progress, internal improvements, and the great influx of immigrants had stimulated the growth of manufacturing in many parts of the country. In the next three decades it would begin to overtake agriculture in attracting capital, providing jobs, and contributing to the gross national product (GNP).

By the end of World War II, Argentina had become Latin America's leading industrial nation. Industries like food and textiles had undergone considerable modernization and were fully capable of satisfying the domestic market. Beyond that, however, heavy industry—paper, chemicals, rubber, metallurgy, and machinery—was starting to make its appearance. Pockets of stagnation like the clothing, wood, and leather industries could not affect the overall picture of a country poised on the verge of taking its place as a fully developed industrial power.

The picture is one of an industrial transformation taking place, although it is difficult to pinpoint exactly when that process reached its crucial stage or takeoff. Indeed, there are many ongoing debates concerning Argentina's history of industrialization. For example, did World War I boost the process of industrialization or slow it down? One thing is certain: the war's disruption of traditional world trade patterns gave an impetus to some industrial sectors while undermining the old assumption that Argentina could always depend on foreign suppliers for its finished goods. When the next major disruption—the Great Depression—came, it was to adopt new policies of import substitution that committed the government to deliberately fostering industrialization.

It is the era of official import substitution, the 1930s, that most writers point to as the time of Argentina's greatest industrial progress, whereas the 1920s are dismissed as a kind of Indian summer for the old agrarian society. In terms of the overall volume of manufacturing, that may be accurate. More factories were started in the 1930s, and more workers found jobs in industry. But if the pace of growth, measured by how much new horsepower was added to manufacturing, is taken as the sign of a takeoff, then the 1920s seem more dynamic.

Indeed, the 1930s may be viewed as a slowing down of industrial progress because the newer factories were smaller, on the average, and more labor intensive. Furthermore, the import-substitution policies of the Conservative governments of the 1930s presaged the more intensive government regulation of the economy that would come with the army's revolution in 1943 and the Peronist regime that eventually grew out of it.

Viewed in this light, the trends of the 1930s all pointed in the wrong direction for Argentina's future development. Manufacturing would emerge technologically backward from the depression and World War II years. Small-scale, poorly capitalized, inefficient, and unable to survive without government aid, the newer industries would become entrenched interests, fighting to keep protection, subsidies, and market regulation. Furthermore, as workers became organized into powerful unions under Perón, it would become all the more difficult to replace them with labor-saving machinery. Workers and new industrialists would become partners in a populist coalition that would transform Argentina's capitalist system into a corporative state.

None of this should obscure, however, the accomplishments of Argentina's many true entrepreneurs. Largely ignored by official policymakers until the depression and by local financiers, they nevertheless accomplished a modest industrial revolution. That they were able to progress as well as they did is testimony to a greater capitalist spirit than they usually are given credit for.

The next chapter will describe the origins, business methods, and political practices of Argentina's leading entrepreneurs. We shall see how they started their businesses, expanded them, and overcame the problems of financing, marketing, and supplies. We shall also see them in relation to both foreign capital and the state. In the process, the Argentine industrialist will gradually change from a background character on the economic stage to a leading protagonist.

## CHAPTER FOUR

# Capital and Capitalists

By the end of the 1930s, Argentine industry was no longer an orphan. It attracted more investment and employed more labor than agriculture, and it enjoyed greater prestige among modern planners and politicians as being the key to national economic independence. But even though it had come a long way, its rate of progress had been uneven: great surges forward were separated by periods of slower growth. Table 4.1, which shows the rate and sources of capital accumulation at intervals between 1900 and 1945, helps to explain why.

Argentine capitalism moved ahead so quickly in the years preceding World War I obviously because it had an abundance of capital to work with. Between 1900 and 1914, capital accumulated at an average rate of about 9 percent a year. Meanwhile, the population grew by only 4 percent a year, leaving an appreciable net gain in the country's per capita wealth. This trend ended with the war. The rate of accumulation dropped sharply and steadily until, between 1917 and 1920, there was a net loss of capital. The war years had an average accumulation rate of only 1.5 percent that was not enough to keep pace with a 3 percent growth in the population.

After the war, the rate of accumulation began to increase again, recording an average of 2.4 percent annually during the 1920s: not as high as before but enough to keep up with the population's growth. Moreover, capital formation began to gather momentum as the decade wore on. Once again, however, progress was halted, first by the Great Depression and then by World War II. There was a net loss of capital in the early 1930s followed by a weak rally that lasted until war broke out again, after which there was almost complete stagnation. Considering that capital accumulation averaged only 1.8 percent a year from 1930 to 1945 while the population increased by about 2 percent, it is evident that Argentine capitalism had lost its earlier dynamism. Small wonder that capital-starved industry turned to labor-intensive methods.

Table 4.1 Capital Accumulation in Argentina, 1900–1945
(in thousands of constant 1950 U.S. dollars)

| Year | Total Capital | Annual Increase (%) | Foreign Capital | Annual Increase (%) | Domestic Capital | Annual Increase (%) | Foreign Capital as Percentage of Total Capital |
|------|------|------|------|------|------|------|------|
| 1900 | 6,347 | — | 2,020 | — | 4,327 | — | 31.8 |
| 1909 | 12,966 | 11.6 | 5,250 | 17.8 | 7,716 | 8.7 | 40.5 |
| 1913 | 17,237 | 8.2 | 8,230 | 14.2 | 9,007 | 4.2 | 47.7 |
| 1917 | 17,517 | 0.4 | 7,980 | −0.8 | 9,537 | 1.5 | 45.6 |
| 1920 | 17,464 | −0.1 | 7,300 | −2.8 | 10,164 | 2.2 | 41.8 |
| 1923 | 19,061 | 3.0 | 7,100 | −0.9 | 11,961 | 5.9 | 37.2 |
| 1927 | 22,030 | 3.9 | 7,580 | 1.7 | 14,450 | 5.2 | 34.4 |
| 1929 | 24,474 | 5.5 | 7,835 | 1.7 | 16,639 | 7.6 | 32.0 |
| 1931 | 25,582 | 2.3 | 7,640 | −1.2 | 17,942 | 3.9 | 30.0 |
| 1934 | 25,479 | −0.1 | 6,920 | −3.1 | 18,559 | 1.1 | 27.2 |
| 1940 | 27,365 | 1.2 | 5,570 | −3.3 | 21,795 | 2.9 | 20.4 |
| 1945 | 27,654 | 0.2 | 4,260 | −4.7 | 23,394 | 1.5 | 15.4 |

Source: ECLA, *El desarrollo económico de la Argentina* (Santiago de Chile: ECLA, 1958), p. 89.

Why did capital accumulation fluctuate so? Again, table 4.1 provides the answer. It is obvious that the boom years preceding World War I were stimulated largely by sizable inputs of foreign investment. That ended with the war years, when there was indeed a net loss. The 1920s saw a very slight recovery in the level of foreign investment, but that was followed by massive withdrawals during the depression and World War II. Given such a close correlation between influxes and withdrawals of foreign capital and the rate of capital accumulation, it is hard to avoid the conclusion that Argentina's development was very dependent on overseas investors. Where, then, were the domestic entrepreneurs?

Domestic capital had been growing before World War I, but at a slower rate than foreign capital. In fact, just before the war it represented a smaller share of the total than it had at the turn of the century. Unlike foreign investors, however, domestic capitalists continued to invest in local industry, although at a much slower pace. Once the war ended, domestic investment suddenly increased very rapidly, making possible the 1920s boom. As with foreign capital, there was a drop in the rate of accumulation during the depression and World War II, but gains were still being registered. In short, Argentine capitalists were active, not idle, but their efforts were not enough to offset the withdrawal of foreign investment.

## The Role of Foreign Capital

Foreign capital may be involved in development directly through investments or indirectly through loans. Argentina's railroads, electric and gas utilities, subway and autobus lines, telephone and telegraph systems, shipping companies, and packinghouses were all financed by direct investments. They were also among the most modern and large-scale enterprises in the nonagricultural economy. Their existence underscored the importance of foreign capital because heavy investment in transportation, communications, and energy allowed agriculture to modernize and industry to take root. Foreign capitalists also underwrote, through loans and the purchase of government bonds, many of the internal improvements undertaken by the Argentine government. Most early foreign investment was British, with lesser amounts coming from France, the United States, and Germany. As table 4.1 shows, foreign capital quadrupled in value between the turn of the century and World War I. The war constituted a watershed, however. The western European countries were forced to liquidate many of their overseas holdings to finance their war effort, and they certainly had no spare capital to lend Argentina. Nor, given the destruction of war, were they able to resume lending on the same scale as before. Meanwhile, United States bankers were only just beginning to take an interest in South America. Thus, foreign lenders made only a modest contribution to the progress of the 1920s.

Direct private investment was another matter. Several foreign companies moved to Argentina after the war. Distinct from earlier investors who were attracted mainly by the opportunities to export Argentine products, these new firms targeted the growing domestic market. In consumer durables, foreign companies included the Ford Motor Company, General Motors, the Dupont-Nemours Company, RCA Victor, and Otis Elevators, all American owned. In metallurgy, the Austrian steel tycoon Thyssen established a large foundry, as did the British firm of Partridge Jones and John Haton. International rubber giants like Pirelli, Goodyear, and Firestone also entered the scene. In pharmaceuticals and cosmetics, American interests were represented by Johnson and Johnson, Parke-Davis, and Colgate-Palmolive; the French by Guerlain; and the Germans by Bayer and by Merck and Company. The French also tried to crack the strongly domestic textile market with their Godde-Badin, Mondin Company, and Seda Artificial Rhodiaseta, a producer of rayon. In food processing, a number of firms with familiar names appeared: Crosse and Blackwell from England, Nestlé's from Switzerland, Cinzano from Italy, and Böls from the Netherlands. In utilities, the Greater Buenos Aires area was served by the Swiss-owned Compañía Italo-Argentina de Electricidad, the British-owned Compañía Primitiva de Gas, and the American-owned Unión Telefónica del Río de La Plata (which originally had been built with British capital). Another American investment was the American and Foreign Power Company, which was responsible for much of the electrification of the interior.

The Great Depression brought even more foreign companies because in 1933 Argentina abandoned the gold standard. The country also began setting official exchange rates lower than the free market and requiring importers to get licenses in order to buy foreign currencies—all of which discouraged imports. Foreign manufacturers either had to write off the Argentine market or locate subsidiaries inside the country. Among those who chose the latter course were American companies like Frigidaire, General Electric, Quaker Oats, Eveready Batteries, and Elizabeth Arden Cosmetics. The British were not far behind with Lever Brothers, the Linen Thread Company, and the Dunlop Rubber Company. From France came Coty Cosmetics and the Michelin Tire Company. In the field of electrical motors and appliances there were Phillips from Holland, and Siemens and Osram from Germany.

In some cases, a foreign company might prefer to buy a local firm rather than start a new one. Such was the case when the Corning Glassworks and the Pittsburgh Plate Glass Company bought controlling interest in Cristalerías Rigolleau in 1942. The Argentine company had been in financial difficulties for years, so the new arrangement allowed it to pay its debts, refurbish its factories, and increase its capital. For their part, the Americans acquired an old and prestigious firm that already enjoyed a commanding position in its field and established connections with both suppliers and buyers.

As of 1940, the distribution of foreign capital in Argentina was as follows: about 41 percent was in railroads, another 21 percent was in public services such as electricity and telephones, 21 percent was in banking and bonds, just under 4 percent was in commerce and insurance, and the remaining 13 percent was in industry, mostly in meatpacking. The total value of these investments was estimated at $3.3 billion, of which one-fifth belonged to Americans.[1]

Direct foreign investment could not make up for a lack of finance capital, however. Moreover, many initial investments were not followed up with more capital. Growing nationalist sentiment that began to manifest itself in the 1930s discouraged foreign companies from sinking too much money into the Argentine economy. Meatpacking was one foreign-dominated sector that particularly attracted local resentment because the handful of American and British companies that controlled it apparently had gentlemen's agreements about the prices they would pay for cattle and how they would carve up the export market. Although strongly in favor of free enterprise in most matters, the Argentine Rural Society (SRA) became almost revolutionary in its denunciations of the "meat trust" and in its insistence upon government action to break the controlling companies' stranglehold on the market. The SRA even waved the flag of populist nationalism, pointing out that over 80 percent of the country's ranchers were small producers with fewer than 200 head of cattle. How could the small rancher, the backbone of Argentina's wholesome rural traditions, stay in business if cattle could be sold only at a single take-it-or-leave-it price previously agreed upon by the packers? If the rancher balked, he risked being left with rapidly depreciating cattle. In 1923 the government, ever responsive to *estanciero* demands, set minimum prices for cattle brought to market, but this proved to be a Pyrrhic victory. The meatpackers forced the government and the *estancieros* to back down by refusing to buy any cattle at all.[2]

The depression, which brought a catastrophic drop in meat prices, heightened the struggle between the ranchers and the meatpackers. This time the government sought to break the meatpackers' buying monopoly by setting up the National Meat Board (Junta Nacional de Carnes) in 1933. All packinghouses were required to register with the board, conform to its system of grading livestock and cuts of meat, and comply with a system of minimum prices. The board also claimed the power to examine the companies' accounts. To prevent the companies from retaliating by refusing to buy, the board created the Argentine Meat-Producers' Corporation (CAP), an autonomous agency that entered into competition with the foreign packinghouses as a purchaser of cattle and exporter of meat. CAP's management was drawn from the *estancieros*, and its operating expenses were financed by a tax on the ranchers and butchers. Thus armed, the National Meat Board was ready to take on recalcitrant companies. When one of the packers refused to submit monthly reports, the board took its case to the Supreme Court, which ordered the company closed down. As time went on the board increased its powers. At first it owned no packinghouses of its own but simply subcontracted those operations to private local slaughterhouses. Prodding by smaller ranchers finally got the board to open its own plants in the early 1940s, however. During World War II, the board extended its controls by placing price ceilings on meat and limiting certain kinds of exports in order to have enough for the domestic market.[3]

The oil industry was another area where nationalist feelings ran high. General Enrique Mosconi, the father of Argentina's state oil company, YPF, related in his memoirs how in 1922, while he was director of the army air force, a Standard Oil subsidiary had refused to deliver gasoline for military airplanes unless it received payment in advance. Considering the cavalier manner in which the Argentine government usually handles its debts to suppliers, Standard Oil's action was perhaps understandable, but it was not politic. The company made an enemy of Mosconi, who became head of YPF the following year after publishing an article about the affair that caught the eye of President Alvear.

Under Mosconi, YPF embarked upon a bitter rivalry with Standard Oil, the largest private oil company in Argentina. In 1923 all oil refineries were privately owned, as were all the tankers; so even though three-fourths of all oil production came from YPF wells, Standard Oil and other private companies could control the flow of oil to the market. Also, Standard Oil produced over 80 percent of the gasoline and 95 percent of the kerosene used in Argentina. With Mosconi as its president, YPF completed the construction of three state oil refineries, purchased a fleet of tankers, built new storage facilities, and set up a chain of service stations all over the country. Mosconi's great personal popularity and his successful campaign to identify YPF with Argentine nationalism convinced the government and the army to purchase their oil and gas supplies exclusively from YPF. In 1929 he took advantage of a worldwide glut in petroleum to force the lowering of prices for oil, gas, and kerosene by starting a price war with the private companies. To insure that they could not retaliate by shutting off all imports of petroleum products to Argentina, Mosconi negotiated an agreement with the Soviet Union to purchase any amount necessary in the event of an international boycott.[4]

Mosconi was only partly successful in his struggle with Standard Oil, for although he raised YPF's production and extended its operations, the private sector grew even faster throughout the 1920s. Labor troubles often plagued YPF because Mosconi, in his desire to maximize profits to reinvest, tried to keep wages low and force workers to submit to military discipline. Despite his appeals to their patriotism, they rebelled. In 1924 and 1927 especially serious strikes were quelled by calling in marines.

Mosconi also failed to prevent Standard Oil from acquiring new concessions in Salta and Jujuy where large deposits were discovered in 1920. Friendly local politicians had too much influence in the Senate. Mosconi's attacks had such great popular response, however, that Hipólito Yrigoyen used them in his 1928 election campaign. Moreover, legislation to nationalize the oil industry was in preparation when the military overthrew Yrigoyen's government on 6 September 1930.[5]

As a pro-Radical officer, Mosconi was forced to resign after the coup and was sent to jail on trumped-up charges of mismanagement. But the battle between YPF and Standard Oil was not over. General Uriburu was succeeded in 1932 by Gen. Agustín P. Justo, who headed a coalition of Conservatives, anti-Yrigoyen Radicals, and maverick Socialists known as the "Concordancia." Having come to power through fraudulent elections, the Concordancia needed an issue to win popular support. Oil seemed to suit the occasion. In 1934 Justo issued a decree forbidding any new concessions to private companies. In retaliation, Standard Oil tried to drive YPF under by flooding the market with cheap imported oil. Forced to lower its prices, YPF accumulated big deficits that required the government to bail it out at great cost to the treasury. Public opinion was aroused. Newspapers excoriated American imperialism and called for nationalization. Students demonstrated in the streets. Justo responded by restricting oil imports and decreeing that any imported oil had to be apportioned equally between YPF and the private sector. He also appointed a commission to study the entire oil question.

The commission's report, issued in 1936, substantiated charges that Standard Oil was guilty of unfair competition, although it rejected related charges that some of the oil dumped on the market had been smuggled in. However, the report also criticized YPF's management for being swollen with political appointees and concluded that the state company should get out of oil production altogether and limit itself to marketing. Finally, the commission recommended the establishment of a permanent regulatory agency.

Justo accepted these recommendations only in part. In 1937 he bowed to nationalist sentiment by giving YPF a monopoly over all oil imports and prohibited any oil from being exported; thus, he guaranteed a sufficient local supply. He would not go further and expropriate, however; but the foreign companies, faced with so many restrictions as well as higher taxes, began winding down their operations anyway. Between 1934 and 1944, Standard Oil's output declined by more than a half, and under the ultranationalistic military government that took power in June 1943 it fell to almost nothing.

YPF thus won the war, but Argentina paid a price. Although YPF doubled its oil production between 1935 and 1937, doubled it again by 1939, and yet again by 1941, those impressive gains were canceled by the drop in private production. During World War II Argentina, already dependent on imports for 40 percent of its oil consumption, was driven to desperate measures to keep going. Herculean efforts by YPF kept production rising until 1943, but lack of machinery, equipment, and parts eventually took their toll. By 1945 oil production had fallen below the 1942 level while imports were less than a fourth of their yearly prewar average simply because of scarcity. It was necessary to resort to "potential combustible residuals"—oils extracted from wheat, corn, linseed, rice husks, and peanuts—to get fuels and lubricants. These accounted for about half of all the oil used during the war years, and they still were not enough: another reason why Argentine industry was driven to more labor-intensive methods.[6]

The railroads provide a third example of how formerly profitable businesses found themselves in trouble under the new nationalism. On 3 February 1942 the foreign railway companies sent a joint letter to the minister of public works asking for relief. According to them, their profits had fallen from 54.7 million pesos in 1935 to only 35.4 million in 1941. They claimed they could raise no money by selling stocks or bonds because they had been unable to pay dividends for the past twelve years. Consequently, they had been unable to replace some 50 worn-out locomotives and 3,000 cars and so had to cut back on service. They blamed their plight on government-controlled freight rates, which had been kept low in order to please the estancieros. They also complained about having to purchase British pounds at artificially high exchange rates in order to repatriate their profits, and they called for a halt in the government's highway building program, which they termed unfair competition because it would encourage trucking. They hinted that the government was out to ruin them deliberately so that it could buy them up cheaply after the war. In such a takeover, the companies warned, the government would only acquire a lot of depleted stock that would require heavy outlays to replace or refurbish.[7]

Such accusations were not without some foundation. In 1940 the Concordancia's finance minister, Federico Pinedo, had come up with an ingenious plan to use his country's favorable trade balance with Britain to buy up the railroads. The current sterling balance would become a down payment, with the balance to be liquidated over sixty years. In the meantime, the Argentine government and the private companies would create a mixed corporation to run the lines. The plan was workable but was killed in the Chamber of Deputies, where the Radical party's majority pounced on the fact that Pinedo had once been a lawyer for the railroads. Accusing him of a conflict of interest, they skillfully took a nationalist stance and branded the Concordancia as a gang of lackeys to foreign capital.[8]

Foreign utility companies had their troubles too. In 1942 the Compañía Italo-Argentina de Electricidad was subjected to a government investigation into its alleged excess profits after it raised its rates. Similar investigations were made of CADE, the German-owned electric company; the American and Foreign Power Company; the ITT-owned Unión Telefónica; and the British-owned Compañía Primitiva de Gas. These last three would eventually be nationalized by Perón.

Nationalism had its price. Without high levels of foreign investment to supplement domestic capital accumulation, the Argentine economy lost its ability to generate savings and investment on a scale large enough to outpace the growth of population. As the petroleum, electrical, gas, communications, and transportation sectors stagnated, bottlenecks appeared that would eventually stifle further growth. For the moment, however, nationalism made most Argentines indifferent to the withdrawal of foreign capital. Claims of economic efficiency were hard for the ordinary citizen to understand, but "Argentina for the Argentines" was a slogan that struck a deep, responsive emotional chord. Politicians were not slow to perceive that flogging the Anglo-Saxon imperialists was a quick route to popularity. As James Buchanan observed concerning the oil issue: "The advantages of adopting a nationalistic oil policy were considerable. The rhetoric of the nationalists refined and simplified the complex petroleum question until it became a choice between 'patriots' and 'traitors' and, therefore, admirably suited for mass consumption."[9] Once unleashed, emotional nationalism would remain for decades in the body politic like a fever, sometimes hot, sometimes quiescent, but never very far beneath the surface. It was to be a crucial factor in shaping the fate of Argentine capitalism.

## Private Domestic Capital

It is not always easy to separate domestic from foreign capital. Many companies involve both local and overseas investors. Furthermore, early census takers classified any firm organized under Argentine laws as domestic, even if the source of its capital and its headquarters lay outside the country. They also failed to distinguish between absentee foreign owners and immigrants, classifying any noncitizen born outside Argentina as foreign. Yet, it is important to know who the "foreigners" were that constituted 65 percent of all the industrial entrepreneurs and 72 percent of all the owners of commercial establishments in 1913.

That they were mainly immigrants seems likely because, outside of fields like meatpacking, petroleum, banking, railroads, insurance, shipping, and utilities, the small size of most manufacturing and commercial enterprises suggests a very limited capital base. In 1913 the average industrial establishment employed fewer than eight workers, and the average commercial establishment fewer than four. That is not the sort of operation likely to attract international capital. Additional evidence to support this theory comes from the 1904 industrial census taken in the city of Buenos Aires that not only classified factory ownership as foreign, Argentine, or mixed, but also classified the source of capital in the same way. According to the census, 89 percent of the city's industrial enterprises had completely foreign ownership (with another 3 percent being mixed), while 86 percent of all enterprises were locally financed. Since banks at that time were reluctant to make loans to small industrialists, it seems reasonable to conclude that local financing referred to the savings of the immigrant entrepreneurs themselves.[10]

The Entrepreneurial Spirit

Many immigrants came to Argentina between 1880 and 1914 seeking land, but finding little available that they could afford, they drifted into the towns. Others settled into urban life directly upon arriving. In either case, the rising population, railroad expansion, and growing trade created many new business opportunities. Census records for Buenos Aires Province show a rapid increase in commercial establishments of all kinds. Every little county seat and railroad junction needed a bar, a hotel, a cafe, a forge, a dry goods store, or a pharmacy. As more immigrants poured in, a variety of new food-processing industries were started: German beer factories, Italian pasta factories, various ethnic sausage makers, bakeries, and dairies.

On a national scale, among the most successful representatives of immigrant background and entrepreneurial spirit are León and Gastón Rigolleau, an uncle and nephew team who founded Cristalerías Rigolleau in 1882. They came to Argentina from Angoulême, where for generations their family had manufactured paper and ink (and possibly was one of the families depicted so savagely by Balzac in *Lost Illusions*). León Rigolleau's original intention upon arriving in Buenos Aires was to start an ink factory, but when he learned there were no locally produced glass bottles for holding ink he turned to glassmaking instead. It was difficult at first because there was no proper sand for making glass; that had to be imported. Fortunately though, some deposits were discovered a few years later in the Paraná River delta north of Buenos Aires, and Cristalerías Rigolleau soon became the first successful glassmaking firm in southern South America. An increasing number of German immigrants and the consequent expansion of the beer industry created a growing demand for Rigolleau's glass bottles. With only two furnaces, and often short of supplies, León Rigolleau worked alongside his nephew and a small staff of workers and managed to turn out 2,000 bottles a day. When León finally retired in 1899, nephew Gastón took over the business, moved it to a modern factory, and raised production to a million bottles a day.[11]

Benito Noel is an even better example of a versatile entrepreneur who was both industrialist and merchant. He inherited a small candy factory from his Basque immigrant father in 1865 and built it up to be the largest producer of chocolates and candied fruits. Noel got a lead on his competition when he began buying large tracts of land in the Paraná River delta and planting orchards, thus guaranteeing himself a cheap and plentiful supply of fruit for his candy. With a fleet of barges originally used to transport his fruit from the orchards to his factory, Noel even branched out into the river transport business. Finally, Noel was one of the first *porteño* businessmen to try mass advertising. When horse-drawn trolley cars began to crisscross the city, he paid for the right to paste signs on them advertising his latest lines of jellies and bonbons.[12]

When it came to industrialists merchandising their products, however, no one could top the ingenuity of Melville Sewell Bagley, an American go-getter from Maine. Bagley, who constantly shocked and amused the *porteños*, arrived in Argentina in the early 1860s as a book salesman. Charmed by Buenos Aires, he decided to stay. Bagley was always bothered by waste, and in Buenos Aires one of the most common forms of waste was orange peels. The fruit was popular, but the streets and parks were littered with its remnants. While working in a pharmacy, Bagley studied various ways to use orange peels and finally succeeded in distilling from them an orange-flavored alcoholic beverage that he called "La Hesperidina." In 1864 he set up a small factory to produce his beverage, which was launched on the market after an advertising campaign the likes of which Buenos Aires had never before witnessed. Bagley hired an army of urchins to go about the city sticking little signs reading "What is La Hesperidina?" on all the walls and scratching the same cryptic question in chalk on the sidewalks. The *porteño* public, bombarded from all sides by these words, became curious and titillated. The press quickly publicized the story. On 21 October 1864, the editor of *La Tribuna* commented, "Public curiosity is fixed upon signs that have appeared overnight everywhere, all over town. 'La Hesperidina!' What is the secret?" The editor thought he knew. "We can almost guarantee our readers that it is an oil which is said to be cheaper and just as good as kerosene."[13]

When Bagley brought out his product in time for the Christmas season, the public was primed for it. La Hesperidina came in little barrel-shaped bottles, each with a label bearing a picture of Bagley's handsome, mustachioed face. It was an immediate success. *La Tribuna*'s editor, unabashed by his wrong guess, was as enthusiastic as anyone else: "Today everyone in Buenos Aires knows it: 'La Hesperidina' is a bitter *digestif* made from sour orange peels. It is an excellent tonic, an agreeable, effective, and quick remedy for dyspepsia, indigestion, constipation, cholic, and nervous attacks." A popular home medicine book published the following year devoted several pages to La Hesperidina's salubrious qualities; and when

Argentina went to war with Paraguay in 1865, hundreds of cases of La Hesperidina went with the army as it marched north, for it was a favorite tonic with the soldiers.

Bagley was annoyed by competitors trying to imitate his product, including the bottle and the labels. At first he went to considerable expense by getting an American firm that printed banknotes to do his labels, making them impossible to copy. Eventually he persuaded President Mitre to set up a patent office. When it opened, Bagley's La Hesperidina was the first product to get a trademark. Since Bagley wanted to be in constant touch with his business, in 1878 he became the first *porteño* entrepreneur to install telephones in his factory, with lines running to his home. The press published the story as an extraordinary news item.

Men like Rigolleau, Noel, and Bagley created large, successful companies by dint of their own energy and ingenuity. Quick to spot new opportunities that others failed to see, willing to spend long hours patiently attending to business, and clever at finding ways to overcome obstacles, they represented the best of the new "self-made men." Nevertheless, they were overshadowed by still more powerful men in the Argentine business world. These were frequently the heads of family dynasties whose interests went beyond manufacturing and merchandising to the control of powerful financial institutions. Though originally of non-Iberian immigrant origins, their families had been in Argentina for two or three generations, had married into the Creole aristocracy, and had built up vast business empires—family-controlled conglomerates called *grupos*—that reached into every nook of the economy. Two such families were the Bunges and the Tornquists.

The Bunges got their start in Argentina in 1827, when Karl August Bunge von Reinessend und von Rauschenbusch, a young nobleman of minor rank and limited means, arrived in Buenos Aires to assume the post of consul general for the Kingdom of Prussia. His brother, Hugo, who made the journey with him, went into the export business. Both of these eligible bachelors soon made advantageous marriages with ladies of the Creole aristocracy. Karl August married a rich widow whose family was prominent in government, banking, and trade. Hugo's wife was from the Ramos Mejía family, which had extensive landholdings. In 1830 Karl August opened a bank whose ostensible purpose was to finance trade with Europe; its capital came, however, from the Bunges's rich Creole in-laws, who were anxious to hide as much as their wealth as possible from the depredations of the recently imposed dictator, Juan Manuel Rosas. By putting it in a bank whose director was a foreign diplomat they hoped to keep it safe.[14]

Karl August had four sons. The first, Emílio (1836–1909), was a military officer who served under the *porteño* leader, Mitre. Later he became president of the Buenos Aires city council, a provincial senator, and a national deputy. Through his friendship with Mitre and his family connections he had entrance to the highest circles, which were helpful when he finally turned to finance. Not only did Emílio have the prestige of the Casa Bunge, his father's bank, behind him, but his maternal grandfather was a former president of the Bank of the Province of Buenos Aires. Emílio Bunge eventually became vice-president of the latter bank. The second son, Ernesto (1839–94), studied to be an architect but is better known as the man who set up one of the country's leading flour-milling and grain-exporting enterprises: Bunge & Born. The company was started in 1884 as a partnership between Ernesto and his brother-in-law, Jorge Born, a Belgian immigrant. Again, family connections, this time with big grain farmers, enabled the firm to control a large share of Argentina's rapidly increasing exports of wheat and corn. From the export of grain it was but a short step to setting up a flour mill, which later grew into the mammoth Molinos Río de La Plata. Not long afterward, Molinos branched out into producing corn oil. Meanwhile, flour had to be put into bags, so Bunge & Born created another company, Centenera, to produce burlap bags. That enterprise also branched out into making soles for *alpargatas*, textile manufacturing, and, eventually, production of tin cans. By the centennial, Bunge & Born had grown into a huge conglomerate. Of the remaining sons, the third, Octavio (1844–1910), went into law and later became a Supreme Court justice; while the fourth, Rodolfo (1848–1919), went from the army into politics and then, after nearly wrecking his career by siding with the Radicals in the 1890 revolt, retired to dairy farming on the western pampa.

The Tornquists descended from a Swedish merchant family whose interests were already worldwide early in the nineteenth century. The founder of the Argentine line, Jorge Tornquist, had been tending the family's interests in Baltimore, his birthplace, when he was sent in 1823 to look after the branch offices in Montevideo and Buenos Aires. Since the Tornquists also had a large office in Hamburg, Jorge was given the additional duty of representing the Hanseatic cities in Argentina and Uruguay.[15]

Jorge Tornquist had only one son, Ernesto (1842–1908), but the boy turned out to be a marvel at business. Sent away at an early age to study in Germany, he returned when he was sixteen and got a job as a commercial agent in the firm of Altgelt, Ferber, & Company. He married the boss's daughter, Rosa Altgelt, and bided his time, learning about trade and finance. Finally, in 1877 his aging father installed him as head of the family firm. After his father's death in 1876, he reorganized the family business entirely and renamed it Ernesto Tornquist & Company. Under his direction, the Tornquist interests diversified: sugar estates in Tucumán, meatpacking (the Sansenina Frozen Meat Company), a refinery in Rosario, various metallurgical plants, and something called the Sociedad General, a mortgage company registered in Antwerp whose purpose was to funnel European capital into Argentina—or vice versa in bad times.

What raised men like Tornquist and Bunge above men like Bagley or Rigolleau was their control of finance capital. Ernesto Tornquist served on the board of directors of several banks, including the Bank of the Province of Buenos Aires and the National Mortgage Bank, both of which brought him into contact with the Bunge family's interests (Emílio Bunge was vice-president of the former, while his cousin Juan Gregorio Peña was a director of the latter). During the protracted financial crisis of the late 1880s, the Casa Bunge ran into increasing difficulties and nearly collapsed altogether when Argentina defaulted on its debts in 1890. Old Hugo Bunge, who headed the Casa Bunge for forty-two years after Karl August's death, was not equal to the crisis, and when he died in 1891 a salvage operation was necessary to save the family's fortune. Exactly what happened is not clear, but through some sort of deal the Casa Bunge became the Banco Tornquist.

Now with its own bank to command, the Tornquist family was ready to expand its investments. After Ernesto Tornquist died his two sons divided the business into two operations. Carlos ran the Banco Tornquist while Eduardo presided over the commercial and investment firm of Ernesto Tornquist & Company. Together they put together an empire that eclipsed even their father's accomplishments. They bought up firms in fields as diverse as insurance, wool textiles, hotels, mining, glass, tobacco, porcelain fixtures, biscuits, motors, farming, metallurgy, real estate, beer, commercial fishing, and bottled mineral water. Among their big acquisitions were Cristalerías Rigolleau and the Bagley Biscuit Company.

Between the great merchant-banking families and the solitary self-made industrialists was a type of early capitalist who displayed some of the characteristics of each. José Menéndez and Elias Hermann Braun, one a Spanish immigrant and the other a German, were pioneer developers of Patagonia at a time when it was a wild and empty frontier region. If Bagley is an example of individual enterprise and the Tornquists represent successful family enterprise, then the stories of Menéndez and Braun and their descendants must qualify as capitalist epics.[16]

Menéndez first went to Patagonia as a commercial agent for a marine equipment company. Traveling aboard a vessel that delivered supplies to fishermen and trappers living in settlements along the coast, he went as far as Punta Arenas at the southernmost tip of the continent. What he saw convinced him that tremendous opportunities lay waiting there, so on returning to Buenos Aires he quit his job, gathered up his family, and returned to Punta Arenas.

In 1875 Punta Arenas was a settlement of about 500 people, most of whom were fishermen, cattle raisers, or drifters, but its value lay in the strategic point it occupied on the north shore of the Magellan Straits. The territory was claimed by both Argentina and Chile, but Chile was in actual possession, having established a naval base and an army garrison at Punta Arenas. Moreover, to bolster its claims even more, Chile encouraged its citizens—or indeed, anyone who would go there under a colonization grant—to settle territory. One of those who accepted Chile's offer was Elias Hermann Braun, who brought his family to Punta Arenas in 1875. By the time Menéndez returned from Buenos Aires, Braun had already set up a hotel and was buying land.

Soon after arriving, Menéndez opened a general store. He also began purchasing large tracts of land outside the town. Land was cheap in that bleak, stony, windswept region, but Menéndez made it pay handsomely by being the first to introduce sheep raising in Patagonia. As profits came in he bought more land and also started a shipping company to carry local products to Buenos Aires. Shortly thereafter, the Argentine government awarded him a contract to service the entire Patagonian coast. With the increased profits Menéndez gradually converted from sailing ships to steamships, taking great pride that his was the first Argentine shipping company to do so.

Navigating Patagonian waters was often risky, so Menéndez needed insurance. Since there was no insurance company, he started his own and offered to insure even the ranchers, fishermen, and traders who sent their products to Buenos Aires. That business proved profitable as well. Meanwhile, Menéndez gained another government concession, this time to build an electric power station in southern Patagonia. He was given broad tracts of land on which to erect transformers and power lines, and on these concessions he also encouraged new settlements—each of which bought his electricity, obtained its supplies from his expanding chain of general stores, sent its products to market aboard his steamships, and insured them through his underwriting company. By the end of the century Menéndez controlled an economic network covering an area larger than some European states.

Building that empire was not easy. Patagonia in the nineteenth century was a wild territory often battered by ice storms, subjected to Indian raids, and inhabited by all manner of violent people. Once while Menéndez was away in Buenos Aires, the Chilean sailors in Punta Arenas mutinied and went on a rampage, burning and pillaging stores and homes including the Menéndez house. Señora Menéndez was so badly hurt that her leg had to be amputated; one of her daughters later died from injuries inflicted during the incident.

While the Menéndez fortune was growing, the Braun family also increased its operations. It too had a chain of retail stores and had quickly followed Menéndez into sheep ranching. Around 1890 Elias Hermann Braun turned over the family business to his son, Mauricio, who quickly displayed exceptional business talent. He imported woollier breeds of sheep in order to improve the quality of his animals and get more wool, thus exceeding Menéndez in that area. He also reorganized the family's various commercial enterprises into a joint-stock company called Compañía Explotadora de Tierra del Fuego (The Tierra del Fuego Development Company). By selling stock he was able to raise much new capital and build a chain of modern-looking general stores that were more attractive than Menéndez's. Thus began a commercial war between the two leading Patagonian families that ended finally in 1908 when Gen. Julio A. Roca brought them together and convinced them that the region's development required their cooperation. Not only did they put aside their feud, but Mauricio Braun married Menéndez's daughter, Josefina. A new holding company was formed, the Compañía Importadora y Exportadora de Patagonia that coordinated the activities of all their enterprises. Menéndez served as president until he died in 1918 and was succeeded by Braun.

The Braun-Menéndez Group thus joined the Bunge & Born Group and the Tornquist Group as one of Argentina's great business empires. In the years that followed the merger, the Braun-Menéndez Group helped to organize, along with the Bunge & Born Group, the country's largest private oil company, Astra. Thus Braun-Menéndez entered the area of industrial chemicals. Meanwhile, its interest in maritime shipping led to the development of shipyards in Patagonia, where navy vessels were also repaired. From there it was but a short step to start a new company, Astarsa, which became Argentina's leading builder of military and merchant ships. Finally, like other Argentine conglomerates, the Braun-Menéndez Group sought to guarantee its capital base by buying into large banks: the Banco Continental, the Banco de Galícia, and the Banco Sirio-Libanés.

## The Problems of Financing

Banking was pivotal to the creation of big business empires, especially those which sought to enter manufacturing. A family or group of investors that controlled its own bank had ready access to the savings of its depositors: an important advantage because most lenders were ultraconservative when it came to industry. Government banks, for instance, almost never lent money for industrial ventures. Not until 1944 was an official industrial credit bank set up. Foreign banks were not much help for local industry either. They bought government bonds or helped investors in their own countries acquire railroads, utilities, or rural property. Local banks also preferred safe investments: land, treasury notes, or the import-export trade. Thus, industrial entrepreneurs had an uphill struggle, and that is where the Bunges and Tornquists had an advantage over the Noels and Bagleys.

*Grupos* also raised money through insurance companies. The insurance business was an ingredient in José Menéndez's success, and later his successors, the Braun-Menéndez Group, joined with the Tornquist Group to establish one of Argentina's largest insurance firms, La Agrícola. Insurance was also the main source of funding for another conglomerate that arose shortly after the turn of the century: the Roberts Group, whose driving force was a Welsh immigrant, Robert William Roberts.

Roberts came to Argentina as a child with his Welsh parents in the late 1880s. He married into a well-to-do Anglo-Argentine family, the Oxenfords, and became a commercial agent for various British exporters, including the Vickers armaments company, which gave him access to government leaders. While still a young man he joined with other British merchants and investors to form Leng, Roberts, & Company, which later became the Anglo-Argentine Investment and Trust Company (Compañía Anglo-Argentina de Inversiones y Mandatos), specializing in representing British exporters and advising would-be investors. As their man on the spot Roberts naturally added underwriting to the other services he offered them. His insurance company, La Buenos Aires, soon had a monopoly on their trade. With this excellent source of capital and an investment company to put it to work, Roberts was able to build quickly a business conglomerate that included sugar estates, the country's largest wine bodega, a paint and varnish factory, a foundry and mechanical works, and a large block of shares in the Alpargatas textile company. He also acquired large interests in two more insurance firms, La Rosario and La Rosario Agrícola. At certain points the Roberts Group interlocked with other conglomerates. It shared participation with the Tornquist Group in Cristalerías Rigolleau; it was a shareholder in Astarsa, the Braun-Menéndez shipyards; and it was a major shareholder in the General Match Company (Compañía General de Fósforos), which was part of the rising new Fabril Financiera Group.

Fabril Financiera was a holding company for a group of investors connected with the Banco de Italia y Río de La Plata, one of the few banks that had occasionally been willing to support an industrialist. Originally, Fabril Financiera was a textile mill, but like many of the bank's debtors, it had defaulted during the early years of the Great Depression and had been taken over. Finding themselves with a heterogeneous group of bankrupt companies on their hands, the Banco de Italia's directors decided to reorganize the lot and try to make them profitable by funneling money into first one firm and then another while giving Fabril Financiera the task of supervising them. In addition to setting old firms back on their feet, however, Fabril Financiera began buying into others that showed good potential but were having cash flow problems. By the end of the 1930s, the Fabril Financiera Group included South America's largest paper company, La Celulosa; two of Argentina's biggest chemical companies, General Match and Electroclor; two machine-building and heavy engineering firms, Talleres Coughlin and Peters Hermanos; the Argentine branch of the Pirelli rubber tire company; and a number of textile and food-processing factories. It also had two large insurance companies, La Inmobilaria and Unión Gremial.

Industrial entrepreneurs outside these big conglomerates were naturally at a disadvantage. With the exception of the Banco Tornquist and the Banco de Italia y Río de La Plata, financial institutions were hesitant to make loans outside their own circle of companies; and when they did they preferred industries closely tied to agriculture like sugar, wine, tobacco, flour, lumber, or cotton fibers. There was little capital to lend in any case because the government constantly claimed a large amount in order to finance its chronic budget deficits. What was left for private investment was available only on short-term financing. Long-term loans for industrial or commercial ventures were almost unknown.[17]

Starved for capital, most industrial entrepreneurs had little choice but to keep their operations on a small scale. Even if a loan were available, the interest rates were high. Thus, the more capital-intensive the venture the greater the risk in taking a loan, because there might be a long interim between investment and profit return. If an entrepreneur miscalculated, he could lose his business. Such was the fate of the Sansenina brothers, two Basque immigrants who founded a meatpacking company in 1884. They were pioneers in freezing meat for export, but the necessary equipment was so expensive they needed help from the Banco Tornquist. In this early, experimental stage, however, machinery often broke down in the factory or on the newly designed freezer ships, resulting in heavy losses. Although the Sanseninas continued to increase their trade, they were always in financial difficulties until the crisis of 1890–91 finally forced the Banco Tornquist to take over the business.[18]

Another example of a conglomerate takeover of a struggling enterprise involved the TAMET metallurgical works. Founded in 1882 by Antonio Rezzónico and Luís Huergo, who merged their machine shop and bolt factory, the company expanded quickly thanks to a Banco Tornquist loan. In this case, however, the bank insisted on being a limited partner. In 1903, the Tornquists arranged a merger with another of their clients, Ottonello & Company, which resulted in Argentina's second-largest metallurgical works. Six years later the Tornquists, who then owned a controlling interest, ordered a complete reorganization of the firm, converting it from a partnership to a joint-stock company. Finally, shortly after World War I, TAMET became the largest metallurgical company by merging with the family firm of Pedro Vasena & Sons.[19]

From the Tornquists' point of view, their actions in the Sansenina and TAMET cases were amply justified by the demands of industrial progress. They financed struggling entrepreneurs, helped them to enlarge and modernize their plants, and created more efficient industries to meet the needs of society. They were not heartless capitalists, eager to gobble up small firms. They were willing to carry their clients through lean years, and if the Tornquists insisted upon an interest in the business it was only fair to grant them some

security for their loans. The limited partnerships that the Tornquists held gave them no management rights; that was a task they
were happy to leave in their partners' hands. But the Tornquists
were also practical. When debts accumulated or when reorganization became necessary to stay ahead of the competition, they did
not hesitate to use their financial leverage to make changes. From
the point of view of the original entrepreneurs who lost control of
their businesses, however, the process of mergers, takeovers, and
incorporations must have been galling and even tragic. Moreover,
from the viewpoint of national control over industry, the gains from
this type of modernization were often dubious. In Sansenina's case,
the Tornquists were instrumental in keeping at least one export-
oriented meatpacking firm under Argentine ownership; but in the
case of TAMET they allowed foreign capital to gain a foothold in the
metallurgical industry by selling large quantities of stock to Belgian
and French investors. Another Tornquist acquisition, Cristalerías
Rigolleau, which was bought up when that company went public in
1906, was sold to American glass interests in 1942.

If a business owner wanted to avoid the banks and conglomerates,
the necessary capital had to come from personal savings. It was a
slow, painful method of financing, but in those days it was not impossible. Fernando Péres, founder of the country's most important
cotton textile mill, started his company from the savings he accumulated by working in an American export firm, although a small
inheritance from his father furnished him with a European education that earned him access to higher business circles. Genaro
Grasso, the Italian immigrant founder of a leading metalworking
company, began as a common laborer. His intelligence and diligence
so impressed his employer that Grasso was promoted to foreman.
After a few years of saving his wages, he used his modest capital to
open a small factory that produced metal tubes. By living frugally
and reinvesting his profits during several arduous years, Grasso
eventually established his firm as one of the largest producers of
metal pipes and tubing. The same was true of Adam Goscilo, the
Polish immigrant who built a lathe-manufacturing business. Beginning as a shop mechanic, he soon rose to foreman and eventually
started his own business with his savings. Similar stories can be
told about Carlos Maria Frigeri, the Italian immigrant founder of
Argentina's leading valve company; or of Johann Matryn, the Aus-
trian-born manufacturer of farm machinery; or of Eduardo Giudici,
who built Argentina's largest construction materials company. Frigeri began as a common laborer; Matryn was a mechanic; and Giu-

dici went to work in a sawmill at a very early age. All three worked their way up to foreman and saved enough from their increased wages to start their own firms. Each man started his firm on a shoestring and built it slowly through many long hours of work and much personal sacrifice.[20]

Other entrepreneurs got started by drawing on their family's resources. Robert Fraser, Sr., the founder of Alpargatas, was helped by his elder brothers who provided the equipment for his canvas shoe factory. He soon became independent of them by converting Alpargatas into a joint-stock company and selling shares, but without the initial capital provided by his family he would not have gotten his start. There is no great difference between a bank loan, a loan from a relative, or the inheritance of some money, on the one hand, and the inheritance of a small shop on the other. In the latter case, the original idea of what to produce comes from the parent, along with the original savings; but in order to survive and grow, the business requires the energy and entrepreneurial talents of the child, who may have more business acumen. Such was the case of the Noel candy company. It became Argentina's biggest candy producer under Benito Noel, but it was started in 1847 by his Basque immigrant father, Carlos Noel. What the father left the son was little more than a rude candymaking operation based on hand labor and housed in an old shed on the docks. It was the son who installed steam machinery, established the orchards to guarantee the fruit supply, bought the fleet of barges to carry the fruit to his docks, hired a French candy expert to develop new product lines, and devised mass advertising campaigns to boost sales. By the same token, Horácio Ejilevich, who built Vitalana into Argentina's leading wool textile company, started with only a lease on a shop and two weaving machines left to him by his father; but that was enough to launch a successful career.[21]

Sometimes a young entrepreneur procured a loan from an older friend who had confidence in him. The bustling Melville Bagley started La Hesperidina with a loan from Marcos Demarchi, one of the three Swiss-Argentine brothers who owned the pharmacy where Bagley worked. Demarchi later figured as one of the founders of the Banco de Italia y Río de La Plata. When in 1877 Bagley decided to expand into the production of cookies and crackers, he brought the Demarchi family into his firm as partners to solidify his financial connections. Torcuato Di Tella, the founder of SIAM, who began working as a shop apprentice when he was fourteen and became a millionaire before he was thirty, had a similar start. When he was eighteen, Di Tella worked as a clerk in a brokerage house owned by the Allegrucci family. The Allegruccis liked the bright young lad, so when he asked for help in starting a small factory to produce a bread-kneading machine he had invented, they made him a 10,000 peso loan, securing their investment with a limited partnership in the firm. Four years later the SIAM Di Tella Company was worth 151,000 pesos.[22]

Di Tella was the most resourceful of entrepreneurs at building up his capital. Knowing the bankers' prejudices against lending to industry, he discovered a way of increasing his sales and getting cash from reluctant bankers at the same time. Bakeries were offered easy credit terms for buying his bread-kneading machines: they needed only a small down payment on a twenty-four-month promissory note backed by property, securities, or even the shop itself. Di Tella would then discount those notes at the banks, which were willing to accept them because they were backed by tangible assets. Thus, unlike many other struggling industrialists, Di Tella always had ready cash. He eventually established such a good reputation with the financial community that he easily got a loan in 1920 to build a foundry that would cast all the parts for his machine. That was the real turning point for SIAM, because after that it was able to produce a wide variety of metal equipment.[23]

On rare occasions the capital to start a business was acquired through pure luck, as when Joaquín Lagos and Enrique Fidanza, two friends in the town of Rosario, pooled their spare cash in 1927 and bought a Christmas lottery ticket. They won and took a trip to Italy. One day while in Rome they read in the newspaper that this particular edition had been printed on paper produced from wheat straw—part of Mussolini's campaign to encourage the planting of wheat in Italy. Since Rosario was located in Argentina's wheat belt, Lagos and Fidanza began to calculate how they could use the large amounts of chaff thrown away after every harvest. On returning home, they looked up an engineer who was willing to experiment with local wheat straw, and the following year they sent him to Naples to interview the man responsible for producing the Italian paper. After examining the sample of Argentine wheat straw, the Neapolitan pronounced the project feasible. Lagos and Fidanza put up the remainder of their winnings, got a loan from a local bank, and began La Celulosa.[24]

Partnerships were another way of raising capital. Argentine commercial law recognized two forms: ordinary partnerships and limited partnerships. The former were more common, requiring only a simple contract. They dissolved automatically at the death, incapacity, or formal withdrawal of any of the partners. They had two major drawbacks, however. First, each of the partners was fully responsible for all of the firm's debts, so if one partner were profligate the others risked ruin. Second, each partner had a right to participate in the running of the business, which raised the possibility of disputes.

Good, responsible friends could make an ordinary partnership fruitful, however, as the success of today's giant conglomerate, Garovaglio & Zorraquín demonstrates. In the early 1920s, Francisco Garovaglio, the owner of a wholesale company dealing in agricultural products, got a small loan from his friend, Federico Zorraquín, to tide him over a difficult period. When business declined, Garovaglio closed the firm, but he assured Zorraquín there was enough in the bank to repay him. Instead of taking the money, Zorraquín went to work in the business, and within a short time profits were coming in again. With that, Garovaglio made his friend a partner, and the two became wealthy in a very short time.[25]

That Garovaglio waited until the business was out of trouble before offering his friend a partnership is testimony to the legal drawbacks of ordinary partnerships, for had Zorraquín been an original partner, he would have been liable for the firm's debts. Clearly, investors who were inclined to bankroll an enterprise but were frightened of risking too much needed some other form of business organization to protect them. The limited partnership, or society in commendum (*sociedad en comandita*), provided that. Under its terms, partners were divided into two categories, special and general. Special partners invested capital and shared in the profits, but had no part in the company's management. Also, they were liable for the company's debts only up to the amount of capital they had subscribed. General partners, by contrast, ran the business and were required to assume unlimited liability. As a rule, wealthy lenders like the Tornquists, Demarchis, or Allegruccis preferred to stay in the background as special, or limited, partners, while allowing their general partners—the Sanseninas, Bagleys, and Di Tellas—full scope for their entrepreneurial talents.

A refinement of this approach was added to the commercial code in 1932 with the creation of the limited liability company (*sociedad de responsibilidad limitada*). To qualify, a firm had to have at least two, but not more than twenty, partners, each of whom would be liable up to a percentage stipulated in the original contract. In companies with five or fewer partners, decisions had to be unanimous;

otherwise a three-fourths majority was sufficient. Although these procedures may seem cumbersome, the limited liability company was common with foreign subsidiaries because, unlike a corporation, it didn't need a state charter, and it didn't have to publish a yearly balance sheet.[26]

For raising capital, no form of business organization was superior to the joint-stock company, or corporation.[27] Other companies could grow only by reinvesting their profits, taking on new partners, or getting current partners to invest more. Corporations, on the other hand, could tap the savings of both small and large investors by issuing stocks and bonds. In addition, corporations offered their investors the protection of limited liability and the security of permanence, since—unlike a partnership—the management of a corporation did not dissolve upon the death or incapacity of one of its members. As the enterprise grew in scale and complexity it was easier to divide its operations among many specialized departments; and while the corporation might sacrifice the genius of the gifted entrepreneur, it was more likely to recruit managers who were experts at their tasks, rather than relying upon friends or family members who might not be qualified.

The movement toward corporations became especially strong after World War I. At the end of the war, there were only 234 corporations operating in Argentina, of which 110 were industrial. By the end of the 1920s, the number had jumped to 925, with 317 in industry. The total amount of capital involved had risen too, from 524 million pesos to 2.6 billion. Most of the new corporations were formed, ironically, just before the great economic crash.[28]

The number of corporations continued to grow throughout the depression. There were 1,203 in 1933 and 2,411 in 1937. However, the total amount of capital invested in them stabilized. After climbing to 3.8 billion pesos in 1933, it reached only 4 billion as of 1937, so the average corporation actually had a narrower capital base. Fortunately, industrial corporations showed a different trend, for they decreased from 391 to 379 while their capital increased from 2 billion to 2.3 billion pesos. However, by 1946 the number of industrial corporations had increased dramatically for the census that year counted 2,825. This probably occurred because the new military government encouraged industry. Unfortunately, the census did not say how much capital was invested.[29]

In any case, there is little doubt that corporations were dominating Argentine industry. In 1935 they accounted for only 6 percent of all industrial firms, yet they employed 40 percent of the labor force and contributed 54 percent of the total value of industrial production; by 1946, given the proliferation of small enterprises, corporations were only 3.3 percent of the total, but still employed 36 percent of the work force and turned out 45 percent of the total value of production. As table 4.2 shows, certain fields like tobacco, chemicals, textiles, rubber, petroleum derivatives, electrical machinery and appliances, and utilities were largely dominated by corporations.

Even fields like food processing and metallurgy that seemed to lack corporations had subfields in which corporations dominated. In food processing, the subfields were the meatpacking, sugar refining, beer, dairy, wine, and flour industries. Under metallurgy, the production of iron and steel was controlled by a few joint-stock companies.

Some entrepreneurs welcomed and promoted incorporation. Robert Fraser began issuing both common and preferred stock in Alpargatas a year after founding it, practically guaranteeing potential investors a return of at least 7 percent annually in dividends. Sound management by Fraser kept administrative salaries modest and profiits steady. There was steady investment in better machinery and a strict no-waste policy: bits of leftover cotton were woven into rag rugs, leftover canvas was used to make beach bags, celluloid from discarded movie films was purchased to make shoelace tips. These business practices produced yearly dividends considerably in excess of 7 percent, making Alpargatas's stock increasingly attractive. By 1900, the original subscribed capital of 150,000 pesos had grown to 680,000.[30]

The Bagley biscuit company also incorporated fairly early. After Melville Bagley's untimely death in 1880 (he was only 42), the firm limped along as a partnership between the Demarchis and Bagley's widow. Leadership was lacking, however, so in 1887 two of Bagley's technicians, Juan León Trilla and Jorge MacLean, were included as partners. In 1898 the company reorganized as a limited partnership and finally incorporated in 1901 with Trilla as president. Each change brought new capital, allowing the company to diversify its production lines and become one of Argentina's food-processing giants.

Not every entrepreneur envied the success of Alpargatas and Bagley, because in going public those companies opened themselves to takeovers by big conglomerates. Although the Fraser family continued to manage Alpargatas until 1946, real control was in the hands of the Roberts Group. Similarly, the Tornquist Group controlled Bagley. The Tornquists also bought controlling interest in

Table 4.2 Relative Importance of Corporations
and Related Organizational Forms
(Limited Liability Companies and Cooperatives)
in Various Branches of Argentine Industry, 1946

| | Percentage of Firms | Percentage of Work Force | Percentage of Total Production |
|---|---|---|---|
| *Fields of absolute dominance* | | | |
| Tobacco | 26.8 | 80.9 | 95.6 |
| Chemicals | 30.8 | 73.5 | 77.1 |
| Petroleum and derivatives | | | |
| (Total) | 55.3 | 92.9 | 96.6 |
| Private | 38.3 | 53.4 | 40.3 |
| State | 17.0 | 39.5 | 56.3 |
| Rubber | 26.0 | 80.7 | 86.4 |
| Electric and gas utilities | 35.8 | 80.9 | 87.6 |
| | | | |
| *Fields of relative dominance* | | | |
| Food processing | 12.5 | 54.3 | 69.5 |
| Textiles | 27.9 | 68.8 | 69.9 |
| Paper | 23.7 | 54.4 | 72.6 |
| Printing and publishing | 9.2 | 47.0 | 51.7 |
| Stone, glass, etc. | 5.5 | 47.0 | 61.6 |
| Metallurgy | 7.9 | 51.0 | 54.4 |
| Electrical machinery | 8.7 | 68.2 | 70.0 |
| Other | 8.4 | 34.0 | 68.0 |
| | | | |
| *Fields not yet dominated* | | | |
| Extractive industries | 19.7 | 33.5 | 27.6 |
| Clothing | 5.2 | 33.7 | 38.4 |
| Wood | 5.7 | 28.1 | 31.7 |
| Leather | 7.3 | 38.3 | 43.2 |
| Vehicles and machinery | 5.6 | 40.8 | 47.0 |

Source: *Cuarto censo nacional* (Buenos Aires: Dirección General del Servício Estadístico Nacional, 1952).
Note: Unfortunately, the census did not separate corporations (*sociedades anónimas*) from limited liability companies and cooperatives when relating them to branches of industry. There were very few cooperatives, however, and none were large. There were twice as many limited liability companies as corporations, but they employed fewer than half as many workers and contributed less than a third as much to the total value of industrial production as did corporations.

the Piccardo tobacco company in 1913 and in the publishing house of Jacob Peuser in 1919, after both firms went public. Together with the Roberts Group, the Tornquists took control of Cristalerías Rigolleau in 1906. Fernando Péres incorporated his textile firm, Manufacturera Algodonera Argentina, in 1928 only to be taken over by the Bemberg Group ten years later when cheap Japanese imports caused a crisis in the textile industry. Later, the Fabril Financiera Group acquired Péres's firm when the Bembergs had trouble. Fabril Financiera also bought out Joaquín Lagos and Enrique Fidanza when La Celulosa went public in 1929. Many businessmen imbued with ideas of loyalty to family interests rebelled at the idea of diluting their personal control over the firm or of bringing strangers into the upper echelons of management. Such feelings were often deeper than a concern for efficiency, profits, or growth.

Not every conversion to the corporate form ended in loss of control. Corcemar, the second-largest cement producer today, began as a partnership between two building contractors in Córdoba. In 1917 Marcelo Garló and Raúl Verzini—the latter a teenager who had just inherited his share of the business from his father—decided to pool their savings and import an electric cement-mixer. The gamble paid off. Soon they were the leading building firm in town; but since they were the only mechanized cement producers, they had an even more lucrative trade in supplying other builders. By 1931 they had expanded their cement operations throughout the province, and in that year they decided to convert from a partnership to a corporation to attract capital for further expansion. Instead of being set back by the Great Depression, Corcemar benefited tremendously from the boom in import-substitution industries by becoming a leading supplier of materials for the construction of new plants. By 1935 Corcemar had factories in several provinces and was one of the largest enterprises in Argentina. Moreover, its management remained in the hands of its two original founders, Garló and Verzini.[31]

Some entrepreneurs turned their firms into joint-stock companies not to raise capital but as a form of insurance against lawsuits. These companies remained closely held corporations with little or no stock offered for sale to the public. With his usual gift for innovation, Torcuato Di Tella discovered an ingenious compromise that allowed him both to raise large amounts of capital and to retain control of his company. In addition to common and preferred stock, he issued "deferred" stock that he parceled out to his family and longtime associates in SIAM's management. Deferred stock paid no dividends, and in the event of SIAM's liquidation its claims would come last; but its holders could vote at company assemblies. When Di Tella died in 1948, there were around 117,000 shares of common stock outstanding, each entitling the holder to one vote; but there were also 20,000 shares of deferred stock with five votes apiece, enough to give the Di Tella family effective control of the company since it was unlikely that the common shareholders would ever vote en bloc. This did not deter investors because SIAM's stock, never having failed to produce a dividend, was considered blue chip.[32]

It is impossible to determine exactly how many of the corporations listed on the Buenos Aires stock exchange (the Bolsa) were of this (essentially) artificial type. The number must have been very high, because available data for boards of directors at later periods indicates a high degree of family control. For 1957 I calculate that 137 of 268 companies listed on the exchange were clearly family controlled, while for 1966 I find that 1,378 of 4,187 corporation executives listed with the exchange had one or more relatives who also were corporation executives. Based on these figures, one may guess that between a third and a half of the corporations registered with the exchange were not really open to public investment. These are conservative calculations because they are based on the appearance of family names on boards of directors, which means that many in-law connections were missed. If there was a high level of family control in the 1950s and 1960s, it seems reasonable to assume an even higher level in an earlier period.

Although devices like Di Tella's were successful in retaining family control, the mentality that prompted them ultimately proved ruinous to Argentine capitalism by confining it in an increasingly rigid and anachronistic organizational mold. In SIAM's case, the modest dividends of the company's bonds and preferred stock no longer attracted investors suffering from runaway inflation in Argentina in the 1960s. SIAM's only hope of raising capital lay in issuing large amounts of common stock whose market value might rise on the exchange. Common stock carried voting rights, however, and the Di Tella family ruled out that option. SIAM stopped raising capital, fell behind its competitors, and eventually was forced into receivership.

The familial nature of Argentine capitalism contributed to the failure of the Buenos Aires stock exchange to develop into an effective capital market. Although the exchange dates back to 1854, its investors traditionally traded in gold, government bonds, mortgages, or grain futures; not until the turn of the century did any industrial or commercial corporation list its stock. Even then, trading was limited chiefly to railroad and bank shares. Of fifty-four companies whose stock was quoted in 1913, only twelve were in manufacturing, strictly speaking. Three others were in meatpacking or meat by-products; six were in transportation or utilities; three were in the mining sector; and fourteen were engaged in the simple processing of rural products (sugar refining, flour milling, coffee and yerba mate roasting, winemaking, dairy products, etc.). The remaining sixteen companies were in real estate, insurance, investments, construction, and storage.[33]

Thus, unlike other industrial countries during their transition toward industry, Argentine investors remained conservative and traditional. As Donna Guy observes, "In most industrializing nations of the time, the growth of public investment and confidence in the stock exchange, even in times of depression prior to 1929, helped to promote the transition from family-owned concerns to professionally managed companies. In Argentina, such confidence in public companies did not exist and they were greeted with a great deal of suspicion even when associated with the prosperous landed sector." And she adds that "due to lack of access to investment capital, most industrial establishments that sprang up in the city of Buenos Aires and elsewhere tended to remain in the category of artisan shops."[34]

In 1943 a government strongly committed to industrialization brought about a change in investors' attitudes. Suddenly, as it became evident that the government intended to pump a great deal of credit, through the Industrial Bank, into the manufacturing sector, there was interest on the stock exchange in industrial stocks and bonds. Between 1941 and 1945, the two dates for which I could find statistics, the volume of trading in industrial stocks and bonds rose from an equivalent of only $32 million a year to over $150 million. As with previous booms in Argentine history, this reflected, to a large extent, the calculations of speculators who hoped to cash in quickly on a new and possibly ephemeral official trend rather than the confidence of long-term investors in Argentina's industrial future. Not many buyers of industrial securities shared the philosophy of capitalism that the Alpargatas textile company expressed in its 1941 annual report to the stockholders: "It is the company's belief that the good investor—that is, the one who holds shares in order to enjoy an income and not for the purpose of speculating in values—has a greater interest in a moderate but certain dividend, rather than in a dividend which may be high in one year and very low in another."[35]

Speculation in industrial securities accelerated even more under Perón, reaching a feverish pitch by the end of the 1940s. Then the bubble burst, leaving behind several ruined companies, lost fortunes, and a permanently scarred stock exchange. To this day, Argentine capitalism has failed to solve the problem of its own financing.

## CHAPTER FIVE

# The State and Industry

The state played a minor role in Argentina's economy until the 1930s. As table 5.1 shows, its share of total investment stayed at around 11 percent until World War I then rose somewhat during the war years because of the drastic drop in private investment (caused by the withdrawal of foreign capital). After the war, the state's role receded again and remained low until the depression. The state then assumed a more active role because of the economic crisis. The establishment of government regulatory boards for meat and farm products, the growth in YPF's activities, and the military's assumption, through Fabricaciones Militares, of certain types of defense-related production combined to increase state investment to unprecedented levels. In the late 1940s, under Perón, it rose to 35 percent of the total. It seems, therefore, that Argentina's early industrialization falls into three phases. The first, which lasted until World War I, was characterized by the leadership of foreign capital. The second, which stretched from the end of World War I to 1943, saw domestic private capital in the vanguard. The third, which began with the revolution of June 1943 and ended approximately with the overthrow of Perón in 1955, was a period of state leadership.

The expansion of the state's economic role was linked to the greater importance accorded to industry. During the depression, falling exports restricted Argentina's ability to import finished products, even though the demand for them remained high. Consequently, local industry was encouraged to meet that demand. Such was the logic of the import-substitution strategy of the 1930s: a far cry from the old days when the governing elites, imbued with the ideas of free trade and comparative advantage, viewed local industry with disdain.

As applied by the old *estanciero* elite, the law of comparative advantage taught the futility of industrializing Argentina. After all, the country had a temperate climate, adequate rainfall, and vast stretches of fertile soil, all of which made it ideally suited to grazing

Table 5.1 Public and Private Investment, 1900–1949
(in millions of constant 1950 pesos)

| Period | Total Investment | Public | Private | Percent Public | Percent Private |
|---|---|---|---|---|---|
| 1900–1904 | 2,789 | 317 | 2,471 | 11.4 | 88.6 |
| 1905–9 | 7,698 | 836 | 6,861 | 10.9 | 89.1 |
| 1910–14 | 8,403 | 944 | 7,459 | 11.2 | 88.8 |
| 1915–19 | 2,490 | 331 | 2,160 | 13.3 | 86.7 |
| 1920–24 | 6,718 | 526 | 6,192 | 7.8 | 92.2 |
| 1925–29 | 11,246 | 1,189 | 10,057 | 10.6 | 89.4 |
| 1930–34 | 7,500 | 1,258 | 6,243 | 16.8 | 83.2 |
| 1935–39 | 9,422 | 2,383 | 7,039 | 25.3 | 74.7 |
| 1940–44 | 8,342 | 2,108 | 6,233 | 25.3 | 74.7 |
| 1945–49 | 13,985 | 4,941 | 9,045 | 35.3 | 64.7 |

Source: ECLA, *El desarrollo económico de la Argentina* (Santiago de Chile: ECLA, 1958), pp. 135–36.

cattle and growing cereals. Conversely, the country had meager deposits of coal and iron. Heavy industry, therefore, was inconsiderable—so the argument ran—and without a heavy industrial base the possibilities for any other type of industry were strictly limited. Only with government subsidies for importing machinery and equipment and government protection in the form of tariffs would most light industry be able to compete with foreign products in the domestic market. And, clearly, such industry would never be competitive on the world market. To coddle it would not only waste resources but would saddle a large part of the community with the unjust burden of supporting a segment that would never be self-sustaining. Finally, to replace free trade with protectionism would cut Argentina off from the civilizing influence of international commerce. The liberal oligarchy was proud of its cosmopolitanism. Some of its members even bragged that Argentina was really a sixth dominion of the British commonwealth.[1]

The liberal oligarchy was not alone in supporting free trade. The Socialist party favored it because mass-produced foreign industrial imports were usually cheaper than the local goods; therefore, the average working-class family had more buying power in a free-trade market. The Radical and Conservative parties liked free trade because customs duties were a major source of revenue with which they could support expanding bureaucracies and lavish public spending. Nevertheless, there was also a long tradition of nationalism in Argentina, dating back beyond Rosas, which challenged the dominant liberal ideology. The *estanciero* who voted Conservative but cursed the foreign-owned railroads, grain companies, and packinghouses that gouged him was—emotionally, at least—a brother to the middle-class nationalist or the disgruntled wage worker who labored fourteen hours a day loading ships or carving up carcasses. By the same token, Argentina's emerging industrialists were quick to use nationalistic arguments to bolster their claims for protection against foreign goods. To counter the argument for comparative advantage that seemed to be supported by Argentina's steady progress until 1929, industrialists pointed to the examples of the United States and Germany, whose even greater progress had taken place behind high tariff walls.

The industrialists' first attempt to create a national lobbying organization was the Industrial Club, established in 1875. Its founders were seventy-eight industrialists, many of Italian, French, and Anglo-Saxon extraction. The Industrial Club was short-lived, breaking up three years later over political issues, but it was successful in getting Congress to approve a steep tariff in 1876 that protected local producers of clothing, dairy goods, cigarettes, perfume, beverages, textiles, furniture, and most foodstuffs. In the preamble to the law, the legislators justified protectionism on the grounds that it would nurture "infant industries," provide needed revenue, and rectify the chronically unfavorable trade balance by reducing imports.[2]

Between 1878 and 1887 Argentine industrialists were divided into two rival organizations, the original Industrial Club and the Center for Industry (Centro Industrial). Of the two, the former represented more strictly manufacturing interests, especially those around Buenos Aires, while the latter reflected the views of agro-industrialists: sugar growers who also had refineries, grape growers who also produced wine, or ranchers who also owned meat-salting or meatpacking plants. The agro-industrialists were more numerous and more influential than their rivals, so when the two organizations finally merged in 1887 to form the Argentine Industrial Union (Unión Industrial Argentina, or UIA) the agro-industrialists occupied most of the leading positions. The first president of the UIA, Antonio C. Cambaceres, was the owner of cattle ranches, yerba mate plantations, and meat-salting plants; president of the Banco de la Província de Buenos Aires; and head of the Western Railway Company. His successors during the next two decades had similar backgrounds. Agustín Silveyra (1888–89) owned *estancias*, processed yerba mate, engaged in shipping, and had a meatpacking plant. Joselin Huergo (1889–90) and Francisco Uriburu (1890–91) were both grape growers and vintners. Uriburu also owned sugar estates and a refinery. Juan Videla (1891–92) had interests almost identical to Uriburu's, but he also manufactured shoes and other leather goods and served as president of the Banco de la Província de Buenos Aires. And so the pattern went, right down to the first decade of the twentieth century. Besides heading the UIA these men were also prominent in the SRA. Francisco Seguí, president of the UIA from 1898 to 1901, was simultaneously editor of the SRA's *Anales*. Alfredo Demarchi, president of the UIA from 1904 to 1908, also served as the SRA's treasurer.[3]

These agro-industrialists naturally adopted a middle position between the agrarian liberal free traders and the industrial protectionists. They argued that it was necessary to make a distinction between "natural" and "artificial" industry. Natural industries were those which used mostly local raw materials. They included wine, sugar, flour, meat, meat by-products, leather, edible oils, dairy products, lumber, furniture, tobacco, alcohol, beer, and nonalcoholic beverages. Besides using local material, such industries needed very little sophisticated machinery; hence their costs were low and their prices competitive enough to meet the standards of the law of comparative advantage. By contrast, artificial industry required much expensive imported machinery, a great deal of imported fuel, and even imported raw materials. Most heavy industry, including iron and steel, machine-building, chemicals, automobiles, electrical equipment, and rubber fell into this category. The agro-industrialists joined with the *estancieros* in considering such industries unsuitable for Argentina and unworthy of protection. By contrast, some temporary protection might be justified for natural industries in order to give them a starting push.[4]

Although real manufacturers recognized their differences with the agro-industrialists there was little they could do. They had little influence with Congress on their own, whereas within the UIA they might hope to prod the agro-industrialists into lobbying for a little more protection. Because of their SRA connections, the latter were often in important government positions. Cambaceres, for example, was vice-president of the Senate. Uriburu was also a senator, and had served as minister of finance. Demarchi was a national deputy and former lieutenant governor of Buenos Aires Province. Estanislao Zeballo, a rancher and packinghouse owner who served on the UIA's executive council, was president of the Chamber of Deputies and had served as minister of foreign relations. Francisco Seguí was a national deputy and member of the tariff commission. Carlos Paz, a landowner and president of various food-processing plants, sat on the UIA executive council and also belonged to the family that owned Argentina's leading newspaper, *La Prensa*. Also on the UIA's executive council were Ernesto Tornquist and Otto Bemberg, the heads of extensive financial and industrial empires.

With that kind of leadership, the UIA was fairly successful in getting protection for at least some industry. Despite agrarian opposition, Congress passed protective tariffs in 1887, 1889, 1891, and 1905. The 1891 tariff was perhaps the pinnacle, following as it did the economic crash of the previous year. Duties were raised to between 50 and 60 percent ad valorem on a long list of items. The tariff was part of Carlos Pellegrini's plan to revive the economy by saving on foreign exchange and creating a larger local market for agricultural goods by fomenting domestic industry.[5] Of course, the UIA also lost some battles. It was unsuccessful, until the 1943 revolution, in getting the government to set up an industrial credit bank. It failed to ward off taxes on industrial production, business property, or corporate dividends or to keep their rates from rising. It also failed in its attempt at preventing the government from regulating labor conditions.

After the turn of the century, a gradual change occurred in the UIA's leadership. Men like Jacob Peuser, publisher; Benito Noel, candymaker; Emilio Bieckert, brewer; Miguel and José Ottonello and Antonio Rezzónico, iron manufacturers, began edging out the agro-industrialists. Although these new leaders were more representative of industry, they were less politically experienced and lacked connections. For instance, they failed to stop the 1905 tariff bill that, though not a complete victory for free trade, moved in a direction contrary to industry's wishes by lowering rates to approximately their 1876 levels. The UIA's fortunes rose again during World War I, however, because local manufacturing gained new importance as the flow of industrial imports was shut off. This disruption of the traditional trading pattern was a rude jolt to the believers in the law of comparative advantage and a boost to those who argued that Argentina must have its own industry. The debate now took a new turn and became even livelier in the succeeding decades.

*The Debate about Industry, 1916–1930*

There was little change in government policy when the Radicals replaced the Conservatives in power. Yrigoyen retained the spoils system and the practice of awarding lavish contracts to friends. The only difference was, as one historian put it, "the hundreds of officials appointed by oligarchic ministers were now swamped by thousands appointed for their service to Radicalism. The result was the creation of an enormously overinflated bureaucracy; even before Perón, one in ten economically active persons was a government employee."[6] Naturally, this was expensive. When the Conservative party left office in 1916 government spending had reached the level of 375 million pesos. By 1922 it was 614 million, with most of the increase coming in the last three years. The public debt rose accordingly, from around 100 million pesos in 1916 to 800 million in 1922. Not only did spending increase, but the money went for different purposes. The Conservatives wasted a great deal in patronage, but they also spent on capital improvements. The Radicals actually cut back on public works spending so they would have more money for patronage and government salaries.[7]

The need for revenue was therefore great, and the primary source of it was customs duties. The trick was to lower duties enough to encourage more imports yet keep them high enough to capture more revenue. Heavy taxes on land or incomes were ruled out, because both Yrigoyen and Alvear were *estancieros* and members of the SRA. The most they would do to satisfy the industrialists was to protect certain natural industries. The 1918 and 1922 tariff acts thus raised duties on shoes, leather goods, cotton and wool textiles, cigarettes, cigars, and edible oils. Even this mild protectionism did not last, however. Great Britain threatened to reduce its purchases of Argentine farm products unless tariffs affecting British goods were lowered. The SRA, alarmed at such a prospect, coined the slogan: "Buy from those who buy from us!" The Radicals began to retreat under Alvear, but it was in 1929, during Yrigoyen's second term, that the retreat turned into a rout. In August of that year, the British sent a tough negotiating team headed by the Viscount D'Abernon who revived the threat that imports from Argentina would be slashed unless concessions were made to British manufactures. Yrigoyen did not fight. In fact, he seemed happy to sign away protection for most Argentine industry. As the British ambassador Malcolm Robertson recalled in his memoirs, "we obtained something for nothing."[8]

The D'Abernon Treaty caused bitter feelings among Argentine industrialists. Even the *RRP*, which usually was pro-British, vented its spleen on the traditional arguments used to justify free trade: "These same traditional theories were being labored fifteen years ago, and in the meantime many important national manufacturing industries have grown up in spite of them. We have yet to meet the individual who would seriously contend that the interests of the country would be served by getting rid of the industries in question."[9]

On the other hand, the SRA's position was well summarized by an editorial in *La Nación*:

> The Argentine Rural Society proposes that its slogan of "Buy From Those Who Buy From Us" . . . is not a declaration of free trade principles, nor does it seek to oppose a discrete protectionism. It neither speaks of buying what we can produce, nor of failing to produce what we can buy abroad. . . . Certainly the gradual perfection of our industries will raise the per capita standard of living. But there is, and always will be, a certain number of manufactured goods that we cannot produce economically. Such limits may be temporary in some cases; but in other cases they are final and insuperable.[10]

The D'Abernon Treaty was never ratified. Before Congress could pass it the Yrigoyen government, overwhelmed by the Great Depression, fell victim to a military coup d'etat. Its passing went unlamented by most of the business community. On 6 September 1930 Gen. José F. Uriburu took control of the government. A year and a half later he turned it over to Gen. Agustín P. Justo and the Concordancia. The Concordancia's rule lasted for the next eleven years under three presidents: Justo (1932–38), Roberto Ortiz (1938–40), and Ramón S. Castillo (1940–43). Two presidents, Justo and Ortiz, came to office by way of fraudulent elections aimed at keeping the mainstream Radical party out of power. Castillo took over when Ortiz, fatally ill with diabetes, was forced to step down. Castillo remained in office until the military coup of June 1943.

Ruling through force and fraud, the Concordancia was never popular. Its period of dominance was called the Decade of Infamy by the opposition Radicals, and the term stuck in the popular mind. Nevertheless, it does not quite do justice to the governments of that period. On the one hand, the Concordancia was politically retrograde, but it managed nonetheless to be compatible with industrial progress.

## The Debate about Industry, 1930–1943

The Justo government made the salvation of agriculture its first order of business. Argentina's exports were plunging rapidly as the industrial countries cut back their purchases. Its best customer, Great Britain, was under much pressure from Australia, Canada, and South Africa—countries whose products were competitive with Argentina's—to purchase goods from commonwealth members only. Justo was willing to offer large concessions to prevent the loss of British trade, while the British wanted to maintain their level of industrial exports and avoid more factory closings. The two countries thus were able to reach an agreement in 1933 which guaranteed Argentina a quota of meat sales that would not fall below the 1932 level, excepting unforeseen circumstances. In return, the Argentine government promised to reduce tariffs on British industrial goods, to grant benevolent treatment to British companies doing business on its soil, and to give preference to British machinery and vehicles over all foreign competitors. In addition, the Argentines were to use the sterling earned from foreign sales to pay their debts to British creditors. Eighty-five percent of the meat-export trade to Great Britain was to be reserved for British packinghouses, with the remaining 15 percent going to any nonprofit Argentine company the government might designate (there was none in existence at the time). Finally, the British promised not to raise their tariffs on Argentine wheat, although they did not promise to lower them either.[11]

In Argentina, an avalanche of criticism greeted the Roca-Runciman Treaty when its details were made public. It was not just industrialists or nationalistic intellectuals who were indignant; protests came even from the upper class. Seldom had Argentina bowed so low to the demands of British imperialism, it was said. But worse was to come three years later when the treaty was renewed. The British then demanded an end to all highway construction and road paving that encouraged trucking to compete with their railway lines. They also demanded that privately owned microbuses (*colectivos*) be suppressed because they were in competition with the British-owned subway and streetcar companies. The public's outrage rose to new heights. Although a success in the sense that it halted the downward slide of Argentina's exports, the Roca-Runciman Treaty deprived the Concordancia of public support and popularized the loathing of foreign capital. Traditional interests dealt themselves a blow from which they never recovered as the humiliating ramifications of "Buy from those who buy from us" were revealed.

One of the most telling critics of the reigning economic orthodoxy was a man whose upper-class credentials were impeccable: Alejandro Bunge, a descendant of the immensely wealthy and influential Bunge family. A former director of the National Statistical Institute and one of the country's leading economists, Bunge adopted the cause of economic nationalism through his books and his influential journal, the *Revista de Economía Argentina*. He demanded a state-supported program of rapid industrialization to make Argentina economically independent.

Bunge was an early proponent of import-substituting industrialization. Through subsidies and tariff protection the state would encourage the formation of industries to produce what formerly was imported. Cost-effectiveness was not a consideration; Argentina must seek to be economically sovereign at any cost. Bunge recognized his policy as an experiment in autarky and accepted the challenge. He advocated stabilizing or even reducing Argentina's exports "until we have a more exact science of the ways of the new international system."[12]

For Bunge, the urgency behind his proposal was not simply to end British exploitation but also to put Argentina in a strong position to confront the threat from the United States, which was emerging as the world's new leading economic power. Argentina had been able to carry on a two-way trade with the British, but it would not be able to do so with the Americans. Not only was the United States a great industrial power, but it also was a major producer of meat and grains and hence Argentina's competitor. In a world of free trade the Argentines might find themselves forced to buy their products from the Americans but would have nothing to sell them in return. That would pose a horrible dilemma: either Argentina would sink deeper and deeper into debt or it would have to stop importing and drastically reduce its standards of living.[13]

Bunge favored an authoritarian technocracy as the most efficient way to reach his goal. The Radical era had left him deeply disillusioned with democratic politics, which he equated with opportunism and demagoguery. He also strongly disliked labor unions, especially those led by communists and anarchists. At bottom, he was a productivist who believed that all classes would benefit as rising productivity created a bigger economic pie. Achieving that level of productivity required social discipline and leadership, however. Economic elites—merchants, farmers, financiers, engineers, and above all, industrialists—had to be encouraged to put their talents and capital to work before any benefits could trickle down to the lower classes.

This was the weak point in Bunge's scheme. If Argentina turned away from the international economy, who would consume the agricultural and industrial goods produced by Bunge's autarkic system? There were only two options. Either the state, and especially the military, would become the chief consumer, as had happened in imperial Germany and imperial Japan; or the government would have to create a mass market in the private sector by raising workers' wages and spending more on welfare, as Perón would later do. Although Bunge recognized the great disparities in living standards between the rich and poor and called for improvements in the latter's housing, education, and medical care, he was too much of an elitist to make this an important element of his strategy. In that respect, he was representative of most of the nationalistic intellectuals of his generation who, by failing to appreciate the working classes' great political potential, made possible the rise of Peronism.

In the meantime, Argentine industrialists found a tough new spokesman to head the UIA. Luís Colombo, president of the UIA from 1925 until 1946, was the quintessential self-made man. Born in Rosario in 1878, of Italian immigrant parents, he was running his own business and sitting on the city council by the age of twenty. A few years later he was elected head of the Rosario Stock Exchange. Such a wunderkind obviously was destined to be more than just a local prodigy. His investments soon spread all over the country and included mining, manufacturing, utilities, real estate, wine, insurance, advertising, importing, and exporting. Having attained a national scale in his operations, Colombo finally moved to Buenos Aires. There he became involved in the UIA and quickly rose to the top of the organization. Under his energetic leadership it grew rapidly from around 300 member firms divided into six industrial chambers to over 3,000 firms and 91 chambers. Almost all of Argentina's big manufacturers joined.

As a leading representative of the nation's industry, Colombo lectured, hectored, cajoled, and pressured successive presidents to win protection for domestic manufacturers. Never a man to mince words, the doctrine of free trade was, in his view, "an effective way to stupefy the Argentine people and kill their economic progress."

We can summarize the argument for protection with the following example: Argentina produces cheaper wheat than the Italians do; the Italians produce silk more cheaply than Argentina can. Therefore, we should exchange our wheat for their silk. We shouldn't worry about improving our silk production or lowering its costs. We have to trade. But suppose it happens someday that some other country starts producing wheat more cheaply than we do; or that Italy decides to intensify its own production of wheat—or hinders the importation of it for economic reasons of its own? We then find ourselves unable to sell them our wheat, but we still have to buy their silk because free trade wiped out our production of that article. A nice fix we'd be in![14]

Colombo brushed aside any distinctions between natural and artificial industry. In his view, any industry was useful which contributed to the nation's economic power. "Economic progress is the supreme concern of wise statesmen. Those nations that attain their economic independence are the ones that can best guarantee their political independence, and are the best prepared to repel any attempts to subjugate them." He also denied that industrial and agrarian interests were opposed. On the contrary, higher living standards in the countryside provided industry with a bigger market for its goods. At the same time, industrial growth created a larger demand for primary products.[15]

Like Alejandro Bunge, Colombo had been an early supporter of Yrigoyen but later turned against him. Both Bunge and Colombo welcomed the 1930 coup and hoped for much from the Concordancia. Colombo even joined the Conservative party (Partido Demócrata Nacional) and ran for a seat in the national legislature in 1932. Although he was a friend of President Justo, who appointed him to head a special economic commission, Colombo put industrial interests ahead of personal or party ties. He publicly criticized the Roca-Runciman Treaty and organized a public demonstration against it. This action, endorsed by the UIA, also enlisted some 70,000 protesting workers.

The influence of business on the Concordancia was not negligible, but it was weakened by disunity. Many UIA members also belonged to other organizations that were less representative of purely manufacturing interests and felt cross-pressured by conflicting loyalties. For instance, there was the Argentine Confederation of Commerce, Industry, and Production (CACIP), which included representation from commerce and agriculture as well as industry. CACIP was chiefly an alliance between agro-exporters, foreign-owned railway and utility companies, and big financiers like the Tornquists and Bembergs. Although Luís Colombo was given a seat on its executive board, he was unable to get CACIP to back the UIA on most issues except those opposing labor unions and social legislation. Given that most of CACIP's membership belonged to nonindustrial enterprises, it is not surprising that it supported free trade. Even as late as 1943, when World War II had shut off most industrial imports, and local industry was struggling to fill the vacuum, CACIP warned that after the war Argentine manufacturers "would have to adapt to the needs of international trade." "This does not mean," CACIP explained, "that industry ought to surrender ground already gained, but it does mean that those industries which are only the result of a transitory situation will be difficult to defend afterwards." Once the conflict was over and normal trade relations had resumed among nations, "if they have not been able to establish a base it would be wrong to pretend that, in order to benefit them, we must perpetuate wartime conditions."[16]

Another rival organization was the Argentine Federation of Entities Defending Commerce and Industry, which was formed in 1932 mainly to represent small business and to fight taxes. On the latter issue, the federation was highly successful in mounting a campaign in 1933 to kill a tax bill that would have affected a wide variety of business transactions. The federation was also very antilabor and formed a solid phalanx with the UIA and CACIP on the issue. It also supported the UIA on the tariff question. Beyond that, however, the federation contained a streak of anti–big business radicalism that frequently set it at odds with the UIA and CACIP. It called for the breakup of monopolies and oligopolies as well as the nationalization of most foreign capital in Argentina. Since UIA members like Alpargatas, the Smithfield Meat Company, and the Duperial Chemical Company contained considerable foreign capital; and since the British railway companies and the ITT-owned Unión Telefónica were in CACIP, cooperation between the UIA and CACIP and the federation could go only so far.

Despite the Concordancia's proagrarian bias, industrial interests gained ground steadily during the 1930s. The Roca-Runciman Treaty halted cutbacks of Argentine farm products, but it could not restore prosperity to agriculture. World prices for meat and grains remained low, squeezing many farmers into bankruptcy. Those who remained in business were usually unable to replace worn-out machinery or hire more labor. In desperation, many of them formed new pressure groups, independent of the SRA, to get government aid for the smaller producers. One of these was CARBAP, whose 10,000 members made it much larger than the SRA. Similar regional associations formed after 1932 in the northwest, the littoral, and the central west.

Beginning in 1933, the government moved to protect smaller farmers by creating regulatory boards to control production of and set minimum prices for meat, grain, wine, yerba mate, milk, edible oils, and cotton. As mentioned previously, the meat board also set up a system of controls over packinghouse practices and founded CAP to compete with foreign meatpackers in the cattle market— hardly the sort of benevolent treatment the British were aiming at through the Roca-Runciman Treaty.[17] By the same token, the National Grain Board served the farmers by offering to buy their crops at guaranteed minimum prices, thereby blunting the power of the big grain merchants, who often conspired to keep market prices low.

Such emergency measures were sufficient to keep many ranchers and farmers out of bankruptcy, but they seldom achieved more than that. By contrast, industry boomed throughout the 1930s. Despite the Roca-Runciman Treaty, British goods were increasingly supplanted in the local market by Argentine manufactures that were accorded protection by a variety of indirect measures including multiple exchange rates, exchange controls, and currency devaluation. Indeed, the government even raised tariffs on competing imports, justifying this increase by a clause in the treaty that required tariff reductions only "so far as fiscal considerations and the interests of national industries permit."

From Argentina's point of view, there was no alternative but to encourage import-substituting industrialization. The decline in its export earnings from agriculture meant a reduced capacity to import, so local industry would have to expand to satisfy demand. Once this decision was made, the Justo government actively supported industrialization. In a speech before Congress, in December 1933, no less a figure than the agricultural minister, Luís Duhau, proclaimed that the era of free trade was over, and Argentina must henceforth depend on its own resources. He was seconded by the treasury minister, Federico Pinedo, who promised to stimulate domestic demand for Argentine manufactures by controlling imports and launching a large program of public works.[18]

This sort of pump priming signaled a new era of active government. From new investments in YPF to the highway building program (in defiance of the British railways), from the creation of a Central Bank to the start of a state merchant marine fleet, and from the establishment of agricultural regulatory boards to the purchase of the British-owned Córdoba Central Railway, the Concordancia governments carved out a more important role for the state in the economy and anticipated many of the measures later taken, on a grander scale, by Perón.

The most ambitious scheme for promoting national industry was formulated in 1940 by Federico Pinedo, then serving as Ramón Castillo's finance minister. The "Pinedo Plan" shows that even Conservative governments had begun to think along lines that would later culminate in Peronist economic strategy. It called for the state to spend large sums on industrial expansion. On the one hand, Pinedo proposed the creation of an industrial credit bank—a pet UIA project—and on the other he wanted a massive program to build low-cost housing. The latter would, he estimated, create 210,000 jobs and stimulate the construction materials industries. Pinedo recognized that Argentina would have to continue importing vehicles and machinery for some time until its own heavy industries could be built up. He proposed the creation of a state agency to buy all cattle and agricultural produce that remained unsold on the private market and resell them overseas, using the profits to pay for the necessary imports. To stop the deterioration of railway and urban transport services, which were being neglected by their British owners, he proposed using Argentina's favorable trade balance with Great Britain to buy those properties. Finally, in his speech before Congress, Pinedo argued that his scheme would not be inflationary because it would be financed by government bonds issued at 2 percent above the going interest rate for savings accounts. To avoid competing with the private banks, however, the bonds would not be offered directly to the public; instead, each bank would be expected to buy a certain number of them that it could then resell. To pay for the bonds, banks would transfer sums from their deposits to the Central Bank.[19]

The Pinedo Plan passed the Senate, enlisting support from both the Right and the Left, but it was killed in the Chamber of Deputies by the Radical party, which saw no reason to support a bill that might make the Concordancia popular. Pinedo was accused of wanting to make himself Argentina's economic czar, of concocting an elaborate bailout of the agricultural sector, and of seeking to enrich the stockholders of the British railroad companies, who (it was alleged) would be paid far more than their property was worth. The

Radicals seized upon Pinedo's former connections as a lawyer for the railroads to accuse him of a conflict of interest. Although the Pinedo Plan failed, it showed how far the dominant thinking, even of the old elites, had moved away from classical liberalism toward the ideas of economic nationalism and state regulation.

## The Debate Resolved: The 1943 Coup d'Etat

Until 1943, the Argentine army traditionally had supported the liberal oligarchy, but now there was a rising generation of officers—of whom Juan Perón was one—that was convinced of the need for a more nationalistic economic policy. Many of those officers were German-trained, had served as attachés either in Nazi Germany or Fascist Italy, and had become ardent admirers of fascism. Fascism's success in Europe demonstrated to them beyond question that a nation's status in the world rested upon military power, which in turn depended upon the level of its industrial development. Like other economic nationalists, such as Bunge and Colombo, these military men felt only contempt for democratic politicians, whom they dismissed as demagogues without vision; but they also were impatient with the Concordancia's half-hearted measures. Why, then, should not the military take over and provide the decisive leadership necessary to marshal the nation's energies and direct them toward the desired goal?

The idea was not so radical. Uriburu, who "saved" the nation from the Radicals' corruption and ineptitude, was a military man. So was Justo, the president who succeeded him. General Mosconi had shown that an army officer was capable of running a vast economic enterprise like YPF. Nor was he unique. The army had been developing its own aircraft industry since 1927, and during the decade preceding the coup it had branched out into the production of explosives, small arms, munitions, chemicals, electrical equipment, and pig iron. In 1943 its various factories were brought together under a single management, called Dirección General de Fabricaciones Militares (General Agency for Military Industry). Gen. Mario A. Savio, who was appointed to head Fabricaciones Militares, proved to be a worthy successor to General Mosconi as a military entrepreneur.

Economic nationalism meant something different for the army than it did for businessmen, however. Not only was industry to be fostered and protected from competition, but it also had to produce in accordance with a national plan. Prices, wages, credit, and the allocation of fuels and raw materials were all to be regulated by the state. Even the location of future factories would come under the state's purview, for the military believed that national integration required that the poorer regions of the interior share in the process of industrialization. Certain areas of the economy considered vital for the national defense, such as fuels, transportation, and energy, would be managed directly by the state.

Businessmen soon found that, under military rule, there was less opportunity than ever for organized interests to influence policymaking. The new government's style was that of the barracks: orders flowed from above, and persons affected were expected to obey without question. That applied even to formerly privileged groups. In November 1943, the rents that big landowners charged their tenants were actually rolled back to 20 percent below what they had been in July 1940. Henceforth, the state would regulate rural rents, and indeed it kept them frozen for many years to come. The same was true of urban rents. To relieve the *porteño* population from the rapidly climbing cost of housing, the military froze all rents on houses, apartments, rooms, and commercial establishments. So long as a tenant paid his rent he could not be evicted, and landlords were forbidden to reduce or discontinue any services.[20]

The military also moved to take over companies that were commonly believed to be overcharging for their services. The grain merchants' oligopoly was dealt a blow in 1943 when the government nationalized all private grain elevators. During the following year it took over the British-owned gas company that supplied Buenos Aires and acquired an American-owned electricity company in Entre Ríos Province. In January 1944 an executive decree was issued empowering the army to expropriate all existing stocks of raw materials or manufactured articles considered indispensable for the nation's defense (except, of course, those that already were in the navy's possession). Especially sought were trucks, rubber tires, motors, spare parts, machinery, tools, leather, canvas, measuring instruments, and optical lenses.[21]

A more active state meant a bigger and more expensive state. In 1940 there were 199,800 national government employees (including those in autonomous units like YPF). By 1945 there were 312,300. Government spending under the Castillo administration had increased from 1.32 billion pesos in 1940 to 1.64 billion by mid-1943, an average rise of about 10 percent a year; under the military, spending hit 2.85 billion by the end of 1945, for an increase of about 30 percent a year. Revenues, despite an excess profits tax, did not keep pace with spending, so there was a growing deficit that was financed partly by borrowing and partly by increasing the money supply— which doubled between 1943 and 1946.[22] Military spending accounted for much of the increased outlay. The military's portion of the total government budget rose from 27.8 percent in 1942 to 50.7 percent in 1946. The expanded government payroll was another factor pushing up spending, and so was the state's growing role as an investor through its enterprises, such as YPF, CAP, Fabricaciones Militares, and the merchant fleet.[23]

Generally, industrialists approved of the new government, at least at the beginning. Naturally they did not like to pay a tax of 30 percent on all profits beyond a stipulated sum, but they enjoyed high protective tariffs and easy, low-interest loans available through the recently created Industrial Credit Bank.[24] Government spending also stimulated private consumption, and the growth of public service jobs increased the size of the urban white-collar class, which sought to solidify its status through luxury consumption. As local business expanded to meet these opportunities import-substitution industrialization seemed to be a great success. Between 1939 and 1945, local manufacturers increased their share of the domestic market from 50 percent to 88 percent in textiles, from 55 percent to 67 percent in paper, from 75 percent to 85 percent in chemicals, from 80 percent to 94 percent in oil, from 67 percent to 90 percent in metal products, and from 60 percent to 90 percent in electrical machinery. Such gains were made in the face of onerous wartime shortages of fuel, machinery, motors, vehicles, and tools.[25]

On the whole, these years of army rule constituted an era of prosperity and opportunity for the small Argentine entrepreneur. Business failures between 1943 and 1946 were at their lowest point since the prosperous 1920s. Total liabilities involved in bankruptcies were (in constant 1960 pesos) 8.1 billion in 1930, 4.1 billion in 1935, 3.5 billion in 1940, and only 1.7 billion in 1945. The war and deliberate government policy combined to shelter an essentially small-scale and increasingly labor-intensive industrial sector from foreign competition.[26]

But what of the long-term prospects for these protected industries? Would they be able to lay down strong roots and survive the postwar challenge of renewed foreign competition? If not, would they be sacrificed to free trade? Or would they continue to enjoy protection, in the national interest? And if protected, would they evolve into effective handmaidens of national power, as the military hoped; or would they eventually justify the old agro-industrialists' dire warnings about artificial industry?

## Summary: The Development Pattern

Argentina's economic development up to World War II owes its success to the quality of leadership during most of that era. Its agricultural elites, far from constituting a closed, hidebound ruling caste, were composed of diverse elements and open to change. Many large ranchers and grain farmers were immigrants or the descendants of immigrants. With the leading Creole families, they carried out an agrarian revolution in the late nineteenth century that commercialized agriculture, diversified production, and incorporated the latest rural technology. This oligarchy was capable of taking the initiative for proposing other changes as well. Like the British upper classes, whom they greatly admired, they accepted the expansion of the suffrage when it was evident that further resistance would only lead to unacceptable levels of political violence. The Sáenz Peña electoral law was a model of political reform rarely seen in Latin America.

With the 1940 Pinedo Plan, the oligarchy also accepted industrialization. Some members had already diversified into agro-industries. The agrarian elites, in their capacity as political leaders or bankers, can be charged with snubbing the nascent industrialists for too long and thus holding back progress. However, their resistance to industry was based on the logical principle of comparative advantage, which had the sanction of leading economic theorists throughout the Western world until the depression. Moreover, the participation of leading agrarian families in the early industrialists' associations proves that progressive elements of the oligarchy were not against industry per se, but only against that which was considered artificial, or inappropriate to Argentina's natural possibilities. This was not an illogical position. The feasibility of establishing heavy industry in Argentina was debated again in the 1940s, and there are many Argentines today who consider that the pattern of development adopted after World War II was a mistake. Much of Argentine industry has never become competitive or self-supporting, nor does it show any potential for becoming so.

Concerning the industrialist class, no serious examination of the careers of such men as Di Tella, Bagley, Péres, Noel, Rigolleau, Grasso, Goscilo, Guidici, Frigeri, Braun, or Menéndez could ever sustain the thesis that they lacked the true capitalist spirit. Most were immigrants and many started out poor. They succeeded because of their energy and their entrepreneurial spirit, but also because Argentina was a land of opportunity. Entrepreneurs were not held down by a hidebound aristocracy; rather, they took advantage of the prosperity afforded by a booming economy to establish substantial manufacturing enterprises like TAMET, SIAM, Alpargatas, and Molinos Río de La Plata. They also used their ingenuity to overcome the challenges posed by two wars and a depression and put their companies on firmer foundations. By the end of the 1930s, the industrialists had forced the oligarchy to accept them as partners in Argentina's economic future.

The rise of nationalist sentiment in Argentina during the 1930s was welcomed by the industrialists, who had long campaigned for protective tariffs and government loans. Yet, it is doubtful whether economic nationalism served their true interests. Like many neglected orphans, industry in Argentina had grown up in adversity and had emerged tough and independent. The earliest established companies were always more securely capitalized, bigger, and more enterprising than those that began under state paternalism in the 1930s and 1940s. Moreover, economic nationalism discouraged the participation of foreign capital in Argentina's growth. It is beyond question that foreign loans and investments were the catalysts behind the country's rapid progress until World War I. The recession that occurred during World War I was a warning of what might happen should foreign capital ever withdraw completely from Argentina; and failure to reach prewar levels of growth in the 1920s showed that local private capital, though willing enough, could not completely replace foreign input. The depression years created another shortage of risk capital from the advanced countries, and the increasingly hostile legislation being directed at foreign firms in the oil, utility, railroad, and meatpacking industries made business more difficult. As fresh capital became harder to find, those industries lost their dynamism. In sum, rather than being a barrier to development, foreign capital was a stimulus. No doubt there had been abuses, and criticism of some of its practices was well-grounded; but it is generally true that Argentina's greatest bursts forward occurred when foreign capital was opening up new opportunities, and that its withdrawal coincided with a reversion of the economy to more small-scale and technologically backward enterprise.

It seems clear, from this survey, that where economic progress is concerned, neither the agrarian upper class, the industrialists, nor the foreign capitalists can be held responsible for Argentina's ultimate failure to achieve the status of a modern industrial nation. A more accurate criticism of them, however, would focus upon their political behavior. However receptive they might have been concerning new ideas about production, their social views were reactionary. Conscious of their position as minorities, they entered the era of mass politics with some misgivings, although the dominant liberal ideology they professed forced them to experiment with democracy. Fourteen years of Radical party rule, especially under Yrigoyen, convinced them that democracy meant demagoguery. The Radicals were indeed guilty of corruption and mismanagement, while often showing little respect for democratic procedures. Nevertheless, the elites also criticized Yrigoyen when he was in the right, as when he tried to protect the rights of workers to organize, strike, and engage in collective bargaining.

As we shall see in the following chapter, the landowners and industrialists opposed almost all progressive social legislation. Their view of society was not just hierarchical and authoritarian; they saw nothing wrong in using their workers merely as instruments of production. To be sure, their hierarchical system was open and ascent was possible—even encouraged. But the liberalism they professed was the social Darwinian variety that treated society's unfortunates, or those who simply failed to rise, as expendable. This was often ameliorated in practice, for even in Argentina the abolition of child labor and the establishment of workers' insurance, factory inspections, pensions, and the eight-hour day gradually became accepted. Even so, the acceptance was grudging, violations were common, and the resentments inherited from the past continued. These class divisions, together with the distorted pattern of development inherited from the import-substituting industrialization of the 1930s, would make Perón's populist coalition possible and bring about the crisis of Argentine capitalism.

As the next chapter will show, that crisis was not inevitable. By the end of the 1930s, progress was being made toward industrial peace between employers and workers. That was before the 1943 military coup, however, which brought Juan Perón to the center of the political stage.

## CHAPTER SIX

# *Labor*

rgentina's first labor unions arose from mutual aid societies organized in the 1850s by immigrant workers from Spain and Italy. People from the same homeland, often from the same towns, banded together in the New World to help one another. The first mutual aid societies were nonpolitical; their original purpose was to provide companionship and succor to their members. With the modest dues they charged they were able to offer some medical assistance, accident insurance, or at the very least, a decent burial. There were over 130 of these societies in Argentina by the end of the nineteenth century.[1]

Even before the end of the century, however, many mutual aid societies were being transformed into, or superseded by, more class-conscious forms of labor organization. Immigrants who arrived during the later decades were more likely to have had some experience with European socialist or anarchist movements and hence were more militant in their outlook. The anarchists were more violent, believing that the world was on the verge of a great upheaval that would abolish all forms of authority, including private property, religion, and the state. The working masses needed only to be ignited through acts of terror, called "propaganda of the deed," against the ruling powers. The socialists, by contrast, were more inclined toward gradual, peaceful, and practical solutions to the workers' problems under capitalism.

The earliest union was the typographers', which grew out of a mutual aid society in 1877. It soon disbanded after losing its first strike for higher pay, but it would reappear in the next decade with many other unions representing workers as diverse as carpenters, bricklayers, railroad engineers, hotel employees, bakers, millers, and waiters. Forty-eight strikes were settled during the 1880s, nineteen of which ended with the workers winning all of their demands; twenty-three were complete defeats and six ended in compromises. Unions would fare worse later on, when the employers got better organized.[2]

The 1890s, for example, were a difficult period for labor unions, because of the financial crisis. With unemployment so widespread, workers who had jobs were afraid to risk them by engaging in union activity. Also, the labor movement was split. The first nationwide federation, the Federation of Workers of the Argentine Region (FTRA), founded in 1890, attracted few members, had almost no money in its treasury, and soon foundered over bitter squabbles between the socialists and anarchists.

A second federation, called the Argentine Workers' Federation (FOA), was organized after the turn of the century but had little more success. Its 9,200 members, about 8,000 of whom were anarchists, all lived in the city of Buenos Aires. Various other unions, all of them small, existed in the interior of the country—chiefly in Rosario—and claimed a combined membership of around 1,780. When added to FOA, they included 11,000 organized workers out of a total industrial labor force of 175,000 in 1902.[3] It is hardly surprising, then, that Conservative governments paid little attention to the labor movement. Strikes were not common, and those that were called involved very few laborers. The dispersal of capital among many small-scale enterprises avoided the concentration of large numbers of workers that facilitates the organization of strong unions. One exception to this was the railroad industry, where strikes involving more than 1,000 workers began as early as 1896. Not until 1902, when the anarchists, inspired by the principles of revolutionary syndicalism recently imported from Marseilles and Barcelona, decided to launch a general strike, did the government begin to take labor matters seriously. Even then, it responded to the strike as a public disturbance and a threat to law and order rather than a symptom of social malfunctioning.

The 1902 strike was preceded by the breakup of the FOA into rival organizations: a socialist General Union of Workers (UGT) and an anarchist Workers' Federation of the Argentine Region (FORA). The latter, restrained no longer by their socialist partners, now sought their Armageddon with the capitalist system through the general strike. It began in the Central Fruit Market of Buenos Aires and spread quickly to the carpenters, metalworkers, mechanics, and bakers. The dockworkers were kept on the job only by generous concessions, although their comrades upriver closed the port of Rosario. The government met the strike by suspending the constitution and calling out the police in full force. Workers' meetings were broken up, hundreds of agitators were arrested, and all subversive publications were shut down. Congress did its part by passing a residency law that prohibited the entry into Argentina of any foreigner with a police record or who might, in the judgment of the authorities, disturb the public order. Undesirable aliens could be deported with ease. Armed with these powers, the government began deporting strikers.

Although the strike was broken, anarchist violence continued. In April 1905, they nearly succeeded in assassinating President Manuel Quintana, and in November 1909 they killed the chief of the Buenos Aires police, Col. Ramón Falcón. There were also more strikes. Between 1907 and 1912, which was the height of the anarchists' influence within the labor movement, there were 986 strikes, involving 241,130 workers. Less than a third (310) ended in outright victories, however. Another 104 strikes resulted in compromise settlements, but in 572 cases the workers suffered total defeat.[4]

Meanwhile, the socialists gradually gained respectability. Employers often preferred dealing with the UGT rather than allowing the anarchists to get a foothold in the shop. The railway companies, for instance, were willing to bargain with the socialist-led engineers' union, La Fraternidad, in order to prevent the anarchists' Federation of Railroad Workers (FOF) from making any headway. Similar considerations induced the marble industry to sign the first industrywide collective agreement with its workers in 1901. The contract conceded not only an eight-hour day, but also the suppression of piece-wages, a guaranteed minimum wage, and a closed shop for the socialist union. The socialists' political moderation also secured some modest legislative gains. At their urging, the National Labor Department (DNT) was established in 1904 to gather and publish information about labor conditions. Between 1905 and 1915 Congress passed laws requiring Sunday rest, prohibiting the hiring of children under ten, prohibiting night work for women and minors, making owners responsible for workplace accidents, and setting up a low-cost housing commission.

Many Conservatives made no distinction between anarchists and socialists, however. All notion of labor unions was alien to Argentina's traditions, in their view. The mild reforms they accepted were inspired by a paternalistic feeling toward the lower classes, but they repressed any sign of independent action from these classes. A government crackdown in 1909 prevented the socialists and anarchists from holding a joint May Day celebration, and in 1910 the government declared a state of siege and used all the state's emergency powers to smash an anarchist general strike aimed at spoiling the nation's centennial celebrations.

The state's willingness to use force discouraged the calling of strikes, which declined between 1910 and 1914 from 298 to only 64. The number of workers involved fluctuated but tended to decline. More importantly, the workers suffered defeat in two of three cases. Strikes ended more quickly too: three-fourths lasted less than a week, and a majority were called off after a day. In addition to government hostility, the workers had to contend with a labor surplus. Continued large-scale immigration undermined their bargaining power, because in many cases an employer could easily replace his entire staff. Workers therefore shied away from unions for fear of being labeled agitators. Of some 410,201 industrial laborers in 1914, only about 3,000 were organized.[5]

Labor's setbacks at this time were often due to bad tactics, too. According to the DNT, many strikes might have been avoided and the causes of discontent quickly eliminated except for the interference of the anarchists. As soon as it was known that the workers at a given plant were discontented, FORA representatives would hurry to the scene and take over. The workers, unhappy but unsure of themselves, would listen to their speeches and usually allowed FORA's "expert" negotiators to represent them. At that point the dispute would become heated. The anarchists would threaten the boss with violence and add fresh demands to the original ones. Whereas the dispute might have arisen over wages or unsanitary conditions, the anarchists would up the ante by demanding a closed shop or worker participation in management. The DNT's report suggested that FORA always seemed to think it had to demand a lot in order to win any concessions at all. Instead, the exasperated employer, stung by the anarchists' abusive language, would usually refuse any further negotiation and threaten to fire his entire work force. Since FORA had no strike funds, and since there was a labor surplus, the strikers were usually forced to settle quickly on the boss's terms.

## Working and Living Conditions

Factory conditions were primitive in the late nineteenth century. The typical small entrepreneur started in an old rented building, often a shed or an abandoned storehouse. Such structures usually had poor lighting and little ventilation. The machinery was almost always old, secondhand, and therefore dangerous. Even when a growing firm moved to larger premises, factory construction tended toward the cheap and simple. The building was usually a square or rectangular brick structure with massive furnaces whose clay chimneys rose above the rooftop. There were few windows to let in air or light. Workers labored in a perpetual dusk penetrated at intervals only by lamps hung along the walls and by the flickering light of the furnace flames. The air was oppressively hot and filled with smoke and soot.

Each industry had its particular health hazards. In the textile, metal, match, and glass factories, the air was always full of a fine dust that irritated the lungs. In leather factories, the curing process required the use of sulfuric, nitric, and muriatic acids as well as arsenic and ammonia, all of which gave off harmful vapors that filled the building. In the packinghouses, workers trod upon floors that were slippery with coagulated blood, entrails, and animal excrement. The stench was overwhelming. The men who carried meat to the freezers had to wrap their hands and faces in rags or old newspapers, being careful not to have any fresh blood on their clothes lest it freeze to their bodies. Rheumatism was a common ailment, and few packinghouse workers lasted more than five years.[6]

Accidents were common. Between 1908 and 1912 some 446 workers lost their lives in industrial mishaps, while another 1,495 accidents resulted in serious injury. These official figures from the DNT did not take into account those workers whose health broke, forcing them to quit, and who were permanently incapacitated or fatally ill. When such things happened the worker was, in most cases, simply out of luck. If a worker died, the family lost a breadwinner. Sickness meant loss of income. Outside of a few miserably funded private charities, there was nothing to tide over a working-class family in misfortune. Until 1915, employers were not responsible for accidents on their premises; therefore, few of them carried any insurance. An investigation by the DNT in 1907 found that of forty-two leather-curing establishments in Buenos Aires only seven had insurance to cover workplace accidents. One had a mutual aid society to which each employee contributed fifty centavos every two weeks; this allowed the employer to hire a doctor in emergencies and to pay sick or injured workers a small daily allowance for up to three months. Conditions in other industries were similar.

Shocked, the DNT campaigned to get more employers to take out insurance. As a result, some 1,500 firms agreed to provide insurance that covered a total of 67,291 workers. Continued prodding by the DNT raised these figures to 4,134 firms, employing 160,452 workers, by 1911. The system was voluntary, however, and many employers refused to spend the little extra money required. Not until Perón's regime did the government finally impose a comprehensive, compulsory system of insurance and pensions to provide security for the working class.[7]

The workweek varied according to the branch of industry, but it was never less than fifty hours. During the early years of World War I, when an economic recession raised unemployment to as much as 30 percent, employers were able to force their workers to put in even more hours. In 1916 it was estimated that the average workweek in industry was fifty-five hours, or between nine and ten hours a day. At the same time, wages were so low that it was necessary for all members to work in order for an ordinary family to survive. Child labor was common, although its incidence varied by branch of industry. For example, the physical demands of the leather-curing industry were too great for children, or even for adult women. On the other hand, many minors were employed in glass factories, where working conditions were exceptionally bad. Children who worked in glass factories grew old very quickly because the air was always filled with a fine glass powder that, together with the smoke from the furnaces, made lung infections commonplace. During its investigations, the DNT discovered that most glass factories had no ventilation. Despite the department's urging, few employers would even provide their workers with face masks to filter out the glass particles. Besides the glass industry, many minors were employed in the match industry, where noxious chemical fumes and powders made the air unhealthy. The shoe industry also employed many minors. Women, on the other hand, constituted a majority of the work force in the garment industry.[8]

Low wages, which never kept up with the cost of living, made the labor of women and children under such conditions necessary. A proletarian family simply could not subsist without this extra income. In 1907, the DNT did a survey of industrial wages in relation to the average working-class household's living expenses. Here are six examples of what it found:[9]

Case 1. A family of seven, with one son old enough to work. The father is a dockworker earning 5 pesos a day, or about 130 a month. The family's monthly expenses average 147 pesos, of which 35 are for rent, 33 for groceries, 60 for clothes, 9 for coal, and 10 for miscellaneous purchases. They can make ends meet because the son earns 20 pesos a month as a messenger boy.

Case 2. A family of four, with two working daughters. The father is a railroad foreman earning 90 pesos a month. Average monthly expenses run to around 132 pesos, distributed as follows: 30 for rent, 49 for groceries, 34 for clothes, 8 for coal, and 10 for miscellaneous needs. Fortunately, the two daughters bring in 35 to 40 pesos a month working as seamstresses.

Case 3. A family of four, with one working son. The father is a common laborer in a glass factory and earns 100 pesos a month. The family's expenses amount to 107 pesos a month: 18 for rent, 53 for food, 20 for clothes, 6 for coal, and 10 for miscellaneous. The son earns 20 pesos a month as a messenger boy, so they manage.

Case 4. A family of seven. The father works for a wholesale firm and earns between 130 and 156 pesos a month. Their expenses average 154 pesos a month, of which 38 are for rent, 58 for food, 35 for clothes, 8 for coal, and 10 for miscellaneous. The mother and eldest daughter take in ironing and earn an extra 40 pesos a month.

Case 5. Here is a childless couple. He works as a chauffeur and earns 150 a month. She brings in 70 as a seamstress. They spend, on the average, about 140 pesos a month, paying 30 for rent, 44 for groceries, 40 for clothes, 6 for coal, and 20 [sic] for incidentals.

Case 6. A family of nine. The father is a "stabber" in a slaughterhouse. He earns 5 to 6 pesos a day, or between 130 and 156 a month. Their monthly expenses of 153 pesos are divided thus: 40 for rent, 55 for food, 40 for clothes, 6 for coal, and 10 for miscellaneous. Two daughters work in a match factory and bring home another 60 pesos a month.

Every one of these cases shows a family struggling to cope. Only the childless couple is actually doing well, but if they have children and the woman's work is disrupted their margin of security will be drastically reduced. In all of the other cases, the family depends on earnings besides those of the father to meet expenses. In any of these families, the sickness or death of a child of working age would create a real hardship, whereas the death or incapacity of the father would be utter disaster.

Yet there is a vicious circular logic inherent in these situations. Although the proletarian family needed its children's wages, child labor was also partly responsible for keeping the father's wages low. Many employers substituted the labor of women and minors for that of adult males whenever possible. If an unskilled adult male earned 4 pesos a day doing simple routine tasks at a shoe factory, the employer could replace him with a female who expected only 2 or 3 pesos, or with a child who would get only 80 centavos. In many of the glass factories inspected by the DNT, men were paid 4 pesos a day, but many jobs were held by boys who earned no more than 2 pesos a day, with some receiving as little as 50 centavos. Even the most progressively minded firms adopted these practices. At the Alpargatas factory, the largest and best-paying factory in the entire shoe industry, men were paid 4 pesos a day, whereas women, who constituted a majority of the employees, got only 2.50, and minors earned 2.20. Moreover, Alpargatas contracted as much of its work as possible to women who worked at home for daily wages of between 1.20 and 1.60. Small wonder, then, that the Socialist party campaigned against child labor and in favor of equal pay for women, although such reforms might have had disruptive effects on working-class families in the short run.

As it was, the urban working class lived in squalid conditions. In the slums that ringed Buenos Aires, families crowded into one- or two-room apartments in tenement houses that were known popularly as *conventillos*. The average room measured about 100 square feet. There were no bathrooms or kitchens, and only about half of the buildings had running water. There was usually a common outhouse, and cooking was done over kerosene stoves or pans of coal set on the floor. The better *conventillos* had sinks for washing, but the others had either a common well or a faucet in the courtyard. Rooms had high ceilings and were unheated, except for the same pan of coal the family used for cooking. The typical furniture consisted of two or three metal cots, perhaps a simple pine table, and some straw chairs. In many homes there might be a sewing machine on a wooden crate shoved against the wall. The wallpaper was stained and peeling. Screaming, romping, unkempt children were everywhere, completing the scene of frustration and chaos. Outside, there were no sidewalks or sewers. The streets were usually unpaved, with garbage rotting in the ruts.[10]

Such conditions encouraged disease and delinquency. Slum conditions taught children early that there were easier ways of getting ahead than by slaving away in a factory for a pittance. A successful prostitute could earn as much in one night as her father could by tending a machine for a whole month. Children left alone during the day by their working parents soon discovered the *mala vida* of the streets, cafes, and dance parlors. Burglars, beggars, pimps, prostitutes, muggers, smugglers, confidence men, drug pushers, drunks, and perverts: every form of the *mala vida* flourished in this noxious environment of poverty, overcrowded tenements, broken homes, violence, and desperation. Crimes against property doubled between 1895 and 1910, while those against persons more than doubled. The fact that most of the criminals were immigrants only convinced the Creole upper class that the residency law was a good thing.[11]

The conditions described thus far pertained only to Buenos Aires. They were even worse in the interior. In 1913 the DNT did a study of labor conditions in the sugar industry which revealed just how close to feudalism the provinces of the distant northwest were.[12] At harvest time, the big sugar mills sent agents down to the Chaco to recruit Indian labor with presents of tobacco, salt, and flour. The illiterate Indians would sign labor contracts on the verbal understanding that certain wages were to be paid on a scale corresponding to the tribal hierarchy, and that the companies would provide food, clothing, and housing. Then the Indians would be marched through the jungle to a railway terminal, put on boxcars, and sent to plantations in Jujuy, Salta, or Tucumán provinces. Many of the older people in the tribe would die during this long journey.

On arrival at the sugar plantations, the Indians were divided into two groups: those needed in the fields and those suitable for work in the mills. Field labor was backbreaking. The Indians worked in a stooping position, chopping the cane close to the ground with squared-off machetes. Those who were quicker to learn and got sent to the mills helped the permanent staff. They were paid about double what a field hand earned: 2.5 pesos a day, as compared to the permanent staff's wage of 4 pesos—which was still less than what the average urban worker got. Both mill and field workers were paid weekly, but only in scrip which could be used at the company store. As for the free food promised by the company, the DNT inspector reported: "Concerning food, this could hardly be more deficient. Besides failing to give them the most basic elements to prepare an ordinary meal, they [the Indians] have to make it themselves out of flour, unground corn, lard, and sugar, from which they make a stew (*locro*), using also a little bit of meat. Clothing and any other food they need must be purchased at the company store, using scrip, or tokens, which they receive for their labor."[13]

The Indians felt cheated. "They make us travel a long way," one of them told another DNT agent. "The *patróns* promise us things and then later they don't do them. They always fool us. The *Patrón Grande* (their name for the President of the Republic) ought to help us." Nevertheless, the inspector was pessimistic about helping the Indians to better themselves. With or without contracts, they were always subjected to trickery and exploitation because they could not understand the companies' system of keeping accounts, nor did they understand the value of the scrip they were paid. Given the Indians' narrow outlook, whatever the companies gave them was more than they were used to, and that was enough to keep them returning year after year for the harvests. The government might legislate on these matters, but it would be impossible to prevent widespread abuses.[14]

Conditions like those on the sugar plantations were fairly typical in agro-industry. Woodcutters in the forests of the northeast were paid between 2.25 and 3.50 pesos a day, which they got in scrip, not money. They had to buy all their provisions at company stores where inferior goods were sold at exorbitant prices. The yerba mate plantations along the Paraná River operated in the same fashion. A DNT inspector who visited several of these in 1913 made a special point of noting that one of them, Puerto Segundo, was the only establishment that supplied free bread to its workers. On other plantations, company stores provided food and other articles of "middling quality" at high prices. Medicine was often unavailable.[15]

Even urban wages in the interior were well below those in Buenos Aires. A master bricklayer who in 1907 earned about 5 pesos a day in Buenos Aires would get only 3 in Corrientes. A tinsmith might earn 4 pesos in Buenos Aires but only 1.50 in Corrientes. In general, a good worker could expect to earn 80 to 90 pesos a month in the interior, as compared with 130 to 150 in the capital. Moreover, wages tended to drop as one got deeper into the interior. That was an important factor in causing a steady stream of migration from the countryside to the big city.

## Employers' Attitudes toward Labor

In 1904 Juan Bialet Massé submitted a report to the Ministry of Interior about labor conditions in the provinces. Besides noting all of the problems described above, he was astonished at the ignorance of employers about matters affecting their own industries. Many owners of machine shops had no understanding of how steam engines worked. There were electricians who did not know the principles of electricity and contractors who could not build in a straight line. Such ignorance on the part of an employer was, in Bialet Massé's opinion, less excusable than that of the workers employed. That same ignorance made it impossible for employers to understand that their workers were not simply instruments of production to be used until exhausted. Try as he might, Bialet Massé could not convince the bosses that laborers were intelligent beings who would produce more efficiently if they were better fed, adequately rested, and well treated. He wrote:

> This hardening of one's ways and this total ignorance of social questions and of the psycho-physiology of labor is not . . . [rare]; unfortunately, it is so general that I have not met a single industrial manager, nor any railway administrator, who, even out of curiosity, had looked at a book on those subjects. Phrases like the "rhythm of work," "adaptation to machinery," "unnecessary waste," and other technical terms are absolutely foreign to them. One sees that they have no notion of themselves as machines of labor, and that they have never bothered to consider how the food and liquid they take in is converted into work.
>
> Many industrialists have told me that it would be impossible to apply labor legislation to the provinces, because they are only theories of some socialist professors in Buenos Aires who don't know what a factory or an industry is.[16]

When they found out that Bialet Massé was not only a professor but also an engineer and successful businessman in his own right and that he believed those same theories, the *patróns* simply shrugged their shoulders and clammed up—"some of them because they did not know what to make of me, and others because they were resolved not to be converted."

In the remoter regions, the exploitation of labor sometimes reached bestial levels. In January 1913, a DNT agent traveling through Misiones Territory had cited Puerto Segundo as a model yerba mate plantation. Its management was efficient; the fields were well tended; all of the buildings, including the workers' quarters, were solidly made of hardwood; there was an infirmary and a medical dispensary; the company store was well stocked with affordable goods; a telephone line connected all parts of the plantation to the central office; a narrow-gauge railroad was being built to speed up deliveries from the fields to the port; and the food and pay were good. In all, the plantation had 270 field hands, 180 construction workers for laying the railroad line, and 80 skilled carpenters, smiths, mechanics, and sawyers. The DNT agent noted that there was "severe" discipline on the job, but the workers seemed happy so his report was positive. Eleven months later, 45 "escapees" from Puerto Segundo staggered out of the jungle into the river town of Posadas and told a different tale.[17]

The men were part of an original gang of Russian, Italian, Spanish, and Argentine workers that had been hired through the DNT's auspices to work for at least six months on the company's plantations. The contract, which the DNT had carefully prepared, had specified the amount of wages to be paid and had required the company to furnish free housing, meals, and round-trip transportation between Buenos Aires and Puerto Segundo. It even had stipulated that the workers were to be fed meat, rice, pasta, and beans. According to the men who fled, however, the company had violated every item of the contract. Instead of being taken north by riverboat, they were packed into the hold of a cargo ship as far as Posadas, after which they were transferred to an open barge for the next five days. After arriving at the plantation, many workers fell sick and asked for their return passage. When the company refused, there was a strike. It was broken by the company police, who beat up the strikers. Their leaders were tied up and sent by canoe to more distant plantations. Finally, some of the men escaped through the jungle. After two harrowing weeks, during which they nearly starved to death, they reached civilization.

The story was played up in the press, but it led to no serious investigation. The local DNT representative accused the press of exaggerating the incident and dismissed the workers' statements as contradictory and incoherent. He concluded that they simply had been unused to working in the tropical climate, could not adjust to the local diet, were resentful of the company's prohibition of alcoholic beverages, and longed for the bright lights of the city. That they had violated their contract by running away proved they were unreliable. The chief of police of Misiones Territory affirmed the DNT agent's report. In closing his investigation he wrote: "This headquarters can guarantee that mistreatment does not exist in this territory, for in no case has it been proven to the police."

Such were the conditions, at their worst, under which rural labor worked. Big city employers were not so uniformly unfeeling. There were moderate men like Gastón Rigolleau, the glass manufacturer, who would have agreed with Bialet Massé that better treatment makes better workers. That did not mean that he and others like him approved of labor unions, but at least they felt a paternalistic responsibility toward their employees. Men like Roberto Fraser, Jr., who ran Alpargatas, believed in paying decent wages, providing medical services, and maintaining clean, safe conditions in the shop. Like a good, humane paternalist, Fraser liked to make the daily rounds of his factory, talking to his men and getting to know them. Torcuato Di Tella was of the same mold. A typical Latin *patrón* of the best sort, he took personal responsibility for running the firm, was honest in his dealings, and was concerned about the people working for him. Although SIAM's wages were not high, its fringe benefits were generous. If an employee got sick, the company continued paying him a stipend, the amount of which increased with the length of service. There were paid vacations, retirement pensions, survivors' benefits, and bonuses for weddings or the birth of a child. Above all, there was job security. No employee was ever fired except under great provocation, and even then the company provided advanced notice and severance pay. Like Fraser, Di Tella enjoyed walking the factory floor and talking with the workers.[18]

Liberals like Rigolleau, Fraser, and Di Tella were a minority within the UIA, however. The typical industrialist was a self-made man who had advanced through years of grueling sacrifice. His capital, his ego, and the efforts of his entire life were completely involved in his business. Given his limited education and his precarious economic position, he was likely to hold the same views toward labor as his counterparts in the interior. Consequently, the UIA fought every type of progressive legislation: compulsory Sunday rest days, the Saturday half day, the eight-hour day, compulsory accident insurance, the prohibition of child labor, the limiting of working hours for women and children, and factory inspections. As for strikes, Bialet Massé summarized perfectly the horror with which the typical industrialist viewed them: "The word 'strike' agitates the nerves of an industrialist. No bargaining or reasoning is possible. The modern worker is an ingrate who wants to impose terms on his employer. Insolence! They are insatiable. If we raise them to ten percent of the forty percent profit we make how much more will they demand? Idlers! They think it's a big deal to work twelve hours a day, when after all we can't even eat or sleep because we're always thinking about the business."[19]

## The Labor Movement Matures

World War I was a particularly severe time for industrial labor. Unable to get fuel, raw materials, machinery, or parts, many industrialists were forced to retrench. Unemployment doubled during the first year of the war and hit a peak of just below 20 percent in 1917. Although the employment situation improved slightly after that, unemployment never dropped significantly until the boom years of the late 1920s. Real wages fell too. Inflation cut them by about a third between 1914 and 1917.

Industrial relations naturally were affected by this erosion of the living standards of laborers. The number of strikes increased as the war continued, and violence was never absent from them. The packinghouse workers' strike of December 1917 climaxed in a gun battle between the strikers and the police, during which the latter invaded the union's headquarters, shooting and sabering the men inside. The railroad workers' strike of August 1917 resulted in great destruction as workers burned railway cars and station houses, tore up rails, smashed signal boxes, and cut telegraph wires. Nonstrikers were beaten up, and even passengers were abused. Similar but less dramatic confrontations occurred in other industries, most notably in the dockworkers' strikes of 1916 and 1917.

The government's attitude was important in determining a strike's outcome. The packinghouse workers' strike was smashed because their union was controlled by anarchists, with whom the government would have no dealings. On the other hand, the railroad workers, who were just as violent, got government backing because their strike was led by the democratic socialist engineers' union, La Fraternidad. The railroad companies were ordered by Yrigoyen to satisfy the workers' demands and reinstate them in their jobs. A month later, when the anarchist FOF called another strike, it failed to get backing from La Fraternidad or the government, so the strike was quickly broken. Similarly, the dockworkers won their strike with support from the government because they were led by political moderates. Political moderation was not enough to win official sympathy for the municipal workers who struck in 1917, however; in that case, the Radicals were eager to fire incumbent employees in order to create job vacancies for their own followers.

It was important for the government to encourage moderate unionism by showing that reasonableness paid but extremism did not. In the Radicals' case, there was also a desire to court public opinion, which was often prolabor so long as the anarchists were not involved. In the 1917 railroad strike, the companies' public-be-damned attitude created sympathy for the workers. Just before the strike, for example, the companies announced wage cuts simulta-neously with a 22 percent increase in fares. There was widespread approval when Yrigoyen rolled back the fare increases and imposed a generous labor contract on the companies that included the eight-hour day, paid annual vacations, sick pay, and time and a half for overtime. The success of politically moderate unionism on the rail-roads, coupled with the inability of the anarchists to make any headway in the face of government hostility, had its desired effect: by 1922 the FOF had lost all support among the workers, who were now represented by the new Unión Ferroviaria. The UF rejected vio-lence in favor of legal tactics.

Employers and their sympathizers in the press were not inclined to take the long view, however. Yrigoyen's intervention in the 1917 railroad strike brought a bitter blast from the probusiness RRP:

The strikers have triumphed. Foreign capital has been humil-iated. The Government is acclaimed by the proletariat as the protector of the poor. Should the Railway Pension Law be ap-plied in its present form, the men who shot engine-drivers, burnt railway wagons, tore down signals and tore up rails dur-ing the successful strike will, in due course, become entitled to pass the afternoon and evening of their days in well-earned re-tirement on pensions paid by the Company they have served so well! Now that it is known what violence and wanton destruc-tion can achieve, it is only reasonable to anticipate that any future workmen's grievances, real or imagined, trivial or tran-scendental, may be ventilated in the same manner. Truly, the railway industry in Argentina is worked under great difficulties these days.[20]

The companies protested the government-imposed contract as a violation of property rights. Rejecting the state's right to interfere in their internal policies, they warned Yrigoyen that "it would not be possible to comply with [the contract's] regulations in their en-tirety," and served notice that they intended to fight the govern-ment in court. They soon backed down, however, because even the British embassy refused to support them. Britain needed steady de-liveries of Argentine foodstuffs during World War I and could not allow the railroad companies to provoke another strike.[21]

Other employers prepared to resist the new prolabor drift, how-ever. The growing number and serious nature of strikes convinced them that capitalism was under attack. In 1915 there had been only 65 strikes involving only 12,000 workers; but in 1918 the number of strikes rose to 196, with 133,000 workers walking off their jobs. It was necessary to show the government who had the real muscle. In 1918 the SRA, the Italo-Argentine electric company, the Braun-Menéndez conglomerate, several big shipping firms, the Buenos Aires Stock Exchange, and the Center for Cereal Exporters founded the Labor Association (Asociación del Trabajo), whose primary function was to recruit strikebreakers from the ranks of the unemployed. It also furnished private police to employers hit by strikes, in the event that the government failed to provide adequate protection.

More aggressive still was the Patriotic League (Liga Patriótica), a paramilitary group founded during the war. Its storm troopers were largely responsible for the events of the "Tragic Week," which occurred in January 1919. That incident, the worst scene of labor violence in Argentina's history, grew out of a strike called early in December at the metal works of Pedro Vasena & Sons. Vasena was a tough employer who often was a spokesman for the UIA's hardliners. Opposing him was a union heavily infiltrated by anarchists. Determined to smash the union, Vasena hired strikebreakers. The strikers, in turn, tried to keep these scabs from entering the plant. Violence ensued, becoming an all-out gunbattle when the police arrived. Five workers were killed. Two days later, another battle was fought as a large crowd of workers was taking the slain men to the cemetery. While that was going on, other police units were fighting workers who were trying to set fire to the factory.

On 10 January the anarchist labor federation, FORA-9, called for a general strike, to which the Patriotic League responded with a blast against "Jewish agitators" who were "corrupting" the workers and subverting the nation. It was true that many anarchist leaders were Jews, so it was the Jewish community that was to bear the brunt of right-wing reaction. Before the day was over, the league's storm troopers rushed into the Jewish quarter, smashing storefronts and invading apartment buildings while shouting "Kill the Jews! Kill the Commies!" Furniture and other personal belongings were thrown into the street and burned. Any Jew who fell into their hands was beaten. Estimates of the death toll from these various acts of violence range from 700 to 1,500. At least another 4,000 people were seriously injured. Yrigoyen, thoroughly alarmed by events, ordered the Vasena company to settle the strike immediately, on the workers' terms. The company grudgingly gave in, and the government, after meeting with a delegation from the union, released all of the arrested strikers.[22]

It was not only nouveau riche industrialists who supported organizations like the Patriotic League and the Labor Association. The Labor Association's president was Dr. Joaquín de Anchorena, a descendant of one of Argentina's "first families." The founder and president of the Patriotic League was Manuel Carlés, an aristocratic lawyer who taught philosophy and literature at the Colégio Nacional, where he recruited many of his young fanatics from Argentina's better families. The league's vice-president was Luís Zuberbuhler, who was also president of CACIP, the agro-industrialist pressure group. The league's executive committee included a retired general, a retired admiral, Carlos Noel (the candy manufacturer), and such *niños bien* of Jockey Club status as Nicolás Calvo, Manuel Calvo, Lorenzo Añadón, and José Saraíva. The presence of these men in such a violent and reactionary organization indicates how thin was the veneer of civilization in the Argentine upper class. The old liberal oligarchy had seen immigration as a civilizing influence; the new generation of aristocrats asserted that, "The country is paying now for the immigration we had between 1880 and 1900," and claimed to possess a list of 43,683 foreign-born subversives in Argentina as proof.[23]

Even more brutal than the Tragic Week was the suppression of a general strike that broke out in Patagonia in 1920. Once again, Yrigoyen was inclined to take a sympathetic view of the workers' claims, but pressure from the SRA (of which he was a member), the British meatpackers, and the Braun-Menéndez empire brought him over to the employers' side. The employers, having failed to break the strike with the local police or hired thugs, demanded that the army be sent in. Early in 1921, Yrigoyen sent the Tenth Cavalry, under Lt. Col. Héctor Varela, with orders to crush what was purported to be an anarchist-inspired rebellion by packinghouse workers, stevedores, *estancia* workers, and commercial employees. Faced with the army, the strikers turned to guerrilla tactics, but their fight was hopeless. Anyone known to favor the strikers was arrested and many were tortured into revealing the ringleaders' whereabouts. Over the next year, an average of five to six guerrillas was killed each day. In some cases, they were shot in cold blood and dumped into mass graves. In all, it is estimated that well over 2,000 strikers were killed, some of them in truly gruesome ways. The strike was eventually broken, but the anarchists got partial revenge by assassinating Colonel Varela with a bomb. The assassin, a German named

Wilckens, was murdered in his cell a few days later by a guard, Pérez Millan, who had been in Patagonia with Varela. Not long afterwards, Pérez Millan too was killed in reprisal.[24]

Despite repression and the division of labor between anarchists, socialists, and (after 1917) communists, union membership continued to grow throughout the 1920s. From only 3,000 unionized workers in 1914 the number rose quickly to around 100,000 in 1920 and reached 230,000 by 1930.[25] These were concentrated in just a few fields, however, with over half belonging to the railroad unions and the remainder composed mainly of municipal employees, dockworkers, and a few skilled trades. In many branches of industry, unions were unknown or almost unknown. Consequently, a growing membership did not lead to winning more strikes, except in the few areas where unions were strong. Indeed, Shipley notes that labor lost three of every four strikes during the 1920s.[26]

On the other hand, the 1920s were a decade of relative calm in labor relations. Compared with the war years, there were fewer strikes and fewer workers involved in them. The decrease was due more to rising prosperity than to the bullying tactics of the Patriotic League. As commerce and industry expanded, there was a greater demand for labor, causing unemployment to drop and wages to go up. As the bargaining position of the workers improved, they were able to improve their lot without resorting to conflict. This was the period when Sunday rest, half-day Saturdays (at full pay), and the eight-hour day became normal for urban workers. The DNT calculated that between 1920 and 1929 labor's real wages rose by about 41 percent. Its surveys of working-class living conditions showed that between 1925 and 1929 the average proletarian family had money left over at the end of the month. In comparison with earlier years when it was difficult to make ends meet, the family could now save a little, or spend a little more on clothes, medicine, or entertainment.[27]

Still, the workers' conditions were far from rosy. Workers continued to be crowded into *conventillos* with four or five people sharing a single room. Medical attention was limited to a few understaffed government or private charitable clinics. The mortality rate, especially from tuberculosis, was much higher in the workers' barrios than in the Barrio Norte. Workplace accidents were still common, as employers constantly evaded the few DNT inspectors. And, despite DNT prodding, most shops still carried no insurance. Employers also found it easy to evade laws regulating the labor of women and children, and if they were caught they almost always escaped unpunished. For example, of some 3,347 employers prosecuted by the DNT in 1927, only 1,007 were convicted; and of those, 705 got suspended sentences. The next year there were only 641 convictions out of 4,281 cases, and every employer found guilty was given a suspended sentence. Often these cases got so tangled in legal machinery that they were never brought to trial.[28]

## Labor under the Concordancia

A rash of business failures and an increase in unemployment to nearly 18 percent were the first effects of the Great Depression. As labor's bargaining position weakened, real wages fell by about 20 percent were between 1929 and 1932. There was a surge of resistance at first, reflected in the increase of strikes from 96 in 1927–28 to 119 in 1929–30, but workers soon realized that such measures might only lead to further unemployment. In 1931–32 there were only 74 strikes, and in 1933–34 there were only 47.[29]

The economy began to improve after the Justo administration took over in 1932. By 1934, thanks to import-substituting industrialization, unemployment was back down to its 1929 level. During the remainder of the decade and all through World War II, 42,000 new jobs were created every year, and 40,000 young people entered the labor force for the first time—in short, there was full employment. Wages failed to rise to reflect this, however, partly because the unions still attracted only a small minority of the urban work force and also because they were not united in a single federation.

The founding in 1930 of a new, nationwide labor federation, the General Confederation of Workers (CGT), was the most ambitious attempt so far to unite all workers in a single, giant phalanx. Like previous attempts, however, it failed to overcome the persistent problem of factionalism. The moderate socialists now had to confront the communists as their main ideological opponents, although there were still some pockets of anarchist influence. Personal ambitions also divided the CGT. José Domenech, head of the Unión Ferroviaria, the country's largest union, wanted to start a Labor party that would be independent of both the Radicals and the Socialists. He was opposed by two leading socialists, Francisco Pérez Leirós of the municipal workers' union and Angel Borlenghi of the commercial employees union. As a result, the CGT split at its March 1943 convention into two rival groups, each having around 160,000 members. Domenech and his union formed the backbone of CGT-1, while the socialists controlled CGT-2. The Communist party aligned itself with the latter organization as the weaker and more easily infiltrated of the two.

In addition to the two CGT organizations, there were 140,000 other unionized workers. About 23,000 of them belonged to the syndicalist Unión Sindical Argentina (USA), headed by Luís Gay, the leader of the telephone workers. The remainder belonged to various unions that were unaffiliated with any federation. Taken all together, 472,828 workers were unionized, or about 10 percent of the nonagricultural labor force. Even in manufacturing, out of 1 million workers employed in 1945, fewer than 150,000 were unionized. While these figures show considerable growth compared with figures from 1914, when there were only 3,000 unionized nonagricultural workers out of 2.3 million, there was still a long way to go before labor could have the muscle it needed to make the employers and the government pay it respectful attention.[30]

Why didn't more workers join unions? To begin with, organization was still hampered by the dispersal of the labor force among many small establishments. Even as late as 1946, the average industrial firm employed fewer than thirteen workers, and 60 percent had fewer than ten. Second, there were more women in the labor force. They not only resisted joining unions; they were also willing to work for lower wages. Third, there was a constant rise in the ratio of white-collar to blue-collar workers. The former were also—with the exception of government employees—less willing to unionize. Fourth, the proportion of workers in commerce and services rose in relation to that of industry. The establishments they worked for tended to be even smaller than those in industry, and their jobs were often more precarious; hence, they stayed out of unions. Fifth, during the 1930s the character of the urban labor force changed considerably as hundreds of thousands of migrants from the interior moved to Buenos Aires. Whereas in 1914 about half of the city's inhabitants were of European immigrant origin, 40 percent were native-born porteños, and only 10 percent originated in the interior, by 1947 European immigrants were only a fourth of the population and migrants from the interior constituted almost a third. Those migrants, or cabecitas negras (little blackheads), as the porteños called them because of their mixed blood and dark complexions, did not blend well with the established work force. They were politically unsophisticated, uninterested in ideological questions, and nonjoiners. For their part, the Europeanized union leaders had little interest in the cabecitas negras and did not try to recruit them.

Thus, the unions missed a great opportunity to convert themselves into truly mass organizations. Not until Perón came along, with his authoritarian, personalistic style, did the *cabecitas negras* find someone able to appeal to them in terms they understood.[31]

## Labor under Attack

General Uriburu, who took over the government from Yrigoyen in 1930, was intensely antilabor. He was determined to purge all subversives and agitators from the country by following a plan designed by his interior minister, Matias Sánchez Sorondo, an admirer of European fascism and its toughness in dealing with the Left. Uriburu set up a Special Section within the federal police for dealing with labor organizers, left-wing propagandists, and Radical party plotters. The Special Section hired sadists like Cipriano Lombilla and José Faustino Amoresano to beat up and torture the government's opponents. It was not abolished after Uriburu left office, either. Justo left it intact and even increased its budget, as did every other government that followed until 1955, including Perón's.[32]

In addition to the Special Section, Uriburu encouraged a new storm troopers' formation called the Argentine Civic Legion, which was created by merging a number of extreme nationalist groups, including the Patriotic League. Like the German SA, after which it was modeled, its members wore brown-shirted uniforms, received regular army training, and were issued weapons and ammunition by the War Ministry. Its propaganda was turned out free of charge by the printing shop of the central post office. In its declaration of principles, the Civic Legion attacked both Marxism and democracy. It favored a corporativist state like Mussolini's Italy and believed that Argentina must fulfill its destiny as a leader of South America by becoming the dominant military power on the continent. Like the Special Section, the Civic Legion outlasted Uriburu's administration. In 1936, Justo appointed Gen. Juan Bautista Molina, a Naziphile fresh from a tour of Hitler's Germany, to head it. Under General Molina, the organization reached a peak of 10,000 members.[33]

Despite efforts by the Civic Legion and the Special Section to weaken the trade union movement, the government was unable to prevent strikes or to keep the workers from winning more and more of them. While it is true that there were fewer strikes under the Concordancia (only 633 between 1934 and 1943, as compared with 1,040 in the period 1920–29), labor had much greater success in getting its demands met. In the 1920s, it lost three of four strikes, but under the Concordancia it won complete or partial victories in two of three cases.[34]

It is surprising that an increasing number of strikes were waged and won by unskilled and less privileged workers. Statistics on strikes and average wages in industry show that after 1933 the average real wage of strikers was constantly below that of the average real wage of industrial workers generally. It was in this lower stratum of the working class that communists were most active, especially in the construction, lumber, textile, metallurgical, and food-processing industries. In the latter sector, the packinghouses and bakeries were hardest hit by union militancy. Communists made little progress in penetrating most of the skilled trades, however. Nor did they succeed in winning over the beer workers or the ladies of the garment workers' union, both of which were tough and skilled at collective bargaining.[35]

About half of the strikes were about wages. After that, the greatest number were called to show solidarity with other striking unions or to demand the rehiring of people discharged for their union activity. In somewhat more than a third of the cases, direct negotiation between management and workers ended the strike. Surprisingly, in about one of five cases the union itself acted as a conciliator between management and the factory work force. Maybe those were only company unions, but if so, it is odd that they got the workers to cooperate. It is more likely that as full employment became the norm, employers were more willing to use the unions' good offices wherever moderates were in control.

### Employers' Attitudes

Businessmen watched the growth of unions with misgivings. While they campaigned in the name of free enterprise to repeal most labor legislation, they succeeded only in preventing the spread of pensions, paid vacations, and insurance to industries not yet covered by them—for as yet there was no comprehensive system of social legislation. In this "spoiling action" they were more successful. As late as 1942, only 647,000 of approximately 4 million workers, of whom 3 million were nonagricultural, were covered by accident insurance or pensions.

Certain other issues were no longer open to debate. The UIA had come to acknowledge that it could not defend child labor or resist the regulation of hours and types of work performed by women and minors without losing public sympathy. Even its feisty president, Luís Colombo, accepted the idea of retirement pensions "on principle." "It is necessary," he admitted in a 1938 speech, "that the working man be secure in his old age, or in sickness, or against the possibility of being incapacitated and unable to support himself and his loved ones. But this should be done in such a way as to avoid causing an excessive and onerous burden on the public treasury, creating social parasitism at the expense of the productive population." At a 1941 banquet celebrating Industry Day, he tried to deflect a government proposal to create a comprehensive social security system by arguing that such a scheme should be left to private enterprise. "Industry desires to protect its employees," he told the ministers of agriculture and of commerce and industry, who were attending the banquet. "It has declared this in no uncertain terms. It wants to do so because it is not only humane, but it's good business as well—so long as we are talking about competent and efficient employees."[36]

One of Colombo's special bugaboos was a 1938 law requiring employers to pay a heavy indemnity when dismissing any employee who had worked more than ninety days for the firm. Theoretically, it was possible to evade the law by using only temporary help; but in those years there was a labor shortage, and skilled labor was always at a premium. Such laws, in Colombo's view, encouraged malcontents in the shop, undermined discipline, and hurt productivity. To the extent that they added to a businessman's costs, consumers would suffer by having to pay higher prices.[37]

The small businessmen's Argentine Federation of Entities Defending Commerce and Industry also complained that the Concordancia was as demagogic as the communists. More strident still was the old Labor Association, which was still trying to break strikes. It protested loudly when Roberto Ortiz, who followed Justo in the presidency, withdrew support from the Civic Legion. Shorn of official backing, the Legion deflated like a punctured balloon, dropping from a peak of 10,000 members to only 1,500 by 1941. Disillusioned by the Concordancia, the Labor Association welcomed the military coup of June 1943, only to take alarm again when the new labor secretary, Colonel Perón, began to court the unions.[38]

It never occurred to Argentine industrialists that there was a basic discrepancy between their hostility to any government regulation of business and their desire to have the government control the labor unions. They argued against labor legislation on the grounds that it would drive up costs and raise consumer prices, but they preferred not to dwell on what effects high protective tariffs would have on the price of goods. Nor did it occur to them that a government strong enough to smother the demands of some 4 million working-class people might not hesitate to extend its power over 116,000 industrial proprietors, 200,000 merchant employers, or the 200 leading *estancieros* as well. Men like Luís Colombo pursued a different logic: if Argentina must industrialize to be great and independent, then infant industries had to be protected, and their owners should be unencumbered by either government regulators or labor agitators. They promised that, in the end, everyone would benefit as the rewards of economic growth trickled down.

Even liberal entrepreneurs believed in this productivist philosophy that viewed the captains of industry as society's farsighted uplifters. Thus, Roberto Fraser, Jr., was sincerely shocked when Alpargatas suffered its first strike in 1946. The company had always paid top wages in the textile field, besides providing its employees with a good array of social services. Fraser, an old-fashioned paternalist, was proud of being a liberal and approachable boss who took an interest in his employees' welfare. It was a bitter moment in his life when he discovered that the privileges he once extended voluntarily to his workers were no longer appreciated as such but had become merely the basis for demanding further rights. Unable to deal with the new militancy, Fraser, at age sixty-four, decided to retire.[39]

Torcuato Di Tella experienced the same bitter lesson. As a good paternalist, he had provided his employees with good pay and excellent fringe benefits, although he also expected them to sacrifice if the company required it. In the early days of the Great Depression, when a bank was making trouble about renewing a loan, Di Tella saved the firm only by decreeing drastic cuts in wages and by selling parts of SIAM's property. Those measures might have been impossible to enforce in an age of strong unions. For that reason, Di Tella battled against unionization just as hard as the most reactionary boss. During a serious strike in 1942, he fired 200 workers who had formed a chapter of the Metalworkers' Union (UOM) in his plant. Eventually the government intervened and ordered him to meet the wage demands that had touched off the strike in the first place. However, Di Tella refused the government's demand that he also take back the dismissed employees.[40]

Di Tella's example points to a common outlook among Argentine entrepreneurs. Most of them were willing to negotiate about wage demands but were inflexible about maintaining their authority over work assignments, job classifications, hiring, firing, and discipline.

When strikes were called over wages, labor was more likely to win. Of 62 strikes that were settled in 1942 involving purely wage issues, labor won 27, lost only 10, and got a compromise settlement in 25. But in 40 strikes where the issue was mainly about work rules, factory conditions, union recognition, or personnel decisions, labor won only 12, lost 20, and achieved a compromise in 8.[41]

By the 1940s, the old paternalistic boss was gradually, but grudgingly, adopting a new outlook that accepted labor unions not only as inevitable, but as potentially useful elements in maintaining industrial peace. In 1942, half of the strikes were settled through conciliation, with the DNT acting as the mediator. Another 37 percent involved the union acting as conciliator between management and the previously unorganized workers. Eight percent were resolved by direct negotiation between the strikers and the company, and only 4 strikes required arbitration. There was evidence, therefore, that capital and labor were beginning to discover the advantages of cooperation on the eve of Perón's rise to power.

At the same time, employers began to form more associations of their own to counteract labor's growing effectiveness. Whereas in 1936 there were only 37 employers' guilds, representing a total of 14,374 firms, by 1941 the DNT had registered 174 covering 50,408 enterprises. The largest number of such associations belonged to the commercial businesses, but in industry the greatest organizational efforts were made in construction, metallurgy, chemicals, and lumber—all of which had experienced serious labor troubles. The largest single association was still the UIA, with 25 subassociations representing different branches of industry and 1,214 individual employers. Considering, however, that there were 60,266 industrial owners and managers in 1941, it is obvious that even the UIA was far short of being comprehensive. The typical Argentine entrepreneur was still too small in scale and too individualistic to join an association, although those who did belong to the UIA were usually the leaders in their fields.[42]

## Living Standards in the Early 1940s

What was the situation of the working class in the period just before Perón? Were the conditions in which the proletariat lived and worked improving or deteriorating? Tomás Roberto Fillol argues persuasively that Argentine workers were not living under miserable conditions and were not filled with class hatred. Except for an urban housing shortage, their living standards were the highest in Latin America and their diet, in terms of per capita calorie intake, compared favorably even with the United States.[43]

In contrast to this view, the DNT published a gloomy report on working class conditions in 1943. The report was issued in April, only two months before the coup that was to launch Perón into prominence, and it concluded, "In general, the situation of the worker in Argentina has deteriorated, in spite of the upswing in industry. Whereas huge profits are being made daily, the majority of the population is forced to reduce its standard of living . . . the gap between wages and the cost of living is continually increasing."[44]

During the first half of the 1930s, wages and prices had fallen at about the same rate. In 1934, both were 22 percent lower than they had been five years earlier. In the latter half of the 1930s, however, wages lagged behind prices, so that by 1940 the average laborer in Buenos Aires had suffered a 9 percent erosion in his buying power. The DNT estimated that a typical porteño working-class family needed 150.28 pesos a month, whereas the average paycheck in industry was only 113.15. As always, the gap had to be filled by sending the wife and children out to work. According to Ysabel Rennie, "Usually it had to be made up by the woman of the family, who might work as a servant or take in laundry. As a servant she would work from seven-thirty in the morning until nearly midnight . . . and would earn 40 to 60 pesos a month. That would be enough to bridge the gap."[45]

Labor recaptured some of the lost ground between 1940 and 1943. Living costs rose by 8 percent in that time, but the expansion of industry and the resulting shortage of workers pushed wages up by 11 percent. Even so, there were wide variations in living standards between skilled and unskilled workers. According to the DNT, the average proletarian family faced a monthly food bill for rent, food, clothes, fuel, and medicine of around 162 pesos. Since the average paycheck was only 135 pesos, an extra breadwinner was still a necessity. The average railroad worker earned 196 pesos, however, besides enjoying excellent fringe benefits such as company housing and free medical care, and so might be considered a "labor aristocrat." An expert bricklayer could earn between 188 and 206; carpenters and electricians averaged 181; plumbers got 184; and linotypists, with an average of 288 pesos a month, topped the list. At the other end of the scale, a bus or trolley conductor almost reached the break-even point with 159 pesos; unskilled factory and construction workers got around 133; packinghouse workers were well below the average wage at 119; and stevedores averaged a miserable 60 pesos a month, probably because of high turnover on the docks.[46]

Wages were even lower outside Buenos Aires. The bricklayer who earned 1.03 pesos an hour in the capital could expect only 0.94 in Santa Fé, 0.88 in Tucumán, and 0.60 in Catamarca. A truck driver earning 0.98 an hour in Buenos Aires would get only 0.63 if he moved to Tucumán, 0.50 if he lived in Entre Ríos, and only 0.38 in Salta. Nor were these lower wages necessarily balanced by cheaper living costs. Even as late as World War II, workers in the northern cotton and yerba mate plantations were paid barely subsistence wages, which they received in scrip, and were gouged by company stores. In La Rioja it was reported that rural laborers lived under brutal conditions. Many of them were housed in thatch-roofed lean-tos; their diet consisted of corn and carob beans; and they drank from the same stagnant pools as the animals.[47]

Foremen, clerical workers, and technicians constituted the upper stratum of the proletariat. Such workers were paid about half as much again what their blue-collar counterparts earned. Foremen earned almost twice as much as the average industrial worker, and qualified technicians were paid about double what foremen got. Although technically proletarians, such people tended to be bourgeois in outlook. Certain categories of skilled workers might earn more than the average clerical employee, but the latter's social standing was higher and his lifestyle was more middle class in nature. He wore a white shirt and tie to work and never got his hands dirty. A shop worker who got promoted to foreman mingled with the bourgeoisie and learned their ways as he acted as a liaison between management and the factory floor. A man who could upgrade his status from mechanic to technician could change his whole way of life. His wife could choose between work or home; his children could stay in school; he could move from his *conventillo* to a decent apartment. He might eventually start his own business.

Such people, though of modest antecedents, were hard on themselves in their drive to ascend the social ladder. They worked long hours, denied themselves comforts, and sometimes went to night school to raise their qualifications. They had little patience with "labor solidarity." They wanted to get out of the working class. If they succeeded, they seldom showed much sympathy for those they left behind because their personal experience proved to them that Argentina was a great land of opportunity—for those willing to make the effort and sacrifice. Their outlook as employers was, therefore, usually that of the most rugged social Darwinism.[48]

What, then, was the situation of the working classes in the early 1940s? On the whole, it was better than it had been a decade before. Union membership was growing, there was full employment, and real wages were crawling upward. The eight-hour day had been won, social legislation protected more workers, and strikes were more likely to yield results favorable to labor. Thanks to a gradual softening of employer attitudes, more disputes were being settled peacefully through the good offices of the DNT.

Such gains should not obscure the fact, however, that Argentine society still had a long way to go to secure real justice for workers. It was still true that only a minority of workers belonged to unions, were covered by accident insurance or pension schemes, or were able to participate more than marginally in the benefits of economic growth. Most working class people in the cities still lived in *conventillos* or shantytowns, and most families still needed more than one breadwinner to make ends meet. Out in the country, some 2 million agricultural workers lived in unspeakable conditions.

It is true, moreover, that revolutions are more likely to occur when things are beginning to improve. Labor, beginning to feel its power in the early 1940s, was gaining confidence. What it lacked was a spokesman, a catalyst who could galvanize it and direct its latent strength toward achieving its long-sought goals. It was the measure of Perón's political genius that he recognized labor's potential power and threw himself into the task of harnessing it to his own career.

# PART TWO

# The Peronist Watershed

## CHAPTER SEVEN

# The Roots of Charisma

In June 1943, Juan Domingo Perón suddenly burst onto the Argentine political scene as the new "strongman" behind the military junta that took power. Previously unknown, save among a clique of army nationalists, he was to become thereafter the pivot around which Argentina's power struggles would revolve for the next three decades. He polarized the society as no man—neither Rosas, Mitre, nor Yrigoyen—had ever done. Even today, more than a decade after his death, a powerful political party backed by the trade union movement bears his name. His speeches and writings are still quoted as gospel by many thousands of Argentines, who nevertheless cannot agree on whether he was a revolutionary of the Left, a champion of the patriotic Right, or a pragmatic reformer who instinctively avoided extremes. By contrast, those who hated Perón during his lifetime agree that he was a demagogue and a tyrant who ruined the country's economy, wasted its resources, and stirred up class hatred.

Whatever view one takes of Perón, there is no denying that, for good or evil, he left his imprint on Argentina. The essential facts about his political career are fairly well known. As head of a secret army lodge called the Group of United Officers (GOU), he helped to mastermind the June 1943 coup and occupied a prominent place in the resulting military government. As under secretary of war, he was in charge of military promotions and assignments, and he used the post to consolidate his power. As secretary of labor and social welfare, he employed all the power of a dictatorial state to overcome opposition to long-overdue labor legislation and to build up powerful unions personally attached to him in every economic field. These became the mass base for the Peronist movement. In 1946 he was elected president of Argentina and was reelected in 1952. Those years constituted a watershed in the country's history in terms of the expansion of government power over the economy, social reform legislation, and the strengthening of the labor movement. The changes that Perón brought about created such opposition, however, that he was finally forced out of office by a military revolt in 1955. But even while he was in exile, Perón's charisma enabled him to control a mass following in Argentina, and with that he was able to prevent any other leader from governing effectively. A political stalemate resulted, lasting from 1955 to 1973, during which the economy stagnated and the anti-Peronist opposition fragmented. Violence spread and became uncontrollable. Finally, in 1973, Perón returned in triumph to Argentina and resumed the presidency, hailed as a savior by practically every segment of the society. He was seventy-seven. It was a remarkable comeback that capped the career of one of the most extraordinary politicians Latin America has ever produced. He died in office the following year.

To some extent, it seems surprising that Perón became so controversial. His opponents charged him with being a dictator, but that was nothing new in Argentina. Democracy had existed there only briefly, sandwiched, as it were, between the liberal oligarchy's long tutelary rule and the Concordancia's thin facade of legitimacy. If Perón's government intervened more in the economy than previous regimes, that was only a matter of degree. Laissez-faire liberalism had already been abandoned by the Concordancia, which had encouraged industry with various kinds of protection and had provided a floor for agricultural prices through its many regulatory boards. And although Perón showered benefits on labor, he also tried, unsuccessfully, to enlist the backing of industry by providing it with more aid and protection than it had ever enjoyed.

More than anything else, it was Perón's fostering of a powerful, united labor movement that divided the country. From the standpoint of the Argentine upper classes, Perón's great sin was the anti-capitalist rhetoric that he and Evita, his spellbinding wife, used to rally labor's support and raise the political consciousness of the lower classes. Not only was that the source of his controversiality, but it was also his most lasting legacy to Argentina.

## The Formation of a Leader

Perón's enemies accused him of opportunism. In their view, he was a demagogue with no fixed ideas beyond some borrowings from the ideological grab bag of fascism. Even his supporters, while rejecting the comparison with fascism, admired him for his cleverness and pragmatism. For them, he was a master politician. What sort of man was Perón, really? Was he truly devoid of principles? Did he believe in any ends that he might use to justify his means? I shall argue here that he did—that Perón's ideas were formed early in his career as an army officer, and that throughout his life he was remarkably faithful to them, despite his Machiavellianism in pursuing them.

It is natural to assume that a person's social background helps to shape his thinking. Unfortunately, like so much of his life, Perón's antecedents are obscured by the mixing of fact and myth. Perón himself was not a reliable source. Ever conscious of his political image, he ignored, distorted, or invented details about his background as it suited his purposes. We know, however, that he descended from a family whose origins in Argentina date back to the 1830s. His great-grandfather Tomás Mario Perón was a Sardinian immigrant who became a successful shoe and button merchant in Buenos Aires and made enough money to send Perón's grandfather Tomás Liberato to medical school.[1] We also know that during the lifetime of Tomás Liberato the Perón family rose to be a part of the proud *porteño* upper bourgeoisie. Perón's grandfather was a well-known physician, academician, and public figure. Had he not died at the age of fifty, he might have established the Perón family securely within the bourgeoisie; but ill health cut short a brilliant career on 1 February 1889.[2] After his death, the Peróns became, in sociological terms, downwardly mobile, for he left behind only a small pension for his widow. Perón's father was a failure who ended up as the overseer of a sheep ranch in Patagonia. Both Perón and his elder brother were born out of wedlock to a half-Indian girl barely beyond puberty. By his own account, Perón grew up among many colorful characters—rugged pioneers, criminals, runaways, loners, misfits—which gave him an understanding of lower-class life that most bourgeois children never get.[3] Fortunately, with the help of his grandmother and aunts, he was able to return to Buenos Aires to get an education, but his family was unable to afford to send him to the university. Thus, he gave up his early hopes for a medical career and, having passed the entrance examinations, entered the Military Academy at the age of fifteen.

As a cadet, Perón ranked in the middle of the class, graduating 43d out of 110. He excelled at sports, however, and was especially adept at boxing and fencing. He was commissioned in the infantry in December 1913, and for the next seventeen years he made his way up the military ladder, serving in a provincial regiment, the War Arsenal, and finally at the Sargento Cabral School for Noncommissioned Officers, where he was extremely popular with the sergeants. In fact, his excellent performance at this latter post earned him an appointment to the Superior War School, a crucial hurdle in the career of a junior officer. By this time Perón had matured; consequently, he took his studies more seriously. No longer content to drift along in the middle of the pack, he strove to excel and spent many extra hours in the school's library. As a result, he graduated near the top of his class. About this time, too, Perón became engaged to a schoolteacher named Aurelia Tizón. They were married at the beginning of January 1929, just a few weeks before Perón graduated. The marriage lasted until her death ten years later (she died on 10 September 1938, of uterine cancer, which also killed Perón's second wife, Evita). The couple had no children, but their marriage is said to have been a happy one.

Perón's good performance at the Superior War School earned him an appointment to the army's General Staff Headquarters. He took up his new post in February 1929, at a time when the general staff was seething with intrigue against the newly elected government of Hipólito Yrigoyen. Toward the end of June 1930, Captain Perón was approached about joining a conspiracy to be led by Gen. José F. Uriburu, the head of the Military Academy. According to his own account of the plotting, Perón had misgivings from the very beginning. For some time, Perón agreed to serve on the operations staff of the movement, but as time went on he became increasingly worried. Convinced that the coup would fail, on 3 September 1930 Perón told his fellow conspirators that he was pulling out. Almost immediately, however, he became involved in another plot organized by the supporters of General Justo. This movement had a much broader base, and its proponents were more certain of success. However, upon learning that he had competition, Uriburu pushed his own timetable forward. The improbable coup was launched on 6 September, and despite Perón's forebodings, it succeeded.[4]

Perón's punishment for abandoning Uriburu was a two-month stint on the Bolivian frontier. Influential friends in the Justo faction got him recalled to Buenos Aires early in 1931, however. Not only was he promoted to the rank of major, but he also got a real prize: a teaching appointment at the Superior War School.

## The Military Intellectual

Perón joined the faculty of the Superior War School as a professor of military history. The appointment was not entirely political because Perón already had established some credentials for the post by publishing, in 1928, a monograph on German strategy on the Russian front during World War I. It was entitled *El frente oriental en la guerra mundial de 1914*, and it contained about twenty sketches drawn by Perón illustrating the armies' battle positions and tactical operations. The work was well received by his military superiors, and in the year following his appointment he brought out volume two, which attempted to draw some theoretical generalizations from the study. That was followed immediately by a lengthy study of the Russo-Japanese War; the first volume appeared in 1933 and the second in 1934. It too was illustrated with Perón's own sketches.

A new Perón was emerging. Underneath his hearty exterior he was proud, sensitive, and very hard on himself. Once involved in a project he would throw his entire energy into it, putting in long hours and studying its minutest details. Previously, however, his talents had been spent on organizing athletic contests or writing manuals on deportment and hygiene. Now it was military history and tactics that absorbed him. Over the next few years he would produce an impressive amount of intellectual work. Some of those studies are especially important for understanding his later career, for they contain, in their theoretical passages, references to certain ideas that were to affect his outlook toward society until the end of his life.

The budding military scholar was not without his critics. One senior officer complained that his writing was unimaginative and unanalytical. On one occasion, Perón and a coauthor were forced to apologize to a general for failing to cite him in a bibliography appended to their article. Nevertheless, Perón's reputation as a military historian was sufficiently established by 1937 to get him an invitation to read a paper on San Martín's crossing of the Andes before an international congress on the history of the Americas. He also received an invitation from the famous historian Ricardo Levine to collaborate on several chapters about the wars of independence for a multivolume history of Argentina.[5] Perón did not accept Levine's offer because an assignment to Europe intervened, but he did coauthor a two-volume history of Argentina's role in the war against Paraguay, *Las operaciones en 1870*. During this time he also published two short monographs about Patagonia: *Toponomía patagonica de etimología araucania* (Patagonian Place Names of Araucanian Origin) and *Memoria del territorio nacional de Neuquén*, which grew out of a lecture he gave on the strategic importance of Neuquén Territory in the event of a war with Chile. Both came out in 1935.

The most important of Perón's works, at least for the student of modern Argentine politics, was his *Apuntes de historia militar* (Notes on Military History), first published in 1932, with a second edition in 1934. It was not a very original book, for as Perón was quick to admit, it drew heavily upon Count Schlieffen's *The Nation in Arms*, but it reveals how Perón's mind was shaping itself: which ideas it drew in and how it linked them to form a coherent ideology to guide him.

It is chapter 3, "Preparations For War," that brings Perón's thought into sharpest focus. He begins by quoting extensively from Oswald Spengler's *Decline of the West* to make his initial point: that any nation has but two choices, either to arm for its defense or accept conquest by another power. Echoing Nietzsche, he dismisses pacifism as a "slave morality." In today's industrial world, according to Perón, it is not enough just to have an army; to survive, the entire nation has to be mobilized, so that every necessary resource within the national territory is capable of being utilized efficiently in the service of defense. That must be true not only during wartime but in peacetime as well, because no one can ever be certain when war might break out. Constant preparedness is the price of national independence. "Today," Perón wrote, "the preparation for war is no longer just the business of soldiers. It involves all the people: governors and governed, soldiers and civilians."[6]

Such ideas were not unique among Perón's generation of Argentine Army officers. He was simply their most articulate spokesman. The concept of total war, as practiced in World War I, and the rise to predominance in Europe of Fascist Italy and Nazi Germany made those ideas seem perfectly suited to the times. Besides, the concept of a nation permanently in arms had its progressive aspects in encouraging even greater efforts toward industrialization. Modern warfare requires industry, Perón argued, and those nations which have a great industrial capacity are at an advantage. That advantage becomes even greater if they also control all the resources that industry needs. At a certain point, of course, the reasoning becomes circular. Perón asserted that modern wars are no longer fought for religious or dynastic reasons but to control markets and sources of raw materials; thus the preparation for war leads to war. Nonetheless, the fundamental point was inescapable: for Argentina to become independent and great it must industrialize; and, moreover, the process of industrialization must be guided by the military. This was the ideological foundation of the government ushered in by the

June 1943 revolution and, to a greater extent, of the Peronist government that followed it.

Still more interesting were Perón's early thoughts about the role of leadership. Industry, natural resources, troops, and arms were all contributors to national power, but they were passive instruments that required leadership to bring them together and make them effective. Although he kept the discussion focused on war, the political implications of Perón's reasoning were plain: in politics as in battle, the quality of leadership makes the difference between success and defeat. Without Alexander, the Macedonians would have succumbed to superior Persian forces; the Romans won battles under Caesar that otherwise would have been lost; the same principle was true of Napoleon's armies. Conversely, the power of Athens declined after Alcibiades left; that of France ebbed after Napoleon was sent to St. Helena; and that of Prussia declined after the death of Frederick the Great. Despite modern technology, the importance of great leaders had not diminished. "Today, as always," Perón wrote, "for an army to continue along the brilliant paths of glory it is necessary to find the man who can guide it." A pessimist, a defeatist, or a coward is fatal to even the best-prepared military organization.[7]

Although *Apuntes* was ostensibly about the art of war, there is little doubt that Perón thought its basic principles could be applied to civilian society as well. Twelve years later, in a speech given while he was minister of war, Perón drew the connection in unmistakable terms. After noting that "total war" necessarily involved the civilian population, he argued that preparing for the nation's defense was not up to the military alone, but that it was necessary to mobilize the nation's moral forces to instill a spirit of national solidarity and patriotism. There had to be a truce with respect to internal quarrels, whether political, social, or economic. National solidarity required government policies of a popular character, but also "a strong machinery capable of carrying out a careful plan of propaganda, counter-propaganda, and censorship that will make the home front invincible." To achieve that, it was necessary "to start with parents in the home, and follow up with teachers and professors in the classrooms, the Armed Forces in their ships and barracks, the governing authorities and lawmakers through their work of government, the intellectuals and thinkers through their publications, movies, theatre, and radio—in their opinion shaping and publicity work—and finally, each individual . . . in the course of his own self-education." The problem to combat, Perón warned, was "cosmopolitanism." Unless the country's search for its independence was guided by the concept of "the Nation in arms," then "lamentable cracks" would appear in the home front. To do its part, the government would have to claim the power to regulate the social, intellectual, and economic life of the country. Concerning the economy, that would include control over finance, foreign trade, industry, and domestic commerce.[8]

The concept of a nation in arms implied all that. The art of government, like war, consisted essentially in the coordination and management of large numbers of people. It meant setting goals, inspiring effort, and maintaining order. Politics, like battle, was a matter of strategy, tactics, and strong leadership. There were battles to be fought, key positions to be gained, masses of people to be mobilized, and enemies to be routed.

But a political career was still far off in January 1936, when Perón was given a new assignment as military attaché to the embassy in Santiago de Chile. His job was to gather as much information as possible about Chile's military preparedness. Apparently, Perón was not very good at espionage because the Chilean authorities quickly learned of his intrigues and set a trap for him. It was Perón's luck, however, that he was recalled to Argentina before the trap was sprung. The job of receiving incriminating documents was left to his replacement, Maj. Eduardo Lonardi. Poor Lonardi was caught red-handed and sent out of the country as persona non grata. Only the intervention of a friend, Col. Benjamín Rattenbach, who was related to the war minister saved his career from this disgrace. Rightly or wrongly, Lonardi retained a lifelong grudge against Perón, whom he suspected of deliberately failing to warn him of the trap.[9]

Perón returned to the Superior War School in March 1938 to resume teaching military history. Meanwhile, he had been promoted to lieutenant colonel. Just as his prospects seemed rosy, however, personal tragedy struck. Aurelia became seriously ill. In July she underwent surgery for cancer of the uterus, but it was too late. After two months of intense pain, she died on 10 September at the age of twenty-nine. Perón seems to have genuinely grieved for his young wife. However, in February 1939, he was shaken out of his doldrums by an exciting new assignment: the War Ministry ordered him to Italy to study mountain warfare with Mussolini's alpine troops.

Perón left Buenos Aires on an Italian liner on 17 February 1939. On arriving in Italy he was attached to the "Tridentina" Alpine Division, but apparently he did not actually join it until July. It is hard to piece together an exact chronology of his movements during his European tour of duty, but he rented a small Fiat and took a trip through northern Italy. It may have been during that interim that he attended tuition-free classes at the University of Turin. It was there, he told his biographer, Pavón Pereyra, that his eyes were really opened:

> When I went to Italy I took a course in Turin on organizational theory that lasted eight months. It involved other subjects too. Later, in Milan, I took another one on organizational practice that lasted another eight months. The first thing that occurred to me was to ask the university heads there why they studied organization so much. They told me, "It's because we are in a time of change, when everything is disorganized, and since we're restructuring everything it is logical to teach our people organization." Then I thought to myself: we, who have been disorganized for the last hundred years, have never thought to study organization.[10]

This is a good example of Perón's unquenchable propensity to exaggerate. He could not possibly have spent sixteen out of twenty-one months in Europe taking university courses and still have carried out his primary assignment. Still, it is obvious that he was strongly impressed by the organization of Mussolini's corporate state. There is little doubt that Perón must have studied the 1926 Fascist Law of Syndical Corporations, the 1927 Labor Code, and the 1934 Constitution of the Corporate State. Their principles—in some cases down to specific details—obviously influenced the social legislation of the Peronist regime a decade later.

After finishing his training with the Alpine troops, Perón got permission to tour Europe. It was an exciting moment because World War II had just started. Perón later claimed that he arrived in Bordeaux only hours before the German columns. From there he went on to Germany, where victory was in the air. After that, he went to Hungary and then down the Dalmatian coast to Albania, which had recently been conquered by Italy. From there he crossed the Adriatic and headed for Rome, where he was posted as an attaché to the embassy. He was filled with vivid impressions of what he had just seen. Germany, especially, struck him as

> an enormous machine that functioned with marvelous perfection, and where nothing—not even a tiny screw—was missing. Its organization was something formidable. And the superhigh-

ways were already functioning: another brilliant miracle. On entering Germany one realized that he had never seen in all of Europe anything so perfect and exact in its performance. I studied this social and political phenomenon a great deal. They had there a great crucible where they were forging something new. The communist revolution was proceeding in Russia and was evolving in conformity with the theories of Marx and Engels, as interpreted by Lenin. But in Germany there had arisen a wholly original social phenomenon which was national socialism, just as in Italy fascism had triumphed. On the American continent, and above all in North America, a lot of superficial people had gone to Germany, taken some notes and photographs, and then, on returning home, had exclaimed "Ugh! Fascism and national socialism are tyrannical systems." And on that they all agreed, without understanding what was incubating over there in that social phenomenon.[11]

Back in Rome, Perón met frequently with other Argentine Army officers. Like him, they were greatly impressed by things they had seen in Europe and were trying to apply them to Argentina's future. One especially friendly comrade was Lt. Col. Enrique P. González, whom Perón had known at the Superior War School. González had been living in Germany and was anxious to talk with someone who shared his enthusiasm for the Nazis. On two occasions when he visited Perón in Rome they spent hours talking politics. Their sympathy for the Nazis and the Fascists was heightened all the more by their hatred for "Anglo-Saxon imperialism," which they considered to be the common enemy of all nations trying to rise.[12]

For Perón, Fascism and National Socialism were living examples of the social theories he had been writing and lecturing about.

My knowledge of Italian allowed me to penetrate, I would say quite profoundly, the fundamentals of the system, and that was how I discovered something that, from the social point of view, was quite interesting to me. Italian fascism achieved effective participation for popular organizations in the nation's life: something which had always been denied to the people. Until Mussolini came to power the nation was on one side and the worker was on the other. The latter had no participation in the former. I saw the resurgence of corporative institutions and I studied them in depth.

I began to see that evolution leads us, if not to corporations or guilds—because you can't go back to the Middle Ages—at least to a formula in which the people might have active participation and no longer be simply the community's step-children. On seeing this, I thought of how the exact same thing was happening in Germany: an organized state that aimed at a perfectly organized community and also a perfectly organized people: a community in which the State was the people's instrument and where their representation was, in my judgement, effective. I thought that should be the political formula of the future—in other words, a really popular democracy, a true social democracy.[13]

If such conclusions sound odd to Anglo-Saxon readers, it must be kept in mind that for Perón there had never been truly popular democracy in the West. What Britain or America called liberal democracy was only a facade behind which capitalists exploited the public. Communism was no antidote for such exploitation, however. Already it was beginning to reveal its monolithic and oppressive character. Besides, both liberal democracy and communism were socially exploitative, with the plutocrats getting the upper hand under the former and the proletariat turning the tables under the latter. Fascism, with its corporative institutions, was superior because it brought all classes together to cooperate for the common good.

Perón's European assignment ended in December 1940. His return to Argentina took him through Spain, where he received another vivid impression that remained with him for a long time and influenced his behavior at a critical point in his career. The Civil War had ended less than two years before and the country was still in ruins. Madrid was devastated and grim. Nothing, Perón concluded, was worth a civil war. All in all, he was eager to move on. By the time he returned, in January 1941, he was intellectually complete. The ideas that he had begun to work out in *Apuntes* had been confirmed by observation. He had greater confidence in them and a greater urge to see them applied to Argentina.

## The Revolutionary (1941–1943)

The story of Perón's rise to power has been told many times, so it is unnecessary to repeat it in detail here. Briefly put, he joined with other nationalist, pro-Axis army officers to form a secret military lodge—the GOU—which took advantage of the Concordancia's unpopularity to launch a successful coup on 4 June 1943. Soon after, Perón, who was the real brains in the GOU, became a pivotal figure in the government. As under secretary of war under Gen. Pedro Ramírez, he was able to influence military promotions and assignments, and when Ramírez was removed in favor of Gen. Edelmiro Farrell, Perón became minister of war and vice-president of the republic. While these changes were taking place in the government, Perón was also building a mass following in the labor movement. In addition to his role as under secretary of war, he took over as head of the DNT and had the job upgraded to the level of an independent secretariat with cabinet status. The DNT's functions also were expanded to include control over public health and welfare, the national pension fund, public housing, rent control, and the Postal Savings Bank. Upon assuming his new duties as labor secretary, Perón announced his intention to take an active part in settling labor disputes. It was the state's responsibility, he said, to find solutions to "problems created by an age of mass change and mass culture, so as to arrive at an equitable division of the fruits of the earth and of labor."[14]

Perón vigorously enforced the labor laws that were already on the books but that had been generally ignored under the Concordancia. Employers who expected the military government to keep the unions quiet soon discovered that they would have to abide by the forty-hour week, pay at least the minimum wage, provide medical insurance and workmen's compensation, pay the required indemnity to dismissed employees, and allow annual paid holidays. Besides enforcing old laws, Perón extended legal coverage to many workers, such as the unskilled, who previously had been left out. Moreover, when strikes occurred he usually backed labor. He invited labor leaders to see him, and when they did he listened while they did the talking. When he learned their requests he would try to comply. Perón always prepared for such meetings. Days before a labor delegation was scheduled to see him, he would contact a union veteran and pump him for information about the organization's problems and its leaders' traits. Thus, when the delegation arrived, Perón appeared very knowledgeable and sympathetic, which always impressed his visitors.

Besides ingratiating himself with the workers, Perón sought allies among the unions' leadership: men who would join his camp and help overcome any resistance to "Peronization." To pry open a resistant union, he was very skillful at playing upon personal rivalries and ambitions. Perón's power to intervene directly in union affairs stemmed from an executive decree issued in July 1943 that made it unlawful for labor organizations to involve themselves in politics or spread ideas "contrary to Argentine nationality." Armed with this edict, he reached into the unions, removing and arresting officials who opposed him and replacing them with Peronist collaborators. Besides the textile workers and meatpackers, he was able to put his own men in charge of the railway, metallurgical, bank, telephone, printing, sugar, and construction unions. In some cases, such as textiles and metallurgy, the takeover was easy because the existing union was weak. In other cases, such as the railway and printers' unions, which were older and better established, Perón's grip was maintained only through constant vigilance and pressure. Peronization had its compensations, however. Backed by the secretary of labor, unions began winning concessions which years of agitation and private negotiations failed to accomplish. Workers had the satisfaction of seeing their employers finally toe the line. They were also proud to see their leaders treated with respect by the government. There were solid material rewards too: between 1943 and 1946 industry's real wages rose by about 7 percent.

Once most of the unions were under his wing, Perón sought to integrate them into a single, massive national confederation. In November 1944, he dissolved the communist-infiltrated CGT-2 and ordered all unions to join the CGT-1. There was resistance, especially from La Fraternidad, the powerful railway engineers' union, and some unions who joined at first later tried to pull out. To such disobedience Perón replied, on 2 October 1945, with a Law of Professional Associations that was almost identical to Mussolini's labor code. No union could claim legal status unless first granted recognition by the Secretariat of Labor. Without such recognition, it could not sign a legally binding contract, represent its members in labor courts, or own property. Only one union was allowed in each economic field. In theory, the government was supposed to recognize the largest union as the most representative, but in practice the Peronist unions were always chosen. Labor policies were not established through free collective bargaining. Instead, wages, hours, working conditions, and fringe benefits were determined by Perón. He would call representatives of the employers and workers to his office where, after some discussion, he would dictate the terms. In order to be valid, all contracts had to be endorsed by him; then they were promulgated as decree-laws so that violators could be prosecuted. Strikes and lockouts were forbidden. Finally, union dues were collected by the government through payroll deductions from each worker. The funds were placed in an account under the control of the labor secretary, who disbursed them to the unions according

to a formula that allocated certain percentages to the local organizations, the national federations, and the CGT. Pension funds were
handled in a similar manner. Thus, any labor organization that opposed the government could be declared outside the law and have
its financial resources shut off.[15]

Perón's concern with labor conditions was not limited to urban
workers. In November 1944 he promulgated the Statute of the Peón,
which regulated minimum wages and fringe benefits for rural labor.
The statute required ranchers and farmers to provide decent housing, medical services, warm clothing, and wholesome food for their
hired hands. The kind of food they had to serve was even specified:
yerba mate or coffee, with cheese and cold or baked meat for break-
fast; a stew (puchero) for lunch; a yerba mate break in midafter-
noon; and a good, thick steak for supper. As in industry, agricultural
workers could not be fired without cause and were entitled to severance pay that increased with each year of employment. Moreover,
regional labor commissions were set up throughout the country to
inspect rural labor conditions and enforce these rules. As in industry, Perón encouraged the forming of rural labor unions, which were
then affiliated with the CGT. This sort of government action put an
end to some of the worst abuses of plantation labor in the sugar and
yerba mate belts. Although the Statute of the Peón still excluded
migrant workers and domestic servants, it greatly improved the lot
of the agricultural laborer.[16]

## Perón Triumphant

Although, as vice-president, Perón was only a heartbeat away from
the top position at the Casa Rosada, he repeatedly denied having
presidential ambitions. No one believed him. Perón was approaching fifty in mid-1945 and was still handsome and athletic with a
magnetic personality and a flair for showmanship. He liked to sport
flashy uniforms that would set him apart from a military crowd. He
also had good coaching from his mistress, Eva Duarte, a minor actress whom he met at a party in January 1944. It was she who
conceived the idea, during a relief drive to help the victims of an
earthquake in San Juan Province, of dramatizing Perón by having
him stroll down the fashionable Calle Florida with an actress on
each arm to solicit contributions. She also arranged for him to make
several appeals over the radio during that drive and helped him
develop a radio manner that served him well in his career.

Not everyone was charmed by Perón, however. Among his military colleagues, some disapproved of his labor legislation and were becoming alarmed about his growing support among the workers. Others were liberals who wanted a return to democracy and mistrusted Perón's intentions in that direction. Still others resented his flaunting of his irregular relationship with Eva Duarte and his bringing her to official parties where she mingled with their wives. By their combined pressure, his detractors finally prevailed on President Farrell to dismiss Perón from all government posts on 9 October 1945. While departing, however, Perón made a public farewell speech expressing his regret at being unable to carry on his crusade for the workers. Thousands of workers chanting "Perón for president!" surrounded him as he left the building.

Realizing their mistake, the anti-Peronist officers had him arrested. The rest of the story is well known: how on 17 October tens of thousands of workers converged on the Plaza de Mayo to demand Perón's return; how the military wavered and finally relented; how Perón finally appeared on the balcony of the Casa Rosada with arms raised and hands clasped overhead like a triumphant champion; how the crowd began to chant "Where were you?"; and how there developed spontaneously an almost mystical dialogue between leader and mass. It was a spectacle of charisma's power.

From that moment, Perón was master of Argentina's fate, and Argentine capitalism entered its crisis.

## CHAPTER EIGHT

# Toward the Corporate State

**B**usinessmen and landowners watched Perón's rise with growing concern. In his campaign to win the workers he frequently abused the nation's capitalists, and they resented him for it. Few could match his eloquence when he chose to play the populist demagogue by hinting at sinister cabals involving certain powerful forces. And he delighted in exposing those forces:

In the Stock Exchange they are some five hundred people who live by trafficking in what others produce. In the Unión Industrial they are some twelve gentlemen who never were real industrialists. And among the ranchers there are other gentlemen, as we all know, who have conspired to impose a dictatorship on this country ever since cattlemen first began meeting together. . . .

This is the notorious behavior, you see, of these gentlemen who have always sold out our country. These are the great capitalists who make it their business to sell us out: the lawyers who work for foreign companies so as to strip us and sell off everything: the handful of men working with certain ambassadors to fight people like me because we defend our country. They include the hired press, which publishes such profound articles, written and paid for by foreign embassies. . . . It is an honor to be opposed by such bandits and traitors.[1]

For Perón, such rhetoric was simply part of the game of politics. He did not expect it to be taken seriously by the capitalists. Consequently, he was surprised and chagrined when they hardened their attitude toward him. How could they accuse him of stirring up class conflict? Had he not wrested control of the labor movement from the communists and socialists? And weren't there fewer strikes than before? Statistics show that from 1940 through 1942 there were 220 strikes, costing a loss of 1.1 million working days; by comparison, from 1943 through 1945 there were only 159 strikes and only 637,637 working days lost. Surely the capitalists were willing to sacrifice a little in higher wages and fringe benefits in return for less labor strife, especially if better working class incomes meant a bigger domestic market!

Perón remained optimistic about winning the capitalists over to his viewpoint. In a speech before the Buenos Aires Stock Exchange on 25 August 1944, he stated his case in a remarkably frank and conciliatory manner.[2] He defended his buildup of the labor movement by arguing that strong unions were less of a danger to capitalism than a poorly organized working class. "Those working masses who are best organized are, without a doubt, the ones most easily led," he claimed. For example, by ignoring labor the Concordancia had allowed the communists to move in. The communists were fanatical and tireless, and they were always better disciplined than rival labor groups. Hence they easily took over weakly organized unions and were far more energetic about starting new ones in previously neglected fields. As a result, Perón said, by 1943 they had achieved a dominant position in the Argentine labor movement. That was the situation he had found upon taking over as labor secretary, and his efforts over the past year had been directed toward reversing that.

Perón reminded his audience that the struggle against communism was all-important. The world was living through a great drama whose first act, World War I, saw the fall of one major state, Russia, to communism. Subsequently, communism had spread throughout Europe's trade unions. Now the second act of the drama was unfolding and would most likely end with communism triumphing all over Europe, while Great Britain—the "capitalist power *par excellence*"—would be reduced to the status of a ruined, debtor nation. After that, communism would quickly become a threat to the Western Hemisphere—even to Argentina. It would not matter that Argentine workers enjoyed relatively high living standards. For, as Perón reminded the businessmen, Spanish workers before the Civil War had earned higher wages than those currently prevailing in Argentina; yet that had not prevented the workers from following the communists. From his personal experience in Spain, Perón drew a vivid picture of the consequences of such a social upheaval. It would, he said, "render useless every kind of property, because we know—and Spain's experience is conclusive in this respect—that in such a cataclysm everything of value is completely lost, or else passes into the hands of others."

How, then, could the spread of communism be stopped? There were three possible strategies. You could try to fool the masses with false promises of reform, but the inevitable frustration would only make the revolution more violent when it finally happened. Alternatively, you could try to hold down the masses by force; but to those who advocated using iron discipline on their workers Perón warned: "I have been fashioned by discipline. For thirty-five years I have disciplined others and have been subjected to discipline myself. And during that time I have learned that discipline must have one fundamental basis: justice. No one can preserve or impose discipline until he has first instituted justice."

Industrial cooperation was the third, and best, alternative. Instead of viewing labor unions as enemies, capitalists should welcome them as an efficient way of settling disputes. An employer could turn his case over to a trade association that would represent his interests, while his workers could negotiate their interests through their labor federation. Through collective bargaining or labor courts, direct confrontations could be avoided, grievances settled, contracts negotiated peacefully. "That's the way to reach agreements without fighting," Perón urged. "That's how you eliminate strikes and partisan conflicts. Of course the working classes will have the same right as their employers to press their interests, but that's only fair. No one can deny someone else the right to join an association that defends his personal or group interests. . . . And the state has a duty to defend one association as much as another, *because it is good to have organic forces that it can control and direct, rather than inorganic ones that escape its direction and control.*"[3]

Therefore, more cooperation from the employers was needed. To overcome their image as reactionaries, they should form a national confederation of their own that would parallel the CGT. Then the two could work together with the state to plan comprehensive economic and social policies. That would spur economic development and foster class harmony.

"My dear capitalists!" Perón pleaded in another 1944 address before the Stock Exchange, "don't be afraid of my labor movement! Capitalism has never been safer, because I too am a capitalist. I own a ranch, and there are laborers on it. What I want is to organize the workers so that the state can control them, and lay down guidelines for them, and neutralize in their hearts the ideological and revolutionary passions that might endanger our postwar capitalist society. But the workers will become easily manageable only if they are given some improvements."[4]

Not only was social justice a political necessity; it made good economic sense as well. Indeed, as Perón explained in yet another speech, it might even be considered an economic necessity:

The Argentine Republic at the present produces twice the amount it consumes. In other words, half of what it produces is sent abroad. Now I ask myself whether, when the war ends, it will be possible to continue selling our products to South Africa, Canada, Central and South America in competition with the United States, England, France, Russia, etc. If we can't export, and if we consume only fifty percent, where will that leave our industry and agriculture? There will be fifty percent paralyzation and then we will see a million Argentines out of work, with no prospect of a job or means to live. There will be no solution other than to increase consumption. And consumption in such extraordinary circumstances as we are going to see can be increased only by raising wages and salaries, so that everyone can consume much more than he is doing at present. That will allow each industrialist, each manufacturer, and each merchant to continue producing the same as now, without being obliged to shut down his machines and dismiss his workers.[5]

Perón failed to budge most businessmen and *estancieros*. What were they supposed to believe: the fine, encouraging words he served up to them, or the anticapitalist diatribes that were the standard fare he offered to the workers? Perón was like a chameleon. He might strike a pugnacious attitude in public, as he did during the packinghouse workers' strike of April 1945 when he ordered the meatpackers to reinstate thousands of laid-off workers even though management pleaded that business was seriously down. Then he would make a deal behind the scenes, as in the same case when he secretly compensated the companies out of the government's treasury. Perhaps such behavior should have convinced the capitalists that Perón was the sort of man they could work with; instead, they were repelled by his tactics. They did not want back-door deals; they wanted the government to leave them alone, unless it meant to offer them protection and subsidies. They most certainly did not want to be controlled and directed by the state, and they did not think the government had any business planning comprehensive social and economic policies. As for trade unions, they were a violation of an entrepreneur's right to do as he wished with his own property.

Argentine property holders could not help but condemn the steady spread of government controls and invasions of property rights that had gone on since the July 1943 revolution. Only a month after the military took over, rent controls were placed on all urban residential, commercial, and industrial real estate. Not only were rents frozen, but first they were rolled back 20 percent. Tenants who paid their rent could not be expelled, and landlords were forbidden to discontinue or reduce such services as heat, water, or elevators. Similar controls on rural property followed in November. Rents were slashed to their levels of three years before. Tenants and sharecroppers could not be evicted.

From the standpoint of Argentina's elites, there were examples of creeping socialism even more serious than these. In 1943 the government took over the private grain elevators, and in 1945 it bought up the British-owned Compañía Primitiva de Gas. Since Perón was considered the éminence grise of the regime, he was inevitably blamed for this increase of state power; and since the takeovers were popular with most Argentines, Perón was not shy about taking credit for them. Thus, he was on hand to represent the government at the ceremonies to nationalize the Compañía Primitiva de Gas, and he also took credit for the creation of the new state enterprise, Gas del Estado. Coming on top of Perón's labor legislation, such actions finally provoked the UIA, the SRA, the Chamber of Commerce, and the Stock Exchange into sending a letter of protest to President Farrell—a letter they also published in the newspapers as an open manifesto. The proximate causes of their ire were Perón's plans to index the minimum wage to inflation, his price controls on a number of industrial goods, and his suggestion that industry should practice profit sharing.[6] However, they really wanted to stop his relentless drive to expand the state's power.

Such protests had little effect on the military, for Perón's ideas about the role of the state were widely shared among the officers. The cutoff of American arms to Argentina during World War II convinced the armed forces that the nation must have its own defense industry. Besides manufacturing armaments, this meant building a steel industry and developing other heavy industries such as machinery, vehicles, and industrial chemicals. Military management, if not full military control, would be crucial to defense development because such enterprises were likely to be either too unprofitable to attract private capital, too costly for private investors to finance, or too strategic for the nation's security to leave in private hands. To arguments that such projects would never pay their own way, the

military countered that national security outweighed any considerations of costs or profitability. Furthermore, the example of the YPF,
which for many years had financed its own growth, was proof that
state enterprises need not lose money.

In 1943, therefore, the military government set up Fabricaciones
Militares under the leadership of Gen. Mario Savio. General Savio,
like Perón, was a nationalist who had been involved in Uriburu's
conspiracy in 1930. His main goal was to create a steel industry.
One of his first acts as head of Fabricaciones Militares was to acquire iron ore deposits in the provinces of Jujuy and Río Negro. In
1945 he built his first steel mill, Altos Hornos de Zapla, in Jujuy. It
was modest in scale, having a productive capacity of only 18,000
tons a year. The experience, however, convinced Savio that a bigger
project was feasible. Two years later he got permission to build a
much larger mill at San Nicolás, a port on the Paraná River north of
Buenos Aires. This mill would have a 150,000-ton capacity. Due to
the enormous cost, the project would be financed through a mixed
corporation in which private capital would own half the shares.
When completed, SOMISA (Sociedad Mixta Siderúgica Argentina)
would be one of the largest steel mills in Latin America.[7]

The move toward heavy industry was not without its critics. The
familiar arguments in favor of natural as opposed to artificial, industry were brought forward again in a slightly modified form in a
report published in June 1944 by a group called the Corporation for
the Promotion of Trade. This innocuous-sounding body was actually a cover for the meatpacking interests, however, and its conclusions must be examined with that in mind.[8] The corporation's report began by recognizing the great spread and diversification of
Argentine industry that had taken place over the preceding years.
This had been possible, it claimed, by the disruption of world trade
due to the war. Since foreign goods were unavailable, local entrepreneurs had filled the vacuum. Although their production methods
were often inefficient, they could succeed because they had no outside competition. But what would happen when the war ended and
world trade returned to normal? Which of the new industries would
survive, and which would go under? The report offered three categories of industry, based on an assessment of their comparative advantage in an open market.

The most favored category included those industries that processed local resources: meat, flour, wine, bakery goods, and pasta.
There was room for much more diversification in those areas too,
the report noted. More could be done to develop the dairy industry

or to produce alcohol. Argentina's great output of corn could stimulate the production of more hogs and might also be the basis of a larger vegetable oil industry. Although poor in some minerals, the country had significant deposits of lead, sulphur, zinc, and lime, which could be used for manufacturing cement or certain industrial chemicals like caustic soda, hydrochloric acid, and sulphuric acid. The leather and lumber industries were also favored, but would require modernizing.

An intermediate category consisted of certain industries which, because of the need to import so much fuel, could be competitive only by holding down other costs, including wages. Such industries included glass, ceramics, porcelain, small appliances, electrical equipment, and simple machinery (but only if made from scrap iron). These lines of production would never be competitive as exports, but the expense of shipping goods to Argentina from the Northern Hemisphere might allow them to retain the domestic market.

Finally, certain industries were considered inappropriate for Argentina because more advanced nations would always be able to produce them cheaply and abundantly. Even with shipping costs added, they would be less costly to import than to produce locally. Iron and steel were the prime examples, given Argentina's lack of the necessary raw materials. Not only would a domestic iron and steel industry be uneconomical, but to the extent that it was protected from foreign competition, it would raise the operating costs of all other industries that used its products. Other examples of industries that fell into this category were most industrial chemicals, pharmaceuticals, and luxury cosmetics. In those cases, foreign technology was so far in advance of local technology that the latter could never hope to be competitive. In sum, the report advised Argentina to produce goods that used local materials, expand the production of those goods, seek new ways of using them, and avoid industries that required large imports of raw materials or equipment. It also recommended that wages be kept down.

Obviously, the report, with its old arguments about comparative advantage and "natural industries," was open to criticism. Moreover, its authors were not unbiased observers of the Argentine economic scene. On the other hand, a similar study of Argentina's newer industries, issued in mid-1945 by the Central Bank, was hardly more optimistic about the ability of most enterprises to survive after the war.[9] The steel industry was given little chance unless the country's many small mills were consolidated into one big complex sustained by large amounts of state aid. The machine-building industry was also slated for a crisis unless costs were kept down. Older establishments that produced small machinery like drills, lathes, cement mixers, gas pumps, electric motors, and floor polishers were fairly well established and might survive; but newer production lines like kitchen appliances, road building and construction equipment, gasoline combustion engines, and heavy duty machinery (like punch presses, drill presses, and riveters) would probably go under when superior foreign goods came back on the market. In the chemical sector, simpler industries producing paints, varnishes, insecticides, and disinfectants might last, but local pharmaceutical firms would not.

Both of these studies predicated their conclusions on the assumption that the postwar economy would be open to free trade. But what if the government adopted a protectionist policy and continued to subsidize import-substituting industry? In early 1946, the Alejandro E. Bunge Institute, which carried on its founder's campaign for economic nationalism, published a series of articles in the *Revista de Economía Argentina* about the import-substituting potential of various branches of local industry. The study concluded that in the areas of food processing, textiles, simple chemicals, and simple metallurgy (such as pig iron or tinplate), the country was fully capable of self-sufficiency. In the areas of paper, porcelain, rubber, machinery, vehicles, and most metal products, much could be done to lower Argentina's dependence on imports, although there would continue to be a need to buy some of these things abroad. Like other reports, however, this one concluded that Argentina would always have to import steel.[10] Even economic nationalists could not ignore the structural weaknesses that prevented the nation from having an efficient steel industry.

Such arguments did not deter General Savio, who continued to press for his steel complex until his death in 1948. The arguments caused reluctance in the private sector to invest in the scheme, however; so in the end almost all the financing had to come from the state. Consequently, SOMISA did not begin production until 1960.

Perón had a prominent place in this debate about industry too. In August 1944, President Farrell appointed him chairman of a newly created National Council on Postwar Planning, which brought together leading government officials, businessmen, financiers, agriculturalists, military officers, and trade unionists to discuss the economic adjustments that Argentina might have to face after the war.

This gave Perón a platform from which to air his economic views to the nation.

Perón's opening speech as chairman, on 6 September 1944, emphasized the theme of organization. Organization, he said, was essential to civilized life. In the modern world the state must "orient, organize, and enliven" society by resolving industrial disputes and subordinating the interests of both capital and labor to the national welfare, and also by coordinating production, distribution, and consumption—processes whose complex linkages could no longer be left unregulated.[11] This did not mean that he was opposed to economic freedom, but that freedom had to be balanced against the demands of social justice. To secure the latter, the state was called upon to play a greater regulatory function than previously. Perón admitted that his argument might seem contradictory, but he insisted that state regulation violated economic liberty no more than its planning of highway routes violated an individual's right to travel. In all systems, the individual is free to operate only within certain rules.

Concerning postwar planning, Perón wanted a state that would actively promote industrialization and do so according to a clear scheme of priorities. Surprisingly, he agreed with those who opposed the fostering of artificial industries whose survival would require a constant drain on the government's resources. Instead, the greatest encouragement should be given to those using local raw materials or whose costs made them competitive with imports. Although he did not express himself directly about the steel industry, Perón recognized that Argentina was poor in iron and coking coal and urged that a search be made for substitutes. For example, he suggested that hydroelectric power replace coal as a source of energy; and since iron was costly, local industry ought to use plastics wherever possible. After all, Argentina's ample petroleum reserves would sustain the development of a large, cost-effective plastics industry.

Finally, in addition to orienting and encouraging industry, Perón indicated that the state would have to do more to promote technical training in order to increase the pool of skilled labor, especially in the interior. Above all, it would have to insure social justice for the workers. A successful industrialization program would require cooperation between classes, and that could occur only as wages and working conditions improved. The state's goal, therefore, must be to "humanize the use of capital."

Capital resisted. Luís Colombo, the UIA's feisty president, refused to have anything to do with Perón or the National Council on Post-war Planning. Instead, he bought space in *La Prensa* and *La Nación* to attack Perón for his demagoguery and his expensive welfare schemes. By the end of 1944, Perón was forced to admit that he had given up any hope of cooperation from the UIA. Henceforth, he said, he would deal with industrialists individually in labor matters. Equally vigorous in his opposition to Perón was José Maria Bustillo, president of the SRA, who represented the *estancieros* on the National Council for Postwar Planning. Bustillo and Perón quarreled bitterly about government planning. By July 1945 Bustillo had had enough and resigned from the council. Shortly afterwards, as president of the SRA, he delivered a speech at the annual rural fair in Palermo Park in which he castigated the government. "It seems," he said, "that productivity doesn't interest them, in their desire to float, momentarily, in the vast waters of popularity." Perón, who had boycotted the fair, was furious when he heard of the speech and ordered Bustillo's arrest. Although the SRA leader was released a few days later, this act served as a warning that Perón was thin-skinned and, if ever in a position of supreme power, would tolerate no opposition.

Perón's enemies stepped up their attacks. On 19 September 1945 they organized a massive "March of the Constitution and Liberty" in downtown Buenos Aires. Estimates vary on the number of participants. The organizers claimed half a million, but the Peronists scaled that down to 65,000. It was, however, the largest demonstration ever seen in Argentina up to that time; thus the turnout must have been closer to the former figure. The demonstration attracted many kinds of notables: aristocratic conservatives like Joaquín de Anchorena, moderate socialists like Rodolfo Ghioldi, and radical socialists like Alfredo Palacios. Prominent at the front of the march was the UIA's Luís Colombo. The demonstration dealt the government a stinging blow and convinced many military men that it was time to return to the barracks. It was this mood that led to the attempt to oust Perón the following month. Only a bigger demonstration by his working-class supporters saved him.

In the meantime, Perón struck back at his enemies. An abortive coup by ex-president Arturo Rawson on 24 September gave Perón an excuse to have Luís Colombo and the UIA's vice-president, Raúl Lamaríglia, arrested as alleged accomplices. The charges were false, and the men were released two days later; but Colombo, who was elderly and declining in health, never resumed his duties as UIA head.

Perón's presidential candidacy forced the UIA and SRA to drop all pretense of being nonpartisan. Lamarúglia, who now led the UIA, spoke openly in favor of the Democratic Union, a slate of candidates supported by the Radicals, Socialists, Progressive Democrats, and Communists. He even violated the electoral laws by giving money to the Democratic Union out of the UIA's treasury. During the campaign, Perón came into the possession of a canceled check that had been sent to the Democratic Union by the UIA treasurer. Waving the check over his head like a captured banner, he accused the opposition candidates of being the minions of big business.

Perón also scored against his opponents in the business world when, during the campaign, he had President Farrell issue a decree providing each wage earner with an extra month's pay (aguinaldo) as a year-end bonus. On 27 December, the leaders of the UIA, SRA, CARBAP, CACIP, and other employers' groups met at the Stock Exchange to plan a joint response. The atmosphere resembled a state of siege. Workers at several stores in downtown Buenos Aires struck to warn their bosses against opposing the bonus. The indignant businessmen drafted a note to the government calling the decree unconstitutional and protesting the "atmosphere of violence and sabotage" that the authorities were encouraging. Finally, to express their displeasure, they voted to have a three-day lockout.[12]

The lockout was successful, in one sense. Downtown Buenos Aires was silent and deserted for three days. So were most suburban shops. Furthermore, the employers had the satisfaction of winning the legal issue when the Supreme Court declared the decree to be unconstitutional. But though the bosses won the battle, they lost the war. The RRP correctly diagnosed the aguinaldo as an election ploy and predicted that if the employers opposed it they would give Perón a propaganda victory. That prediction came true. The workers, feeling cheated of their bonus, rallied all the more behind Perón.

The elections of 24 February 1946 gave Perón 52.4 percent of the vote against 42.5 percent for the Democratic Union's José Tamborini. Moreover, Peronist candidates won majorities in both houses of Congress, won all the provincial governorships, and gained majorities in all but one of the provincial legislatures. There was no question about a democratic mandate. Even the Democratic Union, convinced by early returns that it would win, praised the electoral process as being fair. The fact is, Perón and his followers accomplished the most decisive landslide in Argentine history.

## Building the Corporate State

The size of Perón's victory forced the business community to come to terms with him. Bustillo was replaced as president of the SRA by the more conciliatory José Alfredo Martínez de Hoz. Although descended from one of Argentina's oldest and richest families, the new SRA leader admitted the need for some kind of agrarian reform, although he did not go into details. In the UIA, Luís Colombo's departure forced elections for a new executive council. Those elections were to split the UIA and lead to its takeover by the government.

Three factions were struggling for control of the UIA. At one extreme were the "collaborationists," who favored Perón's plan for converting the organization into a semiofficial counterpart of labor's CGT. They argued that Perón's program for quickly industrializing Argentina was bound to benefit manufacturing interests. Instead of opposing the new government, industrialists ought to participate enthusiastically in its deliberations so they could influence them. The main spokesman for this viewpoint was Miguel Miranda, formerly a pro-secretary of the UIA, who had become friendly with Perón while serving on the National Council for Postwar Planning. Miranda was now Perón's choice to head the Central Bank. Another prominent collaborationist was Rolando Lagomarsino, a hat manufacturer, who frequently fought with Luís Colombo. He was to become Perón's first minister of industry and commerce. Two other former UIA secretaries were in this faction too: José Oriani, who represented the Paper Industry Federation, and Eduardo de Elizade, a member of the board of a large vegetable oil company. Aquiles Merlini, president of the Metallurgical Chamber, and Alfredo Fortablat, the owner of Argentina's largest construction materials firm, Loma Negra, also lent their support to this viewpoint. Nor were the collaborationists without connections to some of the country's biggest conglomerates. Francisco Prati was vice-president of Fabril Financiera, president of La Celulosa, vice-president of Electroclor, and a director of the General Match Company. Roberto Llauró, a former UIA treasurer and president of a soap company, sat on the directorates of two companies in which the Roberts Group had substantial interests. Alberto Dodero was president of a steamship company that was partially owned by the Roberts Group. Miguel Campomar, who had been the UIA vice-president in 1943, was a director in the Tornquists' meatpacking company, Sansenina, and his brother was vice-president in their Banco Avellaneda.

None of these men stood for the executive committee in the UIA's

April 1946 elections, however. Instead, they gave their support to a middle-of-the-road slate called the "White List." That was headed by Ernesto L. Herbín, the president of a mortgage firm called Hipotecaria Argentina. Also included on the White List were Guido Clutterbuck, a member of the SIAM Di Tella executive board who could be considered Torcuato Di Tella's stand-in; Carlos A. Tornquist; Oscar Sassoli, the general manager of Fabril Financiera; and Ladislao Reti, the director-general of Atanor, a chemical company owned partly by the state and partly by the Braun-Menéndez Group. The Roberts Group was represented indirectly through Herbín, who was on the board of directors of El Globo, a large wine producer whose president was Robert W. Roberts.

Those determined to resist any hint of Peronization formed the "Blue List." Although masterminded by Lamarúglia, he was considered too controversial to head it and stepped aside for the young and personable Pascual Gambino, president of the La Cantábrica steel company and managing director of the Piccardo tobacco company. (Since the Tornquists were major shareholders in Piccardo, one may suspect that the family was hedging its bets.) The Blue List also included Edmundo Saint, head of Saint Brothers, Argentina's largest producer of coffee, cocoa, and chocolate; Horacio Celasco of Massalin and Celasco, a large tobacco firm; and Pedro Bardín, a director of Iggam, an up-and-coming construction materials firm.

Naturally, it was a matter of some interest which list Luís Colombo would support. His refusal to declare himself publicly inspired some controversy. Eldon Kenworthy claims that Colombo favored the White List even though he had long been identified with the UIA intransigents. This argument is supported by Rodríguez Goicoa, a member of the UIA's executive committee at the time. Although Colombo had only bitter resentment toward Perón, he recognized the danger of seeking a confrontation with him. To complicate matters, however, Raúl Lamarúglia, in an interview years later, claimed that Colombo secretly supported the Blue List. Dardo Cuneo, taking a middle position, describes Colombo as trying to act as an intermediary reconciling the two sides to preserve the UIA's unity.[13]

In fact, Colombo had close associates and friends on both lists. He and Herbín were intimately involved in many business ventures: Colombo was vice-president of Hipotecaria Argentina while Herbín was a director on the boards of La Rosario and La Rosario Agrícola, insurance companies that Colombo owned (and in which the Roberts Group had substantial interests).[14] On the other hand, Colombo was a close friend of Lamarúglia and a close business associate of Juan Sangiacomo, who was on the Blue List. Sangiacomo was a director on the board of La Rosario Agrícola. At the same time, he was associated with Herbín as a director of Hipotecaria Argentina and of a textile company called Herbín, Incorporated.

Given so many overlapping personal associations, it is questionable whether the two lists were really so distinct. In any case, the Blue List won the April elections. In August, two months after his inauguration, Perón intervened in the UIA, dissolving its executive board and declaring it to be without "juridical personality" (that is, legally non-existent). He justified this on the grounds that the organization had broken the law by spending its members' dues for political purposes and also because it was unrepresentative of industrial interests. Under the Law of Professional Associations both were valid reasons for a government takeover.

## Instruments of Planning and Control

From the standpoint of Peronist populism, the UIA represented only a handful of big businessmen and ignored the average Argentine industrialist just as the SRA reflected only the interests of the largest ranchers. Perón's aim, therefore, was to either bypass or eliminate those organizations. He hoped to replace them with national confederations that would follow the state's economic leadership and act as both technical advisers in the planning process and as agents of the state in seeing to it that their members carried out the general plan.

Central planning was introduced soon after Perón took office. There was a five-year plan scheduled to run from 1947 to 1952. Its architect was José M. Figuerola, a Spanish exile who once had served as secretary of labor under Gen. Miguel Primo de Rivera's quasi-corporativist dictatorship. Figuerola came to Argentina in 1930, shortly after Primo's fall from power, and got a job with the DNT. Soon he was promoted to head its statistical department where he became well acquainted with many aspects of industrial relations and working-class living standards. Because of his high reputation, he was put on the National Council for Postwar Planning where he impressed Perón with his expertise. After Perón took office, he appointed Figuerola his secretary for technical affairs, with the responsibility for drafting the country's general economic plan.

Figuerola's five-year plan was to proceed in stages. First, it was necessary to compile accurate information on the country's needs, especially with respect to vehicles, fuel, machinery, and electric energy. Information was also needed about the level of development, relative efficiency, and location of native industry operating in those fields. Second, the government would assess Argentina's capacity to produce those goods and services and would develop an investment strategy to increase output. Third, the plan envisioned the creation of industrial zones in the interior to bring all regions of the country to approximately the same level of modernity. That would require the building of new roads and the harnessing of new energy sources to support such zones and facilitate interregional exchange. Finally, the plan aimed at improving Argentina's human resources through better schools and health care. It also urged changing the laws regulating investment, thereby cutting red tape and encouraging entrepreneurs to invest.

The plan set a scale of priorities for industry. At the top of the list were those industries having military significance. Special emphasis was put on building up the steel industry—a sharp shift in Perón's position from his more conservative statements of a couple years past. Moreover, Argentina's steel mills were to use domestic iron ore and coal "in so far as possible." Another primary target was self-sufficiency in oil and gas. A third was the development of hydroelectric power. A fourth was an increase in rubber production. A fifth was the development of heavy machine-building industries. After these sectors, considered essential for national defense, came another high priority category which consisted of industries that produced consumer necessities. That covered practically all of the food-processing, textile, lumber, and construction materials producers. Those manufacturers who processed local primary products were to be accorded special protection and encouragement.[15]

Reaching the goals of the plan would require state control of the flow of credit. There was already a state-owned Industrial Credit Bank which the Farrell government had created in 1944 and placed under the direction of Miguel Miranda. Its main function was to make medium- and long-term loans to start new industrial enterprises or modernize existing ones. In the latter case, it would facilitate the importation of machinery and provide technical assistance. The bank also was instructed to allocate its credit on a regional basis in accordance with the military's desire to develop the country's interior. Besides helping private industry, the bank was to make direct investments of its own in areas where the state thought public ownership was necessary.[16]

But where would the Industrial Credit Bank get its loan capital?

Of course the government could print more money, but that would be inflationary. It made more sense to use the private savings already accumulated in Argentina. Also, the profits derived from exports could be directed toward industrial investment. In order to do these things, the Perón regime resorted to two key institutions, the Central Bank and the Argentine Institute for Production and Trade (IAPI).

The Central Bank had been created in 1935 as a mixed enterprise. Its capital came partly from the federal government and partly from Argentina's large private banks. Its president, vice-president, and one of its twelve directors were appointed by the president of the republic; the eleven remaining directors represented the private banks. Its main function was to control the availability of credit—both the total supply of money and the direction of loans. Given the conservatism of Argentine bankers, this meant tight money and safe, traditional investments. That did not coincide with Perón's strategy. Therefore, as president-elect, he got Farrell to nationalize the Central Bank on 28 March 1946.[17]

Once the Central Bank was wholly under government ownership, the state required all private banks to register their deposits with it. Henceforth, the use of all bank deposits would be centrally controlled, meaning that no private bank could make a loan or an investment without first getting the Central Bank's approval. The Central Bank issued guidelines so the private banks would know what to expect and so that all lending and investing would conform to the federal government's five-year plan. To compensate the private banks for their loss of freedom, the Central Bank promised to pay all the financial and administrative costs involved in handling their deposits. Peronists defended this scheme on the grounds that the twin pursuits of economic independence and social justice required the nation to mobilize all its resources, including capital. This, of course, was the logical extension of the nation in arms. Any private banker who was so unpatriotic as to lend money in violation of Central Bank guidelines could have his deposits seized.[18]

Given the government's investment priorities, the Industrial Credit Bank naturally became a major recipient of Central Bank loans. In turn, the Industrial Credit Bank was able to make loans to various private industrialists whose activities (supposedly) accorded with the priorities of the five-year plan. It also extended much financial aid to the IAPI and to a growing list of state economic enterprises.

Created by Perón in 1946, IAPI was a state buying and trading monopoly for agricultural exports. It started as a scheme to eliminate private middlemen and traders from the grain market by buying directly from the farmers and selling to overseas buyers. It resembled the old system of regulatory boards the Concordancia had set up, but with this difference: under the Concordancia, farmers had the option of selling their crops to the government or selling them on the free market if they could get a better price, whereas under the Peronist system they were required to take the government's price. The Concordancia system was aimed at guaranteeing farmers a certain minimum income, even if the taxpayers had to foot the bill. Rather than protecting farm incomes, the Peronist system sought to make large profits for the government by paying producers the lowest possible price and charging foreign buyers the maximum the market would bear. Those profits were then supposed to be used to promote industrialization. In line with that, IAPI was authorized to purchase any materials or equipment overseas that Argentine industry needed.[19]

While IAPI's empire was spreading, the state was creating new public enterprises in a number of fields. According to William Glade, Perón's expansion of government ownership of industry "was perhaps unequalled in Latin America until the Castro regime was installed in Cuba."[20] In addition to YPF, Gas del Estado, and the state merchant marine fleet, which were all inherited from past administrations, the public sector came to include the railroads, which were purchased from Britain and France; the telephone system; a river fleet, bought from the Dodero Steamship Line; most of the nation's waterworks and electrical power plants; some coalfields discovered in southern Patagonia; an airline company; and a heterogeneous conglomerate called DINIE (Dirección Nacional de Industrias del Estado), formed in 1947 from several expropriated Axis properties. DINIE owned ten metallurgical plants that produced goods ranging from machinery and steel storage drums to diesel motors and surgical equipment; four electrical equipment companies; four textile mills; nine firms producing pharmaceuticals, cosmetics, or agricultural chemicals; five industrial chemicals plants; four construction and engineering companies; and two import-export firms.[21]

In addition to these state enterprises, there was the army's growing industrial empire, Fabricaciones Militares, whose operations went beyond the production of armaments and explosives to include mining, chemicals, electrical equipment, and, of course, steel. The navy and air force also had their own factories: Astilleros y

Fábricas Navales del Estado operated shipyards and an explosives factory, and a modest aircraft industry was begun under Fábrica Militar de Aviones.

As the government's responsibilities increased, so did its bureaucracy. Between 1945 and 1955 the number of people employed by the central administration of the federal government rose from 203,300 to 394,900, while the personnel in state enterprises, including IAPI and Fabricaciones Militares, increased from 109,000 to 148,300 (having reached a peak of 186,500 in 1950).[22]

## The Syndicalist State

Mussolini's corporate state, whose organization Perón admired so much, had not come into being all at once. It had evolved in stages. Between the March on Rome in 1922 and the promulgation of the Law of Syndical Organizations in 1926, the Fascist government had gradually drawn workers and employers into vertically organized and officially regulated associations called syndicates. As in Perón's Argentina, their membership, finances, and legal status were all determined by the government. Having succeeded in extending these regulations to every facet of Italy's economy, in 1927 Mussolini proclaimed the country to be a "syndicalist state," which was the first stage on the path to a complete corporative system. As Roland Sarti notes:

> Fascist ideologists began to differentiate clearly between syndicalism and corporativism after the syndical reform. Because the syndical state was an accomplished fact and corporativism could not be renounced, Fascist theoreticians had to devise a system that would give each a logical function. The most authoritative view . . . was that the two were complementary. Syndicalism was now declared to be a necessary pause on the way to the corporative state. Eventually the syndicates would be absorbed by the corporative state, thereby crowning the Fascist revolution.[23]

Mussolini's corporative state finally came into being in 1934. The employers, weakened by the Great Depression, were unable to resist further "fascistization" and accepted being placed, together with workers' syndicates, in twenty-two "corporations" which were supposed to embrace every aspect of the Italian economy. Capital, labor, and the state were represented equally on each corporation's governing board, and, in theory, they shared equally in decisions about production, purchasing, pricing, and wages. In reality, the corporations were firmly controlled by the government.

Perón's regime never reached the stage of fully developed corporations, but it also was in power for much less time than Mussolini's. It took twelve years and a severe depression for the Italian Fascists to break the resistance of big business to state control, whereas Perón came to power in an era of prosperity and was out of power in just over nine years. Nevertheless, his efforts were aimed at producing a corporative state in Argentina, following Mussolini's path. "We are moving towards the Syndicalist State," he proclaimed to a delegation of Latin American trade unionists in November 1951, "the ancient aspiration of the human community, in which all will be represented in the legislature and in the administration by their own people. We shall achieve the Syndicalist State. I still retain the [old] political forms, since we are still in the process of evolution. But the day will come when everything will be done through syndicalism."[24]

Like its Italian model, Perón's syndicalist system justified itself by an eclectic ideology that he called *justicialismo*. The term was first coined by Perón in a paper he read at a philosophy conference held in 1949 in Mendoza. A difficult word to translate into English, it was defined, in the title of a published version of Perón's original paper, as "the organized society." Like fascism, *justicialismo* claimed to be an alternative to both capitalism and communism. It rejected both the egoistic individualism of the former and the class-based sectarianism of the latter, proclaiming service to the nation and the state as the highest ideal. It also rejected collectivism in favor of a plurality of group interests; but unlike openly competitive capitalism, the state would guide the groups toward the common good. "Negative" elements would be eliminated while the rest would be subjected to discipline and control. In brief, *justicialismo* was simply a restatement of the nation in arms idea.[25]

It is questionable whether, even as late as 1951, Perón had succeeded in establishing a syndicalist state, although he had gone a long way toward getting control of the labor movement. All independent labor union leaders had been purged and the CGT was turned into a supervisory body that could intervene in any member organization and remove its officials. Financial mismanagement, fraudulent elections, or the rejection of the *justicialist* doctrine were all excuses for intervention As a result, unions representing the metallurgical workers, sugar workers, maritime workers, dockworkers, construction workers, and the taxi drivers were taken over by the CGT. In May 1951 the railway engineers' union, La Fraternidad, was subjected to intervention because it refused to participate in the campaign to reelect Perón and also because it would not contribute three days of every member's pay to Eva Perón's Social Aid Foundation.[26]

The "organized society" had its advantages for those who "went along." Labor's wages rose by about a third between 1946 and 1950; job security was all but absolute; and there were many important fringe benefits like pensions, health insurance, and maternity benefits. The Argentine constitution, as revised by Perón in 1949, contained a long list of labor's rights: the right to a job; decent, clean, and healthy working conditions; vocational training; social security; protection of the family; and economic betterment.[27] One right that was missing, however, was the right to strike. Workers who did so without the state's permission soon felt the full force of its power. Not only were their unions subjected to intervention, but the government would not hesitate to use mass arrests, strikebreakers, or even martial law to break strikes.[28]

Although Perón was able to conquer the workers, he found himself repeatedly baffled in his attempts to bring the businessmen to heel. The *estancieros* avoided open confrontation by withdrawing from all active participation in the SRA and leaving it in charge of collaborationists. Under Enrique G. Frers and José Gregorio Elordy, the SRA joined the chorus of praise for Perón, pledging to support the government's economic plan, congratulating him on his reelection in 1952, and mourning Evita's death that same year. Another newly prominent SRA figure, Juan Carlos Picazo Elordy, became Perón's first minister of agriculture. A wealthy young man who had inherited several *estancias*, he called himself "a capitalist of the left."[29]

This Peronized SRA could not get the *estancieros* to cooperate with IAPI, however. They refused to raise beef at government prices. In 1946, 296,440 tons of beef, having a value of 889 million (1954) pesos, were exported; but by 1954, only 167,635 tons were shipped abroad, having a value of only 503 million pesos. Similar decreases were registered for the leading grain crops, and the amount of acreage sown actually declined—partly because grain farmers would not produce at government prices, and partly because *estancieros* would not lease their land under the terms of the Rural Rent Law.

Perón's agricultural policies earned him no support in the countryside, even from groups that originally were inclined to support him. In 1945 he campaigned as a radical who would expropriate the holdings of big landowners and even financed a weekly newspaper,

*Hombres del Campo*, to enlist the support of the land-hungry tenant farmers. In the final weeks of the race, he sent in organizers among them with record books and area maps to ask them which parcels they wanted to claim after the election. As president, however, Perón refused to break up the big estates for fear of disrupting production. Instead, he subjected both tenants and owners to IAPI's ruthless policies and ended by alienating the rural masses as well as the elites.

Perón's dealings with domestic industrialists were equally inept. After intervening in the UIA, he appointed an advisory commission that included Aquiles Merlini, Roberto Llauró, Alfredo Fortablat, and Miguel Campomar to organize a new businessmen's association, the Association of Production, Industry, and Commerce (AAPIC). Rather than limiting itself to industry, AAPIC was supposed to represent both merchants and farmers, thus eliminating the need for the UIA, the Chamber of Commerce, and the SRA.[30]

The attempt was an utter failure. None of AAPIC's officers was a prominent or respected figure in the business world. Not even the collaborationists on the advisory commission that formed it would agree to serve. The only officer who appeared on the Stock Exchange's list of company directors was Carlos G. Grether, a board member of a middle-sized insurance company. Among its other officers, only Miguel Miranda and Rolando Lagomarsino were well known, and neither of them had much of a following among businessmen. As of 1948, AAPIC counted only sixty-one member firms, none of which was large.

By 1949 Perón had to admit that AAPIC was not working, but he would not give up the idea of a state-controlled businessmen's association. AAPIC was succeeded by the Argentine Economic Confederation (CEA), which also grouped industrialists, farmers, and merchants into one organization. The CEA's first president was Alfredo L. Rosso, an obscure businessman who also had headed AAPIC. Agriculture was represented by Enrique G. Frers and José Gregorio Elordy, Perón's yes-men at the SRA. But there were weightier figures as well: Francisco Prati, Roberto Llauró, and Aquiles Merlini had been prominent in the UIA. So had Hamleto Borsotti, a former UIA treasurer. Torcuato G. Sozio was a top executive at SIAM.

More significant companies joined the CEA too: Alfredo Fortablat's Loma Negra cement and gravel company; the Pirelli rubber tire company, where Francisco Prati was a director; Herbín, Incorporated; Miguel Campomar's woolen textile firm, Campomar, Incorporated; Philco Argentino, a radio and appliance subsidiary presided over by Enrique O. Roberts; the Roberts' holding company, Compañía Anglo-Argentina de Inversiones y Mandatos; Viuda de Canale, the third-largest biscuit company; Anthony Blank, a large manufacturer of stationery, cellophane, and cardboard; and Sydney Ross, a local pharmaceutical firm owned by the old and prestigious Beccar-Varela family.

How had Perón made this breach in the businessmen's wall of resistance? Apart from the collaborationists, many employers were beginning to doubt the wisdom of continued opposition. In 1949 the regime was at its peak of power and popularity. It was so confident that it had even dared to change the old constitution for a new one that drastically reduced property rights. Property was no longer inviolable. Ownership now had social obligations; failure to meet them could result in loss of the property. Service to the national economy, not private profits, was henceforth the principal goal. The state could "intervene in the economy and monopolize any particular activity" for the general interest. Foreign trade, natural energy resources, and public services fell exclusively within the state's realm; but the new constitution also allowed it to expropriate any private enterprise that tried to "dominate national markets, eliminate competition, or make excessive (usurious) profits."[31]

In fact, Perón never seized much private property. A few *estancieros* who had been prominent oppositionists, such as Robustiano Patrón Costas, suffered; and some newspapers, like the Socialist *La Vanguardia*, were shut down. More shocking to businessmen, perhaps, was the government's closure of two industrial companies, Massone Chemicals and Chocolates Mu-Mu, after they incurred Eva Perón's anger by refusing to contribute to her social aid foundation. But what must really have sent a shiver down the businessmen's spines was the expropriation, in 1948, of the Bemberg Group, one of Argentina's largest conglomerates. If Perón could seize an empire like that, he was indeed a power to be reckoned with.

## The Bemberg Expropriation

The Bemberg fortune dated back to the middle of the nineteenth century, beginning when Otto Bemberg, a young German immigrant, married Luisa Ocampo Requiera, the daughter of a prominent Buenos Aires politician. Through his political connections, Bemberg got appointed as Argentina's commercial attaché in Paris, which allowed him to make his fortune by charging large commissions as a middleman. Since there were no income taxes, he was an immensely wealthy man when he died, and since there were no inheritance taxes either, his fortune descended intact to his heirs. After Bemberg's wife died in 1904, his three children—a daughter and two sons—divided the inheritance.

One of the sons, Otto Sebastián Bemberg, became the family's acknowledged business leader. Through his acumen, the family fortune became even greater. Otto Sebastián followed two main lines of business: government loans and the beer industry. He owned a string of beer factories, one of which, the Quilmes Brewery, became the largest in Argentina. As banker to both the federal and provincial governments, he performed important services, such as arranging the reparation of some $9 million of Argentine gold from Europe when World War I broke out. When he finally died in 1932, the Bemberg empire encompassed several breweries, the Buenos Aires streetcar system, a large textile company, a mortgage company, fifteen *estancias*, and various food-processing plants. Its total worth was estimated in the tens of billions of pesos.

In the meantime, however, Argentina had passed an inheritance tax in 1904; so when Bemberg, died the government's tax collectors demanded an audit of the estate. What they found was that in the last years of his life Bemberg had transferred all his liquid assets to an overseas holding company based in Paris, the Brasserie Argentine Quilmes. The Brasserie, in turn, had been turning over those assets to Bemberg's five children in the form of large gifts of stock. Therefore, upon Bemberg's death there were only 658,313 pesos left in his Argentine bank account. Since the 1904 inheritance law applied only to inheritances or property transfers that took place in Argentina, the Bemberg heirs proposed to pay only 80,000 pesos to the government, which were the taxes due on the bank account. They argued that they were not subject to taxes on any wealth received from the Brasserie Argentine Quilmes, and they refused to turn over the company's books.

The internal revenue office (Dirección General de Impuestos, or DGI) disagreed. It accused the Bembergs of trying to defraud the treasury, and took the case to court. The judicial wheels revolved slowly, however, because the Bembergs had friends in high places: men like President Robert Ortiz and Federico Pinedo. But with the 1943 revolution, matters came to a head. The Bembergs, with their foreign interests and their Jockey Club lifestyle, were perfect symbols of the haughty, spoiled cosmopolites that the military reformers wanted to stamp out. On 26 August 1943, the Ramírez government issued a decree that "clarified" the 1904 inheritance tax law, holding that all transfers involving Argentine wealth or property were subject to taxation regardless of where they took place. The Brasserie's stock was taxable in proportion to its share of the net assets of any Argentine company that it owned. The decree was also made retroactive for the preceding ten years.

In reply, the Bembergs protested the ex post facto nature of the decree and argued that, in any case, they were not affected because the stock transfer had taken place before 1933. But since they still had several properties in Argentina that could be seized, they became more cooperative. They declared their total inheritance to be worth 91 million pesos and offered to put 9 million (the tax on that amount) into an escrow account, pending the outcome of a special judicial investigation. The military government was not appeased, however, because it had estimated the worth of the Brasserie stock at around 250 million. The Bembergs did not reject this figure but argued that they owned only 40 percent of the Brasserie stock, with the other 60 percent being scattered amongst numerous shareholders in Argentina and abroad. The government's reply was to occupy the offices of all the Bemberg companies in Argentina and impound their records.

Shortly after Perón took over as president, he received an appeal from the Bembergs to reconsider their case. He agreed to do so, and named as special investigator a certain Juan Pablo Oliver. This man was a nationalistic fanatic who recently had been involved in a plot to bomb Congress from an airplane because it had ratified the Act of Chapultepec, which set up the United Nations. Perón brushed aside all complaints, however, and put Oliver to work. A few weeks later, Oliver presented his findings, which were highly unfavorable to the Bembergs. With that, Perón ordered the seizure of all Bemberg property in Argentina until the family agreed to settle the government's claims. On 7 April 1947, a Federal court found the Bembergs liable for 97 million pesos in inheritance taxes and another 19 million for other taxes, plus court costs and interest on unpaid taxes.

Since the Bembergs were in Europe, there was no way to make them pay. The government did not really want their shops, farms, and factories; it preferred cash. On their side, the Bembergs did not really want to lose their property. Then, in August 1947, an incident occurred that eventually broke the stalemate. During her "Rainbow Tour" of Europe, Eva Perón visited Switzerland (where she apparently opened a secret, numbered bank account). She was accustomed to riding in an open-top car so she could wave to crowds; but as she was going through the streets of Berne something happened that later came to be known as the *tomatazo*. Out of the gawking throng that lined the streets there suddenly arose a shower of tomatoes that pelted her unmercifully. Furious, she ordered all the Argentine embassies in Europe to investigate the incident. It was discovered that the whole thing had been planned by the wife of one of the Bemberg heirs. Determined on her revenge, she demanded that Perón expropriate the Bemberg properties outright.

Cautious as always, Perón delayed putting the expropriation decree into effect, although the government continued to keep the Bembergs' property under its control. In order to avoid putting workers out of jobs, the companies were managed by court-appointed intervenors, and the cost of running them was added to the Bembergs' bill. Finally, in 1954, Perón declared the properties to be formally under state ownership, after which they were turned over to their employees to run.[32]

## The General Economic Confederation

From Perón's point of view, the CEA was an improvement over AAPIC, but it still embraced only a minority of businessmen. Since joining it was voluntary, many of the largest firms remained aloof. In a speech given on 10 July 1950 at the Stock Exchange, Perón indicated how far businessmen still had to go to fulfill their role in the "organized community." While labor and government were well organized, he said, Argentina fell below the average of other modern nations in its development of efficient institutions to represent all economic interests.[33]

The advantages of having an all-embracing organization to represent employers were obvious, Perón told his audience. A truly comprehensive businessmen's association would act in concert with the CGT to advise the government about economic matters. That would guarantee the business community an equal voice in policymaking. Moreover, the heads of the various federations that would compose this organization would be more effective in bargaining with labor federations over wages and work rules. The state might be involved in such bargaining, or it might not, depending on how labor and capital cooperated. After all, the main purpose of creating such organizations was to relieve the state of some decision-making responsibilities. "Already," Perón said, "the state finds itself with too many things to manage to wish to involve itself in more areas, when others could decide those matters." And, from the standpoint of

businessmen, it surely was better to form self-governing organizations with powers to regulate their own members than to have the
state bureaucracy expand.

Despite such urging, the CEA stalled out. By the end of 1951, all of
the big names on its executive committee had left, except for Francisco Prati who had taken over as president. Five years of Peronist
labor policies had embittered most large- and medium-sized businessmen. Just as in the pre-Perón days, what rankled them most
was not the workers' insistence on higher wages but their challenge
to the entrepreneur's control over his own establishment. Workers
could no longer be fired except for "just cause," which was difficult
to prove in a labor court. And even if the dismissal were upheld, the
worker was still entitled to severance pay equal to a month's wages
for every year that he had served the firm. No worker could be fired
for his union activities; in fact, if he was a union official, the employer had to allow him time off with pay to carry out his duties.
Moreover, the boss had to collect union dues by payroll deduction
from every worker regardless of whether or not the latter wanted to
belong to the union, and he had to provide space in his factory for
union officials to hold their meetings.

Inside the factory, the employer had to struggle constantly with
shop stewards and their committees (*comisiones internas*), which
had to be consulted about every single change, however minor, in
the method of operation. Labor contracts had become extremely
detailed and shop stewards would not allow workers to perform any
tasks not specifically mentioned. Any attempt to change a worker's
classification, switch him to another section, or modify the kind of
work he did had to be cleared with the *comisión interna*. A typical
labor contract would even contain provisions limiting the number
of machines an employer could require a worker to operate. Many of
the newer workers, who were migrants from the interior, resisted
adapting to factory discipline. Feeling themselves immune from dismissal, they were often absent, and even when they did show up
they performed lackadaisically and bragged openly of tricking the
management. The slowdown, once a means of protest, became the
standard of work performance, according to a study by the Chamber
of Commerce. A 1948 report prepared by the Confederation of Light
Industries, in conjunction with a business research outfit, claimed
that many absentee workers were holding second jobs at places
where wages were higher, but, secure in the knowledge that they
couldn't be fired, continued to draw their pay from the first em-

ployer. Some workers, on the other hand, committed egregious acts of misconduct so they would be fired and given their severance pay.[34]

Attempts by employers to maintain discipline on the shop floor brought confrontations and, inevitably, strikes and violence. Since the process of going to a labor court was too slow and cumbersome, the only recourse was to appeal to the local delegation of the Labor Ministry. The result, in most cases, was an investigation by a corps of intervenors known (perhaps appropriately) as the "labor police," who would almost certainly take the workers' side. Factories and shops became battlegrounds instead of production units. An engineer at the SIAM factory described it in the following way:

> After two years of Perón's protection the workers wanted more but wanted to work less. The means and techniques used by labor created many moments of anxiety. Workers accused foremen of being against Perón's regime and it was not long before the role of foremen was affected to the extent that very few people wanted to continue as such. The power extended to the foreman in the structure of the factory was in conflict with the union delegates. There was a vicious cycle of complaints, a struggle, individual uncertainty, and the consequence for industry was less efficiency and less production. Management could not keep out of the situation and spent most of the time arguing, clearing themselves, defending the rights of the organization and faithful employees. Less and less time was available for planning and problems of production. Equality in salary for the labor force was psychologically damaging inasmuch as skilled labor lost the incentive to work well.[35]

Sometimes confrontation led to something more serious than a strike. Mr. Tito Casera, SIAM's director of personnel, was thrown into jail on charges of anti-Peronist activities because he had tried to stop the workers from placing pictures and busts of Eva Perón throughout the factory. A letter of protest, which he wrote from his cell to the Ministry of Justice, illustrates vividly what it was like to be in management during the Perón era. Here is an excerpt:

> In 1945 the delegate of the *Secretaría de Trabajo* arbitrarily prohibited the personnel manager from attending their meetings. In 1946 the *Comisión Interna* of the Avellaneda factory requested from the Ministry of Work [Labor] an order to fire me. Engineer Di Tella would not accept such a proposition and I

remained on my job. Within a few days a bullet was fired at me but I escaped uninjured. In 1949 the National Director of Work and I were bargaining on certain points relating to factory discipline, positions of foremen, etc. I rejected the Director's point of view, and a policeman was called immediately for my arrest. In 1953, I, as General Director of Personnel for siam and its subsidiaries, sent a long letter to the Minister of Industrial Commerce and Work reporting the great number of labor abnormalities. Particularly, I outlined the unacceptable behavior of the *Comisión Interna*, which in turn brought many interruptions to production and, therefore, to the country. . . .[36]

In this kind of deteriorating atmosphere, it is hardly surprising that class hatreds grew up on both sides, forever polarizing Argentine society.

As it became clear to Perón that he could not hope to win over big business, he switched his attention to small businessmen, especially those in the interior. The latter harbored a long-standing resentment against the big financial and economic interests in Buenos Aires which, in their view, monopolized capital and trade. Unlike the *porteño* capitalists, these small entrepreneurs of the interior actively sought government aid and protection in order to overcome their geographical disadvantage. Their spokesman at this time was the very dynamic and ambitious José Ber Gelbard, a businessman and promoter from the northwestern province of Catamarca. The poor son of Polish-Jewish immigrants, Gelbard had started out in business when he was only a boy, literally with a pack on his back. By the time he was seventeen, he owned a small store that sold men's clothing and accessories. "Unlike the *turcos* [local Lebanese merchants], I sold for cash, never on credit," he once recalled in an interview. Gradually his business grew. He bought land and went into construction. Eventually he owned a variety of investments. "Persevere and you'll get ahead," was Gelbard's advice. Even in a small town like Catamarca there were many possibilities for someone with a quick mind. Said Gelbard, "I went along thinking up new ideas."[37]

Gelbard gained prominence through his ability as an organizer of regional businessmen. He was convinced that the poverty of the northwest was the result of insufficient government aid, so he traveled around his province and the neighboring provinces of Tucumán, Salta, Jujuy, and Santiago del Estero urging businessmen to form a political pressure group. His message was simple: the big business interests of Buenos Aires got all the attention because they were organized, so the small businessmen of the interior would get help only when they pulled together and made common demands on the government. Gelbard's persuasiveness paid off. First came a regional convention in 1942, at which the businessmen of the northwest issued their Act of Catamarca, a manifesto calling for more government credit and protection against foreign competition. Various attempts at forming a permanent organization of regional business interests followed, leading in 1950 to the Argentine Confederation of Production, Industry, and Commerce (CAPIC).[38]

It was at this juncture that Perón and Gelbard discovered their mutual interests. Perón needed some organized business group to act as the nucleus of yet another attempt at a national employers' confederation, whereas Gelbard's ambition was to become a national spokesman for business. In 1951 CAPIC agreed to merge with the CEA to form the Confederation of Industry, Commerce, and Agriculture. At its opening meeting, Perón spoke to the delegates of his long-term aims of organizing the nation: "first the government; then the social services and the trade unions; and finally the employers' entities, with a view to establishing a coordinated and progressive system."[39]

Although more broadly based than any previous Peronist business group, the new confederation still met with the resistance of the most important companies in Buenos Aires. By this time, Perón's patience was exhausted. The Law of Professional Associations was invoked, making membership compulsory. To allow the porteños to save face, they were allowed representation at the forming of yet another semiofficial association, the General Economic Confederation (CGE), which came into being in December 1952.

The new CGE was composed of local chambers of farmers, industrialists, and merchants. Local chambers then formed provincial federations, which in turn created three national confederations, for agriculture, industry, and commerce. Finally, those national confederations combined their leadership to form the CGE, on whose executive committee they had equal representation. At every level, enterprises were represented equally regardless of their size, so small business interests were firmly in control. On the other hand, since every enterprise had to contribute one-tenth of one percent of its capital to the CGE annually, big business shouldered the burden of financing the organization.[40]

Gelbard became president of the CGE. On his executive committee were the familiar names of entrepreneurs who had supported the

Peronist cause over the years: José Gregorio Elordy, the Peronist *estanciero;* and Aquiles Merlini and Eduardo Azaretto, two former UIA intervenors. They were proud to finally bring their fellow businessmen under the government's control. "We," said the petition of 18 November 1952, which called for the CGE's creation,

are the same industrialists who signed the petition of 6 August 1946 [for the UIA intervention], the ones who aided in the unprecedented growth of industry brought about by His Excellency, General Perón, in his few years of service; the ones who responded to all his calls; the ones who, believing in justicialist premises, put our utmost efforts voluntarily at his service; the ones who, on 10 August 1951, went to the Presidential Residence in Olivos to ask him to accept renomination in order to prolong his beneficial services at the post of command; the ones who, on that occasion, heard with great emotion, from the lips of his Excellency, the President of the Nation, that he had never dissolved any institution, and that the Union Industrial was obviously stronger for having been intervened. We are the ones, in brief, who embody the tradition of the industrialist class that was formed under the protection of a monitoring influence which plans for the generations to come.[41]

For its part, the government provided the CGE with representation on many important policymaking bodies. Gelbard attended cabinet meetings and sat on the high-level President's Economic Advisory Committee along with the general secretary of the CGT. CGE representatives were also on the boards of the Central Bank, the Industrial Credit Bank, the National Mortgage Bank, IAPI, the Social Security Fund, DINIE, the Customs Bureau, and several other agencies dealing with trade, agriculture, or industry. As a result of this cooperation, the CGE helped to promote a closed economic system in which established businesses were protected and subsidized not only against foreign competition but also against new domestic entrepreneurs who might seek to break into the market. For example, in 1954 the Central Bank established new procedures for obtaining exchange permits to import industrial machinery. Under the new rules, based on plans drawn up jointly by the state and the CGE, importers would have to furnish the bank with a detailed account of their import activities over the previous three to five years before they would be given a permit.[42]

With respect to labor relations, the CGE, CGT, and Ministry of Labor formed regular tripartite commissions which drew up obligatory labor contracts for every economic field. With the businessmen now part of the organized community, Perón had the process of collective bargaining so well controlled that all contracts ran for two years and expired on exactly the same day, March 1. The march toward corporativism was accelerated even more when, in March 1955, the CGE and CGT held their first congress on productivity and social welfare—mainly at the insistence of the employers, who were being squeezed by high wages, absenteeism, and low output. Prodded by the government, the CGT agreed to a pact, called the National Agreement on Productivity, which promised more cooperation from the unions in combating absenteeism, raising work norms, making rules more flexible in assigning labor tasks, and using wage incentives to encourage production. Although employers at the time were said to be skeptical about the workability of the agreement, the government promised them that if they met the CGT's wage demands they would be reimbursed with easy credit, import subsidies, and subventions to cover production costs. The scheme was never tested because Perón's government fell only a few months later, but subsequent experience in Argentina with such pacts between capital, labor, and government indicate that the employers' skepticism was well conceived.[43]

## Other Syndicalist Organizations

Although the CGT and CGE were the main pillars of Peronist economic planning and control, the concept of an organized community dictated that every aspect of public life was to have its state-regulated association. For example, in December 1950 Perón created the General University Confederation (CGU) to replace the independent Argentine University Federation (FUA), which opposed him. In this case, he used the same tactics that later worked against big business. Unable to get control of FUA chapters in Buenos Aires and La Plata, he sought to organize professors and students on the smaller campuses of the interior. Once they were on his side, he formed the CGU and, using the Law of Professional Associations, declared it the only legitimate representative of university interests. About the same time, an official organization was set up to represent high school students: the Union of Secondary School Students (UES).[44]

Other liberal professions were organized under the General Confederation of Professionals (CGP), which the government recognized formally on 8 January 1953. The largest group composing it was the

280,000-member Teachers' Union, which Perón detached from the CGT. There was some speculation that Perón might be trying to split the CGT in order to keep it from growing too strong, but Bernard Silverman argues that the CGP's purpose was simply to gain control of professional groups that had thus far escaped the Peronist net: scientists, technicians, and artists.[45]

The CGP, like the CGE, came into being gradually. One of its components, the National Junta of Intellectuals, dated back to 13 November 1947 when Perón invited a group of nationalistic writers, journalists, historians, artists, and musicians to the Casa Rosada. His purpose, he told them, was to group them into a single organization, under the supervision of the Ministry of Education, to fight for a common goal: the good of the nation. Allowing cultural activities to go unsupervised was wrong and out of date. "We cannot let every man do what he likes in a completely disorganized way," Perón said. "Therefore, I am taking on the task of organizing all aspects of cultural life in which the State is involved, and you are charged to do the same for the private sector. And I assure you that when we combine the two organizations, from that moment on our success will be absolutely guaranteed." Pointing to Mussolini's Italy as his model, he explained that "it is necessary for the State . . . to give a proper orientation that will establish objectives and supervise activities to make sure they are being met."[46]

Two weeks later Perón was already putting pressure on the intellectuals to get organized. On 27 November he met with a group of painters and sculptors and succeeded in getting them to form a commission in charge of "organizing everything referring to the plastic arts." In December he met with a group of writers and elaborated on the need to organize intellectual activity. Analogizing literature to medicine, he asked rhetorically whether it was not the state's duty to protect the public from quacks even if their concoctions were popular. So, then, with writers. Freedom could not be extended to those who wished to poison society; therefore an organization was needed to supervise the national letters and to inspire literature with the doctrine of *justicialismo*. Those who joined this writers' organization and served the nation would be freed from the necessity of writing for commercial gain; they would be taken care of and allowed to devote themselves to spiritual or ideological prose.

The National Junta of Intellectuals came into being in May 1948, and was composed of two syndicates, one for writers and another for artists. It was to embrace, according to the decree giving it legal recognition, "any person who at present devotes, or has formerly devoted, a considerable part of his time to scientific research; or to producing works of culture by means of books, broadcasting, signed newspaper articles, or dissertations; or by theatrical, cinematographic, or musical works; or works in the plastic arts; or architecture." All Argentine citizens falling into one of those categories had to register with the junta. In return, the junta promised to provide protection and solid benefits for the nation's intellectuals. In the following year, for example, it secured legislation that required: (1) that all periodicals would henceforth have to devote at least 2 percent of their space to contributions by registered Argentine intellectuals; (2) that publishing houses would be required to devote no less than 10 percent of their annual production to books written by registered intellectuals, with royalties to be determined by the junta; (3) that every ship in the merchant fleet would have to carry a library containing at least fifty books by living Argentine authors, and every foreign merchant ship arriving in Argentina would have to purchase at least ten such books per visit; (4) that all commercial and industrial enterprises with over half a million pesos of capital would have to establish libraries for their employees, containing at least one book or musical work by a living Argentine for each 10,000 pesos of capital; and (5) that employers, when paying the year-end *aguinaldo*, would also have to furnish each employee with a book or musical composition or phonograph record, from a catalog furnished by the under secretary of culture.[47]

On 12 January 1950, another decree ordered that wherever music was played in public—whether on the radio, at dances, or in restaurants, bars, or night clubs—no less than half must be by Argentine composers. This came after a group of Argentine musicians and composers complained to the junta that an invasion of foreign music was putting them out of work. They appealed to patriotism and demanded that the government protect national culture.[48]

Such decrees were no more absurd than other Peronist legislation that sealed off local industry from foreign competition. In each case, special interests were accorded privileges at the expense of the public's right to choose what it would consume, whether in songs or steel. The organized community, or nation in arms, meant an inward-looking society cut off (as much as possible) from the rest of the world and governed by minute regulations issued in abundance by an all-embracing paternalistic state.

## CHAPTER NINE

# The Rise and Fall of Peronist Economics

**P**erón's administration launched its economic program with advantages that few developing countries ever enjoy. Argentina in 1946 was a semiindustrialized society whose productive capacity had been untouched by the recent war. Moreover, it was one of the world's creditor nations. During the war, Argentina sold its agricultural products to the Allies on credit, since they would not part with their precious foreign exchange. Their debt to Argentina was nearly $1.7 billion—an enormous sum in those days. Britain alone owed about $560 million (or slightly more than 140 million pounds). Argentina also was in a favorable position with respect to world trade, for the war had disrupted agriculture all over the world; yet there were millions of hungry people to be fed, and Argentina was one of the great food producers. It was this advantage that Perón intended to exploit, through IAPI, to help pay for rapid industrial growth. Miguel Miranda put it crudely: "If people need to eat, as I believe they do, then they will have to find dollars and bring them here to buy food from us." Peronists were confident that American aid spent to rebuild war-torn Europe would ultimately make Argentina richer.

That confidence seemed well placed for the first few years. Argentina had trade surpluses that totaled more than $6 billion (in constant 1950 dollars). When added to the credit balances owed the country, there was good reason for exhilaration because such wealth opened up great possibilities. To the average Argentine, the country seemed ready to take its place as a major actor in world events. Even Perón was carried away. In April 1947 he boasted confidently to a delegation from the FAA: "This cannot be said in the newspapers but it is the truth: we have the Central Bank full of gold and we don't know where to put any more. The passages are full of piles of gold. We have 2,000 million pesos frozen so as not to increase inflation."[1]

While that was an exaggeration, it is nevertheless true that Argentina was living through a historic moment. Never before, and never since, did it have such an opportunity to make a quantum leap forward in economic development. Figuerola's five-year plan had been published identifying goals to be achieved by 1952 based on various reports showing an urgent need to reequip both industry and agriculture, where machinery was antiquated and on the verge of breaking down. Those reports also showed that more than half of the trucks, buses, and automobiles in use needed to be replaced. Furthermore, if industry were to grow, there would have to be a parallel expansion in energy output, which was showing signs of stagnation by 1946. But beyond merely replacing obsolete equipment, Argentina would have to invest large sums in new, capital-goods industries if it was to vault the hurdle that divides the world's leading industrial powers from those countries that are merely semi-industrialized. It had the financial resources; would it use them properly?

Perón threw himself into his economic program with all of his usual energy and optimism. He was at work every day by six in the morning and expected to see his cabinet ministers there when he arrived. His role, as he saw it, was to bring creative experts into the government and to use his authority to remove any obstacles in their way. Ramón Cereijo, who served first as president of the Central Bank and then as finance minister, later recalled that Perón almost never overruled his ministers and never quibbled about details. "He always encouraged us. He would say, 'You got past the cannons? All right, open fire!' "

"There was no definite program of government," according to Juan Carlos Picazo Elordy, the agricultural minister. "We were young people, new, unknown, and we all wanted a new and different kind of society. It was a renovating and experimental kind of government. And it was possible to work without obstacles because Perón gave carte blanche to his ministers. He had faith in the people he chose, at least while I was there."[2]

Of all the advisers who surrounded him, none enjoyed Perón's confidence more than Miguel Miranda. Born in 1891 of humble Spanish immigrants, Miranda was the quintessential self-made man: poorly educated but street smart, hustling and confident to the point of arrogance. He was a natural salesman who began his business career as a commercial agent for the Bunge & Born grain company. In the middle 1930s he used his savings to start his own company, a tinplate factory. Canned foods were just becoming popular, and within a short time Miranda had made a fortune supplying the food-processing industry. He joined the UIA and soon got elected to its executive committee as one of the bright new men of industry. He was one of the few men in that organization to understand the real significance of the June 1943 coup and quickly identified Colonel Perón as the coming man. Breaking ranks with a majority of his fellow industrialists, he accepted an appointment to the National Council on Postwar Planning, which brought him together with Perón.[3]

Perón was impressed by this fast-talking operator who, as one person described him, swept you away as he explained his ideas. Like Perón, he was energetic, impatient of details, knew where he wanted to go, and once started on his course would persevere even at the risk of compounding mistakes. Cereijo, his colleague and rival, described him as a "great intuitionist" but a "poor manager." He had, Cereijo said, "a broad vision and knew what he wanted, but he loved to improvise." That appealed to Perón, who often invited Miranda to his office at the Labor Secretariat to discuss Argentina's economic future. One afternoon, while listening to Miranda describe his business successes, Perón interrupted him with a question. "But tell me something," he said, "How do you manage your business so well if you spend all the time talking to me?" Miranda was unperturbed. "Look, Colonel," he replied, pulling a notebook from his pocket, "I carry everything with me here, in this little notebook, see? Here's where it says what I owe and what others owe me, what I've got and what I still have to get. It's right up to date: bank balances, sales, everything."

Perón, who knew nothing about business, was impressed. From that time, he decided that Miranda was the man to run Argentina's economy. "A man who knows how to handle his own business ought to be a good manager for the country," he would tell his colleagues.[4] At his insistence, President Farrell appointed Miranda to head the newly created Industrial Credit Bank; and when the Central Bank was nationalized in the last weeks of Farrell's administration, Miranda took charge of that. In July 1947 he left the Central Bank to become chairman of the National Economic Council, Perón's top economic advisory board. He also took over as president of IAPI. Those two positions made him, in effect, Argentina's economic czar. As chairman of the National Economic Council he supervised subcommittees on production, exchange, commercial organization, and housing construction whose purpose was to translate the goals of the five-year plan into specific projects. As president of

IAPI he had wide-ranging control over agricultural sales, overseas trade, and foreign exchange. He took in and disbursed enormous sums of money which he seldom accounted for.

Perón's economic team during his first term of office consisted mainly of Miranda; Rolando Lagomarsino, the minister of industry and commerce; Orlando Maróglio, president of the Central Bank; and Ramón Cereijo, the finance minister. Perón enjoyed their meetings, which often lasted for hours. Although he usually preferred listening rather than talking, he followed the discussions attentively. His nimble mind immediately grasped the essential details, and he had a knack for bringing a wandering conversation back to the point by injecting a sharp question. Heated arguments would often arise, especially between Miranda and Orlando Maróglio, who as Central Bank president was more concerned with financial responsibility. Maróglio resented IAPI's ability to dodge the bank's attempts to control the money supply. In this he was backed by Cereijo, who criticized Miranda's lax management of IAPI's funds and his questionable practice of shifting money among accounts without keeping records. At the beginning, Miranda, confident of Perón's support, brushed off such complaints as petty quibbling. During 1948, however, serious bottlenecks in production and trade began to show up, putting him increasingly on the defensive. Then the meetings became more acrimonious. At one of them an exasperated Miranda lost his temper and picked up an inkpot to throw at Maróglio. Perón had to grab his arm and warn him: "Don't do a Quixote."[5]

Despite its initial advantages, the Perón administration failed to achieve its goal of making Argentina an industrial power. This lost opportunity has generated a large body of literature, much of it polemical but some of it scholarly, to explain why the Peronist industrial program failed. Perón and his defenders blamed United States imperialism, which, they claimed, pursued a deliberate policy of undermining Argentina's trade and blocking its access to capital. On the other hand, critics of Perón's economic strategy point to at least four serious mistakes.[6]

First, Perón's desire to encourage mass consumption conflicted with the need to make long-term investments in heavy industry, energy, and farm mechanization. Most of the credit extended to industry went to light, consumer goods industries, not to basic industrial development. Then, as light industry grew, it became necessary to import more capital goods. Second, capital goods imports were possible only if agricultural exports could pay for them. But investment in agriculture declined largely because IAPI's pricing policies discouraged it. There were fewer exports and less foreign exchange, which slowed down industrialization. Third, Peronism's extreme nationalism discouraged foreign capital, while its prolabor and anticapitalist rhetoric put off potential investors at home. Those who did invest preferred to put their money into speculative ventures that offered high, quick returns, rather than into long-term growth. Finally, Argentina's large accumulated reserves were misused in acquiring foreign properties such as the railroads and the public utilities. These nationalizations had great propaganda value, but they added no new productive capital. Instead, they used money that might have been spent on building new industries or modernizing agriculture, and they almost always ended by saddling the treasury with heavy expenses for refurbishing companies whose stock had been allowed to deteriorate.

Did Perón squander his opportunities, or was he the victim of foreign interests? To answer this question, it is necessary to examine his critics' allegations in greater detail.

## The Peronist Economy: First Phase

The Perón era can be divided into two phases. The first is characterized by optimism and experimentation; the second by an economic stringency that put the government increasingly on the defensive. During the first phase, labor gained in wages and benefits; but in the second phase, productivity was emphasized and many concessions were made to private, including foreign, capital. No single date stands out as a natural dividing line between these two phases, although in January 1949 Perón showed cognizance of the regime's growing economic troubles by shaking up his ministerial team and dismissing Miguel Miranda. For the purposes of a statistical comparison of industry's performance during these two phases, however, it is necessary to use the 1950 industrial census as the midpoint. That results in two four-year periods to study: (1) from the 1946 general census to the 1950 industrial census, and (2) from the 1950 industrial census to the 1954 industrial census. Taken together, they give a fairly complete picture of the rise and fall of the Peronist drive to industrialize.

Mass Consumption, Falling Production, and Inflation

Real wages in industry rose by around 33 percent from 1946 to 1950. When fringe benefits are added, the increase was 70 percent. Those were not the only benefits labor received, either. Rent freezes, low cost housing, and the Eva Perón Social Aid Foundation helped the position of the lower classes. Indeed, the lower the class the greater, proportionally, were the benefits. Wages for skilled industrial workers rose by only 27 percent, while those for unskilled labor went up by 39 percent. But blue-collar workers as a whole gained at the expense of the middle classes, as labor's share of the gross domestic income increased from 40 percent to 50 percent. Some bourgeois groups, such as rentiers, actually saw their incomes decline drastically.[7]

The class biases of *justicialismo* were obvious, but they at least could be rationalized by arguing that labor's buying power must be enhanced in order to provide a mass market for domestic industry. In the short run, this redistribution of income did stimulate mass consumption. Retail sales in Buenos Aires's large downtown department stores rose in volume by about 20 percent between 1946 and 1950.[8]

This consumer boom, along with easier credit, led to a sharp increase in business investment higher than any Argentina had experienced since the onset of the Great Depression. It might have been higher still, except that foreign capital had been withdrawing steadily. Foreign capital accounted for just under half of all investment in the pre–World War I period; it dropped to only a third during the 1920s, to only a fifth by the end of the 1930s, and finally to only 15 percent by the time Perón took office. By 1949 it was down to 5 percent. This fall in foreign investment was partly offset by more activity from domestic private capital and, even more, by the federal government; but the postwar boom might have been even greater if more foreign capital had been involved. There was a strongly nationalistic mood in Argentina, however, that excluded foreign investors from crucial areas like steel, energy, or transportation.[9]

Domestic private and state investment were helped by more credit. Between 1946 and 1950 the Central Bank expanded the money supply by an average of 35 percent a year, which was a tremendous tonic for business. Nor was the government very discriminating about who got loans. Under such lush conditions, almost any enterprise was certain of survival, if not success.[10]

High wages coupled with easy credit naturally encouraged inflation. That might have been kept under control if productivity had risen apace, but workers were tending to work less while demanding higher pay. New holidays, celebrating Peronism's leaders and significant events in the movement's history, were added to the usual religious or patriotic holidays on the calendar. Trade unions in various branches of industry began declaring their own workless days, "in celebration of that industry's contribution to the Nation." Soon it became the practice to declare the day after one of these holidays to be a "free" day also, in order to allow the workers to rest up from the big rallies they held. By 1951, it was estimated that the ordinary Argentine worker took a day off for every two spent on the job.[11]

High absenteeism, estimated by employers at between 12 and 15 percent, went with rising wages and falling productivity. It is not surprising, therefore, that private companies were unwilling to hire any more labor than was absolutely necessary and sought to replace workers with machines wherever possible. Indeed, there were some 14,500 fewer industrial blue-collar workers in 1950 than in 1946. In that same period, installed horsepower increased by 16.8 percent, and the value of fuels and lubricants used in industry nearly doubled.

As wages outstripped productivity, prices rose, more than tripling in three years. By 1949, the annualized rise in living costs was 68 percent. In his first month of office Perón had announced a "Sixty Days' Campaign" against inflation. Price guidelines were decreed on a wide variety of consumer items, and producers and merchants were warned that unless they cooperated a blanket freeze would follow—along with a large wage increase. "Let those who cannot work this way close up shop," Perón said. Customers were urged to report to the authorities any attempt by store owners to charge more than the stipulated prices. On the opening day of the campaign, Perón assembled some 650 government agents on the steps of Congress and told them they were going to make surprise visits to shops in various parts of the city in order to ferret out price violators. Then, attaching himself to one of the flying squads and appointing his cabinet ministers to head the others he set an example by leading an inspection tour.[12]

The Sixty Days' Campaign failed to stop inflation. Retailers accused wholesalers of deliberately holding back merchandise and diverting goods to the black market. Wholesalers accused manufacturers of deliberately limiting output to keep prices high. Manufacturers put the blame on labor as well as on government red tape, high spending, and the excessive printing of money. By the beginning of May 1947 Perón was forced to take more direct action to control inflation. Price controls were decreed and a squeeze was placed on credit. This latter move created a panic on the stock exchange, however, and tumbling prices forced Perón to beat a partial retreat. Loans became available again at the Industrial Credit Bank, and businessmen were offered government subsidies as compensation for accepting price controls. Thus, consumers got affordable goods; entrepreneurs were recompensed; the money supply continued to expand; and inflation resumed its climb.[13]

During 1948 the Perón administration turned its attention to wages as the main cause of inflation. It did not want to risk unpopularity by declaring a wage freeze, however, so employers were blamed for giving in too easily to labor's demands. Henceforth, Perón told them, any wage increases would have to come from profits. In order to make sure wage increases were not passed on to consumers, the federal police took over the job of catching violators of price controls. The warning had the desired effect. Employers began refusing union demands for wage adjustments; but as the threat of industrial strife mounted, the Ministry of Labor stepped in to back the unions. Once again wages went up, with compensatory subsidies being granted to businessmen to offset their increased costs.

Having failed with the private sector, the government next tried to stop inflation by holding down the prices of goods and services charged by state enterprises. Ceilings were placed on what YPF could charge for oil or what Gas del Estado could charge for gas. Prices on telephone calls, subway rides, railway tickets, water, and electricity were fixed. Not only were these subsidies to the consuming public, but it was hoped that by lowering production costs for private manufacturers the prices of goods would come down. In the meantime, however, the state enterprises began running large deficits. While they were deprived of reinvestment capital that would permit them to modernize and keep up with demand, they also became a constant drain on the treasury, which had to provide them with more money to meet their operating costs.

### Light versus Heavy Industry

Not only were there fewer workers in 1950 than in 1946, but there were also 3,316 fewer factories. The average factory employed about the same number of workers, but it used more machinery. Concentration and modernization had proceeded furthest in such heavy and intermediate industries as machine building, nonelectrical machinery and motors, rubber, paper, glass, and textiles. In the food-processing industry there were strong modernizing trends in meatpacking, flour milling, nonalcoholic beverages, wine, dairy products, and candymaking. Such fields as cement, lumber, metallurgy, cosmetics, paints and varnishes, pharmaceuticals, and nylon thread also made notable progress. Other fields of industry remained more or less stagnant, however: tobacco, sugar refining, petroleum, clothing, vehicles, furniture, leather, alcoholic beverages, electrical motors and appliances, and industrial chemicals.

The gains in industry were thus somewhat uneven. Some progress had been made toward building heavy industry, but there is no indication that the government had made a concerted drive in that direction, despite the First Five-Year Plan. Consumer goods and service industries had received most of the loans made by the Industrial Credit Bank and so had grown faster. Especially favored were housing construction, regional meatpacking plants, the production of 16-mm movies, agricultural machinery producers (who also were granted special credits for importing the necessary raw materials), regional electricity cooperatives, regional "industrial nuclei" (usually consisting of several small factories clustered around electric power stations), experimental nuclear power plants, frozen-food factories, storage facilities for wine and cheese, the purchase of diesel vehicles, any factory that would locate in Tierra del Fuego, and a wide variety of artisan-type industries. It is not surprising, therefore, that Perón's critics describe the period as a "lost opportunity." "What would have happened," Díaz Alejandro asks, "if industries such as steel, oil extraction, petrochemicals, and so on had received priority over the expansion of light consumer goods industries producing for the domestic market?" His answer is that Argentina would, in a short time, have become an exporter of manufactured goods instead of a net importer of them. It would have been freed from its reliance on agricultural exports, whose prices on the world market were not keeping up with the prices of capital goods that Argentina was forced to import, and so would have avoided the foreign exchange bottleneck.[14]

In later years Perón became sensitive to criticism that he had neglected heavy industry. He admitted in his autobiography that the plans for a steel industry had been put aside during his administration, despite their priority in the First Five-Year Plan. But he defended this decision on practical grounds:

We couldn't involve ourselves in such a fabulous investment as that was going to require. The studies that were made showed that it was going to take a long time to complete and that the costs were going to be uneconomic. Our iron was going to cost 25 percent more than what we bought from Luxembourg, Germany, the United States, or Japan. So we thought about it and instead of investing fabulous sums we set ourselves to creating industries that would justify it. We created consumers. Why produce iron just to pile it up? Who was going to use it? At that time Argentina consumed half a million tons of iron a year. So we said, let's use all our efforts to develop light and medium industry. The country already has suffered so much, let's first industrialize in order to help it. The steel mills will come later.[15]

Perón was right about the uneconomical costs of producing iron and steel in Argentina. For example, in 1949 it was calculated that steel could not be produced in Argentina for less than 484 pesos a metric ton; yet steel of better quality could be imported more cheaply than that, even with shipping costs added. It could be bought from Brazil for 427 pesos a metric ton, from Holland for 381 pesos, or from France for 340 pesos. Only if the industry was protected from foreign competition would it be able to sell to local customers, and in that case it would raise the price of any product made from it.

There was less excuse, however, for Perón's neglect of the oil industry. Oil production had declined from a peak of 3.95 million cubic meters in 1943 to only 3.31 million when Perón took office in 1946. In the meantime, however, oil consumption had risen as industry grew, resulting in a sharp increase in oil imports from only 483,000 cubic meters to over 3.5 million. This fall in production was partly due to a deliberate policy of the United States, which during the war had refused to sell Argentina any oil drilling or refining equipment because of the latter's sympathy for the Axis cause. The problem also stemmed, however, from certain policies of the Argentine government itself.

Good management had been lacking at YPF ever since General Uriburu removed General Mosconi. Bureaucratic red tape came to surround every phase of the oil industry, and political interests took precedence over professional criteria in personnel decisions. Managers with no experience in the oil business were hired. Technicians and clerks, many of whom had been with YPF for years, were dismissed to make room for political appointees.

There was also meddling with YPF's finances. During the 1920s the company had made profits from which it financed its own growth since the Radicals had insisted on its becoming self-sustaining. The Concordancia politicians, however, had resorted to the practice of skimming YPF's profits in order to cover deficits in other areas of state activity. It is estimated that between 1932 and 1943 around 30 to 40 percent of the company's profits were turned over to the federal treasury for this purpose. That represented an annual sum that rose from 4.9 to 36.9 million pesos a year. The Ramírez and Farrell regimes were even more rapacious. While the Concordancia plundered YPF for a total of 218.6 million pesos for an average of 19.8 million a year, in just three years those military governments grabbed 129.2 million from YPF's profits for an average of 42.4 million a year.[16]

This practice of skimming YPF's profits continued under Perón. In 1949 alone, the national government got almost 44 million pesos from YPF in the form of taxes and contributions. Another 15 million were claimed by provincial governments. Had those same sums been reinvested in modernizing oil production and if YPF's management been trimmed down for efficiency, Argentina might have become self-sufficient in oil. Instead, between 1946 and 1950 total oil production rose only slightly, from 3.31 million cubic meters to 3.73 million, while imports soared from 3.5 million to almost 6.3 million. Comparing census figures from 1946 and 1950 helps to pinpoint the cause of this growing gap. In both the oil drilling and refining sectors there was an ominous decline in the amount of installed horsepower, which indicates that new investment was being neglected while machinery was wearing out and not being replaced. In the drilling sector there was also a slight decline in the number of workers employed, but in the refineries the work force grew by about 40 percent. In both sectors wage increases far exceeded production gains.[17]

Another major cause of stagnation in oil production was the reduced activity of the private companies. Their output declined from slightly over a million cubic meters in 1946 to only 975,000 in 1950. Emotional nationalism was so pervasive that foreign companies found it difficult to do business. Perón's own behavior was erratic. On the one hand he fanned antiforeign and anticapitalist emotions with his speeches; yet he could be pragmatic behind the scenes. In 1947 he actually opened negotiations with foreign oil companies to form a mixed corporation with YPF for exploring, drilling, and refining. Word of the deal leaked out, however, and Argentine nationalists began complaining loudly. In Congress, a Radical party deputy named Arturo Frondizi denounced Perón for giving away Argentina's subsoil wealth, and a weekly newsmagazine called *Qué*, edited by Rogelio Frigerio, chimed in with a series of articles attacking foreign oil interests. This publicity was so effective that Perón's normally docile Congress began to waver in its allegiance. By September 1947 Perón was forced to disavow publicly any intention of signing a contract with foreign oil firms.

By that time, however, the nationalists and YPF's management decided to go on the offensive with a proposal to expropriate all remaining private companies in Argentina. Pressure from the United States and Great Britain, which supplied Argentina with about a third of its oil imports, blocked the proposal, but YPF still won a major victory. Henceforth, Perón promised, there would be no new private concessions to either foreign or domestic firms.[18] That remained the regime's policy until 1955 when the oil shortage grew so desperate that Perón was forced to brave nationalist sentiment and bring in foreign capital.

### The Foreign Exchange Bottleneck

As table 9.1 shows, Argentina's trade surplus vanished after the first three years of Perón's administration. Only in 1953–54, when imports were reduced sharply, did the balance turn positive again.

The great jump in imports between 1946 and 1948 reflected Perón's industrialization program. Three-fourths of those imports consisted of capital goods, raw materials, fuels, and lubricants.[19] However, Argentina's exports declined at the same time, partly because of adverse terms of trade but also because of a decline in the supply. Not only did exports fall in value, but there was a drop in production. For example, in 1946, 296,440 tons of beef valued at 889 million (1954) pesos were exported; in 1950 only 167,635 tons valued at 503 million were exported. Similar decreases were recorded for wheat, corn, and linseed. Consequently, Argentina's share of world trade in meat fell from 40 to 19 percent; in wheat it dropped from 19 to 9 percent; in linseed it plunged from 68 to 44 percent; and in wool it slid from 12 to 10 percent.[20]

As can be seen from the last column in table 9.1, the stagnation and decline in Argentina's exports led to a nagging foreign exchange

Table 9.1 Argentina's Trade Balance, 1945–1955
(in millions of constant 1950 pesos)

| Year | Imports | Exports | Balance | Gold and Foreign Exchange[a] |
|------|---------|---------|---------|----------------------|
| 1945 | 1,803 | 6,768 | 4,965 | $1,642 |
| 1946 | 3,555 | 7,541 | 3,968 | 1,688 |
| 1947 | 6,272 | 7,378 | 1,106 | 1,080 |
| 1948 | 7,033 | 6,144 | − 889 | 578 |
| 1949 | 5,494 | 4,543 | − 951 | 370 |
| 1950 | 5,357 | 5,013 | − 344 | 416 |
| 1951 | 6,713 | 3,938 | − 2,775 | 395 |
| 1952 | 4,448 | 2,720 | − 1,728 | 342 |
| 1953 | 4,228 | 4,403 | 175 | 419 |
| 1954 | 4,524 | 4,743 | 219 | 438 |
| 1955 | 5,322 | 4,423 | − 899 | 402 |

Source: RRP, 11 September 1956, pp. 21–22; Carlos F. Díaz Alejandro, *Essays on the Economic History of the Argentine Republic* (New Haven: Yale University Press, 1970), p. 486, table 73.
[a] Millions of dollars and other nonconvertible currencies held by the Central Bank at the end of each year.

shortage. That, in turn, required a cutback in imports and a consequent slowing of the industrialization program. Within the domestic economy there were two main reasons why exports failed to play their assigned role of paying for industrialization. First, the encouragement of popular consumption led to government controls that diverted more food to the domestic market. The share of meat and farm produce being sold abroad dropped drastically. Second, farmers and ranchers were cutting back on production. Between 1948 and 1949 alone, the amount of acreage sown to wheat fell by about 5 million acres. Ten million fewer acres were planted to corn, and about 2.5 million fewer to linseed. In the livestock sector, the number of cattle remained virtually at a standstill. Moreover, the ranchers were keeping their cattle off the market. By January 1954, the situation became so alarming that the government decreed that all ranchers with over eighty head of cattle had to inform the authorities by registered letter or certified telegram of the location of their animals and the name of the nearest railroad station. This veiled threat of confiscation nudged ranchers into increasing their deliveries somewhat, but they were still so far below normal that the regime had to decree a temporary suspension of beef exports and to declare that no beef could be sold domestically during two days of the week. That was a shocking decree in a country where it had been customary to eat beef at least once every day.

Farm owners and ranch owners were refusing to invest and were not leasing any more land to tenants. There was no incentive, given IAPI's prices and the Rural Rent Law, to do either. It was better simply to let the land lie fallow or to turn it over to grazing. Thus, an unanticipated revolution took place on the pampa during the Perón era. Some 70,000 tenants and sharecroppers (about 58 percent of the total when Perón came to power) abandoned farming in this period and were not replaced, either by other hands or by farm machinery.[21]

A few examples of IAPI's pricing policies will suffice to show how discouraging they were. In March 1946, when the world market price for wheat was 18.2 pesos per 100 kilograms, IAPI was paying Argentine farmers only 15. Linseed was quoted at between 90 and 100 pesos on the world market, but IAPI would offer only 35. In 1948 IAPI would pay wheat farmers no more than 23 pesos a *quintal* (100 lbs), even though the Chicago grain market was offering 28. The following year, wheat prices dropped to 17.5 on the Chicago market; so IAPI paid Argentine farmers 15.5. Meanwhile, inflation was driving up farm costs. Wages in 1949 had risen by 20 percent, grain bags cost 85 percent more, and fuel prices had risen by 95 percent.[22]

In addition to being paid low prices, Argentine farmers also suffered a myriad of annoying restrictions aimed at forcing them to employ more labor. For instance, 1946 labor laws stipulated that a farm family owning a combine could use it to cut its own crops but could not offer to cut a neighbor's crop without hiring a certain number of men from the local farmworkers' union to run the machine. The combine owners complained, to no avail, that not only were the wages too high but the union-appointed workers were often unfamiliar with the machinery and were careless in using it. If the neighbor offered to rent the combine and operate it himself, he still had to hire the requisite number of men from the labor exchange. Besides paying them, he had to feed them as well. Local unions were also vigilant about preventing any farmers from bringing in combines from outside the district. Any combine found crossing a county (*partido* or *departamento*) line was taxed. Farmers whose property straddled county lines obviously had a perplexing dilemma on their hands.[23]

Another restriction imposed by the Ministry of Labor, at the request of rural unions, prevented farmers from employing members of their own family or even working at certain tasks themselves. For example, when hiring extra hands at harvesttime, a farmer had to take on a certain number of men from the local labor exchange to carry the bags after the cutting and threshing. He could not do this job himself. Similarly, if he rented trucks or other vehicles he also had to hire extra workers to go with them. He was not even allowed to use members of his own family to drive the vehicles.[24] That sort of legislation discouraged mechanization and ran counter to other Peronist objectives, such as the encouragement of the farm machinery industry (which was highly protected by tariffs).

To be fair to Perón, part of the foreign exchange shortage could be blamed on the world market, where the terms of trade were becoming increasingly unfavorable to agricultural nations. But Argentina also tended to price itself out of the market by trying to overcharge its foreign customers. Not only was it trying to earn quickly the capital to industrialize, but IAPI also had to cover the losses it sustained from selling food to domestic consumers at subsidized prices. For instance, the wheat it bought from farmers in 1948 at 23 pesos a *quintal* was sold to local flour millers for 10 pesos in order to keep down the price of bread. Sugar, which it bought for 85 centavos a kilogram, was sold to the public for 45; and vegetable oil, for which it paid farmers 2.5 pesos a liter, was offered to the Argentine consumer for 85 centavos. On the other hand, confident that the postwar food shortage throughout the world had put it in a commanding position, IAPI charged foreign customers 45 pesos a *quintal* for wheat instead of the 28 pesos quoted in Chicago. It also demanded 23.5 pesos a *quintal* for corn at a time when the going world price was only 17.5. At first, Argentina's traditional customers, such as Great Britain, had no choice but to pay because a shortage of dollars prevented them from turning to the United States as an alternative. The inauguration of the Marshall Plan in 1948 was to upset all of Perón's and Miranda's schemes, however.[25]

Perón later referred to the Marshall Plan as a scourge and a disaster for Argentina. Its entire purpose, he said, was to rid the United States of its agricultural surpluses and to extend American power to Europe on a grand scale. It is true, of course, that for several years American farmers had been producing bumper crops that had to be stored by the federal government at considerable expense; and it is also true that massive shipments of those foodstuffs to Europe under the Marshall Plan prevented world food prices from rising to the levels that Argentina had expected. Nonetheless, of the more than $10 billion of economic aid sent to Europe between 1948 and 1951 by the United States, only $3.7 billion were products from America itself. The remaining $6.3 billion worth of goods was purchased from other countries, because the United States Congress clearly instructed the Economic Cooperation Commission (ECA), which administered the Marshall Plan, to buy wherever goods could be had most cheaply.

In fact, IAPI tried to take advantage of the Marshall Plan. Although the American State Department, eager to win over Perón, dangled before him the prospect of large purchases of Argentine foodstuffs, the ECA balked when IAPI insisted on charging $4.86 a bushel for wheat that could be bought in Chicago for $2.50. Despite State Department protests, Argentina was all but excluded from the Marshall Plan. "A sorry episode of bad faith, broken promises, and international duplicity," Perón called it.[26]

## The Uneconomic Allocation of Resources

The foreign exchange bottleneck could have been alleviated if Argentina had attracted investment capital into the country. Instead, however, the political climate discouraged potential foreign investors, and local capitalists sent as much money as they could out of the country.

Argentines who found it difficult to sneak their savings abroad were forced by accelerating inflation to become speculators. Bank accounts were paying negative interest rates; rent controls discouraged real estate investment; and even government bonds were unattractive after Perón, in July 1946, repudiated existing bonds, which bore a face value of 4 percent, and forced creditors to convert them into new bonds at 3 percent.[27] Private shares, on the other hand, paid an average return of 17.7 percent, which brought a stampede of small investors to the Buenos Aires stock exchange. From 1946 to the beginning of 1949 the cash value of trading on the Bolsa, figured in millions of current dollars, went from 446.2 to 1,163.6.[28] While all of that helped the liquidity of national corporations, it was not enough to provide a solid base for development because small stock buyers would withdraw their money quickly at the first sign of political or economic trouble.

What Argentina needed was long-term capital; but, unfortunately, the period from 1945 to 1949 saw a net withdrawal of some $276 million from the country: its first net loss since the World War I years and the largest loss in its modern history up to that time.[29] Most of that loss was due to Perón's decision to buy up foreign transportation, communications, and utilities companies. The British railroads were bought for 150 million pounds, or about $600 million. The United River Plate Telephone Company, an ITT subsidiary, was acquired for $95 million. The American and Foreign Power Company was purchased for $14.6 million. The British-owned subways cost $50 million; their gas companies $37.5 million; and their port facilities in Rosario $8.8 million. Buenos Aires's port facilities, which were in both British and French hands, were bought for $19 million. Finally, Perón repurchased the Argentine foreign debt for around $246 million. At this rate the Argentine government quickly ran through its accumulated reserves. Having started with almost $1.7 billion, by the end of 1949 it had only $370 million left.[30]

Critics have accused Perón of dissipating Argentina's foreign exchange reserves with these nationalizations that added no new assets to the country's capital stock and that, in any case, could have been acquired more cheaply. In later years Perón defended himself against such accusations on the grounds that he had no choice, and his arguments have been supported by social scientists like Jorge Fodor and Pedro Skupch. In their view, Argentina was caught in an inflexible trade triangle in which it depended on Great Britain as a customer for its agricultural exports and upon the United States as a supplier of its capital goods imports. The British could not furnish capital goods because of wartime damage to their industries, and the Americans had no need of Argentine beef and grain since they produced all those things themselves. This triangle created no problems for Argentina so long as British pounds were freely convertible into American dollars; but when, in August 1947, the British declared the pound to be inconvertible, the stage was set for a crisis.[31]

The British at that time held about 140 million pounds (about $560 million) which they owed to Argentina. They would not allow this to be withdrawn, except in very small amounts, and they would pay no more than a half-percent yearly interest on it. Furthermore, there was a growing rumor that the pound was about to be devalued. Seeing its accounts about to be wiped out, the Argentine government hurried to use the money by acquiring the railroads and public utilities and by paying off the foreign debt. In that way, Perón argued, the national patrimony was tripled at a fraction of what it would have cost after the devaluation of the pound, which in fact occurred soon afterward.

Though plausible, this argument is open to criticism. First, it explains only the use of some $560 million worth of pounds sterling out of total assets of around $1.7 billion. One might question why Perón used up his dollar account to purchase American companies as well. Since Argentina usually had an unfavorable trade balance with the United States, that account should have been held back for purchasing capital goods. Second, it may not be true that Argentina was unable to use its blocked sterling to buy British industrial goods instead of the railroads and subways. The 1948 Anglo-Argentine Treaty, which involved the railroad deal, explicitly stated that the blocked sterling accounts were to be used for commercial transactions, such as buying 2.5 million tons of petroleum and petroleum products, 1 million tons of coal, 111,350 tons of steel, and 100 tons of chemicals. The railroads were to be paid for out of the sales of Argentine foodstuffs to Britain. Another treaty, signed the following year, provided for the barter of Argentine food for British fuel, iron, steel, and chemicals. It seems clear, then, that British industrial goods and crucial raw materials and fuels were readily available.[32]

Nevertheless, the railroad purchase was made in February 1948, and the British negotiating team in Buenos Aires was able to telegraph gleefully to London: "We got it!" They could afford to cheer, too, because the Argentine government paid nearly three times what the properties were worth. The price was paid despite the report of a special presidential commission, submitted in secret on 30 January 1947, that the railroads were worth no more than a billion pesos. "To pay more, or to value the railroads' capital higher, would burden Argentine production with impositions that do not represent real values," the report concluded, "especially since we will have to spend another billion renovating them to make them fit for service. Rather than pay more than a billion pesos, it would be better to do nothing and demand that the companies meet the strict requirements of their contracts." This judgment tallied with a similar study made by Miguel Miranda the previous September and also with a simultaneous report by the President's Technical Advisory Subcommittee. The final treaty, however, committed Argentina to paying the British owners the equivalent of two billion pesos ("for sentimental reasons and debts of gratitude," according to Miguel Miranda in a subsequent interview), plus another 700 million was spent in paying off the companies' debts and their legal expenses incurred during the negotiations.[33]

The nationalization of the railroads was very popular in Argentina. Peronist propaganda surrounding the transferal ceremonies emphasized that it was a day of pride, symbolizing the end of Argentina's dependence upon foreign capital. *La Producción*, a journal reflecting entrepreneurial opinion, thought differently, however: "Instead of buying agricultural machinery, automobiles, wagons, locomotives, and industrial machinery to renew the equipment that has been used to the point where it is useless, we have spent the money buying what is old and useless, for the whim of being able to say that it is ours." The railroads were indeed in a dilapidated state and, as all the studies had predicted, their purchase price was only the beginning of an enormous and constant drain on the government's treasury. Within a year after the takeover, Miranda had to confess that they were costing the state about 500 million pesos in operating deficits. Not only was all the property and equipment in sorry repair, but fuel costs were rising and the great number of featherbedding workers on the payroll absorbed 84 percent of the income. Even nationalistic economists, like those in the Alejandro E. Bunge Institute, were forced to admit that perhaps Argentina had acquired a white elephant.[34]

## The Peronist Economy: Phase Two

### The Stock Market Crash

By the end of 1948 Argentina's foreign exchange reserves were running low; inflation was over 50 percent; and the trade balance had turned unfavorable. The meetings that Perón held at the Casa Rosada were becoming more acrimonious. Not only was Miguel Miranda coming under attack for mishandling the economy, but his use of the IAPI to enrich himself was becoming scandalous. The army had removed all its military purchases from IAPI's jurisdiction after it learned that Miranda got a $2 million kickback from a company that was awarded a contract to build a steel mill for Fabricaciones Militares. It turned out that the company in question was not even the lowest bidder. Evita Perón also became furious with Miranda after she discovered that he was using her name to extort money from businessmen who were seeking export licenses.[35]

Finally, on 19 January 1949 after an especially stormy meeting in his office, Perón decided upon a major shake-up of his economic team. The National Economic Council, over which Miranda presided, was dissolved. In its place a secretary of the economy and a secretary of the treasury, both with cabinet status, were created. In the former position Perón placed Roberto Ares, an international trade expert from the Foreign Ministry; and in the latter he placed Alfredo Gómez Morales, an economics professor currently serving as under secretary of commerce. Gómez Morales also took over the Central Bank, replacing Orlando Maróglio, who stepped down, pleading that he was "tired, very tired." IAPI was placed under Ares's supervision, and José Constantino Barros, a friend of Ares, replaced Rolando Lagomarsino as minister of industry and commerce. The only major holdover from the old team was Ramón Cereijo, who stayed on as finance minister. As for Miguel Miranda, he took a leave of absence, pleading reasons of health, and went to Uruguay.[36]

Rumors of the impending shake-up reached the Buenos Aires stock exchange even before the fateful meeting in Perón's office. "Smart money" was predicting that the palmy days of high government spending were over and a period of retrenchment was coming. When the exchange opened its doors on Tuesday morning, 18 January, a large crowd of brokers and traders already had gathered outside. For the first twenty minutes there was pandemonium on the floor as shareholders tried to dump their stock. Panic spread and prices tumbled rapidly. By mid-morning, however, there were signs that the market was firming up again, and by late afternoon there was even a slight rally. Even so, most stocks closed at well below their opening price: Alpargatas lost 12 points, Astra 9, Bagley 12, Celulosa 3, Fabril Financiera 5, Loma Negra 7, Piccardo 17, and SIAM 3, to name just a few. Hardest hit were two very speculative stocks: Globo, a wine company, and Pesca, a whaling company. Both were part of the Roberts conglomerate but were also said to have attracted a great deal of Miguel Miranda's money and therefore enjoyed his favoritism. That had been enough to attract lots of amateur investors eager to make a huge, quick killing on the market. According to the RRP, "investor, speculator, office boy, and bellhop all clamoured to enter the GLOBO-PESCA stakes." Now, with the prospect of Miranda being turned out of office, Globo lost thirty-six points and Pesca thirty-two.[37]

On Wednesday (the day of Perón's last meeting with Miranda and other members of the old economic team) the market showed further signs of recovery. Most stocks rose slightly. So far, nothing was known about Miranda's fall from power. He had been avoiding reporters all week, but his secretary gave an interview in which he assured the press that not only was Miranda staying in the government but Perón was even preparing new tasks for him to undertake. That sounded good, but disturbing rumors still emanated from the Casa Rosada. As the *RRP* surmised, "the weaker hands of amateur speculators . . . must have been shaking with indecision and fright on that day, and many must have resolved during a sleepless night that at the first sign of a further downward move they would be unable to face heavier losses." After all, many of them had bought their stocks on the margin by putting up less than half of the purchase price. Any significant drop would result in demands from their brokers for more money.

They awakened Thursday morning to find the news of Miranda's downfall in all the papers. "On Thursday," the *RRP* reported, "the Bolsa opened at about the same level as the previous night's close, but the atmosphere was tense and after a few liquidations had been tentatively offered without much purchasing response, the storm broke and the public unloaded their speculative hoardings as though they were trying to rid themselves of forged banknotes." Globo plunged 54 points and Pesca dropped by 70. Most other stocks fell too: Alpargatas lost 8, Astra 29, Celulosa 15, Fabril Financiera 15, Loma Negra 3, Piccardo 21, Sansenina 6, and SIAM 10. Some rose, however. Peuser gained 20 points and La Cantábrica 10. Bagley and Garovaglio & Zorraquín remained steady.[38]

Brokers were being hurt as much as investors. Not only were they unable to collect any commissions, but many of them had advanced the credit with which to buy stocks on the margin and now, with their clients facing bankruptcy, they were being dragged to ruin. Their relief was great, then, when the Mixed Commission on Liquid Investments (IMIM) announced shortly after midday on Friday—a day of wild fluctuations—that it was providing 50 million pesos in credits to cover the brokers' debts. The announcement was received with prolonged cheering and applause on the floor of the exchange.[39]

The market opened strong on Monday. Many shares that had plunged in the previous week began to recover. Globo gained 30 points, Pesca 24, Piccardo 10, Astra 6, and so forth. During the days that followed there were further shock waves, which the exchange seemed to absorb, emanating from the government. On Wednesday, 26 January, a large number of government employees, mostly followers of Miguel Miranda, were summarily dismissed. On Thursday Miranda sent in his formal resignation. Despite this, stock prices continued to inch up, largely because of massive buying by the

IMIM. Also, a printers' strike, which broke out in the second week of February, shut down all the city's newspapers, thus sparing shareholders more gloomy information.

The market soon turned down again. The IMIM could not keep buying indefinitely, and those who consulted news sources other than the local papers soon learned that the Central Bank had suspended all foreign exchange permits because the country's reserves were so low. Before the end of the month the government had to place additional controls on imports.

The market hit bottom around 24 February, and by early March it experienced a slight rise. Even so, it was far below where it had been before the crash. When newspapers reappeared on 4 March the stock prices they quoted indicated how much damage had been done. Since 17 January Alpargatas had lost a total of 75 points, Bagley 82, La Cantábrica 58, Celulosa 46, Fabril Financiera 66, Ferrum 51, Molinos Río de La Plata 75, Piccardo 79, and so on. Globo and Pesca were no longer being quoted. The RRP reported that "at the moment of writing the Bolsa presents a disconsolate picture. The storm, it seems, has passed, but the financial wreckage it has left in its trail is, by all accounts, appalling. In many cases a broker's cheque is not accepted unless certified by the bank, and the banks, so long as the situation remains undefined, as it is at present, are understandably reluctant to assume the liability inherent in certifying a cheque."[40]

The crash brought reforms aimed at preventing such disasters in the future. The secretary of the treasury and the Central Bank decreed that henceforth those investors who bought on the margin would have to put up at least half of the stock's value in cash, and in the case of certain stocks they would have to advance the full amount. Also, the contingency fund for the IMIM was increased to 120 million pesos. Nevertheless, it was difficult to restore investor confidence in the Bolsa. Whereas before the crash the cash value of stocks traded had soared from $446.2 million in 1946 to $1.2 billion by the end of 1948, there now began a downward turn that touched bottom in 1952 at $162 million.

The Bolsa, stimulated by the passage of a law making dividends and profits on share trading exempt from taxes, experienced a strong upturn in the last two years of the Perón era. This law, called the *anonimato*, caused the volume of trading to hit the equivalent of $955.8 million in 1955. The upsurge was cut short after Perón's fall, however, when General Pedro Aramburu repealed the *anonimato*. The market promptly slumped again and did not recover for another two decades.[41]

The Decline in Investment

The stock market crash of 1949 marked a watershed in the rate of investment. Between 1945 and 1949 total investment, both public and private, had increased by over 67 percent, as compared with the previous four-year period. By contrast, total investment rose by only 1.8 percent between 1950 and 1954. The state cut back drastically on its financing of public enterprises, condemning them to even greater inefficiency, and the private sector found it increasingly difficult to raise capital. Private banks would make no long-term loans, and only favored customers could get short-term money (and only then at very high interest rates). To get credit from government banks it was necessary to have good political contacts, and in any case inflation so quickly gobbled up the value of money that only very high return investments made sense. James Bruce, the American ambassador, noted that "the most solid firms were offering promissory notes in payment of current bills, and one for 420,000 pesos from a conservative metal-working establishment was discounted at 8 per cent a month. The few individuals with cash available for private loans were collecting up to 15 per cent."[42]

Investment planning was made difficult by the shortage of foreign exchange, and that, in turn, was affected by the sluggish performance of Argentina's exports. Agricultural production, already low, fell even further during two years of drought in 1950–51. The government was now forced to revise its tactics and provide farmers with some incentives. The Second Five-Year Plan, announced in 1952, recommended more credits to agriculture, more imports of farm machinery, and more generous prices from IAPI. The regime made good on those promises, but unfortunately IAPI's generosity came at a time when world market prices were on their way down, which resulted in losses of billions of pesos. For example, in 1954 the IAPI paid 50 pesos a *quintal* for wheat, but could sell it abroad for no more than 30; paid 65 pesos a *quintal* for linseed when the world market price was 62; paid 43 a *quintal* for barley that would fetch only 23 abroad; paid 42 for rye, but was forced to take 21 from foreign buyers; paid 38 for oats and recovered only 18. Thus, the foreign exchange problem was not resolved.[43]

Price controls and import restrictions discouraged investment in private industry. With the stock exchange in disrepute and bank lending restricted, businessmen were forced to finance their companies' growth from profits, which was a slow, painful, and uncertain method. Many joint-stock companies adopted the pernicious practice of paying dividends with new stock issues rather than cash. That left them with more of their profits to reinvest, but it quickly eroded investor confidence (which was low enough already) in those firms. But even reinvesting profits became increasingly problematic as the government, casting about for new sources of revenue, decided in 1951 to impose a tax on "eventual profits." This consisted of a 2 percent levy on the companies' capital and reserves.

The tax on eventual profits was not adjusted for inflation; therefore, as a firm's capital appreciated nominally it was forced to pay more. The effect was to decapitalize industry. The absurdity of this tax may be illustrated by the example of the Piccardo tobacco company. Though listed on the Buenos Aires Stock Exchange, this firm had been in financial difficulties since it began to miss some of its dividend payments to stockholders in 1935. In terms of its real capital, it had stopped growing in 1920. That is, its buildings, furniture, and machinery had not been modified since then, except for minor repairs. Having added nothing in the past thirty years, obviously it was working with antiquated capital. Nor could it raise new capital because, having paid no dividends for the past seven years, nobody wanted its stock. In brief, the firm was immobilized. Yet, because of inflation, the nominal value of Piccardo's property was appreciating. According to tax officials, between 1950 and 1951 its capital grew from 89.28 million pesos to 121.55 million; so it was sent a bill for 645,000 pesos.[44]

Such were the problems of large firms. Small firms could avoid several of them because of their very size. The stock market collapse scarcely affected them because almost all were individually owned. Import restrictions actually aided them by depriving big industrialists of some of their technological superiority. Small businessmen also found it easier to evade taxes, controls, and labor laws. They frequently ignored official wage scales and neglected to send in their social security contributions.[45]

On the other hand, small businessmen, who had little access to private banks, were more dependent on government loans. Thus, when the government tried to restrict the money supply during 1951–52 to combat inflation, small firms began folding by the hundreds. After that, however, the faucet was turned back on, for small businessmen were the backbone of the CGE. Indeed, political criteria counted heavily in the lending policies of the Industrial Credit Bank. Despite the emphasis of the Second Five-Year Plan on heavy industry, the bank continued to favor light, consumer goods manufacturing. In the metallurgical industry, for instance:

Figures from the annual reports of the Banco de Crédito Industrial (1944–1955) suggest that the most important sectors
represented by the anti-Peronist Metallurgical Association (machinery and equipment for industry and the casting of metals)
were disfavored in the distribution of credit during the Perón
years, while such light metallurgical items as stoves, refrigerators, and electrical fans increased their share of industrial credit
after 1950. Furthermore, members of the Confederation [of
Light Metallurgical Industries] benefitted from specific credits
made available to small and medium enterprises and by the
special loans and preferential treatment given to cooperatives
in view of the fact that the Confederation was the first metallurgical association to form such a co-op.[46]

It is not surprising, therefore, that during this second phase of
Peronist economics many small firms proliferated. Between 1950
and 1954 some 68,000 new industrial enterprises came into being,
an increase of 82 percent. At the same time, the average number of
workers involved in an enterprise dropped from 13.1 to 8.4, the
smallest figure since 1913. Most of the new enterprises were located
in the interior, which now claimed 42.4 percent of all industrial
firms, compared with only 39.3 percent in 1950.

## Distorted Investment

Protectionism increased the bureaucracy's web of economic controls. A businessman had to struggle through a labyrinth of officialdom to obtain foreign currency, import a product, or get a loan. This
naturally increased the temptation to shortcut procedures by bribery, smuggling, or blackmarketeering. When Perón, in order to have
more beef for export, decreed two meatless days a week he only
encouraged further an already thriving black market in beef. For
regular customers there were always roasts and steaks at the butcher
shop. These were not displayed in the case at officially set prices, of
course, but were still available from some mysterious source in the
back for a free market price. That gap between the free market (i.e.,
black market) price and the official price was often so large that
butchers felt it was worth taking a risk. Similarly, since many luxury imports like cigarettes, whiskey, cosmetics, and nylon under-
wear were being kept out by high tariffs, a brisk trade in contraband
had grown up. After all, Argentina has a long coastline, a long
mountainous border with Bolivia and Chile, and a long jungle border with Paraguay, all of which are difficult to patrol thoroughly.

Circumventing the closed bureaucratic economy bred a cynical attitude summarized in the popular saying: *Hecha la ley, hecha la trampa* ("Every law is a trap").

Perón raged against these illegal activities that undermined the government's economic controls. In a speech to the CGT on 1 April 1953 he exclaimed: "Some people, those in opposition, say there is a meat shortage because we are selling to the British. But how can we be short of meat? What we are short of here is shame! We have 45 million head of cattle, so how can we be short of meat? We have an abundance of meat here. We can send meat to everybody in the world and still have more than enough." The blame should be laid upon the *estancieros*, he said, who were trying to sabotage the regime by refusing to send their cattle to market. He warned that he would use troops, if necessary, to force them to make their shipments, and he threatened to place a guard in every merchant's shop to enforce compliance with price ceilings "with the butt of a rifle." If all else failed, he said, "I'll sell vegetables myself in the Plaza de Mayo" to prove that a person could obey the law and still make a profit. In his frustration, Perón even began privately to complain about the common people: "eighteen million dunces" who did not have the courage to denounce the black marketeers.[47]

Nevertheless, the government set a poor example. Much potential investment money was lost through graft. John Frikart concluded that "the absolute truth in regard to statistical figures will probably never be ascertained. Too many branches of the Perón government either did not keep books at all, such as the 'Eva Perón Foundation,' or else they doctored their accounts and in some cases even destroyed them as the debacle approached."[48]

The Peróns were deeply involved in corruption. The Eva Perón Foundation, despite its useful work in building schools, clinics, orphanages, and old age homes, and in distributing food, money, medicine, and clothes to the very poor, was also a conduit through which vast sums of money—perhaps as much as $700 million—were funneled into overseas accounts. Starting in June 1948 with a modest 10,000 pesos (about $2,000) from Evita's own savings, the foundation's budget was soon swollen with "voluntary contributions" from business firms and labor unions, a fifth of the proceeds from the national lottery, and special grants-in-aid from Congress. Evita once told Maurício Birabent, a Peronist editor, that Miguel Miranda had taught her how to raise money fast: "You give the 'fat cats' a kick and out comes the cash." And, she explained, "with cash we can get social justice and programs." Birabent describes how she dispensed social justice to a group of poor women: "Many of the old ones knelt at her feet to kiss her; they crossed themselves; they wanted to touch her. Then they began to pray. She patted them maternally and gave each of them a crisp 100-peso bill, which she took from a box where there were dozens of stacks of them. It was a moving spectacle I'll never forget. Some of them didn't want money. They would ask her to solve a problem for them, get them an old-age pension, or a job, or a place to live, and she would order her brother Juan to take notes and see to the requests."[49]

Such personal attention created a tremendous emotional bond between the regime and the masses, and much individual distress was no doubt relieved, at least temporarily. But what would have happened if the billions of pesos the foundation handled had been invested in building up industry or in modernizing agriculture? Evita surely would have replied, as she did to Birabent's urging of a land reform, that "the people want to eat now, not twenty years from now." But it hardly did Argentina much good to squirrel away $700 million in Swiss banks, and real social justice requires basic reforms. For all his ranting against the *estancieros*, Perón never touched the land tenure system; nor did he concentrate on making Argentina a real industrial power, as contemplated in the First Five-Year Plan.

Corruption spread throughout the regime, tainting cabinet ministers, party officials, and trade union leaders. Often the top men worked through go-betweens, such as the notorious Jorge Antonio, who amassed a fortune by making himself "useful" to people in power. The son of Syrian immigrants, he first wormed his way into the Industrial Credit Bank and the president's Technical Secretariat through his friendship with José Figuerola. After losing his government jobs, following a quarrel with Figuerola in 1947, he continued to use his political contacts to pull off shady deals. His first line of business was the buying and trading of new cars, which were extremely scarce in Argentina because of the high tariffs and import quotas. In less than three years he transformed a modest automobile agency into a multimillion-peso dealership that counted even Juan and Eva Perón among its customers. The company was actually a front through which regime officials could acquire imported cars without fear of scandal. In return for the coveted import licenses, Antonio would sell half of his yearly stock of some 22,000 cars to his government patrons at list price, which was far below what they would fetch on the local market. The new owners could easily resell them, if they wished, at a profit of between 70,000 to 120,000 pesos.

Antonio then would sell the remaining 11,000 cars either to the public or to other auto agencies for a similar profit. Moreover, he always demanded an informal "surcharge," which was never recorded and on which he paid no taxes, on every sale. It is estimated that he made over 200 million pesos on those surcharges alone.[50]

In 1951 Jorge Antonio branched out into importing television sets, which were new and rare in Argentina, in collaboration with economics minister Roberto Ares. One of his dummy companies imported the sets and sold them to another dummy firm, which then resold them to dealers at a big markup. Between 1952 and September 1955 Antonio is supposed to have handled more than $90 million worth of television sets, and on the sales between his two dummy firms he paid no taxes at all because no records were kept.

Other highly placed regime patrons of Antonio's were Raúl Mende, Perón's secretary for technical affairs; Antonio Cafiero, the minister of commerce; and Jorge Newton, the head of the Peronist party's Leadership School. Antonio got to know this triumvirate through Sílvio Tricieri, a former Miguel Miranda protege who once worked for IAPI. The group made a killing on the grain market by using Antonio and Tricieri to make an offer to buy IAPI's grain at prices far above any other bidder's. Once the contract was secured, the men in the government would see to it that IAPI would be dilatory and careless about making its deliveries so Jorge Antonio would be justified in demanding discounts and indemnities. His complaints about delays or about receiving grain of a different grade than what the contract called for always received a sympathetic response and an offer to lower the price. Eventually Antonio and Tricieri would secure their grain at much below the going market rate and, having a monopoly on the crop, could then resell it for a handsome profit. It is not certain how much Antonio made on this deal, but Tricieri alone is said to have pocketed over 100 million pesos.

This kind of jobbery, which added nothing productive to the economy, must have netted Jorge Antonio no less than 5 billion pesos between 1950 and 1955. In other words, one man alone siphoned off around $200 million that could have been invested in Argentina's growth. Adding to that the estimated $700 million stolen by the Peróns brings the total to nearly $1 billion. But it is also certain that there were scores, indeed hundreds, of other individuals who were tapping the regime for graft and plundering the public finances; so the actual amount drained off might easily have been $2–3 billion dollars. Nor was most of this reinvested in Argentina.

Rather, it was converted into dollars, no doubt at the official rate of five to one, instead of twenty-three to one, and secretly sent abroad. Seen from this angle, the "lost opportunity" thesis takes on a sharper edge.

### The Retreat from Economic Nationalism

Given the decline in exports, the foreign exchange bottleneck, the falling rate of domestic investment, and the clandestine outflow of capital, attracting foreigners was the only way to revitalize the Argentine economy. Until 1950, however, the Perón regime had striven to eliminate foreign capital, with considerable success. Foreign investment, figured in constant 1950 dollars, fell from $4.26 billion in 1945 to just over 41.74 million by the end of 1949.

By the end of 1949 Argentina's foreign exchange reserves were dangerously low, threatening the country's capacity to import. Until exports revived (and they were to decline even further over the next two years), it would be necessary to get more capital flowing in from abroad if a severe recession in the urban sector was to be averted. Thus, beginning in 1950, and especially after 1953, Argentina began liberalizing its laws on profit remittances, capital withdrawals, and exemptions from customs duties as they applied to foreign investors. However, despite a friendly visit in 1954 by Henry Holland, the assistant United States secretary of state for inter-American affairs, the response from American companies was rather disappointing. By 1955 total foreign investment in Argentina had risen to only $1.86 billion, thanks to the entry of the automobile firms of Kaiser, Mercedes-Benz, and Fiat. The most controversial deal, however, was with Standard Oil of California, which was contracted to take over exploring and drilling in Patagonia.

Perón's previous run-in with nationalists over the oil issue made him aware that he was courting trouble with the Standard Oil contracts; nevertheless, there was little he could do. From the beginning of 1950 to the end of 1954 the consumption of fuels and lubricants in industry had increased by 92 percent while YPF's production had gone up by 42 percent and that of private oil producers by just under 20 percent. Thus, despite fuel rationing, oil imports had grown by 13.5 percent and were costing Argentina some $175 million a year out of its precious foreign exchange. On 29 March 1955, in a speech before Congress on the subject of national security, Perón anticipated the storm of criticism that was certain to come. "If war came tomorrow," he warned, we would be unable to continue importing oil within two months, and we would have to reduce our present level of economic activity by 40 percent. Where would that leave us? The fact is, our problem is to produce oil, and if we can't we are in a terrible situation. We need oil to produce energy. Today we produce about 4 million cubic meters. Within two years we will need to produce 8 million to satisfy our consumption, and in five years we will need to produce 20 million cubic meters.

If this progression continues I must ask myself whether YPF can be equal to the task, producing, as it now does, only 4 million. Therefore, we have offered to whomsoever wishes to, the opportunity to come here and work to extract the oil that we, unfortunately, cannot obtain by ourselves in the period of time that we require. Because if it took YPF 40 years to reach the point where it could supply 40 percent of our needs, we will need to wait many more years before it can increase to another 40 percent. And who knows whether oil will even be needed then, because atomic energy may have replaced it. . . .

We cannot extract our own oil because we haven't got the money to invest in a company capable of doing it. Sure, we have oil, but what good is it if it is two, three, or four thousand meters beneath the ground? In order to get it out we would need a lot of capital, which unfortunately we don't have.[51]

The contract with Standard Oil was signed on 26 April and sent to Congress for ratification on 10 May. The Radicals, led by Arturo Frondizi, leaped upon the issue with glee, accusing Perón of selling out to Yankee imperialism. The Peronist bloc, by contrast, was thrown into dismay. Although possessing an overwhelming congressional majority, it could not bring the issue to a vote. The contract's terms seemed advantageous enough to the government: in return for a 40-year concession over some 49,800 square kilometers in Patagonia, with exclusive rights to explore, drill, pump, and refine oil, Standard Oil agreed to sell its output to YPF at 5 percent below the world market price and to turn over half of its profits to the Argentine state. However, nationalists like Frondizi and Professor Silenzi de Stagni of the Buenos Aires Law School seized upon clauses in the contract which gave Standard Oil the right to build any roads, airfields, docks, or communications lines it needed for its exclusive use; the right to import, duty-free and without foreign exchange restrictions, anything it needed; to repatriate its profits freely; and to have a free hand in hiring, firing, or assigning tasks to workers. These privileges, the nationalists claimed, were serious violations of national sovereignty. Not only could access to the roads, docks, and landing strips be denied the Argentine armed forces, even in a national emergency, but these facilities would become points of penetration for the United States military, which (as everyone knew) had designs on Patagonia and the Argentine Antarctic. As for the exemptions granted from the foreign exchange and labor laws, the government was granting foreigners privileges that its own citizens could not claim besides opening the way to wholesale manipulation of the currency and the brutal exploitation of Argentine workers by outsiders.[52]

Despite the regime's attempts to silence its critics (Silenzi de Stagni's house was ransacked and he was forced to go into hiding for fear of his life), even its faithful followers in Congress dragged their heels on ratifying the contracts. The agreements were still being debated in September when Perón was finally overthrown by a military coup. The new military government prudently declared them void.

## The Erosion of Labor's Position

The Second Five-Year Plan addressed Argentina's mounting economic problems and offered as solutions "an inflexible austerity in consumption and a decided effort in production." "Save, don't waste," workers were told. "Buy where prices are lowest . . . and buy only what is needed." The workers were also reminded that "every Argentine who works is a cog in this great enterprise; his duty is to produce, produce, produce." In his speech introducing the plan, Perón observed, "Sometimes when I am going to my office around six in the morning I am tempted to stop at some house and inspect the stuff that is dumped into the garbage cans. It is common to find in them big chunks of meat and bread. With what Buenos Aires throws away every day into the garbage you could feed another Buenos Aires." The objective was the reduction of current spending, both public and private, by 20 percent. With that, he promised, the country would solve its balance of payments problem, halt inflation, and raise its own investment money.[53]

Perón's call for sacrifice was directed at the population as a whole, but it was easier to force this upon the working classes, whose unions were completely under the government's thumb by the beginning of 1951. Businessmen and landowners were harder to control because they could respond to price controls, inflation, and shortages by turning to the black market or by cutting back production and suspending workers. Such practices were condemned by the authorities as economic sabotage, and some firms who engaged in them were actually seized. Nonetheless, prices rose inexorably while wages were held down, resulting in a decline of about 32 percent in real wages between 1949 and 1953.[54]

With real wages falling, by 1953 the average worker was no longer making ends meet with just one job. During the halcyon years of 1946–50, living standards had risen appreciably; now the family budget had to be pared to necessities. More than half (53 percent) of it was devoted to food, as compared with only 47 percent ten years before. Had it not been for rent control, the working classes would have been badly squeezed indeed. As it was, there was little left over at the end of the month: indeed, there was usually a deficit. Downtown shopping was cut back drastically. Department store sales in 1953 were only half of what they had been in 1949.[55]

Compared to other Latin American workers, however, the Argentine was still well off. In 1954 a basket of food items that included cooking oil, rice, sugar, bananas, coffee, beefsteak, leg of lamb, macaroni, lard, flour, eggs, milk, apples, bread, fish, beans, and tomatoes cost an Argentine bricklayer about 14 hours of labor, as compared with 25 hours for an Uruguayan, 40.5 hours for a Brazilian, and 74 hours for a Peruvian. Compared with workers in more advanced nations, an Argentine might work twice as long as a laborer in Chicago to buy a pound of steak or a pound of bread, but only half as long as a worker in London. Nor was the Argentine worker doing so badly in comparison with most people in the nation's middle class. As table 9.2 shows, the general result of Perón's rule was a shift in income from the self-employed and rentiers to wage and salary earners.[56]

Nevertheless, for the Argentine worker the only real basis of comparison was with the level of prosperity of a few years past. The economic position of the worker had deteriorated, and although the unions were government controlled, their leaders were not always able to maintain order. Shop committees complained about the raises and resisted the authorities' call for greater production. In May 1954 those committees in the metallurgical industries suddenly repudiated their leaders and launched a wildcat strike that tied up production for nearly a month. Although the police finally broke the strike, the government decided to placate the workers by

Table 9.2 Shifts in Average Real Family Income
in Selected Occupational Categories, 1946–1953 (1953 = 100)

|  | 1946 | 1949 | 1953 | Difference, 1946–1953 |
|---|---|---|---|---|
| *Wage and salary earners* | 88 | 113 | 100 | + 12 |
| Industry and mining | 88 | 119 | 100 | + 12 |
| Agriculture | 89 | 81 | 100 | + 11 |
| Commerce and finance | 85 | 111 | 100 | + 15 |
| Services, including government | 84 | 113 | 100 | + 16 |
| *Self-employed persons* | 118 | 122 | 100 | − 18 |
| Industry, mining, and construction | 115 | 148 | 100 | − 15 |
| Agriculture | 111 | 82 | 100 | − 11 |
| Commerce and finance | 162 | 175 | 100 | − 62 |
| Services and professions | 109 | 132 | 100 | − 9 |
| *Rentiers* (income derived from rent, interest, or dividends) | 150 | 122 | 100 | − 50 |
| *Pensioners* | 105 | 130 | 100 | − 5 |

Source: ECLA, *Economic Development and Income Distribution in Argentina* (New York: United Nations, 1969), p. 135.

meeting their wage demands and replacing the union's repudiated leadership. During the following month the government also gave in to the dockworkers, textile workers, coffee millers, and match workers, all of whom were resorting to slowdown strikes to pressure the authorities for wage increases. In all, labor's real wages went up by 6 percent in 1954, thus demonstrating to the government the limits to which austerity could be imposed.

Similarly, Perón's calls for greater productivity met with only a tepid response. Between 1949 and the end of 1954, output per worker-hour increased by 16.5 percent for industry as a whole, for an average of only 3.5 percent a year. Some sectors, such as metallurgy, electrical machinery, and consumer durables did better than that, but their gains were offset by a decline in the garment industry and almost total stagnation in mining, food processing, and textiles. Absenteeism was still very high: about 8.3 percent in 1953–54, as compared to 9.3 percent in 1948–49.[57] On the whole, productivity was such a nagging problem that Perón finally brought the CGT and CGE together in a jointly sponsored congress of productivity in March 1955.

The main purpose of this meeting was to get labor to agree to a list of proposals, drafted by José Ber Gelbard, aimed at increasing industrial output: (1) to switch, wherever possible, from hourly wages to piece-rates; (2) to establish minimum daily production quotas; and (3) to offer bonuses to workers, or work teams, who exceeded their quotas. Gelbard also wanted greater flexibility for management to change work rules and shift workers to different tasks as circumstances required. He also wanted to reduce sharply the powers of shop committees, whose stewards could paralyze a factory merely by blowing a whistle whenever they perceived the minutest infraction of labor's rights.[58]

The CGT did not give in tamely to Gelbard's demands. Eduardo Vuletich, the CGT's general secretary, warned that labor would not sacrifice any of its hard-won conquests and challenged the employers to raise productivity themselves by modernizing their factories. Nonetheless, regime pressure was behind Gelbard, and the CGT reluctantly agreed to the National Pact on Productivity, signed on 31 March 1955, which incorporated the incentive schemes, gave management greater freedom to define work rules, and committed the unions to combating absenteeism.

It is hard to determine how much impact the pact would have actually had on the shop floor, because there was not enough time to put it into practice before Perón fell. It is generally agreed that by 1955 the workers were disgruntled, but on the other hand they had no alternative to Perón. It may be significant that on the day the military coup started only a small number of workers answered the CGT's call to go out into the streets to defend Perón. Whether this failure was due to labor's disillusionment with the regime, as Perón's critics contend, or the workers' waiting for Perón to call them out himself, the absence of proletarian initiative was a far cry from the dramatic upheaval of 17 October 1945, which had made the Perón era possible.

## CHAPTER TEN

# The End Is the Beginning

On Tuesday afternoon, 13 September 1955, Eduardo Lonardi, a retired army general living in Buenos Aires, inconspicuously boarded an omnibus for the city of Córdoba. It was an overnight journey, and as the bus rumbled across the darkening pampa he had plenty of time to think about the plot he was involved in. Lonardi had been conspiring against Perón ever since the latter had the constitution changed in 1949 to permit his reelection. In part, Lonardi shared the alarm felt by other officers at the prospect of one-man rule; but in part he also felt a personal resentment against Perón, blaming him for a scandal that nearly ruined Lonardi's career as a young military attaché in Chile. Moreover, as a devout Catholic, Lonardi was deeply troubled by the recent attacks Perón had made against the church. Though never caught red-handed in his plotting, Lonardi's associations with known enemies of the regime resulted in his forced retirement in 1952. Now he was heading for a rendezvous with a group that, because of the tight security in Buenos Aires, had decided to raise a revolt in Córdoba in the next few days. Lonardi had been picked as their leader.

For months officers involved in the plot had been visiting various provincial garrisons. Their movements were approved by Gen. Eduardo Señorans, the army's chief of operations, who supported them. The navy had been contacted too and had pledged to send both the river fleet and the Atlantic fleet to blockade the capital. Lonardi's raising of the Córdoba garrison would be a signal for the others to go into action.

The choice of Lonardi as leader of the rebel forces had been a last-minute decision. Originally the plot had centered around Gen. Pedro Aramburu, the popular chief of the general staff; but just two weeks previously, Perón's secret police had uncovered a part of the conspiracy which involved the Río Cuarto air base in Córdoba Province. The key man at Río Cuarto, Gen. Videla Balaguer, had escaped and now was in hiding, but Aramburu had decided that the moment was no longer propitious and backed out. The other conspirators were determined to go ahead, however, and had turned to Lonardi as their next choice. In the meantime, Perón's minister of war, Gen. Franklin Lucero, flew to Córdoba to personally inspect the situation, having received reports of a plot brewing there. He was still in the city, meeting with the commanders of the infantry, artillery, and air transport units, when Lonardi arrived on the morning of the fourteenth and checked into a modest hotel.

On 15 September Lucero, having been assured that everything was under control, wired Perón: "I have been in the Córdoba garrison. Only a madman would imagine that these people are about to revolt." Later that day he flew back to Buenos Aires, and Lonardi commenced a series of meetings with artillery and air transport unit commanders to put the finishing touches to the uprising that would begin the following morning. It was his fifty-ninth birthday.[1]

Before dawn on the sixteenth, news reached Buenos Aires that loyal infantry units in Córdoba had been attacked by artillery and air transport troops and had been forced to withdraw from the city. Soon afterward disturbing reports began coming in from other parts of the country: fighting at the Curuzú Cuatiá garrison near the Uruguayan border, a revolt at the Bahia Blanca naval base, a proclamation favoring the rebels from the garrison commander in San Luís.

General Lucero, proclaiming himself chief of the "forces of repression," quickly took measures to secure the capital and stamp out the rebellion. Infantry units marched on Córdoba from Tucumán and Santa Fé. Another regiment lay siege to Bahia Blanca. Antiaircraft batteries were set up around Buenos Aires; public buildings were placed under heavy guard; and the Plaza de Mayo was closed to the public. Movie houses, theaters, and bars were shut down. The police were ordered to break up gatherings of more than two people on the streets. Radio programs were severely censored. Despite this, porteños with shortwave sets were able to pick up "the Voice of Liberty," broadcast from Córdoba, which carried Lonardi's proclamation that his "liberating revolution" favored no party, class, or creed but was aimed simply at freeing Argentina from tyranny.

On Saturday, 17 September, Adm. Isaac Rojas, commander of the Atlantic fleet, announced a total blockade of Argentine ports and warned all foreign vessels to stay away. This bad news was offset, however, by favorable reports from Curuzú Cuatiá, where loyalist forces finally had smashed the uprising. Generals Aramburu and Señorans, who had escaped from Buenos Aires to join the rebels, had fled to Uruguay. Fierce fighting was also raging in Córdoba where the rebels, greatly outnumbered, were desperately holding on. The government, now more confident, admitted to the public that there had been a revolt but claimed that only a few "pockets of resistance" were still holding out. Throughout Sunday the eighteenth, the Voice of Liberty remained on the air, testifying to Lonardi's determination to see the rebellion to the bitter end. His appeals to General Lagos, the rebel commander in Mendoza, for reinforcements were unavailing, however. Lagos could spare no more than 200 men and advised Lonardi to abandon Córdoba for Mendoza, where the rebels could retreat to the mountains if necessary. In the meantime, Uruguayan radio broadcasts announced that the Argentine river and Atlantic fleets had rendezvoused at the mouth of La Plata estuary.

During the night, torrential rains lashed the city, turning to a steady downpour by morning. The river lay under a dense fog, and people who crowded along the waterfront could not see the ships lying just offshore. In the early morning Admiral Rojas wired an ultimatum to the Casa Rosada: either Perón resigned by noon or the city's oil refineries and other military targets would be bombarded. It was no idle threat. On the previous day, the fleet had destroyed the oil refineries outside Mar del Plata. On receiving the wire, Perón called Lucero to his office. He was convinced that a naval bombardment would wreak general destruction all over the city, he explained, and he wanted to avoid that. He handed Lucero a note that stated that he would consider resigning if it would bring peace. Lucero immediately called a meeting of loyalist generals who, after a brief discussion, accepted Perón's resignation and set up a junta to negotiate with the rebels.

Perón was taken by surprise. He had worded his note ambiguously, hoping that by offering to resign he would shock his generals and stiffen their resolve. Instead, they had taken his offer literally and had even read his message over the air to forestall the navy's attack. Perón summoned his officers to his home and explained that his note was not a formal resignation—the constitution required that to be sent to Congress—but simply a suggestion that he might do so, which the generals could use in bargaining with the rebels. Despite this, on Monday night Perón received a note from the army's general headquarters stating that his resignation would be treated as final and that he was to leave the country at once. Before dawn on Tuesday, 20 September, Perón packed a suitcase purportedly containing 2 million pesos and $70,000 and had his chauffeur drive him to the Paraguayan embassy. From there the Paraguayan ambassador conducted him to a Paraguayan gunboat anchored in the harbor, where he claimed diplomatic asylum. It was the end of the Perón era.

## Why the Military Revolted

As in the case of European fascism, many Argentines on the extreme right had attached themselves to a popular nationalist movement with the intention of using it for their own purposes: to promote Argentina's glory, to revindicate Hispanic culture against Anglo-Saxon imperialism, or to defend the Catholic faith against godless materialism. Their eventual fate, like that of similar right-wing generals and clergymen in Italy and Germany, was to be threatened with destruction by the very phenomenon they had hoped to control; for Perón's concept of an organized community, or a nation in arms, contained an impulse to totalitarianism. Just as in Fascist Italy, labor unions, business associations, students, professionals, farmers, and intellectuals were all to be brought under state-controlled syndicates. Similarly, the various groups that had contributed to Perón's electoral victory in 1946—the Labor party, the dissident Radical UCR, Junta Renovadora, and the ultraconservative Centros Independientes—were forced afterward to merge into a single Partido Único de la Revolución (the Single Party of the Revolution), which was rechristened the Peronist party in 1949.

Like the Italian Fascist party, the Peronist party was organized in a military fashion with a supreme leader (Perón) at the top whose infallible will was executed through a supreme council (also known as the strategic command) appointed by him, and through lesser party committees (called tactical commands) that extended downward from the provincial level to every county, town, and neighborhood. At every level, leaders were appointed by those above them, and emphasis was placed on obedience, discipline, and centralized command so as to "avoid confusion of ideas and wills, the dilution of decisions, and the dispersal of efforts."[2] There was also a storm trooper contingent, some 1,000 heavily armed young fanatics called the National Liberating Alliance. Until 1953 they existed as an autonomous organization that cooperated with the Peronist party; after 1953 they were integrated within it.

It seems odd, in retrospect, that any group, even the church or the military, should have assumed that it could escape the Peronist lockstep. From the very beginning, Perón made it clear that he would not tolerate opposition. Within a month after his inauguration his minions in Congress began a successful move to impeach four of the five Supreme Court justices. That effort was duplicated by Peronist-dominated provincial legislatures, which purged the provincial courts. This assault on the judiciary was capped in 1949 when Perón used the rewriting of the constitution as an excuse to declare that all federal court appointments, having been made under the old constitution, were no longer valid unless reconfirmed by the Senate. Some seventy-one federal judges were not reappointed and were replaced by Peronists. As with the courts, so with Congress. In 1948 the Peronist majority passed the Law of Disrespect (*desacato*), making it a crime for any citizen, even a congressman, to disparage a government official. A congressman who violated this law could be deprived of his seat and his political immunity if a majority of his colleagues voted to expel him. Some of the leading Radicals fell victim to this law, including the head of the party, Ernesto Sammartino, and the 1951 presidential nominee, Ricardo Balbín.

Peronists saw to it that their legislative majority would be permanent. Although elections were held in a formally correct manner, laws prohibited the opposition from entering into electoral coalitions and penalized smaller parties that failed to have nationwide organizations. The Peronists really took advantage, however, in their control of the mass media and in their ability to hold mass meetings in convenient places while denying the same opportunity to others. All radio stations were government controlled, and by 1952 all newspapers but one (*La Nación*) were in Peronist hands. Thus, the opposition found it difficult to reach the public. It could not broadcast; its press was closed down; and printers were warned not to turn out its propaganda. Local officials often refused to allow opposition parties to hold public rallies, fearing a "disturbance of the peace"; and when rallies were held they were often broken up by Peronist bullies. Opposition candidates were subjected to all manner of intimidation and persecution. During the 1951 electoral campaign the Radical standard-bearer, Balbín, had just been released from prison; the presidential and vice-presidential candidates of both the Conservative and Socialist parties were in jail or in hiding; and the Communist presidential candidate was first jailed and then, after his release, killed when a Peronist mob shot up one of his meetings. Of the 32 Socialists running for the Chamber of Deputies, 23 were either in prison, in hiding, or were awaiting trial. Small wonder, then, that when the votes were tallied the opposition lost all its Senate seats, and its representation fell from 45 to 14 seats in the 157-man Chamber of Deputies.

It is sometimes said in Perón's defense that his rule became tyrannical only when mounting economic troubles emboldened his enemies and only when their attacks became violent. It is true that the excesses of 15 April 1953, when Peronist thugs sacked and burned the Jockey Club along with the headquarters of the Radical, Conservative, and Socialist parties, occurred when the economy was in a severe recession and immediately after a Peronist rally had been disrupted by bombs planted in the crowd. And it is true that the burning and destruction of many downtown churches, including the National Cathedral, during the night of 16 June 1955 came after an abortive coup by the navy air force and marines, in which many civilians were killed. With the National Liberating Alliance always in the vanguard, however, such mob violence was hardly the product of spontaneous public indignation. Perón himself encouraged the atmosphere of violence, as in his famous speech of 31 August 1955, when he told a mass rally that "anyone, in any place, who tries to change the system against the constituted authorities, or against the laws or the Constitution, may be killed by any Argentine." And he added: "Every Peronist must apply this rule, not just against those who commit such acts, but also against those who inspire and incite them." In conclusion, he promised that for every Peronist who fell in the cause, five of the enemy would die.[3]

Rather than changing his policies during the latter stages of his rule, Perón relentlessly tightened the screws on his opponents from the very outset. The creation of a single official party, the court purgings, the closure of most opposition newspapers, the Law of Disrespect, the elimination of all independent labor leaders, the intervention in the UIA, and the attempts to control the universities and intellectuals all began during the first years of the regime, when it still basked in prosperity. In September 1951 a big step was taken toward totalitarianism when Argentina was declared to be under "a state of internal war"—a wholly new concept not contained in the constitution—which permitted the regime to suspend constitutional liberties. Although it was true that this action was a response to an attempted military coup (which never came close to succeeding), it was retained in force for the next four years. Under this sweeping grant of extraordinary power, the state could arrest anyone it wished, and a list of those jailed under it reads like a selection of Argentina's most honored public figures: Reinaldo Pastor, head of the Conservative party; Nicolás Repetto, a venerable Socialist leader; Alfredo Palacios, a former Socialist senator and presidential candidate; Arturo Frondizi, a Radical congressman and vice-presidential candidate; Carlos Sánchez Viamonte, a famous constitutional lawyer; Victoria Ocampo, publisher and editor of *SUR*, a well-known literary magazine; and Federico Pinedo, former minister of the treasury under the Concordancia, to name just a few. Famous people like them were usually sent to Villa Devoto Prison where restrictions on prisoners were relatively lax, but lesser figures faced the grim rigors of the National Penitentiary or of Patagonian concentration camps. Many were first tortured at the headquarters of the dreaded Special Section.[4]

Although some opposition remained in Congress until the very end of Perón's rule, it had become increasingly meaningless. Nor is it likely that it would have been tolerated indefinitely, as Perón's "five for one" speech indicated. The totalitarian impulse imbedded in the very spirit of Peronism required a politically homogeneous society, as attested by the directives sent out in 1952 by the Peronist Superior Council to all local committees instructing them to compile lists of opponents in every province, county, and neighborhood, with the person's address, occupation, place of work, and party affiliation. Local committees were also to discern which government posts in their district were being filled by non-Peronists, and they were to note all sports and cultural clubs in their area so that competing Peronist organizations could be formed. The goal, according to the directives, was to "undermine the morale and ability to resist of the enemy" and to spread a "sentiment of despair" among them, to "localize, combat, and neutralize" all their actions. It was necessary to create in the public's mind a Peronist "climate of victory" and an image of "meanness and injustice" on the part of the enemy.[5]

### The Desertion of the Church and the Military

As Peronism sought to eliminate all opposition and to submit all followers to a single discipline, its goal of an organized community could exempt neither the altar nor the barracks. Nevertheless, in the beginning the clergy and the military considered themselves autonomous in respect to the regime, although friendly toward it. During the 1946 election the Catholic bishops circulated a pastoral letter forbidding the faithful to vote for Perón's opponents on the grounds that the opposition favored legalizing divorce, banning parochial schools, and separating church and state. Upon assuming office Perón continued the policies of his military predecessors of making Catholic religious instruction compulsory in the public schools, providing generous aid to parochial schools, and making all teaching appointments in the public school system subject to review by Catholic ecclesiastical advisers in the Ministry of Education.

Sooner or later, however, Peronist sectarianism and its demands for the citizenry's total loyalty clashed with the claims of religious faith. Indeed, encouraged by Eva Perón and her followers—like her handpicked CGT general secretary, José Espejo, and the education minister, Raúl Méndez San Martín—Peronism grew into a secular faith that competed with the church. Its practices tapped more primitive sentiments (and therefore more dangerous ones, from the church's point of view) than the fuzzy concepts of *justicialismo* ever could reach, for Evita had an uncanny understanding of the mass mind. "The people surrender themselves more easily to a man than to an idea," she observed. "It is easier for them to love a man than to love a doctrine, because the people are all heart." Thus, the Peronist movement turned to hero worship, which could be inculcated in easily learned and chantable slogans: *La vida por Perón!* (My life for Perón!); *Amar siempre al Perón!* (Always love Perón!); or *Perón, Perón, que grande sois!* (Perón, Perón, how grand thou art!). Inevitably, a cult of the personality grew up around Evita too, given her plebian origins and her extraordinary public presence. Among the common people, for whom the Catholic faith often was reduced to a simple worship of the Virgin Mary as a mother figure, the cult of Evita struck a responsive chord. The Peronist press encouraged this by according her titles like Our Lady of Hope, the Martyr of Labor, and Champion of the Poor. Even Perón once referred to her in a ceremony as Saint Evita.[6]

The popular grief that followed Evita's death was exploited by the regime through the printing of pamphlets extolling her virtues and recounting various miraculous cures she had effected. Perón spent over $100,000 to have her body preserved through a special method of embalming, and a vast tomb was planned for displaying it. School textbooks carried pictures of her with a halo around her head, and classes began with children praying to her: "Our little Mother /Who art in Heaven, / Good fairy / Who smiles among the angels, / Evita, I promise to be good, / As you want me to be: / Respecting God, loving my country, / And cherishing General Perón."[7]

The Peronization of the public schools had begun long before Evita's death, however. As early as 1951 Robert Alexander reported that the Catholic clergy were becoming concerned about the introduction of Peronist propaganda into the curriculum. "The teach-

ers," he noted, "must devote a certain amount of time during the
school day to the discussion of the life and teachings of Perón and
their 'significance' for the country." Alexander also warned, pro-
phetically, that "if the trend toward a totalitarian form of Peronismo
continues, the teaching of that 'one true faith of all Argentines' is
likely to come into conflict with the teaching of the Faith of the
Church."[8] The trend did continue. First grade readers taught children their letters with pictures of Perón and Evita and captions such
as: *Evita mira a la nena. El nene mira a Evita.* (Evita looks at the
little girl. The little boy looks at Evita.) Or, *Perón ama a los niños.
Mi papa. Mi mama. Perón. Evita.*[9] For children in the higher grades
there was Evita's ghostwritten autobiography, *La razón de mi vida,*
which became required reading in the schools after her death.

The popularity of the Peronist cult presented the church with a
dilemma. Although Cardinal Copello might go to CGT headquarters
to say a requiem Mass over Evita's remains, he was not willing to
recommend to the pope that she be declared a saint, as some Peronists were demanding. Nor could he ignore the growing evangeli-
calism of the Peronist party Leadership School, whose director, a
former Jesuit seminarian, referred to the party leaders as apostles
and to the school's instructors as preachers who were exercising an
apostolate. On the other hand, Copello wanted to avoid a confrontation with the regime because that would jeopardize the church's
privileges.

Finally the church adopted the strategy of maintaining correct
relations between the upper clergy and the government while allowing liberal priests more latitude to criticize and combat Peronism.
Catholic Action youth began to set up organizations in the universities and high schools to offer alternatives to the CGU and UES. Other
Catholic Action organizers were busily trying to form workers'
groups. Their first success was achieved when a group of white-
collar female workers started the Catholic Association of Employees. In July 1954 a group of Catholic political activists met in Rosario to launch a Christian Democratic party.

Perón would not allow this challenge to Peronism to pass. He also
felt betrayed by his erstwhile ally. On 10 November 1954 he made
his now-famous speech accusing Catholic Action of seeking to divide Argentina by setting up organizations in competition with all
the Peronist syndicates and the Peronist party. The Church's denial
of these charges, published in an open letter on 25 November,
showed no sign of a willingness to change its course. One side
would have to retreat. Two days later the regime opened its fateful

campaign against the church with a mass rally at the Luna Park Stadium. Called upon to declare their fealty to Perón, the party faithful rose to chant:

Atrás, mercadores de la religión;
Atrás, enemigos del Pueblo y enemigos de Dios.
La Patria tiene un destino: se llama Perón.
La Patria tiene una consigna, siempre con Perón.
La Patria tiene una bandera: la bandera de Perón.[10]

(Begone, traffickers in religion;
Begone, enemies of the People and enemies of God.
The Fatherland has a destiny: it's called Perón.
The Fatherland has a trust: it's placed in Perón.
The Fatherland has a banner: the banner of Perón.)

The deterioration of church-state relations had its parallel in Perón's relations with the military. Many of his fellow officers had resented his flaunting of Evita as his mistress, and after she became First Lady they still found her vulgar and too politically ambitious. Army pressure kept her from being appointed secretary of labor and social welfare, although she in fact ran the organization through a stooge. Her belligerent and vindictive character led her into personal feuds with most of the men who surrounded Perón during his first administration, and when Evita decided that someone was not sufficiently loyal to Perón, that person was usually replaced. The military seethed about her frequent interference in matters of government, especially when the popular war minister, Gen. Humberto Sosa Molina, was replaced because he refused to discipline the cavalry officers at Campo de Mayo who had refused to allow Evita on the base.

Sosa Molina's removal came in 1949, the same year that Perón rewrote the constitution to expand presidential powers and permit his reelection. Sosa Molina's successor, Gen. Franklin Lucero, was much less popular and considered much less independent of Perón. Many officers began to worry about the possibility of a personalist dictatorship and of the Peronization of the Army.[11]

Military spending under Perón was also a source of growing discontent. Under Ramírez and Farrell, the portion of the government's budget devoted to defense had risen from 28 to around 50 percent. Perón brought that down to only 21 percent by 1950. He did this without provoking a revolt by making cuts in troop and reserve strength while simultaneously increasing the officers' pay and providing for more rapid promotion. Despite that, many officers, especially those connected with Fabricaciones Militares, were disappointed by his failure to deliver on promises to build heavy industry and by his cutbacks in purchases of military equipment. They were also annoyed by his resistance to joining the Inter-American Defense System, thus depriving them of military aid from the United States.[12]

The forebodings felt by many officers in 1949 proved correct. With Sosa Molina out of the way, Evita once more felt free to pursue her boldest political ambitions. Her followers in the CGT began a campaign to secure her the vice-presidential nomination in 1951. The military was outraged, for if Perón died she would succeed him as commander in chief. Gen. Juan Pistarini, the public works minister and a friend of Perón's, was delegated to inform him that the officers would not tolerate her on the ticket. Perón respected the advice. Evita's campaign was stopped.

In the meantime, Peronization had begun with the sending of officers around the country to lecture at military bases about the regime's accomplishments. Teachers at the Military Academy also were ordered to inculcate loyalty to Peronism as well as to the Constitution.[13] The pace was accelerated after part of the army revolted in September 1951. Although the revolt failed, Perón was shaken by the attempt and became determined to root out any other conspiracies.[14] Early in 1952 his secret police uncovered another plot, involving a secret military lodge called Sol de Mayo. Another extensive purge of the officer corps followed, along with a change in the defense structure to provide a counterweight to the military. This involved shifting the coast guard, which had been under the navy, and the national gendarmerie, which had been under the army, to the jurisdiction of the Ministry of Interior. At the same time, courses in *justicialismo* were made mandatory as part of the officers' training program, and more scholarships for working-class youth were made available at the Military Academy. In April 1953, about a week after the burning of the Jockey Club, the CGT presented the Círculo Militar with a huge portrait of Eva Perón to hang in its grand hall; and before the year was out a white marble statue of her was erected in its garden.[15]

Efforts to Peronize the army were most effective among the noncommissioned officers. Their pay was raised; their living conditions were improved; and they were given smart new uniforms to wear. Procedures for them to enter the commissioned officers' ranks were liberalized, and they were encouraged to do so. They also were given the right to vote, which previously had been denied them, and were urged to get active in the Peronist party. New instructions issued by General Lucero permitted the singing of Peronist songs and the displaying of Peronist banners in the barracks. Peronist party militants, playing upon the noncoms' class consciousness, encouraged them to spy on their officers and report any disloyal activities to the party or the federal police.[16]

Peronization naturally created unease among the officers—even those who considered themselves Peronists—for it threatened to undermine discipline. More alarming still was talk about forming a militia based on the CGT. Shortly before her death Eva Perón had used funds from her social aid foundation to purchase small arms for the CGT on the grounds that the regime needed "shock troop detachments" as a first line of defense against any possible rebellion. Since this occurred just after the 1951 revolt, it seems evident that she intended to pit armed workers against the military. After her death Perón continued to provide the CGT with weapons, including machine guns and antitank guns. Armed units from the CGT subsequently went into action during the abortive coup attempted by the marine and navy air force on 16 June 1955.[17]

On 7 September 1955, just a week before Lonardi's coup, the question of a labor militia was raised formally at the Casa Rosada by a delegation from the CGT. Hugo Di Pietro, the CGT's general secretary, pledged to Perón the organization's members as an auxiliary force and requested the government to provide them with heavy arms. Considering the increasingly confident attacks being mounted daily by Perón's opposition and the frequent clashes between Peronist and Catholic militants, such an offer must have been tempting to Perón (if, indeed, it did not actually originate with him). In his reply, however, he said that he would have to consult the army. On the following day he discussed the matter with Lucero. According to some sources, Perón was lukewarm to the idea, saying that it was easy enough to arm the workers but that it would be difficult to disarm them afterwards. Years later when he was in exile, however, he blamed Generals Lucero and Sosa Molina for vetoing the CGT's offer. In any case, on 9 September Lucero publicly announced the army's opposition to providing the CGT with heavy weapons, although he thanked the unions for their "noble attitude."[18]

Despite this setback, the CGT continued to press the issue, and Perón is generally believed to have become more favorable to the idea. After Lonardi issued his *pronunciamiento*, the CGT leaders once again called for arms to defend the regime. It is certain that the possibility was discussed on 19 September during Perón's meetings with the generals after receiving Admiral Rojas's ultimatum. In his autobiography Perón claimed that Lucero and Sosa Molina had suggested arming the workers but that he rejected the idea because it "would only have led to a massacre." But elsewhere he accused Lucero and Sosa Molina of overruling his orders to arm the workers because they preferred defeat to placing any trust in the common people.[19]

Perón's vacillation on the question of forming a workers' militia does not necessarily prove that he was first and foremost a military man. Under his influence, the armed forces had became highly politicized, at the expense of professional standards. Peronization had advanced so far by 1955 that, despite Lonardi's revolt, a majority of the army remained loyal to the regime. When Perón offered his resignation the rebels had been defeated in the north and were about to be overwhelmed in Córdoba. A naval bombardment of the capital would have been tragic; but Admiral Rojas did not have the forces to take the city, and in the meantime his bases had been occupied by army units. Eventually the fleets would have had to withdraw, probably to Uruguay, where according to international law they would have been impounded. That would have left Perón with only a mopping-up action in Mendoza. It was lack of will at the top of the system, rather than a wholesale rejection by the army, that allowed Lonardi to win.

## The Politics of Revenge

Despite the chilly, penetrating drizzle, jubilant crowds of anti-Peronists took to the streets of Buenos Aires on Monday night, 19 September, to celebrate the rebels' victory. Meanwhile, in Córdoba, fighting had stopped while Perón's generals negotiated the terms of surrender aboard Admiral Rojas's flagship. General Lagos, flying in from Mendoza, found Lonardi stoically awaiting events, but in great pain: he was suffering from a stomach cancer that would end his life within a few months. When news of Perón's flight arrived, Lonardi promptly declared himself provisional president and named an emergency cabinet. The next morning, the loyalist army having surrendered, he boarded an airplane for Buenos Aires to take over the government. When he arrived at midday a limousine met him at the airport. The ride to the Casa Rosada turned into a triumphal procession as great crowds lined the route, cheering, waving flags, and crying "Death to the tyrant, long live liberty!" That night, army tanks surrounded the headquarters of the National Liberating Alliance, the last redoubt of Peronist resistance, and blew the building to pieces.

Although it is true that well-wishers of the Liberating Revolution were drawn from all classes of the population, the great majority were middle and upper class. Among the proletariat the sudden turn of events produced mainly shock and gloom. "On one of those days," Juan José Real later recalled, "I was returning home with a lady friend. We rode second class on the San Martín line. At Palermo station some 15 or 20 street laborers got on. They sat silently, their heads bowed, not looking at each other. They were the defeated. In the first-class car ahead groups of male and female students were waving Argentine flags and cheering for liberty. They deprecated the fallen regime and thought they were the victors."[20]

In his first public speech Lonardi reiterated the nonpartisan character of his Liberating Revolution and took as his theme a quote from General Urquiza, the conqueror of Rosas: "Neither victors nor vanquished." There would be no reprisals against Peronists, he said, and all legitimate gains of labor would be respected. The rule of law and freedom of the press would be restored, and so would the universities' autonomy. Inflation would be brought down; the bureaucracy trimmed; and political indoctrination in the public schools ended.[21]

Such a conciliatory course wrung a grateful offer to collaborate from the Peronist party's titular leader, Alejandro Leloir, head of the Superior Council, and from Hugo Di Pietro, the CGT's general secretary. It also won the approval of Arturo Frondizi, the head of the left-wing "Intransigent" faction of the Radical party. With Perón out of the way, Frondizi hoped to capture the support of the working class and of nationalistic intellectuals with his own brand of national socialism. Other Argentines, however, were not disposed to forgive and forget. Anti-Peronist labor leaders who had been ousted and jailed by Perón called for intervention in the CGT, the complete de-Peronization of the trade unions, and the abrogation of the Law of Professional Associations. Military men, who feared reprisals if the Peronists ever regained power, demanded the dissolution of the Peronist party and a full investigation into corruption and "high treason" during the Perón administration. Businessmen wanted the cancellation of all current labor contracts and a complete revision of existing labor legislation. They also wanted the 1853 Constitution, with its emphasis on property rights, restored. Liberals from all sectors demanded the dissolution of all Peronist syndicates and the return of *La Prensa*, which Perón had expropriated in January 1951 and given to the CGT, to its original owners. The dominant mood favored action to forestall any resurgence of totalitarianism. Freeing the political prisoners, dissolving the Peronist-controlled Congress, and restoring the original nomenclature of places renamed in honor of Juan and Eva Perón, as Lonardi was doing, was not enough to satisfy this mood. His refusal to intervene in the CGT, cancel the labor contracts, or act on the *La Prensa* case—for fear of seeming too punitive toward labor—was interpreted by liberals as favoring a continuation of Peronism, albeit without Perón. Lonardi's cabinet choices, many of whom had been involved in extreme right-wing activities, also raised liberal suspicions. Mario Amadeo, the foreign minister, was a former Axis sympathizer who resigned in 1945 as director of political affairs in the Foreign Ministry after Argentina broke diplomatic relations with Nazi Germany. Atilio dell'Oro Maini, the education minister, once edited *Critério*, a journal that extolled the virtues of Mussolini, Franco, and Salazar. Juan Carlos Goyeneche, the press secretary, had collaborated with Amadeo in editing a journal called *Sol y Luna*, which specialized in pro-Axis propaganda furnished by the Spanish Falange.[22]

To placate the liberals, who had the powerful support of General Aramburu and Admiral Rojas (now serving as vice-president), Lonardi appointed a National Investigating Committee to look into charges of scandal and treason against the Perón regime. The committee made sensational revelations, fully covered in the press, about the jewelry, clothes, cars, and other luxury items which the Peróns had accumulated. Even more lurid were the accounts of Perón's escapades with teenage girls, especially a certain Nelly Rivas, who was only 14 when she became his mistress. Perón, several former cabinet ministers, and scores of congressmen were indicted for violating the constitution's protection of press, speech, and property. A military court of honor also found Perón guilty of violating his oath of office, inciting his followers to violence, and corrupting a minor. He was stripped of his rank and titles and denied the right to wear the Army uniform.

This was not enough to satisfy the *revanchistes*. High Peronist officials and members of Perón's entourage were placed under military arrest: Leloir; General Lucero; Delia De Parodi, head of the Peronist Women's party; Héctor Cámpora, former president of the Chamber of Deputies; Jorge Antonio; Guillermo Patricio Kelly, leader of the National Liberating Alliance, to name only a few. The Peronist Supreme Court was purged, and new justices were named. The Eva Perón Foundation was closed down. All incumbent CGT officers and union leaders were dismissed from their posts and overseers were appointed in their place.

Anxious to shore up his support among liberals, Lonardi appointed a National Consultative Council, composed of representatives from all the parties except the Peronists and Communists, to advise him about future policy. He also dismissed his war minister, Gen. Justo León Bengoa, whom the liberal army leaders accused of blocking a purge of Peronist officers. Bengoa's departure was followed the next day by the resignation of Goyeneche, who was exhausted from dealing with a hostile press.

Lonardi was determined to maintain a political balance, however. The chief liberal in his cabinet was Eduardo Busso, a law professor who headed the ministries of interior and justice. On 12 November Lonardi took from him the powerful Interior Ministry and gave it to Luís Maria de Pablo Pardo, a prominent reactionary. With that, Busso resigned, and so did all the members of the National Consultative Council, except for the representatives of the far-right Christian Federal Union, Mario Amadeo's party. Lonardi went on the radio to explain his action and make a plea for toleration and forgiveness toward those who had once supported the Perón regime in good faith. They represented important segments of public opinion, he said, which might still make positive contributions to the nation. His alleged leniency toward unions, for instance, reflected a recognition of labor's importance. Not only would he resist policies of vindictiveness that would polarize Argentina's classes, but he urged that Peronist representatives be included on the National Consultative Council.

It was no use. The liberal opposition was aroused. That night a junta of fourteen officers from all three branches of the armed forces removed Lonardi and replaced him with Gen. Pedro Aramburu. To clarify the new government's orientation, it also issued a declaration of principles calling for the Peronist party's dissolution, the disqualification of leading Peronists from voting or holding office, and the early scheduling of elections in order to restore civilian rule.

## Aramburu and Labor

Aramburu's cabinet appointments signaled an end to conciliation. Eugenio Blanco, his treasury minister, had been prominent in the UIA and, as dean of the Economic Sciences Faculty, had resigned from the University of Buenos Aires to protest Perón's interference in campus affairs. Pedro Mediondo, the public works minister, had resigned as professor of engineering for the same reason. The war minister, Gen. Arturo Ossorio Araña, played a key role in Lonardi's revolt. Álvaro Alsogaray, the minister of industry, was a former army officer turned successful businessman and an aggressive proponent of laissez-faire. Juan Llamazares, the minister of commerce, had a seat on the commodities exchange. Sadi E. Bonnet, the transportation minister, was a retired admiral who left the service because of a personal quarrel with Perón. Adolfo Lanús, the press secretary, was an editor at *La Prensa* when Perón expropriated it. Raúl Mingone, the labor minister, was recruited from the International Labor Office, where he had gone after resigning a diplomatic post in protest over "the nazi-fascist farce" in Argentina.[23]

Aramburu aimed at depoliticizing the labor movement by breaking the Peronist union bosses' hold on power, making union elections more democratic, and giving the individual worker a choice about which union (if any) to join. By doing so, he would prepare the working class to take a responsible part in the liberal democratic system that he was pledged to restore as quickly as possible. He was to discover, however, that the proletariat wanted none of those liberal reforms.

Lonardi had already begun the process of de-Peronizing labor by removing Hugo Di Pietro as head of the CGT and replacing him with two cosecretaries: Andrés Framini, leader of the textile workers, and Luís Natalini, general secretary of the power and light union. Both were young and, though Peronists, had come to maturity in the regime's later years. They were used to working within the system and, so long as labor's gains were not threatened, they might be counted upon to go along with the new order. Indeed, the pragmatism with which they accepted the change was one of the bitterest pills that Perón had to swallow in his first months of exile, as he related later in his autobiography:

The unions let me down too. They were supposed to be ready for a general strike, but that never materialized. The leaders, with Di Pietro at the head and the whole CGT ready to paralyze the country—and they didn't paralyze it! Instead, they tried to make a deal with the group coming in. You look at the whole scene and you say to yourself: you mean I've worked so hard and sacrificed so much *for this*! That's when I concluded that the Argentine people deserved a terrible punishment for what they had done. And now they've got it. Now there's hunger there, and desperation. It's the fate they deserve.[24]

After Perón's fall, however, many Socialist, Radical, and Communist labor leaders returned from prison or exile and again sought to take over the unions they formerly headed. That was not difficult in some of the older unions, where Peronism had never penetrated deeply, but in other cases it led to violence. True to his promise to protect the trade unions, Lonardi sent soldiers to the offices of the dockworkers', trolley workers', and bank employees' unions, which had been taken over by "free unionists," to remove the invaders. The Socialist party then accused him of wanting to keep the unions under totalitarian control, and many top-ranking military officers also were disgusted at the sight of troops being used to maintain Peronists in power. To pacify both sides, Lonardi had promised to hold absolutely free union elections within 120 days to let the workers choose their leaders, but in the meantime the government would prevent any more clashes. Despite this, violence continued, resulting in fourteen more unions being attacked by armed invaders who dislodged the Peronists. The fact that Lonardi no longer tried to interfere suggests that the attackers were backed by powerful figures in the armed forces. Meanwhile, the Socialists demanded a postponement of the elections, pleading that they had little time to prepare for them after so many years of repression. Peronists, on the other hand, felt their power slipping away from them and threatened to call a general strike.[25]

By the end of October Lonardi's attempts to pursue a moderate labor policy were in shambles, and his attempt to appear neutral by removing all union officials only provoked the long-threatened general strike on 31 October. The strike was sufficiently successful that Lonardi felt the need to conciliate Framini and Natalini by restoring the Peronist officials to their posts and setting up joint committees of Peronists and non-Peronists in those unions that recently had been invaded. That brought strong protests from both the Socialists and the armed forces.

Aramburu, by contrast, made no attempt to get along with the Peronists. Armed raids of Peronist unions increased, and when the CGT responded with another general strike on 15 November, Aramburu sent in troops to seize its offices. Framini, Natalini, and some 200 other high union officials were sent to a prison camp in Tierra del Fuego. All of the unions were placed under intervention.

To free the workers from their union bosses, Aramburu favored a right-to-work law that would forbid the closed shop. He settled, however, for a modification of the Law of Professional Associations that simply allowed competing unions in the same field. Such a compromise failed to satisfy the liberals, and the Peronists accused Aramburu of trying to weaken labor by dividing it.[26]

Aramburu's most controversial labor policy, however, was his scheme to link wages to productivity. Industrial efficiency already had become a worrisome topic in Perón's last years, as the National Pact on Productivity attested. After Perón's fall a study of the economy commissioned by Lonardi pointed to big wage increases without corresponding gains in productivity as a prime factor in the country's accelerating inflation. Accordingly, the Aramburu government, facing the renewal of some 500 labor contracts in February 1956, issued a decree on the seventeenth of that month which (1) authorized the use of "moral and material incentives" to increase productivity; (2) allowed companies to sign individual contracts with employees that included such incentives; (3) permitted management to shift workers to different tasks and revise job classifications as circumstances required (but without affecting the individual worker's pay, job security, or seniority); (4) allowed management to change any existing work arrangements that might inhibit productivity, so long as those changes did not lengthen the working day or endanger the workers' health; and (5) required that women be paid the same as men.[27]

News of the decree leaked out before the official announcement, giving both labor and management a chance to air their positions in advance. Union leaders, predictably, condemned the government for reintroducing sweatshop practices. Businessmen were generally pleased, although they protested that raising women's pay would cause hardship for employers. From now on, said the RRP, the ruling principle will have to be "one which allows the man who works most to earn most," however much that might offend "the average trade unionist's dislike and distrust of anything savoring of payment by results." There was perhaps just a tinge of gloating in the RRP's adding, "Clearly, however, it will not be easy to convince the labor rank and file to swallow this bitter medicine without kicking; but in their own interests, as well as the country's, it will have to be administered."[28]

It is difficult to measure the actual effects of this decree. DINIE, a state-owned conglomerate, claimed that it achieved increases in output of around 3.5 percent in 1956–57 by introducing bonuses for good attendance and punctuality; but productivity in the private industrial sector rose by only 0.4 percent in that same period. One explanation suggests that many private employers took a "get even" attitude toward their workers by dismissing troublemakers, docking wages for absenteeism, and restricting sick leaves. While understandable in light of past union abuses, such actions made the workers feel like victims. Unwilling to believe that management would not simply pocket any benefits accruing from higher productivity, they resisted en bloc.

Aramburu also undermined his own policy by giving in too easily to strike demands. In his desire to cajole the workers away from Peronism, he often forgot about tying wages to output. Thus, while productivity in private industry actually stalled in 1957, the Labor Ministry granted average wage increases of 38 percent and warned employers to absorb them out of profits, rather than passing them on to consumers. To insure that consumers were protected, price controls were instituted on a variety of goods, and a corps of honorary price control inspectors, drawn from the trade unions, police, and government bureaucracy, was appointed to monitor the stores.[29]

Speaking before the Foreign Press Association on 1 October 1957, Federico Pinedo expressed the businessmen's bitter disenchantment with the Aramburu regime. The government was increasing consumer purchasing power and then expressing its indignation when that led to greater demand and higher prices, he said. It played the demagogue by its "futile and puerile, even grotesque, recriminations and complaints against producers and merchants." Matters would only get worse.[30] But if Aramburu lost the businessmen's support he also failed to win over labor. Price controls failed to stop inflation, which eroded labor's real wages by 6 percent during 1957. Semiclandestine shop committees began to form, and the number of strikes increased. In 1955 there had been 21 strikes costing 114,120 working days; by contrast, there were 52 in 1956 with 5.2 million working days lost, and 56 in 1957 with a total loss of 3.4 million working days.

Aramburu sometimes responded with force. When the railroad and typographical workers struck he drafted them into the army; and when, on 9 June 1956, Peronist elements in the army revolted with the support of armed workers, he crushed the uprising and ordered twenty-seven of its leaders to be summarily shot. But force had its limits. You could use soldiers as strikebreakers against garbage collectors, but they could not substitute so easily for teachers, locomotive engineers, or hospital workers. Nor could they be everywhere when many strikes broke out simultaneously. Some labor leaders were ingenious, too, at passive resistance. When Aramburu sent troops into the power plants in January 1958 to break a strike, Juan José Taccone, the union boss, slipped his followers sleeping pills. One by one the men began to stretch out on benches, tables, and even the floor, despite the soldiers' threats. Knowing it was beaten, the government came to terms within hours, whereupon Taccone called in a second shift and got the generators going again.[31]

By mid-1957 Aramburu was convinced that the non-Peronists had made sufficient headway in the trade union movement to allow him to lift the intervention. He scheduled a CGT convention for late August at which new statutes would be approved and a new executive committee elected. First, however, each union had to elect its officers as well as its convention delegates. The outcome of those elections seemed to justify his optimism. Socialists and Radicals gained control of most of the older, and larger, unions and claimed a majority of the delegates to the upcoming convention. When the convention opened on 29 August, however, a segment of the non-Peronist bloc which followed Arturo Frondizi, leader of the Radical party's left, went over to the other side, thus giving the Peronists a majority. After name-calling and fistfights the remainder of the non-Peronists walked out, depriving the convention of a quorum. With his de-Peronization scheme in shambles, Aramburu had to be content with appointing a Committee of Twenty, composed of eleven "democratic" leaders and nine Peronists to govern the CGT, pending full restoration of its legality. Even this concession failed to mollify the Peronists, however. They refused to show up for the ceremony in which the new leadership was installed.[32]

## Peronism's Revival

True to his original pledge, Aramburu scheduled elections for a constitutional convention to be held in late 1957 for the purpose of restoring the 1853 Constitution, with whatever modifications the delegates might deem appropriate. General elections for president, Congress, and provincial and municipal governments were to follow on 23 February 1958, with the elected officials to assume office on the first of May.

This plan did not please everybody, to be sure. The Peronist party was barred from running, and no one who held high office under Perón could be a candidate on any ticket. Conversely, there were military officers who opposed any elections at all, believing that such an early return to civilian rule was a mistake. For them, a much longer period of military rule was necessary to purge the country of every trace of Peronism. Arturo Frondizi also was critical of Aramburu's timetable, arguing that the general election should be held first, after which the new civilian government (presumably his) could write a new constitution.

Nevertheless, Aramburu pressed ahead, confident of the support of a majority of the armed forces, which favored a return to the barracks. Many of the officers, known as "constitutionalists," wanted to restore the military's professionalism by getting it out of politics. Others, more political in outlook, preferred civilian rule—but only if it was guided by "responsible" people of a liberal outlook who would encourage businessmen and farmers and keep the labor unions under control. These latter officers placed their hopes in the right-wing elements of the Radical party.

The Radicals were riven by factionalism, with the mercurial Frondizi always at the center of the controversy. A leftist who once had led the party's youth organization, he had resisted the temptation in the 1940s to go over to Peronism, preferring to work inside the Radical party to bring it to a more national-socialist position. Now, with Perón gone, he hoped to capture the workers and lower middle class for Radicalism, with himself as president and party leader. Rather than a solid organization, however, the Radical party was a coalition of provincial and local machines. Frondizi's hard-driving and sometimes devious tactics alienated other party notables, who also failed to share his enthusiasm for embracing the Peronist masses. When he packed the national convention and got the presidential nomination, they decided to form a splinter party. The Radical party, which might have provided a smooth transition to civilian rule, was thereby split into two roughly equal divisions: Frondizi's Unión Cívica Radical Intransigente (UCRI), and his opponents' Unión Cívica Radical del Pueblo (UCRP), which nominated Ricardo Balbín as its presidential candidate.

## Perón as the Pivot

Meanwhile, Perón had become a rootless exile. After waiting two weeks aboard a Paraguayan gunboat in the Buenos Aires harbor, where his fate was debated by the victorious rebels, he finally was allowed a safe-conduct pass to Paraguay. But allowing Perón to remain in a neighboring state was obviously too dangerous; so the Argentine government pressured Paraguay's dictator, Gen. Alfredo Stroessner, to send him further away. On 1 November 1955 Perón took off for Nicaragua aboard Stroessner's private airplane, having accepted an offer of asylum from another dictator, Anastasio Somoza.

Instead of going to Nicaragua, however, Perón made a change of plans en route, having learned during a stopover in Panama that Somoza was under a great deal of pressure from the Catholic clergy and the American ambassador to cancel his invitation. On the other hand, he was informed that the Panamanian government was eager to have him stay. Not only did the country's president want to see him, but a suite at the luxurious Hotel Panama would be placed at his disposal.

President Espinosa Arias apparently believed that Perón had escaped with at least $700 million stashed away and hoped to attract some of that money to Panama. What he did not know was that most of Perón's fortune was locked up in numbered Swiss bank accounts under Eva Perón's maiden name. He could not get to it without proving that Maria Eva Duarte was the same person as Maria Eva Ibarguren de Perón (her legal name), and the Argentine government was not willing to furnish the necessary documentation.[33] All he had in hard currency, therefore, was the $70,000 he had stuffed into his suitcase. He was not poor, but he had to guard his resources.

Unwilling to discomfit Somoza, Perón decided to stay in Panama, but when no investments were forthcoming from him the Panamanian government's hospitality began to cool. Perón then moved to the town of Colón, in the Canal Zone, where he took up quarters in the rather seedy Hotel Washington, a great comedown for a man who had known so much luxury and power. Emílio Perina, a Frondizi emissary who visited him there, described the room as plain and shabby: broken tiles on the floor, two iron beds, a rude table in the kitchen, clean but worn curtains. The only luxury was a balcony that overlooked the ocean, from which an occasional breeze entered to cool the room from the awful tropical heat.[34]

Perón was not dispirited, however. In defeat he seemed to recover the iron determination and boundless energy that once had carried him to power. Smarting from his enemies' accusations of corruption and treason, he already had started writing a book in his defense, soon to be published as *La fuerza es la razón de las béstias* (Force is the Reasoning of Beasts). He also was busily writing all his friends and followers who had escaped into exile, asking them for news and urging them to get in touch with one another. As he later told Américo Barrios, a journalist who joined his entourage: "In Panama the climate was infernal. I sat in my undershirt in front of a fan, because the heat was suffocating. And I wrote and wrote. I spent fifteen hours a day writing. Letters were my emissaries. I made terrific efforts to stand the heat. It was like a boiling hot slab, but I worked in spite of it. I had been out of touch with the boys, but little by little we began to communicate more effectively."[35]

During his visit with Perón, Perina was shown a pile of letters that had come from admirers, mostly Argentines, but also some from other countries. Many of them offered him money. One, from a São Paulo industrialist, contained a check for $10,000. Others were from humble workers who offered him their meager savings. But it was not money that Perón wanted most. His main concern was to rebuild his shattered movement.

By the end of 1955, resistance committees were already forming in the lower-class barrios. They turned out crudely handwritten or mimeographed propaganda, held secret meetings, went out at night to paint slogans on the walls, always with the same message: *Perón vuelve* (Perón will return). The problem was coordination. Each barrio committee tended to be independent, and without Perón on the scene, there was no one of sufficient stature to make them work together.[36]

The movement received a great boost in March 1957 when six prominent Peronists, including John William Cooke and Jorge Antonio, escaped from a Patagonian prison near Río Gallegos and successfully made their way to Chile, where they were given asylum. They would be helpful in coordinating and financing the movement. Cooke had been active in the underground after Perón's fall, trying to set up a central command in Buenos Aires. Although extremely fat, he was intelligent, resourceful, energetic, and absolutely fearless. Perón recognized his talents at once and appointed him chief of operations in the newly constituted Peronist Supreme Command. It was largely an empty title, for Perón was jealous about making all the final decisions and would not hesitate to use other agents besides Cooke if it suited his purposes; but it tickled the younger man's vanity. Perón, a shrewd manipulator, reminded Cooke that "from this moment on you will be the center of attention" and lectured him about the responsibilities of leadership. "Forgive me for telling you all these things," he concluded in his letter of 22 June 1957, "but I am like your father and I feel a sincere desire to see you succeed."[37]

By August 1957 Cooke was able to report some gains. In the place of sporadic, uncoordinated acts of violence there was now a regular organization linking exile groups to resistance committees inside Argentina. From Buenos Aires a central coordinating command reached out to provincial committees, which in turn were in contact with Peronist neighborhood and workplace cells. Arms were shipped regularly through Bolivia and Paraguay. Daily acts of sabotage were beginning to sap the government's confidence, while underground Peronist organizations were so full of enthusiasm that there was no shortage of volunteers for direct action.[38]

Nevertheless, there were problems. First, there were the "softliners" or neo-Peronists, who were disposed to cooperate with Aramburu. Since many of them were well known they tended to confuse the masses about the true Peronist position. Second, Guillermo Patricio Kelly, who had escaped to Chile at the same time as Cooke, had resurrected the National Liberating Alliance, secured his own arms, and was carrying on violent activities independently of the movement. Third, the underground Peronist labor committees also failed to consult the movement's chief of operations and elected Andrés Framini as their leader, a decision that caused Cooke "no joy" because he saw Framini as a "weak man, prone to many errors." Fourth, the movement's chronic shortage of money kept it from purchasing all the guns and explosives it needed. Finally, Cooke complained that many prominent Peronists refused to accept his leadership, preferring instead to go directly to Perón—who by this time had moved from Panama to Caracas—and thereby disrupting the proper chain of command. Many of them would come back claiming to have different orders, countermanding his commands and disturbing the movement's unity.

Perón's replies to these complaints were reassuring but vague. He complimented Cooke on his progress in organizing guerrilla activities. The abortive uprising of June 1956 had proven, he said, that the military could not be confronted openly. The only route for Peronism was to go underground and begin the slow process of organizing the masses for civil resistance. To make sure the society remained polarized, the guerrillas should even incite acts of repression. Their job was to "create chaos, which is the only way the people can take matters into their own hands." As for Cooke's authority in the movement, Perón assured him that "at all times the leadership is in your hands and all the decisions are yours. . . . You have me to grant you whatever you need and to call on whenever necessary as a last resort." Nevertheless, Cooke was beginning to experience that organized confusion that Perón deliberately fostered in the movement so as to keep his grip on it from a distance. Cooke was the first of many personal representatives on whom Perón bestowed authority only to undermine it lest the designee become too powerful to control. For the next decade and a half he worked through many separate lines of command whose authority overlapped, issuing contradictory orders that would send his various agents running back to him to referee their disputes. In later years he explained this approach in blunt terms to one of Cooke's successors, Jorge Paladino, when the latter complained to him: "I have two hands and I move them both."

The movement's finances were put on a sounder footing with Jorge Antonio's escape to Chile. Antonio had squirreled large sums abroad where they were easily accessible. He also had an enormous ego that was highly susceptible to flattery. Perón wrote him long letters, filling him in on the latest events in the movement's progress and telling him that his persecution in prison and his dramatic escape put him in the front rank of Peronists. Antonio's political future was bright because he, Perón, was now sixty-three and would not head the movement much longer. "Naturally, I will have to pass the flag on to you, the younger generation," he wrote. "And naturally I expect you to pass it on to men like yourself, who mean for me a guarantee of action. I am an old politician who is coming to the end of his road. You are a young fellow who may just be starting his career. So I am obliged to tell you in all sincerity what I think, as the greatest homage I can offer to friendship and affection for you."

Besides, Perón reminded him, there was the prospect of revenge. The Aramburu government had seized all of Antonio's property in Argentina. Therefore, the best chance of getting it back was to put himself in the vanguard of Peronism, which would surely return to power someday.[39]

A few days later Perón, knowing of Cooke's personal dislike for Antonio, wrote his chief of operations to ask him to treat their potential "angel" with forbearance. Antonio, he said, was a "good fellow" and loyal, albeit a little confused. "He doesn't know much about politics, although he apparently wants to show that he does." Cooke agreed to go along, and by September Perón informed him that Jorge Antonio was beginning to help out with money. Moreover, he said, he was working on some business matters with Antonio which ought to free the movement entirely from its financial pinch.[40] Apparently this referred to Peron's lending his name to some business ventures in Caracas in which Jorge Antonio would be a silent partner.

The constitutional convention elections of 28 July 1957 gave the Peronists their first opportunity to test their strength. They also presented Perón with a dilemma. Since the Peronist party was unable to participate, what were the faithful supposed to do? Perón's first inclination was to order them to stay away from the polls, but in Argentina voting is obligatory and failure to do so is a misdemeanor. That would inflict a hardship on his followers, especially public employees and pensioners. It did not seem worthwhile to place Peronist support behind any of the other parties, however, so eventually Perón instructed his followers to go to the polls and cast blank ballots. And so they did. In the final tally, the blank ballots were 24.3 percent of the total vote, outrunning both the UCRP, which got 24.2 percent, and the UCRI, which came in third with 21.2 percent.[41]

UCRP supporters were crestfallen by the size of the Peronist vote but were consoled by the fact that of all the legal parties they had the best chance of winning in February. Frondizi, on the other hand, was in a jam. His presidential hopes were dim indeed unless he could make a deal with Perón. The Peronists thus held the key to victory: with their votes Frondizi would win handily, but if they cast blank ballots again, Balbín would be the next president.

There were deep divisions in the movement about which strategy to adopt, and Perón was wise enough not to make his decision without consulting leading representatives of the trade union, exile, and underground organizations. Those who favored blank ballots did so for various reasons. Many were sincere fighters for principle, for whom a pact with Frondizi would be a betrayal of the movement's integrity. After all, Frondizi had been a relentless opponent in the past. Others, like Alejandro Leloir, leader of the party organization in Buenos Aires, had become Aramburu's secret collaborators and were working to insure an UCRP victory. This latter group included Jorge Antonio, who hoped to curry favor with Aramburu and thus retrieve some of his sequestered property. Finally, among those who opposed any support for Frondizi were extreme militants like Guillermo Patricio Kelly, who was committed to violent revolution and viewed all peaceful tactics with contempt. At the other end of the spectrum were pragmatists like Cooke, who argued that a Frondizi victory was preferable to one by Balbín. Cooke also pointed out that the UCRI leader was campaigning very hard to sell himself to voters as the only realistic alternative to continuing the policies of economic liberalism. It was an appealing pitch, and if enough voters were attracted by it Frondizi might win after all. If that happened, the Peronists would have no influence in his government, whereas if Frondizi won with their support they could claim the victory as their own.

Frondizi was pressing for an alliance, so early in December Perón convoked a meeting of his top advisers in Caracas. Jorge Antonio was asked to chair the sessions (and was allowed to foot the bill for all expenses too). For two days Perón listened to reports from various representatives of the trade unions, the federal capital and provincial party organizations, exile groups, and special emissaries of the Peronist Supreme Command. Most of those who spoke favored the blank ballot strategy, and after the sessions Jorge Antonio asked Perón for a private interview in order to find out what decision he would make and to press his own arguments in favor of blank voting. Perón, after eliciting a solemn promise of secrecy, gave him a knowing wink and pronounced just a single word: "blank." The following morning the Caracas chief of police, a close friend of Perón's, showed him photocopies of four telegrams Antonio had sent to Argentina the night before, all containing the same message: "The management is expected to invest exclusively in white clothes." Perón treated it as a huge joke and immediately dispatched a courier to Frondizi, inviting him to send a representative to Caracas to discuss the details of an electoral pact.[42]

On 2 January Rogelio Frigerio, Frondizi's closest collaborator and the man believed to be mainly responsible for the idea of seeking Peronist support, arrived in Caracas to negotiate. It took two days to hammer out an agreement. Perón promised to instruct his followers to vote for Frondizi and the entire UCRI ticket. He also agreed to urge all neo-Peronist parties not to run, and he would order all Peronists who might have accepted nominations from other parties to withdraw. In return, Frondizi promised that, if elected, he would restore the Peronist party, the Eva Perón Social Aid Foundation, and the CGE (which Aramburu had suppressed) to legality; restore the Law of Professional Associations to its original form, banning competing unions; lift the intervention of the CGT and release all Peronist labor leaders from jail; drop all criminal charges against Perón and other leading Peronists; renationalize the banking system; replace the current Supreme Court (all Aramburu appointees) with justices more sympathetic to Peronism; take all appropriate measures to insure full employment; and call another constitutional convention to restore the 1949 Constitution. All of those measures were to be adopted within ninety days after Frondizi's inauguration.[43]

This document was signed by Perón and Cooke for the Peronist movement, and by Frondizi and Frigerio for the UCRI. Transmitted by courier to Argentina, Perón's orders were received loyally in some quarters, but with consternation in others. On the whole, however, the February 1958 election results presented an impressive picture of Perón wielding a solid bloc of some 1.2 million voters. Support for the UCRI went up by 23.6 percentage points over its 1957 performance, while the blank vote dropped by 15. Frondizi came in 16 percentage points ahead of Balbín and his congressional candidates won 130 of 187 seats in the Chamber of Deputies.[44]

It was an amazing comeback for Perón, only two and a half years after being overthrown. From thousands of miles away he continued to exert his will over at least a quarter of the Argentine electorate. The incoming government owed its existence to borrowed votes of his, and the outgoing government had been utterly defeated by him in all of its plans. The future would pivot on Perón and his movement.

## *Summary and Retrospect: Argentina's Distorted Development*

We have reached the midpoint of our study and can now review the ground covered so far, summarize the main trends in Argentina's development up through the Aramburu government, and try to identify the sources of stagnation. In Part I we saw a fairly orderly growth in Argentina's economy, beginning in the 1860s and continuing until World War I. Stimulated by demand from European markets for its agricultural products, by foreign capital investment —in the form of loans and direct ventures—in infrastructure, and by a rapid rise in population due in large part to immigration, in about four decades Argentina was transformed from a poor marginal country into one of the world's richest providers of meat and grain. Its so-called oligarchy, the *estanciero* ruling class, contributed to this economic progress by responding to the opportunities of the market, absorbing the latest methods in agriculture and stock raising, diversifying its production, encouraging investment and immigration, and—perhaps most importantly—providing political stability through a governmental system which, if not wholly democratic, at least was not barbaric or retrograde. The rule of law generally prevailed, and in the end the oligarchy even legislated the demise of its own political monopoly.

Industry emerged gradually as a kind of unintended by-product of agricultural and commercial expansion. For the most part, it was the creation of the European immigrants who settled in the towns, principally Buenos Aires. It was unplanned and unencouraged by any official policy, aiming almost entirely at providing for immediate local needs. Nevertheless, it sustained an increasingly large number of bustling entrepreneurs, many of whom were drawn originally from the skilled labor, clerical, and shopkeeper classes. A burgeoning economy, a steadily rising population, and a vast frontier provided opportunities not dissimilar to those discovered by other immigrants in that same period in the United States. Within a generation or two some of these Argentine immigrant entrepreneurs succeeded in establishing large companies—and, in some cases, rather complex conglomerates.

Two features of the Argentine industrialization pattern should be underscored, however, because of their ramifications for the country's development. First, the key industries were almost wholly foreign-owned: the railroads, the utilities, the communications systems, and the principal export industry, meat. Even in oil, foreign capital's share was larger than the state's until the 1930s. This fact was important not because Argentina was exploited—the phenomenal growth of its economic opportunities disproves that hackneyed interpretation—but simply because Argentina was left extremely vulnerable to any changes in the external environment that would disrupt foreign investment or trade. The withdrawal of European capital during World War I demonstrated that vulnerability, and the depression permanently reinforced it. Unfortunately, the conclusions drawn from those experiences were distorted by popular xenophobia; therefore Argentina went to the opposite extreme. In the place of excessive dependence upon foreign capital, the latter was to be excluded from the economy altogether, by design.

The second feature of the industrial pattern worth noting is the late development of Argentina as a nation. It was a full century behind the British when it started its development, and at least a half a century behind the Germans and the Americans. Had this not been the case, the fact that its native industry was oriented toward satisfying the local market would not have been significant. With time, Argentine industry probably would have evolved as industry did in the United States: growing to satisfy domestic demand, eventually becoming influential enough to achieve government protection, and finally emerging as a competitor in the world economy. There is simply no evidence to support the contention that the Argentine industrialist lacked the requisite entrepreneurial instinct or talent to achieve this. On the contrary, the rise of Argentine industry despite official neglect, its forward strides during the 1920s, and its ability to survive the shocks of the depression reveal a toughness that should have led ultimately to a successful capitalist system. But the Argentine industrialist's world was not the slower-paced world of the early nineteenth century with its classical liberal model of development. The recently emergent economic powers, Germany and Japan, had muscled their way to the top of the world hierarchy by using a different formula: one that intertwined the state and private enterprise, economic and military power, trade and diplomacy. In Argentina, men like Bunge and Colombo sensed this, but only imperfectly. As for the oligarchs, as well as the political opportunists in the *Unión Cívica Radical*, most of them still professed the classical economic liberalism they had learned from the British. Industry, for them, was unimportant. Those attitudes would change in the 1930s, especially within the military, but then the reaction would be to go to the opposite extreme: to embrace a hypernationalism that would prevent the formulation of a balanced strategy of development.

The depression years provided a needed respite from competition from the more advanced capitalist powers, but the opportunity to put the full force of the state behind industrialization was lost. First priority was given to saving the oligarchy through the Roca-Runciman pact, currency devaluations, price supports, and the creation of a large number of state regulatory agencies. It is true, of course, that industry benefited from this too, but it did so only inadvertently. The idea of consciously fostering a powerful and independent Argentine private industrial sector did not occur to the conservative elites of the Concordancia until 1940, when the Pinedo Plan was presented to Congress. The scheme was killed, be it noted, not by the *estanciero* oligarchy but by the Radicals.

The military regime of 1943 and, much more importantly, the Peronist regime that arose out of it, were the first comprehensive attempts to promote rapid development through an alliance between the state and private capital along authoritarian lines reminiscent of Bismarck's Germany or imperial Japan. This was truly a watershed in Argentina's history in that it rejected liberalism in toto, establishing in the process a number of institutions, practices, and expectations that have not been eliminated since, despite repeated and often violent attempts by anti-Peronists to do so.

Although there are some resemblances to Bismarckian Germany and imperial Japan, Peronism's development model was closer to that of fascism. The significant difference is the adoption of an inward-oriented, as opposed to an export-oriented, strategy. Germany and Japan were essentially aggressively commercial states, whereas fascist economics aim at autarky—at least in all aspects of production relevant to military needs. Those who may object at this point that Perón was a populist, not a fascist, because he was supported by labor do not sufficiently understand just how populist Italian Fascism or German Nazism was. In terms of social welfare benefits, job security, and psychological gratification there was little difference between Fascist, Nazi, and Peronist labor legislation. The same may be said with respect to official control over the unions, or with the personal popularity of Hitler, Mussolini, or Perón among their respective proletariats. Fascism, as an expression of extreme nationalism, may be aggressive toward foreigners or certain minorities, but within the national group—as defined by the fascists—the emphasis is upon solidarity, cooperation, and the elimination of artificial social barriers. In terms of class relationships, both Nazi Germany and Fascist Italy were more democratic than the regimes they replaced. The idea that fascism is organized upper- or middle-class oppression of the workers is a gross oversimplification, at best.

The development model that Perón followed, therefore, may be considered fascist in its general outline. He had conceived of it while still only an obscure instructor at the War College: the nation in arms. His belief in it was confirmed by his experiences in Nazi Germany and Fascist Italy before the war, and he began applying it as labor secretary even before he achieved full power. Indeed, Perón's career reveals that he was not the cynical opportunist so often depicted by his enemies. He made many tactical switches in his life, but the ideas he believed in remained remarkably consistent: the inevitably of conflict between nations; the need for every nation to prepare itself militarily to the utmost of its capacity; preparedness for modern total war requiring the total mobilization of national resources—political, cultural, and moral, as well as economic; and the necessity of a strong state to direct the process.

From that model came particular policies whose effects continue to shape everyday life in Argentina. Primary among them was the creation of a powerful, politicized labor movement capable of intimidating industry, electing governments, and ignoring the laws. A second set of policies established a corporative political structure in which key occupational groups were organized into semiofficial bodies with the state above them as an active intervenor in their relationships. Third, and flowing out of that corporativism, was state dictation—the word is carefully chosen—of economic behavior. Politics, "considerations of state," not the marketplace, were to determine what is to be produced, financed, imported, and exported. Fourth, a large and important state-owned sector of industry arose, encompassing the most pivotal areas of the economy: transportation, banking, oil and gas, steel, electrical energy, and communications. It has since been expanded to include coal, iron ore, nuclear power, and aluminum. Together with the ordinary administrative bureaucracy, this sector would come to provide jobs for a sizable proportion of the working-age population, without any regard for efficiency or productivity. Moreover, since political considerations were paramount, the state enterprises would be run with scarcely any regard for making them profitable; and because many of them would be administered by the armed forces, which see them as essential to the national defense, it would be all the less likely that they would ever be privatized or subjected to more businesslike management.

Finally, and perhaps most central for a study of capitalism, the Peronist-fascist model produced changes in the business class. Even before Perón's time, the import-substitution approach to industrialization had begun to encourage the spread of small, poorly capitalized, and technically backward enterprises; but this trend was accelerated under Perón. Those new entrepreneurs could never hope to be competitive in foreign markets nor even hold their own in the domestic market without protection and subsidies. Frightened and envious of the larger Argentine industrialists, they clung to Peronism and formed a kind of right wing in the populist coalition: resistant to change, demanding more government support, and encouraging income redistribution in favor of the lower classes in order to maintain high levels of consumer spending. Only when the unions threatened employers' shop privileges did they begin to protest. As for the larger producers, whether industrialists, merchants, or farmers, the Peronist economic strategy first provoked their resistance, then their alienation, and finally their withdrawal of capital. Faith in the future, once destroyed, is difficult to rebuild. That faith was lost during the watershed and has not returned. That is perhaps the fundamental factor in the crisis of Argentine capitalism.

In sum, by following the fascist model, rather than a more Bismarckian one, Perón gave Argentina perhaps the worst of all possible worlds. A vast, corrupt bureaucracy, running unproductive public enterprises and dispensing the country's savings in the form of welfare, armaments, or patronage, rather than investment, is not the way for a late-developing nation to catch up in the capitalist world-economy. Nor was it possible, as Peron and other nationalists imagined, to isolate Argentina from the world economy. By attempting to do so, they simply made their country technologically backward.

This concludes our review of the first half the study. Beginning with chapter 11 we will switch our approach to analyzing the crisis of Argentine capitalism from a historical, or chronological, one, to an examination of the various features of the contemporary system. Chapters 11 through 16 will describe the characteristics and role of the state, economic planning, foreign capital, domestic capital, and labor in the 1960s and early 1970s: roughly, the period comprising the governments of Arturo Frondizi, José Maria Guido, Arturo Illia, Juan Carlos Ongania, Roberto Levingston, and Alejandro Lanusse. That is the period during which Perón's successors tried to reform the system he left behind and return Argentina to its prewar pattern of steady progress. Part IV resumes the historical approach by describing the vicissitudes of the Peronist, military, and Alfonsín governments of the 1970s and 1980s as each grappled with the country's seemingly irreversible drift toward entropy.

# PART THREE

# Political Stalemate and Economic Decline

## CHAPTER ELEVEN

# The Paralysis of the State

Argentina faced many issues—each of them significant enough to divide the country—in the years following Perón's fall. Much debate centered on how to achieve economic development, or more particularly, how to revive a formerly dynamic industrial sector. Everyone agreed that the system was stagnant, but public opinion was sharply divided on the remedies offered for revitalization. Economic liberals, blaming Perón for everything, wanted to reduce the state's role and return to free enterprise. Investment should be encouraged by restricting consumption and encouraging savings, they argued. Moreover, foreign capital should be enticed back to the country, and incentives should be offered to agriculture to produce more for export.

Economic nationalists, on the other hand, looked to a reformed state, purged of Peronist excesses, to lead the revival. They put their faith in a more socially equitable distribution of wealth as the way to encourage industrialization, arguing that a stronger domestic market would provide the incentive for industry to expand. Such industry would have to be protected from foreign competition, and agriculture, rather than producing for export, would be encouraged to supply the home market. Foreign capital had little or no place in this inward-looking strategy. It could not be allowed to penetrate essential areas of the local economy, nor would it be allowed to drain off precious capital through profit remittances. As might be expected, the nationalist position was more popular with the trade unions, smaller businessmen, and tenant farmers, whereas big business and large farming concerns tended to support liberalism.

In politics, the main issue was how to treat the Peronist masses. The military set the parameters of the possible: Perón would not be allowed back, and his party could not be permitted to win power. Beyond that, the military was as divided as the rest of the country. From the outset, military and civilian liberals faced a nagging question: Would democracy be fully restored in Argentina if the largest segment of the electorate was unable to vote for the party it preferred? Those liberals shuddered when they remembered the old Peronist electoral campaigns: the chanting crowds; the deep, rhythmical beating of the Indian *bombo* drums; undershirts hoisted aloft on poles as flags of the *descamisados*; the rallying cry of the masses to "wash our feet in the fountains of the Plaza de Mayo." "But what is dangerous about Peronism," wrote one liberal, "is not what is on the surface: the *bombo*, the undershirt, the language. That is nothing in relation to the desire for revenge and the hatred that inspires it. It is a totalitarian movement and deadly for democracy. That is what is essential."[1] Both of the elected presidents of this period from 1955 to 1973, Arturo Frondizi and Arturo Illia, tried to resolve this dilemma by permitting the Peronist party to run, and in both cases Peronist victories soon resulted in military coups.

This inability to integrate the Peronists led to violence. Between 1958 and 1973 Argentina suffered more military revolts, both successful and unsuccessful, than any nation in the world except Iraq. Only India had more politically inspired labor strikes, and only the United States, racked by Vietnam protests, had more student demonstrations. Countries suffering all-out civil wars, like South Vietnam, Nigeria, or the Congo, had more bombings, armed assaults, and kidnappings, but Argentina ranked just below them. Some 287 people were murdered for political reasons, including ex-president Aramburu and two CGT leaders, Augusto Vandor and José Alonso.[2]

The state was paralyzed and its weakness could be shown with simple statistics. Almost 18 years elapsed between Lonardi's takeover and the inauguration in 1973 of Héctor Cámpora, Perón's stand-in president, and in that time eight men occupied the Casa Rosada: three civilians and five military officers. Six came to office through coups and five left for the same reason. Neither of the two elected presidents finished his term. For about eleven of those eighteen years Argentina was under military rule, either open or disguised. Violence also thwarted all attempts to solve Argentina's economic problems. In those eighteen years some eighteen different men were brought into the government to formulate an economic program, and three of them served twice. So, while there was no shortage of economic talent, no one could stay in office long enough to be effective. Other ministries had high turnover rates too. In that period, Argentina underwent more cabinet changes than any country in the noncommunist world. It also had one of the worst GNP growth rates in Latin America: its average of 1.9 percent a year outperforming only Haiti, Uruguay, and probably Cuba.[3]

Unable to conceive of any civic good that would transcend their own interests, the military, trade unions, businessmen, professionals, farmers, ranchers, universities—everyone—responded to calls for sacrifice with cynicism. Yet, given the weakness of the government and the political party organizations, those interest groups were the only real source of political action and institutional continuity. Although they often were riven themselves by factionalism, they nevertheless had broad, consistent interests to defend; and long experience in politics made them effective at pursuing those interests. In the absence of effective mediative institutions, like courts and legislatures, they acted directly upon the government, using whatever tactics they deemed appropriate. Their struggles with each other and with the state constituted the meat of Argentine politics.

Argentine governments often tried to cloak their weakness by adopting an authoritarian approach to economic policymaking. Unlike democratic societies, where legislators and judges try to reconcile opposing interests and where civil servants normally solicit the cooperation of groups likely to be affected by their decisions, Argentine policymakers seldom consulted with anyone. The usual method was to elevate some prestigious economic "wizard" to head the Ministry of Economy, where he exercised almost dictatorial powers. Programs were formulated from a very theoretical, indeed ideological, perspective, embodying some social philosophy in which every detail dovetailed logically with every other. This ideological and authoritarian style of policymaking is what Torcuato Di Tella, Jr., an Argentine political sociologist, calls *principismo*: "the besetting sin of our cultural elites, who seek to overcome what they regard as materialism, or a regrettable tendency towards accommodation within our society."[4]

*Principismo* made economic ministers and their supporting teams resist any modification of their programs, because to change them would compromise the intellectual coherence of the underlying theory. They likewise resisted involving pressure groups in the policymaking process because they feared the result would be a patchwork of special-interest legislation rather than an integrated approach to the country's problems. On the other hand, pressure groups, having been left out of the deliberations, felt no commitment to conform to the plan. If they benefited from it they felt no particular sense of gratitude because they knew that the government could arbitrarily withdraw those benefits. For the same reason, they felt no compunction about evading those parts of the plan they found onerous.

Groups which feel strongly that they are being hurt by government policy may resort to violence, especially where civic spirit is lacking. In Argentina, the military held the trumps in that game; but labor strikes, employers' lockouts, and farmers blocking the roads were often effective ways of forcing the government to alter its program. Usually, however, the pressure groups preferred noncompliance to confrontation. A weak government lacking a trained administrative corps with high morale found its efforts easily sabotaged by widespread tax evasion, bribery, smuggling, black marketeering, production slowdowns, and capital flight. Such tactics created budget shortfalls, balance of payments crises, inflation, shortages, and unemployment. In short, they made it impossible for government planners to achieve their targets, and they created an atmosphere of general disorder. Hence, the high turnover of governments and their economic wizards.

## The Institutional Vacuum

On 6 April 1962 Argentina's provisional president, José Maria Guido, appointed sixty-seven-year-old Federico Pinedo to be his minister of economics. Just nine days earlier the armed forces had deposed the constitutionally elected Arturo Frondizi because he had allowed the Peronists to run in congressional and gubernatorial elections, which they won. Extreme anti-Peronist officers had wanted to impose a dictatorship, but were thwarted by the moderates. The vice-presidency being vacant, the Supreme Court moved quickly to preserve civilian rule by swearing in Guido, who as president of the Senate was next in line. As their price for accepting this, however, the military's hardliners demanded the cancellation of the recent electoral results, the dissolution of Congress, and intervention in all the provinces where Peronists had won.

Pinedo's appointment was intended to bring prestige as well as talent to the shaky new government. His credentials could hardly be challenged by the most ardent anti-Peronist, for he had suffered imprisonment under Perón. A member of the Jockey Club, the SRA, and the Chamber of Commerce, and twice cabinet minister under the Concordancia, he was in the very highest and most conservative social circles: a prominent symbol of the class that Peronists wished to destroy. Nevertheless, at this juncture Pinedo became the voice of moderation. Argentina's troubles were essentially political, not economic, he asserted. No progress could be made toward an economic recovery until stable political institutions and procedures were established, and for these the 1853 Constitution was a sufficient blueprint. Consequently, he opposed intervening in the provinces and dissolving Congress because such acts, following the overthrow of the country's legitimate president, would destroy any last semblance of constitutional order. He was willing to annul the Peronists' victories, however, because Peronism was a totalitarian movement and therefore had no right to participate in the democratic process. On strictly legal grounds its candidates had not been eligible to run because the party had been outlawed in 1955 and there had been no formal lifting of that ban. Although Peronists might argue that the elections represented the "sovereign will of the people," Pinedo insisted that even popular opinion must respect the rule of law. For the Peronists to run they must first be legalized; otherwise it would be the same as if a popular president decided to violate the constitution by running for immediate reelection. Even if the people wanted him and voted for him, his act would be unconstitutional and therefore invalid. Nor was the ban on Peronism a violation of democratic principles. Both West Germany and Italy outlawed fascist parties, yet were generally considered to be democracies. Democracy had the right to deny freedom to those who were dedicated to destroying it.[5]

Neither the Peronists nor the hardline military accepted Pinedo's legalistic arguments. The navy, bastion of the most extreme anti-Peronism, argued that either all or none of the elected candidates ought to be seated, and since the Peronists were unacceptable that meant that Congress and the provincial governments ought to be dissolved. After much wrangling between the hardliners, the military constitutionalists, and the government, on 20 April the hardliners revolted and presented Guido with an ultimatum: either meet their demands or tanks would rumble in the streets. Guido caved in, whereupon Pinedo resigned. He had been in office for only two weeks, the shortest tenure on record for an Argentine economics minister.[6]

As Pinedo predicted, chaos followed. Over the next twelve months military hardliners and constitutionalists warred openly over who was to control the government. In September, a revolt by the constitutionalists, led by Gen. Juan Carlos Ongania, the commander of Campo de Mayo, led to the removal of many hardliners from their commands and the scheduling of elections for July of the coming year. Although the Peronists would be barred from running or from participating in any electoral coalitions, the hardliners were not appeased and attempted an unsuccessful revolt in April 1963. Their failure permitted elections to be held as planned and a new civilian government, headed by Arturo Illia of the UCRP, to take office in October. But all this was by the grace of the military. By mid-1966 the military mood would be different and the same General Ongania who had made civilian rule possible would take over as dictator.

### The Lack of Mediative Institutions

In the late 1960s Richard Mallon and Juan Sourrouille studied the problems of "semi-stagnation and great cyclical instability" in Argentina's economy and, like Pinedo, found the cause to be chiefly political: the lack of "mediative institutions." Without an effective national legislature and a properly functioning court system, policymakers would have a hard time reaching agreements with powerfully organized interests, they argued. Similarly, political parties, which ought to be "interest aggregators," were unable to perform their proper function because they were so frequently forced to disband or go underground.[7]

Congress, for example, had never been allowed to function independently, as the constitution prescribed. First it was dominated by General Roca and his political machine; then, after the Radicals took over, it fell under the sway of Hipólito Yrigoyen; and finally it was dissolved by General Uriburu. The Concordancia restored it, but corrupt electoral practices robbed most of its senators and deputies of any real mandate. The military closed it down again in 1943; and although Perón revived it he also reduced its powers in the 1949 Constitution, and his faithful majority rubber-stamped nearly all his proposals. It was dissolved again after his overthrow, and by the time it was restored in 1958 it could hardly be said to have had a normal institutional development. It would be shut down during eight of the next fifteen years.

Since most congressmen were products of political machines, of which the president was the visible head, they lacked independent power bases from which to oppose him. Thus he was able to extend his powers, in practice, far beyond what the constitution intended. Emergency powers, such as the right to declare a state of siege or to intervene in a province, though hedged about by constitutional checks, were easily abused if Congress was compliant. Similarly, presidents commonly seized upon the constitutional provision authorizing them to "issue instructions and regulations that may be necessary for the execution of the laws" in order to usurp the legislative power. Acquiescent Congresses grew accustomed to passing laws in a very general form, leaving it up to the president to fill in the details that determined their real content.[8]

Congress was also weakened by the Argentine parties' propensity to fragment and multiply. In the period after Perón's fall, almost every party split over whether to punish the lower classes for supporting him or to try to win them over by adopting much of the Peronist program. Not only the Radicals but also the Socialists, Christian Democrats, and Conservatives were divided on this question. Peronism split too, over whether to remain loyal to the exiled leader or to work within the new system. Those who faithfully followed Perón's orders were orthodox Peronists, while those who argued for "Peronism without Perón" were called neo-Peronists.

The proliferation of parties made legislation more difficult. No party was able to command a solid majority in the Chamber of Deputies after the March 1960 congressional elections, and if the 1962 election results had been allowed to stand, Frondizi's UCRI would have had only 76 seats out of 192. The use of proportional representation, started in 1963, increased the number of parties in the Chamber of Deputies from 13 to 32 in just two years. Thus, Illia, who came to office as a minority president to begin with, saw the UCRP bloc dwindle from only 72 seats to 68. Neither of Argentina's elected presidents had a Congress he could work with, but a greatly divided Congress was unable to lead the country either. This stalemate might have been overcome by a coalition of parties, but Argentine political habits militated against that. As one observer commented, "All Argentine groups and organizations, whether a political party, a football club, an university, or a hospital . . . are affected by the same disease, lack of coordination between members and the fact that individual purposes and ambitions prevail over common objectives." This also extends to attempts to coordinate actions between organizations, he added. No coalition could have lasted in the face of strong personal ambitions and ideological rigidities, for as Federico Pinedo observed, "The calamity that weighs upon this land is the belief in all or nothing—intransigence as a sign of virtue, principles." Mallon and Sourrouille agreed. "Even among Latin societies," they noted, "Argentina has been considered the nirvana of intransigents. Indeed, the conflict is painted so grim in Argentina that it is difficult to conceive how any law could be implemented, except that of Darwin."[9]

Congress lacked the fortitude and coherence to play an effective mediative role; but what about the courts? Four days after he seized power in 1930, General Uriburu informed the Supreme Court that he was setting up a dictatorship and suspending the constitution. Put on the spot, the court caved in and recognized Uriburu's government on the grounds that it had no authority to pass on the constitutionality of a revolution or to assume that the government's acts were necessarily invalid. It did reserve the right of judicial review concerning violations of personal or property rights, however, and subsequently heard a case involving the closure of a provincial newspaper. In that instance the justices (perhaps wisely) upheld the government on the grounds that it had acted in conformity with its state of siege powers.[10]

Under the Concordancia the court attempted a bolder clarification of the lawful powers a de facto government could claim. In 1933 it held that such regimes possess all the normal executive powers but not legislative or judicial authority. In another decision, two years later, it clarified this doctrine by holding that dictatorships might issue decrees that implement existing laws, but they could not legislate by decree. However, when the military assumed power in 1943 the court backtracked from this position, recognizing in a 1945 decision that circumstances might require a dictator to legislate. Even so, the court reserved the right to judge the constitutionality of such decrees, and subsequently it struck down two of them in 1945.[11]

Despite these attempts to preserve some semblance of the rule of law, the judiciary was drawn into partisan politics. The decrees it struck down in 1945 involved social and labor legislation advocated by Perón, then secretary of labor and social welfare. And during the events of October 1945, when Perón was removed from office, some of his enemies called on the military to turn power over to the Supreme Court as the first step toward restoring civilian rule. In the aftermath, a triumphant Perón began to plan his revenge, which he hinted at in his presidential inauguration speech: "I place the spirit of justice above the Judicial Power. Justice, besides being independent, should be efficacious, and it cannot be efficacious if its concepts are not in accordance with public sentiment. Justice must be dynamic, not static, in its doctrines. Otherwise it frustrates decent public expectations and slows down social development, with grave prejudice to the working classes."[12]

In other words, judges had to conform to whatever majority opinion, especially working-class opinion, might hold at the moment. Or, practically speaking, they should uphold whatever laws or decrees the people's representatives might issue. Such a doctrine would have no patience with minority opinion, individual rights, or judicial autonomy. It led directly to Perón's purge of the Supreme Court and the lower courts, and eventually to a wholesale revision of the constitution.

After Perón's fall, Aramburu purged the courts again, to get rid of Perón's appointees. New men were named to the bench ad interim, but since there was no Congress they could not be confirmed. When Frondizi took office he refused to ratify a large number of Aramburu's men and nominated others, some of them Peronists, to replace Aramburu's selections. An uproar followed in which the chief justice and sixty other federal judges resigned; the Supreme Court went on strike ("indefinite recess"), and the bar association accused Frondizi of plotting Perón's return. After a week, Frondizi backed down and accepted all but a few of Aramburu's appointees.

General Ongania went far beyond what Uriburu or even Perón did. Rather than impeach the court he simply abolished it and appointed five new justices. Their new oath did not stress their duty to uphold the constitution but emphasized their obligation to defend the Charter of the Revolution, a manifesto issued by the leaders of the 1966 coup. Under that Charter, the president would usurp the legislative power, just as his provincial intervenors would govern without any legislatures. The constitution was not actually abolished, but the new Supreme Court had to agree that its provisions would be suspended any time they conflicted with the Charter of the Revolution.[13]

A Supreme Court so emasculated was a mockery of the whole idea of the rule of law. When, in 1968, the tiny Progressive Democratic party brought suit to test the government's ban on political parties as a violation of the right of association, the court expressed its sympathy but pointed out weakly that "ever since its establishment, this Court has recognized the ability of a government which is the result of a successful revolution . . . to do those things which are necessary for the accomplishment of its goals." The justices went on to say that the military's revolution was a fact which no one could ignore and that Ongania's government clearly had the power to impose its will. Therefore, the court would not jeopardize its existence by contemplating any act that would challenge the president.[14]

Although the president might overshadow the other branches of government, he was not necessarily free to exert his will. Forces beyond his control hemmed him in. Although the constitution made him commander in chief of the armed forces, with the power to dispose of military units as he thought fitting, in reality the military usually disposed of presidents. Other powerful pressure groups may have lacked the military's ability to get rid of an obnoxious president, but through evasion or sabotage they could thwart him. Nor could a president order foreign bankers and investors to send capital to Argentina or demand that overseas suppliers continue sending their goods regardless of Argentina's ability to pay.

All of the presidents after Perón were flawed by their inability to claim a clear mandate. The military men could not because they were not elected, even though they claimed to be acting in the higher interests of the nation. Guido, though sworn in by the Supreme Court in a constitutional fashion, came to office as the result of a coup. Frondizi owed his election to votes borrowed from Perón, and Illia was elected with only 25 percent of the popular vote.

If Frondizi and Illia had been truly popular they might have been able to face down rebellious military officers, but they were not. Frondizi was defied by powerful armed forces commanders thirty-eight times during his forty-seven months in office, and most of the time he was forced to back down. Both democratic governments seemed ineffectual by their inability to curb inflation, increase trade, keep order, or raise living standards. The exposure of Frondizi's pact with Perón damaged him beyond repair with the military, and his secret meeting with Ernesto "Ché" Guevara at the Casa Rosada in August 1961 only confirmed the officers' suspicions that Frondizi was a dangerous leftist. Those suspicions already were strong when he took office because of his close association with Rogelio Frigerio, a former communist whose friends were given important posts in the government. In Illia's case, his toleration of disruptive strikes and factory seizures by Peronist trade unions and his legalization of the Peronist party (renamed the Unión Popular) put an end to the military's willingness to abide civilian politicians.

The failure of civilian governments to revive the economy also made the military impatient because it was clear that Peronism would never go away unless the conditions of the working class improved. Yet, civilian governments seemed unable to make the necessary hard decisions for fear of losing votes. Inevitably, the officers were drawn into taking positions on social and economic policies where their competence was questionable but their power to approve or veto was decisive. All of the powerful organized interests tried to enlist the military while the officers became convinced that only a strong government, able to ignore the polls, could restore economic confidence and dynamism.

That illusion was destroyed after General Ongania took office. Although his government made progress toward controlling inflation and stimulating growth, in May 1969 his regime was shaken to its roots by several days of rioting and armed resistance which began in the city of Córdoba and spread to other provincial capitals. The *cordobazo* was followed by the assassination of Augusto Vandor, the CGT leader, a neo-Peronist who had been gaining ground against Perón for control of the labor movement. Then former president Aramburu was kidnapped and assassinated. Perceived as unable to maintain order, Ongania was removed as president after forty-nine months in office. Ongania's successor, Gen. Roberto Levingston, lasted only nine months, his departure being speeded by a second *cordobazo* in March 1971. The army's commander in chief, Gen. Alejandro Lanusse, took over mainly to arrange a retreat to the barracks. That was made even more humiliating when Lanusse handed over power to a Peronist, Héctor Cámpora, in May 1973.

All in all, the military's record of economic management was disastrous. The cost of living at the end of Lanusse's term was six times higher than at the end of Illia's; the peso was valued at only about a sixth of its former worth; and the foreign debt had doubled. But much more serious was the damage done to the constitution, governmental institutions, political parties, and public attitudes. Argentina had become a violent place to live, and the scale of violence would grow even more in the next decade. Table 11.1 shows how violence escalated up to 1973.

Relatively peaceful means of registering political protests had been discarded for more violent ones. Strong government not only failed to solve the problems it was meant to tackle, it created new ones. And along the way, Argentina's feeble mediative institutions were destroyed.

## Elephantiasis of the State

The Argentine essayist Ezequiel Martínez Estrada once wrote that throughout his country's history the state weighed upon society like a dead hand. Lacking either strength or mobility, "it did not stimulate life but tamed it by paralysis. . . . It maintained immense armies of employees and soldiers; it manufactured university gradu-

Table 11.1 Domestic Violence in Argentina
under Peronist, Democratic, and Military Rule

|                          | Period |  |  |
| --- | --- | --- | --- |
|                          | 1948–54 | 1959–61 and 1964–65 | 1967–72 |
| Type of Protest          | (Peronist) | (Democratic) | (Military) |
| Demonstrations           | 10 | 31 | 23 |
| Riots                    | 13 | 9 | 45 |
| Armed attacks, bombs     | 45 | 112 | 128 |
| Deaths from political violence | 32 | 38 | 67 |

Sources: Charles Lewis Taylor and Michael C. Hudson, eds., *World Handbook of Political and Social Indicators*, 2d ed. (New Haven: Yale University Press, 1972); and Taylor and David A. Jodice, eds., *World Handbook*, 3d ed., vol. 2 (1983).
Note: Transition years such as 1955, 1958, 1962, 1963, 1966, and 1973 were not included because the data were not disaggregated by regime.

ates in the same way as it did paper money: without control and without solvency. It split its budget in two parts: one to support those who supported the State, and the other for the functioning of the government. Its apparent strength originated in the State's weakening everything to make itself powerful."[15]

During Perón's ten years in power, the national government grew from 312,300 employees to 541,200. The central administration expanded from 203,000 to 369,600, an increase of over 80 percent. In addition, the expansion in the number of state enterprises and regulatory agencies and the creation of new advisory bodies, listed in the budget under "special accounts," added another 62,300 to the previous 109,000 employees included under those categories. Perón was accused of padding the public payroll, but he was behaving no differently than his predecessors. Furthermore, the governments that followed him also created government jobs wholesale for their friends and followers.[16] Statistics vary, according to whether certain categories of people, such as military personnel and teachers, are included or not, but all sources agreed that public employment grew fairly steadily until the end of the 1960s, as table 11.2 indicates:

Greater efforts were made to trim down the public payroll after Ongania took power. The number of national government employees had been growing at more than double the rate of the general population. This growth was not solely a result of the traditional spoils system; it also was an attempt by the democratic governments to provide full employment in the face of sluggish growth in the private sector. Low-paying make-work jobs were a way of disguising unemployment, although they offered no real future to their occupants, who performed their duties with little enthusiasm and often engaged in bribery and moonlighting to supplement their income.

Every administration denounced this state of affairs. Upon taking over as Frondizi's economics minister in 1959, Álvaro Alsogaray vowed to reduce the government payroll, whose ratio to the population was, he claimed, "more than double the corresponding proportion in Italy and Canada, and much greater than in Germany, Belgium, and even Sweden, where socialism and state ownership are highly developed." He aimed at eliminating 80,000 jobs: 30,000 to be trimmed right away and the remainder to be closed out gradually through early retirements and not filling vacancies. He also planned to reduce the number of military conscripts, sell off some state enterprises, and require other state companies to be more efficient. In a subsequent speech, he elaborated on the methods he would follow. All department heads would have to list their employees and rank them according to their efficiency, attendance record, work attitudes, and family responsibilities. That data would then be turned over to a newly created Rationalization and Austerity Plan Committee which would decide which employees to eliminate in each department. Any department head who refused to cooperate would have his budget held up.[17]

Alsogaray found the job of cutting the payroll more difficult than he had imagined. As table 11.2 shows, although 54,000 people were dropped from the central administration between 1958 and 1960, some 57,000 were added to the state enterprises and autonomous agencies, resulting in an overall increase of 3,400 jobs. Alsogaray was even more embarrassed because he had promised to reduce the government's deficit; yet the deficit for 1960 set a record. He vowed to intensify his campaign. More central government employees would be fired; salaries would be frozen; certain state companies would be sold off; the defense budget would be reduced; public utility rates would be hiked; the YPF would return to self-financing; and the state railroads—whose annual losses of around $280 million constituted about 80 percent of the government's entire deficit—would be reorganized, which meant dismissing 75,000 employees and closing some uneconomical lines.[18]

Table 11.2 Government Employment, 1955–1971
(in thousands of employees)

| | | National Government Level | | |
| Year | Source | Central Administration | State Enterprises and Autonomous Agencies | Total |
| --- | --- | --- | --- | --- |
| 1955 | 1 | 394.9 | 148.3 | 541.2 |
| | 2 | | | 477.0 |
| 1958 | 1 | 418.9 | 155.3 | 574.2 |
| 1960 | 1 | 364.8 | 212.8 | 577.6 |
| 1962 | 1 | 330.7 | 210.5 | 541.2 |
| 1966 | 1 | 311.7 | 245.3 | 557.0 |
| | 3 | 294.4 | 502.0 | 796.4 |
| | 4 | 205.3 | 557.0 | 762.3 |
| 1968 | 1 | 312.2 | 257.7 | 569.9 |
| | 2 | | | 898.0 |
| | 3 | 296.1 | 482.7 | 778.8 |
| 1971 | 3 | 294.7 | 468.8 | 763.5 |

Sources: 1. Benjamin Most, "Authoritarianism and the Growth of the State
in Latin America, an Assessment of Their Impacts on
Argentine Public Policy, 1930–1970," *Journal of Comparative
Political Studies*, July 1980, p. 101, table 3.10.
2. Beba Balve et al., *Los asalariados: composición social y
orientaciones organizativas: materiales para su estudio*
(Buenos Aires: Centro de Investigaciones en Ciencias Sociales,
1975), p. 224.
3. *Veritas*, 15 April 1973, p. 10.
4. Juan Carlos de Pablo, *Política antiinflacionaria en la
Argentina, 1967–1970* (Buenos Aires: Amorrortu Editores,
1970), p. 126.

This fresh attempt at belt-tightening had only modest success.
Reductions were made in both the central administration and the
decentralized units, but the cuts were small and the political costs
were high. Alsogaray himself was sacrificed in April 1961 after the
UCRI suffered serious losses in the May 1960 congressional elections and in some by-elections held in February 1961. Alsogaray
had become so unpopular with the working-class and lower middle-

| | | Totals | |
|---|---|---|---|
| Provincial Governments | Municipal Governments | National and Provincial | All Governments |
| 223.0 | 107.0 | 700.0 | 807.0 |
| 409.8 | | 1,206.2 | |
| 412.0 | 169.0 | 1,310.0 | 1,479.0 |
| 412.4 | | 1,191.2 | |
| 424.6 | | 1,188.1 | |

class voters that Frondizi, facing the prospect of another round of congressional races in March 1962, decided to drop him as a liability.

Even before firing him, Frondizi had been unreliable in backing Alsogaray. In September 1960, while the latter was struggling to reduce the deficit, Frondizi granted the employees of the publicly owned Power and Light Company a 10 percent wage increase, retroactive to 1 May, and shortened their workweek from 40 to 35 hours. Alsogaray countersigned this decree, but his colleague Salvador San Martín, the fuel and power secretary, resigned in protest. Frondizi also used sleights of hand which made it seem as if he were pruning the payroll when in fact he was simply shifting workers to different accounts, as when he announced that he was selling the federally owned Lisandro de la Torre meatpacking plant. It was sold to the CAP, a semipublic corporation whose enormous debts were financed each year through the federal treasury. Strictly speaking, the packinghouse workers were no longer on the government payroll, but in reality their jobs were still being subsidized.

Frondizi's most dramatic surrender to political pressure was over

Alsogaray's railroad reorganization plan. The railroads were a classic example of Parkinson's Law. With the rise of the trucking industry and the spread of the private automobile, trains carried less freight and fewer passengers in 1960 than they had ten or even twenty years before. Nevertheless, there were more employees, and wages were rising at more than double the rate of the average industrial wage.[19] In August 1961 Roberto T. Alemann, Alsogaray's successor, announced that 75,000 railway employees were to be laid off, several lines would be closed down, the working day would be increased from three and a half to six hours, and services such as dining cars and station-house restaurants would be turned over to private concessionaires. The railroad workers struck, and remained out for several months. By December Frondizi's resolve began to wane, especially since gubernatorial races were looming in Catamarca, Santa Fé, and San Luís, and congressional races were only four months away. He was planning to gamble on letting the Peronists run, hoping that the anti-Peronists would all stampede to the UCRI out of fright. If the gamble worked, Perón would be permanently deflated; but to win he needed the support of traditionally anti-Peronist unions like the Unión Ferroviaria and La Fraternidad. If he gave in, their votes might be his. Otherwise, they might vote Peronist out of spite.

In the first week of December Frondizi sent Arturo Acevedo, the public works minister who had direct jurisdiction over the railroads, to Washington to talk with World Bank officials about a loan that was contingent upon the successful completion of the railway reorganization scheme. No sooner was Acevedo out of the country than Frondizi left as well, ostensibly to seek more investment and trade from Canada. José Maria Guido, head of the Senate, became acting president in his place, and Juan Ovidio Zavala, Acevedo's under secretary, who was known to be more sympathetic toward the strikers than his boss was, was left in charge of negotiations with the unions. A mediation committee quickly formed which rescinded the reorganization plan, a decision which Guido promulgated as an executive decree on 10 December. With that, the unions lifted the strike. Antonio Scipione, secretary of the Unión Ferroviaria, hailed the decree as "another glowing page" in his union's history. Guido defended it as a "victory for the country," but the probusiness *El Cronista Comercial* said it had "profound political significance" that seemed to signal "the start of a fundamental change in the president's policy." The World Bank seemed to agree with that, because it canceled its loan. Acevedo, unable to get Frondizi to overrule the decree, resigned on 11 January 1962. Zavala, after being "reprimanded" by Frondizi, was appointed technical secretary to the president.[20] Four months later, having been defeated at the polls by the Peronists, Frondizi was under military arrest.

Politicians like Frondizi, always sensitive to election trends, may have lacked the will to fight for real reforms, but military dictators like Gen. Juan Carlos Ongania were not bothered by such considerations. Soon after taking office Ongania commissioned a study of the executive branch which reported that there were 762,300 employees, not counting schoolteachers or military personnel. The report also said that at least 150,000 of those were superfluous.[21]

Who were these superfluous workers? Over 80 percent were white-collar clerical help; another 10 percent were managers; and only 8 percent were manual workers. The average employee was a male with only primary school education and no skills other than typing or working an adding machine, but with ten or more years of seniority. He earned slightly more than the minimum wage so he probably had a second job. Managers earned much more, however. The head of YPF got 200,000 pesos a month, or about ten times what the average government employee earned, and the head of the DGI got 180,000. These salaries put them at approximately the same level as Supreme Court justices and lieutenant generals, who earned 210,000 and 202,720, respectively.[22]

Like Alsogaray, General Ongania focused on the railroads as the place to begin cutting. In January 1967 he appointed Gen. Juan Carlos De Marchi as director of the state railways, with orders to reduce personnel, improve efficiency, and increase profits. De Marchi's first report, shortly after taking over, described a picture of chaos in the railroad system: lack of planning or regular procedures, lack of discipline, inattention to the safety of cargoes or passengers, the absence of any budgetary or rate-setting standards. He promised to impose stricter work rules, cut staff and expenses, introduce central purchasing, sell unneeded equipment, and reduce freight rates to become competitive with the trucking industry. Specifically, he promised to reduce the railways' budget deficit, which was nearly 100 billion pesos in 1966, by reducing the work force from 172,500 to around 108,000.[23]

Like Alsogaray and Alemann, De Marchi made some progress but not as much as he had planned. By 1970 he reduced railway personnel to 146,000 and cut the deficit to 71 billion pesos; he also eliminated 2,848 kilometers of branch lines, closed 237 of 2,710 stations, and reduced services in 875 others. Even so, the railways still accounted for nearly 85 percent of the government's annual deficit. Also, some savings were not genuine: old locomotives and cars had not been replaced; repairs to tracks and roadbeds had been postponed; and some of the railroads' debts had been extended. De Marchi met violent resistance from the workers, who barricaded the tracks, burned locomotives, overturned cars, and shot at policemen and soldiers; but political pressure from above really slowed him down. By 1968 Ongania was voicing concern about the firing of so many workers at a time of high unemployment. Also, De Marchi was not allowed to close down the big money-losing suburban commuter lines because an estimated 1.3 million *porteños* used them every day and Ongania didn't want to provoke an outburst from his middle-class supporters. The army also insisted that certain lines had to be kept going, even if uneconomical, because of their strategic importance.[24]

In other words, there was only so much that any government, whether civilian or military, could do to cut the state's payroll. Deficits could be reduced somewhat, but only temporarily. Sooner or later the government would be faced with the choice of either junking equipment or investing large sums to upgrade services that had been allowed to deteriorate. Any attempt to eliminate personnel or services would cause resistance which eventually would meet with sympathy at the top levels of the administration. If workers were fired, where would they find other jobs? If commuters were stranded, how would that affect the urban economy? These and similar considerations sapped the will of most reform-minded administrations. Small wonder that Ongania's successors, Generals Levingston and Lanusse, gave up altogether and let the railroads' deficits rise from 70.9 billion pesos in 1970 to 291 billion (old) pesos in 1972.[25]

## The State Enterprises, Pro and Con

Economic liberals argued that Argentina's railroads were only an extreme example of what could be expected from any state company, for without the profit motive and the pressure of competition there was no incentive to operate efficiently. Political criteria would always dominate decision making. Thus, liberals located Argentina's economic stagnation in the spread of state enterprises, five of which (YPF, the railroads, the electric company SEGBA, the telephone company ENTEL, and SOMISA) ranked among the top ten companies in terms of sales, while another three (Gas del Estado,

Agua & Energia, and Aereolineas Argentinas) were in the second
ten. State capital dominated the fields of transportation, communications, oil refining, gas, electricity, and warehousing. The largest
steel mill was state owned, and so were many banks and insurance
companies. The state provided about 15 percent of all investment
annually, employed 5 percent of the economically active population, and contributed around 6 percent to the annual GNP. Workers
in the state enterprises, as opposed to those in the central administration, were among the nation's top wage earners. They were much
better paid than civil servants and even most workers in the private
sector. The average public utilities employee, for example, earned
about twice the average national wage and about 73 percent more
than a worker in private industry.[26]

Liberal economists quickly pointed out the relative inefficiency
of state enterprises wherever the latter were forced to compete with
private firms, as in the cases of oil and steel. In the oil industry, for
example, it was easy to demonstrate that private companies, though
employing a small percentage of the labor force, produced a disproportionate share of the oil. In 1963, for example, with only 4 percent
of the employees in the industry they nevertheless produced 33.2
percent of the oil. Zinser, who studied the relative performance of
YPF and the private companies in the early 1960s, concluded that
"relative to YPF, both in terms of sectoral output per unit of capital
expenditure and the contribution to national income per unit of
investment, the difference in capital-output ratios more than en-
sures the relative desirability of private over government production." He noted, however, that this conclusion conflicted with the
bulk of Argentine opinion. Another study, carried out in 1960 by the
Consejo Federal de Inversiones, indicated some of the reasons for
YPF's poor performance. According to the study, the general atmosphere at YPF was one of "low output and disorder" caused by "excessive personnel," half of which was superfluous. The report also
noted a high turnover in management for political reasons, with YPF
directors serving an average of less than a year in office.[27]

It was not just a case, either, of foreign companies having better
technology and know-how. Even local private firms like Astra were
more efficient than YPF. Between 1963 and 1966 Astra raised its
output from 204,700 cubic meters to 346,000: a 69 percent increase.
In that same period, YPF's production rose from 10.3 million cubic
meters to 12.2, or by about 18 percent.[28]

Steel was another area that afforded economic liberals an opportunity to point out the shortcomings of state enterprise. Argentina

consumed about 4 million tons of steel yearly in the late 1960s, of which 2.2 million was produced locally. Three state-owned mills, SOMISA, Altos Hornos de Zapla, and Aceros Ohler, accounted for 60 percent of the domestic output, with SOMISA producing the lion's share. In the private sector four firms, Acindar, Gurmendi, Propulsora Siderúgica, and TAMET, were the leaders.

SOMISA, though the second-largest industrial enterprise in Argentina (after YPF), was no model of dynamism. To a large extent it was crippled by state regulations such as the one that required it to buy as much locally produced iron and coal as there was available. The operation of Argentina's few remote iron and coal mines by Fabricaciones Militares and insistence by the military on making Argentina as self-sufficient as possible for its basic needs, for reasons of national defense, prompted this regulation. Unfortunately, Argentina's iron and coal are of poor quality and require extensive treatment before they can be used in making steel, all of which makes steel production in Argentine a high-cost industry. Repeated studies have shown that it would be cheaper to import steel than to produce it domestically, and local producers need high tariffs to stay in business. Even so, they can supply only half of the country's needs.[29]

The military's insistence on self-sufficiency resulted in other controls that raised the cost of domestic steel. For instance, SOMISA produces most of Argentina's pig iron, and when its output is insufficient to satisfy local demand it must ask the central authorities for permission to import more. Such authorization could be granted only to SOMISA. Private companies were not allowed to import pig iron themselves; they had to purchase it through SOMISA so the government could control how much pig iron was available at any given time. That protected the market for SOMISA and guaranteed that its prices would not be undercut.

Fabricaciones Militares also had the right to veto domestic steel companies' plans for expansion or diversification. It did this indirectly through its consultative role with the ministries of defense, economy, justice, and labor, all of which had to approve such plans. Thus, the steel industry was enmeshed in red tape that forced it to conform to military plans, not the marketplace. This could be maddening to private management, but it also could be used by them to defend their own vested interests. For example, when Agustín Rocca, the owner of Propulsora Siderúgica, offered to build a steel mill in southern Patagonia near the sources of Argentina's coal and iron, he provoked an outcry from the other steel companies for daring to do what none of them ever had attempted. A campaign was orchestrated in both the press and behind the closed doors of ministerial offices against this Italian immigrant interloper. Since Fabricaciones Militares favored Rocca's scheme, the private companies could not stop the negotiations, but they were able to slow them down to a snail's pace as various ministries wrangled over the details. After eight years Propulsora got the contract, but its mill was to be located in Buenos Aires Province and its output was to be limited to 1.3 million tons annually.[30]

Such neomercantilism did not prevent warfare within the system. The generals who ran SOMISA often behaved like robber barons who wanted to eliminate all competition. In their view, steel was so important that it should be a government monopoly. They got angry, too, whenever the private companies did anything to lessen their dependence on SOMISA, as when they installed new furnaces in early 1970 that sharply reduced their need for pig iron. Fabricaciones Militares accused them of a lack of patriotism as SOMISA's falling sales produced alarming deficits that made government ministers begin to grumble. As a counterattack, SOMISA started turning out products in competition with the private sector; and, since it could call upon the state treasury to cover its losses, it sold them at below cost. Within a year Propulsora was in financial trouble, at which point Fabricaciones Militares offered to buy control for $30 million. However, Rocca had an ally in defense minister Rafael Cáceres Monie, who helped put through a rescue operation that included aid from the Argentine government, the Italian state steel company (FINSIDER), and the current Propulsora shareholders. Not only was bankruptcy staved off, but Propulsora was authorized to expand its operations. Fabricaciones Militares fought this bitterly and submitted its own plan to raise SOMISA's production. Both proposals went to the junta of commanders in chief that supervised the military regime. It decided that "the State should . . . only invest in steel production when the private sector shows no intention of doing so." To emphasize their intentions they dismissed SOMISA's president, Gen. Pedro Castiñeiras, and replaced him with Gen. Mario Chescotta, who believed in limiting the state's role in industry.[31]

That was by no means the end of the struggle. In March 1972 General Cáceres Monie went too far when he tried to transfer the authority for regulating steel production from the Fabricaciones Militares to an agency of the Defense Ministry. After an unpleasant scene before the junta, both he and Gen. Alberto Rocatagliatta, the president of Fabricaciones Militares, were forced to resign. In January 1973 the Lanusse administration swung back to the statist side by canceling Propulsora's expansion plans. So the war went on into the 1980s. As late as 1981 Acindar brought suit against SOMISA for selling pig iron at below cost to smaller mills in order to keep them competitive and then covering those losses by overcharging big private companies. It is also interesting to note that by this time Acindar had hired a much respected general, Alcides López Aufranc, to be its new president, a move which surely enhanced its influence within the military regime.[32]

The military was sensitive to criticism that it was unbusiness-like. "The private companies always want to take over after we succeed, but never before," General Aguilar Benítez, a director of Fabricaciones Militares once said in an interview. "They complain that Fabricaciones Militares is interfering with the marketplace, so we abandon that line of business to them and disappear from the market." He cited the San Francisco electric motor works in Córdoba Province, which was started with military capital but turned over to private enterprise once it began to show profits. Other examples were the initiatives taken by Gas del Estado in manufacturing steel containers during the sudden expansion of the bottled gas market and in the production of certain types of drills for YPF, after private capital had backed away from those ventures. Once the product lines were profitable, Gas del Estado was forced to turn them over to private companies. In other words, Aguilar Benítez said, "Fabricaciones Militares profits temporarily from its successes and absorbs permanently its mistakes."[33]

Some military men accepted this role of handmaiden to private enterprise as both natural and proper. Brig. Abelardo Sangiacomo, the head of DINFIA, an air force company producing engines and vehicles, told an interviewer that he tried to run the firm like a private business, but part of its function was to help private industries get started by absorbing some of the initial expenses. In 1955, when Kaiser opened its automobile plant in Córdoba, DINFIA put up 50 percent of the financing. Later, it provided the same sort of aid to Fiat. Also, DINFIA's subsidiary, Industrias Mecánicas del Estado (IME), was for many years a training ground for skilled mechanics, most of whom went into private industry at higher wages. "In other words," Sangiacomo observed, "we've been a substitute for the Industrial Bank in promoting new enterprises."[34]

State enterprises didn't always show deficits, either. Despite all the featherbedding and mismanagement, YPF usually showed a profit. Gas del Estado was another consistent money-maker, and so was ENTEL after telephone rates were hiked in 1962. The worst money-losers were the railroads, the merchant and river fleets, the navy shipyards, Aereolineas Argentinas, and some of the companies belonging to DINIE, a conglomerate of companies taken over from their German owners during the war. The railroads alone accounted for over 90 percent of the total state enterprise sector deficit.[35] Indeed, there was no logical reason why some state enterprises could not be run profitably. Surely all of them could have been more efficient, as IME's example shows. In 1968 air force Brig. Lionel Jansen took over this company, which had been chronically in the red, overstaffed, and inefficient. Despite a tight budget, in four years he turned it into a profit-maker by firing redundant employees and plowing the money saved on wages and fringe benefits into modernization. When Jansen first took over, there were 4,000 employees producing 4,000 trucks in IME's vehicle division; by the end of 1971 there were only 1,300 employees but they turned out 8,000 trucks.[36]

Unfortunately, not many state enterprises followed IME's example. Sometimes the government discouraged efficiency by holding down the prices charged for their goods or services in order to court popularity. The resulting deficits usually were covered by printing more money or borrowing, either of which was inflationary. In the meantime, as an austerity measure, those deficit-ridden enterprises were given no additional funding for updating their equipment, and consequently the quality of their output deteriorated.

## The Tax Stalemate

Deficits might have been covered by raising taxes, but most Argentine governments were afraid to do so because taxes were so unpopular. The usual recourse was indirect methods of taxation, such as sales taxes, import and export duties, and stamp taxes. Those constituted just over half of all the revenue raised every year. Another one-fourth came through social security taxes. The remainder, about 21 percent, was raised from direct taxes on individuals or business enterprises. Under Perón, by contrast, taxes on individuals or businesses accounted for 49 percent of the government's revenues.[37]

One reason for the heavy reliance on indirect taxes was the relative ease with which they were collected. Direct taxes, which fell almost exclusively on the middle classes and the rich, were commonly evaded, and such behavior was socially condoned. Enforcement of the law was difficult because the DGI was badly organized, rich taxpayers had political influence, and many businessmen were self-employed. A study by ECLA concluded that in Argentina "it is not likely that income taxes can ever be fully enforced against [the business class] so long as there is a will to evade payment, and this means that direct taxation will remain of limited importance so long as the self-employed dominate the upper income groups." It also meant that the tax burden would fall more heavily on white-collar and skilled blue-collar workers, whose incomes were easy to verify and who could be taxed at the source.[38]

Tax evasion so starved the state of needed revenues that periodically it was unable to pay its employees or creditors. In 1963 a group of those creditors, whose bills were long overdue, formed a consortium and, supported by the UIA, sent a note to the economics minister reminding him of the seriousness of not paying debts. An acerbic exchange of letters ensued, ending with the minister's reminder that the treasury was empty because too many people like them did not pay their taxes.[39]

When the DGI tried to get tough with evaders, it found itself stymied by the organized resistance of business groups. In 1964 it sent letters to over 100,000 firms, demanding payment on back taxes owed which amounted to a total of 70 billion pesos. Immediately the UIA and the Argentine Chamber of Joint Stock Companies (Cámara Argentina de Sociedades Anónimas) protested, charging the DGI with unfairness for singling out big enterprises and ignoring the smaller ones. They also protested the DGI's charging interest on the unpaid sums and adding legal fees and administrative charges to the bill. They demanded that the government abandon any attempt to collect back taxes owed beyond the previous year. A meeting between business leaders and President Illia failed to produce any compromise. The most he would do was to offer the companies a credit line of 5 billion pesos to help them pay what they owed, but the Chamber of Joint Stock Companies argued that this was no solution because most businesses were unable to meet even their present financial commitments: thus, they would be equally unable to repay a government loan as they would their back taxes. To the DGI's threats to seize their assets, the big businessmen responded that the government would have to socialize all the large firms in the country because none of them could pay.[40]

Faced with this wall of resistance, the government backed down and declared a moratorium that was to run until 31 October 1966. Delinquent firms would then have to pay 10 percent of their debt immediately, plus legal costs, and would retire the balance in thirty monthly installments at 22 percent annual interest. In the meantime, however, Illia was overthrown by General Ongania. As the October deadline drew near, the UIA decided to test Ongania by offering a counterplan by which the businessmen would pay 3 percent of their debt on the thirty-first and the remainder in sixty monthly installments at 12 percent, with no legal fees added. The UIA also appended a survey of its members' current financial status which showed, predictably, that all of them were suffering. Ongania was unimpressed and favored a tough line, but his economics minister, Jorge Salimei, convinced him that the government could not just seize 70 percent of the nation's industrial assets. A compromise was necessary that would save face on both sides.

On 2 November the DGI announced that 42 percent of the delinquent companies had paid their back taxes in full and the rest had agreed to pay in installments of not more than thirty months. The amount collected so far was 8.4 billion pesos, and there was another 22.6 billion still outstanding. Those figures did not tally with earlier estimates by the Ministry of Economy that the total taxes owed amounted to 70 billion; so reporters probed deeper. They discovered that most companies were making small payments in order to keep the DGI off balance but that more than 61 billion pesos was still being held back. Apparently the government was willing to forget about most of it.[41]

Both sides soon were at loggerheads again, because of the *aguinaldo* coming due at the end of the year. Businessmen were in no mood to pay a "thirteenth month's wages" on top of a new bill for taxes which would come due two months later. The DGI again threatened to seize property and the UIA was adamant. A fight was averted when Adalbert Krieger Vasena, the new economics minister, offered the businessmen two long-sought concessions: taxes on capital and profits could now be adjusted for inflation, and replacement costs for worn-out equipment could be written off. But to qualify for these concessions they would first have to settle their back taxes with the DGI. This scheme worked fairly well. Revenues increased during 1967 and 1968, allowing the fiscal deficit to be brought down from 31.6 percent to only 10 percent by 1969.[42]

Farmers were another big group of tax evaders. A study done in 1963 in the south of Buenos Aires Province showed that only 3 percent of the farmers in that region were complying with the income tax laws. In 1968 the government decided to guarantee that farmers paid their fair share by placing a 1.6 percent tax on rural land values, free of improvements. This had a double purpose: to force unused land into production and to make sure that every farmer paid *some* tax to the state. Any income tax a farmer paid could be deducted from his land tax, and so could any improvements made to the property. This tax bill was bitterly resented, however, especially since it followed the reimposition of export taxes (called, euphemistically, "retentions" by the government). The combination of these two taxes cost Ongania his original support in the rural areas. Farmers retaliated by cutting their purchases of domestic agricultural machinery and fertilizers, which caused a crisis in those industries, and by reducing their production for export. In the end, government revenues from those taxes proved to be far less than was anticipated.[43]

Employers and unions also evaded their contributions to the social security fund, which were mandatory for everyone except government workers (who had their own pension plan). Employers were supposed to pay an equivalent of 15 percent of their employees' wages and the unions were supposed to put in another 11 percent. Instead, employers were holding back their share and using the money to invest in equipment. In 1963 Illia's treasury secretary discovered that businessmen owed a total of 50 billion pesos in unpaid social security taxes, but when he demanded that they be paid the UIA protested that the taxes were too high. The businessmen argued that not only did the taxes add to production costs, but they made Argentine products uncompetitive, discouraged the employment of more workers, and saddled long-suffering industries with a financial burden that threatened to submerge them altogether. The government also discovered that union leaders were pocketing social security contributions and that the five largest unions owed a total of 652 million pesos, or about $2 million. As a result of such widespread cheating, some 200,000 pensioners did not get their checks for several months that year because there was no money in the fund.[44]

Employers disliked contributing to the fund for a good reason: they knew the money would be misspent. Although the social security payments were kept in a special account, governments had a habit of raiding the fund to cover other expenses. During the 1963 squabble with the government over social security contributions, the UIA accused the authorities of having squandered some 60 billion pesos of pension fund money over the years. Indeed, they charged, a figure of 60 billion was only a nominal sum, because if adjusted for inflation the real amount owed by the government to the fund would be more in the range of 450 billion. Although no proof was offered at the time, in mid-1970 Francisco Manrique,

President Levingston's minister of social welfare, confirmed the existence of such illegal government practices. He reported that the government owed 101.5 billion "old" pesos to the social security system. There was no accounting for how some of the money was spent: it was simply gone. But 48 billion pesos could be traced. They had been diverted to the Armed Forces' Retirement Fund. In other words, the civilian population had been defrauded of its contributions and stripped of its security in old age in order to insure that military retirees would be well off. Manrique's investigations also revealed that other large sums had been siphoned off to pay contractors for public works projects, or as "loans" to trade unions to buy their political support. Meanwhile, in order to collect any pension money from the system (supposing there was any money in the fund), a typical retiree would have to hire a "fixer" (gestor) to work through the labyrinth of bureaucratic red tape and corruption.[45]

The failure of the fiscal system to achieve a measure of responsibility pointed to the essential weakness of a government that was big but not strong or intelligent. Like a swollen appendage, it could not function properly and was a hindrance to the rest of the body. As such, it impeded economic recovery and prolonged the political crisis. Its cumbersome bulk would frustrate the plans of many clever men, whose strategies for restoring healthy growth to Argentina constitute the subject of the next chapter.

## CHAPTER TWELVE

# Planning under Pressure

Two weeks after Perón's fall General Lonardi appointed noted Argentine economist Raúl Prebisch head of a committee to survey the nation's economy and make recommendations for its reform. Prebisch's report, submitted a month later, began by warning that Argentina was then undergoing "a crisis of unparalleled gravity." In every previous economic crisis the country's great productive potential remained intact, permitting a quick recovery, but now it had become technologically backward as the result of "a dozen years of misrule" during which capital had been discouraged. Recovery would require an "intense and prolonged" effort, as well as sizable investments. Painful sacrifices in the general living standard would be necessary in order to raise capital for those investments.[1]

Argentina was suffering from "stagflation": sluggish production coupled with inflation. On the production side, agriculture had been discouraged by price controls and IAPI while industry had suffered from regulation, restrictive labor practices, and the government's failure to invest in heavy industry and infrastructure. Bureaucracy and corruption had discouraged productive efforts and had channeled investment into speculative activities. At the same time, inflation had been caused by an irresponsible expansion of the money supply and by encouraging wages to rise in excess of productivity. There was a growing demand for a shrinking supply of goods.

Such was Prebisch's analysis of the problem; his recommended cure was a long period of austerity, during which the government would have to trim its budget by firing redundant staff and either selling its loss-producing companies or making them pay their way. Taxes and service charges would have to be raised at the same time that credit was restricted. Many public works would have to be canceled; only the most essential could be funded. The practice of subsidizing all import-substituting industries would have to be discarded in favor of concentrating on those that had export potential (or which at least could compete with foreign imports without the aid of tariffs). Freer trade should be encouraged so as to separate the strong enterprises from the weak and to force down prices. Such measures would attack the problem of inflation.

To encourage production, Argentina would have to go back to what it traditionally did best: exporting meat and grain. That would allow it to earn the capital needed for industrial expansion. Prebisch urged the immediate dismantling of IAPI, the removal of price controls, and the devaluation of the peso. All that would bear hard on the urban sector, but it was necessary to revive farm output. Prices would increase at first, but the rises would be moderate if decontrol were linked to freer trade. As agricultural production climbed there would be enough food to supply both the export and the domestic markets, and prices would level off.

The revival of industry would require a mixture of state, foreign, and domestic private capital. In Prebisch's view, Argentina's consumer goods industries were sufficiently developed, and it was time to move into heavy industry. The state should concentrate on basic fields like oil, steel, transportation, and electrical energy. Foreign capital should be involved in those areas where advanced technology as well as large initial investments were required: chemicals, automobiles, and machine building. Local private capital would probably continue to concentrate on nondurable consumer goods, the demand for which might be expected to rise as a result of this new surge of industrial growth.

The Prebisch report provided a departure point for economic debates for the next fifteen years. Besides resenting its allusions to their alleged mismanagement, Peronists attacked it as a veiled plan to get revenge on the lower classes and a sellout to the *estancieros* and their foreign allies. Liberals, for their part, were skeptical about the future of heavy industry in Argentina, although they applauded the calls for less government, free trade, and growth led by exports. Aramburu, who inherited the Prebisch report from Lonardi, implemented some parts of it, but on the whole he preferred to back away from its more controversial recommendations.

Indeed, for a military man, Aramburu provided weak leadership, although perhaps he may have seen himself as no more than a caretaker president. In any case, IAPI was not liquidated until the last month of his administration; wages were not held in line with productivity; and the money supply was allowed to grow much too rapidly. Attempts were made to devalue the peso and remove price controls, but the government backed down when protests became too loud. The problem, according to finance minister Roberto Verrier, was that Argentines of every class and occupation still thought the country was inexhaustibly rich; therefore they resisted any sacrifice. They might give lip service to the need for restraint, but they really intended that the burden be borne by someone else.

Even that mild criticism drew protests from the leading pressure groups. The Chamber of Commerce replied that the economy was still "semi-collectivized" and called on the government to set an example for others by selling its state enterprises and restoring the free market. The UIA noted that industrialists could not afford to import new machinery that would increase their productivity if the government devalued the currency; and it added that government-imposed wage increases were adding to business operating costs. The rural sector accused Aramburu of continuing Perón's policy of sacrificing agriculture to urban political pressures. Farmers and ranchers were angry that the government had reimposed price controls, taxes on agricultural exports, and tariffs on imported farm machinery. Finally, the labor unions had recovered from the shock of Perón's fall and were resorting to illegal strikes to defend their wages.[2]

## Liberals and Nationalists

The governments that followed Aramburu might be classified according to their economic policies as having either "liberal" or "nationalist" tendencies. Liberal policymakers placed the greatest emphasis on controlling inflation as the sine qua non for restoring healthy economic growth. In pursuing that goal they tried to restrict the money supply, hold down wages, and balance the government's budget by reducing its spending and raising its revenues. As a consequence liberals were unpopular, and even the military governments that practiced liberalism often felt pressured to relent in the application of such bitter medicine. By contrast, nationalists put their greatest emphasis on full employment. They sought to foster this through government spending, easier credit, and higher wages, all of which were supposed to increase demand and thus stimulate production. If inflation appeared as a by-product, nationalists were ready to hold it down with price controls.

Neither liberal nor nationalist policies worked very well in practice. This was partly due to chronic governmental instability. Because no economics minister stayed in power for long, pressure groups simply learned to bide their time and use stalling tactics.

More importantly, however, the political consequences of either approach inevitably caused resistance to build up until a change of policy became inevitable. Liberal austerity measures seemed to lead always to recessions. A domino effect built up in which lower consumer demand led to the retailers' cutting back their orders to consumer goods producers, who might in turn purchase fewer machines or motors from the capital goods sector—thus negating the whole drive to build up heavy industry. During the early 1960s, as Frondizi and Guido battled inflation, idle capacity rose to 40 percent in the automotive industry, 40 percent in steel, 50 percent in metal products, 50 percent in pulp and paper, and 45 percent in machine building.[3] Sooner or later pressure would build up from both business and labor to reinflate the economy.

Nationalists had the opposite problem. It simply was not possible to inject "just a little inflation" into the economy. Twice during this eighteen-year period, at the end of 1958 and at the beginning of 1973, the inflation rate approached 100 percent, making the peso literally not worth the paper it was printed on. Under Ongania, prices being quoted seemed so astronomical that in 1968 the government created the "new peso," which eliminated two zeroes. Inflation was socially disruptive, too, because workers frequently had to strike in order to renegotiate their wages. Businessmen also found it difficult to calculate their future costs, while farmers found their exports priced out of world markets. When nationalists tried to hold down inflation with price controls they inevitably created shortages and encouraged black markets. Pressures would then build up to free the economy from bureaucracy.

### Frondizi's "Developmentalist" Experiment

Arturo Frondizi came to office as a nationalist. One of his first acts was to decree a 60 percent wage increase for the Peronist workers, whose votes had made his election possible. But when inflation promptly shot up to an annual rate of 80 percent (from the 40 percent he inherited from Aramburu) and the Central Bank informed him that its exchange reserves were depleted, he announced a radical switch in his tactics. In return for an emergency loan, he signed an agreement with the International Monetary Fund (IMF) to start an austerity program that would include tightening credit, a thirty-month wage freeze, reducing the public payroll, raising taxes and utilities rates, encouraging freer trade, and canceling several public works projects: all measures advocated by the Prebisch plan.

This "stabilization plan" was never enforced vigorously, however. When austerity measures threatened to have high political costs, Frondizi usually backed off, as in his abandonment of the railroad reorganization plan or his cancellation of electricity rate increases in 1959 after mobs stormed government buildings. Tax reform turned out to be mild increases in personal income taxes for the upper brackets and in sales and excise taxes, but there was only the slightest increase in corporate taxes paid by foreign companies and none at all on domestic firms. Tax collection remained lax. In 1961 it was estimated that only 5 percent of the working-age population ever bothered to file a return. Credit was tightened somewhat, but banking practices were not closely supervised, with the result that a group of Rogelio Frigerio's friends in the Banco de la Nación managed to embezzle several millions of dollars, which they deposited in foreign banks. This was done by making loans to dummy companies which they controlled, using as collateral bills or checks from other dummy firms which they set up overseas.[4]

All in all, austerity was more rhetoric than reality under Frondizi. During his time in office the amount of money in circulation nearly tripled; the cost of living almost quadrupled; and the peso lost half its value relative to the dollar. Only in depressing wages was he really effective, and even then he did it in a roundabout way by granting large increases and then allowing inflation to wipe them out.

Politics got in the way of controlling the money supply. Just before the March 1960 congressional elections Frondizi, having quarreled with Perón and knowing that he could expect no more help from that quarter, ordered a huge increase in government spending for public works that almost doubled the rate of monetary expansion and negated all of Alsogaray's efforts to bring inflation under control. Similarly, just before the 1962 elections Frondizi diverted hundreds of millions of pesos from their original budgeted purposes to both finance more projects and to hire more government employees. Some of the provincial governments controlled by the UCRI borrowed heavily from local bankers, who dared not refuse them, and even ransacked their employees' pension funds in order to expand their patronage. After Frondizi's overthrow, intervenors in Catamarca found that the provincial government owed 600 million pesos in debts against only 64,062 in its treasury. There was literally no money to pay staff salaries or debts to suppliers. In San Luís the public payroll had swollen from 243 employees to 1,600 in the two months prior to the elections. The province's debts exceeded 161 million pesos, and there was no prospect of paying them. The pension fund, insurance fund, and education fund were depleted after being plundered for political purposes. In La Rioja the public works board was greatly overstaffed; the province owed 125 million pesos; and the Provincial Bank of La Rioja was deeply in debt to local private bankers, who had been forced to lend to it.[5]

Such practices made many liberals pessimistic about applying their principles within the context of a democratic system. Perón, then in exile in the Dominican Republic, watched their disillusionment with Frondizi grow and explained its cause to Emílio Perina with sardonic amusement:

> Today there is no middle ground in the country. You either do what the people want, and it seems that Frondizi doesn't feel strong enough for that, or you think of the Nation as a whole, which means you have to govern in a conservative and reactionary way. If Frondizi really wants to implement this policy of development and expansion he's always talking about, there is no other way except to throw himself into the arms of the Right. But he won't do that because he's a prisoner of his leftist background. He doesn't have the courage. He's afraid they'll call him a reactionary.[6]

### Illia's Statist Experiment

Liberalism promised to attack inflation but its policies sometimes had the opposite effect. Devaluing the currency or raising the rates charged for the government's goods and services added to production costs, which then were passed on to the consumer in the form of higher prices. On the other hand, credit restriction discouraged investment and kept the economy technologically backward. It also induced unemployment, which led to a fall in demand and another contraction of production.

Two lines of criticism offered alternatives to the liberal approach. The first, which might be called quasi-liberal, agreed about freer trade and lifting price controls, but rejected the liberals' monetarist policies of restricting credit, reducing government spending, and holding down wages. Like the nationalists, the quasi-liberals believed in stimulating demand in order to put industry's idle capacity back to work. But they also believed that government spending, if properly channeled toward increasing production and not merely toward showcase projects or creating make-work jobs, was an efficient way of restoring rapid growth. To the charge that this would be inflationary they responded that lowering tariffs would keep prices down.[7]

The second group of critics was more nationalist, or populist, in outlook. It favored a big role for the government in the economy through direct controls on prices, foreign trade, investment, and credit. In many areas the state would have to assume the exclusive role of entrepreneur, and to do so it would have to increase its revenues, largely by raising both income taxes and property taxes on the rich.[8]

This latter approach was the one taken by Arturo Illia, the second democratically elected president, who campaigned in 1963 against the stabilization plan, promising that he would brook no foreign interference in Argentina's affairs. Rather than trying to limit the printing of money, his government turned it out at an annual rate of 38 percent. Large increases in wages and pensions allowed workers to recover some of the economic ground lost under Frondizi and Guido. With such pump priming, gross domestic production (GDP) grew by 8 percent in 1964 and 7.8 percent in 1965, while manufacturing output reached 14.4 percent and 11.6 percent. To head off inflation, a National Office of Supply (Dirección Nacional de Abastecimiento) was created, with sweeping powers to control production and distribution. It became a criminal act to raise prices beyond the limits set by this office, or to hoard goods and withhold them from the market. The National Office of Supply had the right to inspect companies' sales records and inventories at any time. To aid it in planning, advisory commissions composed of representatives of management and labor were set up for every branch of production. In the event that these controls failed to work, Congress was empowered to declare a state of economic emergency that would allow Illia to set limits on profits, confiscate merchandise, suspend patent rights, and even decree mandatory production quotas.[9]

For many people these policies seemed like a return to Perón's corporative state, and the déjà vu became all the sharper when, in February 1964, the National Grain Board bought up a million tons of wheat and sold them to communist China for a profit. That brought a cry of protest from the Center for Cereal Exporters, which saw it as a first sign of reviving IAPI. During that same month, the Illia administration sought to correct a domestic shortage of beef by ordering the foreign packinghouses to deliver, at cost, 15 percent of their production to the National Meat Board. This act of confiscation was called, euphemistically, a contribution.[10]

As in Perón's time, controls were not only aimed at creating self-sufficiency, but they were also manipulated to make money in questionable ways. For example, when exchange controls were reintroduced the government set an official exchange rate for the peso that was about 15 percent higher than the free market rate. That enabled the government to realize a tidy profit by requiring exporters to turn in to the Central Bank all foreign exchange they earned abroad. The Central Bank could then resell those dollars, pounds, marks, or francs for their real value on the free market.

Despite all its formal powers, the state was unable to contain inflation for long. By the end of 1965 the cost of living was rising at an annual rate of 32 percent. At the same time, production was slowing down again. Discouraged by export taxes, unfavorable exchange rates, and other controls, agricultural producers were cutting back on their investments. Exports were falling, creating the same sort of foreign exchange bottleneck that stymied Perón's economic strategy. As the government was forced more and more to restrict imports, the industrial sector, which had been growing, began to contract again. By the time Illia was removed from office in June 1966, commercial failures, in terms of total liabilities, were more than triple their highest level under Frondizi. Much of the steel and automobile industries stood idle; sales were off by a third in the machine and tool industry and by 80 percent in the agricultural machinery industry. As industry went into recession, unemployment went up. Only by the wholesale creation of public sector jobs was the government able to prevent the jobless rate from exceeding 7 percent.

## The Ongania Dictatorship: A House Divided against Itself

In the beginning, Ongania's economic policies did not differ much from Illia's. His economics minister, Jorge Salimei, and his Central Bank president, Felipe Tami, were Social Catholics whose corporative state ideas soon caused businessmen, who had hailed Illia's overthrow, to withdraw their support. At the end of December 1966, however, a complete cabinet shake-up brought Adalbert Krieger Vasena to the Economics Ministry, and the pendulum swung back toward liberalism. Krieger Vasena put heavy emphasis on controlling inflation, which he aimed to do by reducing government expenditures, trimming its bureaucracy, raising taxes, and increasing public service rates.

Krieger Vasena's new tax policy was rather innovative. Duties were to be lowered on essential imports of raw materials and machinery, in order to encourage agricultural and industrial modernization, but at the same time sales taxes would be lifted on locally produced machinery in order to help domestic industry compete. To encourage savings and investment, the nontaxable minimum on personal income and capital gains was increased, while to make up for the loss of revenue from those changes, other taxes—on sales, utility rates, and exports—were increased. The export taxes were justified as being designed to prevent windfall profits, since Krieger Vasena coupled it with a sharp devaluation of the peso.[11]

In trying to reduce the government payroll, Krieger Vasena focused especially on the railroads and the ports, where there were many redundant workers and restrictive labor practices. In the private sector, inflation was to be attacked through wage and price restraint. In April 1968 Krieger Vasena decreed a total wage freeze that was to remain in effect until the end of the year; meanwhile, "voluntary" price guidelines were laid down, and companies that signed agreements to abide by them were promised preferential treatment in getting government contracts and loans from government banks. Otherwise, credit would only be extended to manufacturing firms whose products had export potential, or for modernizing agricultural equipment. Government spending was allowed to increase only in the area of urban housing, where the construction of new units was to ease the shortage.

Under Ongania, official policy moved back toward freer trade in order to force domestic industry to become more efficient. As Krieger Vasena put it: "Marginal enterprises now existing only because of high tariff protection will only go when we move from a closed economy to an open, modern, competitive one."[12] In theory, as a dynamic new private sector appeared, workers could be transferred into it from the public sector. During the transitional period, meanwhile, public works projects would be used to prevent massive unemployment.

This scheme seemed to work, particularly after it became clear that Ongania intended to stand firmly behind his economics minister. Unconcerned about his popularity, the crusty general came down hard upon labor unions that struck to protest the new program, and with wages held in check, prices began to come down: from an annual rate of 22.6 percent in December 1966 to just under 4 percent by the end of 1968. Meanwhile, the GNP rose by 2 percent in 1967, 4.6 percent in 1968, and 6.9 percent in 1969. Manufacturing led the way, with an average annual increase of 18 percent be-

tween 1966 and 1969. The fastest-growing industries were metallurgy, chemicals, and machine building, where annual growth rates
exceeded 25 percent. Gross domestic investment rose by over 30
percent between 1966 and 1969, most of it being channeled toward
importing new machinery and equipment.[13]

Most extraordinary of all, growth was achieved without inflation,
and inflation was checked without contracting the money supply.
To avoid recession and arrive at his growth targets Krieger Vasena
carefully increased the currency in circulation and tried, through
the Industrial Bank, to direct it to those industries that fit his priorities. The bank made fewer loans but larger ones. Unlike previous
governments, the Ongania dictatorship was willing to see many
small firms go out of business. This period of big production gains
also witnessed a record number of bankruptcies.[14]

Despite his apparent success, Krieger Vasena had powerful critics,
the most dangerous of which were inside the government. A devout, conservative Catholic himself, Ongania recruited many right-
wing Catholics to his administration. Admirers of Franco's Spain,
Salazar's Portugal, and Mussolini's Italy, they were authoritarian,
nationalist, and corporativist, and therefore looked askance at Krieger Vasena's liberal policies. Most of them belonged to an elitist
club called the Atheneum of the Republic, which was heavily represented at the highest levels outside of the Economics Ministry.
Nicanor Costa Méndez, the Atheneum's first president, became
minister of foreign affairs; Mario Amadeo, its most prominent intellectual (and Lonardi's choice for the foreign affairs portfolio),
was made ambassador to Brazil; Samuel Medrano, its founder, was
named secretary of social security; and Raúl Puigbó, a former Peronist storm trooper in the National Liberating Alliance, became secretary of assistance and support for the community.

Other Atheneum members who got prominent positions were
Guillermo Fals Borda, minister of interior; Mario Díaz Colodrero,
secretary of government in charge of local affairs; Enrique Pearson,
under secretary of government; Ernesto Pueyrredon, under secretary
of interior; General Héctor Repetto, general secretary to the presidency; Jorge Mazzinghi, under secretary of foreign affairs; Rafael
García Mata, secretary of agriculture; José Mariano Aristegui, secretary of culture and education; Pedro Real, president of the Central
Bank; and Máximo Etchecopar, director of the Foreign Service Institute, to name only the most outstanding examples. Of these, Fals
Borda, Díaz Colodrero, Costa Méndez, Medrano, and Mazzinghi
also were members of Opus Dei, a semisecret order of right-wing

Catholic laymen whose parent organization in Spain was a major supporter of the Franco government.[15]

Besides these members of the Atheneum, other authoritarian nationalists formed part of Ongania's inner circle: Federico Frischknecht, former dean of the College of Economic Sciences at the University of Buenos Aires who became secretary of propaganda and tourism; Roberto ("Bobby") Roth, presidential under secretary for legal and technical affairs; and Carlos Vidueiro, under secretary to the presidency. Frischknecht was a favorite of the president and lunched with him almost every day. Roth was Ongania's favorite speech writer and was in frequent conference with him. Vidueiro, whose job was supposed to be rationalizing the government bureaucracy, was really Ongania's contact man with the Vandor wing of the trade unions. All three hated Krieger Vasena and worked closely with the Atheneum group to block his policies. Their primary goal was to prevent any great reduction in the size or expenditures of the government; unless the government was reduced, all other liberal successes were bound to be ephemeral.[16]

The nationalists' other main objective was to prevent the liberals from returning the government to civilian rule. They preferred a military dictatorship that would govern through corporative institutions. As it became clear, by mid-1968, that they were successful in getting Ongania to think in terms of an indefinite stay in power, liberal criticism began to mount against the regime. In May, ex-president Aramburu held a meeting with representatives of the country's leading political parties, including the Peronists, and outlined a plan which involved lifting the ban on party and union activities and the scheduling of general elections. He criticized Ongania for creating an institutional vacuum and for treating labor as a subversive movement instead of incorporating it into the policymaking process. The government was unable to adopt a clear political position, he said, because it was divided between "a liberal economic faction and a political faction with a medieval mentality." Aramburu was acting as though he were about to resume the presidency, which gave rise to rumors that a coup, led by the liberal commander in chief of the army, Gen. Júlio Alsogaray, was impending. Ongania apparently took those rumors seriously because in August he suddenly dismissed Alsogaray and replaced him with Gen. Alejandro Lanusse.[17]

The nationalists reached the height of their influence in May 1969 when the government finally unveiled its proposed Fundamental Charter, a blueprint for creating local, provincial, and national advisory councils that would represent the interests of business, labor, agriculture, professionals, and cultural organizations. At each level the government would select from lists of nominees furnished by officially recognized interest groups the particular delegates who would form these councils. This system would take the place of Congress and, in the opinion of its authors, Guillermo Fals Borda and Mario Díaz Colodrero, would be more truly representative of national opinion.[18] Those who were skeptical about the Fundamental Charter had their attention directed to Córdoba Province, where Governor Carlos Caballero already had a similar system functioning. A few days later, however, the city of Córdoba was shaken by the worst riots in Argentina's history as workers and students seized control of the streets, threw up barricades, and overwhelmed the local police. After four days of street warfare the *cordobazo* left a dozen people dead and the city's center in ruins. Ongania, shaken by this outburst, changed his entire cabinet, dismissing both Krieger Vasena and the most prominent nationalists.

Krieger Vasena's departure was a blow to the liberals, who had seen in Ongania's government their best chance of applying their economic principles. The RRP voiced their alarm in its editorial of June 11:

> It is no good saying that "there will be no going back, no weakness, no giving way, no hesitation," when uncertainty about the immediate future, and the course of economic policy, makes it appear that the Government is guilty of all these things, whether or not it eventually pulls itself together. Nor is it easy to understand why incidents in Córdoba which the President described as "sad episodes, repugnant episodes, upon which we shall turn the page and which tomorrow we shall overcome," should have so undermined what has hitherto looked a strong and successful Government.[19]

Perón, with his usual keen insight into politics, understood better the significance of the *cordobazo*. As he wrote to Rogelio Frigerio: "These events signal the beginning of the end, and I have not the least doubt that they will continue until all government action is paralyzed. That will be the end of the dictatorship, and although I don't deceive myself about what is to follow, things will go on falling apart through various phases until they reach a logical solution."[20]

Perón was a prophet. In June, Augusto Vandor, the principal trade unionist favoring cooperation with the government, was assassinated by terrorists. And in May 1970 Aramburu was kidnapped and executed. Although it was later proven that his murder was carried out by a leftist group, at the time it raised deep suspicions inside the armed forces because Aramburu had become such a vocal critic of the government. On the morning of 8 June 1970 the heads of the three military services presented Ongania with a joint demand for his resignation. After a brief show of resistance, he complied. In the aftermath, one of the liberals in the Economics Ministry summarized the last four years with regret: "The period of the military government was unique in many respects. It was the best opportunity we had and we lost it. One problem was President Ongania. He was unable to understand political economy. He had many merits, but he failed to understand the economic policy of Krieger Vasena. It passed him by."[21]

### Levingston and Lanusse: A Return to Statism

Gen. Roberto Levingston, whom the military chose to succeed Ongania, gave the appearance of wanting to balance his cabinet between liberals and nationalists, as his predecessor had done. His interior minister, Brig. Eduardo McLoughlin, an air force officer, and Francisco Manrique, the new minister of social welfare and a former navy captain who once served as Aramburu's presidential liaison with the military, were liberals. It soon became obvious, however, that they were merely window dressing to disguise the fact that Levingston listened only to the nationalists in his cabinet.

Economic policymaking was largely in the hands of Carlos Moyano Llerena, the new economics minister, and Gen. Juan Gugliamelli, the head of the National Development Council (CONADE). Although a well-known nationalist, once in office Moyano Llerena apparently adopted the view that holding the line against inflation was top priority. That brought him into conflict with Gugliamelli, who proved to have more influence with the president. In August 1970 Moyano Llerena was forced to issue an edict, which he personally opposed, drawn up by Gugliamelli ordering all private banks to increase their consumer credit operations. After one year, they would be required to show in their books that at least 12 percent of their loan portfolio had been devoted to consumer loans. The edict said nothing about where the money was to come from, but either the government would have to print more or else the banks would have to shift their lending from business firms to consumers—that is, investment would have to be sacrificed to short-term consumer gratification. But worse measures were being planned. Gugliamelli already was drawing up other edicts that would nationalize all bank deposits, raise tariffs, impose exchange controls, and grant large wage increases. Unwilling to be a conveyer for this sort of policy, Moyano Llerena resigned on 13 October. His departure came at a time when the cost of living, lowered to a rate of increase of less than 4 percent by Krieger Vasena, had just passed the 10 percent limit that he had set as being a "civilized level."[22]

Brigadier McLoughlin resigned on the same day that Moyano Llerena did. In his case, his discomfiture came when he learned that his under secretary, Gilardi Novaro, was secretly collaborating with Levingston on an amnesty for Perón. Manrique, the remaining liberal in the cabinet, resigned the following February.

Moyano Llerena was succeeded by Aldo Ferrer, an up-and-coming young economist and currently public works minister, who was strongly identified with the nationalist position. The author of two well-received books, *El Estado y el desarrollo económico* (1956) and *La economía argentina* (1963), he argued in both for a larger role for the state in directing the course of development. Ferrer was not an orthodox nationalist, however. Like the liberals, he believed that the only way to foment growth was to increase the country's exports. Unlike the liberals, however, he did not favor devaluing the currency to encourage agricultural exports; rather, he wanted the state to identify those industries with export potential and concentrate on building them up until they were internationally competitive. Ferrer believed that the first phase in promoting nontraditional exports should concentrate on Latin America, and that Argentina should promote a regional common market. Up to that point his thinking did not diverge much from Krieger Vasena's. The critical difference was in their treatment of agriculture. Ferrer not only wanted to reduce the nation's dependence on agricultural exports, which might have been reasonable enough, but he also wanted to expropriate the large holdings and redistribute them in the form of medium-sized farms to those who currently were tenants. That, he argued, would increase farm output so much that domestic food prices would come down and there still would be plenty left over to export. In the same vein, he took the populist position that increasing the demand for domestically produced consumer goods by raising wages and increasing government spending would be a stimulus to industry. Insufficient supply, not excess demand, was for him the real cause of Argentina's inflation.

Unlike other nationalists in Levingston's cabinet, Ferrer wanted a quick return to civilian rule. Democratization was essential to development, in his view, because the masses were more favorable to reform than were the elites. For the same reason, he advocated legalizing Peronism. Ferrer also was determined to set the government's economic policy and not simply be a stooge for Gugliamelli. After a behind-the-scenes scuffle, the latter resigned on 10 November, accusing Ferrer of being insufficiently nationalist. The charge was unfair. As economics minister, Ferrer required all state agencies and industrial enterprises to buy their equipment and supplies only from nationally owned companies. Moreover, only nationally owned contracting and consulting firms could get the government's business. Like any other nationalist, Ferrer increased government spending, added more jobs to the public payroll, and boosted government wages.

In March 1971 there was a second *cordobazo*, indicating that it was the fact of military dictatorship, and not the content of economic policy, that lay at the root of unrest. In the aftermath, Levingston was replaced by Gen. Alejandro Lanusse, the army's commander in chief. Ferrer was retained, but decided in May to resign anyway. His departure had no great effect on the new government's policies. Lanusse was anxious to disengage the military from politics, but without turning power over to the Peronists. His strategy was to negotiate with Perón for a political truce while also pursuing a populist program that would dampen mass discontent. In pursuit of that, government spending rose even more, with the money supply increasing at an average rate of 5 percent a month. Inflation hit 90 percent by the end of 1972 and 100 percent by the following February.

Lanusse's answer to the spiraling cost of living was to put price controls on most consumer goods. At the same time, he prohibited most imports in order to save on Argentina's dwindling foreign exchange and to encourage domestic industry. The effect of this combination of measures was to dry up the supply of goods even more and to give added impetus to inflation.

The military's belief that it could manage an economy by edict was reflected in an even more curious hodgepodge of measures. The soldiers wanted industry to expand; therefore Lanusse ordered that at least half of all new money being invested in the stock exchange had to go into new issues. They wanted more industry to locate in the interior of the country, so a 50 percent surcharge was added to the tax on capital that companies located in the Greater Buenos Aires area had to pay, and a 20 percent surcharge on those located in

Buenos Aires Province. As further inducement, Lanusse promised subsidies to companies that moved their factories and research facilities to the interior. Such intervention provoked the Stock Exchange into declaring "no confidence" in the government. The UIA joined in, protesting the government's "inflexible impositions" and "drastic penalties" that were issued without any consultation with the groups affected by them.[23]

Such criticism was only the pale reflection of a deeper panic. Squeezed by runaway inflation and frightened by the prospect of Perón's return, businessmen were hurrying to withdraw their money from the economy and place it safely overseas. Unofficial estimates put the volume of capital flight at more than $1 billion. Banks, starved for deposits and unable to calculate against inflation, were refusing to loan money except in the short term and then only to favored clients. Cut off from credit, many companies went into bankruptcy. Commercial failures, in terms of liabilities involved, doubled over what they had been under Ongania. Unemployment, which had been held to under 5 percent by Krieger Vasena, rose to over 6.5 percent. Such economic disorder undermined Lanusse's political strategy. By the time he capitulated and handed power over to the Peronists in May 1973, even conservatives were ready to concede that Peronism might be preferable to the chaos fostered by the military's mismanagement.

## Agriculture: The Policymakers' Nemesis

There was broad support in Argentina for Prebisch's call to build heavy industry, but there was great disagreement over the best way to proceed. Both liberals and nationalists agreed that agriculture should play an important role in raising capital to invest in industry, but their approaches were very different. Liberals wanted to induce farmers and ranchers to increase their exports by making it more profitable for them to do so, whereas nationalists wanted to tax the rural sector so the state would have more money to invest.

Fertile soil, temperate climate, and moderate rainfall make Argentina one of the world's great potential suppliers of meat and grains; however, since the Great Depression, investment in agriculture had been neglected. Farm technology had not changed appreciably since the 1930s, and the output of the four major cash crops was only slightly larger than it had been back then. First falling profits then Peronist interference had, in the liberals' view, discouraged

Table 12.1 Argentina's Land Tenure System, 1960

| Size of Holding (in hectares) | Number of Holdings | Percentage of Total | Amount of Land | Percentage of Total |
|---|---|---|---|---|
| Under 25 | 181,404 | 38.5 | 1,759,545 | 1.0 |
| 25 to 100 | 127,463 | 27.0 | 7,710,135 | 4.4 |
| 100 to 400 | 97,072 | 20.6 | 19,697,963 | 11.2 |
| 400 to 1,000 | 24,876 | 5.3 | 15,624,948 | 8.9 |
| 1,000 to 2,500 | 18,899 | 3.2 | 25,774,150 | 14.7 |
| 2,500 to 10,000 | 8,908 | 1.9 | 46,168,620 | 26.4 |
| Over 10,000 | 2,551 | 0.5 | 58,407,136 | 33.3 |

Source: Dirección Nacional de Estadística y Censos, *Censo nacional agropecuario*, 1963, 1:4–5.

the landowners from mechanizing. Unless price controls were lifted and the currency devalued, agriculture would continue to stagnate, and that would hold back industrialization because agriculture still earned about 90 percent of Argentina's foreign exchange. Nationalists were quick to point out, however, that such policies would make a handful of *estancieros*, grain farmers, and exporters rich at the expense of the bulk of the population. Furthermore, incentives would not make the landed elite produce more, because, as Aldo Ferrer argued, their mentality was precapitalist. The typical big landowner was interested more in social status than in working his estate as a business enterprise. He had no incentive to mechanize because a good living could be earned by using traditional methods. In most cases he was even an absentee landlord living off the rents from his tenants, and they, lacking any permanent attachment to the land, had no incentive to invest in long-term improvements either. In such a situation, currency devaluations and price incentives would never succeed in raising production very much. Only expropriation, or punitive taxation of poorly used land, would eliminate the root cause of agricultural stagnation.[24]

The case for land reform seemed buttressed at first by the 1960 agricultural census, which showed the distribution of landholdings as in table 12.1.

Let us call holdings of under 25 hectares *minifundios* and those of between 25 and 100 hectares small farms. At the other end of the scale we shall say that those of more than 2,500 hectares are *latifundios* and those of more than 10,000 hectares are *megafundios*. All those in between are then middle-sized farms. Using those categories, it can be said that *minifundios* and small farms comprised 65 percent of all landholdings but only 5 percent of the total acreage. Conversely, *latifundios* and *megafundios* were less than 2.5 percent of all landholdings but controlled nearly 60 percent of the land. This situation seemed to demand reform.

The problem of very large estates diminishes, however, when it is discovered that a disproportionate number of them are concentrated in the wastelands of Patagonia. Some 36 percent of all the *latifundios* and over 60 percent of the *megafundios* are found in the provinces of Chubut, Neuquén, Río Negro, Santa Cruz, and the territory of Tierra del Fuego. Holdings of 2,500 hectares or more comprised between 72 percent and 84 percent of the rural land in Chubut, Neuquén, and Río Negro, and 99 percent in Santa Cruz and Tierra del Fuego. These were sheep ranches—the only feasible use for the poor soil and grasses of the region, which required extensive grazing.

There was a very different pattern of land tenure on the pampa. In Buenos Aires Province, middle-sized farms constituted 41 percent of all holdings and had 65 percent of the land. Most of those middle-sized farms also were at the lower end of the category, falling within the 100 to 400 hectare range. In the pampa's drier western zone, grazing predominated over farming, and the land tenure pattern looked more like Patagonia's; but on the northern pampa (roughly, the province of Santa Fé) small and medium-sized holdings were the rule. Thus, in the very heart of Argentina's agricultural belt the pattern of land distribution looked fairly equitable. Some writers even went so far as to argue that, strictly speaking, the country had neither *latifundios* nor *minifundios*. The large holdings were not entailed and inheritance was not based on primogeniture. Moreover, the land was used relatively efficiently in conformity with the climate, soil, and market possibilities. Very small holdings were usually found near towns, where their owners had jobs and simply used their *minifundios* to supplement their income. It was generally agreed that, on the pampa at least, there was no rural misery; this was a stabilizing factor in the country's politics. Rural poverty was confined mainly to the distant northwestern provinces, where few people lived anyway.[25]

In 1960 more landholdings were being worked by their owners, as opposed to tenants, than in 1946. In those fourteen years the number of owner-operators had increased by 30,000, while the number of tenant farmers had decreased by around 70,000. Much of this was the result of owners selling out to their tenants in the 1940s as frozen rents made absentee landholding unprofitable. Large estates were broken up, and large numbers of tenants finally realized their ambition of becoming proprietors. All in all, about 2 million hectares changed hands this way in Buenos Aires Province alone. Other tenants, discouraged by IAPI's prices, got out of agriculture altogether. But still others who owned farm machinery found a new source of income as *contratistas*, or rural contractors, who for a fixed amount of cash or a share of the crop would plow and harvest for the burgeoning new class of small and medium landowners whose cash was tied up in land and who could not afford to buy a tractor or combine. A study done by the SRA calculated that a *contratista*, owning perhaps only a single tractor, could earn as much in a year as a middle-sized farmer.[26]

## Incentives versus Controls

Statistics on land distribution gave little support to arguments for agrarian reform; but the evidence on how land was utilized did suggest that large estates were less efficiently run than smaller holdings. The 1960 census did not deal with this question directly except to show that over 95 percent of the country's arable land was actually being used. To measure efficiency, however, investigators at the University of Córdoba calculated the amount of capital invested per hectare for each holding in Córdoba Province. The results, published in 1963, showed that small and medium-sized farms had the highest ratio of capital to land. A similar study, done in 1965 by CONADE, showed that productivity per hectare was highest in holdings of under 100 hectares and lowest in those of over 2,500. Such findings strengthened the arguments of nationalists like Ferrer that price incentives would be ineffective at raising production substantially because the biggest owners had little interest in maximizing profits.[27]

Other statistics, however, supported the liberal view that excessive government controls and taxation were discouraging farm production. In 1960 there were about 3 million fewer acres under cultivation than in 1947 and some 38 million fewer than in 1952. Government surcharges on imported farm machinery, fertilizers, and pesticides—all designed to encourage domestic manufacturers—raised the cost of these essential inputs higher than any compensating increases in food prices. To this the nationalists could reply that the problem was not one of capacity but of willingness to put existing capacity to work. After all, the number of tractors had just about doubled between 1956 and 1960, yet total agricultural output per capita was about 7 percent less.[28]

Stagnant agricultural production meant the domestic food supply failed to keep up with urban population growth, and that helped to fuel inflation; also, exports continually lagged in relation to imports, creating a chronic balance of payments crisis. Concerning the latter problem, Mallon and Sourrouille concluded: "Balance of payments problems have indeed been so persistent under such varying conditions and policies that one is tempted to conclude that unless agricultural export expansion again becomes the main engine of growth of the Argentine economy—a very dim prospect at best in the medium run—the country is condemned to continue suffering from the semistagnation of stop-go development."[29]

What could be done to raise production? The Aramburu government had no clear policy toward agriculture. Though it claimed to favor liberalization, it retained price controls on many popular food items, including beef. IAPI was not dismantled until April 1958, just before Aramburu left office, and in the meantime it was used to control the domestic sale of wheat in order to avoid any sudden rise in the price of bread. Although the peso was allowed to fall to the free market rate (in effect, a devaluation), the government initiated the system of retentions, or export taxes, to prevent the farmers from reaping windfall profits.[30]

The farmers, naturally, were chagrined. In January 1958, over 400 agricultural producers' associations cosponsored a long manifesto that was published in all the Buenos Aires newspapers. "The Revolution has not succeeded in making any impression whatsoever on the vast bureaucratic structure which it inherited from the deposed regime," it asserted. Furthermore, bureaucrats at the Ministry of Agriculture, though knowing nothing about the farmers' problems, "systematically refuse[d] to seek the guidance and advice of the representatives of private trade associations." The manifesto demanded an end to price controls, the abolition of retentions, and the free importation of farm machinery. It also ended with a warning: Argentina's prosperity depended on raising agricultural production, which could be done only by giving farmers incentives to modernize.[31]

The Frondizi administration aroused little enthusiasm among farmers either, although it abolished both price and exchange controls. Like so many governments in the past, it believed in rapid industrialization as a panacea for Argentina's problems and sought to pay for this through taxing exports. So the hated system of retentions was kept. In addition, Frondizi placed heavy surcharges on the importation of agricultural machinery, pesticides, and fertilizers in order to encourage the domestic production of those goods. At the SRA's annual convention in 1959 its president, Juan Mathet, attacked the retentions and surcharges and warned that the government would never meet its balance of payments obligations or succeed in its industrialization plans until farmers were encouraged to produce for export. As it was, he said, taxes were robbing them of half the value of their production.[32]

Mathet predicted correctly. Although cattle stocks increased slightly between 1958 and 1961, the numbers actually sent to market dropped sharply, and meat exports fell from 647,000 tons to only 394,000. Of the four principal grain crops (corn, wheat, oats, and barley), there was a decline in the acreage sown in all but the first. Production dropped, and so did exportable surpluses. Since Frondizi's industrialization strategy depended on export earnings to pay for the importation of capital goods, this cutback in farm output quickly produced a crisis.[33]

Farmers also were embroiled in fights with certain provincial governments whose policies they considered frankly hostile. The worst of these, in their view, was that of Buenos Aires Province, where Governor Oscar Alende was being advised by Aldo Ferrer. Alende, titular leader of the UCRI's left wing, supported Ferrer when the latter devised a land tax which required owners to pay according to their land's potential value, or what it would be worth if exploited efficiently according to the government's standards. Ferrer defended his tax on the grounds that it would force the large owners to either improve their output or else sell out to someone who would. Naturally, the farmers saw the tax as a first step toward expropriation and accused Alende and Ferrer of trying to copy the Cuban Revolution.[34] The farmers were also incensed because Alende had decreed a "gainful activities tax" as well, which placed a 2 percent levy on the value added at every stage of food production. As a result of the tax, it was estimated that a farmer in Buenos Aires who formerly paid 63,500 pesos a year in taxes to the provincial government would now face a bill for 1.44 million. Similar taxes were being adopted in the provinces of Córdoba, La Pampa, Mendoza, San Luís, and Santa Cruz.[35] Farmers responded by refusing to play their assigned role as earners of foreign exchange. In 1961 the value of Argentina's exports was around $205 million less than it had been ten years before.

Passive resistance from the farm sector provoked even liberal economists into exploring ways of forcing agricultural production to rise. Álvaro Alsogaray, though a champion of the free market, proposed a tax on farmland when he returned to the Economics Ministry under Guido. He excused his measure on the grounds that farmers would then have to produce more in order to pay the tax. The SRA attacked its former friend in a blistering manifesto. "You depart from the truth and confuse public opinion," it charged, "when you announce that the 5 percent tax on producers is an emergency measure needed to rescue the 1963 budget, and you depart even further from the truth when you say that the opposition of agricultural groups reflects a lack of understanding and of a social conscience." Supported by other agricultural pressure groups, the SRA organized mass resignations from the Secretariat of Agriculture, the National Meat Board, and the National Grain Board. The agriculturalists also formed an alliance with the UIA, which was fighting with Alsogaray over his proposal to limit credits to industry. Acting together, these entrepreneurs eventually forced him out of office.[36]

Antigovernment resistance was even more solid after Illia came to office. The new administration had strong statist inclinations that led it to impose food price controls, a land tax, export retentions, and even restrictions on the volume of exports so as to insure a plentiful supply of beef locally. In 1964 the CRA and CARBAP, which represented smaller farmers and cattlemen, organized several other regional associations into an united farm front called the Coordinating Committee for Agrarian Entities. By working together, they succeeded in forcing Illia to rescind price controls and export restrictions, and made him back away from a proposed tax on grain production.[37] Even so, relations between the rural sector and the government were worse than they had ever been since Perón's time.

Farmers' hopes were raised by the Ongania regime, especially when Krieger Vasena abolished the rural rent law in April 1947 and allowed landowners to raise rents and evict tenants for the first time since 1948. The farmers were also encouraged by the devaluation of the peso by almost half and by changes in the tax laws that would allow them to write off purchases of locally produced farm machinery and permit their fixed assets to be reevaluated to take inflation into account. But the government lost the farmers' goodwill when it reimposed export taxes and refused to lower the duties on imported farm machinery, fertilizers, and pesticides. In July 1968 the SRA, CRA, the Confederation of Rural Cooperatives, and the Coordinating Committee for Agrarian Entities sent Krieger Vasena a note which stated that export taxes, which ranged between 9.5 percent and 25 percent, were causing agricultural exports to fall. Meat exports were down by 47 percent, grains by 27 percent, and linseed by 53 percent compared to the previous year, resulting in a loss of some $70 million. In reply, the government cut taxes by 3 percent, but the farmers were still unsatisfied.[38]

Disappointment turned to hostility in November 1968 after Krieger Vasena decreed a land tax that would charge owners 1.6 percent on the assessed value of all unused farm- or pastureland. It was Illia's scheme redivivus. Furious, the rural groups announced that they would boycott all future meetings with the secretary of agriculture. This time even the Agrarian Federation—the tenant farmers' group—joined the protest because it would mean rising rents. Krieger Vasena tried to point out that the government was struggling with a large budget deficit created in part by the well-known fact that many farmers evaded their income taxes. The new law would stop evasion yet allow any land tax paid to be deducted from a farmer's income tax. That failed to mollify the agrarians, however.

The government's position would have been more defensible but for the fact that the land tax was imposed in addition to export taxes and high duties on imported agricultural machinery. The farmers felt whipsawed and so responded in their usual fashion by refusing to invest. Although the land tax was supposed to induce owners to utilize their holdings more efficiently, in fact production remained practically stagnant, and both meat and grain exports continued to fall. Consequently, revenues from the rural sector actually declined. Farmers also suspended their purchases of domestic machinery and agricultural chemicals, leaving huge stocks of unsold goods in those industries the government was so eager to promote. They, in turn, began slashing production and laying off workers. Thus, agriculture and its ancillary industries constituted a blight on an otherwise rosy economic picture under Krieger Vasena.[39]

Relations between the government and farmers worsened under Levingston and Lanusse. When Aldo Ferrer became economics minister he attempted to impose the same sort of policies that already had made him the bête noire of the rural sector. To gird themselves for the coming battle, the SRA, CRA, Agrarian Federation, the Confederation of Rural Cooperatives, the Coordinating Committee for Agrarian Entities, and several regional agricultural federations joined in September 1970 to form the all-embracing United Farmers' Movement (Movimiento del Campo Unido). The first test of strength came over a new law which empowered the Economics

Ministry to establish minimum quotas for domestic meat sales. In order to guarantee a meat supply at government-set prices, the law would empower Ferrer to penalize ranchers, middlemen, or butchers if they attempted to withhold meat from the market. From the rural sector's standpoint, it was the opening wedge of a plan to restore a totalitarian command economy.[40]

The indignant cattlemen refused to comply with the law, which was to go into effect on 15 March 1971. When the day arrived, cattle deliveries at the Liniers Market were minimal, and the few steers that arrived were of such poor quality that their owners obviously wanted to get rid of them. The boycott remained in effect for days until finally Ferrer invited the ranchers' representatives to his office to "discuss the next steps to be taken." That meeting was scheduled for 24 March, but before it took place Ferrer made the mistake of trying to raise support among the cattlemen of Buenos Aires Province by making a few appearances at their meetings. At one of these, in the county seat of Trenque Lauquen, he found himself surrounded by an angry crowd that insulted and threatened him. Before he could extricate himself he was called everything from an antinational to a Marxist and was told that if he didn't repeal his law the United Farmers' Movement would descend with thousands of tractors on the federal capital. After this confrontation Ferrer called off the meeting scheduled for the twenty-fourth and announced that the government would revise its price guidelines. That still didn't satisfy the cattlemen, who continued to plan their *tractorazo*. By the end of March, Ferrer was ready to surrender. The minimum quota law was repealed, as were all price guidelines and most rural taxes.[41]

Ferrer's departure from office two months later did not restore good relations between the government and the countryside. In September 1972 the Lanusse government, smarting from a $128 million deficit in the trade balance, declared its intention of bringing back the land tax to prod farmers into producing more. Once again a confrontation was brewing, but before it took place an even greater threat to farmers arose: a triumphant Peronism that won the March 1973 elections and was preparing to take over the government in May. Meanwhile, the rural sector presented a picture of complete stagnation, with the overall per capita product the same at the end of 1972 as it was in 1960.

## CHAPTER THIRTEEN

# The Role of Foreign Capital

Argentine industry underwent considerable change between 1955 and 1973. First, there was a shift from labor-intensive to capital-intensive methods of production. Second, the average industrial enterprise became larger. Third, technological progress and growth in size, while felt in all branches of manufacturing, were especially true of such fields as iron and steel, chemicals, petroleum derivatives, rubber, automobiles, and machine building. Those were known as "dynamic" industries, to distinguish them from more "traditional" industries like food processing, tobacco, textiles, clothing, leather, and woodworking. Fourth, most of those changes occurred as a result of foreign investment, often by multinational corporations. Tables 13.1 and 13.2 illustrate some of these trends.

Although Perón may have initiated some of those changes when he opened the country to foreign capital in 1954, table 13.1 shows that the general effect of his rule was to increase the number of small, labor-intensive establishments. By 1954 the average industrial enterprise was smaller and had less installed horsepower than in 1943. After 1954 there was a slowdown in the appearance of new establishments, and indeed there was a sharp contraction in their numbers after 1964. The industrial labor force continued to grow, but at a slower pace; still, the average factory was larger in 1974 than it had been in the previous twenty years. The greatest gain was in installed horsepower, however. The average amount per establishment, and the ratio of horsepower to hand labor increased dramatically.

Larger firms were playing a more dominant role in industry as employers of labor and producers of goods. Those employing more than 200 workers constituted only six-tenths of one percent in 1964, just as they had in 1946; yet in that interval they raised their portion of the total industrial labor force from 29 percent to 40 percent and that of the total value of industrial production from one-third to one-half.

Table 13.1 Argentine Industrialization, 1943–1974

| Year | Number of Establishments | Number of Workers | Installed Horsepower | Workers per Establishment (avg.) | Horsepower per Establishment (avg.) | Horsepower per Worker (avg.) |
|---|---|---|---|---|---|---|
| 1943 | 59,765 | 820,470 | 1,836,453 | 13.7 | 30.73 | 2.24 |
| 1946 | 84,905 | 1,058,673 | 2,076,531 | 12.5 | 24.46 | 1.96 |
| 1950 | 81,599 | 1,035,765 | 2,661,922 | 12.7 | 32.62 | 2.57 |
| 1954 | 148,371 | 1,217,844 | 3,570,037 | 8.2 | 24.06 | 2.93 |
| 1964 | 190,892 | 1,370,483 | 5,115,913 | 7.2 | 26.80 | 3.73 |
| 1974 | 126,388 | 1,525,221 | 6,753,375 | 12.1 | 53.43 | 4.43 |

Rates of Change (%)

| | 1943–1954 | 1950–1954 | 1954–1964 | 1964–1974 | 1954–1974 |
|---|---|---|---|---|---|
| Number of establishments | +148.3 | +81.8 | +28.7 | −33.8 | −14.8 |
| Number of workers | +48.4 | +17.6 | +12.5 | +11.3 | +25.2 |
| Installed horsepower | +94.4 | +34.1 | +43.3 | +32.0 | +89.2 |

Sources: *Cuarto Censo Nacional* (Buenos Aires: Dirección General del Servicio Estadístico Nacional, 1952); *Censo Industrial 1950* (Buenos Aires: Dirección Nacional de Estadística y Censos, 1957); *Censo Industrial 1954* (Buenos Aires: Dirección Nacional de Estadística y Censos, 1960); *Censo Nacional Económico* (Buenos Aires: Instituto Nacional de Estadística y Censos, 1968); *Censo Nacional Económico 1974* (Buenos Aires: Instituto Nacional de Estadística y Censos, 1975).

The increasing importance of technologically complex dynamic industry is demonstrated by table 13.2. If food and beverages dominated industry in the pre–World War I period, and textiles was the glamour industry of the 1940s, then industrial progress after 1955 was centered in vehicles and nonelectrical machinery, metallurgy, and petroleum derivatives. Also, areas such as scientific, photographic, and optical equipment, and electrical machinery were contributing significantly to the total industrial product.

Within these dynamic industries, foreign capital was concentrated in certain branches where large amounts of start-up capital and advanced technology were necessary: automobiles, farm machinery, industrial chemicals, rubber, electrical motors, pharmaceuticals, plastics, synthetic fibers, synthetic rubber, agricultural chemicals, automotive parts, electronic equipment, gasoline engines, turbines, and industrial machinery generally. Of all the heavy industries in the dynamic sector, only steel and paper were dominated by local capital.

Table 13.2 Traditional and Dynamic Industry in Argentina:
Contribution to the Total Value of Industrial Production,
1913–1974 (in percentages)

| | 1913 | 1946 | 1974 |
|---|---|---|---|
| *Traditional industry* | | | |
| Food and beverages | 53.2 | 31.5 | 25.8 |
| Tobacco | 3.1 | 2.2 | 1.8 |
| Textiles | 2.2 | 12.4 | 9.3 |
| Clothing | 8.6 | 7.8 | 3.5 |
| Wood | 4.7 | 5.0 | 2.2 |
| Printing and publishing | 2.1 | 3.0 | 1.7 |
| Leather | 3.0 | 5.2 | 0.6 |
| Stone, gravel, cement | 12.3 | 3.6 | 3.0 |
| Other | 2.2 | 1.0 | 3.4 |
| Subtotal | 91.4 | 71.7 | 51.3 |
| | | | |
| *Dynamic industry* | | | |
| Paper and cellulose | 0.5 | 2.0 | 2.4 |
| Chemicals | 3.0 | 7.2 | 3.2 |
| Petroleum derivatives | 0.0 | 3.1 | 6.1 |
| Rubber | 0.0 | 0.9 | 1.9 |
| Metallurgy | 5.1 | 7.3 | 13.5 |
| Vehicles and nonelectrical machinery | 0.0 | 5.5 | 15.5 |
| Electrical machinery and appliances | 0.0 | 1.3 | 3.1 |
| Scientific, photo, and optical equipment | 0.0 | 1.0 | 3.0 |
| Subtotal | 8.6 | 28.3 | 48.7 |

Sources: *Tercer Censo Nacional 1914* (Buenos Aires: Comisión Nacional
del Censo, 1916); *Cuarto Censo Nacional* (Buenos Aires: Dirección
General del Servício Estadístico Nacional, 1952); *Censo Nacional
Económico 1974* (Buenos Aires: Instituto Nacional de Estadística y
Censos, 1975).

There was broad agreement among economists, government officials, and military officers that the move toward large, sophisticated
enterprises was desirable, but it became a matter of growing concern that so much dynamic industry was in foreign hands. To others, the parallel growth of state-owned industry was ominous too.
Champions of domestic private capital complained that it was being
squeezed out by these two giant competitors. For example, in 1958
four of the top ten industrial firms, in total sales, were owned by
local private capital (Molinos Río de La Plata, SIAM, Alpargatas, and

Sansenina), five were foreign (Swift, Shell, Esso, CADE, and Frigorí-
fico Anglo), and one was state owned (YPF). A decade later, however,
none of the top ten were local private, six were foreign (Swift, Shell,
Esso, Fiat, Ford, and General Motors), and the remaining four were
state companies (YPF, SEGBA, SOMISA, and Gas del Estado). Local
private capital was being relegated to the increasingly peripheral
area of small, backward, traditional industry.[1]

## The Debate about Foreign Investment

In his report on the economic crisis, Raúl Prebisch anticipated the
controversy that foreign investment would arouse among Argentines, for whom economic independence was a main source of national pride. But, he cautioned, "the prospect of upwards of a decade
ago, that because of the considerable degree of economic maturity
gained then, the country might soon be in a position of relative
independence of foreign capital, has again receded, probably for a
good many years." A decade of Peronist mismanagement had left
the state bankrupt and the local private sector deprived of capital
and technology. Only foreign capital could provide the means to get
Argentina moving forward again.

Foreign capital has been a controversial subject in Argentina
and it is advisable that public opinion should be enlightened
as to its role. In order rapidly to overcome the present crisis
affecting the country's economic development, foreign loans
and capital investment are required. If it is desired to avoid this
recourse to such outside aid, the country will have to resign
itself to the indefinite continuance of its precarious condition.
Such is the nature—and the magnitude—of the problem, and it
cannot be modified.

If the country elects the first of these alternatives, it will
have to create favorable conditions for the influx of foreign
capital by curbing inflation and taking severe measures to
achieve equilibrium in the balance of payments.[2]

Even Prebisch underestimated the extent to which foreign capital
would polarize political opinion. Moreover, the greater the role foreign capital played in the economy the more the hostility toward it
would grow. There were to be sharp zigzags in official policy on the
matter, reflecting the conflicting pressures of economic and political reality.

The Neoliberal Strategy of Frondizi and Frigerio

Rapid industrialization lay at the heart of the Frondizi-Frigerio strategy for winning the Peronist masses to the UCRI. By building up heavy industry Argentina would, once and for all, secure its economic independence, and in the process many new jobs would be created. Like Prebisch, however, Frondizi and Frigerio came to the conclusion that only through the massive involvement of foreign capital could those goals be achieved quickly; and to attract that capital they would have to reduce government regulation, balance the budget, curb inflation, and keep the labor unions under control. For both men this meant a sharp ideological about-face, but they believed the goal of national self-sufficiency justified such means. As Frondizi argued, "It does not matter where capital originates, only its functions matter. If it serves national ends it is welcomed and it is useful."[3]

This neoliberal strategy essentially applied import substitution to capital goods. Top priority was given to increasing the production of oil and natural gas, without which heavy industry would not be possible. The next priority was the establishment of a steel industry. Other key targets were the development of the electrical energy, machine building, industrial chemicals, cement, paper, and cellulose sectors. Much of this was to be financed by direct foreign investment, and in the case of steel, SOMISA was launched with sizable foreign loans. Neoliberalism, like classical liberalism, thus looked to the private sector for leadership and welcomed foreign capital to the country, but it differed from classical liberalism by abandoning the idea of comparative advantage. It did not matter to Frondizi or Frigerio whether it was economic for Argentina to produce steel or build heavy machinery so long as national self-sufficiency was attained. Cost was no object because it would be borne by foreign investors. In this way, Argentina would achieve development without painful sacrifices.

To attract foreign capital, Frondizi began to relax the rules, instituted by Perón, that regulated its entry. Previously, all applications by foreigners to invest or to expand existing investments were closely scrutinized by an Inter-Ministerial Commission on Foreign Investment, which required them to conform to the five-year plan. The same was true with requests to import materials and equipment or to send home profits. Under Frondizi, foreigners only had to agree not to interfere with other industries, invest in the projects agreed upon, and inform the authorities of the source of their capi-

Table 13.3 Production and Consumption of Oil in Argentina,
1952–1962 (in millions of cubic meters)

| Year | Domestic Production | Imports | Total Consumption | Percentage of Consumption Produced Domestically |
|------|---------------------|---------|-------------------|--------------------------------------------------|
| 1952 | 3,946 | 7,053 | 10,999 | 35.9 |
| 1953 | 4,531 | 6,384 | 10,915 | 41.5 |
| 1954 | 4,701 | 7,110 | 11,811 | 39.8 |
| 1955 | 4,850 | 8,291 | 13,141 | 36.9 |
| 1956 | 4,930 | 9,040 | 13,970 | 35.3 |
| 1957 | 5,391 | 9,489 | 14,880 | 36.2 |
| 1958 | 5,669 | 10,268 | 15,937 | 35.6 |
| 1959 | 7,089 | 8,702 | 15,791 | 44.9 |
| 1960 | 10,153 | 4,177 | 14,330 | 70.9 |
| 1961 | 13,428 | 4,100 | 17,528 | 76.6 |
| 1962 | 15,614 | 3,100 | 18,714 | 83.4 |

Sources: Eidlicz, "Combustibles, electricidad, mineria," in *Argentina,
1930–1960* (Buenos Aires: Editorial Sur, 1961), p. 218; and Carl Solberg,
*Oil and Nationalism in Argentina* (Stanford: Stanford University Press,
1979), p. 173.

tal. Profit remittances and the repatriation of capital were freely permitted. Special tax incentives were offered to firms that located in the interior or that reinvested their profits in Argentina; but those conditions were not requirements.[4]

Despite this favorable attitude, the amount of foreign capital actually attracted was much less than the $1 billion a year Frondizi had hoped for. Between 1959 and 1962 the average was closer to $170 million, of which about 60 percent came from the United States. Still, that was enough to give Argentina's dynamic industries a start.[5] Frondizi's most spectacular success was in attracting foreign capital to the oil industry, his highest priority. In August 1958 he concluded what he termed "the biggest oil deal ever made in Argentina" with a consortium of private oil companies from the United States, Great Britain, West Germany, France, Italy, and even Argentina. The contracts called for exploration, drilling, refining, and pipeline construction. Shell and Esso were also to share the domestic retail market with YPF.[6] As table 13.3 shows, the volume of oil imports had been on a steady rise through 1958; in that year alone they cost Argentina over $150 million in foreign exchange. Frondizi estimated that when the private companies went into full-scale operation they would save the country about $300 million a year for the next decade.

Although the oil contracts were an economic success, they were a political liability. Rival politicians quickly reminded the public that only three years ago Frondizi had led a vitriolic campaign against Perón for agreeing to a similar deal with Standard Oil of California. Copies of Frondizi's famous book, *Petróleo y política*, which he subtitled *A Contribution to the Study of Argentine History and the Relations between Imperialism and Our National Life*, quietly disappeared from the bookstores. In a system that fostered pride in rigid devotion to principle (Frondizi's own party was the Unión Cívica Radical *Intransigente*), a switch from advocating state control of all basic resources to inviting in foreigners was viewed as an unpardonable breach of faith. The UCRI's congressmen were so dismayed that it took more than a month, and a great deal of arm-twisting from the Casa Rosada, to get the bill passed. The UCRP excoriated Frondizi as a renegade from the traditional nationalism of Radicalism and the Peronist oilworkers' union called a strike to protest this "surrender to imperialism." The strikers soon became violent, forcing Frondizi to decree a state of siege and send in troops to restore order in the oil fields.

The Frondizi-Frigerio neoliberal scheme was, as Mallon and Sourrouille observed, an "all or nothing strategy" that required a constant forward motion to attain success. "All desireable investment programs could be financed rapidly and simultaneously with a massive inflow of foreign investment, which would also take care of the balance of payments constraint." But if at any time the confidence of foreign investors was shaken, resulting in a slowdown in the inflow of new capital, the entire strategy might collapse. Even a relatively minor problem, if handled improperly, could blow up into a political crisis that might bring disaster.[7]

Foreign confidence in Argentina could be charted by the rise and fall of exchange reserves held by the Central Bank because, exports being stagnant, their fluctuations reflected chiefly the behavior of overseas investors and lenders. When Frondizi first took office, there was $179.1 million in the Central Bank, as against $358.5 million in immediate claims, which is to say that the country was bankrupt. Things did not improve much during Frondizi's first year of office, even with the IMF stabilization plan and the oil agreements. In June 1959, when Álvaro Alsogaray took over as econom-

ics minister, the level of reserves was just over $100 million. Also-
garay, who was more of a classical liberal than a neoliberal, inspired
more confidence among foreign bankers and businessmen. His top
priorities were balancing the budget and stabilizing the currency
rather than building steel mills or locating power plants in remote
districts—projects whose justification was more political than economic. By the end of 1959 Alsogaray managed to quadruple the
Central Bank's reserves to $396.5 million. Even after current press-
ing debts were paid, there was still $4.3 million left.[8]

Argentina's reserves continued to grow under Alsogaray. In June
1960, when he had been in office for a year, they stood at $702.9
million, and at the end of March 1961 they hit a peak of $749.6
million. That was his last full month in office, because Frondizi
dismissed him in April. Although Alsogaray was replaced by the
equally orthodox Roberto Alemann, his prestige was so high in the
international business community that his departure was viewed
with dismay. Moreover, Alemann was not allowed by Frondizi to
pick his own secretaries of industry, commerce, and agriculture as
Alsogaray had. In the months that followed, rumors spread that Alemann was feuding with these nominal subordinates as well as with
other cabinet ministers who did not share his liberal convictions.
All of this was taken as evidence that Frondizi's reforming zeal was
flagging. His abandonment of the railroad reorganization scheme
in December 1961, followed soon after by the resignations of Alemann and the transportation secretary, Arturo Acevedo, killed off
any remaining hopes the business community might have had for
his administration. Money was being withdrawn from the country.
Already, by June 1961, the Central Bank's exchange reserves had
slipped to $650.8 million. By the end of December they were down
to $501.9 million: a loss of $247.7 million in nine months.

Genuine panic began to spread as the March 1962 congressional
and gubernatorial elections approached and it appeared that Frondizi would let the Peronists run candidates. The Peronist victories,
Frondizi's ouster, and the repeated clashes of military factions for
control of Guido's government combined to produce a massive
withdrawal of capital from the country. By the end of 1962, gross
exchange reserves were down to $195.8 million, with pressing debts
amounting to $360.1 million. Almost $500 million of capital had
been lost in a year and a half, leaving Argentina about where it had
been at the start of Frondizi's administration.

Those were only the official figures on capital withdrawal, however. Much more was smuggled out of the country by frightened

Argentines looking for safer havens for their savings. Unofficial estimates of capital flight ran as high as $2.5 billion. The effects were catastrophic. Starved for cash and credit, many companies slashed their operations during 1962–63, throwing thousands out of work and causing the recession to snowball. Weaker firms simply went under. Bankruptcies, calculated in millions of dollars worth of liabilities, rose from $22.3 million in 1960 to $33.5 million in 1961 before soaring to $115.6 million in 1962. Caught in the grip of its worst economic crisis since 1929, the country's economy contracted by just over 5 percent.[9] The neoliberal strategy was revealed as a failure. Its forward motion had stalled, and once the inflow of capital stopped, the fragility of the whole scheme became clear.

## Illia and the Shift Back to Nationalism

By 1963 there was growing concern about overdependence on foreign capital. Liberals might argue that it introduced new technology, created jobs, trained managerial staff, paid taxes, bought local products, and contributed to import substitution; but nationalists insisted that subsidiaries of multinational corporations too often bought up local companies and that their capital-intensive methods created many fewer jobs than the liberals claimed. In addition to denationalizing the economy, foreigners were decapitalizing it because the superprofits they sent back home often exceeded the amount of their investment.

Subsidiaries were often restricted in their operations by parent companies in such a way, the nationalists claimed, as to stunt Argentina's development. The contracts that founded them often contained clauses known as drawbacks that required the subsidiaries to buy equipment and materials from the parent company, or from other subsidiaries in the system, even if the prices charged were higher than could be obtained elsewhere. Drawbacks were often a way of evading local restrictions on profit remittances and also a way of lowering a company's tax liability because net profits were reduced. Another type of drawback forbade subsidiaries to engage in their own research, thus forcing them to depend on the parent company. This, the nationalists insisted, would keep Argentina in perpetual technological dependence. Still another kind of drawback would allow the subsidiary to produce only for the local market, never for export, which nationalists claimed was an invasion of Argentina's sovereignty.

On the issue of job creation, a study by Juan Sourrouille showed that foreign companies were both capital-intensive and large-scale employers. In 1963 they were only one-half of 1 percent of all industrial enterprises (666 out of 142,995), yet they employed a disproportionate 12 percent of the industrial labor force. Nor was this because the foreign companies were all giants. Contrary to their public image, the majority—343 firms—employed between 51 and 500 people, while another 217 firms employed between 6 and 50. Even so, they were larger than the average local industrial enterprise, which still had fewer than 5 employees. More importantly, foreign companies were almost always twice as productive as Argentine ones of the same size, except for the very largest private local firms.[10]

Even productivity was open to criticism, however, as nationalists accused the foreigners of buying up the best workers and managers. It was true that foreign companies paid almost double the wages that local employers offered, but that was the way to get productivity—which is what Argentina needed. Higher wages didn't necessarily buy good will, either. Labor unions always made the heaviest demands on foreign companies, on the assumption that they could better afford to pay.[11] Even so, it was profitable to do business in Argentina in the 1960s. The average American company earned about 12 percent a year, with industrial firms doing a little better and commercial firms just a little worse. Naturally, subsidiaries of multinationals had to send home a portion of this, in addition to royalty payments for the use of patents and franchises. Nationalists accused foreign capitalists of taking more money out of Argentina than they were putting in, especially when drawbacks were included. Although defenders of foreign investment insisted that the savings earned through import substitution more than compensated for those remittances, the popular conviction spread that somehow Argentina was being exploited.

Arturo Illia exploited this mood during his 1963 presidential campaign at the head of the UCRP ticket. He promised, if elected, to cancel the foreign oil agreements and break off negotiations with the IMF saying that he would brook no interference by foreigners in Argentina's affairs. Once in office, Illia was true to his promises. The austerity plan which Frondizi had worked out with the IMF was abandoned. Government spending rose, pensions and other social insurance benefits increased, and real industrial wages went up. The oil contracts were annulled by presidential decree on 13 November 1963, although the foreign companies would be permitted to drill and refine pending a settlement of their claims for compensation.

The oil companies' claims arose out of the original terms of the contracts, which provided for compensation in the event that the government terminated the agreement before the time stated. Taken together, those claims amounted to $270 million. Illia had no intention of paying that sum, however; so to forestall the foreign companies the government began a countersuit for damages, charging them with negligence, bribery, "irrational exploitation" of the oil fields, tax evasion, and a host of other irregularities. Not surprisingly, the companies rejected these charges. The only Argentine company in the consortium, Astra, soon buckled under the pressure, however, and admitted that the government *might* have a case against it for faulty engineering practices. This signed admission, which was the price the government demanded for a settlement, resulted in Astra's being reimbursed not in cash but in four-year promissory notes bearing 6.5 percent interest—at a time when inflation was over 20 percent.[12]

The foreign companies preferred to hold out and count on the government's changing its mind as it became aware of the practical problems it would face in getting enough oil for Argentina's needs. Up to August 1964, when the YPF took over their installations, the foreign companies continued to raise their output of oil and gas, although the drilling of new wells dropped sharply. After that, negotiations dragged on, with each side becoming more rigid. The Argentine government had the advantage of territorial sovereignty and the comfortable knowledge that its appointed judges would almost certainly decide the litigation in its favor. The companies, for their part, were sure that without their capital and expertise Argentina would soon face another oil shortage and balance of payments crisis. They were soon proven right. Under YPF's management, oil production dropped by 320,000 cubic meters in 1965, while imports rose from 2.2 million to 5.1 million cubic meters, at a cost of $43 million.[13] After Illia was overthrown in June 1966, the Ongania regime dropped all charges against the foreign companies and agreed to compensate them with ten-year promissory notes.

The costs of nationalism may be illustrated by the sequel to this story. Shortly after taking office, Ongania set up a government commission to negotiate with the foreign oil companies for their return to Argentina. In June 1967 a new series of contracts again permitted them to enter as concessionaires of YPF for exploring for, drilling for, refining, and distributing oil. The companies would own all they produced but would not be allowed to export any until local demand was satisfied. In addition, they would turn back 55 percent of their net profits to the government as taxes and royalties. Finally, they could not locate their service stations near any of those owned by YPF. Despite those restrictions, foreign companies went immediately into high production and boosted the output of oil from only 16.7 million cubic meters in 1966 to 22.8 by 1970. In that same period, imports fell from 5.4 million cubic meters to 3.2 million. In 1968, a typical year under Ongania, the companies produced $62 million worth of oil (calculated at world market prices), which they sold to YPF for $28 million, yielding a savings to Argentina of $34 million. Of the $28 million earned by the foreign companies, 55 percent or about $15 million went to the government in taxes and royalties. Thus, even if all the remaining $13 million was remitted abroad, the oil companies contributed $47 million to the Argentine economy that year, aside from wages paid and local purchases.[14]

Such were the apparent trade-offs in dealing with foreign capital: economic sovereignty versus economic productivity. But was that really the choice? Liberals argued that a country which sacrificed economic productivity to nationalism would only find itself further behind, and more dependent upon, the advanced industrial powers. The only rights secured by economic sovereignty, they insisted, were the rights to be poor and inefficient.

## Profits, Debts, Denationalization, and Disinvestment

The debate about foreign capital did not take place in a vacuum. Throughout the 1960s there were several examples of foreign capital's methods and their impact on the local economy that provided ammunition for either side. In this section we will consider whether foreign investments and loans really made positive contributions to Argentina's development. We will also discuss whether foreign takeovers of local companies were good or bad for the Argentine economy. Finally, we will describe the celebrated Swift-Deltec bankruptcy case, which occurred in 1969, as a way of reviewing the many angles of the foreign investment question, including the capacity of local governments to regulate effectively the business practices of multinational corporations.

### Profits and Debts

Did foreign capital get more out of Argentina than it put in? The best data available concerning the profitability of foreign business deals with American companies, whose total capital was about 60 percent of the approximately $3 billion of direct foreign investment in 1972. Between 1958 and 1972, American capital raised its level of investment from $740 million to just over $1.8 billion. At the same time, American companies realized profits totaling in excess of $1.28 billion; obviously they did well in Argentina. Moreover, of those profits, some $849 million, or just about two-thirds, was sent out of the country, and only $433 million was reinvested. Coming at a time of sluggish exports and unfavorable trade balances, this sizable repatriation of profits constituted a heavy burden on Argentina's exchange reserves and balance of payments. It was one more reason why Argentina was forced to borrow from abroad.[15]

Considering that profit remittances amounted to about 80 percent of the total American inflow, one might join with the nationalists in wondering whether it really was worthwhile trying to attract foreign investment. Table 13.4 suggests that perhaps it was, but only if a favorable investment climate was maintained.

Foreign investment and reinvestment were heaviest between 1959 and 1961, when Alsogaray was heading Frondizi's economic team. That ended in 1962, and during 1963 there was even a net disinvestment. Foreign capital inflows picked up again after democracy was restored. Despite Illia's treatment of the oil companies and his defiance of international bankers, 1964 and 1965 saw a steady increase in new investment and reinvested profits. By contrast, Ongania was never able to attract long-term foreign capital. Although new investment picked up, the portion of profits being remitted was always very high. Either the new money coming in was of a speculative nature, or else it failed to compensate for a large and steady flight of previously invested capital The same was true of the Lanusse years. Whatever the reason behind those trends, they undercut the military's claim that it could attract business.

Argentina's inability to attract and keep sizable direct investments from abroad meant that it had to fuel its economy with foreign loans. That was a second-best strategy which rested on the assumption that it would be only a temporary expedient—that once heavy industry was built and growth became steady Argentina would easily repay its debts. Unfortunately, the economy stagnated and further borrowing became necessary. The public foreign debt rose from around $1.6 billion under Frondizi to just over $2.4 billion under Illia. Annual payments on the debt became more burdensome too, rising from $372.5 million in 1961 to $526.2 million in 1965, or from 30 percent to 40 percent of export receipts. Ongania managed

Table 13.4 Investment and Profit of U.S. Companies, 1958–1972
(in millions of dollars)

| Era/Year | New Investment | Profits Total | Reinvested | Percent Reinvested | Remitted | Percent Remitted | Net[a] |
|---|---|---|---|---|---|---|---|
| *Frondizi* | | | | | | | |
| 1958 | 3 | 12 | 1 | 8.3 | 11 | 91.7 | −7 |
| 1959 | 36 | 24 | 14 | 58.3 | 10 | 41.7 | 40 |
| 1960 | 106 | 46 | 36 | 78.3 | 10 | 21.7 | 132 |
| 1961 | 188 | 106 | 64 | 60.4 | 42 | 39.6 | 210 |
| 1962 | 139 | 73 | 32 | 43.8 | 41 | 56.2 | 130 |
| Subtotal | 472 | 261 | 147 | 56.3 | 114 | 43.7 | 505 |
| *Illia* | | | | | | | |
| 1963 | 30 | 52 | −3 | −5.8 | 55 | 105.8 | −28 |
| 1964 | 53 | 91 | 29 | 31.9 | 62 | 68.1 | 20 |
| 1965 | 110 | 133 | 87 | 65.4 | 46 | 34.6 | 151 |
| 1966 | 43 | 133 | 65 | 48.9 | 68 | 51.1 | 40 |
| Subtotal | 236 | 409 | 178 | 43.5 | 231 | 56.5 | 183 |
| *Ongania* | | | | | | | |
| 1967 | 47 | 80 | −3 | −3.8 | 83 | 103.8 | −39 |
| 1968 | 74 | 126 | 35 | 27.8 | 91 | 72.2 | 18 |
| 1969 | 90 | 140 | 30 | 21.4 | 110 | 78.6 | 10 |
| 1970 | 35 | 105 | 15 | 14.3 | 90 | 85.7 | −40 |
| Subtotal | 246 | 451 | 77 | 17.1 | 374 | 82.9 | −51 |
| *Lanusse* | | | | | | | |
| 1971 | 72 | 80 | 18 | 22.5 | 62 | 77.5 | 28 |
| 1972 | 38 | 81 | 13 | 16.0 | 68 | 84.0 | −17 |
| Subtotal | 110 | 161 | 31 | 19.3 | 130 | 80.7 | 11 |

Source: Juan V. Sourrouille, *Impact of Transnational Enterprises on Employment and Income: The Case of Argentina* (Geneva: International Labor Office, 1976), p. 60.
[a] New investment plus reinvested profits, minus remitted profits.

to keep the public foreign debt from rising, but failed to check private foreign indebtedness, which climbed from $519 million in 1962 to $800 million in 1966 and $2.3 billion by 1970. Thus, the future of many of Argentina's leading industrial and commercial firms was at risk. Under Levingston and Lanusse, both private and public debt rose rapidly, reaching $2.7 billion for the private sector at the end of 1972 and $3.2 billion for the public sector. Meanwhile, bankers were growing nervous about Argentina's prospects; so from 1970 it became almost impossible to get long-term loans.[16]

Where were the loans going? According to Central Bank figures

for the end of 1972, of the $3.2 billion owed by the public sector
$1.35 billion, or 42 percent, belonged to the chronically loss-produc-
ing state enterprises. The next largest chunk, $1.22 billion, or 38
percent, was owed by the national government's central administration and by related agencies such as the meat and grain boards.
Government banks owed another $570 million, or 18 percent, while
provincial and local governments accounted for a relatively insig-
nificant $73 million. In the private sector, exactly half of the $2.7
billion owed was due foreign banks. Slightly less than a billion dollars (about 37 percent) was owed to foreign suppliers who had
shipped goods on credit. (The Central Bank's figures did not indicate
whether, or to what extent, such credit involved drawbacks from
parent multinationals to their subsidiaries, but Argentine nationalists were entitled to their suspicions.) Finally, some $348.7 million
was owed in royalties, profits, and dividends to foreign parent companies and patent-holders.[17] About two-thirds of the total foreign
debt was owed to American creditors and the remainder to Europeans or international banks. Most of it had to be repaid in dollars and
at variable interest rates. Debt payments in 1972 consumed more
than a third of Argentina's export earnings.

The country was caught in a painful dilemma. In order to repay
its loans it had to maintain a favorable trade balance, which was not
easy to do at a time when both the United States and the European
Common Market were raising tariff barriers. Moreover, it was no
longer easy to make exports more attractive by devaluing the currency, as the IMF urged, because that would make it more expensive
to convert pesos into dollars to repay the debt. Given the high level
of indebtedness of many local companies, a sharp devaluation might
push them into bankruptcy. Cutting back on imports was not an
acceptable method of achieving a favorable trade balance either,
because without new machinery to replace that which was obsolete
or worn out, production would fall, unemployment would grow, and
Argentina would be further behind in its technology. The only way
to avoid that was to attract more foreign investment, but with the
Peronists preparing to return to power there was little prospect of
that.

Looking back over the period since Perón's fall, one cannot conclude that foreign capital helped Argentina very much. Foreign capitalists were not necessarily at fault, however, because Argentina
had seldom provided them with an attractive investment climate.
While foreign involvement in certain areas like oil might have
made sense, a development strategy predicated on such heavy reli-

ance upon outsiders was flawed in its basic concept. Ultimately, for a country to achieve success as a capitalist industrial power, it must develop a domestic entrepreneurial class capable of exercising economic leadership. As Ezequiel Martínez Estrada once put it: "The weight of machinery, like the weight of civilization, should find solid support in society; no machine settles on earth but rather on the shoulders of a state of civilization. The society that incorporates the machine without having achieved a mechanical structure, succumbs under the inert weight or converts it into scrap iron. The nation that adopts the latest forms of progress and of culture, skipping the transitional stages, regresses to the primordial forms even faster than it left them."[18]

## Denationalization

Early in the century, foreign companies located in Argentina to take advantage of low wages and cheap raw materials so as to be competitive in world markets. As the economy grew and Argentines became more prosperous, a domestic market that was also attractive to foreign companies began to develop. But since local industries were protected from outside competition by tariffs, quotas, and exchange controls, it became necessary to locate inside Argentina in order to get access to that market. Then, in the 1960s, the creation of the Latin American Free Trade Area (LAFTA) provided foreign companies with another inducement to set up in Argentina. By doing so, they could participate in Argentina's growing export trade in industrial goods to other LAFTA members. Of the twenty leading exporters of Argentine industrial products in 1972, seventeen were foreign subsidiaries.[19]

The arrival of foreign firms in the 1960s was viewed by many as a mixed blessing. Suppliers and retailers linked to the foreign producers could make great profits, but only by orienting their procedures to conform to the foreigners' demands for punctuality, standardization, and better quality control. On the positive side, foreign investors could be seen as the spearhead of the modernization drive; but on the negative side they drew much of the local economy into the web of multinational influences.

Nationalist critics were especially bothered by the direct takeover of local firms by foreign companies. Between 1962 and 1968, for example, 39 major local businesses were bought up by overseas investors: 9 banks, 4 cigarette manufacturers, 1 automobile plant, 14 metallurgical factories producing various automotive parts and accessories, 3 chemical plants, 1 machine building factory, 1 paper mill, 2 appliance firms, 1 producer of synthetic fibers, 1 manufacturer of veterinary products, 1 ceramics company, and 1 wholesale distributor. Slightly more than half of the purchasers were Americans, who concentrated mainly on the cigarette and auto parts industries; but French, Spanish, Dutch, German, and Swiss capital also was involved in this wave of denationalization. Probably the single biggest sale was the automobile plant, Industrias Kaiser Argentina (IKA), to the French firm of Renault.[20]

Foreign investors saw many advantages in buying up Argentine businesses. They could acquire plants, equipment, valuable contacts, and established markets more cheaply than they could if they started from scratch. They also could eliminate part of the competition and grab a larger share of the market. Local companies often were starved for capital and submitted to gradual takeovers by foreign firms. Often the process began with the foreign company becoming a minority shareholder in return for a loan. If the loan could not be repaid, more shares were transferred. Eventually, if the company failed to achieve a turnaround, the foreign investors would assume its management. The UIA blamed the process on "the profound deterioration in the economic and financial structure of Argentine businesses," which in turn was caused by "the prolonged process of endemic inflation that our economy is experiencing."[21]

The cigarette industry is a case in point. Even though Argentines are heavy smokers, the industry was deeply troubled throughout the 1960s. Manufacturers blamed the government, whose tariffs on imported equipment raised production costs and whose taxes on cigarette sales (amounting to 66 percent ad valorem) boosted the final price to the consumer to the point where it was worthwhile to smuggle foreign cigarettes into the country and sell them on the black market. That cut so deeply into legitimate sales that in order to survive, the five leading local companies—Imparciales, Nobleza, Massalin & Celasco, Particulares, and Piccardo—made a gentlemen's agreement to limit their competition: for example, by not introducing filter-tipped cigarettes they avoided a sales war. Another gentlemen's agreement was to avoid licensing agreements with foreign manufacturers.[22]

All such attempts to lock up the local market failed in the face of growing competition from the black market, which was being supplied by an estimated 10–15 million packs a day smuggled over the Bolivian and Paraguayan borders. First the filter-tip agreement was violated in 1963; then in 1966 the financially distressed Piccardo

Company announced that it had signed a licensing agreement with the American firm of Ligget & Myers to produce L&M cigarettes, one of the more popular brands on the black market. Nobleza, which already was owned by the British American Tobacco Company, immediately countered by introducing Viceroy cigarettes to Argentina and by signing licensing agreements with the American Tobacco Company to manufacture Pall Malls and Lucky Strikes.

With a new sales war on, the other local cigarette manufacturers hurried to protect themselves. Massalin & Celasco sought an agreement with Philip Morris to produce their name brand, as well as Benson & Hedges. In this case, however, the American company demanded a majority interest in the local firm, citing the need for quality control. Imparciales, which also was shopping around for an American ally, ran into the same sort of demand. It finally made a somewhat better deal with the German company, Reemtsma Cigaretten Fabriken, which insisted upon only 49 percent of its stock, in return for which Imparciales would produce a popular European brand of cigarette called Reval. Those deals left only two Argentine cigarette companies free of foreign control: Piccardo, which had struck an initially favorable deal, and Particulares, which remained independent, hoping to keep its share of the market as the only producer of Argentina's traditional dark-tobacco cigarettes. By 1968 even Piccardo was forced to transfer effective ownership to Ligget & Myers in return for another infusion of capital.

All of this was advantageous for the foreign companies, which hitherto had been kept from exporting to Argentina. From the standpoint of the local firms, Manuel Pando, the president of Imparciales, insisted that selling a controlling interest to foreigners was preferable to a licensing agreement because the latter usually contained escape clauses that allowed patent- and trademark-holders to break their contracts at short notice. That could leave a local manufacturer that had become dependent on the sale of those brands in an untenable position, he said. It was much better to involve the foreigners in the company's future by selling them stock.

A few years later, however, it was not so clear that the foreign companies had brought such obvious advantages. It is true that Particulares, the only independent company, had lost some ground in the market, but it was no worse off financially than its competitors that spent large sums in mass advertising and were making large royalty payments to their foreign owners. Indeed, all cigarette manufacturers were suffering because the government continued to raise excise taxes and, therefore, smuggling continued to be profitable. During the decade that followed, all five companies were forced to merge for their survival. In 1978 Piccardo and Nobleza laid aside their old rivalry and became one company; and in the following year the other three companies merged as well, bringing the denationalization process to its culmination.

### Increased Regulation of Foreign Capital

Official attitudes toward foreign capital gradually became less friendly after Frondizi fell, and regulations governing its entry were made more restrictive. All projects for new investment and for expanding existing operations had to wend their way through a bureaucratic labyrinth that might take as long as two years to traverse. During that time a project would be reviewed by more than a hundred minor and middle-level functionaries before it was passed up to the cabinet level. It could be jeopardized at any time by an objection from some government agency.

A typical project would enter the labyrinth with the National Agency for Industrial Promotion, where it would first be studied by the agency's division of procedures (trámites). This division would set up an agenda for further deliberations before sending the project to the legal division, which would examine the project to see that it conformed to existing laws. If the project required imported machinery or equipment, the next step would be to send it to the advisory commission on capital goods (comisión asesora de bienes de capital) to make certain that its requirements could not be satisfied with locally made machinery. After that the project would go to the advisory commission on imports (comisión asesora de importaciones), which would evaluate the project's probable impact on the balance of payments and exchange reserves. If it survived these hurdles, it would then be sent to the agency for industry (dirección de industrias) which would examine it from the standpoint of its likely influence on existing industries, as well as upon the domestic market as a whole. An important part of this stage of review would be the opinion of the department of metallurgical industries, which would have reported earlier to the advisory commission on capital goods about whether some of the project's equipment needs could be met by local firms.[23]

If the project cleared all those obstacles, the next stage would involve its financing. Both the Industrial Credit Bank and the Central Bank would study how the funding was to be arranged. That would require lengthy discussions between those banking officials and the company's management. Once those details were ironed out, the project would be passed along to the under secretary of industry, who screened projects for the secretary of industry. The under secretary would solicit the opinions of CONADE and Fabricaciones Militares, both of which were concerned about how any new industry, or the expansion of an existing one, would affect the economy in general. Their views were likely to be nationalistic and biased against foreign capital; thus, their objections were likely to be the most serious. They could not veto a project outright, but their reports constituted part of the file that was sent on to the secretary of industry. If their opinions were negative, a battle probably was in store at the cabinet level.

In addition to these departments, the under secretary would want to consult many other officials. The many tax angles of foreign investment would have to be reviewed by the national director of tax policy, the DGI, the director of imports and tariffs, and the treasury. Also, once a location for the project had been decided, it was a good idea to get the opinions of the provincial governor and the municipal officials.

Finally, the project was ready for the secretary of industry's perusal. Even at that level, it was necessary to involve other powerful political figures: the secretary of finance, the secretary of labor, the secretary of energy, and in some cases the secretary of public health. Only then would the plan be put before the minister of economics. If he signed the authorization decree, its clearance was practically assured—but not necessarily so. The president of the republic had to sign it too, and before he did it was sent to the Technical Secretariat to the Presidency, where a special high-level staff reviewed it again in every aspect. That gave the project's enemies one last chance to kill or delay it. Sometimes they could make a successful goal-line stand, as we shall see later in the case of a Dow Chemical Company project.

In light of all this, it is hardly surprising that relatively little foreign capital was attracted to Argentina, even when governments like Ongania's encouraged it. Besides, the red tape reflected a distrust and hostility toward foreign capital that pervaded all social classes. For example, there was the success that Fabricaciones Militares and SOMISA had in stopping the entry of foreign capital into the steel industry, on the grounds that it was a sensitive area for national defense. Because of their pressure, Ongania stopped Acindar from completing an agreement it had made with the World Bank and U.S. Steel to sell the latter a minority interest in return for money to expand its production. He issued a decree requiring private companies to get Fabricaciones Militares' permission before selling any shares to foreigners or entering into any other contracts with them. Fabricaciones Militares promptly ordered Acindar to stop buying iron ore from the Orinoco Mining Company, a U.S. Steel subsidiary, because such an arrangement made the local steel industry too dependent on foreign suppliers.[24]

Nationalist pressure also prevented Dow Chemical from building a large ethylene plant at Bahia Blanca. The proposal, made in 1966, provoked fierce resistance from four local chemical companies who argued that the tremendous capacity of Dow's plant would allow Dow to flood the market and drive them out of business. Ongania's government split over the issue. The industry secretary, Mario Galimberti, favored Dow on the grounds that one really modern chemical plant that could meet all of Argentina's needs was worth more than four small, antiquated plants that could not. On the other hand, the energy secretary, Luís Gotelli, backed the local companies and refused to grant Dow a special low price on gas from Patagonia, which was needed to generate the plant's electricity. Five years later Ongania was out of power and the government was still debating Dow's project, which by now had gotten hopelessly lost in the bureaucratic maze. Aldo Ferrer, the nationalist economics minister, was hostile to it, and President Lanusse was seeking a rapprochement with the Peronists and therefore wanted to avoid any appearance of courting foreign capital. In April 1971 an exasperated Dow finally withdrew its offer. A large chemical complex was finally built at Bahia Blanca, with mostly local financing; but it would be another ten years before the private local companies, YPF, Gas del Estado, and Fabricaciones Militares could raise the capital.[25]

Under Lanusse, further restrictions were placed on all direct foreign investments. Foreigners could acquire only nonvoting stock in Argentine companies; their access to local banks was limited; and 85 percent of all managerial and technical personnel had to be Argentine. By themselves, such measures were not very onerous; indeed, they made sense if the object of attracting foreign capital was to increase the amount of capital and technical expertise available locally. But the spirit with which such legislation was passed reflected a growing hostility. In response, potential investors found more attractive places in which to do business while many established foreign companies began to look around for ways of getting their capital out of the country.

*Disinvestment: The Case of Swift-Deltec*

The growing tension between foreign businessmen and economic nationalists led to acts of bad faith on both sides. Nationalist governments hesitated to take the extreme step of outright expropriation, but they sought popularity by sniping at the foreign companies, and sometimes saddled them with requirements that were hardly distinguishable from shakedowns. The foreigners' ultimate weapon was to withdraw their capital from Argentina: no easy task in the case of manufacturers who had sunk large sums in plant and equipment. The Swift-Deltec bankruptcy case, which caught the public's attention in 1970, is one example of how a foreign company went outside the law to evade restrictions on the repatriation of its capital.

On 18 December 1970 Compañía Swift de La Plata, Inc., a foreign meatpacking firm that had operated in Argentina since 1907, was taken to court for failing to pay its debts. Although it was one of country's ten largest enterprises in terms of sales, its creditors numbered over 2,500, and their claims came to some $43 million. Most of them were ranchers who had not been reimbursed for cattle they had sent to the packinghouse. Others were bankers who had lent money. Swift owed local bankers around $10 million and foreign bankers another $8 million. A particularly curious group of creditors were companies that belonged, like Swift, to a multinational conglomerate called Deltec International. These sister companies presented claims for $14 million which they said was owed to them for various goods and services.[26]

Deltec International had bought up Swift two years before, from International Packers, Ltd., another multinational corporation which also owned the Armour and La Blanca packinghouses. Swift thus became part of an empire that spread across North America, South America, Western Europe, and Oceania, with headquarters in the Bahamas. Deltec International's specialty was agricultural products, but it also owned banks, insurance companies, and shipping lines. Its operations were organized in a logical, hierarchical fashion. Radiating out from its central office were regional headquarters for each of the continents, and beneath those were national headquarters in each country where it had investments. Each national headquarters, in turn, became a holding company controlling several firms. For example, Deltec's South American operations were handled by Deltec Panamericana, which controlled holding companies in Argentina, Peru, Venezuela, and other countries. Its holding company in Argentina was called Argentinaría, under which were Swift, Provita (an animal food company), La Esperanza (a large sugar mill and distillery in Jujuy), a navigation company on the upper Paraná River, various *estancias*, the streetcar company in Tucumán, some investment companies, and the Armour and La Blanca packinghouses.[27]

Swift fought the bankruptcy proceedings, arguing that it only needed a little more time to reorganize itself in order to pay its debts. Nevertheless, in November 1971 the court declared Swift bankrupt. Moreover, it took the additional step of deciding that if Swift was unable to pay its creditors they could collect from Argentinaría. The holding company appealed, claiming that it was not responsible for Swift's debts. The appeals court, while affirming the bankruptcy decision, upheld Argentinaría on the matter of liability for Swift's debts. From there, both sides appealed to the Supreme Court. In the meantime, national sentiment was aroused when the lower court judge, Salvador M. Lozada, announced that during the trial he had been asked by the minister of justice to render a verdict favorable to Swift.

The Swift-Deltec case became notorious in Argentina, and is useful for our purposes, because it touched on so many issues surrounding the whole question of foreign investment in Argentina: did it enrich the country or deplete it? to what extent was nationalist hostility responsible for foreign business failures? did foreigners exert too much influence over local officials? and how much collusion existed between foreign subsidiaries and the parent companies to defraud the host country?

### Background: Why Swift Went Bankrupt

Swift claimed that it was the victim of unfair government policies as well as conspiracies by its suppliers to force up cattle prices at a time when the world market for meat was unsettled and the local packinghouses were involved in expensive reorganization schemes. Local creditors responded by accusing Deltec International of deliberately decapitalizing Swift because Deltec had decided to close down its Argentine operations and wanted to evade the laws restricting the repatriation of capital.

Swift's argument was supported by the fact that ever since the Perón era the meatpacking industry had been subjected to everincreasing government controls. Most of those were aimed at limiting exports so as to insure an adequate supply of meat for domestic consumption. Whereas in the 1930s about 40 percent of all beef slaughtered was destined for export, only 20 percent was in the 1960s. That might not have been a problem if Argentina's cattle herds had increased, but they had not. A combination of price controls, taxes on cattle, and labor laws had so discouraged the ranchers that the number of head of cattle in the 1960s (about 44 million) was about what it had been twenty years before. That meant a real decline in the volume of exports as well as a real fall in profits. Added to this were taxes on wholesale and retail sales, taxes on exports (the hated retentions), and various impositions like Illia's 1964 decree ordering the packinghouses to contribute 15 percent of their output, at cost, to the National Meat Board in order to stave off a domestic meat shortage.[28]

Swift was right, too, when it said that the whole meat industry was undergoing a thorough reorganization. Under Perón and Aramburu, the government eased the financial burden of high wages and controls by offering subsidies in the form of soft loans. Alsogaray lifted both the controls and subsidies, however, only to have Illia reimpose the former without restoring the latter. Without subsidies, the meatpackers were forced to modernize their plants in order to compete in world trade, but in trying to do so they ran into fierce resistance from the labor unions, who saw their jobs threatened. All too frequently, especially under Illia, the government sought to court popularity by siding with the workers. In 1961 the Wilson Meatpacking Company shut down its operations after 48 years in Argentina, sapped and disheartened by a particularly violent strike which broke out when it tried to modernize its machinery. Other companies soldiered on, but were faced with falling export receipts and rising costs. Swift lost 847 million pesos (about $4 million) between 1961 and 1965; Armour lost over 450 million; Frigorífico Anglo lost 500 million; and state-controlled CAP ran up losses amounting to 1.7 billion. (In CAP's case, however, the losses were covered from the government's treasury.)

In the meantime, the established packinghouses were faced with a new challenge that eventually proved to be the final blow. A new breed of middle-sized regional packinghouses (frigoríficos regionales) had sprung up in the interior and were cutting into both the foreign and domestic trade of the big meatpackers. They were able to do this because they were nearer the source of supply. In the past, when the export trade was most lucrative, it had been an advantage to locate close to the port of Buenos Aires; now, when the domestic market was more important, these regional packinghouses, located near both the supply and the market, could outbid the exporters because they avoided high transportation costs and could eliminate many middlemen. Eventually they even were able to invade the export trade by pooling their resources and hiring experts to find markets and promote their sales. Since most of those sales were of canned or frozen beef, it didn't matter where they were located. Furthermore, since many of these regional packinghouses were new, they could start their operations with modern canning and refrigeration equipment. By contrast, the older packinghouses near the port would have to scrap their antiquated equipment and redesign their buildings in order to keep up.

What might have been done can be illustrated by an Argentine firm, Frigoríficos Argentinos, S.A. (FASA), which took over the old Wilson plant and completely renovated it. Whereas Wilson had employed 2,400 workers who cut up animal carcasses with knives, the new plant installed pneumatic vibrating machines and doubled production while cutting the labor force to only 600. It was able to make those changes, however, only because the old plant had gone out of business and dismissed its workers. The other big meatpackers could not do that; so one by one they slid into bankruptcy. La Blanca stopped operating in 1964, and Armour was ready to close when Deltec bought it in 1968.

Swift was still struggling to stay in business when, late in 1967, another blow fell. Great Britain, Argentina's principal customer, claimed that recent meat shipments were tainted by hoof-and-mouth disease and placed a ban on further imports. The embargo was extended throughout 1968, lifted temporarily at the beginning of 1969, and then brought down again in April. In this second ban Britain was joined by the United States, Spain, Italy, and the Netherlands. Unlike the previous one, however, it applied only to the regional packinghouses. That allowed Swift to monopolize export sales, but it brought cries of "foul" and "conspiracy" from Argentine nationalists who saw this as an international plot.[29]

As it turned out, Swift was unable to take much advantage of its favored position because in the meantime it had become embroiled in a battle with its suppliers, the *estancieros*. The latter were complaining about the low prices they were getting. Ordinarily the cattlemen were at a disadvantage in dealing with the packinghouses because there were more sellers of cattle than there were buyers, but in October 1970 the SRA, CRA, and other ranchers' organizations met in Rosario and agreed to concert their actions. They began withholding cattle from the market in order to drive up the prices. The strategy worked: at the Liniers Market the price for beef on the hoof rose from 115 to 168 pesos per kilogram.[30] Swift insisted that it could make no profit if cattle prices went over 120 pesos, and to counter the ranchers it refused to buy any of the 9,000 animals that appeared for sale. Only CAP bought any. Swift next turned to the government and demanded that it set a maximum price, warning that unless the ranchers sent more cattle to market the company would have to close its plants. To underline this argument, the company laid off 25,000 workers.

The dispute between the ranchers and Swift became a debate over figures. The former pointed out that a kilo of prime beef cost only 500 pesos, wholesale, in the port of Buenos Aires, compared with 1,500 in New York, 1,930 in Amsterdam, 1,390 in Genoa, and 2,312 in Hamburg. If beef was so cheap in Argentina, why couldn't Swift pay more to its suppliers? Swift responded by claiming that there was much waste in what they bought. Out of a typical animal weighing 450 kilos perhaps only 175 would be export-quality beef. Thus what was paid to the supplier was only the nominal price, whereas the actual price was really much higher.

Each side enlisted powerful, prominent figures in its cause. Roberto Verrier and Júlio A. García, both cabinet members under Aramburu, were on Argentinaría's payroll. So was Adalbert Krieger Vasena, who recently had resigned from Ongania's cabinet. Col. Enrique Holmberg, Swift's president, was a cousin of Gen. Alejandro Lanusse, the army's commander in chief. The meatpackers' union was split. Its secretary, Constantino Zorrilla, sided with the ranchers and threatened to occupy Swift's plants; but Héctor Gauna, the leader of a rival faction, accused the ranchers of trying to manipulate the market. It was time, he said, to back the company and protect the workers' jobs. Weighing in on the side of the ranchers was former secretary of agriculture Tomás Joaquín de Anchorena, from one of Argentina's leading families. He accused Swift of keeping two sets of books in order to fool the public and advocated nationalizing the company. Also on the ranchers' side was Aldo Ferrer, the economics minister. Though no friend of the cattlemen, he was even more opposed to foreign capital. When the ranchers brought an antitrust suit against Swift for conspiring to lower prices on the cattle market, Ferrer backed them up. So did the federal court judge who heard the case. He arrested four top Swift executives and levied a heavy fine on the company. Although he was overruled on appeal, Swift gave in and began buying cattle, insisting all the while, however, that the prices it had to pay were spelling its ruin.[31]

It is not likely that the higher prices Swift had to pay for its cattle were what really sealed its doom. Subsequent investigations by the National Meat Board would show that during 1970 Swift was selling meat to Deltec and its other subsidiaries at much below world market prices. For example, it was selling frozen cooked meat to Deltec Panamericana for $1,800 a ton, whereas other Argentine exporters were selling the same product for $3,000 a ton—which is what Swift charged its other, non-Deltec, customers. Here was a blatant example of a subsidiary subsidizing its parent company and then claiming that it needed to lower the price it paid its suppliers because it was losing money.[32]

It is not clear just why Deltec Panamericana followed policies that inevitably drove Swift out of business. It is curious, however, that shortly after acquiring Swift in 1968 it had Swift purchase two other Deltec-owned subsidiaries, Armour and La Blanca, for a total of $41.4 million. La Blanca already had shut down, and Armour was on the verge of closing; so the only result of the purchase was that Swift acquired two bankrupt properties instead of using the money to modernize its own facilities. In the process, that large sum of money was transferred out of Argentina to Deltec Panamericana's home office. It seems, therefore, that Deltec Panamericana was playing a game by which it aimed at withdrawing as much capital as possible from Argentina. Having liquidated two of its subsidiaries, if it could now get its money out of Swift the success of its strategy would be complete.[33]

In April 1970 Swift's new president, Col. Enrique Holmberg, who had been on Deltec's payroll since retiring from the army in 1961, announced plans to "Argentinize" the company. The idea, he said, was to give Argentines an opportunity to buy control of the country's largest meatpacking firm. In the months that followed, however, there were no takers for Swift's stock. Not even the government could be induced to buy, even though Krieger Vasena was listed on the board of directors. Argentine investors were too well aware that Swift owned a lot of bankrupt packinghouses and was itself on the verge of bankruptcy. Its stock was worthless, and all they would own after Deltec pulled out was a lot of dirty, run-down buildings. Indeed, even as the "Argentinization" campaign was in progress Swift sent more than $6 million out of the country to clear unpaid "debts" to Deltec Panamericana. In short, by using drawbacks the parent company was working fast to empty Swift's coffers before its creditors started bankruptcy proceedings.[34]

## The Bankruptcy Suit

Swift's creditors formed a committee to press their claims as a group. Their suit was initiated in commercial court on 18 December 1970. It charged Swift with questionable financial dealings aimed at deliberately draining it and defrauding its creditors. In support of this charge the creditors' committee cited an investigation by the National Meat Board that showed that over 80 percent of Swift's exports in 1970 were to other Deltec companies and that the prices charged were substantially below those prevailing on the world market, as well as below those Swift charged its other customers. The National Meat Board also characterized as "incomprehensible" Swift's purchase of the Armour and La Blanca plants.

The court began its deliberations by initiating its own investigation of Swift's affairs. Its legal investigator (syndic), Anibal Olives, turned up other evidence of curious dealings with Deltec subsidiaries. For example, Swift recently had "loaned" 1.1 billion pesos to Provita, which was roughly the amount that Swift had in its treasury at the time and also rather close to the sum that it owed its creditors. In Olives's view, the action was "irresponsible" and tended to confirm the charges brought against the company. In the meantime, Swift's creditors, having discovered that Argentinaría owned 99.5 percent of Swift's stock, were now demanding that the holding company be held liable for its subsidiary's debts.[35]

Deltec Panamericana countered with an offer to bail out Swift in return for repayment in dollars. Swift would then pay its creditors over four years: 10 percent the first year and the balance spread over the remaining three years. Meanwhile, to put pressure on the government, Swift shut down its operations, throwing 17,000 people out of work. Thus, when the creditors' committee assembled on 4 October 1970 to consider Swift's offer, two busloads of packinghouse workers showed up at the meeting to plead for its acceptance. Whether their arguments were persuasive, or whether the forlorn creditors saw the offer as their only shred of hope, the committee voted overwhelmingly for it. It was, indeed, a gamble. If Deltec Panamericana were only playing a game, this strategy would give it more time to decapitalize its other Argentine companies.

Although a majority of the creditors had voted for the plan, their decision was not legally binding on the minority. Two creditors immediately challenged it, thus throwing the whole matter back into court. The holdouts claimed that the decision had been based on false information because previously Swift's representatives had been going around the countryside holding meetings with some of the principal creditors, promising that they would be paid off earlier than the others if they would give Colonel Holmberg their proxy votes at the creditors' meeting. The holdouts cited specifically the town of Lincoln, in Buenos Aires Province, where such an offer allegedly was made before an audience of 250 people.

Before deciding whether to approve the Swift rescue plan or declare the company bankrupt, Judge Salvador Lozada ordered a hearing, to be held on 15 October, on the vote-buying charges. Seven people from the Lincoln branch of the SRA volunteered to appear as witnesses, but when the day arrived none of them showed up. It was learned later that officials from Swift, and other persons not identified, had gotten in touch with them and made threats. Consequently, six of the men never left Lincoln. The seventh, Albino Fernández, president of the local SRA chapter, set out for Buenos Aires early in the morning but was stopped on the way by a gang of men who threatened to harm him and his family. He returned home "very nervous" and told the local SRA secretary, Dante Sorgentini, what had happened. With that, Sorgentini drove to the capital where he immediately contacted one of the minority creditors' lawyers, Salvador Bergel. Two days later Bergel went to Lincoln and talked with Fernández, who turned over to him the SRA's records, together with an affidavit signed by 180 members, affirming that Swift had offered them privileged terms of payment in return for their proxies. All of this was turned over to Judge Lozada, who accepted it as evidence. On 8 November he declared the agreement between Swift and the creditors' committee to be illegal. He also declared the company to be in bankruptcy and charged Argentinaría with responsibility for all of Swift's debts.[36]

Within a few hours after Judge Lozada announced his decision, President Alejandro Lanusse appointed the president of the Banco Ganadero (Cattlemen's Bank) as Swift's liquidator. Meanwhile, Swift appealed the decision. In September 1972 the court of commercial appeals upheld Judge Lozada about annulling the creditors committee's acceptance of Swift's offer, which forced Swift into bankruptcy, but the court absolved Argentinaría from any responsibility for Swift's debts on the grounds that each company in the conglomerate had a separate legal identity. The court observed that some of them never had any dealings with Swift; therefore, it would be unfair to make them pay for its debts.[37]

Swift's creditors appealed to the Supreme Court, which on 4 September 1973 reversed the appeals court and upheld Judge Lozada on every point. It affirmed that corporate legal structures could not be used to avoid social responsibilities or to violate the rights of other parties. Argentinaría was held responsible for all of Swift's debts, and the court ordered that all of its properties be seized in order to pay off Swift's creditors. Not until December 1976, however, did the actual liquidation of Argentinaría's holdings begin. In the meantime, Judge Lozada raised a national uproar when he revealed, in the course of an interview, that he had been approached during the first trial by Hortensio M. Quijano, the minister of justice, who asked him to rule in favor of Swift-Deltec. For Argentine nationalists, this was additional proof, if any were needed, of the perfidious link between powerful foreign interests and the country's upper classes.

Certainly the Swift-Deltec affair highlighted many of the unpleasant problems that may arise when developing nations allow large foreign investors to enter. There is little doubt that this multinational enterprise and its subsidiaries intended to defraud their creditors and that they used both prominent politicians and common bullies to achieve that end. On the other hand, Swift-Deltec was not without its own legitimate complaints. For years the government had allowed irresponsible labor unions to force unjustifiable wages and work rules on the company and to practice violence and vandalism whenever they met the slightest resistance. On top of that, the government itself imposed taxes and controls on meat production that made the business unprofitable. Disinvestment was not only a deliberate strategy on the company's part to avoid its debts, but the only strategy that made sense in an increasingly hostile business climate.

Perhaps the most interesting sidelight to the case was the clear evidence that, under certain conditions, domestic capital could compete successfully with even large-scale foreign capital. The regional packinghouses had taken sensible advantage of market shifts and technological changes to run circles around Swift and the other big meatpackers. Swift's bankruptcy put the regional packers in sole possession of the field, save for CAP. Before long, however, they were voicing the same complaints that Swift once had: official exchange rates and export taxes were hurting foreign sales, and the government was currying popular favor by granting excessive wage increases to the packinghouse workers. "While the Government gives away big wages with one hand, with the other hand it makes it impossible for us to pay them and therefore endangers the source of many jobs," a representative of the regional packinghouses told reporters during a 1973 labor dispute. It was an echo from the bad old days of imperialism.[38]

## CHAPTER FOURTEEN

# Local Businessmen and Their Limitations

The failure of foreign capital to play the role assigned to it would not have mattered much if a local capitalist class had undertaken to lead the country. Instead, however, local private capital seemed content to play a relatively modest role, investing chiefly in urban real estate, commerce, and light consumer goods industries. Because Argentine entrepreneurs were willing to leave the development of basic industries to the state and to foreign capital, it was inevitable that these entrepreneurs would become increasingly marginal in the new economy. Why did Argentine industrialists, who had been the leaders of progress in the 1920s and 1930s, now settle for an inferior status? Guido Di Tella suggests that decades of excessive protection under import-substitution strategies made them too conservative. What Argentina needed in the 1960s, he argues, was a Schumpeterian entrepreneur: innovative and daring. What it got instead was a Colbertian type of businessman, inextricably linked to the state in a kind of neomercantilist arrangement. Shielded from competition and assured of making profits, Argentina's capitalists lost their entrepreneurial spirit.[1]

Most observers, both Argentine and foreign, had a poor opinion of the local business class. James Bruce, an American ambassador in the early 1950s, described Argentine industrialists in these terms:

> Some have progressive labor and public relations ideas, but most have the same characteristics as our industrial leaders had a generation or two back. There is little public ownership of shares or accounting of profits. *Porteño* industrialists don't feel the public has a right to know much about their enterprises. Their social behavior and their economic and political creeds are inferior to those of similar groups in the United States, England, or prewar Germany. They make deals where they may, forget scruples when those interfere, and pile up what they can—making certain that as much as possible is invested out-

side Argentina, just in case they lose their influence in government circles or there is a potential crisis.[2]

A few years later Tomás Roberto Fillol, an Argentine student of
industrial management, judged Argentine businessmen in similar
terms. He argued, however, that their behavior was but a particular
manifestation of certain national traits: a lack of any sense of social
responsibility beyond the family, a belief that success came through
luck or personal connections rather than through talent or hard
work, and an aristocratic disdain for manual labor and the people
who performed it. Applied to a business situation, such precapitalist values meant searching for quick, easy profits rather than a patient, long-term strategy of reinvesting profits and working long
hours. Such an industrialist or merchant would prefer getting the
better of a deal rather than building goodwill among his customers,
and his attitude toward his workers would be to treat them simply
as factors of production, like machines, to be bought and used as
cheaply as possible. As a result, under Perón the workers turned the
tables, making unreasonable demands and showing little sense of
social responsibility themselves. Thus arose the current stalemate:

> Argentine industrial managers (and businessmen in general)
> seem to be sitting in a glass cage, watching the day-to-day dete-
> rioration of industrial relations, blaming labor and government
> for Argentina's retardation, but at the same time discharging
> their burden of responsibility for solving the industrial problem
> on the already overloaded shoulders of the state. They know
> that, in the past, government has been conspicuously unable to
> manage the nation's industrial process. But they still insist that
> the state should not only provide the necessary protectionist
> climate to foster industrialization, but also (perhaps by magic!)
> provide industry with a docile, obedient, disciplined, produc-
> tive labor force. Industrialists in general do not seem to have
> given any thought to the fact that the productivity, motivation,
> and cooperation of labor are primarily determined by the man-
> agement that employs it and not by the more or less enlight-
> ened social and economic policies of government.[3]

Marcos Kaplan, an Argentine economic historian, also described
the local businessmen as having a precapitalist outlook. Rather
than possessing the classic capitalist characteristics of asceticism,
self-discipline, innovativeness, and aggressiveness, the typical Argentine businessman shuns industry and "tends to prefer mercan-

tile and speculative activities. He seeks large profits by keeping wages low and prices high, by a great deal of protectionism and the monopolistic control of small and stagnant markets, and by success in getting subsidies and favors from the State (whose intervention in other areas and other matters he rejects). The large profits that result are not used for technological improvements to increase productivity; they are diverted toward sumptuous consumption, influence-buying, speculation, or investing abroad."[4]

Such an attitude made it impossible for the local business class to lead the country's industrialization, Kaplan argued, which is why nationalists looked to the state. He might have added that it is why liberals who shared the same opinion of local capitalists looked to foreign investors.

Finally, Ricardo Mandelbaum, writing in the early 1970s to explain why local private capital had failed to play a larger role, pronounced a similar verdict on the Argentine entrepreneur. The typical Argentine investor, he concluded, had a get-rich-quick mentality that made him shun involvement in capital-intensive industry. Heavy industry required a lot of start-up money and there usually was a long wait before profits came rolling in. Most Argentines wanted big returns on small investments: nothing less than 30 percent or 40 percent annual profit would do. "Why should millions be invested in a blast furnace," Mandelbaum asked rhetorically, "if a much smaller capital investment will bring high and immediate profits when invested in land, elegant buildings, the stock market, or textile industries?"

According to Mandelbaum, the Argentine investor not only hesitated to put up large sums but wanted to be guaranteed a sure thing. It was the state's duty to make sure that he was. For industrialists, that meant protection from foreign competition so they could exploit a captive local market. In such conditions, there was no need to improve the technical efficiency of their operations. All costs, including wage increases to the hated unions, could easily be passed on to the consumer. If consumer demand fell because prices were too high, producers had only to cut back on output, lay off workers, and raise their prices even more to maintain their profits. Then, if demand rose again, they could raise their prices yet another time.[5]

Before accepting these as accurate portraits of the Argentine businessman, it might be worth considering how he views himself. According to Eduardo Zalduendo's pioneering 1962 survey of 27 top executives, the Argentine businessman was indeed a conservative avoider of risks. Although Zalduendo's executives did not think of themselves as traditionalists, they knew they were not innovators either. Rather, they thought of themselves as achievers. They were not traditionalists because, they said, hard work, education, and a pleasing personality were more important for getting ahead in business than one's family background. On the other hand, success—or achievement—was defined mainly as gaining economic security. Social prestige and personal independence were also mentioned as desirable goals, but they lagged far behind security. Zalduendo's respondents also were less opposed to labor unions and state regulation than one might expect. Most of them believed that unions really represented and protected the workers. When approached in good faith they could be a help to the firm, although they sometimes interfered too. Most of the businessmen also accepted the need for some measure of state control of the economy and said that labor should be represented along with business in helping the state to plan its policies.[6]

Of course, these were the views of leading executives of the largest domestic firms, and so might not be typical of the business class as a whole. Moreover, the survey was taken fairly early in the 1960s, when the attitudes of the elite about economic progress and reincorporating the workers into a bourgeois democracy were still optimistic. Later studies reflected more pessimism. For instance, a 1967 survey of UIA and CGE leaders by John Freels found that many representatives from both groups believed that Argentines needed a strong government in order to maintain social peace. They were also more hostile toward labor unions and wanted the government to prevent strikes and factory seizures. A large majority of industrialists thought that unions no longer really represented the workers but were manipulated by labor bosses for their own advantage. The industrialists accepted state planning grudgingly and recognized that unions would have to be involved in it, but they looked to agriculturalists and merchants as natural allies to balance labor's power.[7]

Freels's interviews were held just after the Ongania government was installed and only a few years after the Peronist unions had engaged in a large number of highly publicized factory seizures. Obviously, class resentments had sharpened, and businessmen were beginning to show a sense of frustration with the inability of democratic governments to achieve social peace and economic growth: hence their attitude that the armed forces and the Catholic church were socially constructive forces.

Deepening pessimism and a feeling of impotence were revealed by the findings of another survey carried out the following year by Alberto Sánchez Crespo, who interviewed executives in thirty leading private industrial firms. Industrialists now believed that, because of the stagnant economy, their companies had reached the limits of expansion. Nor did they view the foreign market as an alternative, given the relative inefficiency of their production methods. The dominant mood seemed to be one of isolation and helplessness. There was a general distrust of all politicians, and although the state was recognized as having a role to play in the economy, there was some confusion as to exactly what that ought to be. Previous surveys had shown businessmen to be in favor of a little inflation to stimulate demand; recent experience with inflation, however, now caused them to favor tight money. Although a majority of industrialists still believed that their interests were compatible with those of the agricultural sector, a rather sizable minority expressed the opinion that the *estancieros* were reactionary in their social attitudes and unwilling to take advantage of their economic opportunities. Above all, there was frustration among the industrialists at their own apparent inability to band together to increase their influence. As one of them observed glumly, "There are many entrepreneurs, but there is no entrepreneurial class."[8]

James Petras and Thomas Cook encountered similar attitudes in their 1970–71 survey of executives in Argentina's 100 largest industrial enterprises. They concluded that big businessmen, in general, did not constitute a happy or confident elite group. Most industrialists felt that, as a class, they had achieved only limited success in keeping down taxes, curbing union power, or protecting local industry from foreign competition. They also felt increasingly isolated from other groups. Party politicians, army officers, and clergymen alike had proven to be poor allies. A businessman, operating alone or through an industrial chamber, might occasionally gain the support of a key civil servant who could bend the law in the businessman's favor, but elected officials were usually of no help at all. Curiously, a businessman's best ally in certain circumstances might be a union leader, particularly if it were a question of some government policy affecting the whole industry and therefore threatening jobs.

The lack of class solidarity among businessmen was best illustrated, perhaps, by their different responses to the question about which era in recent history had been best for Argentina's industrial development. Although most respondents picked the Ongania regime, a surprisingly large number—about one-third—answered that the Perón years had been the best. Also, while most industrialists expressed approval of the military regime in neighboring Brazil, they also wanted an end to military rule in Argentina. Perhaps the *cordobazo* had convinced them that the Brazilian model of authoritarian capitalist development was inapplicable to their own country; or perhaps the populist course that Levingston and Lanusse adopted made them distrustful of the military.[9]

Perhaps the most positive picture of Argentina's industrialists emerges from a 1971 survey, conducted by Ruth Sautu and Catalina Wainerman, of 107 top executives of large and medium-sized firms in the plastics, textile, electronics, and steel industries. Half (51 percent) of those interviewed were the founders of their companies; slightly fewer (42 percent) inherited their positions in a family business; and a few (7 percent) were hired managers. Their average age was forty-six, and about half had been to college (although not all had graduated). During these interviews Sautu and Wainerman discovered that these local executives were moderately open, on principle, to innovative production and administrative methods, and were moderately willing to take risks. Most of them, especially the younger and better educated, admitted that Argentine industry was technologically backward, and of those, many had already taken steps to bring their enterprises more up to date. Their preferred solution to catching up, however, was for the government to lower import duties on imported machinery and to provide more credit. The younger and better-educated industrialists were also more likely to believe that no permanent improvements could be made until political stability was achieved and the government ceased interfering with the market. Although labor unions were far from popular among these industrialists, only a few blamed their problems on them. In fact, most of them opposed austerity policies that would reduce consumer buying; others, however, preferred to concentrate on increasing Argentina's exports through a regional common market.[10]

Finally, Frederick C. Turner conducted a survey of executives from the 120 largest firms, just after the Peronists had resumed power. He found businessmen to have a strong antipathy toward Perón, but also to be isolated psychologically from groups normally thought to be their natural allies, such as the *estancieros*. In fact, the average big businessman's identification even with his own class was considerably less than the *estanciero* had for other landowners. At the same time, industrialists had a surprisingly high opinion of their workers, as opposed to union leaders. Although tolerant of foreigners and little inclined toward nationalism, there were no figures, national or foreign, the industrialists admired. The impression gained from Turner's study of the large business executive at the start of the new Perón era was that of a weary, cynical cosmopolitanism.[11]

If opinion surveys give a slightly more liberal image of the Argentine entrepreneur than that conveyed in the general literature, then census data provide an even more favorable impression. Although critics might portray the entrepreneur as hidebound and unwilling to invest in improvements, statistics indicate that every branch of industry, traditional as well as dynamic, became more capital intensive during the 1960s. The amount of installed horsepower increased by an average of 4.7 percent a year in the traditional industries (compared to 8.5 percent for the dynamic ones), and in sectors like clothing and construction materials it doubled and tripled. Between the 1963 and 1974 industrial censuses thousands of small, inefficient, labor-intensive establishments went out of business, leaving all fields in the hands of larger, better-organized, and more soundly financed enterprises.[12]

Despite this evidence that the Argentine industrialist did possess truly capitalist instincts, the role of the industrialist in the development process remained secondary. How could it be otherwise when, ever since Perón, access to money, materials, and machinery had been controlled by the state? Writers who scorned the Argentine businessman's lack of initiative and propensity to evade the laws usually overlooked that.

## In the Grip of the State

Once the Argentine government became committed to industrialization, in the 1940s, it adopted a strategy that might be called state capitalism. Rejecting both laissez-faire and the state ownership of industry, this approach, as practiced by imperial Germany and imperial Japan in the nineteenth century, used the state to put up the original capital for new industries but later transferred their ownership to private hands, usually in the form of large trusts and cartels. "Infant industries" were then protected from competing imports, as well as from competing foreign investments inside those countries, and large military purchases guaranteed them a domestic market for their products. What the state did not consume was largely exported because private consumption was restricted and labor was kept docile by a mixture of coercion and paternalism. The dominant social values were patriotism, sacrifice, and social solidarity.[13]

Argentina's state capitalism differed in important respects from that of Germany and Japan, however, by appealing to labor and small business rather than to large capital. Instead of encouraging savings and investment, Argentine capitalism encouraged consumption. Therefore, at the opening of the 1960s there were powerful vested interests ready to block any attempt to shift development priorities toward capital formation and large heavy industry. There were only three ways to break out of this impasse: (1) invite in foreign investors to build heavy industry, (2) seek foreign loans to help the state expand its economic enterprises, or (3) use the state's power to effect a radical shift in the distribution of income and credit from consumers and small businesses to big local capitalists. As we saw in chapter 13, the first two options were tried but failed to work. The third was politically unrealistic: a form of suicide for elective politicians and even too costly for a martinet like Ongania. Furthermore, government planners usually started from the assumption that local private capital was either inadequate or unwilling to assume the leadership in development. With such a bias, it is not surprising that local private industry lost ground to foreign corporations and state enterprises: the former being favored by liberals and the latter by nationalists.

The automobile industry is a good example of how Argentina, unlike Germany and Japan, failed to nurture its own domestic capitalists. Automobile manufacturing, as opposed to just assembling, got started on a large scale in 1954 when the Henry J. Kaiser Corporation agreed to join with the air force's IME to form a mixed corporation, Industrias Kaiser Argentina (IKA). IME put up part of the financing, furnished a large tract of land near the city of Córdoba, built the factory, and owned two-thirds of the stock. Kaiser supplied the technology, machinery, and patents and owned the remaining one-third. IKA aimed at producing cars, trucks, and buses.

Market analysts estimated that Argentina would absorb about 150,000 new cars a year and that IKA alone would not be able to satisfy the entire demand. Therefore, in 1958 SIAM Di Tella, Argentina's largest metallurgical works, decided to move into automaking. It could boast of many advantages for undertaking this venture. First, as a producer of motors, pumps, generators, and compressors, it already possessed considerable expertise in engineering. Its large foundry, which turned out steel pipe, oil-field equipment, and a variety of machinery for both industrial and domestic use, could be adapted to making automobile bodies and chassis. Second, SIAM had previous experience in making motor vehicles, having for some years turned out motor scooters and three-wheeled vans under a contract with the Italian company of Lambretta. Third, SIAM had secured permission from the British Motors Corporation to be the exclusive manufacturer in Argentina of the Riley and Morris lines. Fourth, the company appeared to be financially sound. Its vice-president, Guido Clutterbuck, was a director of the Banco Popular Argentino; and Mario Robiola, the brother of Torcuato Di Tella's widow, owned a finance company in which the powerful Mackinlay-Zapiola conglomerate was involved. José Negri, another friend of the Di Tella family and a SIAM director, was on the board of the Banco Shaw and also was president of TAMET, a steel mill belonging to the Tornquist family.

With experience and connections of that sort, and with protection and nurturing from the state, SIAM might have provided, along with IKA, an independent, nationally owned source of vehicles for Argentina. If the Argentine government had followed the German and Japanese models it would have placed high tariffs on imported foreign vehicles and would have prohibited foreign manufacturers from locating in the country to avoid those tariff walls. While it is true that General Motors and Ford already had assembly plants in operation, having come to Argentina just after World War I, it would have been easy to put restrictions on their output to leave the lion's share of the market for local manufacturers.

Unfortunately for SIAM, however, its entry into automaking coincided with Frondizi's coming to office. The new official policy was to court foreign capital; thus Chrysler, Renault, Peugeot, Fiat, Citroen and a host of others were allowed into the country. By 1960 SIAM Automotores was but one of twenty-four automotive manufacturers competing for a limited local market. Obviously, only a few companies could survive in this free-for-all, and indeed, by 1970, only ten were still in business. Among the competitors, the foreign multinationals, with their superior access to financing, naturally had an advantage.

Financing was, after all, the key to success because not only were the start-up costs high in this particular industry, but to gain and keep customers a manufacturer and his dealerships had to offer easy terms of payment. Cars and trucks were sold for very little money down with installments spread over several years at low interest rates. When the severe recession of 1962–63 hit, however, even the easiest loans were impossible for a great number of middle-class

Argentines, who defaulted on their payments. All of the auto dealers lost heavily; but the foreign companies had their home offices to tide them over the crisis, whereas SIAM Automotores had only its holding company, SIAM Di Tella, to turn to. The holding company could go only so far in bailing out its automotive subsidiary without weakening the entire conglomerate.

Indeed, SIAM Di Tella's aid to SIAM Automotores went so far beyond the danger point that by the end of 1962 the conglomerate was in financial straits. For the first time in SIAM's history it was forced to pay its stockholders' dividends in company bonds rather than in cash. When it tried to pay its work force with those same kind of bonds, however, it provoked a violent strike that pushed it further towards the brink.[14] Even though SIAM workers earned high wages and enjoyed generous fringe benefits, their union, the Union of Metallurgical Workers (UOM) had a typically Peronist suspicion of the bosses. Its shop stewards shrugged off SIAM's concessions as mere paternalism and carried on the Peronist tradition of skirmishing with management. Productivity studies showed that SIAM Automotores took twice as long as its competitors to turn out vehicles; thus it was often behind in filling orders from its dealers. The UOM's leaders responded to management's pleas for patience by calling a slowdown strike at all of SIAM's large plants, and when that failed to budge the bosses the workers began smashing machines and office equipment. But even that failed to bring the usual concessions from management; instead, SIAM began a drastic reorganization that soon reduced the number of companies in the conglomerate from thirteen to four and allowed it to dismiss half the work force.[15]

Even with all its financial troubles, SIAM Automotores was the fifth-largest company in auto sales. Furthermore, the economy had begun to improve again toward the end of 1964, promising a new jump in the demand for cars. At that point the Illia government, with its *dirigiste* distaste for private markets, entered the picture. CONADE decided that "the buying of cars is a clear misapplication of savings and makes it urgent to keep demand for such goods within certain limits in order to channel the national effort toward other productive activities that are more valuable for the process of development." The auto manufacturers were informed that they could increase their production in 1965 by only 5 percent over the previous year. Also, sales taxes were raised on cars and trucks.[16]

In September 1965 SIAM Di Tella finally admitted defeat and sold SIAM Automotores, its parts factory, its foundry, and its finance company to IKA. SIAM's management admitted that the decision was "traumatic" but insisted that it was unavoidable. Automotores had used up all its capital and no longer had any money for bringing out new models. It was bankrupt, unable to pay accumulated debts amounting to over $30 million, and its stock was no longer being quoted on the Buenos Aires exchange. IKA thus acquired it, and its 10 percent of the auto market, for the bargain price of $4 million—which obligated the new owners, however, to pay off the debts.[17]

The sale of SIAM Automotores didn't really help either SIAM Di Tella or IKA. The burden of bailing out the automotive subsidiary had drained capital from the rest of the SIAM conglomerate, whose various debts now reached around $60 million. Faced with ruin, the Di Tella family prepared to put their business into receivership. But SIAM was too important as a provider of jobs and a producer of equipment for YPF for the state to permit it to close; therefore, a bailout was arranged whereby government loans would keep its remaining factories going in the hope that the company eventually would bottom out of its troubles. SIAM never recovered, however, and in 1971 the state finally purchased it outright. Meanwhile, in March 1967 IKA shut down SIAM Automotores as a hopeless money-loser. A few months after that, Henry Kaiser, who had been facing losses in the auto business in both Argentina and the United States, decided to get out. In November 1967 he sold out his share of IKA to Renault.[18]

Many years later Roberto Roth, who had been one of General Ongania's "braintrusters," placed the blame for SIAM's failure on its own management: "This pioneer industrial concern had followed the classical Argentine road to ruin: accelerated over-expansion with a financial base that would not bear the weight. As the group was important and had political influence, successive governments poured in more and more public funds.... The owners of SIAM found in the Argentine state a more lucrative, safe, and comfortable business than any they had tried before, with adverse results."[19]

Aside from the imputation of unworthy motives to the Di Tellas and their associates, such a judgment may be correct, from a liberal point of view. Once the government decided to open the domestic auto market to foreign manufacturers, SIAM probably should have gotten out. But if the Argentine government had followed a more nationalistic course, then SIAM, as a protected infant industry, might well have possessed the capacity to serve adequately Argentina's modest automotive needs.

## Businessmen's Pressure Groups

The limitations imposed by the state on local private capital do not explain why those capitalists did not exert more influence on the state. Industrialists and merchants together constituted a numerous and economically significant group. The size of this group may be estimated by the fact that in 1974 there were 830,000 industrial and commercial enterprises, of which 60 percent had a single owner and the remainder were either partnerships or some form of limited liability company. Assume, conservatively, that the average number of proprietors in those partnerships and limited liability companies was between two and three. One arrives, then, at an estimate of around 1.5 million business owners. Around that core of support for local capital would most likely revolve an equally large number of technical, managerial, supervisory, and professional people whose interests were linked to domestic private enterprise.

The business community lacked political effectiveness because it was divided into two antagonistic organizations. The larger, older, and more anti-Peronist firms were united under the Coordinated Action of Free Entrepreneurial Associations (ACIEL), an umbrella organization composed of the UIA, CAC, SRA, CRA, the Coordinating Commission of Agrarian Entities, the Chamber of Exporters, the Banking Association, and the Argentine Chamber of Joint Stock Companies. This organization of urban and rural business elites was prompted by the reappearance of the old Peronist CGE, dissolved by Lonardi in 1955 but re-legalized by Frondizi in 1958.[20]

ACIEL was by far the larger of these two rivals, claiming a membership of 1,361 out of a total of 1,675 businessmen's trade associations across the country. Some of those associations belonged to the CGE as well, however. For its part, the CGE never published a membership list. Its head, José Ber Gelbard claimed he was protecting the members from economic retaliation. Such secretiveness spurred the RRP to sarcasm:

> Sr. Gelbard is fond of repeating that his organization "represents" one million business organizations, a figure that seems to have suffered from inflation, because not long ago he used to stop at 600,000. Even he does not claim that all are members, and it is unclear how he defines businesses. The grocer, the corner shop, the tobacco kiosk and the humble shoe-black all must surely be counted in with the same pomp as Onassis, if he still lived in Argentina. In the event of further inflation, it

would not be surprising to see any housewife with a full-time maid included in the count.[21]

The rivalry between these two organizations was fiercest in the industrial sector. The CGE's industrial component, the Confederation of Industry (CI) claimed to be representative of those industries that were truly national: a category that, according to it, embraced practically the entire textile and light metallurgical industries, 70 percent of food processing, 80 percent of the wood industry, and about one-fifth of the heavy metallurgical sector. Like the CGE, however, the CI refused to publish any list of members. The UIA naturally dismissed the CI's claims. Among its own members it counted some 13,000 industrial firms, 176 industrial chambers, and 31 industrial federations. While conceding that the CI might actually represent a sizable number of small firms, the UIA argued that its own affiliates accounted for 90 percent of all industrial sales, 95 percent of the industrial labor force, 91 percent of all industrial output, 96 percent of all industrial wages and salaries, and 85 percent of all capital invested in manufacturing. Certainly the UIA's members were wealthier. In 1963 it was able to raise 37.2 million pesos in dues from its members, who paid in proportion to their invested capital; by contrast, the CI had a budget of only 4.5 million.[22]

Ideologically, the CGE took a nationalist position that favored a close relationship between government, business, and labor. The state would foster and protect national industry and maintain an expansive domestic market by raising working-class living standards. Gelbard's pet scheme for ending inflation was a "social pact" whereby businessmen and trade unions would agree to raise neither wages nor prices. Both would be represented in a social and economic council through which they would advise the government on economic policy. ACIEL, on the other hand, wanted freer competition, freer trade, and a much reduced role for the state. Government protection of small, inefficient industries should be discontinued, and the open market ought to determine which enterprises deserved to survive. Instead of giving unions a voice in policymaking, the government ought to insure that unions did not prevent greater productivity, because more output was the only way to raise the living standards of the common people in the long run.[23]

Within ACIEL, the merchants of the CAC and the *estancieros* of the SRA and CRA were the most deeply committed to this classical liberal outlook. The CAC was so orthodox laissez-faire that it even attacked Álvaro Alsogaray as being too statist. Heavily dominated by banking and import-export companies, its constant themes were the need for monetary stability, the deregulation of interest rates, and a balanced government budget—which could be attained only by selling the state enterprises. The *estancieros* were no less orthodox. In 1965 a National Agrarian Assembly, jointly sponsored by the SRA and CRA, expressed the view that "anything that violates the concept of a free market is unconstitutional, and therefore the Executive and Legislative powers ought to abandon their present statist economic and social policies." The assembly wanted the government to stop dictating wages, scale down the social security system, and reduce its regulatory powers. On the other hand, it wanted the government to restrict the rural worker's right to strike and to provide easy credit to producers who demonstrated their efficiency.[24]

In the early 1960s the UIA's official attitude was not dissimilar to other ACIEL groups, but this changed during the course of the decade. By 1967 John Freels was beginning to discover some evidence of convergence between the UIA and CI viewpoints. Krieger Vasena's tight money program had caused a liquidity crisis in local industry, resulting in several highly publicized takeovers of Argentine firms by foreign multinationals. While still recognizing the importance of foreign capital as a source of technology and progressive management methods, the UIA was drawing closer to the CI in advocating closer state regulation of foreign capital to restrict the repatriation of profits and make sure that foreign activities would complement, not supplant, domestic industry. That was not the position of the SRA or CAC. The CI industrialists were much less positive toward labor unions than was the CGE as a whole. Most significant, perhaps, was the expressed desire of a large majority of both UIA and CI members for a merging of the two bodies so as to enhance industry's political influence. Many members volunteered the opinion that the only reason for the separation was personal antagonism between the leaders, and not any great difference in ideology.[25]

The increasing probability, under Lanusse, of a Peronist restoration softened the UIA leadership's resistance to a merger with the CI. After all, past experience with Perón had shown the futility of resisting him. There were also pressures from some UIA members for a change in the organization's ideological orientation. A "developmentalist" faction, representing more dynamic and heavy industries, had arisen, demanding more protection from foreign competition and more representation for the steel, automotive, and petrochemical centers of Córdoba and Rosario. These developmentalists threatened to break away from the UIA and form a separate organization unless it adopted a more "national" point of view. There also was the danger that they might join the CI, making that body much more powerful.[26]

It was evident that changes were occurring inside the UIA when, in May 1972, some 123 companies affiliated with it agreed to meet with President Lanusse and the leaders of the CGT in order to work out a plan for dealing with inflation. Until then the UIA, in conformity with the rest of ACIEL, had been demanding strong austerity measures to meet the problem; but now, with spreading unemployment, a shrinking domestic market, and a shortage of liquid capital, the big industrialists were ready to try a different method. They agreed to grant the workers a large wage increase and not pass on the cost to the consumers in return for easy government loans and the promise of greater export subsidies. That touched off a bitter public quarrel between the UIA and the rest of ACIEL.[27]

By September, inflation had taken another large jump that prompted Lanusse to call a meeting of employers' groups to get their advice. The CGE took advantage of the occasion to present a plan, already endorsed by the CGT, which called for another big wage hike in order to maintain the workers' buying power. This time a skeptical UIA joined the rest of ACIEL in countering with a proposal that would protect jobs by providing more credit for business expansion while avoiding inflation by holding the line on wages. Lanusse then resolved these opposing views by increasing both wages and industrial credits. The CAC and SRA strongly opposed the compromise, but the UIA accepted it after some soul searching.

This fresh breaking of ranks by the UIA led to an ugly fight inside ACIEL, which ended with the industrialists walking out of the meeting. An emergency conference of the UIA was called for 9 October. By a vote of seventy to sixteen the industrialists resolved to "reaffirm their independence" by separating from ACIEL. After that they put out feelers to the CI about forming a common front of industrialists. To make the rapprochement easier they even published a manifesto proclaiming their support for various measures they formerly had opposed: protection of local capital from foreign competition, closer regulation of multinationals, the necessity of maintaining labor's buying power, and the need for state economic planning.[28]

Thus, as the country prepared itself for a return of Peronism to power, the industrialists were alone among the business class in trying to forge a single pressure group. Without a great, overarching organization to represent all of capital, however, Argentina's entrepreneurs would not be able to impress the government. By itself, each segment of the local capitalist class was limited in the amount of influence it could bring to bear. *Estancieros* were too unpopular; industrialists were too dependent on protection; and small businessmen contributed too little to the economy. Only in concert could they become a formidable political force; yet they were too heterogeneous to achieve more than a temporary unity.

## The Business Community

Businessmen were a diverse lot. Their outlook differed according to whether they were attached to foreign, state, or local private enterprises. Industrialists and merchants often had opposing interests, with the former favoring protectionism and the latter advocating free trade. Large and small businessmen lived in different worlds too. As a rule, larger enterprises found it easier to get private bank loans and to compete with foreign products, whereas small businessmen needed government credits from the Industrial Bank and were the most protectionist group of all. To some extent, the large business versus small business issue overlapped with the old rivalry between Greater Buenos Aires and the interior. The UIA and CAC tended to represent large companies located around the port, whereas the CGE's small business membership was drawn heavily from the interior. Even among *porteño* businessmen, those who belonged to the UIA or CAC lived in the Barrio Norte, while CGE members were more likely to be found in less fashionable neighborhoods. Finally, whatever its size, location, or type of ownership, each enterprise tended to view the economy from the narrow perspective of its own particular line of business.

Businessmen also differed greatly in social background and career experience. No longer did "self-made men" predominate among the top firms, as they had done up to Perón's time. By the 1960s it was common to find companies headed by executives who had inherited their position. In some of the larger firms, even the professional manager was beginning to make an appearance. In 1962, for instance, the Instituto de Desarrollo Económico y Social did a study of 286 top industrialists and merchants listed in *Quien es quien* (Who's Who) and the *Guía de sociedades anónimas* (Corporations Guide) and found that fewer than one of five had worked their way

up from humble origins, unlike the business pioneers of the previous two generations.[29] This tallied with similar findings in the
Zalduendo, Petras and Cook, and Turner studies. The first two studies discovered that the modern Argentine businessman was far
more likely than his predecessors to have been born in Argentina
of second-generation parents and to have attended college. In the
Petras and Cook sample, three-fourths of the executives were children of established merchants, industrialists, landowners, or professionals. Only one-fourth had risen from the working or lower
middle classes. In Turner's sample, about 30 percent came from
white- or blue-collar backgrounds; the remainder were drawn from
what he terms elite backgrounds.[30]

The typical career pattern of an executive in one of the larger
private Argentine firms was to enter a business owned by a relative
and work to the top by proving managerial talents at the head of
various departments. By age forty, the executive had completed his
apprenticeship and was ready to assume the presidency. There were
numerous examples of this new type of executive. Guido Di Tella, a
Harvard-educated economist who took over SIAM after his father
died, fitted the mode. More interested in academic matters than in
business, he and his elder brother, Torcuato Jr., a sociologist, put a
large share of the family fortune into a foundation to support research in economics, sociology, and the fine arts. The foundation
survived the collapse of SIAM so the Di Tellas continued to play a
prominent role in intellectual and political circles. Less intellectual
and more businesslike, but also a representative of the new type of
executive, was Federico Zorraquín. In 1961, at the age of twenty-
seven, he became the third generation of his family to head the
Garovaglio & Zorraquín conglomerate. His grades had not been
good enough to get him into college, so at seventeen he began working in the firm. During the next ten years he worked his way up to
increasingly more responsible jobs, some of which required him to
look into the affairs of some of the more troubled enterprises in the
conglomerate. Those challenges taught young Zorraquín a lot about
management and investing so that upon taking charge of the whole
empire he showed a tough-mindedness and competence rare in
someone his age. He reorganized the business, selling off some divisions, diversifying others, modernizing, and adding on. By the end of
the decade, Garovaglio & Zorraquín had taken its place as one of the
soundest operations in Argentina, and during the 1970s it forged
ahead as a leader in many new fields of industry. As a final example
of the new breed of executives there was the Noel family, owners of

the largest candy manufactory. Three brothers, Carlos, Martín Benito, and Martín Alberto, represented the fifth generation to run the firm. Carlos, the eldest, had degrees in law and economics, had been a director of the Banco de la Nación, and had served as an economic consultant to both the Aramburu and Frondizi administrations. He was also prominent in the UIA, CAC, and Chamber of Joint Stock Companies. Martín Benito, also a lawyer, had been president of the Candy Manufacturers' Association and the Food Products Federation, as well as secretary of the UIA. Martín Alberto, the youngest, had a doctorate in philosophy and letters and taught at the National University while also serving on Noel's board of directors, from which post he obviously was being groomed to take over the company.[31]

But what of the "self-made man"? According to the study by the Instituto de Desarrollo Económico y Social, only one of six UIA members and one of five CAC members could be so classified. The largest proportion of self-made men was in the CGE, but even there they constituted only a third. Nevertheless, there still were brilliant examples of this breed. For example, there was Carlos Alberto Pérez Companc, who as a lawyer in the 1940s began by suing to recover some family property in Patagonia. After setting up an *estancia* on the land, he and his brother went into the coastal shipping business, using capital loaned from the Knights of Columbus to buy war-surplus American landing barges. Next they set up a company that specialized in the repair and maintenance of oil wells. Eventually the firm of Pérez Companc went into drilling and exploration on its own sizable Patagonian properties. When oil was found, the firm was soon established as one of Argentina's fastest up-and-coming conglomerates.[32]

Perhaps the outstanding example of a self-made man, however, was Agustín Rocca, a steel magnate who fit perfectly the old pattern of an immigrant who made good. Born in Milan in 1895 and orphaned at an early age, Rocca originally followed a military career and fought in World War I as an officer in Italy's Alpine troops. After the war, however, he got an engineering degree and went to work for a private steel company called Dalmine. When Dalmine failed in the Great Depression, Mussolini's state holding company, the Industrial Reconstruction Institute (IRI), took it over and hired Rocca to run it. Eventually Rocca rose to become a director of FINSIDER, a division of IRI that operated all the state's steel companies, but because of his high position in the Fascist regime he was forced to emigrate after the war. Arriving in Argentina with about $10,000 in savings, he opened a branch of Dalmine and began to manufacture metal products. After years of hard work, during which he suffered two heart attacks, Rocca managed to attract enough Italian and American capital to establish Dalmine as a major supplier of steel pipes to the local oil industry. In 1962 Dalmine sprouted a sister company, Propulsora, which became the second-largest producer of laminated steel. Above both of these firms Rocca placed Technit, an engineering and construction outfit that also functioned as his holding company. Lifetime experience had taught Rocca the need to maintain good political and financial relationships. Much of his business was with state enterprises like YPF, Agua y Energia, Gas del Estado, and Obras Sanitarias; at the same time he counted among the investors in his companies such names as FINSIDER, the Morgan Guaranty Trust, and Bunge & Born. His experience also taught him to channel a portion of his profits to safe places outside the country, which probably is why Technit's central office was located in Panama, not in Buenos Aires.[33]

The 1962 study by the Instituto de Desarrollo Económico y Social also identified a growing number of modern, professional managers who, though not related to any of the owners, were nonetheless entrusted with running the firm. In most cases, they were hired by foreign companies where (in the words of the study) "real leadership is beyond personal influence, and even beyond strictly national control." In those instances, an employee's promotion to the top was based on his "possession of some skill whose efficient application results in lifting him to some high position."

Such a man was Enrique Krag, who at thirty-seven became the head of Monsanto-Argentina, the subsidiary of a multinational chemical company. His career began as a young employee of the West India Oil Company, whose management, recognizing his intelligence, gave him a fellowship to study chemical engineering at the University of Massachusetts. Upon graduating in 1943, Krag became a traveling technical representative for Monsanto throughout South America. After that, Monsanto promoted him to the board of directors of a new chemical firm in which it shared ownership with Atanor, an Argentine company. Krag's career suffered a setback when, reacting to Peronist harassment of foreign businesses, Monsanto pulled out of Argentina; but when Perón reversed his attitudes during his last years in power, Monsanto returned and opened up a new factory with Krag at its head.[34]

An equally good example of someone who worked his way up without family connections was Rainani Bargagna, another chemical engineer. Educated at the University of the Litoral, Bargagna went to work for Ducilo, a Dupont company that manufactured rayon and nylon locally. Beginning as a plant supervisor, he quickly rose to be a technical supervisor, then head of production and sales, and finally, at forty-one, general manager—the second-highest post in the company.

As highly placed executives in some of the country's largest enterprises, men like Krag and Bargagna constituted a progressive segment of the native business class. They were also among the most highly paid people in Argentina. In 1969 top-level management in big private corporations earned, on the average, around 470,000 old pesos a year, and department heads got 300,000. Compared with them, lieutenant generals in the army were paid only 202,000, heads of state corporations like YPF got 200,000, and Supreme Court justices earned 210,000.[35] Nevertheless, these professional managers remained peripheral to attempts by the Argentine business class to exert group pressure in the political system. Multinational corporations seldom joined any entrepreneurial pressure groups (Ducilo and Fiat, both UIA members, being exceptions to the rule) and generally tried to stay clear of politics.

## The Persistence of the Premodern

Capitalist enterprises in North America and Western Europe have generally evolved from family firms to become corporations. The 1974 census indicated that Argentina was moving along this same path, inasmuch as the number of industrial corporations had grown in the previous twenty years from 3,272 to 10,999. From only 2.2 percent of all industrial enterprises, they were now 8.7 percent; whereas previously they had only a third of the industrial labor force, they now had 54 percent; and rather than 42.2 percent of all production, they now accounted for 69.5 percent.

Those figures were misleading, however. Argentine corporations were still family owned rather than public. As one management consulting firm complained: "In most Argentine private firms, regardless of size, the top executives belong to the family that owns them, while the second layer of executives and the technical staff belong to the professional management type. . . . Private firms run by professional managers of the United States style would be hard to find in Argentina, although slow changes in this direction may be noticed as the industrial tradition of Argentina grows older."[36]

Thus, it was quite common in local private companies for middle management to be better educated and more professionally competent than the top-level executives. Yet, opportunities for advancement were slim. A similar situation existed in the state enterprises, where political influence determined who got the best jobs. Thus, Argentina's good public school system kept turning out bright, young talent which the economic system wasted: a contradiction that may have been the cause of the serious brain drain that the country began to suffer in the 1960s as thousands of skilled people emigrated to seek better opportunities.[37]

Working with a 1966 list of corporations and their executive boards published by the Buenos Aires Stock Exchange, I was able to find empirical evidence to indicate not only that Argentine corporations are still family-owned enterprises masquerading as modern joint stock companies, but also that these family companies frequently had interlocking directorates. At least one out of every three companies had one or more members of the same family on the executive board: a finding that tallied with a similar study by Victor Tokman, an International Labor Office economist who worked with a 1961 list from the Stock Exchange. Tokman discovered that 28 percent of all the corporations, representing 54 percent of all the corporate capital, had board members drawn from at least one of the thirty-two traditional landowning families. My data also showed that 17 percent of all company directors and 29 percent of their presidents were members of the Jockey Club.[38]

Interlocking directorates resulted in the even more curious phenomenon of the family-owned conglomerate. In fact, there was so much interlocking of corporate directorates, both within a single conglomerate and between conglomerates, that any attempt to draw a full diagram of corporate interconnections would result in a confusing welter of crisscrossing lines. Some generalizations can be made, however, that might clarify the system. First, it must be repeated emphatically that most conglomerates, even as late as the late 1960s, were family owned, their components being held together by assigning family members to multiple directorships. In some cases companies, and even conglomerates, were linked together through marriages, as in a feudal system. Second, conglomerates diversified their investments, commonly having interests in agriculture, commerce, and finance as well as industry. This helped to overcome some of the natural divergence of interests those different sectors might have had. Third, each conglomerate was buttressed financially by either owning or having close ties to one or more banks, insurance companies, or investment houses.

The Tornquist Group was a good example of such a conglomerate. Its brain was the holding firm of Ernesto Tornquist & Company, and its financial lifeblood flowed from the Banco Tornquist. Clustered around these were several companies that extended the Tornquists' influence into industry, agriculture, and commerce: Ferrum, a porcelain fixtures plant; Introductora de Buenos Aires, which mined salt and grew tobacco; Cotécnica, a producer and vendor of motors and ball bearings; TAMET, a steel mill; La Agrícola, an insurance company; General de Comércio, a hotel chain; Textiles Oeste, a woolen textile mill; and Cristalerías Rigolleau, in which the family still had a minority interest.

In many cases the Tornquists shared the management of these corporations with other influential family groups. One such Tornquist ally was the De Bary family, with whom they were related by marriage. The De Barys were found on the directorates of Ernesto Tornquist & Company, Ferrum, Introductora, TAMET, La Agrícola, and General de Comércio. In addition, the De Barys had their own investments, which included the IPAKO chemical company, in which they shared control with the Gruneisen family and the Garovaglio & Zorraquín Group; Crédito Mobiliario Argentina; and La Agraria, a real estate investment firm in which another family, the Shaws, had a large interest.

The Shaws also were close allies of the Tornquists. Alejandro Shaw, head of the family, was president of General de Comércio and vice-president of Introductora. The Shaws also had representatives on the boards of Ernesto Tornquist & Company, Ferrum, TAMET, and Cotécnica. They also, even more than the De Barys, had an impressive web of investments apart from the Tornquist Group. There was a Banco Shaw and a Shaw-owned insurance firm, La Continental. Through their bank the Shaws had lines of influence running out to other important families and conglomerates. One of the bank's directors was José Negri, a director of SIAM Di Tella and also president of TAMET. Another director was Ricardo Gruneisen, head of another family conglomerate that had ties to the giant Braun-Menéndez Group as well. Yet another influential director was Eustaquio Méndez Delfino, a former president of the Stock Exchange, former head of Aramburu's Economic Advisory Commission, secretary of finance and president of the Central Bank under Frondizi, and minister of economics under Guido. Méndez Delfino was also a board member of the Shaws' insurance company. Through him the family was connected to the Roberts Group by way of a telecommunications company, Transradio Internacional.

The Shaws also shared the ownership of a publishing house, Editorial Sud America, with the Braun-Menéndez Group; and they were connected to the proud and prestigious Bunge family through marriage. Indeed, Alicia Bunge de Shaw brought together three different family interests by serving on the boards of the Tornquists' General de Comércio and Introductora. The head of the Bunge family, César Bunge, also was closely connected to the Tornquist Group, serving as attorney for the Banco Tornquist and as a board member of both TAMET and Ernesto Tornquist & Company. He was an influential man in government circles, too, having been minister of commerce under Lonardi and secretary of finance under Frondizi. He also was a leader in the CAC, a director in Rocca's Dalmine metal works, and president of his own oil drilling equipment firm. Other members of the Bunge family extended its influence to the chemical industry through Compañía Química, auto parts and accessories, women's clothing, and agrobusiness. In conjunction with the Born family, with which it shared control of the great holding company of Bunge & Born, it participated in the running of more than three dozen other companies, of which the largest was Molinos Río de La Plata—Argentina's biggest producer of flour, rice, yerba mate, vegetable oils, mayonnaise, and margarine. The Bunge & Born Group was connected, in turn, to the aristocratic and powerful Pueyrredon family through La Rural, an insurance company which also gave them access to the Banco Popular Argentino.

Retracing our steps to the Tornquists, we find that six of their companies also included representatives of another powerful family group, the Mackinlay-Zapiolas. Four of those companies (Ernesto Tornquist, Ferrum, TAMET, and General de Comércio) brought in the De Barys and Shaws as well; one (Cotécnica) involved only the Shaws besides; and one (La Agrícola) only the De Barys. Matias Mackinlay-Zapiola was president of this last firm, as well as president of the Banco Popular Argentino and vice-president of Inverco, a loan company that financed auto sales for SIAM Automotores. Through the Banco Popular Argentino, links were tightened between all these families and the Pueyrredons, for Júlio A. Pueyrredon was the bank's executive vice-president. The bank also carried the names of many other old, prominent families on its board:

Gelly y Orbes, Mitre, and Martínez de Hoz. José Martínez de Hoz was an especially powerful connection. Coming from one of the largest landowning families, he had been president of the National Grain Board, secretary of agriculture under Frondizi, and minister of economy under Guido. He soon was to be appointed by Arturo Acevedo, the founder and president of Acindar, to succeed him as head of the largest private steel mill. Eventually he would return as minister of economy under the military government of Gen. Jorge Videla (1976–81).

The Mackinlay-Zapiolas also had interests in the Franco-Argentino insurance company, which in turn connected them to the Banco Francés del Río de La Plata through the company's president, Carlos Grandjean, who also was a director of the bank. The Tornquists had even more direct access, however, through Emílio Van Peborgh, a director of Ernesto Tornquist & Company who also sat on the board of directors of the bank. The Van Peborghs also were business partners with the Lanusse family in a company that owned large tracts of ranchland.

La Agrícola, an insurance company, not only brought together the Tornquists, Mackinlay-Zapiolas, and De Barys, but it also involved the interests of the vast Braun-Menéndez Group. Cristalerías Rigolleau linked the Tornquists to American multinational interests, since Corning Glass owned most of the stock; and it also involved minority participation by the influential Roberts Group. In fact, "the Rigolleau Connection" had many fascinating ramifications. The company's president, Gastón Texier, also was secretary to the board of the Banco Popular de Quilmes and a director of La Buenos Aires, an insurance company connected to the Roberts Group. Two other directorships on Rigolleau's board were controlled by the old and distinguished Beccar-Varela family, which traced its lineage on both sides back to colonial times. In addition to his position at Rigolleau, Horacio Beccar-Varela, the family's head, was vice-president of the Argentine Bar Association, a director in RCA-Argentina, and lawyer for the local branch of Citicorp. The Beccar-Varelas owned *quebracho* forests, whose trees rendered an extract used in tanning leather, and paper mills. They participated with the Shaws and the Roberts Group in Transradio Internacional, and with the Soldati family, a medium-sized conglomerate, in pharmaceutical and electric power companies.

The Tornquist Group and its relationship to other companies and conglomerates illustrates how intertwined Argentina's leading capitalist families were, as well as the importance of personal representation in binding them together. Other giant conglomerates presented a similar picture. Take for example the great Braun-Menéndez empire. Its holding company was Importadora y Exportadora de Patagonia. Radiating out from this power center were two banks (Banco de Galícia and Banco Sirio-Libanés); a coastal shipping company; an insurance company owned jointly with the Tornquists, De Barys, and Mackinlay-Zapiolas; shipyards (Astarsa); an oil company owned in conjunction with the Gruneisens (Astra); a chemical company owned in conjunction with the state (Atanor); a rubber tire company owned jointly with Agustín Rocca (Pirelli); a publishing house owned in conjunction with the Shaws (Editorial Sud America); various landed estates; a mineral water bottling plant; and a metallurgical plant. Through the Banco de Galícia's president, Eduardo Escasany, the group was linked to two other insurance firms, plus a steel mill (La Cantábrica). Another of the bank's directors, Roberto Bullrich, connected the group, through his old and illustrious family, to a variety of commercial interests: publishing (Peuser), dairy products (Saint Hermanos), and ranching. The Bullriches also were partners in various enterprises with the Roberts Group. Through the Banco Sirio-Libanés, in which the Braun-Menéndezes had a lesser interest, links were forged directly with the Roberts Group, as well as with middle-level families like the Gruneisens, the Aguirres, and the Van Tienhovens.

The Braun-Menéndez interests in Astra, Argentina's largest private oil company, cemented its ties to the Aguirres and Gruneisens. Ricardo Gruneisen was president of Astra, director of the Banco Shaw, president of Fiat's distributorship, and president of a *quebracho* company. Other Gruneisen investments were located in such diverse fields as construction, rural real estate, and plastics. Associated with Gruneisen in many of these ventures was the Aguirre family, whose head, Luís Aguirre, was president of Neroli Plastics. The Aguirres also were on the board of the Banco de Galícia and had independent investments that included the production of lead oxide and refractive instruments. The Astra connection also linked the Braun-Menéndezes to yet another middle-level family: the Soldatis. Francisco Soldati was an Astra director but also had been successful in building up an impressive network of firms in the fields of industrial chemicals, pharmaceuticals, and surgical instruments. The Soldatis were also part owners, along with the De Barys and the Garovaglio & Zorraquín Group, of IPAKO, a major chemical firm. They also had a minor interest, along with the Beccar-Varelas, in the Swiss-owned Compañía Argentina de Electricidad (CADE), which provided Buenos Aires with its electricity. Like other solidly established groups, the Soldatis tried to protect their financial base by acquiring interests in banking (Nuevo Banco Italiano), insurance, and investment brokerages.

Through its shipyards, the Braun-Menéndez Group had strong links to the Roberts Group, which had two directors on Astarsa's board. Also on the board, as the company's second vice-president, was Francisco Ramos Mejía, scion of another one of Argentina's oldest and most prestigious families. Other connections to the traditional upper class came through the group's investment in a company that canned and distributed hearts of palm, which made it a partner of the Pueyrredons.

The third great conglomerate in Argentina was the Roberts Group, an Anglo-Argentine empire whose holding company was called, appropriately, Compañía Anglo-Argentina de Inversiones y Mandatos (Anglo-Argentine Investment and Trust Company). On its board, besides members of the related Roberts and Oxenford families, was Horacio Bullrich, through whom the group was linked to the Banco de Galícia.

There were three insurance companies in this conglomerate. Bullrich was second vice-president of one (La Buenos Aires) whose president was the very influential Enrique García Merou. This pivotal figure also presided over Sedalana, a leading textile firm, and Editorial Sud America as well as serving as a director on the board of IPAKO. Therefore, the group was linked through him to the Shaws, the Braun-Menéndezes, the Soldatis, the De Barys, and the Zorraquíns. Also on the board of La Buenos Aires were Ezequiel Bustillo, a board member of the Banco Sirio-Libanés; Gastón Texier, president of Rigolleau; Roberto M. Fraser, president of Alpargatas; Eduardo Bemberg; and two politically influential men, José Martínez de Hoz and Elbio Coelho.

La Rosario and La Rosario Agrícola were the two other insurance companies owned by the Roberts Group. Ernesto Herbín was president of both. He also owned an electrical company, and his son was president of a cement company owned by the Aguirre family. Another influential board member of both insurance firms was Roberto Monserrat, president of the Banco Monserrat. Still another banking connection was Roberto Llauró, a board member of La Rosario and attorney for La Rosario Agrícola. Llauró, the president of a large soap factory, was also a director of the Banco del Interior.

The relationship between the Roberts Group and Alpargatas, Argentina's largest textile company, was very close. Not only did Roberto Fraser sit on the board of Compañía Anglo-Argentina, but two members of the Oxenford family were on the board of Alpargatas. Enrique Oxenford and Roberto Roberts also were vice-president and alternate director, respectively, on the board of Rigolleau, which brought the Roberts Group into partnership with the Tornquists and the Beccar-Varelas. Another connection with the Beccar-Varelas was through Transradio Internacional. The Roberts Group also was involved in the chemical industry through its ownership of Compañía General de Fósforos, and that connected it, through Guido Clutterbuck, Fósforos' president, and Mario Robiola, a director, to the SIAM Di Tella conglomerate. Through those two men the lines of influence also radiated out to the Banco Popular Argentino, of which Clutterbuck was a director, and Inverco, which Robiola headed and in which the Mackinlay-Zapiolas participated.

As might be expected of an Anglo-Argentine conglomerate, there were many connections between the Roberts Group and foreign capital. One was through Cristalerías Rigolleau. Another was through Ehlert Motors, which controlled the importation and sale of British-made cars and trucks. A third connection was through two sugar plantations and refineries. The first, La Esperanza, was owned by Deltec International, which put Charles Lockwood in charge. Lockwood also served on the board of the second plantation, Azucarera Argentina, as well as on the board of Molinos Río de La Plata, a key company in the Bunge & Born Group. Bunge & Born were connected even more closely with Roberts, however, through their common interests in Aranco, a canned food company.

The last of Argentina's superconglomerates was the Fabril Financiera Group. This was more of a true corporation because it was not dominated by any one extended family. Still, it represented the interests of a cluster of families: the Dellachas, the Pratis, the Lavignes, the Gagliardis, and the Scottos. Like other *grupos*, Fabril Financiera's empire was protected by a bank, the Banco de Italia y Río de La Plata, and two insurance companies.

Through its bank, Fabril Financiera had connections with other important conglomerates. Its board of directors included people with connections to the Roberts, Shaw, and Gruneisen groups. There was also an indirect link, through a representative of the Unión de Comerciantes insurance company, to the Banco Supervielle, a medium-sized banking chain owned by the Baron Supervielle family. Several directors of the Banco de Italia y Río de La

Plata were also connected with the Pirelli rubber tire company, in which the Braun-Menéndez family and Agustín Rocca had interests.[39]

Beyond that, however, Fabril Financiera's contacts with other conglomerates tended to be very limited. It controlled an empire that was relatively self-contained. It included several textile firms, paper (La Celulosa), chemicals (Electroclor), alcoholic beverages, machine building (Talleres Coughlin), and a lock factory.

These four great conglomerates, together with their lesser allies, accounted for about 3,400 establishments out of a total of 190,892 in 1963, according to a study by ECLA. Though only a handful of firms, they nevertheless claimed about 80 percent of business profits and constituted, apart from the foreign multinationals and big state enterprises, Argentina's industrial and commercial leadership.[40] But compared with the foreign companies, they were poorly organized because the paramountcy of family interests often kept the country's best managerial talent from rising to the top. Family ownership also stunted the development of a modern capital market, which would have allowed a more efficient financing of business expansion. The relative inefficiency of Argentine family corporations can be seen from the fact that, although foreign enterprises were only 3 percent of all industrial corporations in 1967, they accounted for around 40 percent of all industrial sales.[41]

### The Financial Limitations of Argentine Capitalism

The failure to transcend the family business and create true corporations had its costs, as can be illustrated by going back to the case of SIAM Automotores. Although it might have been futile to try to compete against foreign companies, it nevertheless was true that SIAM Di Tella stopped short of going all out in raising money for the venture. Late in 1959 the holding company began issuing common stock for SIAM Automotores to the amount of 400 million shares, each valued at 100 pesos. Each share was entitled to one vote at the stockholders' meetings; but to insure control by the Di Tellas and their friends 800 million shares of deferred stock, each entitled to five votes, were subscribed by them. Such conservative tactics, which put family control ahead of maximum capital formation, were eventually to tell against the company.[42]

SIAM's decision highlights the dilemma that Argentine capitalists faced when trying to finance their operations. Their choices were (1) to borrow money, either by taking out loans or issuing bonds; (2)

issue new stock; reinvest profits and unpaid dividends; or (3) evade taxes and social security contributions and invest that money. This last option, though illegal, was common. Carlos Díaz Alejandro estimated that, in the period from 1950 to 1960, about 16 percent of all capital for investment came from tax evasion: a figure that, according to Adolfo Dorfman, rose to more than 50 percent after 1960.[43] In SIAM's case, when the state finally took over, the DGI discovered that the company's liability for unpaid taxes amounted to about 60 percent of its capital.

Of course, no business could publicly admit to tax evasion; so the questionnaires periodically sent around by business research outfits like FIEL (Fundación de Investigaciones Económicas Latinoamericanas) and the Consejo Federal de Inversiones probably did not elicit a perfect picture of business financing in Argentina. But for what it is worth, a 1962 survey by the Consejo of 233 corporations on the stock exchange reported that about two-thirds of all funding came from internal sources. That would include profits, undistributed dividends, depreciation allowances, and (presumably) tax evasion. Of the other third from external sources, half was raised from the sale of stocks and bonds while the remainder came from loans. By comparison, a 1971 survey by FIEL of 435 business enterprises in Buenos Aires, Córdoba, and Santa Fé found even less reliance on the stock market but a growing dependence on loans from banks and finance companies. Also, businessmen were trying to solve their cash flow problems by deliberately delaying payments to their suppliers.[44]

The weakness of the stock market as an instrument for raising capital was a major stumbling block in the development of Argentine capitalism. The Buenos Aires stock exchange never fully recovered from the 1949 crash, although it did rally in the later years of Perón's rule, thanks to the *anonimato*, which, by allowing shareholders to remain anonymous, in effect made corporate dividends and capital gains tax-free. However, when the Aramburu government abolished the *anonimato* in order to raise revenue, the market suffered another crash. Frondizi restored the *anonimato* and produced another revival, but the volume of trading never reached the levels it had attained under Perón. The best years of the Frondizi period were, of course, those associated with Alsogaray. His dismissal in April 1961 put an end to the rally and sent stock prices tumbling to new lows. But they had not hit bottom: that came later, during 1962–63, with the Peronist electoral victories, capital flight, Frondizi's ouster, the clashes of armies in the streets, and Guido's repeal of the *anonimato*. The Illia government's generally antibusiness attitude and its imposition of a steep withholding tax on dividends guaranteed that the stock market would stay down. By 1965 the volume of trading had dropped to an equivalent of only $93.3 million, compared with $374.2 million in 1961 and $955.8 million in 1955. The average price of a share was down by 56 percent, and there were ninety-three fewer companies listed on the exchange. About half the shares being traded were selling at around half of their nominal value.[45] A private research outfit, the Consejo Técnico de Inversiones, drew a dreary picture of the exchange during Illia's last months in office: "As the year progressed it became clearer and clearer that not only had the Buenos Aires Bolsa ceased to function as a capital market, but that if it were not for the support provided by the Industrial Bank and the National Postal Savings Fund, the market would have all but collapsed completely. Private investor interest disappeared and even the speculators, usually counted on to provide a steady volume of trading, were staying out of the market."[46]

Ongania's coming to power created excitement on the exchange. Trading was very active and prices shot upward, surpassing even the levels reached under Alsogaray. But another slump came when Ongania named Jorge Salimei, a nationalist, as his economics minister. Another strong rally ensued when Krieger Vasena replaced Salimei, especially as his appointment coincided with a sharp crackdown by Ongania on the unions.

Even so, the volume of trading in private shares was disappointingly low, and the exchange played only a minor role in raising capital for businessmen during the Ongania years. This diminished role was due in part to government competition with the private sector for capturing funds. The government offered bonds at much below their face value—an attractive alternative to raising taxes. Government bonds, which had constituted only 5 percent of all trading under Frondizi and 20 percent under Illia, accounted for 64 percent by the end of Ongania's rule. Discouraged, many private corporations turned away from the exchange. Whereas there had been 660 registered with it in 1961, by 1970 only 414 remained.[47]

Indeed, the situation of most private companies was unenviable. Unable to attract enough investors, they sought loans to keep up their operations. Because profits were low and credit was tight, many of them could not get help from the banks. Therefore, they turned to finance companies, whose interest rates were exorbitant. That drove up the cost of doing business, which entrepreneurs sought to pass on their customers. High prices depressed sales, however, and profits fell. Low profits meant low dividends, and in fact many companies sought to pay their shareholders with new stock issued at below par in order to retain cash for reinvestment. Naturally, the shareholders' confidence was shaken. "All such practices show a lack of understanding of the way to guarantee permanent possibilities of using the Stock Exchange as a funding source," a 1971 report by the Bolsa warned, "and they ultimately boomerang on their authors, making it hard for them to get any new funds from the stock market. But the worst of it is that it hurts investors and the Stock Exchange in general."[48]

Under Lanusse a new law was passed in June 1971 that gave investors a 10 percent tax exemption if they reinvested their dividends in stocks and bonds. That, in conjunction with a moderately successful campaign by the Stock Exchange to get companies to pay regular cash dividends, helped to boost stock prices. During 1971 and 1972 there was a boomlet in share trading, but mostly in that of banks and companies in the service sector. The Argentine investor continued to shy away from mining and manufacturing firms as being risky and unprofitable.[49]

The larger private companies had privileged access to banks and were less concerned about the stock market. About 32 publicly owned banks at the national, provincial, and municipal levels accounted for about 40 percent of all commercial loans, while the remainder came from private banks. Many of the directors in the government banks also sat on the boards of big private corporations and conglomerates, had seats on the Stock Exchange, and were members of the Jockey Club. Within the private sector, the largest banks tended to be foreign owned, but even in those cases their directors were drawn from the boardrooms of the largest local business firms. Smaller private banks usually were a direct part of some family conglomerate, as in the case of the Banco Tornquist or Banco Shaw. This rather incestuous relationship between so many banks and private conglomerates was probably one reason why FIEL, in its 1971 business survey, found no clear correlation between a company's profitability and its access to bank credit.[50]

## The Place of the Small Entrepreneur

The average industrial establishment in 1974 employed 12.1 workers: considerably more than in 1954, when there were only 8.2

workers per establishment, but rather less than the 13.7 recorded in 1943. As we have seen, the Peronist regime encouraged the proliferation of small, inefficient workshops. Frondizi, who was eager to win support among small businessmen, continued to encourage small domestic enterprises while he was seeking to build heavy industry with foreign capital. From 148,371 industrial establishments in 1954, the number increased to 190,892 in 1964; and instead of 8.2 workers per establishment, the average sank to 7.2. Sometime during the next ten years, however, the era of the small industrialist came to a rude end, because in 1974 there were only 126,388; thus, some 64,504 had disappeared. The average number of workers rose to over 12; the amount of horsepower used per factory nearly doubled; and the ratio of horsepower to hand labor rose to an all-time high. One has to assume that most of these changes occurred after 1966 under the military, and that they represented a more or less conscious attempt to create larger, more modern industrial firms.

Even so, an average of 12 workers per factory indicates that there were still many small industrialists. They continued to hang on especially in the traditional sectors. There were thousands of garment makers, bakers, brewers of nonalcoholic beverages, stonecutters, printers, leatherworkers, furniture makers, and tilemakers. Also, there were thousands of small foundries, metalworking shops, sawmills, wine bodegas, and repair shops, all of which employed fewer than 5 workers and used almost no machinery.

Although small manufacturing concerns were on the decline, their counterparts in the commercial and service sectors seemed to be thriving. From 389,750 wholesale, retail, and service establishments in 1954, the number rose to 593,665 by 1964 and to 698,317 in 1974. The average commercial establishment was far smaller than the average factory, employing only 1.2 workers in 1954, 2.5 in 1964, and 2.6 in 1974. Nearly two-thirds of those were retail establishments such as bars, boutiques, juice stands, barbershops, beauty parlors, bookstores, newsstands, drugstores, stationers, groceries, hardware stores, florists, restaurants, and cafes. Often they had no employees except the owner and perhaps some family members. They were able to keep down their costs because their stock was limited, they did not advertise, their owners sometimes lived on the premises, and they invariably paid less than the minimum wage. Since much of their business was on a cash basis, it was easy to evade taxes.

Unlike the corner store, the small industrial entrepreneur could not continue to use primitive methods and stay in business, because of the corporations' inexorable squeeze on his share of the market. The small industrialist had to either improve efficiency of operations or offer customers terms of sale more attractive than those of the bigger competitors. To do this, he was forced to go to lending sources other than banks: savings and loan associations, credit cooperatives, finance companies, or private lenders. Many of these were unofficial lenders operating outside the law. Regimes like Ongania's tried to eliminate them as usurers, but they persisted because they were essential to the small, struggling entrepreneur who had little choice but to pay their rates.

For the small businessman it was almost impossible to get credit from the banks; but money was always tight for all but the very largest entrepreneurs. Tight credit policies aside, one reason for the general shortage of loan capital was the declining propensity of Argentines to put their money into savings accounts, which meant that financial institutions had less to lend. Savings accounts were unpopular because the government, hoping to make credit cheaper for industry, held down interest rates to below the level of inflation. Furthermore, depositors not only received negative rates of interest, but they were taxed on the interest they earned. In 1967 Carlos Moyano Llerena, an economist at the University of Buenos Aires, estimated that if the level of deposits could be raised again to what it had been in 1945, banks would have an additional 90 billion pesos to lend. Instead, declining deposits meant that banks had little to fall back on in hard times if several of their loans went sour.[51] The shortage of capital might not have directly affected the small industrialist, who probably would not have been eligible for a loan from most banks even if the amount of loan capital doubled; but it did create conditions that could suddenly wipe out a small business. It meant that even the apparently powerful business empires, with their captive banks, were operating with relatively little capital and hence were vulnerable. To the extent that the small producer was a supplier of a larger firm, the sudden contraction of the latter would be disastrous. In brief, both small and large industry were starved for capital and had little or no cushion to withstand the shocks that were approaching in the 1970s.

## CHAPTER FIFTEEN

# Capital on Strike

The real problem of Argentine business in the 1960s was not, strictly speaking, a shortage of capital but a lack of willingness to invest. In 1973 a former high official of the Economics Ministry, Juan Quilici, estimated that $10 billion of Argentine capital was deposited in banks in Zurich, London, Paris, and New York. If that money had been channeled into Argentina's economy, the country might have overcome its stagnation.[1]

Money was drained illegally out of Argentina's economy through the informal financial network existing outside the regular banking channels, as well as through the vast underground economy in which individuals of all classes participated. Much of it was raised through tax evasion, which spot investigations by the DGI showed to be extremely widespread. One study, carried out in a rural district of southern Buenos Aires Province, showed that only 3 percent of the farmers there complied correctly with the tax laws. But farmers were no worse than anybody else. A former DGI chief, Elbio Coelho, admitted that other investigations revealed similar levels of tax evasion throughout the population. In some parts of the country, he said, fewer than half of the potential taxpayers even bothered to fill out a form.[2]

Businessmen involved in foreign commerce had ample opportunity to evade taxes by underinvoicing goods they exported and overinvoicing those they imported. Since much local business was on a cash basis, it frequently went unrecorded. As in foreign trade, the blank invoice was commonly used. Since the penalties for tax evasion were so light, companies regularly falsified their records and lied on their tax forms. Another method for hiding transactions from the tax collector was to use a *cheque volador* (flying check). This was either an undated check that served as a demand note payable upon presentation, or a postdated check that could be used as a promissory note. Either way, it allowed businessmen to buy goods and services they needed without ready cash while also keeping the transaction secret. If the signatory's reputation was good, a *cheque volador* could even be passed on to third parties, though usually at a discount. Checks written for dollar amounts on overseas banks circulated widely in the underground economy.[3]

Whether kept in Argentina or sent abroad, these "black funds" circulating in the underground economy created a dilemma both for their owners and for the government. The successful tax evader might amass a considerable amount of undeclared wealth but could not spend it without attracting the attention of the DGI. Undeclared wealth could be invested overseas, but unless the investor intended to expatriate, this solution was not entirely satisfactory; and in the meantime the investor's business was deprived of needed capital. The government was aware that it was losing revenue, of course, but it could not locate the hidden funds. Therefore, it periodically declared a "whitewashing" of black funds by agreeing to charge only a fraction of the original tax if the evaders would agree to declare their illegal hoards of wealth. Those who took advantage of these offers would then be able to invest their hidden capital legally or spend it in lavish consumption. Because whitewashing was a confession of weakness on the government's part, it was done only when the need for revenue became desperate. It also had the disadvantage of encouraging more tax evasion, since those who violated the law were pretty confident that they would be forgiven later. Even so, many operators in the parallel economy would refuse the whitewashing opportunity for fear they would henceforth be placed under specially rigorous scrutiny by the DGI.

Black funds invested abroad might also be enticed back to Argentina by devaluation of the currency, but that involved serious political and economic costs. Any funds that returned that way were likely to be speculative "hot money" rather than true investment capital. Such quick fixes were usually disruptive, inflationary, and ephemeral. Neither whitewashing nor sharp devaluations should have been necessary had the country's affairs been managed competently, the RRP accurately pointed out: "The need for them seems to arise when policy is excessively influenced by the petty bureaucratic mentality, by people who are strongly disposed to State intervention and official control systems, interminably trying, by Byzantine punctiliousness of successive ordinances, to correct faults inherent in a system that is rife with, in fact, Byzantine punctiliousness." And it concluded that:

It may be an exaggeration to say that, in Argentina, things work out not too badly, thanks to the operation of a variety of parallel systems, extra-juridical agreements, credit and loan systems operating outside the banking system, the parallel exchange market, tax evasion, the activities of people claiming to be influential in official circles (the so-called *gestores administrativos*) and people actively engaged in contraband activities of one kind or another. What cannot be ignored is the enormous importance of the extra-juridical facilities on which the country so largely depends.[4]

The underground economy inevitably corrupted and distorted the whole economic system, however, and undermined legitimate trade. The impact of smuggling on the tobacco industry, which was discussed in chapter 13, had its parallels in other areas. In 1968 Roberto Fraser, president of Alpargatas, complained to a stockholders' meeting about growing competition from clandestine textile and shoe factories that were not registered with the authorities, paid no taxes or social security contributions, and ignored the labor laws. He was referring to a host of tiny operations scattered among the shantytowns that ringed the city or spread along its riverbanks. An idea of the type and range of their activities may be gained from a report issued in 1977 by the Buenos Aires municipal housing commission. One shantytown, situated between the Retiro railway station and the port, contained about 35,000 inhabitants, some of them far from poor. They operated furniture and shoe factories, refrigerated plants, hardware stores, parking lots and garages, pharmacies and clinics, a soda water bottling plant and a soft drinks warehouse, and a tire-repairing establishment. They paid no rent or taxes and got free electricity by tapping into nearby power lines. A large number of people in the community spun yarn or knitted at home for a company of South Korean immigrants who furnished them with the materials and machinery and came by periodically in trucks to collect the finished goods. This commercial beehive was serviced by a well-designed plan of interior and access roads. In one grocery store the investigators discovered some 4.3 million pesos lying about the premises.[5]

It was unfortunate that pernicious rules and regulations turned otherwise honest and decent businessmen into white-collar criminals. After all, the *cheque volador* process could not have functioned as well as it did without the pledged word and good faith of the parties involved. Once justified, however, illicit activities became an accepted way of doing business and bred in some entrepreneurs a cynicism that could not help but destroy capitalism's development. This attitude was reflected in the rash of fraudulent bankruptcies, or *vaciamientos*, that occurred in the late 1960s. The perpetrators used methods were similar to those used by Deltec in the Swift case. The managers of a joint-stock company would set up a dummy firm overseas, to which they would sell a controlling interest in the company—sometimes with, and sometimes without, the stockholders' knowledge. The new "owners" would then proceed to sell all the company's property: buildings, machinery, land, furniture, inventory, everything. The former owners would be paid out of the proceeds of these sales for their shares and the rest of the money would be transferred abroad to the home office. In the meantime, the company would be slow in paying its bills. When the process was finished the owners would declare bankruptcy, after first leaving the country. The workers, suppliers, and tax collector were then left holding an empty bag. Each step taken might have been legal, strictly speaking, but the end result would be to defraud hundreds, perhaps thousands, of people.[6]

## A Social Stalemate

Labor does not have a monopoly on the strike as a weapon; the refusal of private entrepreneurs to invest in Argentina's economy can be considered a strike by capital. Potential investors reacted not just against onerous taxes and regulations; they were resentful of Argentina's militant labor unions and feared what might happen if Perón ever returned to power.

Organized labor, representing around 2 million workers, was a force to be reckoned with. In the utilities, transportation, and communications fields the closed shop was the rule. The same was true of health services, public agencies, state enterprises, banking, insurance, and large-scale manufacturing. Many union bosses were no better than extortionists. Payoffs were the way management avoided trouble. Despite pledges by Aramburu and Frondizi to make labor more efficient, wherever unions were strong they tended to set the conditions of employment and the pace of work. Employers often felt, with some justification, that they had lost control over their own factories and offices.

An extreme example of this is how the longshoremen's union, the Sindicato Unido de Portuarios Argentinos (SUPA) ran the docks. Only union members could work there, and the union kept its membership restricted. Hundreds of unemployed nonunion workers (*changas*) hung around the wharves, hoping for an occasional job; but there was work for them only if there was an exceptionally big task that required more labor than the unions could provide. A *changa* had little hope of getting into the union unless someone died or retired. On the other hand, the 15,000 or so who did have SUPA membership were among the best-paid workers in Argentina and enjoyed the protection of a union that was vigilant about protecting every one of their rights. SUPA would not hesitate to call workers off the job if it thought there was too much dust in a ship's hold, or if it detected strange odors, or if it discovered leaky containers. If the union charged that working conditions were unhealthy, the ship's captain would have to take immediate measures to rectify the problem; in the meantime the stevedores would still be drawing their wages. Shipowners often alleged that workers deliberately punctured containers, threw blood obtained from nearby meatpacking plants over bags, or released insects in the holds in order to get time off with pay. Owners also complained that work rules were interpreted so strictly by the union that if a crew of stevedores were led to the wrong section of the dock they would remain there and refuse to go where the ship was actually located. "They stay there, looking at the water, and demand their pay," one maritime agent reported, "because they say they were hired to work in this particular place and, since the mistake was made by the company, the company ought to pay for it."[7]

Because of the supposedly unhealthy nature of dock work, the law prescribed a six-hour workday divided into two periods: from 8 to 11 in the morning and from 2 until 5 in the afternoon. If a shipowner did not want the work interrupted, he had to pay an extra full day's wage to keep the workers on the job from 11:00 A.M. until noon and another full day's wage between noon and 2:00 A.M. If the work was not finished by 5, another day's wage was needed to continue until 6, a fifth day's wage to keep the crew on the job until 7:30, a sixth day's wage for any work done until 11, and a seventh day's wage to make them continue until midnight. Theoretically, a dockworker could earn seven days' pay in one, and if he could keep it up for a month he would earn more than an industrial manager, a Supreme Court justice, or top-ranking army officer. SUPA officials were always quick to explain, however, that no one could keep up such a pace for a whole month. According to their estimates, the average dockworker only worked about fifteen normal days every month and could last as a common laborer for only about five years. Either a worker rose to become a supervisor or sank to the level of a "wharf rat," good only for light, auxiliary work. A union doctor explained that the average man was quickly worn down by dock labor. After a few years he would suffer so from hernias, wounds, and bruises that he would hardly be able to work two full days a week.[8]

Although SUPA was quick to defend the workers' pay and health, it certainly did nothing to discourage them from pilfering. Owners complained that the stevedores stole openly from the ships' holds, and if caught they would pull a knife and threaten violence. To some extent the union actually encouraged pilferage by requiring companies to hire SUPA workers as tallyclerks. These clerks were notorious for their complicity in thievery. The usual modus operandi was for the clerks to turn in dishonest tallies and attribute the missing goods to short deliveries by the shippers. While the vessel owners were calculating how much such claims would cost them, the missing items would be loaded onto trucks for delivery to certain shops in downtown Buenos Aires that specialized in moving stolen goods. Because such shops never gave their customers a bill of sale, the merchandise could not be traced. The RRP reported a typical incident that happened in 1961:

> Early in December a Dutch ship docked 60 meters away from the fiscal warehouse where her cargo of bales of virgin rubber had to be lodged. A truck with 35 bales (each worth 10,000 pesos), instead of going to the nearby warehouse, was making for the port exit. It was stopped at the request of a private detective and was found to have the necessary papers duly signed by a customs guard to leave the area. Truck driver, customs guard, and talleyclerk were arrested. The consequent court proceedings will no doubt follow their habitual pattern: release on bail; and eventually the verdict: not guilty.[9]

If, as alleged, the Argentine business class lacked a sense of social responsibility, the same could be said of labor. This lack of a conscience on both sides may well lie at the heart of Argentina's failure to develop a full-grown capitalist system. As Max Weber observed in *The Protestant Ethic and the Spirit of Capitalism*,

> The universal reign of unscrupulousness in the pursuit of selfish interests by the making of money has been a specific characteristic of precisely those countries whose bourgeois-capitalist development, measured by Occidental standards, has remained backward. As every employer knows, the lack of

*conscienziosità* of the laborer of such countries, for instance Italy as compared with Germany, has been, and to a certain extent still is, one of the principal obstacles to their capitalist development. Capitalism cannot make use of the labor of those who practice the doctrine of undisciplined *liberum arbitrium*, any more than it can make use of the business man who seems absolutely unscrupulous in his dealings with others.[10]

It was not only union corruption that capital reacted against, however, but a deep-seated fear that the workers eventually would claim the right to comanage the enterprise. Beyond that lay outright expropriation. Since the average Argentine worker was a Catholic, a patriot, and far from a revolutionary, the likelihood of that happening may not seem so great to an outside observer. Nevertheless, there was a tendency to violence and thuggery within the unions which, when wedded to the exalted classist rhetoric of some labor leaders, could easily give the impression that capital was no longer safe.

Indeed, there was a vocal leftist element inside the Peronist block of labor unions. Late in 1957 the Peronist unions issued a resolution calling for government control of prices, credit, investment, and foreign commerce; the expropriation of large landed estates, large foreign companies, and all energy sources; comprehensive state economic planning; higher wages and more social services; worker control of production and profits; and "the reinforcement of a national popular state aimed at destroying the anti-national oligarchy and its foreign allies, recognizing that the working class is the only force in Argentina whose interests are identical with those of the country as a whole."[11]

Five years later another meeting, held at the resort of Huerta Grande in Córdoba, brought forth another manifesto that went even further. While reiterating all of the demands above, it specifically pointed to steel, oil, electricity, meatpacking, and banking as targets for nationalization. New demands included the abolition of all commercial secrets, the prohibition of all transfers of capital out of the country, and heavy taxation of business. No compensation would be paid for property seized, and central economic planning would include establishing both minimum and maximum production goals.[12]

By the mid-1960s Peronist unions were indulging in factory seizures as part of a so-called Plan de Lucha (Battle Plan), which smacked of a campaign of class warfare. Within the next few years a guerrilla movement, calling for revolutionary socialism, would make its appearance on the Peronist left—and would be endorsed by Perón himself. All of that made Argentina seem a much less secure place for capital to invest. But the most dramatic event to traumatize capital was the *cordobazo*, which seemed to many Argentines as the harbinger of a fast-approaching Armageddon.

## Confrontation in Córdoba

The bitterest conflicts between capital and labor happened in the newly industrialized city of Córdoba, hub of the automotive industry. Until the 1950s Córdoba was known as a conservative, Catholic city run by a proud old oligarchy. Those leading families, drawing their wealth from the surrounding countryside, had dominated the government, the liberal professions, and the academic chairs at the local university, whose founding dated back to colonial times. Then the Kaiser automobile company, enticed to Argentina by Perón, decided to install a factory in the sleepy satellite village of Santa Isabel, about ten kilometers (six miles) from downtown Córdoba. That revolutionized the city.

From a quiet colonial town, Córdoba quickly became a bustling, aggressive industrial center. Its population grew from 370,000 in 1950 to 580,000 in 1960 and 798,000 by 1970. Following closely upon the heels of IKA came Fiat, which soon surpassed it in size. IKA was the third-largest auto producer out of a field of twenty-four, but Fiat was number one. It was a giant company, by Argentine standards, employing 11,000 people among its five plants: Fiat Concord, which manufactured cars, trucks, and buses; Materfer, which built railroad and trolley cars; Fiat Someca, which produced tractors; Grandes Motores Diesel, which made ship and locomotive engines; and Metakor, a foundry for turning out metal parts. But the local auto industry went beyond this to embrace also a galaxy of some 200 satellite companies producing rubber tires, glass windshields and mirrors, electrical equipment, cushions and seat covers, gears, ball bearings, and various plastic parts. In all, the automotive industry in Córdoba employed around 50,000 people.[13]

The ramifications it had for the local economy went much further than that, of course. Shops, gas stations, groceries, bars, cinemas, and restaurants sprang up to accommodate the influx of new people. The city spread rapidly outward as new industrial and residential neighborhoods gobbled up the countryside, erasing the boundaries of the former satellite villages. Electrical power, water lines, telephone service, garbage collection, bus lines, sewers, and schools had to be extended to those new areas. The construction industry boomed. New businesses and a rapidly rising population meant more money being pumped into the economy. Córdoba's older population felt a certain ambivalence about all of this. It was a bonanza for merchants, bankers, laborers, and the owners of urban and suburban real estate; at the same time, the comfortable old colonial city was being swamped by change, much of which was ugly. The old elites were resentful, too, that pride of place was passing to a richer, more aggressive group of automotive executives brought from outside. These new economic leaders preferred to live apart and took little interest in the community. The same was true of the new middle class of supervisors and technicians, whose salaries were enormous by local standards. Córdoba's traditions and the social prominence of its old families meant nothing to these people who considered such things quaint—if they thought of them at all. Even the factory hands at IKA and Fiat were considered by other workers in the community to constitute a privileged group because the automotive companies were highly selective and paid the best wages.

The impact of these changes was especially great upon the youth of Córdoba. It was suddenly apparent to them that the old way of life and its values were antiquated and parochial. They became critical of their schooling, particularly of the university, which had equipped them so poorly for this new world. Extremists among them found various outlets for their frustration: the aggressive rejection of traditional Catholic beliefs, the embracing of some of the crasser tastes and attitudes of the consumer society, or the adoption of a revolutionary Marxist outlook. Whatever the choice, a great deal of friction was created between generations by this erosion of traditional authority.[14]

Above all, there was resentment at the growing realization that the city was increasingly dependent upon just one industry, whose decisions were made by people living thousands of miles away: people with no knowledge of, or interest in, Córdoba. Moreover, that industry was far from healthy because there were too many companies competing for a limited market. Automobile manufacturers consequently limited their output, and most of the time their factories were not working at full capacity. Furthermore, Argentina's economy tended to fluctuate erratically between inflation and recession, and when the economy turned downward so did auto sales.

Then would come drastic retrenchments: orders from suppliers would be canceled and workers would be laid off. During the 1960s many auto firms went out of business or merged. Kaiser itself abandoned the field, selling its interest in IKA to Renault.[15] Roberto Nágara, an official in the Automotive Mechanics' Union (SMATA), expressed the growing conviction that the automobile industry

> didn't come to solve the needs of the people, to help Argentina develop an independent industrialization process. It came because the machines it brought down were already obsolete back home and couldn't compete. So it came to shove off part of its problems on a dependent country. It decided to make automobiles for the Argentine market to absorb, and once that was accomplished it would accumulate stocks. In short, all the problems of capitalism were duplicated here.
>
> To that, add all the collateral and subsidiary industries, dependent on the automobile industry, like rubber, foundries, and others, like the production of screws, etc.: things that don't interest the imperialists and that they'd rather not bother to make (although some auto parts are made outside the country). Sometimes, of course, the monopolies take these over, when they feel like it, under conditions of exploitation and sub-exploitation, the former owners being a very typical local bourgeois servant of the monopolies, who impose their prices and conditions on him, etc. And when he finally goes crazy they take him to court and then do business with someone else.[16]

This antiforeign, anti–big business mood became more open and widespread as industry in Córdoba began to lose ground to other regions in Argentina, especially Buenos Aires. At the beginning of the 1960s over half of all cars made in Argentina came from Córdoba, but by 1970 fewer than one-fifth did. Part of the reason lay in Córdoba's militant trade unions, which commonly produced leaders like Nágara. Indeed, Córdoba had developed a notoriety among industrialists which made them instinctively avoid the province as a hotbed of Marxists. Let us examine why industrial relations there were so exceptionally bad, despite the fact that autoworkers were the most highly paid laborers in the country.

### The Industrial Workers of Córdoba

The industrial proletariat of Córdoba was newly created. Moreover, it was highly concentrated in a few large factories, which greatly facilitated its ability to organize on a mass scale. Those two facts go a long way toward explaining why the labor movement there became so radical. Political sociologists often have argued that working-class radicalism usually appears during periods of rapid industrialization as a reaction to the painful adjustments necessitated by accelerated, fundamental change. Moreover, where unions are nonexistent or are swamped by huge influxes of new members they are unable to perform the vital function of helping workers adjust to new work habits.[17] As applied to Argentina, this theory would explain why the most radical expression of working-class protest occurred in Córdoba and not in the older industrial areas around Buenos Aires.

Most of Córdoba's work force, which doubled in size between 1958 and 1964, was drawn from nearby small towns and rural areas. Many of the workers had no previous experience in industry. Meanwhile, industrial unions in Córdoba lacked both tradition and organizational experience. SMATA was a new union, not even a member of the CGT, having been encouraged to expand by both the government and IKA's management as a preferable alternative to the thug-ridden UOM. But SMATA was at least a nationwide organization; the unions at Fiat were all creations of the company itself. Each of Fiat's five plants had its own union unaffiliated with any outside labor organization. Other unions in Córdoba, such as the Power and Light Union, had more history behind them but had been forced to take in so many new members that their internal processes were in flux.

Just as Córdoba resented its dependence on outsiders, so the local unions were jealous of their autonomy from the big national federations quartered in Buenos Aires. Indeed, the labor establishment was viewed with contempt as being bureaucratic and conservative by men like Agustín José Tosco, chief of the Córdoba power and light union. For Tosco, a Trotskyite Marxist, labor bureaucrats were as evil as capitalism itself. He took care to avoid bureaucracy in his own union by building up the power of the shop stewards at the utilities plants and keeping a minimum of staff at the central headquarters so the stewards could reach him directly. Elected directly by secret ballot, the stewards were encouraged to take initiative on the shop floor and be combative in their dealings with management.[18]

Córdoba's radicalism stemmed not only from the strains of rapid industrialization, however. It also reflected the failure of the development process to reach a satisfactory conclusion. The transition from traditional to industrial society had stalled out after a brave start. Val R. Lorwin, an economic historian, has argued that, in the European experience, whenever the industrialization process stalls out the working classes' alienation from capitalism takes extreme forms. "Sluggish economic growth," he claims, "may generate the deepest and longest-lasting protest by reason of the society's inability to provide the well-being to match social aspirations and by reason of the economic elite's failure to inspire confidence."[19]

There is evidence to indicate that something like this may account for Córdoba's turbulent labor relations. Although a survey of autoworkers' attitudes, taken by Richard Gale in 1967, showed that most of them liked their jobs, it was clear that many of them aspired to a still higher position in society. In comparing them with autoworkers in Michigan, Gale found that they were much more likely to describe themselves as middle class instead of working class, and he discovered that a lot of them had given up white-collar jobs elsewhere to take advantage of the high pay being offered in this particular branch of industry. For about a third of the Córdoba autoworkers, their current job was just a stepping stone. They planned to save their wages to pay for further schooling. More than half of them already had a high school degree. Because most of them were younger than thirty-five and were either unmarried or childless, they had every reason to expect to ascend the social ladder.[20]

Those expectations, which were raised in the initial stages of Córdoba's industrialization, were frustrated by the subsequent economic malaise. During recessions many workers lost their jobs, and although they might be rehired when things got better there was a general trend toward replacing hand labor with automated equipment. Thus, during the 1962–63 downturn, IKA reduced its blue-collar work force from 6,351 to 4,736; and although an upswing the following year allowed much rehiring, the total work force only reached 6,235. Other economic fluctuations during the remainder of the 1960s had the same effect, with each recovery producing a work force whose numbers were just below the previous peak.

In addition to this, the autoworkers suffered from a peculiar kind of status deprivation. Among other workers in the local community they enjoyed tremendous prestige; but inside the factory they were at the bottom of the chain of command. Francisco Delich noted that one of the principal demands they made when they turned to radical politics was "greater participation, if not outright control, over the factories—or, as Marx would put it, over the means of production (which is probably why Marxism has appeal for them)." Given their education and intelligence, it must soon have dawned on these workers that their place in a complex production process gave them the power to paralyze the whole industry, to say nothing of the regional economy. A heady sense of potency and disappointed social aspirations made them a volatile group, susceptible to the urgings of extremists who sought to use them as the shock troops of revolution.[21]

## Labor Troubles before 1969

Auto workers first struck in Córdoba in 1959, when the workers at IKA walked off their jobs after the management refused them a 10 peso per hour raise. SMATA's leader, Elpídio Torres, timed the walkout to coincide with a visit to Córdoba by Henry Ford, who was looking for a site to open a new plant. Embarrassed local politicians, who wanted very much to impress Ford, pressured IKA into meeting the union's demands.

More serious was the 1963 strike protesting the growing number of layoffs. Although IKA's management pleaded that the economic recession and declining sales made these necessary, workers took over the factory. The seizure was sprung without warning and resulted in 284 of the administrative and supervisory staff being captured as prisoners by the strikers. SMATA warned IKA's management that it would not be responsible for what might happen to the plant's equipment or the hostages if the layoffs were not rescinded. IKA's American-born president, James McCloud, promptly conceded the strikers' demands and obtained the hostages' release and the return of his factory. Amazed by their success, SMATA officials boasted that "the rights of the workers have triumphed" and that henceforth "the sources of work belong to those who produce the goods." A week later, however, McCloud announced that the plant would be closed temporarily, timing this for a late Friday afternoon after the staff had gone home. Elpídio Torres told the workers to ignore this and report for work on Monday as usual. But on Monday morning the plant's gates were locked and the premises were under a heavy police guard. This lockout lasted ten days, after which the plant opened with a much reduced work force, the chief perpetrators of the recent strike having been dismissed.[22]

In August 1966 IKA, facing another sharp drop in sales, again decided to cut its work force, this time by about 20 percent. The workers seized the plant once more and finally got the management to agree to a compromise by which no dismissals would occur until next January, in return for which the union accepted a shorter workweek. When January arrived, however, the recession had worsened, making it necessary to lay off even more workers than originally planned. With unemployment already at very high levels, the workers decided to resist. Not only was IKA affected, but autoworkers at other plants put down their tools for twenty-four hours in sympathy. Despite that, some 6,100 blue- and white-collar IKA employees were dismissed. The unemployed retaliated by stoning the homes of some of IKA's top executives, and in a few cases homemade bombs were planted.[23]

Six months later there was more trouble at IKA. After an accident occurred at the plant on 12 August 1968, some 200 IKA workers walked off their jobs to protest the lack of safety precautions. Even before this, tensions had been building because of rumors that more layoffs were coming. All of the protestors were fired, whereupon SMATA called a strike. IKA's management responded with a lockout. The workers then put the factory under siege. Prevented from breaking into the building, they proceeded to stone it, breaking all the windows. A melee ensued with the police, during which five workers and four cops were hurt and one of the IKA executives' car was burned. Later in the day, in an act that presaged the *cordobazo*, the workers marched to the city's center for a public protest rally. Joined by radical students from the university, the rally turned into a rampage. Store windows were smashed, and cars and buses were turned over and set afire. Driven back by tear gas, the mob took refuge on the university campus. The next day they were downtown again, after failing to get into the factory. There were ugly scenes of violence before the police drove them off again.[24]

## The *Cordobazo*: The Motives behind the Events

From labor's point of view, the proximate cause of the May 1969 uprising in Córdoba was Governor Carlos Caballero's decision to abolish the so-called English Saturday. This was a local practice, dating from early in the century, by which workers received a whole day's pay on Saturday but only worked until noon. It always was unpopular with employers, and as more and more industry located in other provinces where the custom was not practiced, their arguments for abolishing it gained force. For labor, however, that meant extending the workweek from forty-four to forty-eight hours. So, when Governor Caballero issued his decree at the beginning of May, the SMATA workers at IKA and all the workers at Fiat's plants scheduled a strike for the fifteenth.[25]

Meanwhile, another serious strike, by the Córdoba Transport Workers' Union, was already in progress. This strike arose over seniority rights after Governor Caballero had arranged for the consolidation of fifty-five small transportation companies throughout the province into seven larger firms. The transport workers and the auto workers quickly agreed to form a common front to pressure the government.

About this time, too, Augusto Vandor, head of the UOM and acknowledged leader of a majority of the country's Peronist unions, arrived in Córdoba. His purpose was to meet with SMATA's Elpídio Torres, the transport workers' Atilio López, and Agustín Tosco of the power and light union—whose members were facing wage freezes and massive layoffs as a result of recent provincial government budget cuts. Though ideologically diverse, these men had a common interest in combating the austerity measures which General Ongania and Krieger Vasena seemed determined to impose on labor. Vandor, known popularly as El Lobo, had said recently that he was going on the offensive, to "show his teeth" to the regime. As a consequence of these union leaders' talks, by 17 May all of the principal unions in the province declared a general strike, bringing the economy to a halt.[26]

This power struggle between government and labor was serious enough, but it need not have become an outright rebellion had it not been for other groups that moved in to escalate it. Two such groups were the radical students and third world priests.

University politics had become violent in the 1960s, with communists often clashing with right-wing groups. An example of the latter was Tacuara, drawn from children of upper- and upper-middle-class families. Its ideology was a compound of extreme nationalism, preecumenical Catholicism, and anti-Semitism. One of the more curious political phenomena of the decade was Tacuara's gradual march from the extreme Right to the extreme Left, prompted primarily by a hatred of the United States. For Tacuara, not only did American imperialism threaten Argentina's sovereignty, but it threatened to inundate Hispanic culture with the mediocrity and crass materialism of its consumer society. Also facilitating this leftward shift was the Catholic church's increasingly critical attitude toward the capitalist nations, as exemplified in papal encyclicals like *Mater et Magistra* (1961), *Pacem in Terris* (1963), and *Populorum Progresio* (1967), for their alleged exploitation of the third world. The Second Episcopal Conference of Latin American

Bishops, held in 1968 in Medellín, Colombia, put the church on record as a supporting a social revolution in the region.

All of this had a powerful effect on young, politically minded Catholics, who later formed the Montonero movement: people like Emílio Maza, a student leader at Córdoba's Catholic University; Mario Firmenich, ex-president of Catholic Action's youth group; Juan García Elorrio, an ex-seminarian who started the radical journal *Cristianismo y Revolución* in 1966; Rodolfo Galimberti, son of a wealthy family, who later headed the Peronist Youth; and Fernando Abal Medina. Unable to embrace "godless" and "antinational" communism, these young revolutionaries concocted their own brand of radical national socialism and eventually attached their Montonero movement to Peronism as its left wing.

In the course of their brief but violent history, however, the Montoneros showed themselves willing to adopt a pragmatic outlook toward strategy, often collaborating with communist groups like the Trotskyite People's Revolutionary Army (ERP), the Guevarist Revolutionary Armed Forces (FAR), the Maoist Armed Forces of Liberation (FAL), or the rival Peronist Armed Forces (FAP). The Montoneros were unquestionably the largest of these underground movements, however. Moreover, they concentrated on urban terrorist tactics, whereas many of the others tried to apply the Maoist or Castroite principles of rural guerrilla warfare. All of them sought to forge an alliance with the labor unions in order to bring off a proletarian socialist revolution. The idea was not so farfetched, either. Many of the university students in Córdoba worked as part-time factory hands for the automobile companies, which allowed them to mingle with the workers and talk to them about the class struggle. Nor was this strange talk to the workers, who had been hearing similar ideas from prominent local labor leaders like Tosco. Now, as labor's confrontation with the authorities was coming to a head in Córdoba, these radical students were busy everywhere, fanning the workers' indignation and organizing other students on the campus for a protest march.[27]

Radical priests, the other catalytic element in turning labor's general strike into a social explosion, also were products of the Catholic church's newfound commitment to social activism. Calling themselves third world priests, or *tercermundistas*, they too attached themselves to Peronism and operated a network of clandestine clubs throughout the country, which they used for consciousness-raising (*concientización*) among students and workers. Their ties to the Church did not prevent them from cooperating with Marxist groups, either, and although they insisted that they were nonviolent, some of them were closely involved with the Montoneros, providing safe houses to hide guerrillas, arms, and underground presses. One, Father Alberto Carbone, was indicted as an accomplice in the kidnapping and murder of ex-president Aramburu. During the *cordobazo*, third world priests were conspicuous organizers of barricades and pickets.[28]

The real nexus between these radical groups and the labor movement was the so-called CGT of the Argentines, led by Raimundo Óngaro, head of the printers' union. Óngaro's labor confederation, created in 1968 as the result of a power struggle between himself and Vandor, took an uncompromisingly militant line toward the military regime and enjoyed Perón's official backing. Óngaro, a former seminarian and music student, preached an ideology that blended Marxism, nationalism, and primitive Christianity. Evita Perón, Fidel Castro, Camílo Torres, and the early church fathers were referred to constantly as model revolutionaries. He drew large crowds of students and left-wing intellectuals with his lyrical and visionary speeches:

> Those Christians who despise money, especially when they have to buy or sell with money gotten from exploiters, now have a chance to belong to a revolution that will convert all goods into common property, as the ancient fathers of the Church, like Tertullian, wanted. . . .
>
> They have a duty, at least once in the history of humanity, to go and take Christ down from the Cross. Because Christ is still nailed to the Cross: nailed through the workers, the poor, the shirtless ones, the humble, whom we keep nailed, whom we keep crucified. But we're going to rescue Christ in order to put Him at the head of our struggle: Christ triumphant, our Revolutionary Banner, the True Hope of Liberation![29]

When it was first launched, Óngaro's CGT of the Argentines had broader labor support than Vandor's CGT. Moreover, since Vandor had been dallying with neo-Peronism, Perón had put his stamp of approval on Óngaro. This, together with Perón's endorsement of guerrilla tactics as being justified by Ongania's suppression of democracy, had enabled Óngaro to forge a close relationship with the students and *tercermundistas*; but it had not prevented a steady erosion of his support among the more practically minded union bosses, who found Vandor's pragmatism more to their liking. The approaching confrontation in Córdoba might change all that, however, if the Radical Left gained control of events and inflicted a major defeat on the government. On 26 May, Óngaro's contact man in Córdoba, Miguel Angel Correa, announced that the CGT of the Argentines was pledging its support to the general strike.

## The May 1969 Upheaval

The *cordobazo* began on 29 May with a march by some 13,000 workers and students on the center of town. Feeling among the students was very high because earlier in the month clashes between police and students in the towns of Corrientes and Rosario had resulted in the deaths of three young protesters. Militants of the revolutionary Peronist University Commandoes for Organized Combat (CUCO), who infiltrated the march's student organizers, had something more than a demonstration in mind, however. Dismissing their cohorts as "petty bourgeois babblers" and boasting that CUCO was "further along in the struggle," they were engaged in "writing the first lines of a vast revolutionary process." As the march proceeded they took it over, turning it from a peaceful demonstration into a riot.[30]

If the *cordobazo* was not a spontaneous event, neither did it catch the government by surprise. Governor Caballero and his superiors in the Interior Ministry had ample evidence that a blowup was brewing and deliberately failed to take precautions to head it off. The explanation for this seeming paradox lies with the right-wing nationalists in Ongania's government who were hoping for a dramatic outburst of this sort so they could blame it on Krieger Vasena's liberal economic policies. Even after the violence erupted, Governor Caballero repeatedly refused offers of military support from the nearby Third Army Corps, insisting that his police could handle the situation. Only when it became clear that subversive groups were leading the rioters and the police were being overwhelmed did the government in Buenos Aires order the army to move in and restore order.[31]

It is also noteworthy that observers as far apart in their views as the RRP and Rogelio Frigerio agreed that reports on the violence in Córdoba were greatly exaggerated. The RRP asserted that, despite press reports of "civil war" and of Córdoba being "an occupied city," the mobs were in control of the streets for only five hours, from noon until late afternoon on 30 May. After that, the army had taken charge and soon confined the resistance to a few snipers. Only fifteen people died in the fighting: not the sort of casualty figures to suggest a civil war. Frigerio wrote Perón that the government itself was overplaying the level of violence in order to frighten the middle classes. State-controlled television channels kept showing the same few burning buildings and exaggerated the reports of street clashes. The UIA was taking advantage of the situation too, he claimed, to say that the *cordobazo* was proof that communists were in control of the unions.[32] But if the nationalists or liberals had deliberately used the *cordobazo* to weaken their opponents, their strategy worked much too well because Ongania swept his entire cabinet out of office, liberals and nationalists alike.

## Labor Moves Further to the Left

Labor relations did not improve after order was restored in Córdoba. Between June 1969 and July 1970 IKA-Renault lost about 2 million work-hours in strikes and factory seizures. SMATA workers called a wildcat strike on 12 May 1970, against the advice of their leader, Elpídio Torres, who warned that continued violence might force IKA to close for good. Over the next three weeks they took over a total of seven factories, protesting alleged plans by IKA to transfer its operations to another province.

Torres's warnings were based on evidence of a real danger that thousands of Córdoba workers would be out of jobs if labor violence continued. General Motors recently had canceled a project to build a plant there, and companies already located in the area were beginning to hive off their operations to branch plants in other provinces. Production had fallen in comparison with the previous year by 24 percent at IKA and by 6 percent at Fiat. That had a devastating effect on the auto parts and accessories industry. A lawyer for one of those companies summed up the situation glumly: "The profit margins of small *cordobés* industrialists depends on their ability to evade taxes and labor laws. This is a town where 'blank receipts' are common. There are no capitalists here, only lumpen-capitalists." One might have thought that such ubiquitous evidence of economic deterioration might have moderated the autoworkers. Instead, they turned against Torres as an "opportunist" and unseated him as head of SMATA in favor of the more radical José Rodríguez.[33]

Labor troubles were as serious at Fiat as they were at IKA. After years of isolating their workers from outside labor organizations, management there had lost control of its company unions. In March 1970 a coalition of left Peronists, Trotskyites, and communists took over the Fiat-Concord union, SITRAC (Sindicato de Trabajadores de Concord) and the Materfer union, SITRAM (Sindicato de Trabajadores de Materfer). One strike after another brought production to a virtual standstill. SITRAC-SITRAM defied management, the police, and the provincial government as they openly proclaimed their commitment to class warfare. "Elections may be a solution for the bourgeoisie's problems," one of their manifestos proclaimed, "but for the working class the only solution is a revolution that will destroy the present society, based as it is upon exploitation, and create socialism. That objective can be achieved only with weapons in our hands."

Not only did SITRAC-SITRAM attack capitalism, but they also refused to have anything to do with other unions, who were seen as being "tainted by bureaucracy." Consequently, SITRAC rejected support from the national CGT when the former decided to occupy the Fiat-Concord plant on 14 January 1971, although it did keep lines of communication open with the local branch of the CGT, which was headed by Maurício Labat of the taxi drivers' union, a Marxist and a close ally of Agustín Tosco. Thus, a Radical Left labor front began to form in Córdoba, consisting of SITRAC-SITRAM, Labat, Tosco, and SMATA. A heady sense of power and a shared commitment to overthrowing capitalism impelled those labor spokesmen to more extreme actions and eventually led Córdoba to its second *cordobazo* in March 1971.[34]

## The *Viborazo*

The second *cordobazo*, of 12 to 15 March 1971, was called the *viborazo* by some because the new provincial governor, Camílo Uriburu, had once bragged that he would cut off the head of the poisonous snake (*vibora*) of subversion that was threatening Córdoba. An ultraconservative from one of Argentina's aristocratic families, Uriburu attracted the hatred of the labor unions and the Left. The only local figure who was more unpopular was Oberdán Sallustro, Fiat's director, who was considered the very personification of capitalist power.

SMATA played a less important role in the *viborazo* than it had in the *cordobazo* because the ouster of Elpídio Torres had left the union badly split. Student activists were less prominent too because the university was still on vacation and only a few of them were in town. However, the dedicated revolutionaries, who had contacts inside the unions, were aware that another confrontation was sched-

uled and were on the scene helping to organize resistance committees in the lower-class barrios. The Fiat workers, who had played
only a marginal role in 1969, were the backbone of this new uprising. Tosco's power and light union was deeply involved too, shutting
off the power plants at night to create a citywide blackout that
spread confusion among the authorities and helped the revolutionaries control the streets.[35]

The *viborazo* began on 12 March with the workers' seizure of the
Concord and Materfer plants, after which they marched on the city
center and started erecting barricades. Meanwhile, students began
taking over the university buildings, which they turned into revolutionary command posts and factories for manufacturing Molotov
cocktails. As in the *cordobazo*, third world priests were much in
evidence, haranguing the crowds and helping to cut down trees to
block the streets.

At the Materfer plant Beba Balve, a social scientist, mingled with
the crowds of workers and students, who were carrying signs that
read Revolutionary Violence Against Reactionary Violence and
Power Grows Out of a Gun-Barrel. They had gathered around a
SITRAM leader who was making a speech without the aid of a micro-
phone from atop an improvised platform. An oil drum, converted
into a *bombo*, was banged furiously each time the speaker stopped
for a breath. His words set the theme for the event:

> Comrades! We say that we live in a society divided into
> classes. And that anyone who's not in the service of one class
> must be in the service of the other. [Shouts of approval] We're in
> the service of the working class, the class that produces. Now,
> there's another class, the class of the exploiters, who are the
> owners of the means of production, who manipulate the state,
> who control education, who have the power of guns. One class
> is on one side, and the other class is on the other side. And
> there's no possibility of compromise between them. [Applause]
> We, the workers, are the class that's historically destined to
> overthrow the system of exploitation—this system of repres-
> sion, this system of misery. And change it for another, which
> undoubtedly will be socialist. [Prolonged applause][36]

Though spirits were high, it is questionable whether the ordinary
factory hand really understood what his leaders were urging. After
the speech, Balve approached one of them. The exchange that followed, which he taped, says a great deal about the differences in
perceptions between the leaders and the rank and file.

*Balve*: Some people say your new union is made up of Marxists. You workers, what do you think?

*Worker*: No, no. We say we are not Marxists. We are nationalists. We don't have anything to do with any kind of politics. We think that what has to come here is some kind of socialism, sure—but nationalist, not Marxist, like people say we are. They also say that we're on the Communists' side, but no: they're wrong. Those are the same capitalists that are trying to propagandize against us, to say that we're communists or something. What happens here at Fiat is that the honest worker, or honest union delegate, they smear him by calling him a communist. Guys have been fired, you see, and weren't backed up by the majority of the union committee because they're all bureaucrats, always sitting on their butts. . . . "

*Balve*: Now, what does "socialism" mean to you?

*Worker*: Well, you see . . . look, uh . . . I myself see it as . . . you see, I really don't know how to explain it. . . . I wouldn't even want to try because I'd probably get it all wrong. The way I see it is good enough for me. Now me, probably I . . . let me see if there isn't someone else around here that can tell you better.

*Balve*: But I'd like an ordinary worker's opinion.

*Worker*: Well, I believe . . . I interpret socialism, like they say around here . . . that socialism's got to be on the left, see? If you get a socialism that's on the right . . . or in the center, see . . . it's like . . . any other party. . . . I think that the kind of socialism . . . that the people want . . . they want to have work . . . so we can all work, not just four or five guys. Because there are some people who think that socialism's all right for one bunch, but that the others . . . they're going to live better, right? It's like if you go to a hospital and you need help . . . I mean, you really need help, they ought to have a bed for you. Because if you go to a hospital these days they don't even look at you. And not just because they're on strike, but they don't even have a pill to give you, not even an aspirin! That's why I say, under socialism that's going to be all different. There's equality of classes . . . I don't know how you want to take that, but that's socialism for me.[37]

Other workers that Balve spoke to also rejected the idea that SITRAM was Marxist. One man volunteered the observation that union leaders could not be communists because, like all the other workers, they wore crucifixes on their chests. All of the workers denied any interest in politics, but many expressed the hope that by taking over Fiat they would bring about the downfall of the Levingston government (which in fact happened). They also showed a cunning awareness that the company's property and the hostages they had seized could be used to force concessions. More than one person interviewed expressed a willingness to burn down the factory if the army tried to intervene or starve them out.[38]

During the *viborazo*, Córdoba was in the hands of strikers for two and a half days. After nightfall, looters and rioters went on rampages throughout the darkened city, emptying stores, offices, banks, and bars. In the end, four heavily armed units of police infantry cleared away the barricades and, with little opposition, began restoring order. By the evening of 15 March most of the ringleaders were under arrest, along with 400 other people. Only one death was recorded during the events.

Although the government fell, as the strikers had hoped it would, the new government of Gen. Alejandro Lanusse was hardly an improvement for them. In October, Lanusse ordered Gen. Alcides López Aufranc, the local army commander, to suppress a fresh wave of factory occupations and crush SITRAC-SITRAM once and for all. The operation was carried out with dispatch. While provincial police occupied key points leading out of downtown Córdoba to prevent students or other workers from interfering, soldiers entered the worker-occupied Concord and Materfer plants and ordered the strikers to leave. Meanwhile, the union leaders were rounded up and taken away. There was no resistance. Afterwards, Lanusse issued a pair of decrees that merged SITRAC with SMATA, and SITRAM with the UOM, thus placing those unions under the control of the despised labor bureaucracy. While the local CGT condemned such action, the national leadership, secretly pleased, only lodged a mild protest.

The following month saw one last flurry of resistance. Remnants of the old SITRAC-SITRAM organization called for a strike on 2 November. This time General López Aufranc countered by inviting all unemployed workers in Córdoba who wanted jobs to report to the Concord and Materfer plants on the appointed day. Some 3,000 showed up to apply for the vacancies already created by the dismissal of some 400 who refused to go to work. The other factory hands, realizing that their jobs would be given away immediately if they joined the strike, filed obediently through the gates.

## The Heightening of Tensions

The suppression of classist unions like SITRAC-SITRAM did little to restore confidence to the business community. If labor violence tended to taper off, a yet more sinister specter arose in the form of terrorism by guerrilla bands of the Peronist and communist Left. Instead of factory seizures, businessmen now had to fear kidnapping, extortion, and assassination. Although the military was in power and unrestrained by law, the state seemed less and less able to protect those whom the Left singled out as its targets. In 1971 leftist guerrillas were involved in 527 shooting affrays that left 406 dead and 339 wounded. They also staged 414 armed robberies. In 1972 they were involved in another 417 shootings that resulted in 356 killed and 286 wounded. There also were 277 bank robberies, from which the guerrillas got more than 20 million pesos.[39]

Kidnapping was another lucrative line for the terrorists. In May 1971 the Trotskyite ERP guerrillas captured Stanley Sylvester, an honorary British consul and manager of the Swift packinghouse in Rosario. His crime was the dismissal of 4,000 workers the previous year. He was released after Swift distributed $50,000 worth of food and clothing to the poor. The kidnapping gained so much notoriety for the ERP that, after the squelching of the *viborazo*, they kidnapped Fiat's director, Oberdán Sallustro. This time they demanded that $1 million in food and clothing be distributed to Córdoba's poor and unemployed. They also insisted on the release of fifty political prisoners—captured guerrillas and SITRAC-SITRAM leaders. President Lanusse forbade Fiat to meet any demands and launched a full-scale search for Sallustro. Eventually a government patrol did locate the "people's prison" where the businessman was being kept, but during the ensuing gunbattle the guerrillas executed him before fleeing.[40]

Two other businessmen were kidnapped in 1972: Ronald Grove, the director of the British-owned Vesty meat corporation, who was released after the payment of a half-million-dollar ransom; and Vincenzo Russo, an ITT executive, who cost his company nearly $1 million in ransom. By this time the guerrillas were no longer content to demand a distribution of goods to the poor but were keeping the money to buy arms in preparation for bigger operations.

The early months of 1973, before the Peronists returned to power, saw a flurry of kidnappings, of which the most notable were those of[41]

1. Norman Lee, a Coca-Cola executive, seized in February and later released for $1 million;
2. Gerardo Scalmazzi, a Rosario banker, seized in February and released two months later for $750,000;
3. Héctor Ricardo García, owner of the Buenos Aires daily newspaper, *Crónica*, who disappeared in March;
4. Anthony de Cruz, a Kodak executive, seized in April and released after the payment of $1 million;
5. Victor Brimicomte, manager of the Nobleza tobacco company, captured by terrorists in April;
6. Santiago Soldati, son of a prominent local banker-industrialist, kidnapped in April and released for $1.5 million.

Nor was labor violence entirely dead. On 4 April 1972 the western regional capital of Mendoza had its *mendobazo* as workers and student radicals took to the streets to protest a rise in local electricity rates. They overwhelmed the local police and took control of the downtown. Looting and burning went on until the following day when troops were sent in to quell the rioting. Even then it took all day to smother all resistance.

The guerrillas were effective because they were supported by a large part of the educated and vocal public. At their height, the combined forces of the various guerrilla groups ranged between 15,000 and 30,000 hard-core militants. They in turn could count upon a support network of perhaps 300,000 more or less active sympathizers willing to provide them with money, information, supplies, and hiding places. There was an even greater number of passive sympathizers who acted as apologists for terrorism, many of whom were connected with the arts, the media, the schools, or the church, and therefore in a position to affect public opinion. It was not that these intellectuals were themselves kidnappers or assassins. "Nothing of the kind!" the conservative journalist, Roberto Aizcorbe conceded.

In fact, none of them would kill a fly. But they are fascinated by violence against established things and people. Above all, they love the language of violence. Thus, Nicolás García Uriburu in a "revolutionary" gesture dyes with paint the fountains of the Palais Chaillot in Paris! Oh! The priest Alejandro Mayol plays guitar on television, singing songs of protest. The millionaire Diego Muñiz Barreto declares to *Time* (September 10, 1973) that he is spending $50,000 a year in donations to arm partisans. The draftsman Miguel Brasco combines "eroticism" and

politics. Another priest, Carlitos Mújica, talks about his connections with the partisans to his girlfriends of the sophisticated Buenos Aires Lawn Tennis Club. Cacha Corral exhibits
the drawings of the Mexican Bolshevik Guadalupe Posada in
her gallery. Yuyo Noe is already painting with shit. How bold!
Nacha Guevara is performing her latest coffeehouse song,
"The Kick in the Ass." Lia Gelín stages the ballet "Viet Rock."
Pony Micharvegas monopolizes the broadcasting stations with
his ballads against capitalism. The Indian Mercedes Sosa asks
for another revolution. Mario Trevo launches his play *Liberty
and Other Intoxications*, and Joaquín Lavado, making fun of
the stupidity of parents, shows the wisdom of their children in
his comic strip *Mafalda*.[42]

"Are they fashionable because they are revolutionary Peronists,"
Aizcorbe wanted to know, "or are they revolutionary Peronists in
order to be 'with it'? It is difficult to find out."

Was all this intellectual posturing harmless? In the context of
rising violence it helped to sharpen tensions. While the terrorists
were confirmed in feeling like a heroic revolutionary vanguard, society's traditional elites were made to feel isolated and beleaguered.
Within the business community, fear and uncertainty led to a cessa-
tion of investment and increasing capital flight. In that respect, the
guerrillas succeeded in attaining one of their aims: the undermining
of the capitalist economy.

The guerrillas also succeeded in demoralizing the government,
and thus paving the way for Perón's return. What neither they nor
the businessmen perceived, however, was that the revolutionary fer-
vor had not yet penetrated the main body of the Argentine working
class, which might oppose the military regime but was not ready to
embrace socialism. The loyalty of the workers was to Perón; and
Perón, for all his recent encouragement of the guerrillas, was no
revolutionary either. Perón, then, was the one solution that all
could agree upon to restore order. And when he failed—as he eventually did—the panegyrists of violence would have their fill of it,
with a vengeance.

## CHAPTER SIXTEEN

# The Erosion of Union Power

Superficially, labor in the 1960s seemed a force second only to the military in power. Over 2 million workers, most of them skilled or semiskilled, belonged to unions. A majority were city born, streetwise, and felt a strong loyalty to Juan Perón, who continued to direct their political actions from exile. The unions they belonged to were relatively mature, having been formed a generation or two earlier, and had attained a considerable degree of experience in dealing with employers, government officials, and each other. They also were united by a comprehensive labor confederation, the CGT, which enhanced their ability to call general strikes.

Although unions usually were strong enough to fight back against austerity policies, essentially they were on the defensive. Bit by bit labor's share of the national income fell, from a high of 50.8 percent in 1954, under Perón, to only 35.9 percent in 1972.[1] The unions did not accept this trend passively. As table 16.1 shows, the early years of this period following Perón's fall saw a record number of strikes.

Nevertheless, labor fought a losing battle. Although the population only grew by a very modest 1.6 percent annually, employment in manufacturing, transportation, and communications rose by an even lower 1.2 percent. Most of the jobs found by people entering the work force each year were in construction, commerce, or services. Many of those were poorly paid, part-time, or seasonal. This trend toward a labor-surplus economy was further accentuated by a relentless substitution of capital-intensive for labor-intensive methods in industry. Strikes might slow down the introduction of new technology here or there, but they also spurred on efforts by employers to find any means to reduce their dependence on hand labor. In some cases, employers actually welcomed strikes, because emptying the factory gave them a chance to install new machinery.

Two other things helped to undermine labor's political effectiveness: its fragmentation into warring factions, and corruption among

Table 16.1 Strikes Recorded in the Federal Capital, 1932–1971

| Period | Number of Strikes | Number of Workers | Days Lost | Average Duration (in days) |
|---|---|---|---|---|
| 1932–35 | 268 | 116,126 | 4,728,672 | 37 |
| 1936–39 | 284 | 164,020 | 2,331,908 | 14 |
| 1940–43 | 305 | 65,946 | 1,193,765 | 18 |
| 1944–47 | 280 | 968,613 | 6,065,202 | 7 |
| 1948–51 | 192 | 420,747 | 5,853,369 | 14 |
| 1952–55 | 93 | 153,012 | 1,966,254 | 13 |
| 1956–59 | 239 | 2,846,646 | 24,881,227 | 9 |
| 1960–63 | 104 | 249,968 | 4,497,832 | 18 |
| 1964–67 | 92 | 584,286 | 2,233,225 | 4 |
| 1968–71 | 36 | 79,850 | 357,884 | 4 |

Source: Ministerio de Trabajo, *Conflictos de Trabajo* (Buenos Aires: Ministerio de Trabajo, 1966–72).

union bureaucrats that tended to divorce them from the rank and file. It is to these last two aspects of the labor movement that we must now give our attention.

## Rivalries in the Labor Movement

Working-class solidarity was relative in Argentina. First, there was a gap between the 2 million people who belonged to unions and the 4 million who did not. Second, there were status differences between white-collar *empleados* and blue-collar *obreros*. Third, among *obreros* there were status differences between the skilled and the unskilled. Fourth, there were differences in pay, job security, and future prospects between people who worked in industry, commerce and services, and agriculture. Fifth, although industrial workers were the most highly paid, those in dynamic industries usually earned between one-third and three-fourths more than those in the traditional industries.[2]

The division of the CGT into warring factions really blunted labor's power to defend itself, however. The first partisan split came immediately after Perón's fall, when socialists, communists, and Radicals succeeded in recapturing some of the unions from the

Peronists. By the time Aramburu called his "normalizing convention" of the CGT in 1957, the labor movement was polarized between a bloc of "62 Peronist Organizations" and the anti-Peronist
"32 Democratic Majority" unions. The former tended to be stronger
in the big industrial unions, such as the metalworkers' UOM and the
textile workers' AOT that grew up in the 1940s; the latter had their
base in older, craft unions, such as the printers' Federación Gráfica
and railwaymen's UF and La Fraternidad, that had won a place for
themselves in the system before Perón.[3]

Both of these blocs eventually fragmented. The militant anti-
Peronism of some of the 32 Democratic Majority leaders provoked a
reaction among their allies, leading to the formation of an Independent bloc that claimed to be politically neutral. This bloc had the
support of the powerful Unión Ferroviaria, the Power and Light Federation, the Commercial Employees' Confederation, and the Bank-
workers' Association. The 62 Peronist Organizations also broke up
in the mid-1960s, with a neo-Peronist group led by Augusto Vandor
rejecting Perón's right to dictate labor strategy from exile. Also,
besides anti-Peronists, Peronists, neo-Peronists, and Independents,
there were a number of nonaligned unions that belonged to no
camp.

Many attempts were made to overcome this fragmentation and
reunite the labor movement. They always failed, however, because
the 62 Peronist Organizations were as much an appendage of a political movement as they were a labor association, and they could
never resist the temptation to turn any alliance to their own partisan ends. The first attempt, after the breakup of the 1957 convention, to reestablish a united CGT came in 1960 following the separation of the Independents from the 32. A Committee of 20, composed
of ten Peronists and ten Independents, was formed to negotiate with
the Frondizi government to lift its intervention in the CGT. To back
up its demand, the committee staged a very successful one-day general strike on 7 November. The government was sufficiently impressed to agree to recognize the committee as the CGT's interim
directorate while plans were formulated to hold elections for another normalizing convention. The committee assumed those functions on 3 March 1961, but the political agitation that attended
Frondizi's last months in office and the chaos that broke loose after
his fall delayed the normalizing convention until January 1963.

By that time, as table 16.2 shows, the Peronists had gained in
strength while the non-Peronists had weakened. Consequently, the
62 were able to elect a majority to the convention and to the CGT's

executive committee. José Alonso, of the Peronist garment workers' union, was made general secretary and Avelino Fernández, of the Peronist UOM, became secretary of organization—a post that controlled the membership lists, managed the CGT's internal operations, and supervised its provincial branches. The Independents had to be satisfied with three seats on the seven-member executive committee, and with getting Riego Ribas of the Federación Gráfica accepted as adjunct general secretary.[4]

The CGT's unity soon fell apart when it became apparent that the Peronists intended to use the organization as a weapon against the newly elected government of Arturo Illia. Even before Illia was inaugurated, Augusto Vandor, head of the UOM and one of the most influential CGT figures, denounced the July 1963 elections as fraudulent because the Peronist party had been excluded from running. On 6 December, just after Illia took office, the CGT met with him to present their demands: (1) a minimum wage, adjustable to inflation; (2) price controls on basic necessities; (3) the creation of government jobs, to eliminate unemployment; (4) more consumer credit, on easier terms; (5) more public housing; (6) the rehiring of workers dismissed during recent strikes; and (7) the payment of pensions that recently had been suspended by the government for lack of funds. Although Illia seemed receptive, the CGT held a rally on the steps of Congress afterward to dramatize their demands.

In reality, Vandor and the other CGT leaders had little respect for the new government and were consciously working to bring it down. Elected with only a quarter of the popular vote, Illia's position was weak. Álvaro Abós, a Peronist historian of the contemporary labor movement, claims that Vandor's aim from the beginning was to replace Illia's regime as quickly as possible with a prolabor military government. Andrés Framini, head of the AOT, also admitted in an interview years later that there was an agreement between the 62 and the army's nationalistic wing to undermine Illia; and Paulino Niembro, a close collaborator of Vandor's in the UOM, confessed afterward that:

For us, each government that falls is a step closer to power. Experience indicates that Peronism will never get control of the government through institutional means. They all block us— even the Radicals. So we have to produce events. It was not in vain that we tried to bring Perón back. We had to destabilize things. At bottom, we knew that his return would not be meekly accepted, either by the Radicals or by the Armed Forces.

Table 16.2 Unions and Their Dues-Paying Members, 1957–1972

|  |  | 1957 | 1960 |
|---|---|---|---|
| *Peronists* |  |  |  |
| The 62 | unions | 46 | 46 |
| Peronist Organizations | members | 881,600 | 1,304,500 |
| Neo-Peronist | unions |  |  |
| (Vandor) | members |  |  |
| Orthodox Peronists | unions |  |  |
| (Alonso) | members |  |  |
| NCO and "the 8" | unions |  |  |
| (post-Vandor participationist) | members |  |  |
| Subtotal | unions | 46 | 46 |
|  | members | 881,600 | 1,304,500 |
|  |  |  |  |
| *Non-Peronists* |  |  |  |
| The 32 Democratic | unions | 29 | 9 |
| Majority | members | 1,339,800 | 90,900 |
| Independents | unions |  | 25 |
|  | members |  | 970,214 |
| Nonaligned | unions |  | 1 |
|  | members |  | 15,000 |
| National Intersyndical | unions |  |  |
| Movement | members |  |  |
| MUCS | unions |  | 8 |
| (Communist) | members |  | 155,000 |
| Subtotal | unions | 29 | 43 |
|  | members | 1,339,800 | 1,231,114 |
| Totals | unions | 75 | 89 |
|  | members | 2,221,400 | 2,535,614 |

Source: Rubén Zorrilla, *El liderazgo sindical argentino, desde sus origenes hasta 1975* (Buenos Aires: Editorial Siglo Veinte, 1983), pp. 129–30 (based on Dimase, *Nucleamientos sindicales* (Buenos Aires, 1972), p. 41.

We wanted to produce reactions. In order to keep up the pressure there was no other path open to us but to ally with the military.[5]

As early as May, while Guido's provisional regime was still in power, the Peronists had succeeded in getting the CGT executive to approve the Plan de Lucha, which called for street marches and protest meetings to pressure the government for prolabor measures.

| 1963 | 1966 | 1969–72 | 1972 |
|---|---|---|---|
| 53 | 13 | 24 | 77 |
| 1,266,900 | 98,400 | 474,900 | 1,766,930 |
| | 20 | | |
| | 408,350 | | |
| | 21 | | |
| | 417,700 | | |
| | | 42 | |
| | | 613,660 | |
| 53 | 54 | 66 | 77 |
| 1,266,900 | 924,450 | 1,088,560 | 1,766,930 |
| | | | |
| 3 | 1 | 1 | 1 |
| 24,400 | 2,000 | 2,000 | 2,000 |
| 28 | 7 | 1 | |
| 839,600 | 392,600 | 14,000 | |
| | 25 | 22 | 13 |
| | 489,600 | 734,600 | 171,300 |
| | | | 1 |
| | | | 3,000 |
| 5 | 2 | | |
| 43,100 | 18,100 | | |
| 36 | 35 | 24 | 15 |
| 907,100 | 902,300 | 750,600 | 176,300 |
| 89 | 89 | 90 | 92 |
| 2,174,000 | 1,826,750 | 1,839,160 | 1,943,230 |

The plan had gained a good deal of publicity for the unions but had been suspended during the elections and the interim before the new government took office. Now the Peronists wanted to resume the attack, escalating the plan to include seizing control of factories. The Independents disagreed, arguing that the new government was, after all, a democratic one and that it already was meeting some of the CGT's demands. Recent decrees had raised labor's real wages; a minimum wage bill was being prepared for congressional approval; unions were being consulted on economic matters; and much more legislation that labor wanted was making its way through the legislative process.

Such arguments failed to deter the Peronists, who on 18 May 1964 pushed a resolution through the CGT executive committee announcing that the second phase of the Plan de Lucha was about to start. Between 21 May and 24 June nearly 4 million workers participated in taking over more than 11,000 factories and shops all over Argentina. Each of these occupations lasted only twenty-four hours and were scheduled at different times and different places in order to gain maximum publicity and keep the authorities off balance.[6]

Conservatives were outraged. The UIA and CAC demanded that police be sent in to expel the workers. Obviously, that was not a practical solution, given the strategy and scale of operations of the plan. In any case, Illia preferred to move cautiously. To have used force would have solidified labor's ranks; instead he appealed to the moderate unions, pointing out that, since most of the strikers' demands were already being turned into law, it was obvious that the Peronists' aims were political. That argument had the desired effect. When the CGT's executive committee met again on 14 July to vote on continuing the plan, the Independents refused to approve it. When they were overridden, they announced that they were withdrawing from the CGT.[7]

This new schism robbed the CGT of much of its effectiveness. The 62 bloc was still too narrow a base to rest on. By itself it could not paralyze the economy or wring concessions from the government. Moreover, the CGT was deeply in debt, since the Plan de Lucha proved to be a more costly strategy than anticipated. At this point, Illia switched his tactics, freezing the Peronist unions' bank accounts and sending in the police to dislodge the strikers. When the 62 tried to hold a protest rally on 20 November, they were dispersed.

Not only did the Plan de Lucha fail to bring down even a weak government like Illia's, but it ended the brief period of unity that labor had managed to achieve after so many years of careful negotiation. The 62 were slow to admit their mistakes, however. Throughout 1965 there were more factory seizures, strikes, slowdowns, and sabotage. To the extent that the Peronists, by creating an atmosphere of perpetual crisis, paved the way for the military coup of June 1966, they achieved their original ends; but they did so at the cost of dividing the labor movement. Moreover, they soon were to be disillusioned by the very army officers whose return to power they had encouraged.

## Vandor versus Perón

Relations between Perón and the 62 Organizations were complicated. Labor was Perón's mass base, and Perón was labor's great
political symbol. Each needed the other; and on labor's side at least,
there was a degree of sincere admiration. Tension arose, however,
because Perón was in Madrid, while union leaders in Argentina had
to make decisions on the spot. There was not always time to wait
for *El Líder* to establish his position, and even when he did, his
information and criteria sometimes differed from what the Peronist
union leaders considered appropriate. Occasionally some of the
younger members, who did not know him from the old heroic days,
questioned his decisions. In 1962, for instance, Perón wanted the
Peronists to cast blank ballots in the March elections, but changed
his mind and allowed Peronist candidates to run after a labor delegation called on him in Madrid.

Absentee leadership inevitably caused pragmatic Peronists who
were willing to work within the given political system for immediate benefits to view *El Líder* as a stumbling block to participation.
Their inclination to adopt a neo-Peronist position of "Peronism
without Perón" was strengthened by the knowledge that their exiled chief was in his late sixties and that his prospects for returning
to power were growing dimmer. By the 1963 elections, it was clear
that Perón's grip on his followers was beginning to slip. Only 19
percent of the electorate obeyed his orders to cast blank ballots, as
compared to 24 percent in 1957 and 25 percent in 1960. Meanwhile,
legalized neo-Peronist provincial parties garnered a total of 7.7 percent of the vote in 1962 and elected 16 deputies to Congress. In
some provinces they were the dominant force.[8]

The majority of ordinary Peronists still believed, however, that
Perón eventually would return in triumph. But as the years passed,
the danger of disillusionment grew, so orthodox Peronist leaders in
Argentina hit upon a scheme to bolster the hopes of the masses.
"Operación Retorno" was simple in the extreme. First, Perón would
announce his imminent return to Argentina; then rallies would be
staged to generate excitement about the coming event. When expectations reached the fever pitch, Perón and a select entourage of top
figures in the movement would board an airplane in Madrid and fly
to Argentina. Illia would not dare arrest him. He would cave in to
public opinion and allow Perón to remain; then it would be impossible to keep Perón from returning to power.

This brainstorm was conceived by Augusto Vandor, spokesman

for the 62; Agustín Iturbe, Perón's personal delegate in Argentina; Delia de Parodi, leader of the Peronist Feminist party; Carlos Lazcano, general secretary of the Justicialist party; Andrés Framini, head of the AOT and spokesman for the left wing of the Peronist trade union movement; and Jerónimo Remorino, Perón's former foreign minister and his most trusted adviser. We do not know how enthusiastically Perón embraced the scheme, but he agreed that something dramatic had to be done to retain his prestige among the rank and file. In August 1964 he announced his "irrevocable" decision to return to Argentina before the end of the year, having already called for the army to desert Illia and reestablish its former alliance with the workers.

As finally carried out on 2 December, Operación Retorno was a comic-opera escapade. Both the Spanish and Argentine authorities knew, even before Perón left his mansion on the outskirts of Madrid and drove to the airport, which Iberia Airlines flight he would take. The airplane was stopped en route at Rio de Janeiro where the Brazilian government, at Argentina's request, ordered Perón and his entourage to disembark and put them on the next flight back to Spain. Generalissimo Franco, Spain's dictator, let Perón know that any more adventures of that kind would result in his being asked to leave the country. All in all, it was a silly scheme that did Perón's prestige little good.

But if Operación Retorno failed, the Peronists soon were able to claim success elsewhere. Illia allowed them to run in the March 1965 congressional elections, and although Perón raised objections to their participation, he wisely backed down when it became clear that Vandor, who favored the electoral strategy, had a majority of the Peronist Coordinating Council with him. This surprising challenge to Perón's authority arose from the jealousy felt by many Peronist politicians of their neo-Peronist cousins, quite a few of whom were enjoying the fruits of political office. Vandor, sensing that more defections to neo-Peronism would follow unless the Peronist party (then known officially in Argentina as the Unión Popular) accepted Illia's challenge to contest the elections, was even able to convince Perón that it was in the movement's interest to participate. The outcome confounded previous predictions that Peronism was in decline. The Unión Popular got 29.6 percent of the vote to 28.5 percent for Illia's UCRP. When that was added to the approximately 10 percent won by the neo-Peronist parties, the picture looked more like resurgent Peronism.

It was probably the combination of the Operación Retorno debacle and Peronism's electoral success that converted Augusto Vandor to neo-Peronism. On the one hand it seemed likely that Perón would never return. He was now seventy, and his political career appeared to be drawing to a close. On the other hand, the Unión Popular stood a good chance of getting a majority in the Chamber of Deputies in the next elections, scheduled for 1967, if they improved their organization. Organization would be the big stumbling block, however, because Perón—though he wrote copiously about the organized society—was instinctively hostile to any regularization of procedures within the movement that would limit his personal role. Vandor's desire to institutionalize Peronism and form an independent cadre of leaders put him at odds with Perón.

In this struggle, Vandor began with the support of a majority of the Peronist Coordinating Council in Argentina. The heads of the party organization, the feminist wing, and the trade unions were behind him. Moreover, the orthodox Peronist congressional bloc had already begun to form a front with the neo-Peronists. There was opposition, however, led by Andrés Framini, the AOT boss. After a brief, bitter skirmish, Framini and a few supporters were expelled from the Coordinating Council. They then set up a rival National Revolutionary Peronist Movement (MNRP) and accused Vandor of disloyalty to Perón. He in turn accused them of being more Marxist than Peronist. The question was, which side would the 62 Organizations support?[9]

Unable to go to Argentina to confront Vandor himself, Perón hit upon the idea of sending his wife, Maria Estela (Isabel), in his place. From October 1965 to July 1966 Isabel traveled about the country, meeting Peronist party politicians and labor bosses, mending fences, but also forcing them to display their subordination to Perón by paying homage to her. Vandor responded with more purges from the Coordinating Council, which Perón then countered by ordering the Coordinating Council dissolved and replacing it with a Supreme Delegated Command for Unity and Solidarity, whose composition he alone would determine.[10] Vandor, speaking for the 62 Organizations, refused to recognize the Supreme Delegated Command, which he said was composed of mere decorative figures who were not representative of Peronism's popular bases. That produced a schism inside the 62, with José Alonso, head of the garment workers' union and general secretary of the CGT, joining with Andrés Framini and Amado Olmos, the leftist head of the health workers' union, to form a breakaway group called the 62 Organizations Standing With Perón (De Pie con Perón). In January 1966 Vandor's segment of the 62 voted no-confidence in Alonso as head of the CGT, and a few weeks later the CGT's executive committee replaced Alonso with Fernando Donaires of the paperworkers' union.

Meanwhile, the struggle between Vandor and Perón shifted to the electoral arena. Attention was focused on two provinces that were holding off-year elections. Jujuy was holding gubernatorial and congressional races on 30 January; Mendoza was to have a gubernatorial election on 17 April. In Jujuy, Vandor was backing the Partido Blanco de los Trabajadores, led by José Humberto Martiarena, while Perón's surrogate was José Nasif's Partido Justicialista. Vandor's stock soared when Martiarena's list won 52 percent of the vote in a multiparty election, gaining 45,996 votes to Nasif's miserable 4,192. The bandwagon effect was instantaneous. A majority of the Peronist congressional bloc, which had been waiting nervously to see which way the political winds were blowing, now declared its loyalty to Vandor and, as a slap at Isabel Perón who was still in the country, repudiated all outside interference in the party's affairs.

The neo-Peronist euphoria was short lived. Throughout February and March, Isabel and her loyal entourage stumped every village and working class barrio in Mendoza Province in a do-or-die effort. It paid off. Although the Peronist split allowed a Conservative to get elected governor, the orthodox Peronist candidate came in a close second while the neo-Peronist ran a poor fourth behind the UCRP candidate. Now the herd of Peronist *políticos* stampeded back to Perón. The congressional bloc's unity evaporated as one Unión Popular deputy after another hastened to declare unswerving loyalty to the Grand Old Man in exile. Provincial party organizations in Chaco and Santa Fé suffered upheavals as orthodox Peronists threw out the neo-Peronists. The telephone workers, brewery workers, SMATA, and the stevedores deserted Vandor's 62 for Alonso's.

Partly offsetting those desertions was the fact that Vandor, by distancing himself from Perón, was able to entice many important Independent unions, like the printers' and the Unión Ferroviaria, back to the CGT. To encourage still more, Francisco Prado, a moderate from the power and light union, was named general secretary, replacing Donaires, who had joined the rush back to Perón. Vandor could also take some comfort in the fact that some conservative Peronists, like the construction workers' union, continued to stand by him. Nevertheless, the tide was running against him as the number of Peronist desertions grew. Only Ongania's coup prevented further erosion of his position.

Labor under Ongania

The June 1966 coup gave Vandor some breathing room and restored to him a modicum of importance, since it was known that he was friendly with some of the plotters. His CGT immediately pledged its support for the new government, which in turn decreed a very favorable wage increase for the metalworkers. Talk began to spread throughout the labor movement of a possible rapprochement with the military.

Perón tried to make the best of the coup. "For me, this is a fine moment," he told a reporter from PP, "because it ended a situation that could not go on." But he warned that it was Argentina's last chance to avoid a civil war. Unless Ongania prepared the country for a quick return to democracy, including the legalization of Peronism, there would be violence. As he warmed to the topic, Perón dropped his guard and admitted that he hoped Ongania would adopt a repressive line. "This is our last opportunity," he said. "It is necessary that the new government lack grandeur. In that case we can try a civil war, and in that war everybody's going to have to take sides."[11]

Perón got his wish. Moderate union leaders soon discovered that Ongania had no intention of sharing power with labor or favoring labor's interests in his economic policies. On the contrary, Ongania was determined to impose a barracks-like discipline on the whole country, the unions included. Labor got its first shock in August 1966 when the government decreed that labor disputes would henceforth be subject to compulsory arbitration. The next big shock came in October, when the government intervened in the operation of the ports, dissolved the dockworkers' union (SUPA), and began reforming existing labor practices. The third blow fell in January 1967 with the announcement of a new railway reorganization plan that would slash services and personnel. When the Unión Ferroviaria tried to hold a protest strike it was put under military intervention. Meanwhile, the government was forcing the closure of a great many inefficient sugar mills in Tucumán by withdrawing its subsidies; and when the sugar workers' union tried to demonstrate against this it too was subjected to intervention, and its leaders were arrested.

The government's reform of the ports showed what might be in store for the rest of labor. Determined to end the notorious corruption and restrictive labor practices on the docks, Ongania appointed a captain for each port with plenary authority to decide on all disputes involving loading and unloading. Any complaints about un-

healthy conditions had to be referred to him, and work had to continue in the meantime. SUPA lost its closed shop. Henceforth, all
hiring would be done by the port captain, including the appointing
of tallyclerks. Above all, the work day was changed. Instead of a
long midday break that allowed a stevedore to earn three days' pay
in overtime for nine hours of work, there were to be three staggered
shifts. While workers were getting three-hour breaks between work
periods a new shift would come on; thus loading was uninterrupted.
Furthermore, a laborer could earn overtime only by working one of
the two nighttime shifts. Night work, previously prohibited by the
union, was another innovation.[12]

When SUPA struck on 14 November, the port captains immediately hired nonunion *changas* to replace the stevedores who walked
off their jobs. Next, Eustaquio Tolosa, SUPA's general secretary, was
imprisoned because he went to an international longshoremen's
conference in London to urge foreign unions to boycott all ships
that called at Buenos Aires. After four months the dockworkers
were forced to lift their strike, and even then fewer than half of the
15,000 who struck were able to get their jobs back.[13]

Confronted by this unexpected attitude on the government's part,
Vandor decided to show labor's muscle by another battle plan, this
time called the Plan de Acción. On 3 February 1967 the CGT's executive committee voted to put the plan into effect. Despite Ongania's warning that this would be considered subversive, both the
pro-Vandor and the pro-Alonso unions agreed upon a nationwide
general strike for 1 March. With that, the government withdrew
legal recognition from the UOM, AOT, Chemical Workers' Union,
Sugar Workers' Union, and Telephone Workers' Union, and then
followed up by freezing their bank accounts.

This sort of forceful action demonstrated the negative side of the
Law of Professional Associations, so far as labor's interests were
concerned. Without legal recognition (juridical personality), a union
could hardly carry on any of its chief functions. For instance, the
contracts of both the AOT and the chemical workers' union were
about to expire; yet without legal standing they could not sign new
ones. Nor could they go to court to enforce the existing ones. In the
meantime, an employer could suspend his contributions to the social security fund and refuse to deduct union dues from his workers'
paychecks. Big unions might lose millions of pesos this way, since it
was highly unpopular for them to dun the members for dues later.
Shop stewards no longer were protected by the law and might be
fired if the boss were daring enough. Meanwhile, frozen bank ac-

counts meant that the union could not pay its officers' salaries, pay wages to its staff, pay its contractors, or pay out pensions. For a big union like the UOM, which employed over 200,000 people in its various offices, clinics, and resorts, and which owed hundreds of suppliers as well as the banks holding mortgages on its many properties, the financial squeeze was extremely painful.

It is not surprising, therefore, that the Plan de Acción collapsed under Ongania's tough tactics. In the wake of defeat, a confused and demoralized labor movement split again, this time into three camps. First, there were the collaborationists, led by Juan José Taccone of the power and light union and Rogelio Coría of the construction workers' union, who counseled cooperation with the government in hopes that such an attitude would win occasional benefits: rewards for rejecting extremists. Sharply opposed to them were the militants, headed by hardline Peronists such as Andrés Framini and certain Independent unions like the Unión Ferroviaria, which were under intervention. Between these two groups were the dialoguers, led by Vandor, who recognized the need to treat with the government but refused to pledge their cooperation in advance. The dialoguers gained an important ally in 1967 when José Alonso quit as head of the Standing With Perón faction of the CGT, because of his concern over what he considered Marxist infiltration of the militant unions, and sided with Vandor. A realist, Alonso also recognized that labor's efficacy under Frondizi and Illia had been due to its potential voting power, and that nothing could be gained by being intransigent toward a government that cared nothing for elections.

In March 1968 the CGT held a convention to elect new officers. The collaborationists refused to attend, however, and only 239 of the 477 eligible representatives were actually present. The militants recently had suffered a psychological setback when one of their most admired figures, Amado Olmos of the health workers' union, died. But in the course of the convention they were to discover another electrifying figure to lead them: Raimundo Óngaro, head of the printers' Federación Gráfica, whose passionate, evangelical style of speaking brought the delegates to their feet time and again as he called for a crusade against capitalism and imperialism. His magnetism helped the militants to sway wavering delegations and so gain an unexpected victory over Vandor's dialoguers. It was a pyrrhic victory, however. The vandoristas refused to accept the convention's verdict on the grounds that, the collaborationists being absent, it was not truly representative of the labor movement. After walking out of the convention they reassembled at CGT headquar-

ters and elected a rival executive committee. Faced with two organizations, each of which claimed to be the true CGT, General Ongania
did not hesitate to grant legal recognition to Vandor's side. Óngaro's
group, which called itself the CGT of the Argentines, had to settle
for the status of an unofficial but tolerated organization.

In fact, the CGT of the Argentines soon went into decline. Though
a spellbinding speaker, Óngaro had little regard for organizational
details. He had a mystical streak that left most hardbitten labor
organizers cold, although it made him extremely popular with student activists and third world priests. Vandor, meanwhile, threw
his tremendous energies into fence-mending. Realizing that the established unions had neglected the interior, he and his lieutenants
began to crisscross the country, getting to know local labor leaders
from the interior and speaking at local rallies. Although he lacked
Óngaro's charisma, Vandor had more solid virtues. His courage was
unquestioned, having been tested in dozens of battles; he was
known as a tough bargainer who won substantial benefits for his
men; and though no intellectual, he was undeniably devoted to
building up labor's power in the political system and, practically
speaking, was the most competent person after Perón himself to
accomplish that. Ultimately, those characteristics counted for more
in this macho world of labor than Óngaro's dreamy mysticism. Bit
by bit the local organizations came over to Vandor's side, even
though Perón gave Óngaro his endorsement. By early 1969 Vandor
was once again able to claim the support of a majority of the labor
movement, the collaborationists having swung behind him as well.

Such was the labor scene on the eve of the *cordobazo*. The events
of May, however, suddenly threw everything into confusion while
opening up new possibilities. Vandor and the dialoguers, together
with the collaborationists, were forced to review their strategy,
which was based on the assumption that Ongania would be in
power for a long time. For Perón, there was the possibility of engineering Ongania's fall and driving a bargain with the next government—but only if he could find someone more effective than Óngaro at uniting the unions and using them as a battering ram. Thus,
Perón and Vandor suddenly discovered their need for each other.

On 23 June 1969 Vandor flew to Spain and joined Perón in Ali-
cante, where they negotiated for the next two days. According to
one report, published in *PP*, Perón finally agreed to switch his support from Óngaro to Vandor in return for the latter's pledge of loyalty. Vandor, arriving back in Buenos Aires on the twenty-sixth,
announced that he would not support Óngaro's call for a general

strike to follow up the *cordobazo* and instead called upon the government to make concessions to moderate unions before it was too late. He also suggested that both he and Óngaro resign their positions as rival CGT leaders in order to facilitate labor's reunification. But if all this was part of a strategy worked out with Perón, it came to nothing, for Vandor was gunned down by Montonero terrorists four days later as a traitor to the working class. It was a grievous blow to the government. Ongania retaliated by arresting Óngaro and shutting down the CGT of the Argentines, which until then had been permitted to carry on its activities in a legal twilight.[14]

But General Ongania, chastened by the *cordobazo*, was wise enough not to rely solely on force to master the situation. In September he announced that he was lifting the government's intervention of the CGT and returning control to the workers. To prepare for that, he appointed a Committee of Twenty-Five, made up of leading collaborationists and dialoguers, to act as a provisional directorate until elections could be held. Ongania himself was out of office by the time the process was completed, having fallen victim to a coup. A reunited CGT elected José Alonso as its general secretary, but he was not allowed to enjoy his position for long. He too was considered a traitorous union bureaucrat by the Montoneros, who assassinated him in an ambush on 27 August 1970 as he drove to work.

There was a certain irony to this drift of events, because just as the labor movement began to reunify itself after the painful factional struggles of the 1960s, the Peronist movement was dividing along new lines. A bitter and bloody struggle was about to begin between its trade unions and the leftist guerrillas.

## Union Bureaucracy

To an Argentine leftist, a union bureaucrat was a loathsome creature: corrupt, unrepresentative, a tool of the capitalists, and a traitor to his class. The Montoneros dealt their version of justice to men like Vandor and Alonso in the belief that they were vindicating the proletariat, who so often had been fooled and exploited by these false leaders. Part of the romanticism that characterized that generation of Argentine youth involved a stated belief in "direct democracy" and a corresponding antagonism toward hierarchies.

It was impossible, of course, to have unions without hierarchies. Unless there were leaders and chains of command, the unions could not be at all effective in battling management. Organization not only required bureaucracy but a lot of solidarity and conformity as well. Moreover, to the extent that the Law of Professional Associations encouraged nationwide labor organizations, it was inevitable that the topmost leadership stratum would become distant from the workers on the factory floor. The very process of building powerful organizations to promote working-class interests created the problem of how to keep those organizations responsible to their members.

The ordinary labor union hierarchy offered an attractive avenue of ascent for bright young people in the working class. A University of Belgrano survey of top labor union officials, carried out in 1969, showed that the average age was only forty-four, which suggests that they left the factory floor for a union job fairly early in life. In addition to ambition, education seems to have been an important factor in an individual's ascent into the hierarchy. The same survey found that a majority of officials had completed primary school and that almost a third had finished high school as well, whereas in the working class as a whole only about one of five had finished primary school. Energetic workers who could articulate their comrades' frustrations and present their demands forcefully to the management were more likely to get elected shop stewards, the first rung on the union's ladder of power.[15]

A shop steward's job was demanding. In addition to union duties, he continued to hold a regular job in the plant and drew the same pay as the other workers. Except in a few cases where the union was rich enough to buy up its shop stewards' time from the management, union work would have to be relegated to after-hours, which meant that most shop stewards put in long days. Often their weekends were taken up, too, with meetings. They enjoyed few advantages over ordinary workers. They could not be fired for acts done in the course of carrying out their duties, nor could they be punished in other ways, such as through pay cuts or reassignments to unpleasant tasks. Indeed, it was usually considered an act of war for an employer to try to fire or discipline a shop steward for any cause.

The shop steward, standing between the leadership and the workers on the floor, played a delicate and pivotal role in the union's organization. Therefore, the importance accorded him by the union bosses was a good measure of how democratic the organization was. Shop stewards were also frequently on the front line in conflicts between labor and management, since most grievances originated at the factory level. A worker who felt unfairly treated went first to one of the shop stewards, of which there were several in most enterprises of any size. If the complaint seemed serious enough, the steward might call a plant assembly of all the workers to discuss what should be done. In that event, the law required management to provide space on the premises for the meeting to be held and to continue paying the workers while they met.[16]

To get elected shop steward usually required the help of a political patron further up in the union hierarchy. Many unions were divided into political factions, each headed by a *caudillo* and his lieutenants. Elections at all levels tended to be contests between rival lists of candidates representing these factions. At election time, these lists would be color coded to help the poorly educated workers chose among them, and slogans would be painted on the factory walls, or throughout the surrounding neighborhood, in the appropriate color: Vote the Blue List! or Vote the Orange List! It was particularly important to have the patronage of a *caudillo* to rise beyond the shop steward level. There were various possibilities for ascent, depending on where one could secure patronage. The usual route was from the shop floor to the local union branch committee, then to the provincial committee, and finally to the national federation. An alternative might be to work on the staff of the CGT's provincial office before moving up. Yet another channel of ascent, if the union was Peronist, would be to serve as a delegate to the bloc of 62 Organizations, from which one might become active in the labor wing of the Peronist party.

On the way up the union ladder, the energetic former shop steward came into contact with top labor officials, politicians, and representatives of capital. These contacts broadened the aspirant's perspectives and provided opportunities for gaining experience in negotiation, acquiring knowledge about how politics operate, and picking up organizational skills. Within the union bureaucracy, he might be in charge of distributing social assistance, dealing with labor courts, managing union property, handling personnel, purchasing, or making investments. As he rose, he would acquire his own personal following and as its *patrón*, he would get increasingly out of touch with former colleagues on the shop floor and with their daily concerns. Even with the best of intentions, this was inevitable: "The . . . estrangement between the leaders and their base is not necessarily because the union leadership is unrepresentative or unenergetic in defending the interests of its members. The fundamental cause lies in the fact that it is increasingly more difficult for the bases to understand the attitudes of its leaders, who are obliged to negotiate and to 'see the adversary's point of view.'"[17]

This incomprehension sometimes led to wildcat strikes, which became more common in the late 1960s and early 1970s as real wages deteriorated. The alienation of the proletariat from its leaders was also encouraged by the highly centralized process of collective bargaining. Negotiations for labor contracts were handled through the Labor Secretariat, which brought representatives of employers' and workers' federations together to sign industrywide agreements. Although the two sides were allowed some leeway in the process, the final agreement had to be within limits laid down by the government's economic plan. In the event of disagreement, the Labor Secretariat would simply impose a solution.[18] To the workers on the shop floor, the resulting contracts often seemed outrageous, especially when real wages continued to decline. Workers blamed the national leaders for selling them out and put pressure on the shop stewards to either stick to a militant line or seek ways of evading the contract's terms by pushing ambiguous clauses to their limit or by interpreting the contract so literally ("working to rule") that production slowdowns would result. The national union leadership was thus placed in a dilemma: they hesitated to repudiate their own rank and file; yet their credibility as negotiators depended on their ability to maintain union discipline. Management too preferred dealing with top-level labor leaders, who, though "credited with being hard bargainers," were nevertheless "considered relatively able and reasonable, politics apart." Shop stewards, on the other hand, were viewed as "a mixed bag. Distinct anatagonism [existed] in some cases."[19]

Union bureaucracies dealt with large sums of money, valuable properties, and diverse social services. The Power and Light Federation, for example, managed an investment account of 3.5 billion pesos (about $14.7 million) in 1966, which was about twice the amount invested by the entire SIAM conglomerate that year. It owned an insurance company, a construction company, several housing subdivisions and apartment blocks, a number of resort hotels, a golf course with a country club, a furniture store, and a chain of self-service department stores. It also furnished its members with kindergartens and day-care centers, clinics and retirement homes, libraries, recreational centers, cultural activities, and technical training. Nor was this union peculiar. The Unión Ferroviaria managed an annual investment fund of 2.2 billion pesos ($9.6 million), and even smaller unions like the state oilworkers' (SUPE) owned luxury hotels and other valuable property. It was estimated in 1972 that half of the first-class luxury hotels in the beach resort of Mar del Plata were owned by labor unions.[20]

The handling of these obligations required the employment of large staffs including well-paid professionals: lawyers, doctors, nurses, accountants, investment counselors, and management specialists. The responsibilities that went with tending such an economic empire naturally tended to make the top leadership more conservative and pragmatic. There was also an inevitable temptation to use union funds for private purposes. Union officials commonly provided themselves with high salaries and lavish expense accounts. The general secretary of the bank workers' union, through an annual salary plus expenses, made about three times what a senior bank employee earned. The Unión Ferroviaria executive committee paid themselves the equivalent of $2,000 a month plus another $1,200 for expenses and were allowed to hire assistants (i.e., close friends or relatives) at another $1,200: all at a time when the average railroad employee earned $800. In addition, many employers paid labor leaders under the table to avoid strikes. The head of the telephone union in Córdoba got, in addition to his annual salary of $60,000, another $40,000 for travel and was drawing yet another $100,000 for serving on the company's board of directors.[21]

It was easy to manipulate the union's administrative machinery for private gain. Lorenzo Miguel, the UOM's treasurer, and Paulino Niembro, another high official in the union, got rich by forming a company to handle all the organization's insurance. Every UOM member had to carry both life and accident policies, which cost 1.5 percent of his wages. Since the average metallurgical worker earned around $2,000 a year, Miguel and Niembro could expect to gross about $6.6 million. On top of that, they had the exclusive contract to supply medical equipment to UOM clinics.

Rogelio Coría, a Peronist who wrested the construction workers' union from the Communists in 1966, built up an immense fortune in just a few years by setting up a collection agency, with government approval, to raise special levies from the workers. His agency charged a 20 percent commission on all the money it was able to extort from the luckless proletarians, which brought him $2.5 million in 1969 alone. Coría lived in a luxury apartment in the Barrio Norte, operated out of a sumptuous downtown office, and eventually retired to a large *estancia* in Paraguay.

Although raised in a *conventillo*, José Alonso, head of the garment workers' union and at various times secretary of the CGT, was residing in a mansion when terrorists gunned him down in 1970. His modest salary of $3,500 a year could not account for his five-bedroom house that included two dining rooms, servants' quarters, and spacious surrounding gardens. Nor could it have paid for his beautiful downtown apartment, his weekend chalet, or his two big limousines.

Probably the most notorious grafter of all was Armando March, the suave, manicured boss of the commercial employees' union. As a prominent anti-Peronist he enjoyed unofficial support from Aramburu, Frondizi, Guido, and Illia, each of whom tolerated his brazen plundering of the union's funds. For example, Frondizi let him take about $64.3 million from his union's retirement fund to build housing for workers; but of the 3,950 units that were to be built, only 257 were ever finished. The rest of the money was invested, under March's name, in banks and mining companies, leaving almost nothing for the union members' old age. Although March drew a paltry salary of only $657 a year he lived in a beautiful mansion in a fashionable Buenos Aires suburb, dressed like an English lord, collected expensive paintings, and raised prize-winning cocker spaniels. In 1969 he fell afoul of the rather prudish Ongania government and was sent to jail after an investigation revealed that over the years he had diverted almost $30 million from the union's account at the Banco Sindical, where he was a director, into a dummy insurance company he owned.

The manner by which unions were financed gave their officers a certain amount of independence with respect to the membership. Dues, the most obvious source of union funds, ranged between 1 and 5 percent of a worker's wage and were withheld from paychecks by the employer, who then turned the sum over to the Labor Secretariat. The money would then be deposited to the union's account. Since workers were powerless to keep back their dues, they had no financial hold over their leaders. And the leaders, so long as they cooperated with the Labor Secretariat, were not closely monitored as to how they drew on their accounts. But even dues accounted for only 35 percent of a typical union's income, according to a 1965 study by *Análisis*. In some of the big industrial unions, that percentage might be as low as 20 percent. The rest came from returns on their investments and from special levies.

Another way of raising money, which was deeply resented by the membership, was to get permission from the Labor Secretariat and levy a surcharge on dues. For instance, in 1966 the UOM took in 650 million pesos ($2.7 million) in dues but then asked for the right to assess its members an additional charge on the grounds that its operating expenses required over a billion pesos. A more common way for national leaders to get additional funds was by skimming off a percentage of every official wage increase granted to their union, as a premium for their lobbying efforts. Usually the leaders pocketed the entire increase from the first monthly paycheck. Since the actual amount that any individual worker had to kick back was small, there was usually no resistance to this practice; but the total amount garnered by union leaders could often be considerable. In 1971 the garment workers' union raised about $1 million in this fashion.

With so much opportunity for corruption on a grand scale, it is not surprising that competition for union offices often got violent. Prominent labor leaders were surrounded in public by scores of bodyguards. Some of them, like Augusto Vandor and José Rucci (the GGT's general secretary from 1970 to 1973), adopted the practice of having several hideouts around Buenos Aires and moving constantly from one to another. Given such an atmosphere, it could be expected that incumbent officers would use their private armies to insure their reelection. Since incumbents also determined the procedures, kept the registration lists, decided on the eligibility rules, controlled the finances, and counted the votes, opposition candidates had an uphill struggle, to say the least. If the latter controlled powerful local or provincial organizations, they might have a chance to score an upset; otherwise, their odds were slim unless the dominant group broke up. Then the contest might really get bloody, as it did in the UOM after Vandor's assassination in 1969. Indeed, the two factions contending to succeed him actually fought a gunbattle in front of the union's headquarters in downtown Buenos Aires.

When the struggle pitted Peronists against non-Peronists, other unions sometimes got involved in order to keep the national balance of power from tilting against their bloc. During the 1964 elections in the commercial employees' union, the Peronist challenger, Juan José Minchillo, sought help from Vandor's UOM to unseat the anti-Peronist incumbent, Armando March. During the voting at the federal capital headquarters March's pollwatchers called in the police to arrest sixty people who had just cast their ballots, accusing them of being nonmembers carrying false credentials. The arrested group eventually confessed that their union cards had been manufactured by the Peronist Union of Plastics Workers and that they were made out in the names of confederation members who had never voted, from a list furnished by the UOM. Naturally, when their envelopes were opened they were found to contain ballots from Minchillo's "yellow list."[22]

Union democracy was the exception, not the rule. One student of Argentine labor politics, Juan Carlos Torre, found only two instances out of 175 elections held between 1957 and 1972 in which an incumbent leadership lost. Francisco Pérez Leirós, longtime boss of the municipal workers' union, was unseated in November 1966 because the Ongania government appointed pollwatchers to make sure the registration lists were not altered and the ballots were counted fairly. Also in 1966, Raimundo Óngaro won control of the Federación Gráfica when the incumbents split and supported different lists in the elections. Long incumbencies were no proof, of course, that a union was undemocratic. The Power and Light Federation, led by Juan José Taccone, was reputed to have fair, honest elections in which over 90 percent of the membership voted. Still, there were very few unions that could boast of such democratic reputations.[23]

One reason why union elections tended to be fraudulent was government permissiveness. Just as governments sometimes overlooked corrupt financial practices for political reasons, so they also tolerated the most blatant electoral frauds. In 1972, for example, the Lanusse government was trying to curry favor with the CGT's general secretary, José Rucci, who also headed the UOM's local branch in San Nicolás. A street-smart punk with a sarcastic grin and a cigarette usually dangling from his lips, Rucci was so high-handed that a serious revolt against him had broken out in San Nicolás. Alarmed that he might lose the forthcoming elections in March, he got the UOM's national executive committee to cancel the contests and simply appoint him for another term. The Lanusse administration approved of this coup without a murmur, all the more so because the opposition was considered too far to the left.[24]

Even when the government did try to reform union practices, it was no easy matter to make them democratic. Andrés Framini dominated the AOT for almost a generation using fraud and intimidation; yet, his being jailed by Aramburu and put under investigation by Illia failed to shake his hold on the union.[25] Even when given an opportunity to vote freely, thanks to government supervision of the elections, the AOT membership continued to support Framini's "green list." The Ongania government got him out, however, by using questionable tactics itself. First it intervened in the AOT and appointed a provisional committee to manage the union and hold new elections. The provisional committee was controlled by Framini's former lieutenant, Juan Carlos Loholaberry, who now headed a rival, neo-Peronist faction. In the May 1967 elections Loholaberry's men used the familiar tactics of stuffing the ballot boxes to keep themselves in power and defeat Framini's bid to regain control. Framini's protests about fraud were undoubtedly true but certainly sounded lame coming from the man who had taught Loholaberry how to play the game. Two years later the government engineered Loholaberry's replacement by Adelino Romero in the same way: intervention followed by the appointment of an interim committee and fraudulent elections.

Often unions were undemocratic because most workers, having little education or civic experience, were apathetic. So long as they were reasonably satisfied, or at least not driven to desperation, they took little interest in what their leaders were doing. A 1970 report by the Labor Secretariat, covering the previous five years, showed that fewer than half of all union members eligible to vote actually exercised that right. The average turnout for a union election was 45 percent. Single-slate elections had also become more common.[26] Interviews with members of Agustín Tosco's power and light union in Córdoba give an excellent insight into the ordinary worker's attitude about union politics and loyalty toward leaders. A manual worker in the city's electric company said that he supported Tosco because "he doesn't put his hand in the till." Also, he added, while in other unions they sell out the workers and use the threat of strikes to extort money from the management, "here they consult the local membership in the assemblies, and there aren't any killers like they have in the UOM." Did he participate in elections and assemblies? "I hate to admit it, but the majority . . . see . . . are like me, pretty well-off. We don't bother going to meetings. . . . I've got a small garage at my house and I work there in the afternoons, so I'm too busy to go. But we all answer the strike calls: 100 percent."[27]

Another worker at the central power plant said he voted for Tosco because of his honesty, not for his political views, which he thought were in a minority among the members. Did union members go to the assemblies? "There are all kinds of people in my section. . . . Lots of them are apathetic, except if they're touched in the pocketbook—then they get combative. Others think that the whole working class ought to get together, not just the Power and Light Union. . . . They're living well and they want others to live well too. I agree, but some comrades don't see it that way yet, but at least they don't bother us and they go along with the decisions, out of discipline."

Why didn't people go to the assemblies? "It depends on the topic.

But I think they just trust 'the Gringo' [Tosco] and figure he'll decide all right after all. So why bother? They already know, through the *Electrum* [the union newspaper] what they're going to talk about and they have a notion of who's going to speak and what they're going to say. Lots of them figure it's not worth going unless they're going to deal with something that affects their section. But if a strike is called, they'll obey—like I said, out of discipline."[28]

A female employee in the central office of the electric company was probably typical of the apathetic member. She said that she had no interest at all in politics, nor did her friends. They voted for Tosco because he always defended the union, no matter what sort of government was in power. How did she view the union's affairs? "Um . . . there's a lot of discipline. Everybody obeys the assembly's decisions. Personally, I never go because I've got the house to look after . . . and anyway, like I told you, political discussions at the assemblies don't interest me."[29]

By the early 1970s formerly apathetic union members all over Argentina were beginning to turn militant because of the steady deterioration in their real wages. Public sector unions, especially, were becoming radicalized because of the military's attempts to prune the government payroll and hold down spending. It was telephone, postal and telegraph, and civil servants' unions—not the blue-collar industrial unions—that formed the backbone of Raimundo Óngaro's CGT of the Argentines.[30]

In some cases, where union bosses tried to ignore the new current of opinion, there were open rebellions. In 1972 the Union of Restaurant Personnel met resistance when it decided to levy a special tax on its 50,000 members. An assembly called to ratify the decision turned into a brawl after the leaders announced that the measure had passed by 146 votes to 34, when only 150 delegates were present. Many locals subsequently refused to pay. Similarly, the Tucumán Federation of Sugar Workers was forced to revoke a special levy after its members rose up in protest. In 1972 Rogelio Coría, of the Construction Workers' Federation, sent gunmen to Rosario to quell a revolt by the local union, which refused to pay a special levy. There was a gunbattle, ending in the local's surrender, but Coría was forced by the government to resign the following year. He retired to his Paraguayan *estancia*, but, not surprisingly, he was assassinated by left-wing terrorists as a traitor to the working class on a return visit. In 1973 Jerónimo Izzeta, head of the Buenos Aires Provincial Federation of Municipal Workers, touched off widespread protests when he announced that he was pocketing the first month of the

Table 16.3 Dues-Paying Members of the Largest Unions
in the CGT, 1963 and 1970

| Union | 1963 | 1970 |
|---|---|---|
| Unión Ferroviaria | 222,978 | 178,443 |
| UOM | 219,000 | 125,759 |
| Commercial employees | 200,000 | 171,000 |
| UPCN (civil servants) | 190,000 | 50,100 |
| AOT (blue-collar textile workers) | 150,000 | 105,000 |
| ATE (state workers) | 150,000 | 111,237 |
| Construction workers | 95,000 | 75,143 |
| Garment workers | 80,000 | 43,000 |
| Bank workers | 65,000 | 62,500 |
| Gastronomic workers | 60,000 | 26,500 |
| Meatpackers | 55,000 | 43,706 |
| *Buenos Aires municipal workers | 55,000 | 65,000 |
| Wood workers | 50,000 | 33,000 |
| Bus and trolley workers | 50,000 | 10,000 |
| *Power and light workers | 41,250 | 50,590 |
| Health workers | 38,000 | 30,700 |
| Food-processing workers | 36,800 | 25,172 |
| Sugar workers | 36,354 | 19,142 |
| Rural workers | 35,000 | 25,000 |
| Printers | 32,000 | 23,494 |
| *State oilworkers | 30,000 | 30,000 |
| *Telephone workers | 28,000 | 30,000 |
| La Fraternidad | 25,500 | 22,133 |
| Commercial travelers | 22,050 | 11,000 |
| Wine bodega workers | 21,050 | 11,000 |
| *Municipal confederation | 20,365 | 56,884 |
| Merchant marine | 20,000 | 13,117 |
| Glassworkers | 15,000 | 10,878 |
| Textile employees (white-collar) | 14,000 | 9,045 |
| Dockworkers | 13,696 | 6,429 |
| Newsvendors | 12,143 | 7,000 |
| Miners | 12,000 | 11,576 |
| Vegetable oil workers | 12,000 | 10,612 |
| Chemical workers | 11,500 | 10,140 |
| Racetrack staff | 10,500 | 7,000 |

Source: Rubén Rotondaro, *Realidad y cambio en el sindicalismo* (Buenos Aires: Editorial Pleamar, 1971), pp. 371–72; based on CGT statistics.
*Did not decline in membership.

new wage increase won by the union. The amount in question was about a billion pesos, or around $900,000. Representatives of several union locals converged on the labor secretary to demand that Izzeta be overruled while municipal workers in Avellaneda and Morón went on strike to back them up. Although Izzeta sent in squads of goons to intimidate the protesters, he finally was forced to forego the money.[31]

By the time the Peronists returned to power, the labor movement was in decline, having lost some 600,000 dues-paying members between 1960 and 1972. Table 16.3 shows the extent of this erosion in the largest unions and illustrates that only some of the militant public sector unions were able to hold their own.

High levels of unemployment, and underemployment, played a part in demoralizing the working class. Organized labor had no effective weapons to oppose the introduction of labor-saving technology in industry. Nor did it have any power to prevent the shrinking number of employment opportunities in both the private and public sectors as the economy stagnated. It could lay the blame elsewhere—on the imperialists, the oligarchy, or the politicians—but that was not enough to prevent cynicism or radicalism from affecting the unions' lower echelons and threatening the whole system of labor bureaucracy and bossism.

Still, labor was to have one last fling under the new Peronist regime from 1973 to 1976. As it became clear that the military dictatorship was fading and Perón's return was imminent, there was renewed interest in union membership, since it was assumed that labor would enjoy a privileged position. Dues-paying membership rose from about 1.84 million in 1970 to over 1.94 million in 1972. The enthusiasm did not last, however. The long-awaited *retorno* was to end in fresh disillusionment for the Argentine working class.

# PART FOUR

# Descent into Chaos

CHAPTER SEVENTEEN

# The End of an Illusion

The elections of March 1973 brought Peronism back to power. Although Perón was barred from running for president, his stand-in, Héctor Cámpora, got 49 percent of the vote to only 21 percent for the runner-up, Ricardo Balbín of the Radical party. In April, Peronists also won large majorities in both houses of Congress and all but two provincial governorships. It was a resounding repudiation of all the attempts since 1955 to win the masses away from Perón.

For Argentine capitalism it was a fateful hour. Would the Peronists demand revenge? The RRP was pessimistic on the day of Cámpora's inauguration:

> Let there be no doubt that a return to the recent past, to established order, to the rules of a clean game, and to bourgeois well-being, no longer appear likely. We are moving into a future that oscillates between anarchy and oppression. Historically speaking, again, it may be remarked that most of the lifespan of humanity has been spent in such circumstances, so that the prospect should not be too upsetting. The human race—since the problem is by no means exclusively Argentine—will carry on. We may consider ourselves lucky to have lived in an era when human beings demonstrated that it is possible to coexist in a climate of tolerance and mutual respect. This is over. This style of life is finished. Future generations will envy us for having known it.[1]

If conservatives were cast into gloom, the Peronist Youth, drawn from several underground groups and their sympathizers, were jubilant. For them, Cámpora's election was their own special victory. The military's retreat from power had been brought about through guerrilla violence—not by Peronist labor leaders or party politicians, who were compromised by shady deals with the other side. Perón's choice of Cámpora as his presidential candidate was viewed by Peronist Youth as a tribute to them, for with two of his sons active in the Montonero underground Cámpora was considered to be the senior spokesman for the leftist faction of the movement. The same could be said for Perón's appointment of Fernando Abal Medina, whose brother was a Montonero leader, as general secretary of the Justicialist party. Other leftists, many of them lawyers who had defended captured guerrillas, had achieved high office in the Peronist government: the ministers of interior, education, and foreign affairs, as well as the governors of Buenos Aires, Córdoba, Mendoza, Salta, and Santa Cruz, to name only a few.

Not surprisingly, the Peronist Youth considered the new government to have a mandate to create a *Patria Socialista*. They were convinced that Perón was committed to such a goal. He had described them as idealistic youth fighting against a capitalist system that wanted to turn them into "mere numbers in the commercial calculations of foreign monopolies." He had said that if he were fifty years younger he would be planting bombs too, and taking vengeance into his own hands. And he had claimed that if Russia had come to his aid in 1955 he would have become "the first Fidel Castro on the continent." "We'll have to demolish everything in order to build from scratch," he remarked once in an interview, and the young Peronists remembered his words.[2]

Exhalted by the belief that their moment had arrived, the Peronist Youth forced Cámpora to sign an amnesty agreement freeing all political prisoners, which included the assassins of some prominent civilian and military figures. They also organized armed takeovers of government offices, factories, schools, hospitals, university buildings, and radio and television studios. Rodolfo Galimberti, the Peronist Youth leader, announced plans to form "popular militias" to defend the revolutionary government and threatened to exterminate the union bureaucracy "like cockroaches."[3]

In behaving that way, the Peronist Youth completely miscalculated their importance in Perón's political strategy. He had been willing to use them as shock troops against the military regime and as a balancing force to keep his increasingly difficult labor and party factions in line; but his style of leadership within the movement was always to divide and rule and not to allow one person or group to claim too much authority. When the news reached him in Spain of the liberties that were being taken in his name, he was furious. He refused to meet Cámpora at the airport when the latter arrived to escort him back to Buenos Aires. Nor would he attend any of the receptions given by the Spanish government for the new Argentine president. Instead, Cámpora was greeted coldly and later given a

dressing-down in Perón's private study. Perón got only evasive an-
swers to his demands that the Left be reined in, which provoked
him all the more.[4]

The fundamental mistake of the Peronist Youth was their refusal
to acknowledge that Perón was not, and never had been, a true
revolutionary. They ignored all the evidence to the contrary, such as
the economic plan he had proposed for Argentina the year before. It
had been studied with interest in labor, business, and military circles and was to become the official program after his return. The
plan was vintage Peronism: protectionism for national industry,
controls on capital outflows, wage increases, easy credit for small
businesses, the regulation of agricultural exports, large public works
projects, and economic planning to develop certain priority sectors
such as steel, chemicals, paper, energy, and transportation.[5] That
this was no mere smoke screen to fool the bourgeoisie should have
been evident when Perón made Cámpora appoint José Ber Gelbard,
the mastermind of the CGE, as his economics minister. Gelbard's
pet scheme was the "Social Pact," by which inflation would be
brought under control and productivity revived through wage and
price freezes agreed to by the leaders of business and labor. That was
certainly not socialism but rather a return to Peronism's traditional
corporativism.

Although Perón's economic approach was the same as twenty
years before, in political terms he had become more moderate. Since
1970 he had cooperated with his former enemies, the Radicals, in
an antimilitary alliance called La Hora del Pueblo (The People's
Hour), and he continued to have excellent rapport with the Radical leader Balbín. Furthermore, the winning ticket in 1973, the Justicialist Liberation Front (FREJULI), was actually a coalition that
incorporated splinter parties from several points on the political
spectrum: Frondizi's Radicals (the Movement for Integration and
Development), the Popular Christian party, the Socialist Movement
for National Liberation, and the Popular Conservative party. If Perón
had learned anything from experience, it was to avoid polarizing the
opposition. Before leaving Spain he had told a journalist admirer,
Esteban Peikovich, "Ideologies are of no use anymore. Marx was the
last of the ideologues, the Z of ideologues. . . . Ideologies fail nowa-
days because the problems are different. People don't want to be
stupefied or pushed around. They want to be treated as human beings." This change of attitude was lost on the Peronist Youth, who
were charmed by the rhetoric, as well as the practice, of revolutionary violence.

Perón returned to Argentina on 21 June 1973, but the occasion was ruined by a shootout near the airport between armed gangs of left-wing and right-wing Peronists. Faced with a power struggle inside his movement, he soon made it clear that his sympathies were not with the Left. Now that Peronism was in power, guerrilla violence had to stop. "Nobody is going to tell me," he said, "that those who assault a bank are doing it for superior ideological motives: they're doing it to rob it. I don't care what they say their motives are; the main thing is that they are crooks. . . . Some people say they want a violent revolution. I'd like to know how we are going to straighten out the economy of a country like ours, which we found with a seven billion dollar foreign debt when we took over, with bullets. And I can say this even though I'm a general, because I'm a pacifist general: something like an herbivorous lion."[6]

Cámpora's fate, and that of the Peronist left, was sealed as soon as Perón came back to the country. Over the next two and a half weeks, Perón met with military and labor chiefs, obviously testing the climate of opinion. On 10 July Gen. Jorge Carcagno met with Perón to inform him of the army's concern over the government's ineptitude and the growing influence of the left. Labor's attitude was displayed by posters that suddenly appeared all over town bearing Perón's picture and proclaiming Perón to Power! The day after Perón's interview with General Carcagno, the vice-governor of Buenos Aires Province, Victorio Calabró, who also was the provincial head of the UOM, declared that "with Perón back in Argentina no one except he can be the president of the Republic." José Rucci, the head of the CGT, backed this up by threatening a general strike unless Cámpora resigned. After a brief meeting with him on the eleventh, Rucci crudely announced to waiting reporters that there would be "no more screwing around" (se acabó la joda). Cámpora resigned the following day. Raúl Lastiri, a right-wing Peronist who presided over the Chamber of Deputies, was sworn in as provisional president and new elections were scheduled, with Perón and his wife, Isabel, making up the ticket. On 23 September the predictable happened: Perón was elected president for the third time in his life.

## The Corporative State Revisited

In their economic policies, Perón and Gelbard, like the French Bourbons described by Talleyrand, "had learned nothing and forgotten nothing." The Social Pact, which constituted the cornerstone of

the regime's program, was designed to reconcile the opposing interests of capital and labor. After an initial increase of 40 percent, to
be absorbed by businessmen out of their profits, wages were to be
frozen for two years. At the same time, the prices of all goods and
services were to be held constant. A National Commission of
Prices, Incomes, and Living Standards, consisting of representatives
of labor, business, and government, was set up to monitor the system.[7] It should be emphasized that this was not considered by Perón
and Gelbard to be an emergency program to halt inflation, but a
fundamental structural solution to Argentina's chronic social conflict: the first step toward building the organized community that
Perón had been advocating over the years.[8]

Controls were extended beyond wages and prices to include investment, interest rates, production, and trade. As in his previous
administration, Perón nationalized all bank deposits, thus concentrating all credit decisions in the Central Bank. Local banks would
have a line of credit at the Central Bank for the purpose of making
loans, but the amount they would get would depend as much upon
the purpose of their loans and the region in which they were located
as on the amount of the deposits they collected. This policy reflected a traditional Peronist desire to channel more investment
toward the interior. As in the 1940s, loans to the private sector were
to favor small and medium-sized businesses.[9]

Peronism's old suspicion of foreign capital was embodied in the
Foreign Investment Law of 1973, which forbade any foreigner from
purchasing more than 50 percent of any enterprise doing business in
Argentina and prohibited foreign investment altogether in areas
considered vital to national security. Those included steel, aluminum, industrial chemicals, oil, public utilities, banking, insurance,
agriculture, the mass media, advertising and marketing, and fisher-
ies. It also limited profit remittances to 14 percent of net returns. A
company that chose to remit the maximum, moreover, might have
to pay as much as 65 percent of its profits in taxes, as opposed to a
normal tax rate of 22 percent. Nor could foreign companies deduct
payments of royalties or other charges by their home offices from
their tax bill. In addition to the usual corporation tax, they also had
to pay taxes equal to those of local shareholders in the highest income bracket. To add insult to injury, Argentine directors of foreign-
owned companies had to register as foreign agents. Finally, several
foreign-owned banks were nationalized: the Banco Argentino de
Comércio, owned by Chase-Manhattan; the Banco Francés, owned
by Morgan Guaranty Trust; the Banco Argentino del Atlántico,

owned by First National City Bank; and the Banco Popular Argentino, owned by the Banco Central de España.[10] Given this obviously hostile attitude of the regime, it is not surprising that not a single foreign investment was recorded for the next three years, although Perón claimed that he was interested in attracting European capital to Argentina.

National industry received protection from foreign competition, and the Industrial Promotion Law of 1973 provided incentives for national industries capable of exporting. State enterprises were ordered to "buy Argentine" whenever possible. Interest rates were reduced by fiat, in order to encourage borrowing for improvements. To compensate businessmen for price controls, the government provided cheap credit. Between the end of 1972 and the end of 1973 the money supply doubled from 28.8 billion to 56.2 billion pesos, with most of the increase occurring during the latter half of 1973. The RRP was alarmed: "Never in the financial history of the country has paper been churned out on such a scale."[11]

Government, not private business, was the chief recipient of the Central Bank's profligacy. Government agencies and enterprises received 69 percent of all bank loans in 1974, up from 64 percent in 1973; local private firms received 22 percent, down from 25 percent the year before; and foreign recipients dropped from 11 percent to 9 percent. The same proportions held through 1975. On the other hand, the source of deposits in 1975 was as follows: government, 52 percent; local private, 32 percent; and foreign private, 16 percent. So it could be said, on balance, that the private sector was subsidizing the growth of government.[12] And indeed the government grew. From the end of 1972 until the end of 1975, the number of national, provincial, and municipal employees rose from 1,421,000 to 1,760,000: an increase of 339,000 in three years, as compared to the relatively modest 95,000 added in the ten years from 1961 to 1971. Political patronage got so out of control that government revenues were frequently insufficient to meet the payroll or the costs of services. In 1975, cities like Santa Fé, Rosario, and Bahia Blanca were cutting services like street cleaning, garbage pickup, and street lighting—but no municipal employees were fired; to the contrary, more were being added each week. In Rosario the opposition protested the sudden raising of local taxes (by 110 percent) to pay for a swollen bureaucracy and under-the-table payments amounting to 4 million pesos a day to favored companies working on contract for the city.[13]

Establishing the organized society meant returning to the semiofficial associations that characterized Perón's attempts to control labor, agriculture, and business in the 1940s. The Law of Professional Associations was revised in November 1973 to strengthen the powers of the CGT and the national federations to impose discipline on the local unions. The top leadership would now be able to intervene and remove local officials as well as impose obligatory contributions on the members without the latter's consent. Union officers had their terms lengthened from two to four years, and labor congresses were to be held every two years instead of annually. Most astonishing of all the changes in the law, however, were Articles 58 and 59, known collectively as the *fuero sindical* (labor's special rights). These gave union officials immunity from prosecution. Labor leaders could not be tried for crimes unless a National Tribunal of Professional Relations—composed of seven members, two from the CGT, two from the CGE, and three appointed by the president—first agreed to lift their protection. They could not even be arrested unless caught in the act of committing a crime, nor could the police search union offices without a court order based on evidence that a crime had been committed. This protection extended even to the squads of gunmen who customarily accompanied the top union leaders as bodyguards.[14]

Armed with these powers, the Peronist labor bureaucracy began centralizing power in the union movement. Perón's labor secretary, Ricardo Otero, a former UOM official, first focused his attention on the Marxist unions. Throwing his support behind the moderate national federation, he had SMATA's Córdoba branch subjected to intervention and its communist leader, René Salamanca, was deposed. When, in August 1974, Salamanca ganged up with Agustín Tosco of the Córdoba power and light union and Mario Firmenich of the Montoneros to try to turn an IKA strike into another *cordobazo*, warrants were issued for their arrest. All three became fugitives. That allowed Otero to break Tosco's previously impregnable hold on his union and replace its Trotskyite leadership with loyal Peronists. Raimundo Óngaro was removed from control of the printers' union in a different manner. Although Óngaro's list won reelection easily, Otero withdrew the union's juridical personality and eventually recognized a rival group of orthodox Peronists. When the Federación Gráfica called a strike in protest, the federal police raided their headquarters and arrested their leaders. Similarly, the non-Peronist teachers' federation (CTERA) lost its legal status in favor of a much smaller Peronist group, which the Labor Secretariat insisted was "the only entity capable of analyzing the concerns and proposals of the teachers." More brutal methods were used on the meatpackers' union. Its non-Peronist leader, Constantín Zorrilla, was forcibly removed from the union's headquarters by a group of unidentified armed men. Immediately afterward, a Peronist organization got legal recognition.[15]

While the workers were being "verticalized," steps were taken to gather the industrialists into a single, Peronist-dominated association. Having learned from previous bitter experience, the UIA did not try to resist this time. It had already separated from ACIEL in 1972, and its president, Elbio Coelho, had even publicly welcomed Perón's return in July 1973, saying that Argentina needed, above all else, the political stability that only the great *justicialista* leader could provide. Earlier in the year, the UIA's leaders had protested their being left out of the government's top economic advisory body, the National Social and Economic Council (CONES).

Unlike the UIA of thirty years before, the big industrialists, fearing the loss of all influence within government circles, did not call for abolishing CONES but rather for their inclusion within it. They found, however, that the price of admission was to merge with the CI, one of the three components of the CGE. That, in turn, would require changing the UIA's constitution to provide for representation of industries by their location rather than by their economic field and to provide more representation for small and medium-sized enterprises, as well as territorial federations, on the executive committee.[16]

The UIA had anticipated such a requirement. Right after breaking with ACIEL, Coelho had appointed a commission to revise the constitution along those lines. In November 1973, a year after the commission was set up, its report was presented to the UIA general assembly for approval. It proposed the creation of a territorial council that would give more weight to enterprises from the interior; in addition the UIA's traditional sectoral council would be reorganized to reflect the interests of smaller establishments. It also pointed out that the new constitution would facilitate the UIA's fusion "with other associations, to form a new entity" if an extraordinary assembly of the whole organization voted to do so.[17]

There was little doubt that the UIA would vote for a merger. Not only were the big industrialists bowing to political realities, but merchants and farmers were hurrying to get on the bandwagon. Since mid-1972, ACIEL had been losing members to the CGE. By the time Cámpora was inaugurated the CGE could claim—probably with little exaggeration—that 58 percent of all business enterprises belonged to it exclusively, 19 percent to ACIEL only, 4 percent to both, and 19 percent to neither. In June 1973 some 500 prominent business and agrarian leaders from the UIA, SRA, CAC, CRA, the Stock Exchange, and the Federation of Export Chambers met to pledge their support for the Social Pact. The meeting was hosted by the CGE. It came as no surprise, therefore, when a joint commission composed of representatives of the UIA and CI was formed in February 1974 to draft a constitution for a new industrialists' organization to be called the Argentine Industrial Confederation (CINA). In mid-April assemblies of both the UIA and the CI approved the merger, which was formalized the following month. Meanwhile, the government was considering a law that would require all industrial establishments to join CINA and pay dues to maintain it.[18]

As under Perón's previous rule, the principle of corporativism was extended to the professional classes. Early in September 1973 the old CGP was revived by executive decree. An organizing committee was created to prepare for the incorporation of doctors, lawyers, engineers, and intellectuals. Also, the CGE announced in May 1974 that its Confederación de Comércio (CC) was carrying on negotiations with other associations representing commerce, services, and finance. The CC's president, José Piva, commented affably, "There always exists on the CGE's part the most ample willingness to integrate all sectors."[19]

Agriculture was to be represented through the Confederation of Production (CP). Shortly after Perón was inaugurated, Gelbard launched a drive to enroll all farm groups into the CP and have them sign an equivalent of the Social Pact called the Act of Commitment With the Countryside. This act promised government credit, price supports, and tax incentives in return for the agriculturalists' promise to accept price controls. The SRA, CRA, FAA, and Agricultural Cooperative Confederation (CONINAGRO) all agreed to do so, but CARBAP, an affiliate of the CRA representing the provinces of Buenos Aires and La Pampa, held out. Though isolated at first, CARBAP's pluck gained it prestige, particularly as the farmers and ranchers found themselves increasingly enmeshed in government controls. Those controls included the monopolization of overseas meat and grain sales by the National Meat Board and the National Grain Board. Like IAPI in the past, these agencies required agricultural producers to sell to the state at prices set far below those being quoted on the world market. Goods not covered by these regulatory boards were still subject to export taxes: the hated system of retentions, which the Peronist government revived as a source of revenue.

To prevent farmers from withholding their goods, the government resorted to a tax on potential production. After a visit from the Secretariat of Agriculture, a farmer or rancher would be charged a tax that would vary with the size of the holding and its estimated economic potential. Since the tax was heavy, a landowner who failed to send a lot of goods to market would be faced with a sizable penalty. Another law, called the Supplies Law, applied to industrialists and merchants as well and was aimed at preventing hoarding and profiteering. Under its terms, the government would supervise every stage of the economic process, from production to retailing. It could establish maximum prices and profit margins and could set quotas for production and distribution, or the provision of services, based on estimated normal levels as well as estimated capacity. Proprietors who hoarded goods or destroyed them rather than sell at fixed prices, who refused to render services or buy goods from suppliers at fixed prices, or who failed to raise their production within three days after being ordered to do so by the Ministry of Economy would be subject to heavy fines, confiscation of their property, or jail. Finally, the government kept in reserve, as a last resort, the threat of an agrarian reform law that would provide for outright expropriation if land was not "fulfilling a social purpose." Although never actually passed by Congress, this law was kept under legislative consideration as a warning that owners had better exploit their holdings to their fullest potential.[20]

## The Social Pact Unravels

The Social Pact seemed to work at first. During the latter part of 1973, inflation was cut by two-thirds, economic growth nearly doubled, and unemployment was practically eliminated. Such gains were only temporary, however. The heartening statistics on growth and unemployment were the results of stimulating consumption and putting idle capacity back to work, while the drop in inflation could be maintained only so long as capital and labor restrained themselves. Unfortunately for the Peronists, forces outside their control were soon to upset the delicate truce. Before the year was out, the effects of the world oil crisis were being felt in Argentina—not directly, since the country had enough of its own oil—through the rapidly rising prices of most of its imports, especially the capital goods, raw materials, and semifinished products that local manufacturers needed. Caught in a squeeze between climbing costs and the price freeze, businessmen began to clamor for a revision of the Social Pact. At the same time, prices of goods not covered by the pact were going up sharply, fueling demands from labor for higher wages. The government's first reaction was to extend price controls to more goods, but by March 1974 Gelbard conceded that some modifications were necessary in the wage and price levels, even though the Social Pact was supposed to remain unchanged for two years. Wages were raised by 13 percent to mollify labor, but businessmen could pass on only part of this increase to consumers. Once breached, the Social Pact quickly crumbled. In June the unions demanded and got another wage hike to keep up with inflation. This time businessmen were not allowed to adjust their prices, but by way of some compensation were allowed special government credits to cover the wage increase. By November 1974 Gelbard was out of office, but a new economic team granted a wage increase of 15 percent without allowing businessmen to pass on the costs. Still another wage adjustment was granted late in February 1975, again without any price adjustment.[21] By that time it was clear that the Social Pact had been reduced to rubble.

Despite all the wage adjustments, the workers' buying power decreased by 7 percent during the first year of the Social Pact. That created pressure on the union leaders from below. Violent strikes, the most spectacular being the March 1974 metalworkers' strike at the Acindar plant in Villa Constitución in Santa Fé Province, served warning that the national leadership was losing control. Supported by sympathy strikes at other steel mills in the region, the Villa Constitución workers not only won large wage concessions but also forced the UOM's national leaders to withdraw the officials they had imposed on the local union and return control to the old classist shop stewards. Events at Villa Constitución influenced other unions. Resistance to centralization took the form of overturning orthodox Peronists in local union elections or, when that avenue was blocked, engaging in wildcat strikes. Over the next two years internal strife within the labor movement would become so general and so intense that, according to Elizabeth Jelin, there was no longer any certain identification between the leadership and the rank and file. All that the former could do to shore up their position was to demand more from the government.[22] No matter what they did, however, they could not keep up with inflation. Naturally, both labor and government blamed the businessmen. All would be well, they reasoned, if only the capitalists would do their patriotic duty by investing more, producing more, and exporting more. Instead, the level of investment in manufacturing fell by 30 percent between 1973 and 1974, and was to fall by another 28 percent the following year. Industrial construction dropped by about 70 percent over those same two years, and purchases of machinery and equipment were off by about 45 percent. Production rose by 15 percent, but that was mainly in nondurable consumer goods and public works construction. As with industry, so with agriculture. Although agricultural exports rose during 1973, by about 50 percent in volume and 65 percent in value, investment did not increase at all in that sector. Obviously farmers were rushing to get rid of their stocks. Between the end of 1973 and the end of 1975, there was a steady drop in exports.[23]

Prices were out of control as early as March 1974 partly because so many small businessmen were able to evade regulation. The government might successfully monitor the big companies because there were so few of them, but it lacked the personnel to insure that small entrepreneurs adhered to price controls. Indeed, there was considerable gloom among the industrial leaders; not only were they rigorously policed, but they were forced by the threat of slowdowns and sabotage to give their workers under-the-table wage increases. Caught in this painful vise, the big companies became desperate. By the end of 1974 they, along with the farmers, were resorting to falsified records, hoarding, black marketeering, and smuggling to get around government controls.[24]

Perón and Gelbard fulminated against "speculators," "negative elements," and "enemies of the people" who were allegedly collaborating with sinister "foreign interests." Certainly they were unfortunate in taking office during the world oil crisis, and their misfortune increased in July 1974 when the European Common Market closed its doors to Argentine meat; but they made matters worse by refusing to adapt their economic program to reality. Faced with the loss of their European customers, they might have devalued the peso in order to pick up export orders elsewhere. That was politically unacceptable, however, because it would benefit the *estancieros* while increasing living costs in the cities. Faced with rapidly climbing inflation, they might have cut back on government spending. But to curtail public works and trim the public payroll was unthinkable for a populist government, and the deficit was allowed to rise precipitously from 4.8 million pesos at the end of 1972 to 19.1 million at the end of 1973, and 27 million at the end of 1974. And to continue fueling the economy, money was churned out at a dizzying rate. There were 28.8 million pesos in circulation at the end of 1972, 56.2 million at the end of 1973, 88.9 million at the end of 1974, and 260.3 at the end of 1975. Inflation, which had been brought down from around 100 percent at the time Cámpora took office to just over 30 percent when Perón was inaugurated, climbed again to over 74 percent by May 1974. In the next two years it was to reach 954 percent.[25]

It was one thing to stimulate the economy through easy credit, but runaway inflation destroyed businessmen's ability to calculate costs and profits. The government also discouraged private investment by other ill-considered measures. Placing a cap on interest rates to lower the cost of borrowing money only caused bank deposits to shrink. For a time, private investors preferred to take their money out of the banks and speculate in the stock market. For stocks and bonds, 1973 was a "boom" year. The volume in trading rose by 29 percent (calculated in constant 1960 pesos), and prices took off. Companies like Alpargatas, Acindar, the Ledesma Sugar Estates, Celulosa, Gurmendi Steel, Santa Rosa, IPAKO, Molinos Río de La Plata, Sasetrú (a food-producing conglomerate), Pérez Companc, Fabril Financiera, Atanor, and Lombardi (a metal can manufacturer) led the industrials, with mining stocks and new service enterprises attracting a still greater number of investors. Nominal gains were impressive. Some stocks doubled their value while the average recorded a 70 percent increase. With inflation factored in, however, the real rise, in 1960 pesos, was only 12.8 percent—but that was still something, considering how long the exchange had languished in the doldrums. Nevertheless, something was wrong with the market. According to a survey of twenty-two selected industrial leaders, most companies were making less than 5 percent net profits on their sales; and some key enterprises like Celulosa, Molinos, Rigolleau, Tamet, Corcemar, Noel, and Pirelli had registered net losses between 1973 and 1974. Interest in the market, therefore, did not reflect investor interest in profitability so much as a desperate speculative search to find a way to keep ahead of inflation.[26]

State enterprises were as stagnant as the private sector, despite the government's heavy spending. The railroads continued to lose enormous sums, as they had done every year. So did CAP, Agua y Energia, and SEGBA. Somisa was another loss producer in 1974. After registering a profit the year before, it obviously reflected the general economic downturn. On the other hand, YPF registered larger profits in 1974 than in 1973, even though its output was down by more than 400,000 cubic meters (and by over a million cubic meters compared with 1972). Those profits were more than wiped out, however, by the fact that Argentina was forced to raise its oil imports at a cost of $468 million.[27]

## The Center Fails to Hold

While the Social Pact was falling apart there was a parallel deterioration in the political system. Perón's return had been welcomed by a large segment of the public that thought he could restore order. Some guerrillas, like the Trotskyite ERP, never intended to lay down their arms, however. For them and their political arm, the Revolutionary Workers' party, Perón was simply a transitional phenomenon, a bonapartist who represented the interests of the national bourgeoisie. The Trotskyites felt that Perón's movement would soon pass away as the proletariat became more conscious of its true revolutionary role.[28] Other guerrilla groups, like the FAP, while nominally identifying themselves with the movement, insisted on operating independently as well. Their role, as they saw it, was to carry on the war against the imperialists, the bourgeoisie, and the trade union bureaucrats, under the protection of a friendly government like Cámpora's. Neither they nor the Montoneros took Cámpora's fall gracefully. The Montoneros remained within the movement until mid-1974 but were increasingly estranged from it by Perón's conservative policies.

Kidnappings, robberies, and assassinations continued under Peronist rule. Dirk Henry Kloosterman, general secretary of SMATA, was gunned down in May 1973; José Rucci, the CGT general secretary, was murdered in September just two days after Perón's election; and Rogelio Coría was killed in March 1974. At the same time, the guerrillas discovered a profitable occupation in seizing business executives and holding them for ransom. Some 170 were kidnapped in 1973 alone. Kodak paid $1.5 million to ransom an assistant general manager; the Vestey Company ransomed its manager for $1 million; the First National Bank of Boston got off fairly lightly, paying only $750,000 for the return of the manager of its Buenos Aires office; Firestone was charged $1.5 million for the ransom of its local manager; and Esso had to pay a whopping $14.2 million for one of its executives who was abducted from the company's lunchroom. With the exception of Kloosterman's murder, which was generally attributed to the FAP, these crimes were carried out by the ERP.[29] Bolstered by these successes and by such an impressive inflow of cash, the terrorists became bolder. Late in the evening of Saturday, 19 January 1974, between sixty and seventy ERP guerrillas attacked the cavalry barracks at Azul, killing the base commander and his wife and forcing the fifty defenders to call for reinforcements. Supported by a small contingent of marines from the nearby navy arsenal, by early morning the soldiers succeeded in driving off their attackers who nevertheless eluded roadblocks set up by the Buenos Aires provincial police.[30]

This latter incident finally forced Perón into declaring all-out war against the terrorists. Already the CGT had begun to organize young trade union toughs into a well-armed paramilitary organization called the Peronist Syndical Youth (JSP), which had shown its muscle during the gunbattle at the Ezeiza airport on the day of Perón's return to Argentina. Assaulted by the ERP, Montonero, and Maoist guerrillas of the FAR, the JSP had routed the leftists, killing several of them. Its success was due to the arms it received from the powerful Social Welfare Ministry, then under the control of rightwing Peronists. In addition to the JSP, the Social Welfare Ministry was backing other armed groups, such as the University National Concentration, which were instructed to get the "bolshies" out of the Peronist movement. From those roots sprang the dreaded Argentine Anticommunist Alliance (AAA), early in 1974. The AAA was a death squad that would eventually claim responsibility for killing hundreds of left-wing terrorists and their sympathizers.

The strong man behind the Peronist Right was José López Rega, Perón's personal secretary whom he imposed on Cámpora as minister of social welfare and retained in that post in his own cabinet. Unlike most of the people in the Peronist regime, López Rega was no longtime loyalist; rather, he was a recent interloper who had wormed his way into the camarilla that surrounded Perón in Madrid. A former police corporal, he had been picked to form part of Isabel Perón's bodyguard when she came to Argentina as her husband's emissary in 1965. When she returned to Spain the next year, he followed her and managed to secure a position in the Perón household as her all-purpose factotum. At that time the personal influence of Jorge Antonio, Perón's principal financial backer, was very high; within a couple of years, however, Jorge Antonio would be out in the cold and López Rega would be running the Peróns' villa, the Quinta 17 de Octubre. The secret to his success was his knowledge of the occult. For years a practicing spiritualist and astrologer, he was known as the brujo (sorcerer) around the Perón household and was treated at first as the butt of humor. However, with the help of Isabel's stepfather, José Cresto, who was Perón's gardener and a spiritualist himself, López Rega gradually acquired influence over Señora Perón. Through her, he was able to influence Perón, who also had an interest in spiritualism.[31]

It would be amusing to imagine daily life at the Quinta 17 de Octubre, with a crazy wizard spouting nonsense to an aging demagogue and his ignorant dance-hall wife—except that the consequences were to be so horrifying. In a letter dated 16 July 1966, López Rega described Perón to his spiritualist friends in Buenos Aires as "strong, youthful, and intellectually sharp" and admitted that it was going to be a struggle to break Jorge Antonio's grip. It may have been some unfortunate investments the latter made, forcing him to reduce his financial aid, that hurt his influence with Perón. Or it may have been Jerónimo Remorino, a close friend of Perón's but an enemy of Jorge Antonio's, who undermined him. But Isabel also hated Jorge Antonio, and it is reasonable to assume that she was probably instructed by López Rega on how to whittle away at his influence. Argentine journals like *PP* and *Análisis* took note of growing rumors of factional fighting around Perón. By the end of 1968 Jorge Antonio was routed, and López Rega had been named Perón's private secretary.[32] After that, the measure of López Rega's growing influence may be gauged from a passage in a letter that Perón wrote to Rogelio Frigerio late in 1971: "In a few days Isabelita, accompanied by López Rega, will go to Buenos Aires. I have asked them both to get in touch with you and say hello for me. López, with whom I have talked at length about our affairs, can inform you personally of the situation, as I see it from my viewpoint. He also can explain, with a wealth of details, what we are doing and what we hope to do in 1972."[33]

About this time Perón's health began to deteriorate. In March 1970 he underwent an operation for a bladder ulcer and also had a tumor removed from his prostate. His heart was not good, either. At seventy-five, he was finally beginning to show his age. During interviews he would launch into long, rambling lectures. López Rega seldom left his side on public occasions and increasingly cut in on Péron's monologues to bring him back to the point. Published verbatim accounts of the famous interview with Colonel Francisco Cornicelli, Lanusse's emissary, at the Quinta 17 de Octubre in 1971 reveal Perón as a peevish, loquacious old man more concerned with displaying his superior knowledge and long pent-up resentment than with negotiating a political bargain. López Rega, Jorge Daniel

Paladino (Perón's personal representative in Argentina), and even Cornicelli repeatedly interrupted him to steer him back to the main topic.[34] Nevertheless, it is a matter of debate whether López Rega really dominated Perón. *La Prensa,* looking back on those times with hindsight, claimed that he did and pointed to the fact that Perón's private secretary contradicted him in public, interrupted his conversation, and limited access to his house. Perhaps recalling Evita Perón's influence in the earlier regime, *La Prensa* asserted that Perón's will "was never really powerful in the face of another more headstrong or imperious." Yet, during his twelve months back in Argentina, Perón conducted sensitive political negotiations with the military and trade unions without López Rega. His public speeches do not give the impression of a cloudy mind or a weak will. One of a group of Spanish visitors who met him informally in one of the salons of the Colón Opera House at the end of May 1974, just a month before his death, recalled that "nothing about the General's physical presence presaged his coming death. His erect bearing, his good disposition, his smiling face, his strong, deep mellow voice . . . were those of a healthy man in the fulness of his faculties."[35]

Clearly, though, López Rega was a powerful figure. The Ministry of Social Welfare commanded an enormous budget that allowed him to dispense a great deal of patronage and build up a large personal following in addition to financing his private militia, the AAA. Directly in charge of those assassins was Col. Jorge Osinde, the ministry's secretary for "sports." A former intelligence officer who had served Perón in the old days, Osinde had excellent contacts inside the government's security agencies. The AAA's usual tactics were to send anonymous warnings to its intended victims, telling them to leave the country. Many took the hint; those who did not generally died, gangland-style, in a hail of machine-gun bullets. Since it was a secret organization, it is hard to say exactly how many people the AAA killed, but one unofficial source estimated that 248 leftists died by violence from right-wing terrorists between July 1974 and September 1975—more than were killed by the army or the police. Among the more notable victims were Júlio Troxler, Cámpora's chief of police; Atilio López, vice-governor of Córdoba and prominent leftist union leader; Silvio Frondizi, brother of the ex-president and former rector of the National University; and Gen. Carlos Prats, a Chilean exile who had served in Salvador Allende's government.[36]

As the campaign mounted against the Left, the government also began to restrict the freedom of the press. Not only did it close down papers known to be sympathetic to the guerrillas, but it also tried to stop investigations into its actions by the more respectable dailies. Sanctions ranged from cutting off official advertising to death threats and actual physical attacks. Ana Guzzetti, a reporter for the leftist daily *El Mundo*, made the mistake during a press conference of asking Perón whether the police were going to investigate the fascist death squads. Perón not only ordered the Justice Ministry to begin proceedings against her, which led to her arrest for disrespect, but she was later abducted and beaten up. *El Mundo* itself was closed for carrying a report on a press conference given by the underground ERP. (When *El Mundo* got a court order overruling the government on constitutional grounds, the police ignored the judgment; and, to make sure that the paper stayed closed, a bomb was set off on its premises, causing extensive damage.) The conservative press had its share of trouble too. *La Prensa* and the weekly magazine for businessmen, *Mercado*, were harassed by printers' strikes. In La Plata, *El Día's* editor was kidnapped and murdered. *Clarín* was attacked by JSP thugs using machine guns and incendiary grenades after it printed an ERP ad that scoffed at López Rega's practice of black magic. These tactics had the desired effect. By mid-1974 the press had given up any real investigative reporting and was assiduously censoring itself by not printing stories that might bring reprisals. Rumor, which fed paranoia, filled the vacuum. Those who wanted to know what atrocities were being committed had to look in either the underground leftist guerrilla press or the AAA-funded *El Caudillo* and read between the lines of their slanted reports.[37]

A brief pause in the escalation of violence came with the shock of Perón's death on 1 July 1974. His health had been poor since his return to Argentina; the dampness of the Buenos Aires climate bothered him, and he had contracted a viral infection of the heart lining. There had been reports in February that the demands of office were taking too great a toll on the seventy-eight-year-old man and that he was considering a return to Spain for a rest cure. He was deeply disillusioned by his failure to bring the nation together, and the last weeks of his life were especially embittered by an open break between himself and the Peronist Youth. During a May Day speech from the presidential balcony, he had been interrupted by crowds of young people chanting from the Plaza de Mayo. Instead of "Where were you?"—their question in 1945—they demanded to know, "What's wrong, General—the people's government is full of gorillas." When Perón lashed back, calling them "beardless types," "malicious persons," and "infiltrators" who were "more dangerous than those who operate outside," they turned their backs on him and left the plaza. Perón had contrasted their treachery with the loyalty of the labor movement, but on 12 June, at a rally organized by the CGT, he made it plain that his patience was wearing thin with all those who called themselves Peronists but failed to support him with deeds. "The time is past for shouting '*la vida por Perón!* '" he told the workers. "We live in times that call for honest and concrete actions." He warned: "When I agreed to govern, I did so because I thought I could be useful to the country, even though it meant great personal sacrifice. But if I see the slightest indication that this sacrifice was useless, I will not hesitate for an instant to turn this post over to whomever can fill it with a greater likelihood of success.[38]

Within three weeks he was dead. Had he lived longer he might have been able to hold his government together, although there is reason to doubt it. Even Perón's charismatic personality had been unable to keep both labor and capital from gradually abandoning the Social Pact. Moreover, the vicious war between the Left and the Right that was to erupt with full force after his death had begun already with his acknowledgment and blessing. Having done all he could over the years to make it impossible for anyone else to rule Argentina, Perón in his turn had come to find Argentina ungovernable. By dying when he did, however, he escaped having to deal with the consequences.

## Things Fall Apart

Political violence escalated after Perón's death. From the day he died to September 1975 some 248 leftists were assassinated by the AAA, another 131 were shot by the police, and 132 unidentified bodies (most of them probably leftists) were discovered. At the beginning of February 1975 the army launched Operation Independence against ERP and Montonero guerrillas in Tucumán and Formosa provinces, where they had been responsible for an estimated 800 deaths. The so-called dirty war against subversion that was to be associated with the military regime that came to power in March 1976, and which resulted in more than 10,000 people "disappearing," had its beginnings under Isabel Perón, who succeeded her husband as president. One unidentified officer summed up the army's grim determination, as well as its past frustration: "We have to act drastically. *Operación Independencia* can't only consist of a roundup of political prisoners, because the Army can't risk the lives of its men and lay its prestige on the line simply to act as a special police force. Nor can it end its task by turning over x-number of political prisoners to some timorous judge who will apply inadequate measures, whose consequences can also be overturned by amnesties granted by functionaries with political ambitions. We're at war, and war obeys another law: he who wipes out the enemy wins."[39]

The army's chief of staff, Jorge Videla, put it more bluntly: "As many people will die in Argentina as are necessary to achieve peace in our country." The army did not intend to limit its antisubversive campaign to just a few provinces, either. Action, including "preventative" action (i.e., the arrest and holding of suspected terrorists or their supporters), would have to be carried out on all fronts: in the rural areas, the cities, the factories, the universities—everywhere that evidence of subversion might be found.

This willingness to sacrifice any number of people for a higher ideal naturally was shared by the guerrillas. The ERP, having failed to make significant inroads into the industrial proletariat, was determined to impose a socialist revolution "with the masses, without the masses, or against the masses." Having launched its guerrilla operations in Tucumán in March 1974, it now fought back against the army with night raids and ambushes. Although it had only 5,000 fighters, they were heavily armed and could depend on a support network of perhaps 60,000 sympathizers. The ERP was also able to recruit remnants of the Chilean MIR and the Uruguayan Tupamaros. Meanwhile, in September 1974 Mario Firmenich, the Montonero leader, said that his movement had decided to go underground and declare war against the government. This was a serious threat because the Montoneros were estimated to have 250,000 members, of whom perhaps 25,000 were bearing arms. Unlike the ERP, the Montoneros preferred urban terrorism. Once again their hit men got busy picking off union bureaucrats, businessmen, military officers, and policemen. Some 135 died from left-wing terrorist reprisals between 1 July 1974 and 1 September 1975. Through their vast network of sympathizers, the Montoneros had an efficient intelligence network that extended even into the police and army; furthermore, they operated a number of munitions workshops, printing establishments, training facilities, safe houses, and "people's prisons." They were well fixed financially, too. Their kidnapping of Juan and Jorge Born, heirs to the Bunge & Born conglomerate, in September 1974 netted $60 million. Mercedes-Benz paid another $5 million for the ransom of one of its executives.[40]

The biggest clash between the army and the guerrillas came on Christmas Eve 1975 when a combined force of about 1,000 ERP and Montonero guerrillas tried to capture the arsenal of Monte Chingolo on the outskirts of Buenos Aires. The guerrillas used high-powered weapons, and the battle lasted a full five hours until, just before midnight, the attackers retired leaving some 100 dead on the field to only 9 lost by the defenders. Most of the dead guerrillas were younger than twenty, and a large percentage were women. As the violence mounted, the Catholic bishops appealed to both sides: "Can we keep up this war of extermination? Is there no other path that will lead to a reconciliation among all Argentines, as children of God? The clergy appeals to the conscience of the Nation and asks for a clear and positive effort—even an heroic one, if necessary—to return to peace and domestic tranquility. It insists that violence is un-Christian."[41]

## Union Power and the Microclimate

Perón's death unleashed a power struggle inside the regime. Isabel Perón was too intellectually limited and weak willed to fill his place, as perhaps someone like Evita might have done; therefore, she became a pawn of ruthless men who battled to control her. López Rega had the inside track, of course, because of his intimate association with the president. He not only retained his posts as minister of social welfare and presidential secretary but succeeded in getting the top echelons of the Justicialist party purged so he could put his own followers in their place. What might have happened had he succeeded in eliminating all his opponents can only be surmised, but it may be significant that he used his control of the party to block any attempt in the Senate to find a permanent presiding officer for that body—a strategy that kept the way clear for his son-in-law Raúl Lastiri, president of the Chamber of Deputies, to succeed Isabel if anything happened to her.

López Rega's chief rival was Lorenzo Miguel, boss of the UOM and head of the 62 Organizations. To command the government he first had to get control of the CGT, which Perón deliberately put in the hands of Adelino Romero of the AOT in order to keep the UOM from becoming too strong. Within a week after Perón's funeral, Miguel mounted a challenge to Romero at an extraordinary congress of the CGT. Although it failed, the strain of battle apparently proved too much for Romero; he died of a heart attack two days later. That led to a second struggle, in which Miguel backed Casildo Herreras, a rival of Romero's in the AOT, while the anti-UOM forces voted for Segundo Bienvenido Palma of the construction workers' union. The result was a stalemate which was resolved by naming the two rivals joint secretaries. But fate played into Miguel's hands a second time; Palma fell sick a short while afterwards, leaving Herreras to run the CGT alone.

Controlling the top levels of the labor movement was not sufficient, however. To be effective, Miguel had to command the support of a well-disciplined force, which meant crushing all pockets of resistance to the labor bureaucracy. In this, he had the support of Ricardo Otero, the labor minister, who also came from the UOM. A rash of union interventions, justified on the grounds that communists were plotting to paralyze the nation's industries, removed the leftist leadership of the Villa Constitución steelworkers' local, the printers' union, the telephone workers' union, the Córdoba auto-workers' and power and light unions, the journalists' union, and the Tucumán sugar workers' union.

Miguel was too shrewd to rely wholly on repression, however. Deprived of their local leaders and unable to strike, the rank and file of labor tended to sink into sullen, passive resistance reflected in a rapidly rising rate of absenteeism. During the latter part of 1974 and throughout 1975 it was estimated at between 20 and 30 percent, as compared to a normal rate of around 6 to 8 percent. The effect was a cut in production in some branches of industry by more than 60 percent.[42] Obviously, that could not go on. Businessmen complained bitterly to the Labor Ministry, which could only reply lamely that their estimates were exaggerated. The next step would be massive layoffs, which might lead to an explosion. The solution, as Miguel saw it, was to reverse the deterioration of real wages, which were no longer keeping up with inflation; but that meant replacing Gelbard, who was still trying to rehabilitate the Social Pact, with a more prolabor economics minister.

Getting rid of Gelbard was fairly easy because López Rega was jealous of him and wanted him out of the way too. On 21 October 1974 Gelbard was replaced by the Central Bank president, Alfredo Gómez Morales, an old Peronist who had previously served as economics minister in 1952. Gómez Morales believed in fiscal responsibility and orthodox economic measures. His first aim upon taking over was to revive the Social Pact. The CGT and CGE were duly brought together to sign a new agreement on 1 November, which was to extend until June 1975. The deal was sweetened for labor by a big increase in wages and fringe benefits, but that could not hide Miguel's failure to get the sort of change in economic policy that he had hoped for.

On the other hand, Gómez Morales was not free to pursue his own policies either. Under constant pressure from both business-men and workers, he was forced to concede price and wage adjust-ments long before the new Social Pact expired. Despite his attempts to limit imports and raise government charges for utilities and transportation services, deficits continued to mount in the balance of payments and the annual budget. Although the government took pride in the reduction in unemployment figures, from 4.2 percent in April 1974 to only 2.3 percent in April 1975, this was achieved only by padding the public payroll. That may have stimulated consump-tion somewhat, but it failed to have the desired effect of encourag-ing more production. In fact, investment had just about ceased alto-gether. The GDP, which increased by 6.8 percent during the last three months of 1974, slowed to only 1.4 percent by mid-1975. Infla-tion was running at an annual rate of 100 percent, thanks mainly to a cheap-money policy imposed on Gómez Morales in order to ap-pease labor, and the Central Bank's foreign exchange reserves were almost depleted. In brief, the economy was headed for a dramatic crash.[43] On 2 June 1975 Gómez Morales was replaced by a friend of López Rega's, Celestino Rodrigo, the third of six men who were to head the Economics Ministry during Isabel Perón's twenty-one months in office.[44]

Rodrigo was an engineer and professor of economic geography who began his career in the 1940s as an assistant to Gen. Mario Savio, father of the Argentine steel industry. A longtime Peronist, Rodrigo was also, like López Rega, an enthusiastic believer in astrol-ogy and spiritualism. That gave him access to the *microclima* (mi-croclimate), as the select entourage that surrounded Isabel Perón was called by its opponents. But he lasted only seven weeks in office because he attempted to attack the growing economic crisis by rais-ing prices and holding down wage increases. Labor responded to these measures by launching a wave of spontaneous strikes and street demonstrations. Taken aback, Isabel agreed in late June to wage increases ranging as high as 130 percent. On 24 June the CGT organized a rally in the Plaza de Mayo to thank the president for her concessions. However, two days later she changed her mind. The CGT leaders were outraged. Not only had they been made to look foolish, but the government's austerity package put their positions in jeopardy. While Isabel addressed the nation over television, urging the people to accept the necessary sacrifices, workers were walking off their jobs. All across the country factories, schools, offices, transport, and shops were closed down. Desperate to retain its credibility before the workers, the CGT leadership called a forty-eight-hour strike—the first CGT strike ever against a Peronist government—to begin on 7 July.

On the day appointed for the strike to begin, unruly crowds gathered in the Plaza de Mayo. Interspersed among them were Lorenzo Miguel's own UOM heavies, armed and carrying walkie-talkies. Instead of directing his thugs against the Casa Rosada, which was heavily guarded, Miguel sent them to break into the Economics Ministry building, to the left of the palace, where Celestino Rodrigo and a few gunmen loaned to him by López Rega had barricaded themselves. The doors were forced, the guards overwhelmed, and the offices ransacked. Rodrigo barely managed to escape through an underground passageway and found refuge in the Casa Rosada; meanwhile, the workers took over the building, raiding the cafeteria and appropriating the minister's private stock of wines and liquors.[45]

Following the *rodrigazo*, Isabel's entire cabinet resigned, including López Rega who was removed both as social welfare minister and presidential secretary. That was not enough to satisfy his enemies, however, who were determined to remove his influence entirely. Isabel herself had suffered a nervous collapse and had retreated into seclusion at the presidential home in Olivos, where López Rega personally barred anyone from seeing her. Facing a complete governmental paralysis, the new cabinet conferred with the armed forces chiefs, and on 18 July units of the mounted grenadiers took control of the presidential grounds, removing López Rega's thugs. The following day López Rega was sent abroad on an extended official mission. A week later, his son-in-law Lastiri resigned as president of the Chamber of Deputies.[46]

Although the UOM got a 190 percent wage increase as a payoff for showing its muscle, Lorenzo Miguel soon found his victory to be a hollow one. He had aimed at controlling the president, but events had shown her to be such a weak and pathetic figure that her authority was all but gone. Victorio Calabró, the UOM boss of Buenos Aires Province and that province's acting governor, had declared in May 1973 that no one could govern the country but Perón; now, a year after Perón's death, the truth of that assertion was even more evident. Indeed, Calabró himself, as a longtime rival of Miguel's, now began an "antiverticalist" movement within Peronism against the monolithic claims of the party and the CGT. Even before the *rodrigazo*, antiverticalists, in collaboration with the Radical party, had elected one of their own, Italo Luder, as president of the Senate in order to head off any move by López Rega to move Raúl Lastiri back into the Casa Rosada. (Isabel had immediately condemned Luder as a Judas.) After the *rodrigazo*, antiverticalists had gotten Lastiri out of the way in the Chamber and had obtained seats in the Cabinet. Although Miguel was able to get Calabró expelled from the Justicialist party and the UOM, those were unsubstantial victories. Calabró was gaining plenty of support both in the CGT and the army, which recently had forced the resignations of two populist generals: Vicente Damasco as minister of interior, and Alberto Numa Laplane as commander in chief (to be replaced by Jorge Videla). All of these activities more than slightly resembled the flirtation that Augusto Vandor had carried on with the military a decade before. As then, rumors of an impending coup were all around.

## The Entrepreneurs' Rebellion

"The general scene is one of penalizing the entrepreneur's efforts and the unprecedented advance of chaos, unproductivity, indiscipline, and intimidation in the manufacturing centers—to a degree that surpasses anything imaginable." Such was the opinion expressed by the CGE at the close of 1975.[47] What could be done with a government whose labor minister insisted that the CGT leaders, as spokesmen for the people, "are always right, and even more when they're not"? What confidence could businessmen have in the current economics minister, Antonio Cafiero, whose background included being manager of IAPI in 1955 and, as minister of foreign trade from 1952 to 1954, having close business dealings with Jorge Antonio? Cafiero's sympathies had always been with labor, and they were again when he took over the Economics Ministry in mid-August. While acknowledging that inflation was a problem (it had reached an annual rate of 233 percent when he took office), he placed greater emphasis on reversing the upward trend in unemployment, which had gone from just over 2 percent in April to about 6 percent. His formula was classic Peronism: price controls together with monetary expansion to encourage spending and borrowing. The peso was devalued, but controls were extended to some forty-six items that were considered essential to an ordinary family's shopping basket. These included chicken, beef, rice, spaghetti, fish fillets, sausages, milk, eggs, butter, cheese, carbonated water, table wine, sugar, bottled gas, and soft drinks. There was an equally long list of items—such as coffee, tea, deodorant, margarine, concentrated soup, soap powder, beer, toilet paper, and canned sardines—for which the possibility of price increases remained, but only if the manufacturers could justify them to the Economics Ministry. In place of wage increases, Cafiero preferred to triple the amounts that employers paid in fringe benefits. Even so, workers in the private sector continued to force up their wages by threatening to bring all production to a halt. It did them little good because the resulting inflation, which reached 335 percent in December, left real wages about 20 percent lower than they had been in August.[48]

The government might dictate—indeed, it told employers that they could lay off no more workers, even if they lacked the means to pay wages—but it could not enforce compliance. By the end of the year, unemployment had edged up further to around 10 percent. At the same time, production was falling, at least in terms of official statistics. Indeed, the ubiquitous web of government regulations, which defied all economic sense, had given such a great boost to the underground economy that statistics were becoming hardly more believable than poetry.

It was traditional, of course, for much of the country's business to take place outside of regular channels, but under Peronism this became even more widespread. Frozen interest rates had caused a shortage of loan capital at the banks; thus it became necessary to find informal, nonregulated sources—naturally at a much higher cost. Wages and fringe benefits had been pushed up far beyond what employers were willing to pay; therefore, workers were laid off whenever possible and young people could not find jobs. The result was a rapid rise in the number of self-employed workers (*cuentapropistas*) who worked without contracts on a cash-only basis. In fact, the cash-only economy extended far beyond the proletariat to include many small businessmen and professional people who could thereby avoid declaring their income. In response to price controls sellers demanded under-the-table surcharges, if indeed they made their goods available at all. Fearful of future shortages, housewives began hoarding durable items like paper goods, cleaning supplies, aerosols, and canned goods. They had reason to do so: more and more goods were being smuggled out of the country, where they would fetch better prices.

As early as 1974 both Gelbard and Gómez Morales had estimated the annual value of illegal exports at more than $600 million—a modest figure compared to the $2.5 billion which the army intervenors who replaced Isabel Perón estimated for 1976. In the latter year, it was calculated that the entire soybean crop, worth $60 million, had been smuggled to Paraguay and then transshipped to Brazil where it sold for at least 60 percent more than the officially set prices in Argentina. Also, out of an 8.5-million-ton wheat harvest, half a million tons worth $65 million were missing—sold abroad illegally for three times the official price at home. Further estimates of smuggled goods included 2,000 tons of tobacco, about $72 million worth of onions, $1 million worth of wool, about 500 head of cattle and a quarter-million kilograms of birdseed *daily*, and vast quantities of flour, spaghetti, vegetable oils, powdered milk, fruit, sugar, rice, soap, lard, timber, tannin, wine, and pharmaceuticals. The volume of this trade was so great that trucks carrying the goods, in broad daylight, created traffic jams in the towns of Clorinda, on the Paraguayan frontier, and Paso de los Libres, on the Uruguayan border. Not all the goods were shipped by truck, either. Much was flown across from large *estancias* equipped with airstrips. Occasionally there were arrests; but Argentina's northern frontier was not easy to police, and besides, corruption was rife among customs guards and border officials.[49]

The money earned was certainly not plowed back into the Argentine economy, either. Capital flight reached record proportions from 1974 through 1976, insofar as it is possible to estimate this. According to one economist, Ricardo H. Arriazu, the best way to get an idea of the volume of "unregistered capital outflows" is to use the category of "errors and omissions" in the official record of the balance of payments. Using this method, it is possible to calculate that slightly over $2 billion left the country between the beginning of 1974 and the end of 1976. That came on top of an estimated $10 billion already deposited abroad by Argentines as of 1973. Small wonder that there was a shortage of investment capital. Those who did have money preferred to speculate in black market currency, buying up dollars whenever possible in the expectation that the peso would continue to tumble. The black market in turn was fed by tax evasion in the form of overstated imports, understated exports, and false statements about dividends, royalties, and expenses.[50]

Although smuggling may have served to release some of the pressure on businessmen, it was not enough in the long run to head off a confrontation with the government. The most discontented group were the smaller farmers of the CRA, among whom the most pugnacious were in CARBAP. They accused the government of reverting to

IAPI policies whereby farmers were forced to sell their produce to the government at low prices so the latter could reap big profits on the world market. So angry were the dairy farmers, for instance, that they withdrew from the CGE's Confederation of Production, after twelve years of membership, claiming that the confederation existed only to facilitate the government's control rather than to protect farmer interests. Finally, in May 1975, the CRA, the SRA, CONINAGRO, and the FAA launched a strike during which their members refused to send their products to market. The results were disappointing, chiefly because only the CRA participated wholeheartedly. CONINAGRO, which depended on government aid, collapsed under pressure after a few weeks; the SRA, whose members feared being branded as oligarchs and having their land expropriated, had little stomach for confrontation; and the FAA failed to coordinate its actions with the other groups.[51]

Nevertheless, the May strike was significant, for never before had so many different farm interests ever come together for a single purpose. The CRA, determined to carry on the fight and backed by thousands of small and medium-sized farmers, set up its own action committee and began new talks with the FAA. The latter, infuriated by the announcement of a new tax on the potential income of farmers, had just pulled out of the CGE (which also wanted to raise compulsory membership fees) and was in a fighting mood. Another strike was called for September, and it was so successful that the SRA joined it in progress and afterward asked to be included on the action committee. Meanwhile, the government raised its support prices.

Even so, the prices being offered for corn, wheat, and beef lagged far behind the rising cost of domestically produced fertilizers, agricultural implements, fence wire, and machinery. The CRA and FAA went back on strike in October. The government threatened expropriation, but on 6 November it finally gave in and met the strikers' demands for higher prices, easier credit, and a promise to promote private exportation. No sooner had the strike ended, however, than the National Meat Board announced a lowering of meat prices. Immediately the action committee met, only to discover that it was deeply divided between the hawkish CRA, whose members talked of blocking the roads with tractors and blowing up rails, and the dovish SRA, which feared a government crackdown—perhaps a repeat of the Córdoba scene in 1973 when gangs of thugs from the rural unions (and even Montoneros) had been sent to *estancias* to seize the cattle. As if to underscore the SRA's point, word was sent in to the meeting that the mayor of a nearby town was sending in trucks, manned by armed men, to collect some cattle. As one participant described the scene: "At that moment there was not a hawk to be found within miles, and any committee member who received the news did an excellent imitation of an ostrich looking for the right-sized hole in the sand for his head."

The rumor was false, and the action committee soon recovered its composure; indeed, its anger reached new heights when it learned that a nearby *estancia*, owned by a couple of industrialists, had ordered twenty railway wagons to ship its cattle to market. Here was the test: either act or be broken. Within a few hours nearly ninety trucks and tractors converged on the *estancia*, blocking all the roads and preventing the shipment. "We had a most enjoyable hate-in of the Government and all its works," one of the participants related. The results were mixed, however. Cattle prices doubled between December and February; other prices were higher too, but not so high as they were during the peak of the strike-caused shortage. To keep the farm front divided, the secretary of agriculture included SRA spokesmen on his advisory committee but no one from the CRA or FAA.

Perhaps the most impressive display of employer strength came from an even broader front of industrialists, merchants, and agriculturalists that called itself the Permanent Assembly of Employers' Trade Associations (APEGE). This group included mainly the die-hard liberal elements of the ex-UIA, and the Chamber of Commerce, plus the bolder spirits within the SRA. Driven to desperation by the collapsing economy, on 29 January they met at the grain exchange to denounce the CGE as "a gang of delinquents" and demand an immediate return to a free-market economy. The meeting hall was packed, with standing room only, and latecomers filled the hall outside. Inside the chamber, emotions ran high as employer after employer rose to vent frustration against a proposed new tax on "lucrative activities," another proposed value-added tax, "labor terrorism," and alleged government intentions to sovietize the economy.

The government should have taken notice because these were normally prudent individuals, not used to drawing public attention to their political views. Its failure to do so provoked APEGE to declare a nationwide lockout on 16 February, a Monday. The CGE was put on the spot. Although it would not support APEGE's action, it could not condemn it either without losing all credibility as a businessmen's association. It straddled the issue by leaving it to each member to decide whether to join the lockout and proposed to hold its own week of protest later in the month. The CP and the CC chose almost unanimously to observe the lockout; only CINA, the industrialists' chamber, refused to go along. The government threatened to prosecute participating businessmen with the "full rigor of the law." Nonetheless, the lockout was a great success. Practically all the commercial establishments in the country shut down for twenty-four hours, with signs on their doors reading "Closed in Defence of Our Survival," "Closed In the Face of Excessive Taxes, Inflation, Instability, and Corruption," or "Closed Due to Social and Economic Chaos." No agricultural products were brought to market, and all across Argentina farmers took a holiday. Transport services and banks continued functioning, but there was little business and their operations were noticeably slower. In industry, most small and medium-sized establishments closed, as did many large ones, but some of the big steel and textile mills kept going. On the day of the lockout, APEGE's leaders invited other businessmen to join them at the Church of Our Lady of the Immigrants to hear a Mass in honor of all their colleagues killed by terrorists.[52]

APEGE felt triumphant, even though the CGT called its action "anti-national" and contrasted the lockout with "the prudence and sensitivity of the ranks of labor, always capable of seeing further than their sectoral interests." The CGE was crushed. In the heady atmosphere of defiance following the lockout, nine provincial businessmen's federations withdrew their membership to protest the organization's failure to support APEGE. They agreed with Robert Meoli, APEGE's secretary, that this new group, "with no 'vertical' structure, no compulsory membership or compulsory dues, and with no political ties, has managed to fill a great gap in the expression of entrepreneurial interests . . . after a long and painful period during which the only voice heard was that which was compromised with the collectivist, statist, and demagogic system which reigns and which is the cause and origin of the economic, political, social, and moral collapse that menaces our very existence as a nation."[53]

On 8 March the CGE's president, Júlio Broner, resigned. He was bailing out of a sinking ship. With or without the lockout, the government's fate was sealed. The leading newspapers were predicting the government's imminent fall, while cabinet ministers scurried about, drafting plans which they only half-heartedly thought might save the situation. The government, sunk in corruption and graft from the president on down, was bereft of friends. It came to an inglorious end on the night of 23 March when Isabel was taken from the Casa Rosada in her private air force helicopter, not to her home as she intended, but to a military base where she was made prisoner.

# CHAPTER EIGHTEEN

# The Agony of the Open Market

Gen. Jorge Videla, head of the military government that supplanted Isabel Perón, was Argentina's twenty-first president since 1930. His task was to restore order to a political economy in which violence and chaos had become endemic. Terrorism had reached the point where political assassinations were happening on the average of one every eighteen hours. At the same time, the economic picture could not have been more dismal. The annual rate of inflation had reached 920 percent; gross domestic production was down by 4.4 percent in the first quarter of 1976; and fixed gross investment was down by 16.7 percent. The budget deficit was enormous (equaling 13.5 percent of the GDP), and a balance of payments deficit of around $600 million exceeded the treasury's exchange reserves, making a default quite possible.

The government's answer to terrorism was the so-called dirty war, or counterterrorism, whose aim was to isolate and root out the urban guerrillas by creating a climate of fear that would paralyze their support network. The strategy of urban guerrilla warfare was based on small nuclei, or *focos*, operating in the anonymity of a great metropolis but supported by many sympathizers who furnished money, information, and hideouts. The most effective countermeasures for dealing with this network were death squads manned by policemen, military intelligence personnel, and even criminals who kidnapped and interrogated anyone suspected of having knowledge of the guerrillas' whereabouts. Such kidnappings were frequent, often occurring in broad daylight and carried out by men wearing civilian clothes. The victims were taken to police or military installations; sometimes any friends or relatives who were with them were also taken. Torture was routine for anyone unlucky enough to fall into this net. Afterward, the victims disappeared into special detention camps where many of them were killed. The actual number of *desaparecidos* is a matter of guesswork: estimates range from 6,000 (the OAS Inter-American Human Rights Commission) to 20,000 (Amnesty International, based on various exile sources).

Relatively few of them were actual terrorists; most were suspected of being sympathizers, or were targeted as being responsible for spreading ideas that aided the Left. Newspapers naturally were not allowed to report any stories about kidnappings; indeed, the entire subject of human rights violations was forbidden by the government. Habeas corpus proceedings were futile: no records were kept of the victims and no one knew where they were sent. Even people with influence were powerless because each army district conducted its own raids and ran its own detention camps; the decentralized nature of the antiguerrilla campaign, therefore, made it unlikely that even the high military commands knew everything that was going on.[1]

It was a dark, clandestine struggle, very different from the war unleashed in the jungles of Tucumán the year before. This time the confrontation occurred in an urban setting and lacked the cleanness of other episodes. Public opinion was filled with stories and rumors of detentions and of disappearances that occurred with frequency. A climate of fear, identical to that which had reigned under Mrs. Martínez de Perón, but more extensive and diffuse, settled upon the country—especially on students, intellectuals, and artists, as well as labor unions infiltrated by extremist ideologies, or sectors especially apt for repression, like journalists, psychoanalysts, and sociologists. It was no exaggerated sentiment, either.[2]

Such indiscriminate tactics made most people, even left-leaning sympathizers, shun any sort of contact that might in any way involve them with the urban guerrillas; thus the latter were robbed of their cover. Moreover, some of the guerrillas themselves were picked up in the dragnet and forced to talk. Bit by bit the authorities unearthed the underground. By 1979 the guerrilla Left was broken, with most of its members either dead, disappeared, or in exile.

Political pacification was paralleled by a determined attempt to reform the economic system. Videla's economics minister was José A. Martínez de Hoz, descendant of a proud old *estanciero* family that had been prominent in Argentina since the eighteenth century. Educated at Cambridge, an outstanding law student and, later, professor of rural property law at the University of Buenos Aires, Martínez de Hoz had served as president of the national grain board under Aramburu, secretary of agriculture and minister of economy under Guido, and president of Acindar, the nation's largest private steel company. His analysis of the economic crisis pointed to two great evils: excessive state intervention in the economy and the recurrent attempts by nationalists to build a closed economy. The first led to the creation of a vast, costly bureaucracy that strangled all private initiative. The second cut off Argentina from contemporary economic and technological developments, discouraged the inflow of capital, and reduced trade. Highly protected and subsidized domestic industries were able to make big profits without producing a great deal or making their prices competitive. Meanwhile, a formerly efficient agricultural sector was discouraged by so many controls from modernizing itself. The results were shortages and high costs, or stagflation.[3]

To attack those evils, Martínez de Hoz proposed to reduce the economic role of the state, rationalize the public administration, and encourage a free market economy and free trade. To achieve the first goal, he aimed at privatizing many state enterprises and turning the rest into autonomous, self-financing corporations. He also intended to do away with price controls and deregulate banking. Rationalizing the public administration not only implied cutting the public payroll and reducing government spending, but also improving tax collection. A free market economy required encouraging private capital formation, which Martínez de Hoz intended to do by reducing taxes on exports and dividends and by eliminating controls on interest rates. Freeing exchange rates and lowering tariffs would not only promote more foreign trade but would also force local industry to become more efficient.[4]

A fragile-looking man but a tireless worker and a true believer in capitalism, Martínez de Hoz threw himself into the task of dismantling the procedures of the past forty years, even suffering hospitalization for an ulcer during the process. He would remain in office until the end of Videla's administration, a total of five years—the longest tenure for an economics minister since 1952. Unlike Krieger Vasena in the Ongania regime, he enjoyed the complete confidence of his president and there was no longer a strong Peronist movement that needed placating. Therefore, his policies may be considered the most clear-cut test of whether free enterprise could be revived in Argentina.

## Reducing the Role of the State

The challenge of trimming big government involved several related tasks. First, there was a need to cut the public payroll, in terms of both the number and expenses of employees. Second, there was a need to cut public expenditures with respect to the operation of state enterprises, either by selling them to the private sector or by rationalizing their procedures. Third, spending on military purchases, public works, and pensions had to be limited if there were to be any chance of balancing the budget.

Public employment had grown slowly and steadily over the years. Both Frondizi and Ongania had attempted to reduce it, but to little avail (see table 11.2). Inevitably, a slash in the central bureaucracy would be balanced by an increase in the work force of state enterprises; or a cut in national public employees would result in more operations being taken over by provincial and municipal governments, with a consequent rise in jobs at those levels. When Martínez de Hoz took over in March 1976 there were an estimated 1.8 million people working for the national, provincial, and municipal governments, plus state enterprises and autonomous agencies; that was out of an economically active population of 10 million. Approximately 400,000 people had been added to the public payroll since Ongania left office.[5]

Public expenditures, as a percentage of the GDP, had risen too. From just under 30 percent during the early Perón years the proportion shot up to over 35 percent under Frondizi and Illia, was lowered slightly by Ongania to 33 percent, then rose sharply again with Lanusse and Perón to 40 percent. In part, this was a natural outgrowth of increasing public employment, but it also reflected a real expansion in the state enterprise sector. One factor in that expansion was the propensity of Fabricaciones Militares to engage in new projects for the purpose of national security without counting the costs. Indeed, those costs could only be estimated in a very rough manner because Fabricaciones Militares published no figures about how much money it spent, how many people it hired, or how much it produced: all was kept secret in the interests of national security. No accounting was made even to the Ministry of Economy. However, it was estimated that this army-operated conglomerate swallowed up about 7 percent of the national budget annually (more than was spent on health services or scientific research and development combined), had sales amounting to over $2 billion, and was a major loss producer.[6]

Another factor in the expansion of state enterprise was the takeover of about thirty bankrupt companies, such as SIAM, the La Cantábrica steelworks, and Swift, over the previous decade in order to preserve the workers' jobs. Finally, the growth of state expenditure was due partly to an aging population, the result of both a low birth rate and the emigration of many young people.[7] That put considerable pressure on the pension system. Thus, in 1960 there were 799,600 pensioners, representing 3.9 percent of the total population and 10.7 percent of the economically active population; but by 1977 there were 2,031,000 pensioners, who comprised 7.9 percent of the total population and 20.3 percent of the economically active population. But it was not only aging that caused the pensioner class to grow. Under the recent Peronist regime, politicians and civil servants were granted extremely liberal pension plans that allowed them to draw full benefits, with only a few years of government service, without waiting until they reached sixty-five. About one of five pensioners was under sixty. On the other hand, the pension fund was always in deficit because its funds were frequently borrowed by the government to finance other projects (the cash would usually be replaced with worthless bonds). Evasion of obligatory contributions by both private and public sector employers also kept the pension fund in deficit. Of the two, the public sector was the more serious offender: its evasion rate was estimated, in a study carried out by the Buenos Aires Stock Exchange, at around 60 percent, as compared to only 8 percent for the private sector. Almost all of that public sector evasion came from the armed services and police.[8]

Martínez de Hoz had only modest success in tackling this governmental leviathan. By the end of 1980 he had managed to trim the bureaucracy by about 200,000 and the state enterprises by around 103,000. It had not been an easy fight because at first he found, like all his predecessors, that firing employees in one part of the government only led to personnel increases in other areas. During the first few months of the new regime, 7,228 people were cut from the payroll, but at the same time 7,874 others were hired, resulting in a net gain of 646. Fortunately, Martínez de Hoz had an intelligent and determined treasury secretary, Juan Alemann, to supervise the budgetary process. It was due largely to him that real reductions eventually were made.[9]

Public sector wages, which had averaged around 12 percent of the GDP from 1961 to 1973 but had climbed to 16.5 percent under the Peronists, were brought down temporarily to 9.5 percent by a wage freeze. By 1980, however, they had crept back up to 13 percent. Other public expenditures continued to rise by about 10 percent a year in real terms—which was even faster than the rise under Perón. The result was the creation of huge deficits because, on the one hand, the military chiefs would not allow Martínez de Hoz to raise the prices for public services, believing that to be inflationary, and on the other hand, Martínez de Hoz himself had lowered or eliminated many businesses taxes in order to encourage capital formation. Moreover, tax evasion continued to be rife. The business community justified this on the grounds that the government was already too large and that more revenues would only encourage further growth. A debate sprang up in the press as Armando Braun, of the Braun-Menéndez family, warned that if the financing of the huge state deficit "is done through the emission of money this will pour fuel on the fire of inflation. If it [the state] resorts to internal borrowing it will deprive the private sector of resources and distort interest rates, making it dearer for the whole community to borrow money. And if, finally, it turns to foreign capital markets it will increase our external debt, result in the emission of more money because of the inflow of capital, and alter the free play of forces in the exchange market."[10]

In reply, treasury secretary Alemann insisted that:

If you want to reduce public spending to the extent that many people think is possible, you have to adopt one of the following decisions: (a) sharply reduce the real wages of the public sector (Do you really think that is possible, or even desirable?); (b) reduce public investment, which means, frankly, that you'll have to cut back in spending on telephones, with the result that you won't solve the shortage for many years; or that you wont build Yaciretá [a hydroelectric project] or Atucha II [a nuclear power station], which means that in the foreseeable future there will be an electrical energy shortage. Our plan for public investment is based on a profound and minute study. No one has suggested to us which projects we ought to leave out; on the contrary, everyone wants new and expensive investments, which generally get the press' support. Then there is (c) reduce military spending. Obviously, that's not an economic decision.[11]

Public sector wages were reduced a little, but were still high by past standards. Public works, on the other hand, cost the country about $40 billion between 1976 and 1980, largely at the insistence of the armed forces, which considered them vital to the national defense: hydroelectric projects, a suspension bridge across the Paraná River, the opening of new iron mines in Patagonia (whose ore was full of phosphate, creating an enormous expense for Somisa to separate it out), and nuclear power stations. Nor would the military allow the closure of other public enterprises—such as the Río Turbio coal mines, which cost $140 a ton to produce coal as compared with the world market price of between $30 and $40 a ton—again, on the grounds that these were essential for the nation's defense. National pride, not security, lay behind the $520 million spent on construction projects in connection with the 1978 World Cup soccer championships.[12]

Military spending also lay beyond the jurisdiction of the Economics Ministry. Although the actual level of such expenditures were kept secret, the Stockholm International Peace Research Institute estimated in 1983 that since 1978 Argentina had occupied first place among all Latin American countries in arms purchases, and that at least a third of its $40 billion foreign debt in that year had been borrowed to pay for military equipment. The threat of a war with Chile over the Beagle Channel, at the southern tip of the continent, prompted a flurry of purchases that were made on short-term credit and at high interest rates, thus saddling the country with enormous debts.[13]

The military was also reluctant to see the state enterprise sector reduced. Fabricaciones Militares was exempted from any closures or privatization schemes even though its losses were estimated, in 1980, at over $600 million. The idea of privatizing the steel or oil industries ran counter to the armed forces' doctrine of national security, even though both SOMISA and YPF had excessively high costs and ran up annual losses. Indeed, the officers refused to allow a reduction in tariff protection for those sectors, which would have forced them to lower their prices and operate more efficiently. Some progress was made toward rationalizing railway service, however. According to Martínez de Hoz, between 1976 and 1980 the number of employees was reduced from 155,000 to 97,000, about 8,500 kilometers of track was taken up, the number of stations was cut from 2,417 to 1,405, and some passenger and freight services were reduced. In addition, railroad workshops for maintaining tracks, roadbed, and rolling stock were privatized. All of this, he claimed, cut the railway deficit by half. That may have been an exaggeration, however. When Martínez de Hoz first came to office, he estimated the railroads' losses at the equivalent of $2 million a day; at the beginning of 1980 the railroads reported a loss for the previous year of 806 billion pesos, which was the equivalent of around $620 million, or about $1.7 million a day. A good part of the deficit was due to a 214 percent increase in wages and fringe benefits for that year (in which inflation averaged an annual rate of 140 percent), and to the continuance of artificially low passenger fares and freight charges. The military, it seems, did not wish to alienate suburban commuters, and it hoped by keeping freight rates low to attract more business to the railroads. Despite that, it was estimated that 85 percent of all grain was sent to market in trucks, as well as practically all cattle. In fact, about 95 percent of all overland freight was hauled in trucks, not trains.[14]

None of the really big state enterprises were privatized. Even supposing that the military would have permitted it, what private local capitalist could have afforded to buy YPF, ENTEL, Gas del Estado, Agua & Energia, the railroads, the merchant fleet, or Aerolineas Argentinas, each of which possessed property valued in the hundreds of millions and billions of dollars? Indeed, even foreign buyers—if any had been allowed to bid—would have been unwilling to take on such enterprises considering that they would also have had to assume enormous debts and shoulder the formidable expense of modernizing their equipment. And even if those obstacles could have been surmounted, avoiding future deficits would have entailed reorganization schemes that reduced personnel, thus bringing on a nasty battle with the unions. The new owner would also have to run the risk that some future populist government would renationalize the company. Consequently, it is not surprising that even when a government enterprise went up for sale there were usually few takers. The same was true of most of the formerly private companies taken over by the state, such as SIAM, Swift, and La Cantábrica. Of about thirty such companies, only a few were sold—and even then they usually had to be sold piecemeal. After all, most of them had gone bankrupt originally because their plants were obsolete and had been taken over by the state in order to preserve the workers' jobs. As such, they were hardly attractive properties. In a few cases, speculators were willing to take a risk at bargain-basement prices, but almost all such sales ended in fresh bankruptcies a short time later.[15]

For the most part, the military resisted the idea of privatization. Efficiency was only one factor they considered. National security dictated that certain kinds of production and services had to be guaranteed. It also indicated a need for developing the poorer regions of the interior, which might be done through locating branches of the state enterprises there. Finally, the armed services were worried that a high rate of unemployment might create opportunities for the guerrilla Left to infiltrate the labor movement; therefore, the military put a higher priority on maintaining full employment than on reducing economic costs. Indeed, they even insisted in some cases on adding to the state enterprise sector. In 1979 they forced the government to purchase the Swiss-owned Compañía Italo-Argentina de Electricidad for $93 million, and in 1980 they forced the acquisition of Austral, a private airline company servicing the interior of the country. Also, in 1979–80 there were several bankruptcies that required the government to take over the management of those companies. All of that wiped out any gains made from the sale of other enterprises.[16]

Given these limits on his freedom of action, Martínez de Hoz had to settle for selling smaller factories, sugar mills, paper mills, hotels, and warehouses: about 43 in all. The Postal Savings Bank and the National Development Bank also sold the shares they had been holding (sometimes amounting to 40 percent of the total) in certain leading companies like Celulosa, Bagley, Alpargatas, Squibb, Ledesma, Ipako, Schcolnik, Astra, Pérez Companc, and Fabril Financiera. Beyond that, the economics minister had to settle for what came to be called "peripheral privatization," in which many services performed by state enterprises were contracted to private companies. Just as the state railroads turned over maintenance of cars, rails, and roadbeds to private contractors, so ENTEL did the same with the maintenance of telephone equipment, YPF with the management of certain oil fields, and Gas del Estado with the maintenance of its pipelines and treatment plants. The government also contracted the building of its nuclear power plants to private firms like Pérez Companc and Garovaglio & Zorraquín.[17]

Some critics, such as Jorge Schvarzer, accused Martínez de Hoz of favoritism and even of deliberately encouraging big conglomerates to grow even bigger by granting them special loans from the National Development Bank and the Banco de la Nación. They had no competition and incurred little risk in these contractual arrangements. For Schvarzer, the creation of a web of influence between the state and selected capitalists was a major policy departure that occurred without any public debate.[18] Be that as it may, the failure to actually reduce the state enterprise sector and the uncontrolled spending on armaments meant that public spending actually rose sharply under Videla, from about 43 percent of the GDP in 1977 to over 60 percent by 1979. At the same time, the money supply expanded at a truly dizzying rate. Under the Peronist government, the number of pesos in circulation had risen from 67 billion to 1 trillion, but under Videla that rose to 2.7 trillion.[19] That made it extremely difficult to combat inflation, although to Martínez de Hoz's credit the rate was reduced to around 90 percent by 1980. The price for that, however, was a set of policies that created a serious recession and a large number of bankruptcies—including some of the country's leading private companies.

## Opening the Closed Economy

After nearly forty years of import-substitution industrialization policies involving subsidies, protection, and the systematic redirection of investment from the rural to the urban sector, the chief characteristic of Argentine industry was its inability to produce goods at internationally competitive prices. Not only had most Argentine industrial firms failed to develop the efficiency required to compete in the world market, but they still needed tariffs and subsidies to fend off foreign competition at home. Meanwhile, farmers and ranchers—who lacked capital for modernization, were burdened with export taxes and unfavorable exchange rates, and had to purchase their industrial inputs from costly local manufacturers—still provided the bulk of Argentina's exports. Between 1972 and 1977 agricultural products accounted for 51 percent of the value of all exports. Although that was down from 63 percent from 1960 to 1966, the drop was caused entirely by the European Common Market's cutoff of meat imports from Argentina. Moreover, if industrial exports were subdivided into those that were processed agricultural products (food, beverages, tobacco, textiles, wood, leather, and paper) and those that were nontraditional manufactures, it would be clear that the former constituted a steady 30 to 32 percent of total export value from 1960 to 1977. Thus, agriculture and agro-industry still accounted for over 80 percent of Argentina's exports when the Videla government took over.[20] To be sure, nontraditional industrial exports had grown, but only with the help of government subsidies.

Having discarded the law of comparative advantage, Argentina's nationalistic policymakers had stopped evaluating economic undertakings on the basis of their efficiency. Santiago Cuquejo, a liberal economist, once complained that their "only yardstick for judging an activity was the amount of work it provided: the same criterion used by a prison director in finding its inmates something to do." He concluded, "What we have done is to evolve an economic system divorced from the rest of the world. If all restrictions on foreign trade were removed tomorrow, our economic system would be destroyed as swiftly as a winter garden exposed to temperatures below zero. But the defenses that have been erected against such a happening are no more than a system which permits gradual stagnation instead of sudden ruin."[21]

Martínez de Hoz rejected the idea of protectionism or import substitution. No country can produce everything it needs, he argued, nor should it try to. Under him, only competitive industries would be encouraged. In certain cases, brand-new infant industries might receive temporary protection, but the level would be decreased over time. He insisted that this did not imply that he was antiindustry. To the contrary, he rejected the law of comparative advantage because it was increasingly evident that developing nations were often in a better position to produce certain industrial goods more cheaply than the advanced nations. For the same reason, he rejected the dichotomy, posed by many leftist economists, of an industrial center versus an agricultural periphery in the modern world economy because it was too obvious that much industry was migrating to the third world. The important thing for attracting such industry was to keep costs down.[22]

Would Argentina's industrialists support a free-market strategy? In the very recent past the UIA had pulled out of the anti-Peronist employers' front, ACIEL, in order to join the CGE. It even surrendered its autonomy and merged with the CI to form CINA, thereby accepting a greater degree of government economic regulation than its erstwhile partners, the SRA and CAC. Among the employers, industrialists had been the least supportive of APEGE's nationwide lockout, and even those who railed against the state in the name of free enterprise elicited considerable skepticism from orthodox liberals. How many of them would support an end to protectionism, the RRP wanted to know. How many still believed "in the multinational conspiracy against the economy," and how many still thought that Argentina would "reach great power status when she becomes self-sufficient in steel, aluminum, soda ash, paper and oil? How many of them would approve the return to private enterprise of deficit-ridden state enterprises, that is to say, all of them? And how many of them would be ready to applaud a harsh monetary policy with positive rates of interest in currency of constant value?"[23]

In truth, industrialists were very conservative and traditionalist in outlook, as revealed by a 1976 survey taken by FIEL, a business research outfit. FIEL sent questionnaires to 230 manufacturing firms considered to be leaders in their specialty but who were not quoted on the Buenos Aires stock exchange, asking them why they did not participate. Out of more than 100 responses received, about one of five explained that they were closed corporations and did not wish to open up ownership to outsiders. Slightly more than half said that they did not like the kind of regulation—the examination of accounts, for example—that the Bolsa and the National Commission on Shares (Comisión Nacional de Valores) exercised over members. Over 60 percent used a circular argument: joining was not worthwhile because not enough companies used the Bolsa anyway (about 320 did). If more companies became members, so would they. About half said they saw few possibilities for economic growth in the near future and it was hardly worth the effort to seek new capital. Around 80 percent were holding back, they said, because political and economic instability were so bad that one had to be cautious. Most companies were frank in admitting, too, that if they needed to raise more capital they preferred to take out a loan rather than sell shares. That made sense, so long as inflation kept rising and interest rates were kept low.[24] Given the recent turbulent past, such cautious attitudes were understandable perhaps, but they did not portend a dynamic response by manufacturers to the opening of the economy.

Sensitive to the industrialists' lack of real enthusiasm about free enterprise, the Videla regime moved slowly on restoring the UIA's autonomy. Meanwhile, it could afford to take its time dismantling the thoroughly defunct CGE, whose top leaders, José Ber Gelbard and Júlio Broner, were fugitives in exile. On 13 July 1977 it finally decreed the dissolution of the CGE, CINA, the General Confederation of Commerce (CGC), and the agriculturalists' CP, on the broad grounds that all were guilty of "economic delinquency and subversion." At the same time, it restored the UIA's juridical personality and appointed the president of Alpargatas, Enrique Oxenford, to be its intervenor. His job was to reform the organization and prepare it for elections of a new executive committee and governing council. He and his transition committee revised the UIA's statutes, but it was not until Videla and Martínez de Hoz left office that elections actually were held.[25]

The UIA was restored slowly to full-functioning status because of factional fighting inside the industrial community and the government's desire for a completely free hand. The UIA's merger with the CI had never been popular with the larger industrialists in the Greater Buenos Aires region; therefore, with the fall of the Peronist regime, they immediately launched a movement—the Movimiento

Industrial Argentina, or MIA—to take over CINA and convert it to orthodox liberal principles. In its first declaration, MIA announced that its aim was to promote private enterprise and free, competitive markets, both at home and abroad. It also placed itself firmly against state "bureaucratic paternalism, whose autocratic, interventionist, and collectivist tendencies smother growth and enterprise."[26] The smaller industries of the interior had their organization too, however: the Movimiento Empresario del Interior, or MEDI, which had been formed in 1974 by businessmen from the northwest. Because MEDI had been opposed to Gelbard personally, it escaped the anti-Peronist purge when Videla took over. There was even a third industrial faction, the Movimiento Unido del Interior, or MUI, representing the larger firms from the Córdoba region. Both MEDI and MUI wanted a closer relationship with the state than MIA did. Oxenford and his transition committee thus had a difficult problem to grapple with, for their aim was to recreate the UIA as a single umbrella organization for all industrialists.[27]

## The Strategy

Martínez de Hoz began with classical stablization measures aimed at curbing demand and encouraging exports. He devalued the peso, removed price controls, and froze wages. To encourage agriculture, taxes and restrictions on exports were removed, while at the same time duties were lowered on imports of fertilizers, pesticides, and agricultural machinery. Farmers were allowed to bypass the meat and grain boards and sell directly to foreign buyers. The combination of record harvests and an export boom led to a rapid improvement in the balance of payments.[28]

Inflation was more difficult to control. As we have seen, the military resisted cutbacks in government spending. Martínez de Hoz was forced, therefore, to attack the problem from a different angle. He concentrated on encouraging savings by removing controls on interest rates, which immediately shot up to very high levels. Savings rose as a result, but there were unpleasant side effects. The reform was partly aimed at discouraging excessive borrowing by business firms, which had gotten used to cheap credit in the past; but businessmen continued to borrow, thinking that Martínez de Hoz—like previous economics ministers—would soon be out of office or forced to reverse his policies. In fact, they were so convinced that the Videla regime would be strongly probusiness that investment in plants and equipment rose by 20.4 percent in the first twelve months after the coup. Consequently, industrialists got very deeply in debt. To cover the costs of servicing those loans, as well as the higher costs brought on by devaluation, industrialists raised their prices, thus pushing inflation higher.[29]

Toward the latter quarter of 1977, however, the economy began to feel a recession. The combination of rising prices and a wage freeze had reduced labor's share of the national income to its lowest level (31 percent) since 1935. As a result, consumption and sales fell off sharply, resulting in a sudden explosion of bankruptcies. Whereas in 1976 some 134 companies went out of business, involving assets worth approximately $700,000, in 1977 that rose to 318 companies and $53.7 million. Businessmen blamed the high interest rates and low wages and called for a loosening of government policies; the government replied that the real cause was bad business habits, engendered by a long history of inflation. It argued that manufacturers and retailers had been borrowing in the expectation of paying back later with cheaper pesos and had been stocking inventories in the expectation of price rises. Now, with falling sales, businesses would have to liquidate at much lower prices.[30]

The government was close to the truth, but it was wrong in one respect: prices in general did not go down. Operating for the most part in captive markets, producers had only to limit their output and raise their prices in order to maintain their profit margins. Frustrated, the government sought to force down prices by freeing the exchange rate, in May 1978, and allowing the peso to float, expecting thereby that imported goods would become cheaper. Instead, the dollar fell relative to the peso, which hurt farm exports.

Frustrated, Martínez de Hoz made a radical policy switch on 20 December 1978. Contrary to his laissez-faire ideology, he abandoned free exchange rates in favor of fixed ones, but announced that there would be constant devaluations at levels just below those of domestic inflation. Devaluations, in turn, would be related to world inflation. Thus, foreign goods would enter the Argentine market at competitive prices—so long as domestic producers kept their own prices high. The idea was to bring domestic inflation down to world levels by forcing Argentine industry to produce more cheaply and efficiently. In effect, it was an attempt to force down prices without reverting to price controls and by introducing foreign competition.[31]

It was a bold and imaginative move by a desperate man trying to fight inflation with one hand tied (by the military) behind his back. Like many other brilliant strategies in Argentina's history, it failed.

One obvious drawback was that the rural sector's exports were hurt as devaluation lagged behind inflation. Second, prices in the public enterprises continued to rise because (1) they were not competing with foreign goods, and (2) the government was determined to eliminate their deficits. That blunted the antiinflation drive. Third, public expenditures for armaments and social welfare remained high. Fourth, the military's insistence on maintaining full employment made fighting inflation difficult. In fact, by 1979 there was a labor shortage, especially for skilled workers, and employers were forced to violate government wage guidelines and pay "black wages" in order to keep their help. Fifth, and most serious of all, in the months following the announcement of the new policy the dollar began to slump while the peso got stronger; nevertheless, Martínez de Hoz refused to devalue. In consequence, the peso became extremely overvalued. Foreign goods became very cheap, as did packaged vacation tours to foreign lands, and consumers went on a buying binge. Domestic industries, on the other hand, were put in a perilous situation. Heavily in debt and faced with competition they could not, or would not, meet, they tottered toward collapse.[32]

## The Crash

The impending economic crisis gave off warning signals in the form of a rapidly mounting foreign debt—signals which most Argentines preferred to ignore. Between the end of 1975 and the end of 1980, foreign debt rose by 236 percent, from $8.1 billion to $28.2 billion. The biggest increase was in debts to international lending agencies, which increased from $3.2 billion to $18.9 billion. Debts owed to private banks also increased, however, from $4.9 billion to $8.3 billion. The public debt just about tripled, from $4.9 billion to $15.5 billion, but the private sector debt quadrupled, from $3.1 billion to $12.7 billion.[33]

What did the Argentines do with the loans they got? Many of them imported luxury goods, took vacations, or bought dollars and deposited them overseas. Private business firms took advantage of the government's deregulation of foreign borrowing to contract debts whose interest charges were lower than those prevailing locally. In most cases, however, they had to go through a local bank. That was not difficult in the case of larger companies, especially those that belonged to a conglomerate that owned its own bank. Once the loan was obtained, the company would sell the note to the bank and deposit the pesos in that bank at a lower interest rate than the one prevailing. The bank thus had more capital to lend and made money from the spread in the interest rates while the company obtained ready working capital at an interest rate below what it would have to pay locally.[34]

The government used loans for expensive public works projects, military equipment, and—in increasing measure—to make up for the consequences of overvaluing the peso. The overvalued peso had created a very unfavorable trade balance as Argentine exports became expensive while imports got cheaper. Furthermore, the expensive peso had encouraged a drain of capital from the country as dollars became cheaper relative to the peso. Only by contracting new loans to replace its shrinking gold and dollar exchange reserves could the Central Bank continue to finance the state's commitments. At an early stage in this questionable process it would have made more sense simply to have devalued the peso, but once the foreign debt began to take off for the sky (it doubled between the end of 1978 and the end of 1980) the costs of devaluation became frightening. After all, the debts were payable in dollars, and anything that would make the dollar more expensive relative to the peso might force the state into default and push many private companies into bankruptcy.

Indeed, the collapse came quickly as many businesses, their debts far outweighing their assets and their loan repayments outstripping their profits, could no longer keep afloat. Bankruptcies, whose total assets had been $265.4 million in 1978, shot up to $509.4 million in 1979 and to a staggering $1.05 billion in 1980. Most of the victims were small and medium-sized firms, but some large ones were included. In the tractor industry, Deutz and John Deere shut down; Chrysler, General Motors, and Citroen closed their plants in the automotive industry, while Fiat, Ford, IKA, and Peugeot were practically idle; in the electrical machinery field, the Singer Sewing Machine Company went out of business; in aviation, Austral Airlines went bankrupt; in steel, La Cantábrica, recently privatized, folded again, while Tamet, a part of the Tornquist conglomerate (reorganized under the name of Arbol Sol), would soon collapse, along with the rest of the grupo; in metallurgy, CAMEA, a rolling mill for lead and aluminum products, whose origins went back to 1904, failed; in chemicals and petrochemicals, SNIAFA, a long-established producer of rayon and cellophane, closed its doors, and Petrosur shut down its sulphuric acid plant; in food processing, Liebig's meat extract company, a British concern, stopped operating after 80 years in the country, and Sasetrú, a large wine, vegetable oil, and flour conglomerate, would be forced into bankruptcy a few months after Martínez de Hoz left office. Perhaps most shocking of all, the Fabril Financiera conglomerate was thrown into confusion when its leading company, La Celulosa, declared itself unable to meet its creditors' demands in mid-1980.

Celulosa's case may well illustrate what had gone wrong with Argentine industry, because its troubles were partly its own fault and partly due to a long series of unfavorable government policies. Until 1973, Celulosa was one of Latin America's industrial success stories. Its timber forests, scattered throughout the northern provinces, covered a total of 90,000 hectares (225,000 acres), and its various offices, camps, and paper mills employed over 5,000 people; it had successfully replaced all imports of paper. In 1970 a market survey projected that consumption of paper products in Argentina would double by the end of the decade; at that point Celulosa's president, Edmundo Paúl, decided to expand. About $160 million was borrowed to build new paper, pulp, and cellulose plants. Celulosa also acquired Editorial Júlio Korn and Editorial Abril, which made it the country's largest publisher. The expansion plan was a gamble because the money was borrowed through short-term loans, whereas the new operations would start to pay off only in the longer term. Nevertheless, because Celulosa's reputation and credit were good, it was able to get loans; and from the company's standpoint, inflation was expected to make repayment easy. The first difficulties were encountered when Celulosa's profits were badly hurt by the price freeze imposed by the Social Pact in 1973. The company took out more loans to cover those that were coming due and managed to stay afloat for a while longer; but that strategy became more risky when Martínez de Hoz deregulated interest rates, making it much more expensive to borrow. Then import duties were lowered and the peso was overvalued, which introduced cheap foreign products into the Argentine market and led to declining sales for Celulosa. By 1979, the company was forced to reschedule its debts, with the help of a $55 million credit from a foreign bank. In 1980 the National Development Bank stepped in with another rescue operation costing $90 million. It was no use. The struggle became hopeless when Gen. Roberto Viola succeeded General Videla as president in 1981 and the new economics minister, Lorenzo Sigaut, finally decreed the long-awaited devaluation. In January 1982, Celulosa finally defaulted and called in its creditors after failing to obtain an emergency loan of $130 million from the state.[35]

A more serious case of questionable business practices made

headlines shortly after Martínez de Hoz left office. On 5 March 1981 a commercial judge refused a request by the directors of Sasetrú for more time to meet their debt repayments, thus placing this important holding company and its thirty-six subsidiaries, including its powerful Banco Internacional (which itself had twenty-eight branches throughout the country) in bankruptcy. On 7 March, plainclothesmen from the federal police entered the offices of Sasetrú and the Banco Internacional and arrested a half-dozen top executives on charges of economic subversion. Although the conglomerate's total assets were estimated at around $75 million, its total debt was in the neighborhood of $1.2 billion. The Central Bank, which brought the charges against Sasetrú, accused it of arranging illegal loans through the Banco Internacional.

An investigation of Sasetrú's books showed that the conglomerate had been staving off bankruptcy for some time by using its various companies to obtain loans, ostensibly to modernize their production. The money, however, was turned over to Sasetrú's central directorate, which used it to pay previous loans. In order to keep getting loans, those directors had falsified company records by using phony sales receipts and expense vouchers (for large capital investments that, in fact, were never made) to impress potential lenders. One favorite tactic was to puff up profits through phony stock sales from one Sasetrú affiliate to another. For example, in November 1979 Sasetrú bought from one of its subsidiaries, Ayllú, 24 million pesos of stock in another subsidiary, Caucan, for 15 million. Two days later it sold the stock to another subsidiary, Lufre, for 35 million and recorded a 20-million-peso profit in its books. Fortunately for Sasetrú, its creditors were always impressed by the size of its empire and never bothered to investigate its operations very closely.[36]

Why did lenders not look more closely into their borrowers' finances? The answer is obvious in the case of banks whose role was to service a particular conglomerate. In other cases, however, the fault is traceable partly to speculative fever and partly to shortsighted government policies. Martínez de Hoz had intended the deregulation of banking to push up interest rates, encourage saving, and permit a greater degree of domestic capital formation. What happened instead was a fierce competition between banks to capture more deposits by raising the interest paid. Following the banking reforms of December 1978, there also was an explosion in the number of new banks being created as many finance companies petitioned for an upgrading of their status—for only as banks could they be eligible to engage in foreign exchange transactions or offer savings and checking accounts. Their entry into the field sharpened the competition all the more, pushing interest rates even higher. That was the point at which even foreign lenders became interested in Argentina. Influential men, like the former American ambassador Robert Hill, acted as go-betweens in attracting a large amount of foreign loan money. In Hill's case, the link was to a particular institution, the Banco de Intercambio Regional (BIR), Argentina's largest private bank, in which Adm. Emílio Massera, one of the members of the ruling junta, had an interest.[37] At a time when most banks were offering depositors 58 to 60 percent on their money, the BIR paid 64 percent. In that way the BIR's president, José Trozzo, quickly brought it from ninety-fifth place among private banks, in terms of deposits, to first.[38]

Naturally, banks paying high interest to their depositors had to seek investments that paid even higher returns in order to make profits. As a rule, however, the higher the rate of return, the riskier the investment. Bankers could assuage their consciences, however, by reflecting on the fact that since January 1979 the Central Bank was offering to insure 90 percent of all savings deposits in return for a small fee. This was another attempt by Martínez de Hoz to encourage small domestic private banks, since such insurance was already available at state banks and big private foreign and domestic banks had sufficient reserves and prestige to attract investors. From the outset, this law of guaranteed deposits had its critics. They argued that such guarantees were dangerous unless the Central Bank was prepared to heavily police local private banks to ascertain their financial soundness and the quality of their loan portfolios. The government's supporters, such as the RRP, retorted that the measure was necessary in order to promote competition and give the newer banks a fair chance to attract depositors.[39]

In the case of many new, small banks, a process rapidly developed by which they were absorbed into the network of a conglomerate and became prisoners of their depositors. These small banks had been forced to increase their capital beyond a minimum required by the Central Bank in order to be upgraded from finance companies, and many of them had recourse to the conglomerates to do this. The conglomerates, for their part, were looking for places to put their money at high interest while they waited for the proper time to borrow it back. Indeed, it may be said that the conglomerates were loaning the banks money, rather than the reverse. Thus, although some of the former finance companies quickly rose to become big banks, their success rested on a very narrow base, making them vulnerable to a panic.[40]

The whole scheme of banking deregulation came crashing down in March 1980 when the Central Bank was forced to intervene in the BIR, the most successful of the new banks. At the time of its closure, the BIR had 101 branches, including some in New York, Washington, and Paris. Its depositors included 50 of the country's top 150 firms, it employed 1,600 people, and in the year and a half since the new banking laws went into effect, its capital had increased to around $1.2 billion. José Trozzo, the BIR's president, was a kind of financial P. T. Barnum who grabbed the public's attention with gimmicks like opening a Baby Bank that offered twenty-one-year deposits indexed to inflation. Its walls were decorated with life-sized pictures of lions, giraffes, zebras, and elephants. He also started an exclusively women's bank—the Joan of Arc Bank—in the Barrio Norte and placed his wife in charge of it. It catered to the rich widows and divorcees of the neighborhood. Each of his overseas branches opened in a blaze of publicity.[41] *Mercado*, the businessmen's weekly magazine, was impressed by the BIR's "aggressive policies of expansion and growth" which "put it almost permanently in the news." Its success was attributed to Martínez de Hoz's banking reforms, which brought about positive interest rates and which "increased competition, encouraged the efficiency of enterprises, and allowed them greater freedom of action."[42]

No one but Trozzo knew, however, that the BIR's aggressive policies included loaning out more money than it had on deposit or in its reserves. In March 1980 it had about $3 billion in outstanding loans, many of which were extremely shaky. The law stated that bad debts could not exceed 30 percent of a bank's capital, but since policing by the Central Bank was lax in this new laissez-faire atmosphere, it was not hard to juggle the books and appear financially solid. Trozzo knew that a crisis was coming in his affairs, and he accepted a bid by Raúl Pinero Pacheco, one of the bank's directors and head of an investment holding company, to buy the BIR. To fix a price, however, it was necessary to examine the books. Pinero Pacheco's auditors found a series of bad loans. One debtor, owing 27 billion pesos, had gone bankrupt in January; another went bankrupt in February and defaulted on a loan of 14 billion; another 6 billion had to be written off in March. The auditors concluded that the BIR might be holding the equivalent of 270 billion pesos in unrecoverable loans. Meanwhile, insiders in the financial district had heard rumors of these disasters, and a run on deposits had begun. In

March alone, between 3 and 5 billion pesos were withdrawn daily from the BIR's various branches. Although shaken by these discoveries, Pinero Pacheco was willing to try a salvage operation if he could get government backing. On 14 March he went to the Central Bank with a plan, but two weeks later Martínez de Hoz made it clear in a public statement—without naming the BIR—that the government would not bail out mismanaged companies. Free enterprise meant, unfortunately, the freedom to fail. The following morning, the Central Bank turned down Pinero Pacheco's request and declared the BIR to be in liquidation.[43]

The BIR's collapse touched off a panic that spread to other banks with similar aggressive strategies. On 25 April 1980 the Central Bank took over the administration of the Banco Oddone, the Banco de Los Andes, and the Banco Internacional. All three lay at the heart of industrial empires, and all had attracted numerous deposits by paying higher rates of interest than normal. Luís Oddone was a boy wonder who had worked his way up from being a runner in a brokerage firm to being the head of a conglomerate that owned banks, finance companies, *estancias*, factories, construction companies, a grain export firm, a shipyard, and 36 percent of the Bagley Biscuit Company. His methods were always somewhat suspicious, since he had made his fortune originally by helping foreign firms evade laws restricting their access to credit by setting up dummy local companies. He was now put under arrest by the federal police for violating laws forbidding banks from making most of their loans to companies whose ownership overlapped with their own. It turned out that he had overspeculated in oilseed futures and was unable to meet his depositors' demands when they rushed to draw out their savings. Police also arrested Héctor and José Greco, two brothers who owned the Banco de Los Andes, the pivot of an empire that controlled much of Argentina's wine production. Like Oddone, they had used their depositors' savings to finance their own companies and got caught in the panic. The Banco Internacional was, as we have seen, the key to Sasetrú's network of interests. The failure of that empire a few months later led to the arrest of its president and founder, Juan Rómulo Seitún, for breaking the banking laws.[44]

The collapse of these big banks spurred the panic. Conservative banks, which had kept their loans below their level of deposits, weathered the storm that battered the financial district for the next six months; but the less prudent went under. By the end of the year, the Central Bank had been forced to decree the liquidation of more than forty financial institutions. The extent of the wreckage undermined all confidence in the government's economic program and, indeed, in the private sector as a whole. Men like Trozzo and Oddone, who only a short while before had been viewed as heroes breathing new life and confidence into Argentine capitalism, were now discredited as con men. Money was tighter and dearer than ever, because those banks which had survived were nervous about making any loans. The saving and investing public was deserting the private banks, whose deposits dropped sharply in 1980 as a percentage of the total, while those of the government-owned banks rose. Martínez de Hoz might blame the debacle on the unbusiness-like mentality of many financial entrepreneurs—and certainly their behavior might rightly be characterized as precapitalist—but for the Argentine public, free-market economics was discredited. Even the progovernment RRP was forced to admit that capitalism did not seem to work in Argentina. In an editorial entitled "The Invisible Hand Is On Strike," the RRP noted that although the government had created incentives to save, Argentines were spending more than ever on amusements and restaurants; instead of using cheap dollars and cheap imports to invest in new manufacturing equipment, Argentines preferred to go abroad on their vacations and bring back luxury appliances and television sets; and instead of using high interest rates for productive investment, Argentine financial institutions simply indulged in speculation, if not outright fraud. Perverse as always, the Argentines had taken advantage of the open economy to violate all the rules in the textbook.[45]

## The Balance Sheet

Martínez de Hoz's policies inspired a number of criticisms by Argentine economists. Orthodox liberals like Álvaro Alsogaray, Horacio García Belsunce, and the editors of the RRP criticized him for not cutting the public payroll, closing down or selling state enterprises, canceling unnecessary public spending plans, or limiting the emission of currency. They put the blame for failure primarily upon the military, which refused to allow the drastic reduction in state spending that the situation called for. Without that, the government was unable to contain inflation, which pushed up costs too fast for Martínez de Hoz to adjust the peso to the dollar. The overvalued peso, in turn, had disastrous consequences. On the other hand, nationalists like Aldo Ferrer accused Martínez de Hoz of wanting to sacrifice local industry to foreign interests and make Argentina revert to being an agricultural nation.[46]

There is no doubt that a large number of industrial establishments went out of business during the decade following the 1976 coup: approximately 15,000 in all. That was not a new trend, however. The number of industrial establishments had decreased drastically in the previous decade too. However, the distinguishing factor in the 1974–85 period was the lead again taken by domestic private capital in industry. During the 1963–74 period, domestic private capital had been shoved into the background by foreign capital. Foreign capital's contribution to total industrial output decreased during the Videla years and under the military governments that followed from about 50 percent to 46 percent, while that of both state and domestic private capital increased. State capital's rise was due almost entirely to government takeovers of bankrupt private firms rather than any increase in dynamism. In the case of domestic private capital, however, an interesting thing occurred: output by independent companies declined, but that of big conglomerates rose considerably.[47]

Spectacular failures like those of Sasetrú and La Celulosa should not hide the fact that other big companies—especially those favored by the "peripheral privatization" process—surged forward: Pérez Companc, Garovaglio & Zorraquín, and Technit (the engineering holding company of the Rocca conglomerate) became the new industrial-commercial-financial giants of the 1980s, replacing the Tornquists and the Robertses as the country's economic leaders. Conversely, their gains came when many smaller establishments were disappearing. Indeed, using their superior access to credit, they often expanded by absorbing the latter. Seen in that light, Martínez de Hoz's policies, rather than being antiindustrial, or leading to deindustrialization, resulted in making domestic industry larger in scale and more modern.[48]

The iron and steel industry led all others in improving its productivity during this period. Output rose by 60 percent while the labor force was trimmed by 16 percent. In early 1981 the biggest merger in the nation's history took place, with Acindar, Gurmendi, Santa Rosa, and Genaro Grasso agreeing to form a single giant enterprise, Acindar. As a result, the private steel sector finally achieved a high level of integration. Impressive gains in productivity were made in the areas of petroleum refining, petrochemicals, trucks, tobacco, and metal products. In fact, as the less efficient enterprises went to the wall, throwing workers out of jobs and leaving only the more capital-intensive in the field, every branch of Argentine industry except food processing, clothing, leather, and paper registered a gain in worker productivity.

The small entrepreneur did not disappear from the economic scene, however. The disappearance of 15,000 small industrial enterprises was more than balanced by the appearance of over 90,000 commercial and service establishments. Another phenomenon was the continued growth in the number of *cuentapropistas,* an occupational category that rose from 12 percent of the economically active population in 1960 to 17 percent in 1970 and 19 percent in 1980. Many commentators on the contemporary Argentine labor market have suggested that this was a reflection of disguised unemployment. Census figures show, however, that white- and blue-collar workers have remained a very steady proportion of the economically active population: 72 percent in 1960, 74 percent in 1970, and 72 percent in 1980. However, the proportion of employers and partners *(patrones o sócios)* has declined sharply from 13 percent to 6 percent, which suggests that the self-employed are former small businessmen—and probably former owners of tiny industrial shops.[49]

## The Labor Situation

With the concentration of industry went a decline in the number of workers employed, from 1,525,221 in 1974 to 1,359,519: a drop of almost 11 percent. Moreover, many of those who had jobs apparently worked only part-time, inasmuch as the number of hours worked by the average blue-collar industrial employee fell by 30 percent. This was offset, in certain respects, by an increase in the number of workers in commerce and services, from 1,845,488 to 2,183,157: an 18 percent rise.[50] That suggests not only a shift in the composition of the labor force but also that the tertiary sector offers the only opportunities for most young people entering the labor market for the first time. Although hard data on wages during this period is not currently available, it is a commonly known fact that wages in this sector are much below those of industry. Much of the employment in commerce and services also consists of dead-end jobs. Given the small size of most commercial shops (fewer than 3 employees, on the average), unionization is not common and labor laws are often evaded.

An increase in the value of the output of the big conglomerates between 1973 and 1983 from $2.3 billion to $2.7 billion indicates that the disappearance of small firms was not the only cause of the contraction in industrial employment. More important was the incorporation of advanced technology in the larger companies. While industrial payrolls were being trimmed, industrial productivity rose by 30 percent and electricity consumption by 50 percent.[51]

Insecurity of employment naturally had a depressive effect on wages, which tended to lag behind the cost of living. Moreover, in order to contract the money supply and bring down inflation, the government adopted the practice of granting raises in the form of increased fringe benefits rather than take-home pay. About 51 percent of an ordinary industrial worker's wage was set aside for the pension fund, family allowances, the national housing fund, and medical insurance. The cash a worker got to live on, with the removal of price and rent controls, was often not enough. This was particularly true since wage increases usually lagged behind the cost of living. In mid-1977, labor's share of the national income was only 31 percent, its lowest level since 1935.[52]

Videla and Martínez de Hoz did not aim only at redistributing income in favor of capital; they wanted to discipline the labor movement as well. Immediately after the coup, the CGT was subjected to intervention, and its leaders were arrested. The *fuero sindical* that accorded privileges and immunities to union officials was abolished, as was the system by which employers had to collect the unions' dues for them. The Law of Professional Associations was retained at first, but in 1979 it was replaced by a Law of Workers' Trade Unions. This new law guaranteed the right to form unions and engage in collective bargaining, but unions were to stay out of politics and could not receive subsidies from political groups or foreign sources. They also were charged with maintaining order and discipline among their members and with preventing the "carrying out of any acts which might take any form of violence, coercion, intimidation, or threat." The number of shop stewards in any factory was limited, and they were expected to "maintain a relationship with the employers on a basis of cooperative and social solidarity." Unions still had to get legal recognition from the Ministry of Labor, and they were subject to intervention if they violated the law, failed to be truly representative of the membership, or mishandled their finances. All union funds had to be deposited in government banks. Union officials would have three-year terms, with the right of only one immediate reelection. They had to hold annual assemblies, and voting in union elections was obligatory.[53]

Naturally, the unions tried to resist the new government. The power and light federation provided the most dramatic test of wills when it called a strike in October 1976 to protest a rule by SEGBA, the state electric company, that would dock a worker's pay for failure to show up on the job. In addition, the power and light workers were, like the telephone workers, bank workers, and stevedores, determined to resist having their workweek increased from thirty-five to forty-two hours. The strike came to a grim climax in mid-January when the power and light leader, Oscar Smith, was kidnapped. His body was never found. A week later, the strikers went back to work on the government's terms. Not only did the workers concede on the original issues, but their union lost long-held privileges such as the right to have union officials on SEGBA's management board and payment by the company for their union work. Fringe benefits such as maternity pay, sick leave, and extra holidays were cut back too. After disciplining the power and light workers, the government turned next on the telephone workers. These workers had carried on a particularly violent strike at ENTEL, in which there was widespread sabotage of equipment. Some 8,000 were fired, and the rest were forced to accept the longer work week. With the breaking of these two strikes, those of the bank workers and the stevedores soon collapsed.[54]

Those were not the last strikes to be attempted, however. The railroad workers struck later in 1977, and the auto industry was plagued by strikes during 1979 and 1981. One of Alpargatas's factories suffered a strike in 1979 too, but the management soon broke it by threatening to close down all the plants. Without the CGT and the 62 Organizations to coordinate action, labor was relatively ineffective. The Peronists were divided by their recent experience under Isabel and could not even form an underground. Two unofficial blocs competed: the orthodox, or "verticalist," Committee of 25, and the neo-Peronist, or "anti-verticalist," National Labor Commission (CNT). Not until September 1979 did the two finally come together to set up the United Leadership of Argentine Workers (CUTA), but the new organization remained so factionalized that it made little impression on the government. Predictably, it urged the lifting of the CGT's intervention, demanded the release of Lorenzo Miguel and other arrested labor leaders, defended the state enterprises, and called for a return to civilian rule.[55]

Table 18.1 Absenteeism in Selected Industries, 1974 and 1978

| | Rate (%) | |
| | 1974 | 1978 |
| Industry | (Perón) | (Videla) |
| --- | --- | --- |
| Iron and steel | 12.7 | 12.3 |
| Automobiles | 18.3 | 16.4 |
| Large home appliances | 15.5 | 15.6 |
| Cigarettes | 13.0 | 14.6 |
| Synthetic cellulose fibers | 16.2 | 17.4 |
| Cement | 15.3 | 13.4 |
| Plastics | 11.7 | 12.4 |
| Rubber tires | 14.6 | 14.8 |
| Paints and varnishes | 13.1 | 11.6 |
| Beer | 17.2 | 15.2 |
| Paper and cardboard | 12.2 | 12.1 |
| Sulphuric acid | 15.0 | 15.7 |
| Leather tanning | 14.1 | 13.9 |
| Matches | 15.3 | 14.2 |
| Soap | 14.1 | 16.5 |

Source: INDEC, *Indicadores industriales*, 4:46–47, 6:74–75.

Union membership was still high, however. Having reached a low point in 1970, it had picked up again under the Peronist government, surpassing in most cases the levels reached in the early 1960s. Nevertheless, by 1980 most unions had lost members in comparison with a few years before. The UOM lost between 12,000 and 13,000 between 1977 and 1980, although it had about 100,000 more than in 1970. State employees, health workers, restaurant personnel, autoworkers, and commercial employees suffered similar losses in comparison with 1977, although all but the commercial employees' union were larger than they had been a decade before. On the other hand, construction workers, textile workers, and bank workers had either gained members or stayed about the same.[56] The labor movement was by no means a spent force.

Nor could it be said that the workers had become truly disciplined by their adversity. Absenteeism rates were still in the double-digit range for a great many industries, as table 18.1 shows. Unable to strike effectively and forced to watch their living standards decline, many workers showed their displeasure in the only way left to them: by not showing up at the factory and by working badly when they did go to their jobs. Such behavior only strengthened the deter-mination of capital to further reduce its dependence on the workers by introducing more labor-saving machinery. So Argentina, at the opening of the 1980s, was still locked in a class struggle that proved to be Perón's most lasting legacy to the country.

## CHAPTER NINETEEN

# Dynamic Stagnation

## The Military's Retreat

The military's "Process of National Reorganization" quickly fell apart after Videla and Martínez de Hoz left office. Their successors, Gen. Roberto Viola and Lorenzo Sigaut, ended the partial opening of Argentina's economy, restored the familiar controls that protected the country's "hothouse capitalism," and borrowed heavily abroad to keep tottering banks and industries from collapsing altogether. Rather than restoring order, this reversal of policy undermined the financial community's confidence and led to an enormous outflow of capital. In 1981 alone, domestic investment dropped by an estimated 27 percent and foreign investment by 13 percent. It is difficult, if not impossible, to know the exact amount of capital flight, but the World Bank estimated that nearly $20 billion left the country between 1979 and 1982—while others put the figure at more than $30 billion. Since an ECLA study of American investment in Argentina pinpointed 1981 as the year in which the largest capital withdrawals, by far, took place, we may assume this was the peak for other investors as well.[1]

Whatever shortcomings the Videla-Martínez de Hoz economic policies may have had, they at least had the virtue of being consistent and of giving people a stable set of conditions upon which to base their planning. Even before General Viola took office at the end of March 1981, the prospect of a change in the economic team provoked a panic buying of dollars in the exchange houses along the Calle San Martín. In anticipation of a return to instability, interest rate controls, and peso devaluations, depositors went rushing to the banks to withdraw their money to convert it into dollars while other frantic speculators were buying dollars with money borrowed at usurious rates in the expectation of a sharp devaluation of the peso. Their gamble paid off. Within a week after taking office, Sigaut announced a 30 percent devaluation along with a 12 percent export tax that was designed to catch windfall profits from agriculturalists.[2]

The devaluation was a mistake because it destroyed all confidence in the peso. Despite assurances from Sigaut that no further devaluations would be needed—that indeed the peso now was undervalued and hence attractive to dollarholders—the public took no notice. Despite Central Bank efforts to prop up the peso by using some $310 million of its exchange reserves, the stampede continued. At the end of May, *La Nación* carried rumors of another impending devaluation. The news sent panic buying to a new peak, emptying the exchange houses on San Martín of all their dollars. In a single day, 29 May, there was an unprecedented run on the exchange market of $308 million. On the next street, the fashionable pedestrian mall called Calle Florida, desperate buyers crowded into cozy *confiterias* (cafés) like the Richmond and El Ciclista to bargain with black market holders of dollars. Once again their instincts were correct. On 2 June, Sigaut decreed a second 30 percent devaluation, which he promised would be the last. That, coupled with compensatory wage increases and restrictions on buying foreign exchange, convinced those with investment capital that the military had now given up all intentions of reforming Argentina's *dirigiste* system. Nor was it possible to stop the trading of pesos for dollars, despite heavy borrowing by the Central Bank to support the local currency. Although Argentina ended the year with a favorable trade balance of $541 million, its exchange reserves had dropped by $3 billion, and its foreign debt had risen to to $32 billion. Gross fixed investment was down by 16.4 percent, the GNP had dropped by 5.3 percent, and industrial production had fallen by 14.4 percent. "Does the government have a future?" the conservative weekly magazine SOMOS asked after the second devaluation. It did not, because on 12 December the military removed Viola and, a week later, replaced him with Gen. Leopoldo Galtieri.[3]

The first actions of the Galtieri government temporarily restored investor confidence. The new economics minister, Roberto Alemann, had served in that post under Frondizi and was a trusted figure in the financial community. He promised to privatize state enterprises "where necessary" and to reestablish a free-market economy. But, like Martínez de Hoz, he was to discover that the Argentine military was an unreliable ally. In February 1982 he proposed a 10 percent reduction in the defense budget, which had hit an all-time high of 45 billion pesos (about $4.5 billion) the previous year. Military appropriations, which were about 2.5 percent of the GDP until 1975, climbed to over 5 percent under the Process because of the "dirty war" against the guerrillas and the threat of a war with Chile over the ownership of some islands in the Beagle Channel. Alemann wanted to decrease the budget deficit, but in April 1982 Galtieri confounded his plans by plunging Argentina into the Falkland Islands War. In the aftermath, Argentina found itself with triple-digit inflation, a $35.6 billion foreign debt, a GDP at 6 percent below the 1981 level, industrial production down by 16 percent, and unemployment up by 6 percent.[4]

Humiliated by defeat, unpopular with the public, and baffled by their failure to reform the economy, the military decided to return to the barracks. A caretaker government under retired general Reynaldo Bignone scheduled elections for October 1983. In the meantime, controls were placed on interest rates in order to encourage businesses to borrow and expand. In the weeks that followed, Argentines went on a buying spree: cars, television sets, condominiums, vacation homes, clothes—all in anticipation of the inflation that was certain to follow. Rather than making it easier for businessmen to borrow money, the government's policies made money scarce because so many depositors emptied their savings accounts in order to join the consumer spending frenzy. By the time Bignone stepped down, price controls had again become necessary as a temporary expedient, since cost of living increases had reached an annual rate of 400 percent.

## The Radicals in Power

### The Alfonsín Administration

On 30 October 1983 the UCR won an unexpected electoral victory over the Peronist Partido Justicialista (PJ) to gain control of the presidency and the lower house of Congress. Its standard-bearer, Raúl Alfonsín, got 52 percent of the presidential vote to only 39 percent for the Peronist candidate, Italo Luder. In the Chamber of Deputies, the UCR had 129 seats to 111 for the Peronists, with 14 seats scattered among minor parties. The Peronists, who had never lost a national election, were shocked by the results and had to content themselves with controlling the Senate.

Raúl Alfonsín was a lawyer and longtime party activist from Chascomús, in Buenos Aires Province. He had learned his politics as a protege of Ricardo Balbín. In the late 1960s, however, he began to distance himself from Balbín in the belief that the UCR was failing to gain popular support because its leadership was too conservative. At the time of the *cordobazo*, Alfonsín was publicly supporting Raimundo Óngaro's maverick movement of leftist workers and students, a stance which earned him the nomination of the Radicals' youth organization for the party presidency in 1971. Though easily beaten by Balbín, Alfonsín found fresh allies from other sectors of the party, including parts of the Buenos Aires and Córdoba provincial organizations. In 1973 he campaigned at the head of a left-wing faction to wrest the party's presidential nomination from Balbín. Although beaten again, Alfonsín made a good showing and had the satisfaction of seeing Balbín soundly whipped twice during the year by the Peronists: by Cámpora in March and by Perón in September. In 1974 Balbín retained control of the party leadership only with the greatest difficulty, for by then even ex-president Illia was calling for a change. Only the military's proscription of all political party activity in 1976 allowed Balbín to stay on as UCR president.

With Balbín's death on 9 September 1981, the Radical party quickly fell into the hands of Alfonsín and his faction known as the Movimiento de Renovación y Cambio. During the Process, when open party activity was forbidden, Alfonsín had solidified his support on the left, defending regime opponents (including Roberto Santucho, head of the ERP terrorist organization) and authoring articles under a nom de plume in defense of human rights. The party's youthful leftists, meanwhile, had busily set up informal organizations in many districts, which provided the Movimiento de Renovación y Cambio with an efficient grass-roots network that was able to capture the party congress in 1983, when the Bignone government restored the UCR to legality. At last the younger Radicals were able to campaign on the democratic socialist platform that they had long argued for as the only hope for winning the public away from Peronism. The UCR's big victory in 1983 seemed to prove them right.[5]

On many issues there was little difference between the UCR and the PJ. Both were suspicious of foreign capital and were opposed to paying off the foreign debt. Both favored financing development with domestic savings. Both wanted the state to lead the process, and both promised to protect local industry from foreign competition. Both, in short, favored a closed, corporativist economy with key economic activities controlled by the state. The only difference was that the Radicals were "clean" on the issues of democracy and human rights while the Peronists were not. Peronist rule from 1973 to 1976 had been marred by such corruption, economic mismanagement, labor union arrogance, and state terrorism in the form of the Argentine Anticommunist Alliance that the PJ was widely blamed for creating the conditions that inevitably led to the Process. The UCR, on the other hand, could conveniently forget that Ricardo Balbín had collaborated with the Peronist and military governments alike; instead, they emphasized that the last Radical government was Illia's—a government with clear democratic credentials, whose overthrow in 1966 had started the horrid slide into violence. Alfonsín himself had earned a reputation for forthrightness and courage and moreover enjoyed the endorsement of famous European socialists like François Mitterrand, Bettino Craxi, and Felipe González.[6]

Alfonsín drew support from all classes. Not only did he carry middle-class districts where Radicals always are strong, but he also received a surprising number of votes from Peronist working-class barrios. Electoral analyses of the Greater Buenos Aires area indicate, however, that his big margin of victory may have been provided by voters traditionally identified with the Right. Conservative parties received only 4 percent of the vote in 1983, as compared with 20 percent a decade earlier; this suggests that many people cast their ballots for Alfonsín in order to prevent a Peronist victory. The combination of anti-Peronist conservatives and traditional Radical voters, who backed him out of party loyalty, indicates that Alfonsín's supporters stood considerably to the right of him.[7]

The new government faced a formidable challenge. At the end of 1983, inflation had reached an annual rate of 400 percent. The foreign debt stood at $46 billion, with annual payments on it absorbing 60 percent of all export earnings. The GDP had ceased to grow and, in fact, was contracting at a annual rate of 4.3 percent (1980–83). Government expenditures, which—thanks to military spending, debt servicing, and large subsidies from the treasury to the deficit-ridden state enterprises—continued to grow while every other sector of the economy shriveled, constituted 50 percent of the GDP. Obviously, forceful action would be necessary to reverse this situation. On the bright side, Alfonsín's opponents, the Peronists, were demoralized and split. In the aftermath of their defeat they quarreled among themselves. A youthful, renovationist wing that wanted to create a more democratic image for the Justicialist party broke away from the old-line orthodox leaders. The former were willing to work with the Radicals to make democracy succeed, whereas the latter were blamed for the party's defeat and lost support even among many trade unions. The unions themselves were badly weakened. The industrial work force was between 30 and 40 percent smaller in 1982 than it was in 1975, and fewer workers were unionized; real wages were about 15 percent lower and unemployment (including underemployment) affected about 10 percent of the economically active population. Finally, the military, that other traditional check on presidential initiative, also was demoralized and, for the moment, passive.[8]

Alfonsín had only two real options. He could adopt a nationalist position and defy Argentina's foreign creditors. As the newly elected head of a democratic government, he could justify a refusal to pay back loans contracted by the military dictatorship on the grounds that the latter was not a legitimate representative of the nation. Furthermore, he could question the good faith of the creditor nations, who loan money freely enough but then, through their own protectionist policies, make it impossible for the debtors to repay. Such a course of action, if pursued boldly, might have earned Alfonsín even greater popularity than he already enjoyed. But it would have been a leap into the dark. The creditor nations might have frozen Argentina's overseas assets, impounded its exports, or at least forced the country to pay cash for its imports.[9] A siege economy and an even worse recession would have resulted.

Conversely, Alfonsín, who was elected for a nonrenewable six-year term, might have attacked the huge government deficits that are the main source of inflation. That would have meant trimming the national, provincial, and municipal government payrolls, which provided jobs for one of every six Argentines. That would have angered Radical party colleagues, who viewed the state as a source of patronage to reward supporters. It also would have meant privatizing the state enterprises, which ran up total losses of about $3 billion in 1982. To do so, however, would require going beyond peripheral privatization. Really tackling the deficit meant focusing on the eight largest companies—YPF, the railroads, the merchant fleet (ELMA), Gas del Estado, the telephone company (ENTEL), the electric power company (SEGBA), Agua y Energia, and Aerolineas Argentinas—which together accounted for about two-thirds of the drain on the treasury from the state enterprise sector.[10] Privatizing state enterprises however, would mean taking on formidable enemies in the unions and the military. It would also increase unemployment and would require braving an outburst of nationalist opinion, which was strong even inside the Radical party.

As a man of the Left, Alfonsín naturally favored the first option. His first economics minister, Bernardo Grinspun, had been a cabinet secretary, Central Bank director, and member of CONADE in the Illia government. He had also worked with ECLA, which stands ideologically to the left and favors a leading role for the state in development. The public works appointee, Roque Carranza, had been secretary to CONADE under Illia and had also worked for ECLA. Antonio José Mucci, the labor minister, was a former printers' union boss and Socialist party activist. Dante Caputo, the minister of foreign affairs, though a relative political unknown, was a sociology graduate of the Sorbonne and, because he had gone into self-imposed exile in Paris during the Process, was said to have leftist sympathies. With a team like that, Alfonsín was most unlikely to adopt orthodox liberal policies.

What emerged, however, was a series of timid and contradictory measures that added up to no policy at all. The government seemed to lose its courage after suffering defeat in its first attempt at reform: a bill, rejected by the Peronist-controlled Senate, designed to democratize trade union procedures. According to Argentina's constitution, the Chamber of Deputies might have overridden the Senate's veto, but Alfonsín's party lacked the two-thirds majority required to do so. In the wake of their setback, the Radicals apparently decided that the only way to approach policymaking was through what they called *concertación*: a process somewhat like the old Peronist Social Pact, by which leaders of capital, labor, government, and opposition are encouraged to produce a consensus on what should be done. The method was democratic, but it also tended to create an atmosphere of sluggishness and uncertainty that was inappropriate in such a time of crisis.

Given the broad public support for the new democracy, *concertación* might have overcome the traditional self-centeredness of Argentina's pressure groups—at least to some extent—if the government had provided more leadership. The nation needed a new vision, a break with the past, a redefinition of Argentina's future. What the country got instead were the same policies that had been practiced for the past forty years, as if they were proven successes. Real wages were to be raised, especially for the lowest income groups. A federal council for exports was created to study how to increase exports, although devaluing the currency and removing export taxes were ruled out. Interest payments were suspended on the foreign debt, but creditors were temporarily mollified by prompt payments for current imports. Industry was to be reactivated through an industrial promotion law that would include affordable interest rates and easy credit. Such credit would be directed by the government toward productive activities, in order to avoid speculation. Priority would be given to import-substituting industries. The state enterprise sector would remain intact, but would be made to run more efficiently. Its deficits would be eliminated through higher charges for its goods and services. Similarly, the government's budget would be balanced by higher taxes, especially on upper income groups, and more efficient tax collection. Inflation would be tackled, *concertación*-wise, by creating committees composed of business, labor, and government representatives for each facet of the economy. Each committee would, after discussions, agree on guidelines for wages, prices, production, and credit; then each committee's agreement would be coordinated by a general committee into an overarching plan for the whole system.[11]

In the face of such inaction, inflation continued to rise. It had been at an annual rate of 402.5 percent when Alfonsín was inaugurated at the end of December 1983. By March 1984 it reached 449 percent; at that point the government imposed price controls and a rationing of beef. At the close of 1984, inflation was running at 713.4 percent, and in April 1985 it reached its four-digit stage, at 1,020.5 percent. In the meantime, Alfonsín's popularity was eroding rapidly. The year before, crowds used to turn out to hear his speeches from the balcony of the Casa Rosada; now he was being assailed from all sides as a do-nothing president. The Radicals were worried because elections to renew half the seats in the Chamber of Deputies were to be held in November.

In February Alfonsín had tried to give his administration an appearance of activity by replacing Grinspun as economics minister with Juan Sourrouille, the young (at age forty-four) secretary for planning. Sourrouille, who held a degree in accounting, had served as undersecretary of economy to Aldo Ferrer, director of the National Statistical Institute and research director for ECLA. He was the forty-third minister of economics, or the equivalent, in the forty-two years that had elapsed since the 1943 military coup. Not until June, however, when inflation hit 1,122.9 percent was he allowed to make a fresh start in dealing with Argentina's desperate situation. On 14 June 1985, Alfonsín made a dramatic speech over television and radio in which he announced the inauguration of a bold, new program which he called the Austral Plan.

## The Austral Plan

The principal features of the Austral Plan were (1) wage and price controls; (2) a promise to reduce the government's deficits by increasing its revenues and cutting its expenditures; (3) a promise to impose discipline on state enterprises by requiring presidential approval of their budgets and by ordering the Central Bank to stop printing money to cover their losses; (4) the encouragement of exports; (5) a reduction of protective tariffs; (6) the encouragement of foreign investment; and, (7) to dramatize the fresh departure that the plan represented, the issuance of a new currency, called the austral.[12] Fearing that the new program might cause a panic and a run on bank deposits, Alfonsín ordered the banks to close before he made his announcement. There was no panic, however; following the speech, according to Gary Wynia,

> an uncharacteristic calm fell over the nation, followed by praise from nearly every sector for the president's courage and common sense. Argentines, it seemed, were relieved that something had been done to stop the economic insanity into which they had plunged. In a few days trading on the stock market picked up, the dollar stabilized, and, most impressive, prices rose only 3 percent in August and 2 percent in September (compared to 30 percent in June). And, as inflation came down, Alfonsín's popularity ascended to levels it had not seen since his election eighteen months before.[13]

Taken at face value, the Austral Plan was an extremely bold attack on inflation. Could it work? There was at least one successful historical precedent: the stabilization program applied by Hjalmar Schacht in 1923–24 during Germany's runaway inflation. As president of the Reichsbank, Schacht, like Sourrouille, introduced a new currency—the rentenmark—when inflation had caused the old mark to be worthless (its exchange rate at the time Schacht took office was 4.2 trillion to the dollar) and when Germany was saddled by foreign debts it could no longer pay. Like Sourrouille too, he promised to limit the quantity of rentenmarks that the Reichsbank would print. Despite intense pressure from government officials and industrialists, state ministries and private banks were strictly rationed as to the amount they could have each month. Schacht, who had a veto power over government spending requests, thus forced the cabinet to raise taxes, cut subsidies to business, dismiss thousands of public employees, and balance the budget. As for the private sector, he gave export agriculture most of the limited credit available, with the remainder going to export industries. Other sectors were simply cut off, and many enterprises collapsed as a result. Nevertheless, for Schacht, public confidence in the currency was more important than saving weak, inefficient companies. In a few years Germany rode out this recession, raised its exports, and began paying off its foreign debt. Inflation was beaten, production resumed, and there were more jobs. Such was the sort of performance that Alfonsín and Sourrouille seemed ready to repeat.[14]

Unfortunately, the Austral Plan was nothing more than an attempt by Alfonsín and the Radicals to buy time with the foreign banks and the Argentine public. After a year and a half of resistance to paying its debts and unsuccessful attempts to form a debtors' cartel with other Latin American countries, Argentina was forced by a lack of foreign exchange to sign a letter of understanding with the International Monetary Fund as the prerequisite for more loans. The IMF insisted on drastic antiinflation measures, however: hence the Austral Plan. To the foreign creditors it would seem as though Alfonsín was finally embracing orthodox economics regardless of political costs. Such bravery could justifiably claim the right to be rewarded with fresh money as well as liberal terms for the renegotiation of old loans. To the Argentine public Alfonsín seemed a statesman, willing to court unpopularity in order to take the initiative for a breathtaking departure from the status quo. His initiative earned him another victory in the November congressional elections. Although the Radicals' congressional vote dropped from 48 percent in 1983 to 43.2 percent, they gained one seat while their Peronist opponents lost eight and fell from 39 percent of the vote to a historic low of 24.2 percent.

It was only after the elections that the public gradually realized that, in fact, the government was not really applying the Austral Plan. New taxes had raised revenues by 105 percent, but public spending had been cut by only 3.8 percent, mainly by delaying payments to suppliers. Lower-level public servants, such as teachers and policemen, had their paychecks held up, although political appointees were paid. There were plenty of the latter, too, for the number of public employees was on the rise, as table 19.1 shows.

Table 19.1 Government Employees, 1976, 1983, and 1986
(in thousands)

| Sector | 1976 | 1983 | 1986 |
|---|---|---|---|
| National administration | 684 | 611 | 647 |
| Public banks | 46 | 36 | 36 |
| State enterprises | 431 | 290 | 313 |
| City of Buenos Aires | 79 | 70 | 84 |
| Provinces | 568 | 681 | 757 |
| Total | 1,808 | 1,688 | 1,837 |

Source: "El Cronista Comercial," 2 December 1986; quoted in RRP, 10 December 1986, p. 533.

Obviously, much of the good work achieved during the Process toward reducing the public payroll was being undone. Although the military might have cut more, it nevertheless made the state smaller. But under Alfonsín the public sector was growing again, although the increases at the provincial level were largely the result of local Peronist governments.

Without large reductions in government spending, the wage and price controls imposed by the Austral Plan could not be maintained. Even before the elections, the government had allowed exceptions to its 5 percent wage guidelines, but by April 1986 it had to admit its complete inability to enforce either wage or price controls. Why, indeed, should labor or capital exercise restraint when the government was unwilling to set them an example? The RRP dismissed the Austral Plan with bitter irony:

The Austral Plan is finished. No follow-up in the form of privatization of state-run industries, utilities and services ever came, and no effort was made to reduce state expenditure. Some effort was made to balance income and expenditure—at the expense of the private sector through dubious devices such as forced savings. They worked for a few months, and trusting people said that confidence was being restored. Not now. An opportunity has been lost, and only Heaven knows how the next one can be created. . . . Privatization simply never figured in any meaningful manner, and no one ever really meant to cut down the size of the state. Indeed, state employment has expanded, and with it, far from gratitude, more people demanding higher wages. Exports are being discouraged by every possible means, but the Treasury cannot manage without its easy source of income, retentions on farm exports—although it is unable to compel YPF, a bankrupt bureaucracy, to pay over fuel tax collected from motorists. The list could be continued, but there is not much point. The message is: Austral R.I.P.[15]

The monthly rate of inflation indicated the gradual unraveling of the Austral Plan. In May of 1985 it had been 25.2 percent, having begun the year at 16.1 percent. After the plan was announced in mid-June, inflation quickly plunged to 1.8 percent in July. There was another rise just before the November elections, reaching a peak of 4.4 percent in October, but that was followed by a postelection drop to 2.5 percent. With the new year, however, there was another surge in prices that brought January's rate to 6.6 percent. Government pressures gradually worked that down to 4.7 percent in March, but when Sourrouille confessed in April that wage and price freezes were no longer working, the monthly inflation rate was back up to 7.1 percent. In August it hit 16.3 percent, which was a pre-Austral level. For the next twelve months the government strove mightily to convince business and labor to restrain their behavior, while showing little inclination to restrain its own. Monthly inflation rates zigzagged up and down the chart, now between 8 and 9 percent, now between 3 and 4 percent. In February 1987 the annualized rate once again reached three digits—at 102.4 percent.

By midyear the government was losing its will to carry on the hopeless fight. Only three months before the September congressional elections the monthly rate was 7.9 percent for June, 9.1 percent for July, and 12.3 percent for August. On 6 September 1987 the voters handed the Alfonsín administration a stinging defeat. The Radical vote dropped from 43.2 percent to 37.3 percent, while that of the Peronists went up from 24.2 percent to 41.4 percent. The Radicals gave up twelve seats in the Chamber of Deputies, thus losing their majority, while the Justicialist party gained five. In the most publicized election of all, the governorship of Buenos Aires Province, Antonio Cafiero, the Peronist candidate, soundly whipped the Radicals' Juan Manuel Casella with 46.4 percent of the vote to 39.5 percent. In 1983 the Radicals had won the governorship with 52 percent. In all, the elections showed the public's repudiation of four years of Alfonsín's do-nothing administration.

Dynamic Stagnation

In their postelection gloom, the Radicals seemed resigned to drifting aimlessly until the 1989 general elections, when they will probably be replaced in power by the Peronists. To be sure, there were bold words about tough new schemes and a cabinet shakeup to emphasize the claim that Alfonsín was about to make a fresh start. In terms of real action, however, little was forthcoming other than renewed efforts at *concentración*. The Peronists, who now saw themselves on the rise again, made polite responses to the government's overtures. But they were not going to cooperate to the extent of helping Alfonsín out of his jam.

So far as the economy was concerned, no turnaround was possible unless drastic surgery was performed on the state. The old debate over the proper role of the state in the economy was being narrowed by harsh reality to a single option: either cut government spending at all levels or see the private sector of the economy, starved for capital and burdened by taxes, grind slowly to a halt—that is, that portion of the private sector that operates legally. A few figures may suffice to describe the situation as of 1987. A recent study by FIEL, a private research outfit, concluded that government spending constituted nearly 60 percent of the GNP from 1983 to 1987. Of that, about 40 percent went to financing state enterprises, about a fourth was given to the social security system, 17 percent was spent on the national administration, and an equal amount went to the provinces and the Buenos Aires city government. The remainder was scattered among the municipalities in the interior.[16]

All of these categories demand increasing expenditures. We have seen already how the Alfonsín administration added personnel to every level of government. The social security system's demands on the budget have grown most rapidly because of Argentina's aging population, and because of the generosity of past governments in granting early pension rights to public employees.[17] As for the state enterprises, there were 305 in 1987, of which 117 were owned by the national government and 188 by the provinces or municipalities. In recent years their losses have amounted to $2.5–3 billion, and their debts constitute the lion's share of the $52 billion currently owed to foreign bankers.

Financing all of these obligations has called for the utmost creativity on the part of government leaders. Tax increases are the most responsible method for financing, but evasion is so widespread in Argentina that the treasury loses about $20 billion a year, a figure that is on the rise since an increasing number of people are working on their own and not declaring their income. Estimates indicate that about 40 percent of the labor force have second jobs which are not officially registered so as to avoid social security taxes. Furthermore, about $2 billion a year leaves the country illegally, through over- or underinvoicing of exports and imports, and perhaps another $5 billion (in cash dollars) is hidden away in safety deposit boxes or in mattresses. In sum, the official GNP is only a rough approximation of total economic activity in Argentina, which may be as much as 60 percent higher than the published statistics.[18] But because the hidden economy escapes taxation, the government must rely on taxes that are relatively easy to collect, such as export and import tariffs and sales taxes. This explains why it insists on keeping retentions on agricultural exports even though it realizes that Argentina must export in order to pay its bills. Such taxes have their limits, however, and do not begin to cover the government's needs. Therefore, other means of financing its operations have to be used.

Borrowing money is, in the short term, a seemingly painless way to meet expenses. The military governments of the Process resorted heavily to foreign borrowing, raising the debt from $18.8 billion in 1978 to $46 billion by 1983. During the next four years the foreign debt rose by another $6 billion as unpaid interest accumulated. Until he launched the Austral Plan, Alfonsín was unable to get any more money from abroad, and even since then the new loans go chiefly toward paying back the old ones, rather than representing fresh money for investment. Indeed, the rate of investment went down every year since 1981 and was responsible for Argentina's negative growth rate. When coupled with the annual outflow of dollars in the underground economy, it is obvious that the country is being bled of capital.

Unable to get foreign loans or to attract investment, the Alfonsín government increased the internal debt through forced savings schemes, the deliberate nonpayment of debts and wages, and the issuance of bonds. Periodically, bonds—known variously as BONEX, BAGON, BARRA, TACAM, TIDOL, etc.—were placed on the market at rates of return higher than those expected from stock dividends or savings deposits. A certain percentage of each issue was also reserved for purchase by the private banks, which were required to buy them. Until 1987 those bonds elicited a favorable public response, but this strategy may soon run its course. Just before resigning as secretary of industry and commerce, Roberto Lavagna criticized what he called the "festival of bonds," because, he said, it was competing with the private sector for scarce investment capital and thus keeping the economy stagnant. He also warned that the level of internal debt would finally reach such a high level that people would begin to doubt whether the government would be able to pay them back. At that point, the system would collapse.[19]

Finally, the government could print money to finance its operations, which it did at the rate of about 1,700 percent a year until the adoption of the Austral Plan. Thereafter, the money supply merely doubled between mid-1985 and mid-1986. After all, if the railroads lose $430 million a year; if YPF loses another $108 million; ELMA $83 million; ENTEL $68 million; Gas del Estado $47 million; Agua y Energia $35 million; ENCOTEL $10 million; and Aerolineas Argentinas $5.5 million; those deficits have to be covered. The alternative is to not provide more cash from the treasury to keep them going. That would mean shutting down the railroads, oil wells, ships, telephones, gas pipelines, water works, telegraph system, and airlines. It is hardly surprising that politicians back down when faced with such a choice.

Privatization could, theoretically, offer an alternative. However, there would hardly be a local private company able to afford YPF or ENTEL, but that obstacle might be overcome by following the earlier example of Japan: the state could simply turn over its enterprises to private owners. It might also add a proviso to the contract that a majority of the stock would have to remain under national ownership. That would allow foreign capital to be incorporated, either through minority shareholding or through subcontracting. The debts of those enterprises would constitute still another stumbling block, but that problem might be overcome by a combination of methods that would include the state's assumption of some debts while others were refinanced in return for making shares and franchises available to foreign investors. The money saved annually by the state through divesting itself of its so-called patrimony would probably be sufficient to reduce the debt to manageable levels within a fairly short time. The thirteen largest state enterprises, which in early 1987 were placed under a newly created holding company called the Directorate of Public Enterprises (DEP), account for about two-thirds of the almost $3 billion lost every year and in 1983 had over $14 billion in outstanding debts to foreign creditors.

Do these enterprises perform essential public functions in a responsible manner? Yacimientos Carboníferos Fiscales (YCF), which produces low-grade coal that no one really needs, owed $247 million in 1983 and has never been able to balance its books, according to a

DEP report issued in May 1987. The same report also noted that the state railroads owed $964 million in 1983 and cost the state $1.2 million a day in losses. More than half of the railway network was deemed to be in bad or unusable condition. Trucking has made most lines uneconomical; only the losses on the suburban commuter lines might be defended as being preferable to clogging Buenos Aires's downtown with more cars and buses. The merchant fleet, which lost $83 million in 1986, is unnecessary. It is kept only as a matter of national pride, to avoid the carrying of Argentine goods in foreign ships. Its reported assets are twice what they would be if the ships were carried on the company books at their true value. Their value is not accurately recorded because whoever bought them paid, for whatever reason, a far higher price than they were worth. ELMA ships are old-fashioned and poorly designed, carrying only about 10 percent as many containers as ships in other fleets, and because of the powerful seamen's union their crews are much larger than needed. What is said about ELMA could be applied to Aerolineas Argentinas as well: it is not really needed because there are other air carriers. Its main function is to provide patronage and a place for retired air force officers to supplement their pensions. In doing so, it lost over $5 million in 1986, and in 1987 it requested another $43 million from the Central Bank to pay the interest on its debts totaling more than $1 billion.[20]

Those companies could be given away or even shut down, with no hardship to the general public. The only losers would be the approximately 117,000 people employed by them as of 1987.[21] But what about the other companies under DEP? Since 1967 ENTEL has failed to get its accounts approved by the Accounting Office for Public Enterprises (Sindicatura General de Empresas Públicas). Meanwhile, more than 60 percent of the telephone network is either obsolete or out of order, and it often takes ten years or more to have a telephone installed. Oil production at YPF has fallen steadily since 1981, even though demand is rising; therefore, Argentina was forced to import oil in 1987 at a cost estimated in August of more than $400 million. On its own wells YPF lost around $647 million in 1985–86, although it made a profit of $240 million from oil delivered to its refineries by the private companies, who produce about 30 percent of Argentina's total petroleum output. Thus, YPF registers an annual loss of about $400 million and also is in debt to its employees by an estimated 300 to 500 million australes (approximately $200 million at the free market rate), which it cannot pay. Such is the patrimony which Congress, in 1987, specifically exempted from any privatization schemes because it was considered basic to the economy. What is truly miraculous is that a supposedly bankrupt economy like Argentina's can go on taking such a blood-letting.

Argentine nationalists argue that the state enterprises can be made more efficient. Forty-five years of experience would seem to cast serious doubt on such a contention. But, if it were possible to rationalize the public sector it could be accomplished only with the same methods Hjalmar Schacht used. The president of the Central Bank would have to be isolated from political pressures and possess almost dictatorial powers to turn down all requests for financing beyond the levels established in the budget. Sooner or later the moment of truth would come when one of the major enterprises would announce that unless it got a supplementary allocation it would have to stop operating. At that juncture the president of the republic would have to order the dismissal of the company's management and a sizable part of its middle- and lower-ranking personnel. The prospects are not likely that any Radical, Peronist, or army general will undertake that.

What is economically sensible, or necessary, is certain to be resisted. Modern politics is about buying support, rewarding followers, and enjoying popularity. Argentina is but an extreme example of the sickness that permeates all modern states whose authority is derived, more or less, from popular sovereignty. "The shadow on the wall for all of us, I fear, is not the totalitarian revolution of a Lenin or a Mao," Paul Samuelson once wrote. "It is not a relapse into the *laissez-faire* of Queen Victoria or President Coolidge. Argentina, I dare to suggest, is the pattern which no modern man may face without crossing himself and saying, 'There but for the Grace of God. . . . '"[22] Samuelson also pinpointed the underlying cause for the disease:

I suspect the answer has to be found in populist democracy. If in the time of England's industrial revolution men had had the political power to try to rectify within a generation the unconscionable inequities of life, in which a privileged few live well off the sweat of the multitude, it is doubtful that the industrial revolution could ever have continued. . . . The outcome would have been legislated increases in money wages of as much as 40 percent per year . . . pretty much like that we have seen in those Latin American countries which have reached the brink of economic development while being, so to speak, fully or overly developed in the political sphere.[23]

Economics and politics thus have their own brand of rationality. What is rational in economic terms—increased efficiency in production—may be politically suicidal. If 83 percent of Argentina's population lives in urban areas, and if 87 percent is employed in nonagricultural activities, many of which could not survive without government protection and subsidies, what politician is going to rationalize the economy? Although the nation might be much better off in the long run, in the short run such a policy might well produce an economic Hiroshima.

Of course, it also is true that what is rational in political terms—getting elected, consolidating one's power—may wreck the economy. But in this case it is often possible, with emergency measures, to postpone for a while the bad effects of an irrational economic policy. It is also possible, in the short run, to distract attention from a deteriorating situation. General Galtieri did so by starting a war with Great Britain. Alfonsín has done so by putting on trial the military officers who agreed to that war, as well as all those who—as leaders of government or commanders of key units—were accused of human rights violations during the antiterrorist campaign. The Radicals also have proposed schemes to move the nation's capital from Buenos Aires to Patagonia and to change the constitution so as to create a prime minister. By departing from established traditions, such notions attract public attention, give rise to debate, and convey the impression that the government is bold and innovative. They do not, however, confront the real, immediate, and fundamental problems of the society. They are part of the tactics of dynamic stagnation, a situation best conveyed by imagining a car sunk deep in mud, its motor racing, its wheels squealing and spraying dirt in every direction. There is much noise and action, but every minute the car sinks a little deeper.

Sooner or later the public catches on to dynamic stagnation and the political leaders using it quickly fall in popularity. Their opponents take over. If they too shy away from real reforms, as is likely, they are apt to adopt the same tactics in order to cover up the fact that they have no policy to correct the country's problems. Once again the public is disillusioned, and the political cycle turns a few more degrees. And so the Radicals, having missed their opportunity, await their overthrow by the Peronists, who are not expected to depart from the old politics of statism and patronage either. And if they fail it is likely that the military will return to power. And so on. And so forth—through more and more cycles of dynamic stagnation, as Argentina sinks further and further.

## CHAPTER TWENTY

# The Permanent Stalemate

## Sources of the Stalemate

**A**rgentina is but an extreme example of the huge corporate state that has emerged gradually almost everywhere in the world, but particularly in the industrial and semiindustrial West. Two major wars and the Great Depression have led to the growth of a vast, active, interventionist bureaucracy that is buttressed by various *clientela* who accept its existence in return for the security and favors it offers. Whether operating behind the facade of a parliamentary system or more openly through the rule of a military-technocratic alliance, the interaction of high civil servants and organized interests increasingly generates official policy. Such a corporativist system has an innate tendency to grow, in Parkinsonian fashion, as it seeks to create an ever more perfect steady state through the control of all conceivable variables that might disrupt society's equilibrium. Its growth, however, must be nurtured by larger and larger inputs of revenue and credit. In the process, it consumes an increasing amount of capital that might otherwise go toward productive investment in the private sector while simultaneously burdening private citizens with higher taxes. Therein lies the real contradiction of this pluralistic, bureaucratic system: by its voracious consumption, its profligate spending, and its complicated red tape it ruins the nation's currency and credit. The result is stagflation—stagnant production coupled with high inflation. Yet, to reform the system is extremely difficult, and perhaps impossible. No group is willing to give up its niche in the corporate state, especially when a deteriorating economy makes life more precarious. Moreover, to the extent that reform requires political action, the bureaucrats are in a position to prevent its implementation. The great political challenge of Western capitalism in the last decades of the twentieth century is to trim down the state and revitalize the private sector; but for the present our concern is to summarize this phenomenon as it pertains to Argentina.

How did the Argentine state get out of hand? Argentine politicians, whether Conservative or Radical, customarily used government jobs to reward their followers; but in the pre-Perón era, when liberal ideas prevailed, the state's role in the economy was limited. It padded its payroll, spent beyond its means, and ran up debts—and occasionally brought on a financial crisis, such as those that occurred in 1874 and 1890. But those crises were quickly overcome because the private sector of the economy was still attractive to investors and therefore basically sound.

The pre-Peronist economic era can be divided into two phases. Until World War I, growth was stimulated by foreign capital, which concentrated on transportation, utilities, and meatpacking for export. Foreign demand also brought about the commercialization of agriculture, in which both local landed elites and immigrants took part. Domestic industry had only a peripheral role. Small in scale and oriented entirely to local demand, it had almost no access to credit and was largely ignored by officialdom. During the second phase, from World War I to 1945, the roles of foreign and domestic capital were reversed. Most foreign investment and loans had come from Britain, and with the latter's decline Argentina was forced to look more to its own resources. The world economic slump during the 1930s deprived the country of export receipts with which to pay for imported finished goods; therefore domestic industry, enjoying the natural protection brought about by the disruption of foreign trade and responding to continued demand for certain products, expanded. By the eve of World War II, Argentine officialdom had come to view domestic industry in a different light. To save on foreign exchange, it began to protect local industry through the manipulation of exchange rates and other trade barriers.

Although state economic regulation had its origins in the official policies of the 1930s, the Peronist watershed that began in 1943 and lasted until 1955 extended controls so much further—and for such different purposes—that it can be said to have implemented an entirely different strategy. Previous regulation by the Concordancia was to stabilize an essentially free-enterprise economy. Peronist regulation, by contrast, aimed at creating a corporativist system whose ideal, the nation in arms, was essentially a powerful barracks state.

In rejecting liberalism, Perón might have adopted what we earlier called a Bismarckian approach to building Argentina's industrial and military power. That would have involved him in an alliance with military, industrial, and agrarian leaders to create an elitist system by which capital accumulation would have occurred at the expense of the working class. Such an approach would not have been too great a departure from the Concordancia's Pinedo Plan. Currency devaluations would have encouraged the farmers to export, and incentives could have been constructed to draw more domestic savings toward industry. Certain natural industries with export potential would have been designated to receive special protection and credits. The military's role would have been to force the labor movement to accept low wages: not a difficult task at the time, given the low number of organized workers and the influx of tradition-minded rural migrants to the cities. Such a strategy probably would have worked, if the experience of Germany and Japan is any guide.

It was the path not chosen, however, for obvious reasons. To become the powerful, independent political figure he wanted to be, Perón needed a base that would be more beholden to him personally. Although he was an authoritarian like Bismarck, Perón lacked the latter's diplomatic skills which enabled him to knit disparate groups into a single alliance. He resented his social superiors and was unable to tolerate equals; thus, he never would have been able to head a coalition of the economic elites and the armed forces. The workers, however, were still organizationally weak and unincorporated into the mainstream of Argentine political and economic life. He could make them grateful to him.

Therefore, a populist strategy was followed. The burden of accumulation was placed on the landowners, whose profits were appropriated by the state. Industry was encouraged in its exploitation of the domestic market by easy credit and protection from foreign competition. No distinctions were made as to which industries would be especially promoted because the aim was not to export but to supply all conceivable local wants. To the extent that it could displace a previously imported product or provide employment, any given industry qualified for official help. It was not considered important whether a particular enterprise could ever become competitive in the world market, or even hold its own in the domestic market against foreign products. The idea was to achieve autarky: to be self-sufficient. In this way Argentine capitalism was transformed from a late-developing but vigorous phenomenon into what Carlos Waisman has termed hothouse capitalism.[1]

Such a strategy required keeping local demand high through state-dictated wage increases and fringe benefits for labor, the maintenance of full employment, and high levels of government spending. Some attempt was made to direct the industrialization process by nationalizing the Central Bank, buying out the foreign utilities and transport companies, and using state capital to start up or expand industries considered as essential (e.g., oil and steel). Perón's liberal critics have condemned those policies as a waste of Argentina's financial resources, but in fact some of them would have made sense if applied in a Bismarckian context. Nationalizing the Central Bank would have suited a strategy of encouraging certain industries to become national champions in world markets, and using the state to initiate heavy industry would have made sense if such industries had been turned over to private ownership later. Instead, the rapid growth of a state enterprise sector proceeded without regard to efficiency or profitability. State companies became receptacles for patronage jobs, and their prices were kept artificially low in order to subsidize consumption, either directly by the public or by private industries that bought the state's goods and services. So began the *clientela* system. Meanwhile, deficits were covered by printing money; when that led to inflation, the government decreed price controls while mollifying producers with compensatory subsidies in the form of more newly printed currency.

By now we are aware of the shortcomings of the populist strategy. The disincentives to agriculture caused a fall in investment and production, leading in turn to a fall in export receipts, domestic food shortages, and more inflation. A foreign exchange bottleneck resulted, preventing Argentina from importing necessary machinery, fuels, and raw materials to keep its industrial sector going. Rather than achieving autarky, Argentina became more dependent than ever upon imports as its consumer-oriented industries required overseas purchases of capital- and intermediate-goods.

Moreover, import-substitution industrialization had built-in limitations in a country like Argentina, where the total population in 1960 was only 20 million. Such a small market was quickly saturated, leaving domestic industry with no further stimulus to grow. That produced a sharp, and increasingly strident, debate over what policies were appropriate for restoring dynamism to Argentina's industrial economy. For nationalists, the dead end could be vaulted by further increases in consumer buying power and a greater share for labor of the national income. However, that threatened to cause even greater inflation, as well as capital flight. For liberals, the only way out was to dismantle a good part of the state, deregulate the domestic economy, and throw the country open to free trade. That, they promised, would allow potentially competitive industries to grow while ridding the public of inefficient industries whose high prices and shoddy goods would be driven out of the market. Unfortunately, such an approach entailed high political costs, since a considerable portion of the working population was dependent upon the state sector or upon those noncompetitive industries for its income.

The moral effects of a corporative order upon the capitalist system were at least as important as its economic effects. Moral decay was especially fatal to capitalism, which depends for its effectiveness upon the entrepreneurial spirit. The crazy mass of regulations produced by the corporate state encouraged businessmen to evade them by corrupting government officials or retreating into the underground economy. Political influence or criminal skills naturally became more important for survival than hard work and enterprise. The more the state could affect one's chances for success, the more it became necessary to influence the state's decisions—or, failing that, to evade them. Perón's organization of the labor unions into a single umbrella organization provoked the employers to do likewise after his fall from power. Farmers, merchants, and industrialists, who previously had quarreled over how Argentina ought to develop, put aside their differences in order to defend themselves against Peronist labor. Furthermore, as the economy turned stagnant, political friction became harder to assuage. Politics became more of a zero-sum game, with the losers refusing to accept their defeats. For labor, the strike, the factory occupation, and sabotage became weapons to employ when decisions went against them. Employers responded with the lockout and the withdrawal of capital from the country. Argentines had less and less sense of common purpose, despite the clamorous nationalism that often crept into public debates.

Who is to blame for all this? To revert to the scheme set forth in chapter 1, the oligarchy, the military, foreign capital, domestic industry, Perón, and the Argentine national character have all been cited as causes for the nation's failure to progress. This study has shown that, so far as capitalist development is concerned, the *estanciero* oligarchy and domestic industry had, in the pre-Perón era, embarked on a path of development which, had it been followed, would probably have led to a system that would have been fragile and flawed in many respects, but essentially successful: somewhat like that of Italy. Foreign capital also played a positive role in laying down the basic infrastructure. With the proper mix of encouragement and regulation it might have provided the extra impetus that Argentina needed in the postwar period to establish itself as a solid member of the first world. Instead, Argentina opted to become a third world nation. For that, Perón must shoulder much of the blame; it was he who held up capital—both foreign and domestic—to scorn. The corporativist, bureaucratic state that weighs so heavily upon today's society is his creation, as is the prehensile labor union movement that constitutes the bulk of popular support for that state. But it is superficial to blame one man for everything. Perón, after all, was a product of an institution: the military. His admiration for fascism, his belief in the nation in arms, and his xenophobic preference for a closed, autarkic economy were values widely shared by his fellow officers. They sustained him in power for a decade, and after his departure they continued to set limits to the sort of reforms that might have restored Argentina to the path of capitalist development. It was the military that insisted upon creating a vast empire of state enterprises in the name of national security, and it is still the military that prevents any serious attempt to dismantle that empire.

As for the role of national character, it is undeniable that Perón was a political genius who understood the Argentine public. He polarized the community because he understood the common people and gave voice to their prejudices in colorful, pungent speech. For three decades the common people gave their wholehearted loyalty to Perón and got, in the end, the kind of society they deserve.

## The Fractured Community

The ordinary Argentine, whether politician, journalist, or trade unionist, views the country's politics as a Manichaean struggle between "the people" and "the oligarchy." It is an attitude consistent with the traditions of the Mediterranean culture of which Argentina is a branch, and while it oversimplifies, it nevertheless expresses a certain fundamental reality that does not require one to be a Marxist to appreciate it. Argentine society can be divided into two very different worlds. There are, first of all, the privileged few who inhabit Buenos Aires's Barrio Norte and the plush suburbs just beyond. They patronize the chic cafes and boutiques of the Avenida Santa Fé or the Calle Florida, attend glittering performances at the Teatro Colón, and weekend at fine country homes. They have university degrees, domestic servants, and foreign bank accounts. They constitute the oligarchy. The people, by contrast, include the factory workers, the store clerks, the shopkeepers, the rural peons, the schoolteachers, the office help, and the inhabitants of dusty towns on the pampa and the run-down barrios of Buenos Aires and lesser industrial cities.

The oligarchy is cosmopolitan, which is one reason why it is unpopular. The oligarchs are as at home in New York, London, Rome, or Paris as they are in Buenos Aires. Their children study at Ivy League or "Oxbridge" universities. As bankers they are linked to world financial centers, as agriculturalists they produce for export, and as industrialists or merchants they often depend on foreign franchises and distributorships.

Being cosmopolitan, the oligarchs are liberals. They can turn nationalist when packinghouses do not pay enough for cattle or when foreign competitors threaten to undercut their prices, but in general they are receptive to foreign capital because it provides jobs for well-educated, well-connected, and multilingual managers and lawyers. As economic liberals, the oligarchs favor reducing the state and allowing more freedom to private enterprise. The private sector, in turn, must be made more competitive by government curbs on the labor unions. Because they admire Western civilization, the oligarchs would like to be politically liberal too, but they are caught in a dilemma. On the one hand, they defend individual liberty, the freedom of the press, and the idea of a pluralistic society; but on the other hand, being an unpopular minority, their spokesmen cannot win enough electoral support to rule democratically. Yet, the oligarchs fear turning over the state to the people, who are certain to use it to redistribute the wealth. Hence the oligarchs' guilty support for military regimes.

The people embrace wage and salary earners as well as small producers. What these people have in common is a fear of the free market, free trade, and free competition—indeed, of all economic modernization, with its efficiency and its labor-saving technology. For them, the state is their hope for saving their jobs or their modest share of the local market. Despite occasional classist rhetoric, the people are not really revolutionary. Because Argentina is rich in resources and has a small population, even its lower classes traditionally have been well fed. Rather, the people are populist, in that they envy and resent the powerful, privileged oligarchs and would like to force them to share the wealth. But they are also radically conservative in the sense that they want the state to shut Argentina off from the world and create an insulated economy within which every person will have a secure place.

Such an outlook requires that all economic activity be regulated minutely so that no disturbing changes can threaten jobs or business investments. Every enterprise, whether efficient or not, has a right to exist in the name of national self-sufficiency and full employment. The ideological justification for this is, of course, nationalism, which in Argentina, "claims to find its roots in the 'Hispanic-Creole' tradition [and] expresses a democratic sentiment that rejects institutional forms and emphasizes, rather, the fraternal sentiments of the people. It puts its accent on the State, out of which a society is formed that remains under its watchful eye. Civil liberty is negated, political liberty restricted, and social pluralism accepted only partially."[2]

This attitude expresses not only the sentiments of the lower and lower middle classes but is quite congenial to elements normally associated with upper strata as well—for example, the armed forces and technocrats. It also appeals to many politicians, who like to see the state expand because expansion provides more opportunities for patronage. In practice, though, nationalism quickly runs into economic problems. In the first place, Argentina is not a self-sufficient country; to import the things that it needs it must export enough to pay for them. At that point, matters such as efficiency, incentives, and competitiveness begin to challenge the planners and regulators. In the second place, neither the people, the armed forces, nor the government's many officials can force the oligarchy or foreign capital to invest in Argentina—and it is those people who have the necessary money. Popular sovereignty's limits are set by those who have capital and who can decide where, how, and whether to invest, because they hold the key to satisfying economic wants.

Between the oligarchy and the people are the party politicians and the military, who try to act as brokers in this political standoff. Whether Radicals or Peronists, party politicians are more pragmatic than their populist rhetoric would suggest. They are attentive to issues that might win or lose votes, but they are also aware that their popularity depends on the economy's performance. Once the elections are over, they are often to be found negotiating out of sight with the oligarchy and foreign capitalists to coax more investment back to Argentina. Their opponents delight in exposing this hypocrisy, only to practice it themselves when they get into power. The result is that the public becomes disillusioned with all politicians. When that happens, the military usually steps in. Unlike its popular image, the military is not really an appendage of the oligarchy. It has its own corporate interests that often parallel those of the oligarchy when populism threatens to destroy social discipline; but in economic matters the military often leans in the direction of statism, as the example of Fabricaciones Militares shows. Moreover, a significant part of the Argentine military believes in the sort of extreme nationalism that holds capitalism and cosmopolitanism in suspicion.

The lack of any trust or sense of common purpose between the oligarchy and the people defeats both the politicians and the generals. The oligarchs have their money safely overseas because they have little faith in the country's future. For them, the politicians are prehensile demagogues, the military are inept and untrustworthy, and the people have been permanently corrupted by Peronism into preferring plunder to hard work. On the other hand, the people remain unmoved when liberal economic planners call for sacrifice and more productivity because they are convinced that the oligarchs will only pocket the profits and not reinvest them. Thus, the perpetual standoff: the people cannot raise their living standards and the oligarchy cannot enjoy its wealth securely. The state cannot break this stalemate, regardless of what sort of regime is in power. It may threaten, and even try to punish. The victims bend for the moment, knowing that the storm will pass and that economic realities will soon bring the authorities to heel—either by a shortage of capital or by a subtle disruption of the institutional processes. Each apparent breakthrough proves temporary; the standoff is reasserted. Attempts to escape this impasse by resorting to foreign capital, as in Frondizi's neoliberal program, come to grief because sooner or later nationalist xenophobia drives away such investment.

## The Political Cycle

We are now in a position to understand that Argentina's apparent anarchy actually follows a pattern. The political and economic systems are like two connected wheels that rotate together with a certain degree of predictability. In describing the cycle it does not really matter where we begin, since we ultimately will arrive back at the same point. However, let us use the foreign exchange bottleneck as our starting point. This bottleneck develops because of the combination of stagnant or falling export receipts and a rising bill for imports; the result is a serious, and chronic, balance of payments deficit. Such a deficit may be financed in the short run by foreign loans, but eventually bankers will insist upon reform measures as a prerequisite for further credit. At that point the sovereign Argentine government must either slash its imports or agree to the reforms. If it slashes imports it deprives local producers of needed machinery, fuels, parts, tools, raw materials, etc., whose lack cannot be made up domestically. Obviously, such a strategy cannot be pursued in-definitely without causing production cutbacks with severe atten-dant consequences for employment. Thus, some attempt must be made at reform.

The sort of reforms that foreign bankers insist upon are aimed at encouraging more exports, which entails devaluing Argentina's cur-rency to make its goods cheaper and attacking inflation so as to lower production costs. In the orthodox view, inflation is caused by excessive demand—which in turn is caused by too much money in circulation. To reduce inflation, the government must cut its spend-ing programs, tighten up on credit, and keep wages in line with productivity.

This sort of austerity program is widely unpopular. Currency de-valuation is a boon to the agricultural sector, which can therefore sell more of its goods; and if Argentina had export industries they would profit too, of course. But Argentina's industry is just "hot-house capitalism," so devaluation only raises the cost of everything that is imported. Add to that labor's disgruntlement over wage con-trols, and you have the basis for an urban, populist reaction. If the government is based on democratic elections, there will be a back-lash at the polls; and even a military government will be faced with strikes, slowdowns, protests, and sabotage, in both the private and public sectors. Since less than 20 percent of the working population is in agriculture and more than 80 percent is connected to the urban sector, such protests are difficult to ignore.

Sooner or later, austerity is abandoned for a return to populist, corporativist policies. The agrarian exporter oligarchy gets thrust back, nationalism takes over, and foreign interference is repudiated. The recession in the urban sector, brought on by the belt-tightening, gives way to a new feeling of prosperity. Idle capacity is put back to work; unemployed workers are rehired; loans are once again avail-able at the bank; and the government begins issuing contracts for internal improvements. The political leaders of the moment bask in popularity.

Within perhaps a year and a half or two years, however, the economy shows signs of overheating. Government printing presses have been so busy that the economy is awash in pesos, resulting in their rapid depreciation. Full employment has made the unions aggressive, and wage settlements far outstrip what employers consider prudent. In fact, with the cost of living shooting upward again, each settlement tends to dwarf previous ones, provoking demands for a revision of their contracts from unions that negotiated earlier. When hard-pressed employers refuse, there are strikes. The faster inflation rises, the more resistant employers get. Meanwhile, agricultural exports are stagnant again, leading to worse and worse balance of payments deficits. The government treasury is depleted of foreign exchange, and foreign lenders are once again making tough demands.

At some point in this scenario the military will step in to restore order. Its first task is always to demobilize the populist organizations, in order to once again force the bitter medicine of austerity down the country's throat. Trade unions are subjected to intervention and political parties disbanded. The press is censored, naturally. For perhaps two or three years, the tough approach works. Exports rise; loans are renewed; industry reequips itself. But eventually the urban middle-class and business sectors become disenchanted with the military for its repressiveness, its puritanism, and its censorship—and also because the continuance of austerity deprives "hothouse capitalism" of the only market it can exploit. There is a certain hypocrisy about the military's austerity program too, because the budgets of the armed forces are exempt from cuts, as are the budgets of those state enterprises managed by military officers, such as the entire Fabricaciones Militares complex. As Gary Wynia notes with perfect accuracy:

> The military's economic power creates all sorts of problems for anyone who wants to set policy in Argentina, as every president has discovered. Officers who make their careers running government corporations as well as their service enterprises are among the first to block intrusions into their domains, no matter how necessary administrative reform and fiscal austerity may be. In the end little gets changed and everyone blames someone else for the failure, the military complaining of the power of public employee unions in nonmilitary enterprises,

economists pointing to sabotage by subsidized industries in the private sector, and military presidents blaming the indiscipline of the entire society. But the fact remains that no obstacle is larger than that of the military's protection of its own territory.[3]

Eventually the military begins to quarrel within its own ranks and finally returns to the barracks. Civilian rule is restored, to public applause, and the political cycle is ready for another turn.

# NOTES

## Chapter 1

1. Good examples of this school of thought are Rodolfo Puiggros, *Pueblo y oligarquía* (Buenos Aires: Jorge Álvarez, 1965); Miguel Murmis and Juan Carlos Portaniero, *Crecimiento industrial y alianza de clases en la Argentina, 1930–1940* (Buenos Aires: Instituto Torcuato Di Tella, 1968); and Raúl Scalabrini Ortiz, *Política britanica en el Río de la Plata* (Buenos Aires: Fernandez Blanco, 1957).

2. See Carlos A. Florit, *Las fuerzas armadas y la guerra psicologica* (Buenos Aires: Ediciones Arayú, 1963). For a foreign viewpoint along similar lines, see Alain Rouique, *Poder militar y sociedad política en la Argentina,* 2 vols. (Buenos Aires: Emece, 1978).

3. The literature on dependency theory is truly voluminous, but certain writers on the subject may be considered as "central" (as opposed to "peripheral"). Perhaps the most central of all is Immanuel Wallerstein, whose *The Capitalist World Economy* (Cambridge: Cambridge University Press, 1979), or his shorter *The Politics of the World Economy* (Cambridge: Cambridge University Press, 1984), give a stimulating treatment of the theory. Also worthwhile, especially for their application to Latin America, are André Gunder Frank's *Capitalism and Underdevelopment in Latin America* (New York: Monthly Review Press, 1967); Helio Jaguaribe's *Political Development: A General Theory and a Latin American Case Study* (New York: Harper & Row, 1973); and Fernando Henrique Cardoso and Enzo Faletto, *Dependency and Development in Latin America* (Berkeley: University of California Press, 1979). Dependency theory is really a modern restatement of V. I. Lenin's *Imperialism, the Highest Stage of Capitalism* and was produced by the marriage of Leninism to Raúl Prebisch's concepts of "center" and "periphery" in modern trade and financial relationships. And of course it takes Prebisch's notions to a far more radical extreme than he intended. See United Nations, Economic Commission for Latin America, *Development Problems in Latin America* (Austin: University of Texas, Institute of Latin American Studies, 1970).

4. See Rogelio García Lupo, *Mercenarios y monopolios en la Argentina* (Buenos Aires: Editorial Legasa, 1972) or his *Contra la ocupación extranjera* (Buenos Aires: Editorial Centro, 1971). A more scholarly and less overtly ideological example is Jorge Fodor's "Perón's Policies for Agricul-

tural Exports, 1946–1948: Dogmatism or Commonsense?" in *Argentina in the Twentieth Century*, ed. David Rock (Pittsburgh: University of Pittsburgh Press, 1975).

5. See Dardo Cuneo, *Comportamiento y crisis de la clase empresaria* (Buenos Aires: Editorial Pleamar, 1967); Carlos Ramil Cepeda, *Crisis de una burguesía dependiente* (Buenos Aires: Ediciones La Rosa Blindada, 1972); and Mónica Peralta Ramos, *Acumulación de capital y crisis política en la Argentina (1930–1974)* (Mexico: Siglo Veintiuno Editores, 1978).

6. Federico Pinedo, *Trabajoso resurgimiento argentino* (Buenos Aires: Editorial Fundación del Banco de Galícia y Buenos Aires, 1968); and Álvaro Alsogaray, *Bases para la acción política futura* (Buenos Aires: Editorial Atlantida, 1968). For a similar foreign viewpoint, see Carlos F. Díaz-Alejandro, *Essays on the Economic History of Argentina* (New Haven: Yale University Press, 1970).

7. David Rock, "The Survival and Restoration of Peronism," in *Argentina in the Twentieth Century*, ed. Rock, pp. 194, 218.

8. James Scobie, *Argentina: A City and a Nation*, 2d ed. (New York: Oxford University Press, 1971), pp. 219, 221, 247–50, 253.

9. Robert Crassweller, *Perón and the Enigmas of Argentina* (New York: W. W. Norton, 1987).

10. Juan Corradi, *The Fitful Republic* (Boulder: Westview Press, 1985), pp. 111, 114.

## Chapter 2

1. *The World Almanac*, 1913, p. 266.

2. James Bryce, *South America: Observations and Impressions*, 3d ed. (New York: Macmillan, 1916), pp. 317–18, 346.

3. Ibid., pp. 331–32, 341.

4. Ibid., p. 320.

5. Ibid., p. 341.

6. 1869, 1895, and 1914 censuses. Oscar Cornblit, *Inmigrantes y empresarios en la política argentina* (Buenos Aires: Instituto Torcuato Di Tella, 1967), pp. 15–17.

7. José Luís De Imaz, *La clase alta de Buenos Aires* (Buenos Aires: Editorial Universitaria de Buenos Aires, 1962), p. 13. See also any *Nómina de socios* of the Jockey Club.

8. James Scobie, *Argentina: A City and a Nation*, 2d ed. (New York: Oxford University Press, 1971), pp. 83–87, 119–20. Also, Dirección General de Estadística, *Anuario, 1913*, pp. xxiv–xxix; Horacio Gilberti, "El desarrollo agropecuario," *Desarrollo Económico*, April–June 1962, pp. 74–75, 81–82, 84; Ernesto Tornquist & Company, *The Economic Development of the Argentine Republic in the Last Fifty Years* (Buenos Aires: Ernesto Tornquist, 1919), pp. 26, 30–31; Miguel Teubal, "Policy and Performance of Agriculture in Economic Development: The Case of Argentina" (Ph.D. diss., University of California, 1975), pp. 15–16.

9. *Tercer censo nacional,* vol. 5 (Buenos Aires: Comisión Nacional del Censo, 1916.)

10. Carl C. Taylor, *Rural Life in Argentina* (Baton Rouge: Louisiana State University Press, 1948), pp. 396–400; Peter H. Smith, *Politics and Beef in Argentina* (New York: Columbia University Press, 1969), pp. 48–50. According to Smith, between 1910 and 1943 five out of eight presidents of the republic were members of the SRA, as were four out of five vice-presidents, four finance ministers, and almost all the ministers of agriculture and foreign affairs. So were approximately 15 percent of the members of Congress.

11. ECLA, *Economic Development and Income Distribution in Argentina* (New York: United Nations, 1969), p. 34; Taylor, *Rural Life,* pp. 195, 201.

12. ECLA, *Economic Development,* p. 34.

13. Taylor, *Rural Life,* pp. 174–75, 192, 195, 202, 205, 395.

14. Gilberti, "El desarrollo agropecuario," p. 86; Gary W. Wynia, *Argentina in the Postwar Era: Politics and Economic Policymaking in a Divided Society* (Albuquerque: University of New Mexico Press, 1978), pp. 23–24; Taylor, *Rural Life,* pp. 384–87.

15. Taylor, *Rural Life,* p. 48.

16. Winthrop Wright, *The British-Owned Railways in Argentina* (Austin: University of Texas Press, 1974), chaps. 1–5.

17. Ibid., pp. 60, 103–4; Felix J. Weil, *The Argentine Riddle* (New York: John Day, 1944), pp. 115–16, claims that railroad companies commonly hid their profits by setting up dummy equipment and construction firms that charged outrageous prices and were paid in high-interest bonds that had to be amortized before any profits could be distributed. In this way the railway companies defrauded both their stockholders and the Argentine government.

18. Aldo Ferrer, *The Argentine Economy* (Berkeley: University of California Press, 1967), pp. 89, 93, 103–4; Vicente Vásquez Presedo, *El caso argentino: Migración de factores: comércio exterior y desarrollo, 1875–1914* (Buenos Aires: Editorial Universitaria de Buenos Aires, 1971), pp. 25–30, 68–86.

19. Banco de Italia y Río de La Plata, *100 años al servício del país, 1872–1972* (Buenos Aires, 1972), pp. 231–34.

20. William Lowenthal, "The Expansion and Modernization of Argentina: Society, Economy, and Politics, 1880–1916" (Ph.D. diss., Georgetown University, 1967), pp. 201–3; Teubal, *Policy and Performance,* pp. 27, 40.

21. Lowenthal, "Expansion and Modernization," pp. 316–26; Banco de Italia y Río de La Plata, *100 años,* p. 113.

22. Roberto Cortes Conde, "Problemas del crecimiento industrial de la Argentina, 1870–1914," in *Argentina: sociedad de masas,* ed. Torcuato S. Di Tella, Gino Germani, and Jorge Graciarena (Buenos Aires: Editorial Universitaria de Buenos Aires, 1966), p. 67; Ferrer, *Argentine Economy,* p. 96n; Guido Di Tella and Manuel Zymelman, "Etapas del desarrollo económico argentino," in *Argentina: sociedad de masas,* ed. Di Tella, Germani, and Graciarena, pp. 190–91; H. S. Ferns, *The Argentine Republic* (New York: Barnes & Noble, 1973), pp. 45–46; *Gran enciclopedia argentina* (Buenos Aires: Ediar, 1960), 1:365–67.

## Chapter 3

1. Ernesto Tornquist & Company, *The Economic Development of the Argentine Republic in the Last Fifty Years* (Buenos Aires: Ernesto Tornquist, 1919), pp. 26–28, 106.

2. Eusebio García, "Consideraciones sobre el censo de las industrias," in *Tercer censo nacional* (Buenos Aires: Comisión Nacional del Censo, 1916), 7:3.

3. Walt W. Rostow, *The Stages of Economic Growth* (Cambridge: Cambridge University Press, 1961), pp. 21, 39. Rostow uses, as a rule of thumb, an investment rate of 10 percent or more of national income to define a level of activity sufficiently energetic to be called a takeoff. Unfortunately, statistics on Argentina's national income in the nineteenth century are unavailable, but the head of the statistical office, Alejandro Bunge, estimated the national income at 5,419 million pesos in 1913 (see Tornquist, *Economic Development*, p. 258). According to the third national census, total fixed capital in industry was 1,788 million pesos, or about a third of the national income. There had been an average increase of 8.2 percent a year in industrial investment between 1895 and 1914. Since this was a period of sustained growth, it is logical to assume that the pace accelerated over time and that in the years just preceding 1914 the average increase exceeded 10 percent.

4. Guido Di Tella and Manuel Zymelman, *Las etapas del desarrollo económico argentino* (Buenos Aires: Editorial Universitaria de Buenos Aires, 1967), pp. 104, 423–24, 456–60.

5. Javier Villanueva, "El origen de la industrialización argentina," *Desarrollo Económico*, October–December, 1972, p. 458. Villanueva identifies three peaks of capital investment in industry prior to World War II: 1913, 1929, and 1937. But the longest series of high-investment years came in the 1920s.

6. Rostow, *Stages*, p. 36n.

7. These figures are given in Adolfo Dorfman, *Evolución industrial argentina* (Buenos Aires: Editorial Losada, 1942), pp. 11, 67. The largest gains were in the vegetable oil, fuel oil, dairy, cement, and textile industries. See ibid., pp. 26–31, 34–37, 42–49, 55–56. Also, Oscar Cornblit, *Inmigrantes y empresarios en la política argentina* (Buenos Aires: Instituto Torcuato Di Tella, 1967), p. 22; James Scobie, *Argentina: A City and a Nation*, 2d ed. (New York: Oxford University Press, 1971), pp. 180–82; Eugene G. Sharkey, "The Unión Industrial Argentina, 1887–1920: Problems of Industrial Development" (Ph.D. diss., Rutgers University, 1977), pp. 5, 169–70; Tomás Roberto Fillol, *Social Factors in Economic Development: The Argentine Case* (Cambridge: MIT Press, 1961), pp. 43–44; and Arturo Frondizi, *Petroleo y política* (Buenos Aires: Editorial Raigal, 1954), p. 56. Besides heading the National Statistical Office, Alejandro Bunge, an economist and historian, edited and published the *Revista de economía argentina*, considered for many years to be the most reliable source of statistics in the country.

8. Joseph Tulchin, "The Argentine Economy During the First World War," part I, *RRP*, 19 June 1970, pp. 901–3; part II, 30 June 1970, pp. 965–67; and part III, 10 July 1970, pp. 44–46; ECLA, *El desarrollo económico de la Argentina*, part 1 (Santiago de Chile: ECLA, 1958), pp. 135–36; Ezequiel Gallo, *Agrarian Expansion and Industrial Development in Argentina (1880–1930)* (Buenos Aires: Instituto Torcuato Di Tella, 1970), pp. 10–11.

9. *RRP*, 9 September 1942, p. 15. The report is based on Central Bank figures.

10. W. Arthur Lewis, *The Theory of Economic Growth* (London: Allen & Unwin, 1956), pp. 142–62.

11. Alberto Conil Paz and Gustavo Ferrari, *Argentina's Foreign Policy, 1930–1962* (Notre Dame: University of Notre Dame Press, 1960), pp. 1–7, 11–15, 23; Daniel Drosdoff, *El gobierno de las vacas (1933–1956): Tratado Roca-Runciman* (Buenos Aires: Editorial La Bastilla, 1972), pp. 101, 104; Fillol, *Social Factors*, pp. 44, 46; José Alfredo Martínez de Hoz, *La agricultura y la ganadería argentina en el periódo 1930–1960* (Buenos Aires: Editorial Sudamerica, 1967), pp. 15, 25–27; Laura R. Randall, *An Economic History of Argentina in the Twentieth Century* (New York: Columbia University Press, 1978), p. 128; Peter H. Smith, *Politics and Beef in Argentina* (New York: Columbia University Press, 1969), pp. 142–46.

12. On Goscilo and Frigeri, see *Historia de la industria argentina*, ed. Enrique Gustavino (Buenos Aires: Editorial Mercury, 1951), pp. 109–13, 153–56.

13. Thomas C. Cochran and Ruben Reina, *Capitalism in Argentine Culture: A Study of Torcuato Di Tella and SIAM* (Philadelphia: University of Pennsylvania Press, 1971), pp. 39–61, 72–111.

## Chapter 4

1. Carlos Moyano Llerena, *Argentina social y económica* (Buenos Aires: Editorial DePalma, 1950), p. 433; Luís V. Sommi, *Los capitales yanquis en la Argentina* (Buenos Aires: Editorial Claridad, 1945), p. 80.

2. Roger Gravil, "La intervención estatal en el comércio de exportación argentino entre la dos guerras," *Desarrollo Económico*, January–March 1971, pp. 396–97; Simon G. Hanson, *Argentine Meat and the British Market* (Stanford: Stanford University Press, 1938), pp. 229–30; Peter H. Smith, *Politics and Beef in Argentina* (New York: Columbia University Press, 1969), p. 50, notes of the SRA: "Notwithstanding its official claim to stand for all the nation's ranchers, the Society represented limited interests. Controlled by a secret admissions procedure, membership fluctuated between 2,000 and 5,000 from 1900 to 1946, usually hovering around the 2,500 mark. So if estimates taken from the 1937 census are correct, the Society included only about 10 per cent of the ranchers engaged in the livestock trade."

3. Gravil, "La intervención," pp. 418–19; and Roger Gravil, "State Inter-

vention in Argentina's Export Trade between the Wars," *Journal of Latin American Studies* 2 (November 1970): 163–69; Smith, *Politics and Beef*, pp. 197–98, 214–18, 232.

4. Enrique Mosconi, *La batalla de petróleo: YPF y las empresas extranjeras* (Buenos Aires: Ediciones Problemas Nacionales, 1957), pp. 25–29; Carl Solberg, *Oil and Nationalism in Argentina* (Stanford: Stanford University Press, 1979), pp. 90–98, 136–38; James E. Buchanan, "Politics and Petroleum Development in Argentina, 1916–1930" (Ph.D. diss., University of Massachusetts, 1973), pp. 150–52, 157–58; Marcos Kaplan, "La primera fase de la política petrolera argentina, 1907–1916," *Desarrollo Económico*, January–March 1974, pp. 790–91; Arturo Frondizi, *Petróleo y política* (Buenos Aires: Editorial Raigal, 1954), pp. 154–57, 161–62.

5. Gravil, "La intervención," pp. 63–64; David Rock, "Radical Populism and the Conservative Elite, 1912–1930," in *Argentina in the Twentieth Century*, ed. David Rock (Pittsburgh: University of Pittsburgh Press, 1975), p. 83.

6. Abraham Eidlicz, "Combustibles, electricidad, minería," in *Argentina, 1930–1960* (Buenos Aires: Editorial SUR, 1961) p. 218; Eduardo I. Rumbo, *Petróleo y vassalaje* (Buenos Aires: Ediciones Hechos e Ideas, 1957), p. 126; *RRP*, 13 September 1946, pp. 3–4.

7. *RRP*, 20 February 1942, pp. 21–25; and 11 December 1942, pp. 24–25. See also Winthrop Wright, *The British-Owned Railways in Argentina* (Austin: University of Texas Press, 1974), pp. 145, 151–53, 157; and Adolfo Dorfman, *Evolución industrial argentina* (Buenos Aires: Editorial Losada, 1942), p. 204.

8. Ministerio de Hacienda, *El plan de reactivación económica ante el honorable Senado* (Buenos Aires, 1940), pp. 49–54; Wright, *British-Owned Railways*, pp. 224–29.

9. Buchanan, "Politics and Petroleum Development," p. 303.

10. Municipalidad de la Capital, Dirección General de Estadística Municipal, *Censo general de población, edificación, comércio e industria de la ciudad de Buenos Aires, 1904* (Buenos Aires, 1906), pp. 164–87.

11. *Gran enciclopedia argentina* (Buenos Aires: Ediar, 1960), 7:147; *PP*, 28 December 1965, p. 54.

12. *Mercado*, 20 April 1972, pp. 32–33; and 29 September 1977, pp. 63–64.

13. On Bagley, see Casa Bagley, *Bagley: 100 años produciendo calidad* (Buenos Aires: Casa Bagley, 1964). I am very indebted to Donna Guy for providing me with this hard-to-get publication. See also *PP*, 14 July 1964, p. 152; and 8 December 1964, pp. 55–56; *Camoatí*, March 1951, pp. 88–89; *Gran enciclopedia argentina*, 1:344; and Donna Guy, "Commercial Law, the Stock Market, and Foreign Capitalization of Argentine Industry, 1870–1940" (unpublished study), p. 21.

14. On the Bunge family, see *Gran enciclopedia argentina*, 1:644–45; and Vicente O. Cútolo, *Nuevo diccionario biográfico argentino* (Buenos Aires: Editorial Elche, 1978), 1:559–61.

15. On the Tornquists, see *Gran enciclopedia argentina*, 8:145–46; and Cútolo, *Nuevo diccionario*, 7:352–54.

16. On Menéndez and Braun, see *Gran enciclopedia argentina*, 1:246–47; Cútolo, *Nuevo diccionario*, 1:529 and 4:540; Mateo Martinic Berros, *Presencia de Chile en la Patagonia austral, 1843–1879* (Santiago de Chile: Editorial Andrés Bello, 1971), chap. 5, pp. 146–85.

17. David S. C. Chu, "The Great Depression and Industrialization in Latin America: Response to Relative Price Incentives in Argentina and Colombia, 1930–1945" (Ph.D. diss., Yale University, 1972), pp. 143–44, 158–59; Adolfo Dorfman, *Evolución industrial argentina* (Buenos Aires: Editorial Losada, 1942) p. 310.

18. Simon G. Hanson, *Argentine Meat and the British Market* (Stanford: Stanford University Press, 1938), pp. 54, 68–70, 137.

19. Dorfman, *Evolución*, p. 18; *Camoatí*, June 1949, p. 182; and July 1955, p. 184; Naum Minsburg, *Multinacionales en la Argentina* (Buenos Aires: Editorial Quipó, 1976), p. 146; and *PP*, 9 February 1971, p. 20.

20. Enrique Gustavino, ed., *Historia de la industria argentina* (Buenos Aires: Editorial Mercury, 1951), pp. 33–37, 78–86, 101–13, 153–56, 178–86.

21. On Alpargatas, see Donna Guy, "From Wicks to World Markets" (unpublished study), p. 4; and *RRP*, 26 July 1961, pp. 21–22. On Noel, see *Mercado*, 20 April 1977, pp. 32–34; and 29 September 1977, pp. 63–65. On Vitalana, see Gustavino, *Historia de la industria*, pp. 19–32.

22. On Bagley, see Guy, "Commercial Law," p. 20; and *PP*, 8 December 1964, p. 55. On Di Tella, see Thomas C. Cochran and Ruben Reina, *Capitalism in Argentine Culture: A Study of Torcuato Di Tella and SIAM* (Philadelphia: University of Pennsylvania Press, 1971), pp. 40–42, 56–57.

23. Cochran and Reina, *Capitalism in Argentine Culture*, pp. 42, 52.

24. *Mercado*, 20 December 1973, pp. 94–98.

25. Daniel Azpiazu, Eduardo M. Basualdo, and Miguel Khavisse, *El nuevo poder económico en la Argentina de los años 80* (Buenos Aires: Editorial Legasa, 1986), pp. 147–49; *Mercado*, 11 December 1975, pp. 96–100. Garovaglio died in a shipwreck in 1929 and his share of the business went to his widow. Since they had no children, after her death the stock—for the company had been incorporated in the meantime—was divided among many distant relatives, with much of it going to charity. Zorraquín died not long after his partner, and his son took over as president of the firm. It still is managed by the Zorraquín family.

26. Guy, "Commercial Law," pp. 4–5; Felix J. Weil, *The Argentine Riddle*, (New York: John Day, 1944), p. 124; and *PP*, 7 December 1965, pp. 72–74.

27. Strictly speaking, joint-stock companies and corporations are not the same thing. The former, which was an earlier form of organization, did not always include the advantage of limited liability. Common usage today makes no distinction between the two forms, however, and I am going to use the terms synonymously.

28. Dorfman, *Evolución*, p. 96. Between 1928 and 1929 the number of corporations jumped from 283 to 925 while the amount of subscribed capital doubled from 1.3 to 2.6 billion pesos.

29. Dorfman, *Evolución*, pp. 98–100; Ministerio de Justicia e Instrucción Pública, Inspección General de Justicia, *Estadística de sociedades anónimas nacionales, años 1930 y 1931* (Buenos Aires, 1932), no page numbers;

*Cuarto censo nacional* (Buenos Aires: Dirección General del Servício Estadístico Nacional, 1952), 3:52.

30. *Camoatí*, April 1949, pp. 108–9; and June 1956, p. 170. Also, RRP, 2 April 1943, pp. 5–6; and 1 December 1950, pp. 18–19. Alpargatas's statutes guaranteed that any time the dividends from preferred stock fell below 7 percent its holders would have a voice and vote in the company's meetings.

31. *Camoatí*, October 1942, pp. 20–21; and December 1944, p. 38; *Mercado*, 16 December 1976, pp. 166–72.

32. Cochran and Reina, *Capitalism in Argentine Culture*, p. 217.

33. Ernesto Tornquist & Company, *The Economic Development of the Argentine Republic in the Last Fifty Years* (Buenos Aires: Ernesto Tornquist, 1919), pp. 209–24; Deltic Panamerica, *El mercado de capitales en Argentina* (Mexico: Inter-American Development Bank, 1968), pp. 51–52.

34. Guy, "Commercial Law," pp. 7–9.

35. Quoted in *Camoatí*, 5 April 1941, p. 11.

## Chapter 5

1. L. Beccaria and R. Carciofi, "The Recent Experience of Stabilizing and Opening Up the Argentine Economy," *Cambridge Journal of Economics*, June 1982, p. 146; Mark Falcoff, "Economic Dependency in a Conservative Mirror: Alejandro Bunge and the Argentine Frustration, 1919–1943," *Inter-American Economic Affairs*, Spring 1982, p. 58; Felix Weil, *The Argentine Riddle* (New York: John Day, 1944), pp. 175–76.

2. Dardo Cuneo, *Comportamiento y crisis de la clase empresaria* (Buenos Aires: Editorial Pleamar, 1967), pp. 43, 50–63; Eugene G. Sharkey, "Unión industrial argentina, 1887–1920" (Ph.D. diss., Rutgers University, 1977), pp. 38–40; Vicente Vásquez-Presedo, *El caso argentino* (Buenos Aires: Editorial Universitaria de Buenos Aires, 1971), pp. 212, 214.

3. Cuneo, *Comportamiento y crisis*, pp. 63, 75; Sharkey, "Unión industrial," pp. 53–55, 60–66.

4. Donna Guy, "Carlos Pellegrini and the Politics of Early Argentine Industrialization, 1873–1906," *Journal of Latin American Studies*, May 1979, p. 124; Sharkey, "Unión industrial," pp. 56–57.

5. Carlos F. Díaz-Alejandro, *Essays on the Economic History of the Argentine Republic* (New Haven: Yale University Press, 1970), p. 217, argues that many industries enjoyed "substantial protection" under the old liberal oligarchy; and Ezequiel Gallo, *Agrarian Expansion and Industrial Development in Argentina (1880–1930)* (Buenos Aires: Instituto Torcuato Di Tella, 1970), p. 13, points out that on the eve of World War I the general tariff level in Argentina was higher than in Australia or Canada and only slightly lower than in the United States. See also Vásquez-Presedo, *El caso argentino*, p. 212.

6. Francis Lambert, *Planning for Administrative Reform in Latin Amer-*

*ica: The Argentine and Brazilian Cases* (Glasgow: University of Glasgow Press, 1971), p. 5.

7. David Rock, "Radical Populism and the Conservative Elite, 1912–1930," in *Argentina in the Twentieth Century*, ed. David Rock (Pittsburgh: University of Pittsburgh Press, 1975), pp. 74–75; David Rock, "Machine Politics in Buenos Aires and the Argentine Radical Party, 1912–1930," *Journal of Latin American Studies*, November 1972, pp. 243–45; Oscar Cornblit, *Inmigrantes y empresarios en la política argentina* (Buenos Aires: Instituto Torcuato Di Tella, 1967), p. 45; Roger Gravil, "La intervención estatal en el comércio de exportación argentino entre las dos guerras," *Desarrollo Económico*, January–March 1971, pp. 80–81; and *Revista de Economía Argentina*, October 1942, p. 344.

8. Quoted in Carl Solberg, "Tariff and Politics in Argentina, 1916–1930," *Hispanic American Historical Review*, May 1973, p. 283. For more on the D'Abernon Treaty, see Gravil, "La intervención" pp. 47–50, 54–55; and Falcoff, "Economic Dependency," pp. 66–67.

9. *PRP*, 29 November 1929, pp. 11–12.

10. *La Nación*, 28 February 1929, quoted in Cuneo, *Comportamiento y crisis*, p. 111.

11. Simon G. Hanson, *Argentine Meat and the British Market* (Stanford: Stanford University Press, 1938), pp. 267–68; José Alfredo Martínez de Hoz, *La agricultura y la ganadería argentina en el periódo 1930–1960* (Buenos Aires: Editorial Sudamerica, 1967), pp. 25–27; Miguel Murmis and Juan Carlos Portaniero, *Crecimiento industrial y alianza de clases en la Argentina, 1930–1940* (Buenos Aires: Instituto Torcuato Di Tella, 1968), pp. 10–11; Alberto Paz and Gustavo Ferrari, *Argentina's Foreign Policy, 1930–1962* (Notre Dame: University of Notre Dame Press, 1966), pp. 1, 7, 11–15; Peter H. Smith, *Politics and Beef in Argentina* (New York: Columbia University Press, 1969) pp. 141–49.

12. Alejandro Bunge, *Una nueva Argentina* (Buenos Aires: Guillermo Kraft, 1940), pp. 231–32.

13. Ibid., p. 479; also, Falcoff, "Economic Dependency," pp. 62–63.

14. Quoted in Juan José Real, *30 años de historia argentina* (Buenos Aires: Ediciones Actualidad, 1962), pp. 49–50. On Colombo's background, see *Gran enciclopedia argentina* (Buenos Aires: Ediar, 1960), 2:388; Jose Luís De Imaz, *Los que mandan* (Buenos Aires: Editorial Universitaria de Buenos Aires, 1972), pp. 127–28; Gilbert D. Storey, "Industrialization and Political Change: The Political Role of Industrial Entrepeneurs in Five Latin American Countries" (Ph.D. diss., University of Indiana, 1978), p. 199.

15. Real, *30 años*, pp. 49–50; *Revista de Economía Argentina*, September 1941, pp. 285–89.

16. Quoted in Javier Lindenboim, "El empresario industrial argentino y sus organizaciones gremiales entre 1930 y 1946," *Desarrollo Económico*, July–September 1976, p. 190.

17. CAP was also used to get around the Roca-Runciman Treaty's provision that only nonprofit companies could take advantage of the 15 per-

cent of the British market reserved for Argentine domestic producers. Until 1941, when the smaller *estancieros* took over CAP's management, CAP bought all of its meat from the Tornquist-owned Sansenina meat company. (Interestingly, CAP's president Horacio Pereda was also on Sansenina's board of directors.) After 1941 CAP operated its own slaughterhouses.

18. Ministerio de Hacienda y Agricultura, *El Plan de reactivación económica ante el honorable Senado* (Buenos Aires, 1940), pp. 89, 163–67.

19. Ibid.

20. *RRP*, 9 July 1943, pp. 13–14; and 19 November 1943, pp. 13–17.

21. Ibid., 21 January 1944, p. 19; and 14 July 1944, p. 15. See also George Blanksten, *Perón's Argentina* (New York: Russell & Russell, 1953), pp. 240–42; and Real, *30 años*, p. 67.

22. *RRP*, 16 November 1945, p. 4; and 22 February 1946, p. 18. See also *Veritas*, April 1964, pp. 6–18.

23. Dino Jarach, *Estudio sobre las finanzas argentinas, 1947–1957* (Buenos Aires: Editorial Roque DePalma, 1961), pp. 15, 39; ECLA, *El desarrollo económico de la Argentina*, part 1 (Santiago de Chile: ECLA, 1958), p. 113; *RRP*, 7 January 1944, pp. 5, 23.

24. The excess profits tax applied to any profits exceeding 10 percent gross for joint-stock companies and 12 percent for all other firms.

25. David Chu, "The Great Depression and Industrialization in Latin America" (Ph.D. diss., Yale University, 1972), p. 65; Carlos F. Díaz-Alejandro, "An Interpretation of Argentine Economic Growth Since 1930," part 1, *Journal of Development Studies*, October 1966, pp. 36–37.

26. *RRP*, 11 January 1972, p. 16.

## Chapter 6

1. Samuel J. Baily, *Labor, Nationalism, and Politics in Argentina* (New Brunswick, N.J.: Rutgers University Press, 1967), pp. 11–12.

2. Júlio Godio, *Historia del movimiento obrero argentino: inmigrantes asalariados y lucha de clases, 1880–1910* (Buenos Aires: Editorial Tiempo Contemporáneo, 1973), pp. 74–80.

3. Godio, *Historia del movimiento obrero*, pp. 199–200. The *Segundo censo de la República Argentina, 1895* (Buenos Aires: Comisión Directiva del Censo, 1898), 3:xcii, was used to estimate the total number of industrial workers.

4. DNT, *Boletín*, no. 24 (1912): 619. Occasionally workers won their demands without any need for organization. In 1904, the Buenos Aires waiters protested the lowering of their wages and their employers' insistence that they shave off their mustaches for hygienic reasons ("those precious adornments," the waiters' manifesto read, "that nature has accorded to the manly visage"). Instead of striking, however, the waiters fought back by serving each bowl of soup with a few hairs floating on top. The owners soon caved in, leaving both wages and mustaches intact. See Santiago Sénen

González, "90 Years of Argentine Trade Union Activities, 1891–1981," *RRP*, 9 December 1981, p. 750.

5. DNT, *Boletín*, no. 24 (1912): 601, 619; no. 30 (1914): 7–71; no. 31 (1916): 77–110.

6. Ibid., no. 3 (1907): 319–22, 329–34, 337–41; Júlio Mafud, *La vida obrera en la Argentina* (Buenos Aires: Editorial Proyección, 1976), pp. 165–75.

7. DNT, *Boletín*, no. 24 (1912): 671, 682.

8. Ibid., no. 3 (1907): 319–22, 328–41; José Panetierri, *Los trabajadores* (Buenos Aires: Editorial José Álvarez, 1967), pp. 83–84, 207.

9. DNT, *Boletín*, no. 3 (1907): 346–61.

10. Panetierri, *Los trabajadores*, pp. 48–49, 51–52, 70, 74–75; Mafud, *La vida obrera*, pp. 177–89.

11. Panetierri, *Los trabajadores*, pp. 53, 56; Mafud, *La vida obrera*, pp. 238, 240.

12. DNT, *Boletín*, no. 28 (1914): 8–9; and no. 31 (1915): 37–41.

13. Ibid., no. 28 (1914): 8.

14. Ibid., pp. 61, 71. In fairness to the companies, the DNT report observed that the articles for sale at the company store were of generally good quality and were priced reasonably. Also, the permanent staff seemed to have been paid in currency. A Spaniard who worked in the mill told the DNT inspector that he had saved enough of his wages to invest in a small business back home and to buy his passage on the boat.

15. Ibid., no. 25 (1913): 31–36; Panetierri, *Los trabajadores*, p. 104.

16. Juan Bialet Massé, *El estado de las clases obreras argentinas a comienzos del siglo* (1904; reprint, Córdoba: Universidad Nacional de Córdoba, 1968), p. 33.

17. DNT, "El caso de Puerto Segundo," *Boletín*, no. 26 (1914): 201–41.

18. Eugene G. Sharkey, "Unión Industrial Argentina, 1887–1920" (Ph.D. diss., Rutgers University, 1977), p. 198; Thomas C. Cochran and Ruben Reina, *Capitalism in Argentine Culture: A Study of Torcuato Di Tella and SIAM* (Philadelphia: University of Pennsylvania Press, 1971), pp. 85–87; *RRP*, 21 January 1961, pp. 21–22.

19. Bialet Massé, *El estado de las clases*, p. 449.

20. *RRP*, 24 August 1917, p. 447.

21. Ibid., 16 November 1917, pp. 1197–1201; and 23 November 1917, pp. 1271–72. Also, Winthrop Wright, *The British-Owned Railways in Argentina* (Austin: University of Texas Press, 1974), pp. 117–18.

22. On the Patriotic League and the events of the Tragic Week, see especially Sandra McGee Deutsch, *Counter-Revolution in Argentina, 1900–1932: The Argentine Patriotic League* (Lincoln: University of Nebraska Press, 1986). Also, Baily, *Labor, Nationalism, and Politics*, pp. 36–38; John Raymond Hebert, "The Tragic Week of January, 1919, in Buenos Aires" (Ph.D. diss., Georgetown University, 1972), pp. 52, 62–63, 65–66, 83–89; Sénen González, "90 Years," p. 752; *Análisis Confirmado*, 17 April 1973, p. 4.

23. *Análisis Confirmado,* 17 April 1973, p. 4; *PP,* 29 April 1969, pp. 55–56.

24. Osvaldo Bayer, *La Patagonia rebelde* (Mexico: Editorial Nueva Imagen, 1980). Also, Sénen González, "90 Years," p. 752; and Alberto Belloni, *Del anarquismo al peronismo historia del movimiento obrero argentino* (Buenos Aires: A. Peña Lillo, 1960), pp. 35–36.

25. Moises Poblete Troncoso, *El movimiento obrero latinoamericano* (Mexico: Fondo de Cultura Económico, 1946), pp. 71, 83.

26. Richard Edward Shipley, "On the Outside Looking In: A Social History of the 'Porteño' Worker During the 'Golden Age' of Argentine Development, 1914–1930" (Ph.D. diss., Rutgers University, 1977), pp. 75, 301, 305. When labor did win, the consequences of victory often undermined labor in general. For example, a general strike in 1924 forced Congress to rescind a "Pensions Law" that guaranteed retirement, sickness, accident, and death benefits to industrial and commercial employees, workers in the graphic arts, seamen, and journalists. The communists and anarchists attacked it as dividing the proletariat between the privileged and nonprivileged, thus weakening its struggle against capital. See Sebastián Marotta, *El movimiento sindical argentino: su genésis y desarrollo* (Buenos Aires: Editorial Calomino, 1970), 3:153–73.

27. DNT, *Estadística de las huelgas, 1940* (Buenos Aires, 1941), p. 19; *Crónica mensual,* June 1929, pp. 2796–2801; Panetierri, *Los trabajadores,* pp. 209–10.

28. Panetierri, *Los trabajadores,* pp. 196–97.

29. Louise M. Doyón, "Conflictos obreros durante el régimen peronista (1946–1955)," *Desarrollo Económico,* October–December 1977, p. 442; David Tamarin, "The Argentine Labor Movement in an Age of Transition, 1930–1945" (Ph.D. diss., University of Washington, 1977), p. 51.

30. DNT, *Organización sindical: asociaciones obreras y patronales* (Buenos Aires, 1941), p. 2.

31. Baily, *Labor, Nationalism, and Politics,* pp. 80–82; Walter Little, "The Popular Origins of Peronism," in *Argentina in the Twentieth Century,* ed. David Rock (Pittsburgh: University of Pittsburgh Press, 1975), pp. 164–68; Tamarin, "The Argentine Labor Movement," pp. 63, 65; Peter Van Hove, "Working Class Crowds and Political Change in Buenos Aires, 1919–1945" (Ph.D. diss., University of New Mexico, 1970), pp. 212–32, 243.

32. *PP,* 11 April 1967, p. 38; Juan José Real, *30 años de historia argentina* (Buenos Aires: Ediciones Actualidad, 1962), p. 36.

33. Robert Potash, *The Army and Politics in Argentina, 1928–1945: Yrigoyen to Perón* (Stanford: Stanford University Press, 1969), pp. 59, 67–68, 78, 90, 119n; Marysa Navarro Gerassi, *Los nacionalistas* (Buenos Aires: Editorial Jorge Álvarez, 1968), pp. 93–95; Ray Josephs, *Argentine Diary* (New York: Random House, 1944), pp. 266–67; Baily, *Labor, Nationalism, and Politics,* p. 54; Frank Owen, *Perón: His Rise and Fall* (London: Cresset Press, 1957), p. 11.

34. Celia Durruty, *Clase obrera y peronismo* (Córdoba: n.p., 1969), p. 120.

35. Ibid., pp. 114–22.

36. Dardo Cuneo, *Comportamiento y crisis de la clase empresaria* (Buenos Aires: Editorial Pleamar, 1967), p. 136; *Revista de Economía Argentina,* September 1941, pp. 288–89.

37. *Revista de Economía Argentina,* September 1941, pp. 285–87; *PP,* 17 September 1968, p. 52.

38. Javier Lindenboim, *Organización gremial y expresiones del empresariado industrial argentino (1930–1946)* (Buenos Aires: Instituto Torcuato Di Tella, 1975), pp. 191–92; Navarro Gerassi, *Los nacionalistas,* pp. 93–95. Ortiz also angered the Radical Right by removing from office the fraudulently elected governor of Buenos Aires Province, Manuel Fresco. Fresco, a brawling reactionary bully, was so high-handed in his tactics that in the 1940 gubernatorial elections he forced voters to stand in the street outside the polling places and give their votes orally. See Navarro Gerassi, *Los nacionalistas,* pp. 151–53.

39. *RRP,* 21 January 1961, pp. 21–22.

40. Cochran and Reina, *Capitalism in Argentine Culture,* pp. 89–90, 161–63.

41. DNT, *Investigaciones sociales, 1942* (Buenos Aires, 1943), pp. 90–91.

42. DNT, *Organización sindical,* pp. 40–44; *Cuarto censo nacional,* Censo Industrial (Buenos Aires: Dirección General del Servício Estadístico Nacional, 1952), p. 26.

43. Tomás Roberto Fillol, *Social Factors in Economic Development: The Argentine Case* (Cambridge: MIT Press, 1961), p. 77.

44. Quoted in Tamarin, "The Argentine Labor Movement," p. 70.

45. DNT, *Estadística de las huelgas, 1940,* p. 19; Ysabel F. Rennie, *The Argentine Republic* (New York: Macmillan, 1945), p. 311.

46. DNT, *Investigaciones sociales, 1942,* pp. 66–81, 117, 119; *Camoatí,* May 1944 (abridged edition), pp. v–viii.

47. Baily, *Labor, Nationalism, and Politics,* p. 81; Adolfo Dorfman, *Evolución industrial argentina* (Buenos Aires: Editorial Losada, 1942), pp. 226–27; Tamarin, "The Argentine Labor Movement," pp. 53–54.

48. Sergio Bagú, "La clase media en la Argentina," in *Materiales para el estudio de la clase media en America Latina,* ed. Theo R. Crevenna (Washington: The Pan American Union, 1950), 1:54–64; Gino Germani, "La clase media en la Argentina, con especial referencia a sus sectores urbanos," in Crevenna, *Materiales,* pp. 6–14.

## Chapter 7

1. Torcuato Luca de Tena et al., eds., *Yo, Juan Domingo Perón: relato biográfico,* (Barcelona: Editorial Planeta, 1976), p. 19; Enrique Pavón Pereyra, *Perón: preparación de una vida para el mando, 1895–1942* (Buenos Aires: Ediciones Espiño, 1953), p. 235, claims that Perón's grandfather Tomás Liberato was born in 1838. Vicente O. Cútolo, in his *Nuevo diccionario biográfico argentino* (Buenos Aires: Editorial Elche, 1978), 5:456–57, dates Tomás Liberato's birthday on 17 August 1839. Diego Abad de Santi-

llán, in his *Gran enciclopedia argentina* (Buenos Aires: Ediar, 1960), 6:331, claims that Tomás Liberato was born on 12 September 1833. I have chosen to follow Cútolo, as the most recent source. According to Pavón Pereyra, Perón's great-grandmother was a Scotswoman with the surname of Mac-Kenzie; but Cútolo gives her name as Ana Hughes.

2. *La Prensa*, 2 February 1889, p. 5, devoted nearly a whole column to Tomás Liberato's obituary, describing him as a "distinguished Argentine" and a "talent of the first order."

3. Luca de Tena et al., *Yo, Juan Domingo Perón*, p. 20; Pavón Pereyra, *Perón: preparación*, pp. 17, 20; *Gran enciclopedia argentina*, 6:331; Joseph Page, *Perón: a Biography* (New York: Random House, 1983), p. 19.

4. Juan Domingo Perón, "Lo que yo ví de la preparación y realización de la revolución del 6 de septiembre de 1930," in Juan Domingo Perón, *Tres revoluciones* (Buenos Aires: Ediciones Escorpión, 1963), pp. 10–86.

5. Page, *Perón*, pp. 32–33; Pavón Pereyra, *Perón: preparación*, p. 155; Arthur P. Whitaker, *The United States and Argentina* (Cambridge: Harvard University Press, 1954), p. 119.

6. Juan Domingo Perón, *Apuntes de historia militar: parte teorética* (Buenos Aires: Círculo Militar, 1934), pp. 138–39.

7. Ibid., pp. 233–35.

8. Juan D. Perón, "Significado de la defensa nacional desde el punto de vista militar," published as a preface to a 1982 edition of his *Apuntes de historia militar* (Buenos Aires: Editorial Volver, 1982), pp. v–xxxii. The speech was given at the University of La Plata on 10 June 1944, at the inauguration of a chair in National Defense Studies.

9. Page, *Perón*, pp. 34–35; Robert A. Potash, *The Army and Politics in Argentina, 1945–1962: Perón to Frondizi* (Stanford: Stanford University Press, 1980), p. 113n, based on an April 1970 interview with Rattenbach.

10. Pavón Pereyra, *Perón: preparación*, p. 204.

11. Luca de Tena et al., *Yo, Juan Domingo Perón*, p. 28.

12. Pavón Pereyra, *Perón: preparación*, p. 205.

13. Luca de Tena et al., *Yo, Juan Domingo Perón*, pp. 28–29.

14. Walter Little, "La organización obrera y el estado peronista," *Desarrollo económico*, October–December 1979, p. 333; RRP, 3 December 1943, p. 13.

15. Bertram Silverman, "Labor and Left Fascism: A Case Study of Peronist Labor Policy" (Ph.D. diss., Columbia University, 1967), pp. 151–57, 219–20, 228; Robert J. Alexander, *Labor Relations in Argentina, Brazil, and Chile* (New York: McGraw-Hill, 1962), pp. 177–79. It gradually became standard practice to sign industrywide contracts, rather than settling terms on an enterprise-by-enterprise basis. Minor contract violations were handled by a system of labor courts, which was set up in November 1944. Those courts also dealt with cases involving severance pay and workmen's compensation.

16. RRP, 3 November 1944, pp. 17–22, for the full text of the Statute of the Peón. See also Samuel J. Baily, *Labor, Nationalism, and Politics in Argentina* (New Brunswick, N.J.: Rutgers University Press, 1967), p. 77; George

Blanksten, *Perón's Argentina* (New York: Russell & Russell, 1953), p. 265; Ray Josephs, *Argentine Diary* (New York: Random House, 1944), p. 257; Silverman, "Labor and Left Fascism," pp. 173–76; and Ian Rutledge, "Plantations and Peasants in Northern Argentina: The Sugar Cane Industry of Salta and Jujuy, 1930–1943," in *Argentina in the Twentieth Century*, ed. David Rock (Pittsburgh: University of Pittsburgh Press, 1975), pp. 94–100.

## Chapter 8

1. Alberto Belloni, *Del anarquismo al peronismo: historia del movimiento obrero argentino* (Buenos Aires: A. Peña Lillo, 1960), p. 2. Perón's speech was made on 7 August 1945, at the Military Academy. The ambassador he refers to was, of course, Spruille Braden.

2. See Juan Domingo Perón, "En la Bolsa de Comércio de Buenos Aires," in Juan Domingo Perón, *El pueblo quiere saber de que se trata* (Buenos Aires, 1944), pp. 157–68.

3. Ibid., p. 161. Italics added.

4. Dardo Cuneo, *Comportamiento y crisis de la clase empresaria* (Buenos Aires: Editorial Pleamar, 1967), p. 72.

5. Quoted in Mónica Peralta Ramos, *Acumulación de capital y crisis política en la Argentina (1930–1974)* (Mexico: Siglo Veintiuno Editores, 1978), p. 80.

6. *Camoatí*, June 1945, pp. 24–26.

7. Ernest Arthur Boas, *Latin America's Steel Industry, Present and Future* (Berlin: Duncker and Humbolt, 1968), pp. 86–89; Juan Manuel Areca de Codes, *La industria siderúgica en hispanoamérica* (Madrid: Ediciones Cultura Hispánica, 1958), pp. 21–25; Curtin Winsor, Jr., "National Security and Armament Policies of Argentina" (Ph.D. diss., The American University, 1971), pp. 4–5, 27, 29.

8. The report was actually prepared by the Armour Research Foundation of Chicago. See *RRP*, 23 June 1944, pp. 13–19.

9. See *RRP*, 3 August 1945, pp. 14–22, for the Report of the Economic Research Department of the Central Bank.

10. "Bosquejo de una economía argentina para 1955," *Revista de Economía Argentina* (May 1946), pp. 143–53.

11. Perón, "El estado de afianzar los princípios de libertad económica," in Perón, *El pueblo quiere saber de que se trata*, pp. 174–81.

12. *RRP*, 18 January 1946; Samuel L. Baily, *Labor, Nationalism, and Politics* (New Brunswick, N.J.: Rutgers University Press, 1967), pp. 94–95; Cuneo, *Comportamiento y crisis*, p. 178f; John William Freels, Jr., *El sector industrial en la política nacional* (Buenos Aires: Editorial Universitaria de Buenos Aires, 1970), pp. 25–26; Eldon Kenworthy, "Did the 'New Industrialists' Play a Significant Role in the Formation of Perón's Coalition, 1943–1946?" in *New Perspectives on Modern Argentina*, ed. Alberto Ciria (Bloomington: University of Indiana, Latin American Studies Program, 1972), p. 21.

13. Kenworthy, "Did the 'New Industrialists'," pp. 15–28; J. Rodríguez Goicoa, *El caso del cheque y el problema creado a los industriales argentinos: lapso historico 1943–1952* (Buenos Aires: Plantíe, 1952), pp. 37–38; Raúl Lamarúglia, interview, Instituto Torcuato Di Tella Oral History Project, Buenos Aires, July 1971; Cuneo, *Comportamiento y crisis*, p. 178–80.

14. To make the relationship even more complex, Colombo was also a director on the board of the Roberts' wine company, El Globo.

15. Ernest J. Wilkins, "The Industrial Aspects of Argentina's Five-Year Plan: Why It Did Not Succeed" (Ph.D. diss., Stanford University, 1953), pp. 69–84; RRP, 1 November 1946, pp. 10–17.

16. Oscar Altmir et al., "Los instrumentos de la promoción industrial en la postguerra," part 1, *Desarrollo Económico*, April–June 1966, pp. 91–93; John M. Frikart, "Effects of the Perón Regime on the Argentine Economy" (Ph.D. diss., University of Colorado, 1959), pp. 45, 89.

17. Mario Alberto Cichero, *Introducción a la economía política y la legislación económica y laboral argentina* (Buenos Aires: Editorial "El Ateneo," 1979), pp. 470–71.

18. Bertram Silverman, "Labor and Left Fascism: A Case Study of Peronist Labor Policy" (Ph.D. diss., Columbia University, 1967), p. 117; *Camoatí*, April 1946 (abridged ed.), p. ii; and May 1946, pp. 1–4.

19. Dino Jarach, *Estudio sobre las finanzas argentinas (1947–1957)* (Buenos Aires: Editorial Roque DePalma, 1961), pp. 13–14.

20. William P. Glade, *The Latin American Economies: A Study of Their Institutional Evolution* (New York: The American Book Company, 1969), p. 425.

21. Altmir et al., "Los instrumentos," part 2, *Desarrollo Económico*, July–December 1966, pp. 469–88. Also, PP, 2 August 1966, pp. 36–37; 9 August 1966, p. 38; and 9 September 1966, p. 17; *Camoatí*, October 1966, p. 5; and Arthur P. Whitaker, *The United States and Argentina* (Cambridge: Harvard University Press, 1954), pp. 191–93.

22. Benjamin Most, "Authoritarianism and the Growth of the State in Latin America, an Assessment of Their Impacts on Argentine Public Policy, 1930–1970," *Journal of Comparative Political Studies*, July 1980, p. 101.

23. Roland Sarti, *Fascism and the Industrial Leadership in Italy, 1919–1940* (Berkeley: University of California Press, 1970), p. 77. On syndical and corporative organizations under Fascism, see also G. Lowell Field, *The Syndical and Corporative Institutions of Italian Fascism* (New York: Columbia University Press, 1938).

24. RRP, 27 November 1951, p. 7.

25. Juan Domingo Perón, *Conferencia del Excmo. Sr. Presidente de la Nación Argentina, Gral. Juan Perón, pronunciada en el acto de clausura del primero congreso nacional de filosofía* (Mendoza, 1949), pp. 75–77; and Perón, *Conducción política* (Buenos Aires, 1953), pp. 53–55.

26. Pedro Santos Martínez, *La Nueva Argentina* (Buenos Aires: Ediciones La Bastilla, 1976), 1:330–31.

27. 1949 constitution, article 37, sections 1–10.

28. Robert J. Alexander, *The Perón Era* (New York: Columbia University Press, 1951), pp. 95–96, 98; Baily, *Labor, Nationalism, and Politics*, p. 115; George Blanksten, *Perón's Argentina* (New York: Russell & Russell, 1953), pp. 326–27; John T. Deiner, "ATLAS: A Labor Instrument of Argentine Expansionism Under Perón" (Ph.D. diss., Rutgers University, 1969), pp. 57–58; Carlos M. Echagüe, *Las grandes huelgas* (Buenos Aires: Centro Editor de América Latina, 1971), pp. 90–92; *HAR*, March 1949, pp. 19–22; and April 1949, pp. 17–18.

29. Cuneo, *Comportamiento y crisis*, pp. 159, 216f; José Luís De Imaz, *Los que mandan* (Buenos Aires: Editorial Universitaria de Buenos Aires, 1972), p. 87; *PP*, 10 May 1966, p. 36.

30. Rodríguez Goicoa, *El caso del cheque*, pp. 61–78.

31. See articles 38, 39, and 40 of the 1949 constitution. Article 17 of the 1853 constitution had declared private property to be "inviolable."

32. *PP*, 22 October 1968, pp. 59–61; *Camoatí*, July 1944 (abridged ed.), pp. v–vi. After Perón fell from power, the Bembergs sued for indemnification and won. Pressure was put on the Argentine government by a group of creditors known as "the Paris Club." In December 1966 a federal court held Buenos Aires Province liable for some 400 million pesos of property that it had taken over from the Bembergs, and a month later the court ordered the federal government to repay some 100 million pesos. The beneficiaries of these suits were not only the Bembergs but also thousands of French, Belgian, and Swiss stockholders. See *HAR*, March 1959, p. 50; and Rogelio García Lupo, *Contra la ocupación extranjera* (Buenos Aires: Editorial Centro, 1971), p. 18.

33. Juan Domingo Perón, *Peron señala la necesidad de organizar las fuerzas económicas del país* (Buenos Aires: Presidencía de La Nación, Subsecretaría de Informaciones, 1950).

34. Robert J. Alexander, *Labor Relations in Argentina, Brazil, and Chile* (New York: McGraw-Hill, 1962), pp. 195–97; James Bruce, *Those Perplexing Argentines* (New York: Longman's, Green, 1953), p. 149; Thomas C. Cochran and Ruben Reina, *Capitalism in Argentine Culture: A Study of Torcuato Di Tella and SIAM* (Philadelphia: University of Pennsylvania Press, 1971), p. 264; Tomás Roberto Fillol, *Social Factors in Economic Development: The Argentine Case* (Cambridge: MIT Press, 1961), pp. 65–67; *RRP*, 29 October 1948, p. 9; and 19 March 1954, pp. 7–8; Silverman, "Labor and Left Fascism," pp. 168–70, 186–91, 248–49, 252, 254, 273, 277.

35. Cochran and Reina, *Capitalism in Argentine Culture*, p. 162, from an engineer whose name was withheld by request.

36. Ibid., pp. 227–28.

37. *PP*, 27 October 1970, p. 26.

38. Cuneo, *Comportamiento y crisis*, pp. 194–205; John William Freels, *El sector industrial en la política nacional* (Buenos Aires: Editorial Universitaria de Buenos Aires, 1970), pp. 27–29; Alexander, *Labor Relations in Argentina, Brazil, and Chile*, pp. 187–89.

39. *RRP*, 28 December 1951, p. 17.

40. CGE, *Memoria* (Buenos Aires: CGE, 1955), pp. 34, 36; Cuneo, *Comportamiento y crisis*, pp. 187–89; Freels, *El sector industrial*, p. 31; HAR, March 1954, p. 32.

41. Cuneo, *Comportamiento y crisis*, pp. 189–90.

42. Carlos F. Díaz Alejandro, *Essays on the Economic History of the Argentine Republic* (New Haven: Yale University Press, 1970), p. 261. On CGE representation in the government, see CGE, *Memoria*, pp. 7–13; Silverman, "Labor and Left Fascism," p. 265; Judith Teichman, "Interest Conflict and Entrepreneurial Support for Perón," *Latin American Research Review*, 16, no. 1 (1981): 150.

43. Santos Martínez, *La Nueva Argentina*, 2:149; Baily, *Labor, Nationalism, and Politics*, p. 140; and Ramón Prieto, *El Pacto* (Buenos Aires: Editorial En Marcha, 1963), p. 11, for the Congress on Productivity. On the process of tripartite negotiations, see Alexander, *Labor Relations in Argentina, Brazil, and Chile*, p. 195; Fillol, *Social Factors*, pp. 66–67; and Silverman, "Labor and Left Fascism," pp. 248–49, 252, 254.

44. PP, 4 October 1966, p. 39; HAR, April 1951, p. 40; Santos Martínez, *La Nueva Argentina*, 1:209–10.

45. Silverman, "Labor and Left Fascism," pp. 219–20; Bernardo Rabinowitz, *Sucedió en la Argentina, 1943–1956* (Buenos Aires: Ediciones Güré, 1956), p. 159; RRP, 20 November 1953, p. 9; HAR, December 1953, p. 38; and May 1954, p. 38.

46. Juan Domingo Perón, *El presidente de la Nación Argentina, General Juan Perón, se dirige a los intelectuales, escritores, artistas pintores, y maestros* (Buenos Aires, 1947), pp. 19, 21–22, 24, 26.

47. RRP, 22 July 1949, pp. 12–13.

48. Ibid., 20 January 1950, p. 7.

## Chapter 9

1. RRP, 4 April 1947, p. 16.

2. PP, 10 May 1966, p. 37.

3. Robert J. Alexander, *The Perón Era* (New York: Columbia University Press, 1951), p. 156; Eldon Kenworthy, "Did the 'New Industrialists' Play a Significant Role in the Formation of the Peronist Coalition, 1943–1946?" in *New Perspectives on Argentina*, ed. Alberto Ciria (Bloomington: Indiana University, Latin American Studies Program, 1972), pp. 17–18; PP, 3 August 1965, p. 40; and 19 July 1966, pp. 41–42.

4. PP, 19 July 1966, p. 40.

5. Ibid., 10 August 1965, p. 42; and 17 August 1965, p. 42.

6. The most serious scholarly critiques may be found in Carlos F. Díaz Alejandro, *Essays on the Economic History of the Argentine Republic* (New Haven: Yale University Press, 1970); and his "An Interpretation of Argentine Economic Growth Since 1930" *Journal of Development Studies*, part 1, October 1966, pp. 14–41, and part 2, January 1967, pp. 155–77; also, Eprime Eshag and Rosemary Thorpe, "Las consecuencias económicas y sociales de

las políticas económicas ortodoxas aplicadas en la República Argentina durante de los años de post-guerra," *Desarrollo Económico*, January–March 1965, pp. 287–344; and Aldo Ferrer, *The Argentine Economy* (Berkeley: University of California Press, 1967).

7. Bertram Silverman, "Labor and Left Fascism: A Case Study of Peronist Labor Policy" (Ph.D. diss., Columbia University, 1967), pp. 162–66, 270–72, 300–301, 315–19; Samuel L. Baily, *Labor, Nationalism, and Politics in Argentina* (New Brunswick, N.J.: Rutgers University Press, 1967), pp. 98–99; Díaz Alejandro, *Essays*, pp. 124–25; George Blanksten, *Perón's Argentina* (New York: Russell & Russell, 1953), p. 266; Mario Alberto Cichero, *Introducción a la economía política y la legislación económica y laboral argentina* (Buenos Aires: Editorial "El Ateneo," 1979), p. 303; Tomás Roberto Fillol, *Social Factors in Economic Development: The Argentine Case* (Cambridge: MIT Press, 1961), p. 64; ECLA, *Economic Development and Income Distribution in Argentina* (New York: United Nations, 1969), pp. 135, 169; RRP, 30 April 1954, p. 19; and 10 November 1966, p. 191.

8. RRP, 20 March 1953, p. 13; 9 April 1954, p. 21; and 9 November 1954, p. 27.

9. ECLA, *El desarrollo económico de la Argentina*, primera parte (Santiago de Chile: ECLA, 1958), pp. 89, 135–36; Silverman, "Labor and Left Fascism," pp. 331–32.

10. CGE, *Informe económico* (Buenos Aires, 1955), p. 148; Oscar Altmir et al., "Los instrumentos de la promoción industrial en la postguerra," *Desarrollo Económico*, part 1, April–June 1966, pp. 91–93; John M. Frikart, "Effects of the Perón Regime on the Argentine Economy" (Ph.D. diss., University of Colorado, 1959), pp. 45, 89; RRP, 20 January 1953, p. 12; 19 January 1954, p. 10; and 11 January 1972, p. 16.

11. James Bruce, *Those Perplexing Argentines* (New York: Longman's, Green, 1953), p. 148; Frikart, "Effects of the Perón Regime," pp. 92–94; Hugh Harold Schwartz, "The Argentine Experience With Industrial Credit and Protection Incentives, 1943–1958" (Ph.D. diss., Yale University, 1967), 1:55; RRP, 9 January 1948, p. 6.

12. Silverman, "Labor and Left Fascism," pp. 279–80; RRP, 21 June 1946, pp. 6–8, 13.

13. Frikart, "Effects of the Perón Regime," pp. 88–89; Hugh Harold Schwartz, "The Argentine Experience," 1:73; RRP, 16 May 1947, pp. 30–31. Schwartz, p. 110, suggests that compensatory subsidies were paid mainly to large producers and merchants. Smaller businessmen turned to tax evasion to make up their losses.

14. Díaz Alejandro, "An Interpretation," part 1, pp. 22–23; Oscar Altmir et al., "Los instrumentos," *Desarrollo Económico*, January–March, 1967, pp. 727–29.

15. Torcuato Luca de Tena et al., eds., *Yo, Juan Domingo Perón: relato biográfico* (Barcelona: Editorial Planeta, 1976), p. 211.

16. Adolfo Silenzo de Stagni, *El petróleo argentino* (Buenos Aires: Ediciones Problemas Nacionales, 1955), pp. 86–87, 92–93; Carl Solberg, *Oil and Nationalism in Argentina* (Stanford: Stanford University Press, 1979),

pp. 164–65; Abraham Eidlicz, "Combustibles, electricidad, minería," in *Argentina, 1930–1960*, (Buenos Aires: Editorial SUR, 1961), p. 218.

17. Silenzo de Stagni, *El petróleo argentino*, p. 152 (Appendix B); Eidlicz, "Combustibles," p. 218.

18. Robert A. Potash, *The Army and Politics, 1945–1962: Perón to Frondizi* (Stanford: Stanford University Press, 1980), pp. 62–75. Potash relates that the army, though originally sympathetic toward the nationalization scheme, was persuaded to change its mind by the threat of a cutoff of American arms sales if Standard Oil was taken over.

19. Arthur P. Whitaker, *The United States and Argentina* (Cambridge: Harvard University Press, 1954), p. 198.

20. Horacio Gilberti, "El desarrollo agropecuario," *Desarrollo Económico*, April–June 1962, p. 109; Richard D. Mallon and Juan V. Sourouille, *Economic Policymaking in a Conflict Society: The Argentine Case* (Cambridge: Harvard University Press, 1975), p. 39; José Alfredo Martínez de Hoz, *La agricultura y la ganadería argentina en el periódo 1930–1960* (Buenos Aires: Editorial Sudamericana, 1967), pp. 54–56; HAR, December 1951, p. 33; RRP, 22 April 1955, p. 9; and 11 September 1956, pp. 21–22.

21. Robert J. Alexander, *The Perón Era* (New York: Columbia University Press, 1951), pp. 148–50; Díaz Alejandro, *Essays*, p. 187; Colin Lewis, "Anglo-Argentine Trade, 1945–1965," in *Argentina in the Twentieth Century*, ed. David Rock (Pittsburgh: University of Pittsburgh Press, 1975), pp. 124–25; RRP, 3 September 1948, p. 10; 15 April 1949, p. 7; 9 February 1954, pp. 3–5; 10 August 1954, p. 13; and 22 April 1963, p. 93.

22. Alexander, *The Perón Era*, pp. 148–50; RRP, 17 December 1948, p. 13; and 22 April 1949, p. 14.

23. RRP, 29 November 1946, pp. 29–30.

24. Ibid., 7 March 1952, p. 7.

25. Guido Di Tella and Manuel Zymelman, *Las etapas del desarrollo económico argentino* (Buenos Aires: Editorial Universitaria de Buenos Aires, 1967), p. 496; Alberto Conil Paz and Gustavo Ferrari, *Argentina's Foreign Policy, 1930–1962* (Notre Dame: University of Notre Dame Press, 1966), p. 154; RRP, 24 December 1948, p. 13; HAR, January 1949, p. 20.

26. Juan Domingo Perón, *Política y estrategia* (Buenos Aires, 1951), pp. 71, 103, 175–79, 191; Antonio Cafiero, *De la economía social-justicialista al regimén liberal-capitalista* (Buenos Aires: Editorial Universitaria de Buenos Aires, 1974), pp. 243–46; Conil Paz and Ferrari, *Argentina's Foreign Policy*, pp. 153–54; Harold F. Peterson, *Argentina and the United States, 1810–1960* (New York: State University of New York Press, 1964), p. 476; HAR, November 1948, p. 17; and December 1948, p. 19.

27. For each old bond of 100 pesos, the creditor got a new one valued at 108. Moreover, he could buy them at slightly below par. The RRP calculated that those adjustments raised the effective yield to 3.25 percent. See 26 July 1946, p. 6; and 2 August 1946, pp. 11–12.

28. RRP, 30 August 1969, p. 315.

29. ECLA, *El desarrollo económico*, p. 92. The loss was computed in

terms of constant 1950 dollars. The comparable loss during World War I had been $59 million.

30. Díaz Alejandro, *Essays*, p. 486; Alexander, *The Perón Era*, pp. 157–58; Blanksten, *Perón's Argentina*, p. 241; Martínez de Hoz, *La agricultura*, p. 65; Pedro Santos Martínez, *La Nueva Argentina* (Buenos Aires: Ediciones La Bastilla, 1976), 2:16–21; Percy D. Warner, "The Impact of the Service of the Foreign Debt on the Monetary Structure in Argentina, 1955–1965" (Ph.D. diss., Michigan State University, 1970), p. 46; *Camoatí*, October 1966, p. 5; *PP*, 2 August 1966, pp. 36–37.

31. Perón, *Política y estrategia*, pp. 187–88; Jorge Fodor, "Perón's Policies for Agricultural Exports, 1946–1948: Dogmatism or Commonsense?" in *Argentina in the Twentieth Century*, ed. Rock, pp. 146–51; Pedro R. Skupch, "Nacionalización, libras bloqueadas, y sustitución de importaciones," *Desarrollo Económico*, October–December 1972, pp. 478, 483.

32. Conil Paz and Ferrari, *Argentina's Foreign Policy*, pp. 161, 163, 165; Daniel Drosdoff, *El gobierno de las vacas (1933–1956): tratado Roca-Runciman* (Buenos Aires: Ediciones La Bastilla, 1972), pp. 135–37, 207–12; *RRP*, 20 February 1948, pp. 12–16; 27 February 1948, pp. 8–9; and 5 March 1948, pp. 13–14.

33. *PP*, 26 July 1966, pp. 34–35.

34. *La Producción's* views were translated and quoted by *RRP*, 11 July 1947, pp. 3–4; the Alejandro E. Bunge Institute's change of attitude was expressed in the *Revista de Economía Argentina*, March 1948, pp. 77–83.

35. Potash, *The Army and Politics, 1945–1962*, p. 93n; Alexander, *The Perón Era*, p. 122.

36. *PP*, 19 July 1966, pp. 41–42; *HAR*, February 1949, p. 23.

37. *RRP*, 25 February 1949, pp. 32–33; *La Prensa*, 17–18 January 1949.

38. *RRP*, 28 January 1949, p. 31; *La Prensa*, 19–20 January 1949.

39. *La Prensa*, 22 January 1949, p. 5.

40. *RRP*, 4 March 1949, p. 24; *La Prensa*, 4 March 1949, p. 14.

41. Deltec Panamerica, *El mercado de capitales en la Argentina* (Mexico: Inter-American Development Bank, 1968), pp. 57, 180; *RRP*, 30 August 1969, p. 315.

42. Bruce, *Those Perplexing Argentines*, p. 263; Frikart, "Effects of the Perón Regime," p. 89; *ECLA*, *El desarrollo económico*, pp. 135–36.

43. *Camoatí*, May 1954, p. 115; and June 1954 (English language supplement), p. ii; *RRP*, 28 November 1952, p. 18; and 20 April 1954, p. 12; Ferrer, *The Argentine Economy*, pp. 187, 189; Baily, *Labor, Nationalism, and Politics*, p. 141; *HAR*, January 1953, pp. 29–30.

44. *Camoatí*, June 1951 (English language supplement), p. 11; December 1951, pp. 410–11; and May 1952 (English language supplement), p. ii.

45. Ruth Sautu, *Poder económico y burguesía industrial en la Argentina, 1930–1954* (Buenos Aires: Instituto Torcuato Di Tella, 1969), pp. 37–39.

46. Judith Teichman, "Interest Conflict and Entrepreneurial Support for Perón," *Latin American Research Review*, 16, no. 1 (1981): 151–52.

47. Juan V. Orona, *La dictadura de Perón* (Buenos Aires: Juan V. Orona,

1970), p. 163; *HAR*, May 1953, pp. 33–34.

48. Frikart, "Effects of the Perón Regime," p. 6.

49. *PP*, 16 August 1966, p. 36. On the funding of the Foundation, see Blanksten, *Perón's Argentina*, pp. 102–4; Alberto Ciria, *Perón y el justicialismo* (Buenos Aires: Siglo Veintiuno, 1971), pp. 111–13; Julie M. Taylor, *Eva Perón: The Myths of a Woman* (Chicago: University of Chicago, 1979), pp. 67–68. *PP*, 27 December 1966, pp. 37–38, claims that Ramón Cereijo, the finance minister, was Evita's chief agent for shaking down the business community.

50. On Jorge Antonio's career, see his autobiography, *Y Ahora Que?* (Buenos Aires: Ediciones Verum y Militia, 1966); also, Argentine Republic, Comisión Nacional de Investigaciones, *El libro negro de la segunda tiranía* (Buenos Aires, 1958), pp. 22–39, 171–77; and *PP*, 27 August 1968, p. 51.

51. Silenzo de Stagni, *El petróleo argentino*, pp. 79–80.

52. Ibid., pp. 123–28; *PP*, 27 August 1968, p. 52; and 10 September 1968, pp. 49–50; *HAR*, June 1955, p. 236. For Standard Oil's version of the matter, see the letter from Mr. Arturo Ojeda to John M. Frikart, dated 29 August 1957, quoted in Frikart, "Effects of the Perón Regime," pp. 35–36.

53. Consejo Económico Nacional, *Plan económico de 1952*, pp. 11–14, 26; Partido Peronista, *Directivas básicas del Consejo Superior* (Buenos Aires: Partido Peronista, 1952), pp. 59–61.

54. On government controls and the black market, see Frikart, "Effects of the Perón Regime," p. 119; Bruce, *Those Perplexing Argentines*, p. 262; *HAR*, April 1952, p. 34; and July 1953, p. 36. On the decline of real wages, see Silverman, "Labor and Left Fascism," p. 315; and Baily, *Labor, Nationalism, and Politics*, p. 142, who puts the decline at only 20 percent.

55. *RRP*, 18 April 1952, p. 7; 19 August 1952, p. 10; 10 February 1953, p. 9; 27 February 1953, p. 7; 20 March 1953, p. 13; 30 April 1954, pp. 19, 21; 22 June 1954, p. 17.

56. Ibid., 9 April 1954, p. 21; and 9 November 1954, p. 27.

57. Silverman, "Labor and Left Fascism," pp. 274, 315, 318–19; *RRP*, 19 March 1954, pp. 7–8.

58. Daniel James, "Rationalization and Working Class Response: The Content and Limit of Factory Floor Activity in Argentina," *Journal of Latin American Studies*, November 1981, pp. 380–81, 384–88.

*Chapter 10*

1. There is a great deal written about the revolt of 16 September 1955, but see especially Juan V. Orona, *La dictadura de Perón* (Buenos Aires: Juan V. Orona, 1970), pp. 97–118; Pedro Santos Martínez, *La Nueva Argentina* (Buenos Aires: Ediciones La Bastilla, 1976), 2:239–308; and for Lucero's views, his *El precio de la lealtad* (Buenos Aires: Editorial Propulsion, 1959). In his autobiography, Perón dismissed Lucero as a bungler: "When you have to rely on types like that, what are you going to do? You haven't got a chance."

Torcuato Luca de Tena et al., eds., *Yo, Juan Domingo Perón: relato biográfico* (Barcelona: Editorial Planeta, 1976), p. 230.

2. Partido Peronista, *Directivas básicas del Consejo Superior* (Buenos Aires: Partido Peronista, 1952), pp. 47–49; and Alberto Ciria, "Peronism and Political Structures, 1945–1955," in *New Perspectives on Modern Argentina*, ed. Alberto Ciria (Bloomington: Indiana University, Latin American Studies Program, 1972), p. 5. See also George Blanksten, *Perón's Argentina* (New York: Russell & Russell, 1953), p. 388; and Santos Martínez, *La Nueva Argentina*, 2:40–41.

3. Orona, *La dictadura*, pp. 263–65. Marysa Navarro Gerassi, *Los nacionalistas* (Buenos Aires: Editorial Jorge Álvarez, 1968), p. 211, specifically blames the burnings of 15 April 1953 on the National Liberating Alliance. Santos Martínez, *La Nueva Argentina*, 2:222–25, says that the church burnings of 16 June 1955 were planned in advance by the Peronist party's general secretary, the general secretary of the CGT, and the minister of education and worship.

4. *PP*, 11 April 1967, pp. 38–41; and 10 December 1968, pp. 57–60; Alberto Caride, "Inside Perón's Secret Torture Chambers," *Colliers*, 28 June 1952 and 5 July 1952; George Blanksten, *Perón's Argentina* (New York: Russell & Russell, 1953), pp. 182–84; *HAR*, June 1953, p. 31.

5. Partido Peronista, *Directivas básicas*, pp. 66, 70–71, 74, 77.

6. Eva Perón, *La razón de mi vida*, 17th ed. (Buenos Aires: Ediciones Peuser, 1953), pp. 14, 16; Noreen F. Stack, "Avoiding the Greater Evil: The Response of the Argentine Catholic Church to Juan Perón, 1943–1955" (Ph.D diss., Rutgers University, 1976), pp. 330–31, 338–39.

7. Stack, "Avoiding the Greater Evil," pp. 344–45.

8. Robert J. Alexander, *The Perón Era* (New York: Columbia University Press, 1951), p. 132.

9. *SOMOS*, 6 October 1978, p. 13.

10. Orona, *La dictadura*, p. 206.

11. Sosa Molina was retained in the cabinet as minister of defense, a post specially created for him, but the appointment was seen as being essentially decorative.

12. After 1951, when military discontent was more pronounced, Perón allowed defense spending to rise to about a quarter of the budget, or from 1.27 billion pesos to 2.76 billion; but big-time military outlays were not the rule again until after his fall, when General Aramburu raised spending to 5.1 billion pesos, or 34 percent of the budget. See Dino Jarach, *Estudio sobre las finanzas argentinas, 1947–1957* (Buenos Aires: Editorial Roque DePalma, 1961), pp. 15, 39, 50; Robert A. Potash, *The Army and Politics, 1945–1962: Perón to Frondizi* (Stanford: Stanford University Press, 1980), pp. 83–84, 108; ECLA, *El desarrollo económico de la Argentina* (Santiago de Chile: ECLA, 1958), p. 113; *RRP*, 22 February 1946, p. 18; and David L. Feldman, "Argentina, 1945–1971: Military Assistance, Military Spending, and the Political Activity of the Armed Forces," *Journal of Inter-American Studies and World Affairs*, August 1982, p. 328. Robert Alexander, *The*

*Perón Era*, pp. 118–19, claims that the size of the armed forces was cut from 105,000 men to 70,000, while in almost every grade Argentine officers were paid more than their counterparts in the United States. See also *PP*, 18 July 1967, pp. 37–38.

13. About this process of "peronizing" the military, see Potash, *The Army and Politics, 1945–1962*, pp. 98–99, 107, 112, 115–18, 127; and Marvin Goldwert, *Democracy, Militarism, and Nationalism in Argentina, 1930–1966* (Austin: University of Texas Press, 1972), pp. 104, 111, 119, 126.

14. Perón demanded the death penalty for the 120 or so officers arrested, but the army's Superior Council only sentenced the ringleader, Gen. Benjamin Menéndez, to 15 years and his chief aides to sentences ranging from 3 to 6 years. The other officers were simply retired. Subsequently, a bomb exploded in the offices of the Superior Council and at the home of the Council's president. Congress meanwhile rushed a bill through making the death penalty mandatory for all future military rebels. See *HAR*, November 1951, p. 30. Perón denied ever demanding the death penalty in his autobiography, *Yo, Juan Domingo Perón*, ed. Luca de Tena et al., p. 224.

15. Orona, *La dictadura*, pp. 171–74; Potash, *The Army and Politics, 1945–1962*, pp. 140, 153–54, 158. The *HAR*, December 1951, p. 33, estimated that half of the Academy's entering class would be covered by these scholarships.

16. Goldwert, *Democracy, Militarism, and Nationalism*, p. 104; Raymond Estep, *The Argentine Armed Forces and Government* (Maxwell Air Force Base, 1970), p. 16; Arthur P. Whitaker, *Argentina* (Englewood Cliffs: Prentice-Hall, 1964), p. 129.

17. Goldwert, *Democracy, Militarism, and Nationalism*, pp. 113, 117–18, 129; Arthur P. Whitaker, *Argentine Upheaval* (New York: Praeger, 1956), pp. 8–9; *HAR*, July 1955, p. 284.

18. Joseph Page, *Perón, a Biography* (New York: Random House, 1983), pp. 317–18; Milciades Peña, *Industria, burguesía industrial, y liberación nacional* (Buenos Aires: Ediciones Fichas, 1974), pp. 153–55; Santos Martínez, *La Nueva Argentina*, 2:286; Whitaker, *Argentine Upheaval*, pp. 25–26.

19. See, for example, his letter of 12 June 1956 to John William Cooke, in *Perón/Cooke correspondencia* (Buenos Aires: Gránica Editor, 1972), 1:7

20. Juan José Real, *30 años de historia argentina* (Buenos Aires: Ediciones Actualidad, 1962), p. 163

21. *HAR*, October 1955, p. 431.

22. Marysa Navarro Gerassi, *Los nacionalistas* (Buenos Aires: Editorial Jorge Álvarez, 1968), pp. 109–12, 123–25, 179; Whitaker, *Argentine Upheaval*, pp. 48–49, 109.

23. *RRP*, 22 November 1955, pp. 21–22; Jorge Niosi, *Los empresarios y el estado argentino (1955–1969)* (Buenos Aires: Siglo Veintiuno Argentina Editores, 1974), pp. 42–47.

24. Luca de Tena et al., *Yo, Juan Domingo Perón*, p. 231.

25. Robert J. Alexander, *Labor Relations in Argentina, Brazil, and Chile* (New York: McGraw-Hill, 1962), p. 212; Samuel L. Baily, *Labor, Nationalism, and Politics in Argentina* (New Brunswick, N.J.: Rutgers University

Press, 1967), pp. 165–67; Miko Mandilovich, "Group Conflict and Political Change in Argentina, 1955–1966" (Ph.D. diss., University of Michigan, 1976), pp. 112–16.

26. Alexander, *Labor Relations in Argentina, Brazil, and Chile,* pp. 216–17; Baily, *Labor, Nationalism, and Politics,* p. 176; Peter Ranis, "Parties, Politics, and Peronism: A Study of Post-Perón Argentine Development" (Ph.D. diss., New York University, 1965), p. 38; Santiago Sénen González, *El sindicalismo después de Perón* (Buenos Aires: Editorial Galerna, 1971), p. 13; *HAR,* June 1956, p. 257.

27. Daniel James, "Rationalization and Working Class Response: The Context and Limits of Factory Floor Activity in Argentina," *Journal of Latin American Studies,* November 1981, pp. 390–91; Tomás Roberto Fillol, *Social Factors in Economic Development: The Argentine Case* (Cambridge: MIT Press, 1961), pp. 67–68.

28. *RRP,* 10 February 1956, p. 14.

29. Ibid., 11 October 1957, p. 13; *Panorama de Economía Argentina,* May 1957, pp. 12–13.

30. *RRP,* 11 October 1957, pp. 25–28.

31. *Confirmado,* 2 February 1967, p. 25.

32. On political blocs inside the labor movement at this time, see Edward C. Epstein, "Control and Co-Optation of the Argentine Labor Movement," *Economic Development and Cultural Change,* April 1979, p. 460; and *HAR,* April 1958, p. 168. For events at the convention, see Baily, *Labor, Nationalism, and Politics,* pp. 181–82; *HAR,* October 1957, p. 488; and John William Cooke's letter to Perón, 14 November 1957, in *Perón/Cooke,* 1:16.

33. Julie M. Taylor, *Eva Perón: The Myths of a Woman* (Chicago: University of Chicago Press, 1979), pp. 67–68.

34. Emílio Perina, *Detrás de la crisis* (Buenos Aires: Editorial Periplo, 1960), p. 46.

35. Américo Barrios, *Con Perón en el exilio: lo que nadie sabía* (Buenos Aires: Editorial Treinta Dias, 1964), p. 17.

36. Ricardo Guardó, *Horas difíciles* (Buenos Aires: Ricardo Guardó, 1963), pp. 59–61.

37. *Perón/Cooke,* 1:189.

38. Cooke to Perón, 28 August 1957, in ibid., pp. 273–305.

39. Perón to Antonio, 23 May 1957, quoted in Jorge Antonio, *Y ahora que?* (Buenos Aires: Ediciones Verum et Militia, 1966), pp. 336–52.

40. Perón to Cooke, 5 June 1957, in *Perón/Cooke,* 1:160–61. Cooke replied that Antonio was difficult to take because "he has the habit . . . of thinking he's infallible." See Cooke to Perón, no date, but between 11 and 21 June 1957, in *Perón/Cooke,* pp. 181–82. Emílio Perina, who met Antonio in Chile, thought he was egotistical to the point of outright lunacy. See *Detrás de la crisis,* p. 106. Finally, Perón to Cooke, 1 September 1957, in *Perón/Cooke,* 1:323; and Rodolfo Martínez, *Grandezas y miserías de Perón* (Mexico: Rodolfo Martínez, 1957), pp. 86–87.

41. Eduardo Zalduendo, *Geografía electoral de la Argentina* (Buenos Aires: Ediciones Áncora, 1958), pp. 31–32.

42. Ramón Prieto, *El pacto: 8 años de política argentina* (Buenos Aires: Editorial En Marcha, 1963), pp. 110–11.

43. Ricardo Guardó, *Horas difíciles*, pp. 109–11.

44. For the election results, see Dario Cantón, *Materiales para el estudio de la sociología política en la Argentina* (Buenos Aires: Instituto Torcuato Di Tella, 1968), 1:72, 196; and see Zalduendo, *Geografía electoral*, to compare them with 1957. Perón's contribution to Frondizi's victory was somewhat exaggerated by the national vote totals. In ten of twenty-three districts the UCRI's gains were less than 50 percent attributable to Peronist support, and in three others the drop in the blank vote exceeded the rise in the UCRI vote, implying that parties other than Frondizi's benefited. In all, a maximum of 73 percent of the UCRI's gain over 1957 could be attributed to Peronist support; the other 27 percent or more came from people who previously had voted for some other party, most likely one of the minor ones. See Paul H. Lewis, "The Durability of Personalist Followings: The Vargas and Perón Cases," *Polity*, Spring 1973, pp. 408–14.

## Chapter 11

1. Estanislao del Campo Wilson, *Confusión en la Argentina* (Buenos Aires: Editorial Guillermo Kraft, 1964), p. 68.

2. Charles Lewis Taylor and David A. Jodice, eds., *World Handbook of Political and Social Indicators*, 3d ed. (New Haven: Yale University Press, 1983), 2:16–106.

3. Taylor and Jodice, *World Handbook*, pp. 96–99.

4. Torcuato S. Di Tella, *Reflections on the Argentine Crisis: Are We at the End of an Epoch?* (Washington: American Enterprise Institute, 1982), p. 4. See also Gary W. Wynia, *Argentina in the Postwar Era: Politics and Economic Policymaking in a Divided Society* (Albuquerque: University of New Mexico Press, 1978), pp. 70, 119, 175; Richard D. Mallon and Juan V. Sourrouille, *Economic Policymaking in a Conflict Society: The Argentine Case* (Cambridge: Harvard University Press, 1975), pp. 34–35; and *HAR*, February 1963, p. 1148.

5. *RRP*, 30 April 1962, pp. 133–34.

6. *Análisis*, 3 November 1970, p. 20. Guido did not actually dissolve Congress right away, but simply declared it to be in recess. Formal dissolution did not occur until 6 September, when another hardliner revolt forced him to take this last step.

7. Mallon and Sourrouille, *Economic Policymaking*, pp. 34–35, 114.

8. Carlos Sánchez Viamonte, "Introducción a los poderes del gobierno," *Argentina, 1930–1960* (Buenos Aires: SUR), pp. 101–7.

9. On national character, see E. A. C. Wetzler, "National Character and the Crisis," *RRP*, 20 November 1964, pp. 289–90; *Análisis*, 3 November 1970, p. 20; Mallon and Sourrouille, *Economic Policymaking*, p. 166.

10. Peter Snow, "Judges and Generals: The Role of the Argentine Supreme

Court During Periods of Military Government," *Jahrbuch des Offentlichen Rechts der Gegenwart* (1975) 24:610.

11. Snow, "Judges and Generals," pp. 611–12.

12. *PP*, 5 July 1966, p. 36.

13. Snow, "Judges and Generals," p. 615. See also articles 3, 5, and 9 of the Charter of the Revolution, in *RRP*, 13 July 1966, pp. 22–23.

14. Snow, "Judges and Generals," p. 616–17.

15. Ezequiel Martínez Estrada, *X-Ray of the Pampa*, trans. Alain Swietlicki (Austin: University of Texas Press, 1971), p. 179.

16. Benjamin Most, "Authoritarianism and the Growth of the State in Latin America, an Assessment of Their Impacts on Argentine Public Policy, 1930–1970," *Journal of Comparative Political Studies*, July 1980, p. 101.

17. *RRP*, 21 July 1959, pp. 23–24, 41–42; and 31 August 1959, pp. 11–12. Dismissed employees would be able to appeal and would have the right to severance pay.

18. Ibid., 11 April 1961, pp. 5–10.

19. James Edward Zinser, "Alternative Means of Satisfying Petroleum Demand: Importation, Government Production, or Foreign Private Contractual Production" (Ph.D. diss., University of Oregon, 1967), p. 107; Salvador Treber, *La empresa estatal* (Buenos Aires: Ediciones Macchi, 1968), pp. 84, 87–91; *Panorama de la Economía Argentina*, 1st trimester, 1970, pp. 229–34.

20. *RRP*, 12 December 1961, pp. 16–17. The government still encouraged voluntary resignations with severance pay, and in fact some 35,700 workers accepted those terms.

21. There were approximately 256,000 public school teachers, 90 percent of whom were in primary or secondary schools, based on estimates from Thomas E. Weil et al., eds., *Area Handbook for Argentina* (Washington: U.S. Government Printing Office, 1974), p. 124. The total strength of the armed forces was around 137,000, a figure that had not changed appreciably since Aramburu left office. See Weil et al., *Area Handbook*, p. 391; Curtin Winsor, "The National Security and Armament Policies of Argentina" (Ph.D. diss., The American University, 1971), p. 284; Raymond Estep, *The Argentine Armed Forces and Government* (Maxwell Air Force Base, 1970), pp. 75–76; and David L. Feldman, "Argentina, 1945–1971: Military Assistance, Military Spending, and the Political Activity of the Armed Forces," *Journal of Inter-American Studies and World Affairs*, August 1982, p. 328.

22. N. Ericksson, "Wages, Salaries, Prices—And the Leap in the Dark," *RRP*, 12 August 1969, pp. 189–92; also *RRP*, 30 September 1969, p. 469. See also Juan Carlos de Pablo, *Política antiinflacionaria en la Argentina, 1967–1970* (Buenos Aires: Amorrortu Editores, 1970), pp. 41, 126; and Beba Balve et al., *Los asalariados: composición social y orientaciones organizativas: materiales para su estudio* (Buenos Aires: Centro de Investigaciones en Ciencias Sociales, 1975), pp. 225–27.

23. *PP*, 4 July 1967, pp. 18–19; and 28 January 1969, p. 10. Frondizi had reduced railway personnel from 211,000 to 176,000, and Guido reduced it

further to 149,000. But the Illia administration used the railroads for political patronage and increased the work force to 172,500.

24. *PP*, 4 July 1967, p. 20; 30 January 1968, p. 18; Kenneth Johnson, *Argentina's Mosaic of Discord, 1966–1968* (Washington: Institute for the Comparative Study of Political Systems, 1969), p. 22; Salvador Treber, *La empresa estatal*, p. 80; *Panorama de la Economía Argentina*, 1st trimester, 1970, pp. 229–34.

25. *RRP*, 31 January 1974, p. 114. A study by the ECLA has shown that state enterprises in the manufacturing, commercial, transport, and communications sectors had their personnel trimmed sharply between 1960 and 1970; but those cuts were more than offset by the addition of jobs in state enterprises in the areas of petroleum, coal, electricity, gas, and banking. Unfortunately, ECLA did not disaggregate civil service employees in the national, provincial, and municipal governments, but there was a steady annual rise, from 1950 to 1974, in the total number of bureaucrats (as opposed to employees in state enterprises). See ECLA, *La empresa publica en la economía: la experiencia argentina* (Santiago de Chile: ECLA, 1983), pp. 21, 25, 29.

26. Túlio Alberto Ceconi, *La economía argentina: un análisis de su funcionamiento* (Buenos Aires: El Ateneo Editores, 1975), pp. 55–56, 67–69; Treber, *La empresa estatal*, p. 2; Guillermo S. Edelberg, "Managerial Resource Development in Argentina," in *Latin American Management, Development and Performance*, ed. Robert R. Rehder (Reading, Mass.: Addison-Wesley, 1968), p. 45.

27. Zinser, "Alternative Means," pp. 107, 167–68; *Panorama de la Economía Argentina*, Spring 1960, pp. 113, 117, 119, 128–29, 263; Carl Solberg, *Oil and Nationalism in Argentina* (Stanford: Stanford University Press, 1979), p. 175.

28. Zinser, "Alternative Means," pp. 69, 101.

29. In 1976 it was estimated that 1.7 million tons of steel was imported at a cost of $295 billion, which works out to $173.50 a ton. In that same year the government subsidized steel exports, which were quoted at $210 a ton for steel bars and $310 for steel plate, which presumably meant that local steel consumers were paying much more. In 1978 the Association of Automobile Manufacturers complained that its members were paying 300 percent more for steel than auto manufacturers in the United States or Japan. See Ernest Arthur Boas, *Latin America's Steel Industry, Present and Future* (Berlin: Duncker & Humbolt, 1968), pp. 85, 88; Juan Manuel Checa de Codes, *La industria siderugica en hispanoamerica* (Madrid: Ediciones Cultura Hispanica, 1953), pp. 17–18; Ronald H. Chilcote, "Integrated Iron and Steel Industry for Argentina?" *Inter-American Economic Affairs*, Spring 1963, pp. 33–36; Ernest J. Wilkins, "The Industrial Aspects of Argentina's Five-Year Plan: Why It Did Not Succeed" (Ph.D. diss., Stanford University, 1953), p. 133; *Análisis*, 2 October 1961, pp. 5–7; *Mercado*, 22 November 1974, pp. 32–34; and 25 November 1976, p. 30; *Confirmado*, 28 September 1978, pp. 12–13.

30. *PP*, 7 March 1967, pp. 49–50; *Mercado*, 19 December 1974, pp. 90–94; *Periscópio*, 6 January 1970, pp. 20–22. Rocca asked for a two-and-a-half-year exemption from sales taxes and import duties, plus a monopoly in supplying Fabricaciones Militares with certain steel products as part of the deal.

31. *Mercado*, 22 April 1971, p. 18; 23 March 1972, p. 15; and 30 March 1972, pp. 40–42; *PP*, 14 September 1971, p. 19; *SOMOS*, 17 July 1981, pp. 54–55.

32. *Mercado*, 30 March 1972, p. 42; *Análisis Confirmado*, 2 January 1973, p. 24; *SOMOS*, 17 July 1981, pp. 54–55.

33. *PP*, 9 September 1966, pp. 18–19.

34. Ibid., 9 September 1966, pp. 18–19.

35. Frondizi attempted some privatization by selling 32 of DINIE's 39 companies. Illia stopped further sales, but they resumed under Ongania, who sold the remaining companies. See Treber, *La empresa estatal*, pp. 3, 60–68; *PP*, 9 September 1966, p. 17; *RRP*, 30 June 1958, pp. 9–11; 22 July 1958, p. 34; 31 July 1958, p. 37.

36. *PP*, 21 March 1972, p. 19.

37. Mario S. Brodersohn, "Elasticidad-Ingreso del impuesto a la renta en la Argentina," *Desarrollo Económico*, January–March 1964, p. 576; *Periscópio*, 23 December 1969, p. 24.

38. ECLA, *Economic Development and Income Redistribution in Argentina* (New York: United Nations, 1969), pp. 143–44. Also, *RRP*, 10 April 1963, p. 509; and 10 August 1963, p. 212. This latter source estimated that more than half of all income taxes due were not paid and that the evaders were mostly middle income groups.

39. *RRP*, 30 March 1963, pp. 429–30.

40. Ibid., 9 June 1964, p. 50; 7 July 1964, p. 50.

41. *PP*, 3 May 1966, p. 58; 25 October 1966, p. 20; and 8 November 1966, p. 61.

42. Ibid., 18 July 1967, p. 19; Jorge Niosi, *Los empresarios y el estado argentino (1955–1969)* (Buenos Aires: Siglo Veintiuno Argentina Editores, 1974), pp. 151–52.

43. Wynia, *Argentina in the Postwar Era*, pp. 181–82; Carlos Ramil Cepeda, *Crisis de una burguesía dependiente: balance económico de la "Revolución Argentina," 1966–1971* (Buenos Aires: Ediciones La Rosa Blindada, 1972), pp. 76, 84–87; *PP*, 26 November 1968, pp. 22–23; *RRP*, 11 January 1969, pp. 12–14, 20–21; 13 May 1969, p. 645; 31 May 1969, pp. 765–67; 11 December 1969, p. 909; 21 August 1970, p. 260. "Retentions" required that exporters turn over a certain percentage (normally 20 percent) of their foreign exchange earnings to the Central Bank for pesos at the official, not the free market, rate. See *RRP*, 20 September 1957, pp. 9–13; 21 January 1958, pp. 19–21; and Organization of American States, Secretary General of the Pan American Union, *Sistemas tributarias de América Latina: Argentina* (Washington: Pan American Union, 1966), pp. 3, 90. "Retentions" were first imposed by Aramburu in 1957.

44. Robert Lucas, "Recent Developments in the Argentine Pension Pro-

gram," *Social Security Bulletin*, June 1968, pp. 14–16; RRP, 11 November 1963, pp. 211–13; 31 August 1970, p. 335.

45. RRP, 11 November 1963, p. 213; 22 July 1970, pp. 79–80.

## Chapter 12

1. For the full text of the Prebisch report translated into English, see RRP, 31 October 1955, pp. 25–35; and 11 November 1955, pp. 19–30.

2. John M. Frikart, "The Effects of the Perón Regime on the Argentine Economy" (Ph.D. diss., University of Colorado, 1959), pp. 128–29; Eprime Eshag and Rosemary Thorpe, "Las consequencias económicas y sociales de las políticas económicas ortodoxas aplicadas en la República Argentina durante los años de post-guerra," *Desarrollo Económico*, January–March 1965, pp. 306, 308; ECLA, *Economic Development and Income Distribution in Argentina* (New York: United Nations, 1969), pp. 252–53; Jorge Niosi, *Los empresarios y el estado argentino (1955–1969)* (Buenos Aires: Siglo Veintiuno Argentina Editores, 1974), p. 22; Samuel L. Baily, *Labor, Nationalism, and Politics in Argentina* (New Brunswick, N.J.: Rutgers University Press, 1967), p. 174; Marysa Navarro Gerassi, *Los nacionalistas* (Buenos Aires: Editorial Jorge Álvarez, 1968), pp. 217–18; RRP, 22 March 1957, p. 22; 20 September 1957, pp. 9–13; and 21 January 1958, pp. 19–21.

3. Adolfo Dorfman, *Cincuenta años de industrialización en la Argentina, 1930–1980: desarrollo y perspectivas* (Buenos Aires: Ediciones Solar, 1983), pp. 586–87.

4. Guillermo O'Donnell, *Modernization and Bureaucratic Authoritarianism* (Berkeley: Institute of International Studies, University of California, 1973), pp. 141–42; Niosi, *Los empresarios*, pp. 56–59; HAR, February 1959, p. 693; March 1959, pp. 49, 52–53; April 1959, p. 112; and May 1959, p. 167; RRP, 10 May 1962, pp. 193–95; 31 May 1962, p. 337; and 22 June 1962, pp. 468–69.

5. RRP, 22 May 1962, pp. 258–59.

6. Emílio Perina, *Detrás de la crisis* (Buenos Aires: Editorial Periplo, 1960), p. 168.

7. Juan Carlos de Pablo, *Política antiinflacionaria en la Argentina, 1967–1970* (Buenos Aires: Amorrortú, 1970), pp. 14–16, 110–11, 114; Carlos Ramil Cepeda, *Crisis de una burguesía dependiente: balance económico de la "Revolución Argentina," 1966–1971* (Buenos Aires: Ediciones La Rosa Blindada, 1972), pp. 13–14, 18–21, 39–43, 45.

8. See, for example, the essay by Alfredo Gómez Morales in Ministerio de Economía, Comisión Honoraria de Reactivación Industrial, *Informe sobre la industria argentina y los medios para su reactivación* Appendix II (Buenos Aires, 1963), p. 5.

9. RRP, 7 February 1964, p. 204.

10. Ibid., 17 February 1964, pp. 199–204; and 29 February 1964, pp. 249–50.

11. Argentine Republic, Presidencia, *Argentine Economic Policy* (Buenos

Aires, 1967), pp. 11–29; de Pablo, *Política antiinflacionaria*, pp. 24–25, 31–32, 35–40; Niosi, *Los empresarios*, p. 146–47; Richard D. Mallon and Juan V. Sourrouille, *Economic Policymaking in a Conflict Society: The Argentine Case* (Cambridge: Harvard University Press, 1975), p. 30; *RRP*, 21 March 1967, pp. 367, 377–80, 387.

12. Argentine Republic, *Argentine Economic Policy*, p. 29.

13. Guillermo O'Donnell, "Comentario a la nota de M. Brodersohn," *Desarrollo Ecónomico*, October–December 1973, p. 611; de Pablo, *Política antiinflacionaria*, p. 119; Ramil Cepeda, *Crisis de una burguesía*, pp. 68, 73–74; Niosi, *Los empresarios*, p. 149; *Periscópio*, 4 August 1970, p. 25; *RRP*, 30 January 1971, p. 138.

14. Niosi, *Los empresarios*, p. 151; *Panorama de la Economía Argentina*, 2d trimester 1970, p. 278; Banco Central, *Boletín estadística*, 1965–1969; *RRP*, 22 September 1970, p. 454.

15. Raymond Estep, *The Argentine Armed Forces and Government* (Maxwell Air Force Base, 1970), pp. 52–53; *Análisis*, 9 January 1967, pp. 8–10; 16 January 1967, pp. 12–15; 6 February 1967, pp. 16–20; and 19 February 1969, pp. 6–7; *Confirmado*, 3 November 1966, p. 25.

16. Francis Lambert, *Planning for Administrative Reform in Latin America: The Argentine and Brazilian Cases* (Glasgow: University of Glasgow Press, 1971), pp. 7–8; *PP*, 12 September 1967, p. 13; 20 February 1968, pp. 15–19; and 30 April 1968, pp. 13–14; *Quarterly Economic Report*, February 1967, pp. 1–3.

17. *PP*, 14 May 1968, pp. 20–22; and 27 August 1968, pp. 13–15.

18. Ibid., 13 May 1969, pp. 8–11; and 20 May 1969, p. 36.

19. *RRP*, 11 June 1969, pp. 829–30.

20. Perón to Frigerio, 18 June 1969, in Ramón Prieto, *Correspondencia Perón/Frigerio, 1958–1973* (Buenos Aires: Editorial Machacha Güemes, 1975), p. 87.

21. Adriana N. Bianchi, "The Politics of Economic Policy Making: A Case Study of Argentina" (Ph.D. diss., University of Texas, 1978), p. 135.

22. *RRP*, 31 August 1970, pp. 318–20; and 23 October 1970, p. 629.

23. *PP*, 28 September 1971, p. 18; *RRP*, 11 August 1972, pp. 190–91; and 31 October 1972, p. 656.

24. Aldo Ferrer, *The Argentine Economy* (Berkeley: University of California Press, 1967), pp. 160–61. See also Ramil Cepeda, *Crisis de una burguesía*, pp. 13–14, 45; and Miguel Teubal, "Policy and Performance of Agriculture in Economic Development: The Case of Argentina" (Ph.D. diss., University of California, 1975), pp. 6–7, for similar views.

25. ECLA, *Economic Development and Income Distribution in Argentina* (New York: United Nations, 1969), pp. 28, 31, 34; Saturnino M. Zemborain, *La verdad sobre la propriedad de la tierra en la Argentina* (Buenos Aires: Sociedad Rural Argentina, 1973), pp. 45–46. A form of entail (perhaps) did make its appearance in the mid-twentieth century with the frequent incorporation of family holdings by Argentina's rural elites. This was a way of avoiding inheritance or gift taxes, and it also kept the family estates intact because, according to the law, land owned by a corporation could not be

divided or sold off unless three-fourths of the voting shares approved. See Zemborain, *La verdad*, pp. 33–34, 46.

26. Zemborain, *La verdad*, pp. 36–39, 49, 52–55; RRP, 12 September 1968, p. 363.

27. Zemborain, *La verdad*, pp. 33–34, 38; RRP, 19 November 1965, pp. 280–81, for the CONADE report.

28. Zemborain, *La verdad*, p. 2; Dirección Nacional de Estadística y Censos, *Censo nacional agropecuario* (Buenos Aires, 1963), 1:1, 52; *Statistical Abstract for Latin America, 1970* (Los Angeles: U.C.L.A. Latin American Center, 1971), pp. 194–95; RRP, 9 February 1960, p. 7; 30 March 1963, p. 425; and 22 April 1966, p. 73.

29. Mallon and Sourrouille, *Economic Policymaking*, p. 92.

30. José Alfredo Martínez de Hoz, *La agricultura y la ganadería argentina en el periódo 1930–1960* (Buenos Aires: Editorial Sudamericana, 1967), pp. 58, 70–82; Colin Lewis, "Anglo-Argentine Trade, 1945–1965," in *Argentina in the Twentieth Century*, ed. David Rock (Pittsburgh: University of Pittsburgh Press, 1975), p. 122; Consejo Técnico de Inversiones, *La economía argentina* (Buenos Aires: Consejo Técnico de Inversiones, 1962), p. 229; *Camoatí*, January 1959, pp. 15–16; RRP, 30 October 1956, p. 15; 9 November 1956, pp. 9–10; and 29 April 1958, p. 27.

31. RRP, 21 January 1958, pp. 19–21. For the impact of Aramburu's policies on agricultural production, see RRP, 7 February 1959, p. 7; 9 February 1960, p. 7; 20 October 1961, p. 15; and 19 February 1966, p. 228.

32. Ibid., 9 June 1959, pp. 21–22.

33. United Nations, *Statistical Yearbook*, 1958–1962; RRP, 13 January 1961, p. 7; and 20 October 1961, p. 15.

34. RRP, 27 October 1970, pp. 19–20.

35. Clarence Zuvekas, "Argentine Economic Policy, 1958–1962: The Frondizi Government's Development Plan," *Inter-American Economic Affairs*, Summer 1968, pp. 68–69; Consejo Técnico de Inversiones, *La economía argentina*, 1962, p. 229; RRP, 31 July 1959, pp. 9–13.

36. Niosi, *Los empresarios*, p. 102.

37. Ibid., p. 128; PP, 9 June 1964, p. 47; 21 July 1964, p. 49.

38. RRP, 21 April 1967, pp. 71–72; 22 July 1967, pp. 77–81; 31 July 1967, pp. 151–54; and 22 July 1968, p. 79.

39. Ramil Cepeda, *Crisis de una burguesía*, p. 69; United Nations, *Statistical Yearbook*, 1965–1969; INDEC, *Boletín estadística*, 1966–1969; RRP, 11 December 1969, p. 909; 21 August 1970, p. 260.

40. RRP, 22 September 1970, p. 443; and 20 March 1971, pp. 389–90.

41. Ibid., 31 March 1971, pp. 454–57.

## Chapter 13

1. Juan V. Sourrouille, *Impact of Transnational Enterprises on Employment and Income: The Case of Argentina* (Geneva: International Labor Office, 1976), pp. 6, 8–9, 25; Túlio Alberto Ceconi, *La economía argentina:*

*un análisis de su funcionamiento* (Buenos Aires: Libreria El Ateneo Editores, 1975), p. 59; Miguel Khavisse and Juan Piotskowski, "La consolidación hegemónica de los factores extranacionales: el caso de 'las cien empresas industriales mas grandes,' " in Jorge Abot et al., *El poder económico en la Argentina* (Buenos Aires: Centro de Investigaciones en Ciencias Sociales, 1973), pp. 78, 81; *Panorama de la Economía Argentina*, 2d trimester 1970, pp. 257–65.

2. *RRP*, 11 November 1955, p. 20; See also James W. Foley, "Balance of Payments and Import Substituting Industrialization in Argentina, 1945–1961" (Ph.D. diss., Michigan State University, 1969), pp. 39–50.

3. *La Nación*, 2 July 1961, quoted in Guido Di Tella, *Argentina Under Perón, 1973–1976* (New York: St. Martin's, 1983), p. 23.

4. Fundación de Investigaciones Económicas Latinoamericanas (FIEL), *Las inversiones extranjeras en la Argentina* (Buenos Aires: FIEL, 1971), pp. 233–37; *HAR*, December 1958, p. 574.

5. Sourrouille, *Impact*, pp. 13, 33–34; Ceconi, *La economía argentina*, pp. 25–27, 34–37, 68; FIEL, *Las inversiones*, p. 40; Oscar Altmir, Horacio Santamaria, and Juan Sourrouille, "Los instrumentos de la promoción industrial en la postguerra," *Desarrollo Económico*, October–December 1967, pp. 372–74; Jorge Niosi, *Los empresarios y el estado argentino (1955–1969)* (Buenos Aires: Siglo Veintiuno Argentina Editores, 1974), pp. 72–73; *PP*, 3 September 1968, pp. 60–61 (based on a study by Javier Villanueva).

6. For the terms of these contracts, see Gertrude Edwards, "The Frondizi Contracts and Petroleum Self-Sufficiency in Argentina," in Raymond F. Mikesell et al., *Foreign Investment in the Petroleum and Mineral Industries* (Baltimore: Johns Hopkins University Press, 1971), pp. 157–88. See also *PP*, 9 March 1945, p. 53; and *HAR*, July–December 1958.

7. Richard D. Mallon and Juan V. Sourrouille, *Economic Policymaking in a Conflict Society: The Argentine Case* (Cambridge: Harvard University Press, 1975), p. 21.

8. Percy D. Warner, "The Impact of the Service of the Foreign Debt on the Monetary Structure in Argentina, 1955–1965" (Ph.D. diss., Michigan State University, 1970), p. 6, based on the annual *Memoria* of the Central Bank.

9. Clarence Zuvekas, "Argentine Economic Policy, 1958–1962: The Frondizi Government's Development Plan," *Inter-American Economic Affairs*, Summer 1968, p. 55; and his "Economic Growth and Income Distribution in Postwar Argentina," *Inter-American Economic Affairs*, Winter 1966, pp. 31–33. Also, *RRP*, 20 October 1962, p. 76; 22 May 1963, p. 268; and 22 September 1970, p. 454.

10. Sourrouille, *Impact*, pp. 6, 8–9, 15.

11. Ibid., *Impact*, pp. 36–40, 66, 83, 88; Elsa Cimillio et al., "Un proceso de sustitución de importaciones con inversiones extranjeros: el caso argentino," in Abot et al., *El poder económico*, pp. 64–65.

12. Edwards, "The Frondizi Contracts," pp. 178–79.

13. Carl Solberg, *Oil and Nationalism in Argentina* (Stanford: Stanford University Press, 1979), p. 173; Edwards, "The Frondizi Contracts," pp. 182, 188; James E. Zinser, "Alternative Means of Meeting Argentina's Petroleum

Demand: Importation, Government Production, or Foreign Private Contractual Production" (Ph.D. diss., University of Oregon, 1967), p. 76.

14. Edwards, "The Frondizi Contracts," p. 185; Solberg, *Oil and Nationalism*, p. 173; PP, 30 January 1968, p. 22.

15. Sourrouille, *Impact*, pp. 60, 73.

16. Niosi, *Los empresarios*, p. 215; Warner, "Impact of the Service," pp. 2, 62–72, 79; Banco Central, *Boletín estadística, 1958–1973*; *Mercado*, 27 January 1972, pp. 18–19; and 14 December 1972, pp. 66–68; *Veritas*, 15 July 1973, p. 12; and 15 December 1975, p. 81; *Competencia*, May 1973, p. 2.

17. Banco Central, *Boletín estadístico*, supplement to the March 1973 issue.

18. Ezequiel Martínez Estrada, *X-Ray of the Pampa*, trans. by Alain Swietlicki (Austin: University of Texas Press, 1971), p. 361.

19. Sourrouille, *Impact*, pp. 53–55.

20. PP, 3 September 1968, p. 67.

21. Ceconi, *La economía argentina*, p. 41; PP, 3 September 1968, p. 57.

22. On the Argentine cigarette industry and denationalization, see Business International Corporation, *Solving Latin America's Business Problems* (New York, 1968), pp. 31–32; PP, 30 July 1963, p. 58; 23 January 1968, pp. 21–23; 20 August 1968, p. 68; and 1 April 1969, p. 16; RRP, 31 January 1970, pp. 113–15.

23. This description of the bureaucratic process is from PP, 18 July 1967, pp. 22–23.

24. Rogelio García Lupo, *Contra la ocupación extranjera* (Buenos Aires: Editorial Centro, 1971), pp. 35–36. Ongania acted too late, however, to prevent Acindar from selling its auto parts subsidiary, Acinfer, to the Ford Motor Company.

25. Jorge Schvarzer, "Estrategia industrial y grandes empresas: el caso argentino," *Desarrollo Económico*, October–December 1978, pp. 320–21; PP, 13 May 1969, p. 16; and 20 April 1971, p. 16; *Periscópio*, 30 December 1969, p. 79; RRP, 22 May 1973, pp. 718–19.

26. Pepe Treviño, *La carne podrida: crónica en torno de la quiebra Swift-Deltec* (Buenos Aires: Ediciones del Salto, 1972), pp. 7, 12, 15, 93, 121; PP, 8 December 1970, p. 24, has slightly different figures: $12.7 million to foreign bankers, $20 million to local creditors, and $10.5 million to other Deltec International subsidiaries.

27. Junta Nacional de Carnes, *Swift, DELTEC y las carnes argentinas* (Buenos Aires: Editorial El Coloquio, 1974), pp. 78–79; Carlos Alconada Aramburu, *El caso Swift-Deltec* (Buenos Aires: La Ley, 1973), p. 18.

28. Clair William Matz, Jr., "Argentine Interest Groups: The Export Beef Sector, 1958–1968" (Ph.D. diss., University of Virginia, 1970), pp. 118–21, 125–28; Colin Lewis, "Anglo-Argentine Trade, 1945–1965," in *Argentina in the Twentieth Century*, ed. David Rock (Pittsburgh: University of Pittsburgh Press, 1975), p. 21; PP, 8 June 1965, pp. 68–70; RRP, 22 April 1963, p. 93; 21 May 1964, pp. 257–59; 20 August 1965, p. 277; 10 September 1965, p. 400; *Camoatí*, October 1951, English language supplement, p. ii.

29. Matz, "Argentine Interest Groups, pp. 165–96; *PP*, 5 March 1968, p. 21; 23 April 1968, p. 23; and 6 May 1969, p. 15; *Periscópio*, 26 May 1970, pp. 78–81; *RRP*, 12 February 1968, p. 196; 29 February 1968, p. 246, 301–2; 12 March 1968, p. 331; 22 April 1968, pp. 567–68; and 12 August 1968, pp. 184–86.

30. *PP*, 13 October 1970, p. 22.

31. Treviño, *La carne podrida*, pp. 59, 61–62, 67; *PP*, 13 October 1970, pp. 22–26; 20 October 1970, p. 25; and 17 November 1970, pp. 30–31; *Periscópio*, 14 July 1970, p. 25; *Competencia*, 22 January 1971, p. 11; *RRP*, 10 July 1970, p. 21; and 31 July 1970, pp. 135–36.

32. Treviño, *La carne podrida*, p. 43; Junta Nacional de Carnes, *Swift*, p. 21.

33. Junta Nacional de Carnes, *Swift*, pp. 23, 67–68.

34. Treviño, *La carne podrida*, pp. 69–79, 82.

35. Ibid., pp. 122–23.

36. Ibid., pp. 166–173; *PP*, 16 November 1971, p. 13.

37. Junta Nacional de Carnes, *Swift*, pp. 24–25.

38. *RRP*, 28 February 1973, p. 277. See also Schvarzer, "Estrategia industrial," p. 331.

## Chapter 14

1. Guido Di Tella, "La Argentina económica, 1943–1982," in *1943–1982, Historia política argentina*, ed. Carlos A. Floria (Buenos Aires: Editorial del Belgrano, 1983), pp. 177, 187.

2. James Bruce, *Those Perplexing Argentines* (New York: Longman's, Green, 1953), p. 52.

3. Tomás Roberto Fillol, *Social Factors in Economic Development: The Argentine Case* (Cambridge: MIT Press, 1961), p. 75. But see also pp. 1–26, 57–61, 73–74.

4. Marcos Kaplan, "El estado empresario en la Argentina," *Aportes*, October 1968, p. 38.

5. Ricardo B. Mandelbaum, "Sectoral Distribution of U.S. Private Direct Foreign Investment in Manufacturing Industries of Argentina, Colombia, and Ecuador: Its Determinants" (Ph.D. diss., University of Pennsylvania, 1979), pp. 56–61.

6. Eduardo Zalduendo, *El empresario industrial en la Argentina* (Buenos Aires: Instituto Torcuato Di Tella, 1963).

7. John William Freels, *El sector industrial en la política nacional* (Buenos Aires: Editorial Universitaria de Buenos Aires, 1970), pp. 83–91, 111, 113, 119–21, 125, 147–48, 150–51, 153, 160.

8. Alberto Sánchez Crespo, "La burguesía industrial y el desarrollo de la Argentina," *Revista Latinoamericana de Sociología*, July 1968, pp. 210–33.

9. James Petras and Thomas C. Cook, "Componentes de la acción política: el ejecutivo industrial argentino," *Desarrollo Económico*, July–September 1972, pp. 389, 391–96.

542 Notes to Pages 334–40

10. Ruth Sautu and Catalina Wainerman, *El empresario y la inovación: un estudio de las disposiciones de un grupo de dirigentes de empresas argentinas hacia el cambio tecnológico* (Buenos Aires: Instituto Torcuato Di Tella, 1971).

11. Frederick C. Turner, "Entrepreneurs and *Estancieros* in Perón's Argentina: Cohesion and Conflict Within the Elite," in *Juan Perón and the Reshaping of Argentina*, ed. Frederick C. Turner and José Enrique Miguens (Pittsburgh: University of Pittsburgh Press, 1983), pp. 223–36.

12. Besides the 1963 and 1974 censuses, see Bolsa de Comércio de Buenos Aires, *Agro e industria en la Argentina* (Buenos Aires: Bolsa de Comércio, 1980), pp. 80–85, 87–88.

13. On Imperial Germany, see: W. O. Henderson, *The Rise of German Industrial Power, 1834–1914* (Berkeley: University of California Press, 1975); J. H. Clapham, *The Economic Development of France and Germany* (Cambridge: Cambridge University Press, 1968); Theodore S. Hamerow, *The Social Foundations of German Unification, 1858–1871*, 2 vols. (Princeton: Princeton University Press, 1969); Thorstein Veblen, *Imperial Germany and the Industrial Revolution* (Ann Arbor: University of Michigan Press, 1939). On Imperial Japan, see: William W. Lockwood, ed., *The State and Economic Enterprise in Japan* (Princeton: Princeton University Press, 1965); Jon Livingston et al., eds., *Imperial Japan, 1800–1945* (New York: Pantheon Books, 1973); Robert E. Ward, ed., *Political Development in Modern Japan* (Princeton: Princeton University Press, 1968).

14. *PP*, 18 December 1962, pp. 56–57. See also interviews carried out through the Instituto Torcuato Di Tella Oral History Project with Leandro Anidjar, former assistant director of SIAM's economic and financial section (22 June 1973), and Guido Clutterbuck, former president of SIAM (January 1973).

15. *PP*, 4 August 1964, p. 55.

16. Oscar Altmir, Horacio Santamaria, and Juan Sourrouille, "Los instrumentos de la promoción industrial en la postguerra," *Desarrollo Económico*, April–June 1966, p. 104; *PP*, 30 November 1965, p. 14.

17. *PP*, 14 September 1965, p. 69; and 20 April 1966, p. 60; *RRP*, 30 September 1965, p. 535; and 9 February 1966, pp. 170–71.

18. *PP*, 21 March 1967, p. 52; 9 August 1967, p. 57; and 24 October 1967, pp. 22–23; *Competencia*, May–June 1972, p. 29; *Quarterly Economic Report*, January 1972, p. 11.

19. *RRP*, 26 February 1982, pp. 207–8.

20. Lonardi abolished the CGE under pressure, and in the following year Aramburu outlawed it altogether and also decreed that some 1,000 formerly prominent officers could never again hold office in any employers' association. Only the national organization was affected, however. The CGE's provincial federations escaped, to become the roots for this new flourishing. Meanwhile, in 1957 the UIA held its first elections since Perón's dissolution of it and chose Pascual Gambino as its president. Gambino led the victorious anti-Peronist ticket in 1946, which provoked the dissolution. Robert J. Alexander, *Labor Relations in Argentina, Brazil, and Chile* (New York:

McGraw-Hill, 1962), p. 218; Dardo Cuneo, *Comportamiento y crisis de la clase empresaria* (Buenos Aires: Editorial Pleamar, 1967), pp. 231–32; Freels, *El sector industrial*, pp. 35–37; Jorge Niosi, *Los empresarios y el estado argentino (1955–1969)* (Buenos Aires: Siglo Veintiuno Argentina Editores, 1974), p. 40.

21. *RRP*, 31 October 1972, p. 657. On the relative size and representativeness of the two organizations, see also Mónica Peralta Ramos, *Acumulación de capital y crisis política en Argentina (1930–1974)* (Mexico: Siglo Veintiuno Editores, 1978), p. 244; and *PP*, 20 November 1962, p. 59.

22. *UIA, Guía de socios* (Buenos Aires: UIA, 1970), p. 1; *PP*, 3 September 1963, pp. 64, 66.

23. José Luís De Imaz, *Los que mandan* (Buenos Aires: Editorial Universitaria de Buenos Aires, 1972), pp. 126–38; Niosi, *Los empresarios*, p. 77, 79–80; Cuneo, *Comportamiento y crisis*, pp. 254, 257–76; Freels, *El sector industrial*, pp. 54–58, 61–63, 65–67, 80, 86–89; *Veritas*, 15 March 1965, pp. 22–23.

24. *PP*, 19 March 1963, pp. 48–49; *Veritas*, 15 March 1965, p. A27.

25. Freels, *El sector industrial*, pp. 83–96, 125, 147–48, 150–51, 153, 160. On the impact of Krieger Vasena's policies on UIA attitudes, see Roque Caggiano, *Notas sobre el desarrollo de la burguesía nacional: la Confederación General de la Industria y la Unión Industrial en el periódo 1957–1973* (Buenos Aires: Instituto Torcuato Di Tella, 1975), pp. 82–87.

26. Caggiano, *Notas*, pp. 54–60, 91–92, 94; *Mercado*, 26 October 1972, pp. 16, 18, 20.

27. Peralta Ramos, *Acumulación de capital*, p. 246.

28. Ibid., pp. 246–47; *Mercado*, 26 October 1972, p. 22; *RRP*, 20 October 1972, p. 597.

29. De Imaz, *Los que mandan*, pp. 126–38.

30. Zalduendo, *El empresario industrial*, pp. 8–15; Petras and Cook, "Componentes," p. 389; Turner, "Entrepreneurs," pp. 232–33.

31. Thomas C. Cochran and Ruben Reina, *Capitalism in Argentine Culture: A Study of Torcuato Di Tella and SIAM* (Philadelphia: University of Pennsylvania Press, 1971), pp. 254–55; *Mercado*, 11 December 1975, pp. 96–100; and 20 April 1972, pp. 32–34.

32. Daniel Azpiazu, Eduardo M. Basualdo, and Miguel Khavisse, *El nuevo poder económico en la Argentina de los años 80* (Buenos Aires: Editorial Legasa, 1986), pp. 141–42; *PP*, 30 April 1963, pp. 2–3; 14 May 1963, p. 8; 11 June 1963, p. 6; and 15 July 1969, p. 24.

33. Naum Minsburg, *Multinacionales en la Argentina* (Buenos Aires: Editorial Quipó, 1976), pp. 152–70; *Mercado*, 19 December 1974, pp. 90–94.

34. *PP*, 7 December 1965, pp. 76–77.

35. *Mercado*, 21 September 1972, p. 65, based on a survey conducted by the Instituto para el Desarrollo del Ejecutivo Argentino (IDEA); and N. Erickson, "Wages, Salaries, Prices—And the Leap in the Dark," *RRP*, 12 August 1969, pp. 189–92.

36. Guillermo S. Edelberg, "Managerial Resource Development in Argentina," in *Latin American Management, Development and Performance*, ed.

Robert R. Rehder (Reading, Mass.: Addison-Wesley, 1968), pp. 38, 44, 46, summarizes studies done on the management of Argentine firms.

37. On this brain drain, see Enrique Otieza, *Emigration of Highly Qualified Personnel from Argentina: A Latin American "Brain-Drain" Case* (Buenos Aires: Instituto Torcuato Di Tella, 1967), pp. 12–15, 19, 28–29; and Fundación de Investigaciones Económicas Latinoamericanas (FIEL), *Las inversiones extranjeras en Argentina* (Buenos Aires: FIEL, 1971), p. 182.

38. See Victor Tokman, "Concentration of Economic Power in Argentina," *World Development*, 10 October 1973, pp. 33–41. In my case, I took as being related all persons in a company having the same surname, after checking with *Quien es quien*. This method probably underestimated family influence, as it would not have identified male in-laws.

39. Rocca, in turn, was rapidly building his own conglomerate. Besides his holding company, Technit, and his metallurgical firms, Dalmine and Propulsora, he had branched out into textiles, cellulose fibers, and paper. A shrewd operator who understood the local rules, he also acquired an interest in the Banco de Crédito Provincial and in an insurance company.

40. ECLA, *Economic Development and Income Distribution in Argentina* (New York: United Nations, 1969), p. 213.

41. Juan V. Sourrouille, *La presencia y el comportamiento de la empresas extranjeras en el sector industrial argentino* (Buenos Aires: Centro de Estudios de Estado y Sociedad, 1978), p. 49.

42. Cochran and Reina, *Capitalism in Argentine Culture*, p. 238.

43. Carlos F. Díaz Alejandro, *Essays on the Economic History of the Argentine Republic* (New Haven: Yale University Press, 1970), p. 250; Adolfo Dorfman, *Cincuenta años de industrialización en la Argentina, 1930–1980: desarrollo y perspectivas* (Buenos Aires: Ediciones Solar, 1983), p. 352.

44. Altmir, Santamaria, and Sourrrouille, "Los instrumentos," *Desarrollo Económico*, April–June 1966, p. 142, and January–March 1967, pp. 710–13; *RRP*, 31 December 1971, pp. 1014–15.

45. Deltec Panamericana, *El mercado de capitales en Argentina* (Mexico: Inter-American Development Bank, 1968), pp. 58, 182; Consejo Técnico de Inversiones, *The Argentine Economy* (Buenos Aires: Consejo Técnico de Inversiones, 1962), pp. 53, 55, 57, 59; Banco Central, *Boletín estadística*, December 1963, p. 39; Banco de Italia y Río de La Plata, *100 años al servicio del país, 1872–1972* (Buenos Aires: 1972), p. 282. *RRP* carried prices of representative stocks in all its issues; for the volume of trading in constant dollars from 1946 to 1968, see its issue of 30 August 1969, p. 315.

46. Consejo Técnico de Inversiones, *The Argentine Economy* (Buenos Aires: Consejo Técnico de Inversiones, 1966), p. 107.

47. Banco Central, *Boletín estadística*, December 1970, p. 71; Comisión Nacional de Valores, *El mercado de valores en la decada del sesenta: sintesis estadística* (Buenos Aires: Comisión Nacional de Valores, 1971), no page numbers, table 8; Consejo Técnico de Inversiones, *The Argentine Economy* (Buenos Aires: Consejo Técnico de Inversiones, 1972), p. 41; *RRP*,

20 May 1967, pp. 243–44; 31 July 1968, pp. 129–31; and 31 March 1969, pp. 422–23.

48. Comisión Nacional de Valores, *Memoria*, 1971, p. 43.

49. Comisión Nacional de Valores, *Evolución de las empresas que cotizan en la Bolsa de Comércio de Buenos Aires, excepto bancos y compañías de seguros*, 1970–71:1, 4; and *Memoria*, 1972, pp. 2–3, 57, 63, 68–69; *Mercado*, 24 August 1972, pp. 21–26.

50. *RRP*, 31 December 1971, p. 1015. On public sector banking, see Adolfo Dorfman, *Cincuenta*, pp. 361–62; *Veritas*, 15 December 1975, p. 85.

51. *RRP*, 21 October 1967, pp. 81–82; 12 December 1967, p. 369; 12 September 1972, p. 363; and 29 June 1973, p. 953.

## Chapter 15

1. Daniel Muchnik, *De Gelbard a Martínez de Hoz: el tobagán económico* (Buenos Aires: Ediciones Ariel, 1978), pp. 310–11.

2. *RRP*, 10 April 1963, p. 509; and 29 June 1968, p. 988.

3. Ibid., 10 January 1970, p. 9; and 22 January 1965, p. 65.

4. Ibid., 10 January 1970, pp. 9–11.

5. Ibid., 22 May 1968, p. 768; and 9 June 1977, p. 743.

6. *Periscópio*, 11 August 1970, p. 25; and 25 August 1970, pp. 18–21.

7. *PP*, 18 October 1966, p. 18.

8. Ibid., pp. 16, 18.

9. *RRP*, 10 January 1962, p. 49.

10. Max Weber, *The Protestant Ethic and the Spirit of Capitalism* (New York: Scribner's, 1958), p. 57.

11. Osvaldo Calello and Daniel Parcero, *De Vandor a Ubaldini* (Buenos Aires: Centro Editor de América Latina, 1984), 2:197–99.

12. Calello and Parcero, *De Vandor*, 2:206; *Cuadernos de Marcha*, March 1973, p. 70.

13. *Periscópio*, 1 September 1970, p. 25.

14. On social change in Córdoba, see Juan Carlos Agulla, "Aspectos sociales de industrialización en una comunidad urbana," *Revista Mexicana de Sociología*, May–August 1963, pp. 747–72; Delbert Miller, "Community Power Perspectives and Role Definitions of North American Executives in an Argentine Community," *Administrative Science Quarterly*, December 1965, pp. 364–80; and Horacio Palmieri and Rinaldo A. Colome, "La industria manufacturera en la Ciudad de Córdoba," *Desarrollo Económico*, April–December 1965, pp. 231–72.

15. Iris Martha Roldán, "Sindicatos y protesta social en la Argentina (1969–1974), un estudio de caso: el Sindicato de Luz y Fuerza de Córdoba" (Ph.D. diss., University of Leiden, 1978), p. 76; *Periscópio*, 1 September 1970, p. 79.

16. Quoted in Calello and Parcero, *De Vandor*, 2:137.

17. Seymour Martin Lipset, *Political Man* (Garden City, N.Y.: Anchor

Books, 1963), pp. 54–57; and William Kornhauser, *The Politics of Mass Society* (Glencoe, Ill.: Free Press, 1959), p. 152.

18. Roldán, "Sindicatos y protesta," pp. 136–37, 142–43, 174, 180–81. For more on Tosco, see *PP*, 11 January 1972, pp. 13–15.

19. Val R. Lorwin, "Working-Class Politics and Economic Development in Western Europe," *American Historical Review* 63 (1958): 338–51.

20. Richard P. Gale, "Industrial Man in Argentina and the United States: A Comparative Study of Automobile Workers" (Ph.D. diss., Michigan State University, 1968), pp. 130, 142–43, 164, 203–5, 240.

21. Francisco Delich, *Crisis y protesta social: Córdoba, 1964–1973* (Buenos Aires: Siglo XXI, 1974), pp. 39–43; Gale, "Industrial Man," p. 40; and Roberto Massari, "Le cordobazo," *Sociologie du Travail*, October–December 1975, pp. 403–19.

22. *RRP*, 22 January 1963, p. 73; *PP*, 22 January 1963, p. 52; 12 February 1963, p. 51; and 23 April 1963, p. 54.

23. *PP*, 31 January 1967, pp. 12–13.

24. *RRP*, 20 August 1968, p. 20.

25. *PP*, 20 May 1969, p. 8.

26. Calello and Parcero, *De Vandor*, 2:130; *PP*, 20 May 1969, p. 9.

27. Beba Balve et al., *Lucha de calles, lucha de clases: elementos para su analisis—Córdoba, 1969–1971* (Buenos Aires: Ediciones La Rosa Blindada, 1973), pp. 105–6; Calello and Parcero, *De Vandor a Ubaldini*, 2:137; Richard Gillespie, *Soldiers of Perón: Argentina's Montoneros* (Oxford: Clarendon Press, 1982), pp. 55–57, 76, 78, 87; Marysa Navarro Gerassi, *Los nacionalistas* (Buenos Aires: Editorial Jorge Alvarez, 1968), pp. 225–31; David Rock, "The Survival and Restoration of Peronism," in *Argentina in the Twentieth Century*, ed. David Rock (Pittsburgh: University of Pittsburgh Press, 1975), pp. 212–13; *Confirmado*, 18 December 1975, pp. 20–25.

28. Jimmie M. Dodson, "Religious Innovation and the Politics of Argentina: A Study of the Movement of Priests for the Third World" (Ph.D. diss., Indiana University, 1974), pp. 41–43, 45, 57–58, 172–200, 244; Antonio Castagno, *Tendéncia y grupos en la realidad argentina* (Buenos Aires: Editorial Universitaria de Buenos Aires, 1971), pp. 27–31, 33; *Confirmado*, 29 June 1967, pp. 19–20.

29. From an April 1969 interview, reprinted in *Cuadernos en Marcha*, a Peronist publication, June 1973, p. 55.

30. *Análisis*, 10 June 1969, pp. 14–17.

31. Roberto Aizcorbe, *The Peronist Myth: An Essay on the Cultural Decay of Argentina After the Second World War* (Hicksville, N.Y.: Exposition Press, 1975), p. 222; *Análisis*, 10 June 1969, p. 15.

32. *RRP*, 31 May 1969, pp. 773–74; Frigerio to Perón, 2 October 1969, in Ramón Prieto, *Correspondencia Perón/Frigerio, 1958–1973* (Buenos Aires: Editorial Machacha Güemes, 1975), pp. 91–92.

33. *Periscópio*, 1 September 1970, pp. 24–25; *PP*, 29 September 1970, p. 23; and 13 October 1970, p. 15.

34. Balve et al., *Lucha*, pp. 105–6; Calello and Parcero, *De Vandor*, 1:120; Elizabeth Jelin, *La protesta obrera* (Buenos Aires: Ediciones Nueva Visión,

1974), p. 72; *PP*, 19 January 1971, p. 11; and 26 January 1971, p. 12.

35. Roldán, *Sindicatos y protesta*, p. 191.

36. Balve et al., *Lucha*, p. 31.

37. Ibid., pp. 34–35.

38. Ibid., pp. 41–42, 44.

39. *RRP*, 31 January 1973, pp. 118–19.

40. James Kohl and John Litt, eds., *Urban Guerrilla Warfare in Latin America* (Cambridge: MIT Press, 1974), pp. 329–30, 356–57.

41. Ibid., pp. 359–60.

42. Aizcorbe, *The Peronist Myth*, pp. 123–26.

## Chapter 16

1. Lorenzo J. Siguat, *Acerca de la distribución y niveles de ingreso en la Argentina* (Buenos Aires: Ediciones Macchi, 1972), p. 20. See also Carlos F. Díaz Alejandro, *Essays on the Economic History of the Argentine Republic* (New Haven: Yale University Press, 1970), p. 129; Edward C. Epstein, "Politicization and Income Redistribution in Argentina: The Case of the Peronist Worker," *Economic Development and Cultural Change*, July 1975, pp. 624, 628; ECLA, *Economic Development and Income Distribution in Argentina* (New York: United Nations, 1969), pp. 122, 169; *Statistical Abstract of Latin America, 1981* (Los Angeles: U.C.L.A. Latin American Center, 1982), p. 189; and 1984, p. 285.

2. ECLA, *Economic Development*, p. 75; Guillermo O'Donnell, "Comentario a la nota de M. Brodersohn," *Desarrollo Económico*, October–December 1973, p. 611; Adolfo Canitrot and Pedro Sebess, "Algunas características del comportamiento del empleo en la Argentina entre 1950 y 1970," *Desarrollo Económico*, April–June 1974, p. 71; Juan Carlos Torre, *La tasa de sindicalización en Argentina* (Buenos Aires: Instituto Torcuato Di Tella, 1972), p. 11; Rubén Zorrilla, *Estructura y dinámica del sindicalismo argentino* (Buenos Aires: Editorial La Pleyade, 1974), pp. 159–60; Ministerio de Economía, Comisión Honoraria de Reactivación Industrial, *Informe sobre la industria argentina y los medios para su reactivación* (Buenos Aires, 1963), p. 20; *RRP*, 31 July 1961, p. 16; 10 November 1966, p. 191; and 21 January 1967, p. 61.

3. Robert Alexander, *Labor Relations in Argentina, Brazil, and Chile* (New York: McGraw-Hill, 1962), p. 221; Samuel L. Baily, *Labor, Nationalism, and Politics in Argentina* (New Brunswick, N.J.: Rutgers University Press, 1967), pp. 181–82; Edward C. Epstein, "Control and Cooptation of the Argentine Labor Movement," *Economic Development and Cultural Change*, April 1978, p. 460; *HAR*, April 1958, p. 168; *PP*, 22 January 1963, p. 11.

4. Rubén Rotondaro, *Realidad y cambio en el sindicalismo* (Buenos Aires: Editorial Pleamar, 1971), pp. 289–99.

5. Quoted in Osvaldo Calello and Daniel Parcero, *De Vandor a Ubaldini* (Buenos Aires: Centro Editor de América Latina, 1984), 1:57, 76. See also

Álvaro Abós, *La columna vertebral: sindicatos y peronismo* (Buenos Aires: Hyspamerica Ediciones, 1986), p. 31.

6. Rotondaro, *Realidad y cambio*, pp. 304–6; Santiago Sénen González, *El sindicalismo después de Perón* (Buenos Aires: Editorial Galerna, 1971), p. 62; Jorge Niosi, *Los empresarios y el estado argentino (1955–1969)* (Buenos Aires: Siglo Veintiuno Argentina Editores, 1974), p. 141; Calello and Parcero, *De Vandor*, 1:70–71; Business International Corporation, *Solving Latin American Business Problems* (New York, 1968), p. 111.

7. Rotondaro, pp. 306–9.

8. Peter Ranis, "Peronismo Without Perón: Ten Years After the Fall," *Journal of Inter-American Studies*, January 1966, pp. 112–28; and Paul H. Lewis, "The Durability of Personalist Followings: The Vargas and Peronist Cases," *Polity*, Spring 1973, pp. 408–14.

9. Niosi, *Los empresarios*, pp. 139, 141–42; *PP*, 7 July 1964, p. 8; 18 August 1964, p. 8; and 22 December 1964, p. 8. Political insiders alleged that Illia was actually funneling money through the Labor Secretariat to the MNRP in order to build it up as a counterweight to Vandor, whom he now perceived to be more dangerous than Perón.

10. *PP*, 8 March 1966, pp. 12, 18.

11. Ibid., 30 June 1966, p. 7.

12. Ibid., 24 January 1967, p. 23. The new shifts ran as follows: (1) from 7 to 10 A.M. and from 1 to 4 P.M., (2) from 10 A.M. to 1 P.M. and from 4 to 7 P.M., (3) from 7 to 10 P.M. and from 1 to 4 A.M., (4) from 10 P.M. to 1 A.M. and from 4 to 7 A.M.

13. *PP* (1967), 3 January, p. 14; 10 January, p. 3; 17 January, p. 20; 24 January, p. 23; 28 January, p. 14; 25 April, p. 22. The government estimated that its reforms would save the ports nearly $70 million a year in operating costs and pilferage.

14. *PP*, 8 July 1969, p. 13.

15. Rubén Zorrilla, *El liderazgo sindical argentino, desde sus origines hasta 1975* (Buenos Aires: Editorial Siglo Veinte, 1983), pp. 76, 78, 87–91.

16. Abós, *La columna vertebral*, pp. 107–8.

17. Torcuato S. Di Tella, *El sistema político argentino y la clase obrera* (Buenos Aires: Editorial Universitaria de Buenos Aires, 1964), p. 28.

18. "The Settlement of Labor Disputes in Argentina," *International Labor Review*, July 1971, pp. 77–96; Business International Corporation, *Solving Latin American Business Problems*, p. 110; Daniel James, "Power and Politics in Peronist Trade Unions," *Journal of Latin American Studies*, February 1978, p. 27.

19. Business International Corporation, *Solving Latin American Business Problems*, p. 110.

20. *Confirmado*, 2 February 1967, pp. 24, 26; *Mercado*, 15 February 1973, pp. 29–31. A good idea of the power and light federation's investments can be had from its official publication, *Dinamis*, from 1969–1971.

21. Jorge Correa, *Las jerarcas sindicales* (Buenos Aires: Editorial Obrador, 1974), pp. 58–59.

22. James, "Power and Politics," pp. 4–11; *PP*, 29 September 1964, p. 10; *Periscópio*, 10 March 1970, p. 9.

23. Juan Carlos Torre, *El proceso político interno de los sindicatos en Argentina* (Buenos Aires: Instituto Torcuato Di Tella, 1974), pp. 10, 52.

24. Ibid., p. 13.

25. Ibid., pp. 6–9, 22–30, 43–50, for the history of relations between the government and the AOT.

26. The Labor Secretariat's study was reported in *RRP*, 21 August 1970, pp. 269–71. On single-slate elections, see Torre, *El proceso*, pp. 6–9.

27. Iris Martha Roldán, "Sindicatos y protesta social en la Argentina (1969–1974), un estudio de caso: el Sindicato de Luz y Fuerza de Córdoba" (Ph.D. diss., University of Leiden, 1978), p. 274.

28. Ibid., pp. 275–76.

29. Ibid., p. 274.

30. Abós, *La columna vertebral*, pp. 45–47; Zorrilla, *Estructura y dinámica*, pp. 176–78.

31. Correa, *Las jerarcas*, pp. 56–58.

## Chapter 17

1. *RRP*, 11 May 1973, p. 647.

2. Gregorio Selser, ed., *Perón, el regreso y la muerte* (Montevideo: Biblioteca de Marcha, 1973), 1:15, 101; *Periscópio*, 14 July 1970, p. 20; Revista "Somos," *Historias y personajes de una época trágica* (Buenos Aires: Editorial Atlántida, 1977), pp. 46, 50–52.

3. Selser, *Regreso y la muerte*, 1:18; Richard Gillespie, *Soldiers of Perón: Argentina's Montoneros* (Oxford: The Clarendon Press, 1982), p. 121; Revista "Somos," *Historias y personajes*, pp. 46, 51–52; *Análisis Confirmado*, 8 May 1973, p. 18.

4. Revista "Somos," *Historias y personajes*, p. 52.

5. Ramón Prieto, *Correspondencia Perón/Frigerio, 1958–1973* (Buenos Aires: Editorial Machacha Güemes, 1975), p. 162.

6. Liliana De Riz, *Retorno y derrumbe: el último gobierno personista* (Mexico: Fólios Ediciones, 1981), p. 105.

7. Robert L. Ayres, "The Social Pact as Anti-inflationary Policy," *World Politics*, July 1976, pp. 474–75; Adolfo Canitrot, "La viabilidad económica de la democracía: un análisis de la experiencia peronista, 1973–1976," *Estudios Sociales*, no. 11 (Buenos Aires: Centro de Estudios de Estado y Sociedad, 1978), p. 17.

8. Guido Di Tella, *Argentina Under Perón, 1973–1976* (New York: St. Martin's, 1983), p. 86.

9. *Empresas Argentinas*, 16 (1974): 5–8.

10. Roberto Aizcorbe, *Argentina, the Peronist Myth: An Essay on the Cultural Decay of Argentina After the Second World War* (Hicksville, N. Y.: Exposition Press, 1975), p. 307; Di Tella, *Argentina Under Perón*, p. 102;

Juan V. Sourrouille, *The Impact of Transnational Enterprises on Employment and Income: The Case of Argentina* (Geneva: International Labor Office, 1976), pp. 16–17; *RRP*, 10 October 1975, p. 540.

11. *RRP*, 11 January 1974, p. 11. Figures on the money supply are based on Banco Central, *Boletín Estadística*, May–June 1977, p. 1. The *RRP*'s figures are: 15.7 billion at the end of 1972, and 32.4 at the end of 1973, with 11 billion of the 16.7 billion increase coming in the second half of the year.

12. *Mercado*, 15 May 1975, p. 115; and 29 April 1976, p. 13.

13. *RRP*, 21 November 1975, p. 804; and 9 April 1976, p. 459.

14. Elizabeth Jelin, *Conflictos laborales en la Argentina, 1973–1976* (Buenos Aires: Centro de Estudios de Estado y Sociedad, 1977), p. 17; Mónica Peralta Ramos, *Acumulación de capital y crisis política en Argentina (1930–1974)* (Mexico: Siglo Veintiuno Editores, 1978), pp. 315–16; Revista "*SOMOS*," *Historias y personajes*, pp. 142–43; Ernesto Krotoschin and Jorge Ratti, *Código del Trabajo, anotado* (Buenos Aires: Ediciones DePalma, 1975), pp. 993–1021 (but see especially pp. 1009–17). The *fuero sindical* was later clarified by a *reglamentación* issued on 9 April 1974, which limited it to protecting officials from being prosecuted for crimes committed in the course of carrying out their duties. Also, it did not apply to unions that had lost their juridical personality or to officials who had been removed from their posts or expelled from their unions. See Krotoschin and Ratti, *Código de Trabajo* pp. 1022–26, for the full text of this *reglamentación*. Even so, it was easy to interpret the carrying out of union duties to cover a wide number of cases.

15. Santiago Sénen González, *El poder sindical* (Buenos Aires: Editorial Plus Ultra, 1978), pp. 77, 99–100, 128; *RRP*, 9 August 1974, pp. 201–2; 21 August 1974, pp. 261, 263–64; 31 August 1964, pp. 317–18; 22 October 1974, pp. 598–99; 21 May 1975, p. 360; and 31 October 1975, p. 673.

16. Peralta Ramos, *Acumulación de capital*, p. 247; *Veritas*, 15 April 1973, pp. 12–13.

17. *Mercado*, 22 November 1973, pp. 45–47.

18. Ibid., 7 June 1973, pp. 16–19; 21 June 1973, pp. 13–14; 28 February 1974; 7 March 1974, p. 7; 11 April 1974, p. 6; and 9 May 1974, pp. 29–31.

19. *PP*, 20 September 1973, p. 58; *Mercado*, 9 May 1974, pp. 29–31.

20. Aizcorbe, *Argentina, the Peronist Myth*, pp. 203, 307; Ayres, "The Social Pact," p. 408. Di Tella, *Argentina Under Perón*, pp. 89–90; ECLA, *La empresa pública en la economía: la experiencia argentina* (Santiago de Chile: ECLA, 1983), p. 58; *RRP*, 11 September 1973, p. 353; 20 September 1973, pp. 429–31, 445–46; 28 June 1974, pp. 917–22; and 23 March 1976, p. 358.

21. Ayres, "The Social Pact," pp. 475–76; Juan Carlos de Pablo, *La economía política del peronismo* (Buenos Aires: Editorial El Cid, 1980), pp. 81–83.

22. Osvaldo Calello and Daniel Parcero, *De Vandor a Ulbaldini*, (Buenos Aires: Centro Editor de América Latina, 1984), 2:147–48; Canitrot, "La viabilidad económica," p. 47; De Riz, *Retorno y derrumbe*, p. 96; Jelin, *Conflictos laborales*, pp. 5–6; 16–17, 22–23; Sénen González, *El poder*

*sindical,* p. 101; Juan Carlos Torre, *Los sindicatos en el gobierno, 1973–1976* (Buenos Aires: Centro Editor de América Latina, 1983), pp. 87–88. Concerning the Villa Constitución workers, in May 1975 the government seized the plant, claiming the discovery of a communist plot to paralyze the entire industrial belt along the Río Paraná, with its center in the UOM local. All of the leftist leaders installed the year before were removed and kept under arrest. See Jelin, *Conflictos laborales,* pp. 29–30.

23. Torre, *Los sindicatos en el gobierno,* pp. 75, 81; *Quarterly Economic Reports,* October 1975, pp. 8–9.

24. Ayres, "The Social Pact," p. 489; Canitrot, "La viabilidad económica," p. 47; De Riz, *Retorno y derrumbe,* pp. 99–101.

25. Di Tella, *Argentina Under Perón,* p. 125; and his "La Argentina económica, 1943–1982," in *1943–1982, Historia política argentina,* ed. Carlos Floria (Buenos Aires: Editorial del Belgrano, 1983), p. 200. See also Banco Central, *Boletín estadística,* May–June 1977, p. 1; and *Veritas,* 15 December 1975, pp. 80, 84.

26. Comisión Nacional de Valores, *Evolución de las empresas que cotizan en la Bolsa de Comércio de Buenos Aires, excepto bancos y compañías de seguros* (1973), pp. 72–73; and Comisión Nacional de Valores, *Memoria* (Buenos Aires: Comisión Nacional de Valores, 1973), p. 1; *Mercado,* 19 July 1973, p. 26; 20 December 1973, p. 140; 19 December 1974, p. 127; and 20 November 1975, p. 50; *RRP,* 31 May 1974, pp. 742–43.

27. De Pablo, *Economía política,* pp. 85–86; *Quarterly Economic Report,* April 1975, p. 10; *RRP,* 10 April 1975, p. 459; and 9 January 1976, p. 21. Crude oil imports alone cost $343 million in 1974, but the importation of refined oil, as well as natural and liquid gas, raised that amount to $468.

28. Partido Revolucionario de los Trabajadores, *El peronismo ayer y hoy* (Mexico: Editorial Diogenes, 1974), pp. 7, 67–69.

29. James Kohl and John Litt, eds., *Urban Guerrilla Warfare in Latin America* (Cambridge: MIT Press, 1974), pp. 355–63; Gillespie, *Soldiers of Perón,* pp. 155, 165; *RRP,* 31 May 1973, p. 779; 23 October 1973, pp. 596–97; *PP,* 27 September 1973, pp. 26–27; *Time,* 23 April 1973, pp. 32–33; 3 December 1973, p. 56; and 14 January 1974, pp. 24–25.

30. *RRP,* 22 January 1974, p. 73; 31 January 1974, pp. 117, 121–22.

31. Revista "*SOMOS,*" *Historias y personajes,* pp. 156–66. In his taped autobiography, Perón recalled that while he was president in the early 1950s he had been visited by a Brazilian spiritual medium named Anael. According to Perón, Anael went into a trance during which "he made me some predictions, and many of the things he said came true. Maybe he had great intuition. But it wasn't anything to laugh at, not at all." (Torcuato Luca de Tena et al., eds., *Yo, Juan Domingo Perón: relato biográfico* [Barcelona: Editorial Planeta, 1976], pp. 188–89.) It so happens that Anael was also the name of the secret spiritualist lodge of which José López Rega was a member.

32. *La Prensa,* 29 January 1976, p. 1. Also, *RRP,* 12 March 1976, p. 297.

33. Prieto, *Perón/Frigerio,* p. 146.

34. For the Cornicelli interview, see *La Prensa,* 4 July 1972, pp. 1, 6.

35. *La Prensa*, 27 January 1976, translated in RRP, 19 February 1976, pp. 225–26; Luca de Tena et al., *Yo, Juan Domingo Perón*, pp. 279–80.

36. RRP, 19 September 1975, p. 427. See also Alejandro Dorrego and Victoria Azurduy, *El caso argentino* (Mexico: Editorial Prisma, 1977), pp. 90, 92–94; *Confirmado*, 18 December 1975, p. 25; Gillespie, *Soldiers of Perón*, pp. 154–55.

37. Alexander Graham Yool, *The Press in Argentina, 1973–1978* (London: Writers and Scholars Educational Trust, 1979), pp. 14–16, 35, 42–44, 46, 49, 52–53, 78; Aizcorbe, *Argentina, the Peronist Myth*, p. 286; Gillespie, *Soldiers of Perón*, p. 156; RRP, 19 June 1974, p. 862.

38. Juan Domingo Perón, *Juan D. Perón, 1973–1974: todos sus discursos, mensajes, y confrencias completos* (Buenos Aires: Editorial de la Reconstrucción, 1974), 2:274. For the May 1 speech, see ibid., pp. 192–93; and Rodolfo Terragno, *Los 400 dias de Perón* (Buenos Aires: Ediciones de la Flor, 1974), p. 182.

39. *Confirmado*, 3 December 1975, p. 23.

40. Aizcorbe, *Argentina, the Peronist Myth*, pp. 1–3; Gillespie, *Soldiers of Perón*, pp. 176–83, 224; Donald C. Hodges, *Argentina, 1943–1976: The National Revolution and Resistance* (Albuquerque: University of New Mexico Press, 1976), p. 184; Kenneth F. Johnson, "Guerrilla Politics in Argentina," *Conflict Studies*, October 1976, pp. 12–15; *Latin America*, 7 November 1975, p. 347; *Quarterly Economic Reports*, November 1974, pp. 2–3; and April 1975, p. 2; RRP, 23 July 1974, p. 90; 31 July 1974, p. 141; and 19 September 1975, p. 427.

41. Statement of the Argentine Episcopal Conference, October 1975, quoted in *Confirmado*, 3 December 1975, p. 20.

42. Di Tella, *Argentina Under Perón*, p. 107, puts the absenteeism rate at 17 to 18 percent; Torre, *Los sindicatos en el poder*, p. 119, estimated it at 20 percent in early 1975; RRP, 22 January 1975 said it was between 20 and 30 percent; and *Latin America*, 31 January 1975, p. 33, reported it as between 25 and 30 percent.

43. De Pablo, *Economía política*, pp. 139–41, 146–47, 150, 152.

44. Isabel Perón's government saw a record number of ministerial changes: thirty-six in all. Besides the six economics ministers, she had four different ministers of foreign relations, six interior ministers, five defense ministers, three education ministers, three ministers of justice, four labor ministers, and five social welfare ministers. See Pablo Kandel and Mario Monteverde, *Entorno y caida* (Buenos Aires: Editorial Planeta Argentina, 1976), p. 177.

45. Revista "*SOMOS*," *Historias y personajes*, p. 35. For other aspects of the *rodrigazo*, including events leading up to it and following it, see de Pablo, *Economía política*, pp. 179–84; Di Tella, *Argentina Under Perón*, pp. 71, 76; Dorrego and Azurduy, *El caso*, pp. 295–96; Jelin, *Conflictos laborales*, pp. 31–32; RRP, 8 July 1975, pp. 17–18, 25, 27–28, 30–31; and 22 July 1975, pp. 81–82; *Latin America*, 13 June 1975, p. 179.

46. Kandel and Monteverde, *Entorno*, pp. 79–83.

47. Ibid., p. 129.

48. Ibid., pp. 194, 196, 214–19, 227; RRP, 21 August 1975, p. 253; 29

August 1975, pp. 311, 317; and 30 September 1975, p. 483.

49. *Latin America*, 21 November 1975, pp. 364–65; and 16 January 1976, pp. 22–23; *RRP*, 31 January 1974, p. 111; 19 February 1975, p. 199; 12 March 1975, p. 302; 21 August 1975, p. 251; 30 September 1975, p. 507; 19 February 1976, pp. 209–10; 30 April 1976, p. 571; and 30 April 1976, pp. 573–74.

50. Ricardo H. Arriazu, *Movimientos internacionales de capitales* (Santiago de Chile: ECLA, 1979), p. 13; Consejo Técnico de Inversiones, *Argentina Económica*, 1972, pp. 31, 79; and *Argentina Económica*, 1974, p. 29; Daniel Muchnik, *De Gelbard a Martínez de Hoz: el tobagán económico* (Buenos Aires: Ediciones Ariel, 1978), pp. 310–11.

51. Concerning the clash between farmers and the Peronist government, see *RRP* (1975), 10 January, p. 19; 31 January, p. 113; 7 February, p. 157–58; 19 February, pp. 201, 204; 28 February, p. 249; 12 March, p. 310; 21 March, pp. 362–63; 10 April, p. 465; 30 April, p. 584; 9 May, p. 643; 30 May, p. 747; 10 September, p. 379; 19 September, p. 430; 30 September, p. 490; 10 October, p. 551; 31 October, pp. 663, 675; 12 November, pp. 724–25, 731; 21 November, p. 795; 28 November, p. 845–46; 10 December, p. 903; 18 December, p. 963; and 10 February 1976, p. 171.

52. Kandel and Monteverde, *Entorno*, pp. 92–93n, 165, 169; *La Prensa* (1976), 29 January, p. 1; 12 February, p. 7; 13 February, p. 1; 14 February, p. 1; 15 February, p. 1; 16 February, p. 1; 17 February, p. 1; *RRP* (1976), 10 February, p. 162; 19 February, p. 203; 27 February, p. 255.

53. *La Prensa*, 29 January 1976, p. 1. Also, *RRP*, 12 March 1976, p. 297.

## Chapter 18

1. James Kohl and John Litt, eds., *Urban Guerrilla Warfare in Latin America* (Cambridge: MIT Press, 1974), pp. 17–20; Richard Gillespie, *Soldiers of Perón: Argentina's Montoneros* (Oxford: Clarendon Press, 1982), pp. 245–46, 250–51; Charles Maechling, Jr., "The Argentine Pariah," *Foreign Policy*, Winter 1981–82, pp. 72–73; Organization of American States, Inter-American Human Rights Commission, *Report On the Situation of Human Rights in Argentina* (Washington: Pan American Union, 1980), pp. 55–56, 136, 199–200.

2. Félix Luna, "El 'Proceso' (1976–1982)," in *1943–1982, Historia política argentina*, ed. Carlos Floria (Buenos Aires: Editorial del Belgrano, 1983), p. 151.

3. José A. Martínez de Hoz, *Bases para una Argentina moderna* (Buenos Aires: Compañía Impresora Argentina, 1981), pp. 21–25.

4. Martínez de Hoz, *Bases*, pp. 30–38, 59–63, 66, 72–75, 134–35, 151, 157, 159.

5. *RRP*, 20 August 1976, pp. 253–54; 21 October 1977, pp. 646–47; 29 August 1980, pp. 307–8; 10 September 1980, pp. 364–65; 28 November 1980, pp. 815–16; 20 May 1981, pp. 647–48.

6. *RRP*, 31 May 1978, p. 769; 30 March 1979, pp. 428–29; 11 June 1980, pp. 822–23; *Latin America*, 30 November 1979, pp. 56–57. *SOMOS*, 22 Janu-

ary 1982, p. 5, reported that in 1980 Fabricaciones Militares suffered a 28 percent deficit as operating costs, financing costs, and inflation far outstripped revenues from sales.

7. *SOMOS*, 2 October 1981, p. 47, claimed that in 1980 some 2,125,000 Argentines were living abroad, as compared with only 4,500 in 1960. In recent years, this article calculated, for every three Argentines born, one Argentine left the country,

8. On the growth of the pensioner class, see *RRP*, 10 January 1979, p. 17; and 30 December 1980, pp. 958–64. For a summary of the Stock Exchange's study of evasion, see *RRP*, 11 October 1979, pp. 582–83. The *RRP* pointed out that many employees in the private sector receive remuneration in the form of under-the-counter payments which do not show up in official wage figures, so the true level of private sector evasion is surely greater than what the Stock Exchange estimated.

9. *RRP*, 20 August 1976, pp. 253–54; and 10 September 1980, pp. 364–65.

10. *SOMOS*, 19 December 1980, p. 5.

11. Ibid., p. 6. Also, Jorge Schvarzer, *Expansión económica del estado subsidiario, 1976–1981* (Buenos Aires: Centro de Investigaciones Sociales Sobre El Estado y La Administración, 1981), p. 22.

12. *SOMOS*, 27 August 1982, pp. 40–41; 3 September 1982, p. 45; and 10 September 1982, pp. 8–12; Martínez de Hoz, *Bases*, pp. 185–86.

13. *SOMOS*, 12 February 1982, pp. 4–8; *Latinamerica Press*, 6 October 1983, p. 7.

14. On Fabricaciones Militares, see *Latin America*, 30 November 1979, pp. 56–57; *RRP*, 19 December 1979, p. 988; 10 April 1980, p. 476; *SOMOS*, 22 January 1982, p. 5. On the railroads, see Martínez de Hoz, *Bases*, p. 200; *RRP*, 30 December 1976, p. 1088; 21 January 1977, p. 62; 9 June 1977, pp. 741, 747–48; 21 December 1977, p. 1003; 17 February 1978, p. 233; 28 February 1978, pp. 277–78; 28 March 1980, pp. 424, 430–31.

15. Schvarzer, *Expansión económica*, pp. 34–35, 56, 61; *SOMOS*, 22 January 1982, pp. 4–9; *RRP*, 10 August 1977, pp. 191, 194, 198; 12 October 1977, p. 557; 11 December 1980, pp. 867–68; and 26 February 1982, pp. 206–8.

16. Schvarzer, *Expansión económica*, pp. 39–47, 52, 57–59, 134.

17. Ibid., pp. 61–68; Martínez de Hoz, *Bases*, pp. 50–52, 169, 182, 184, 200, 206; *RRP*, 20 April 1979, pp. 547–48.

18. Schvarzer, *Expansión económica*, pp. 99, 101, 103–5, 108, 112. See also Daniel Azpiazu, Eduardo M. Basualdo, and Miguel Khavisse, *El nuevo poder económico en la Argentina de los años 80* (Buenos Aires: Editorial Legasa, 1986), pp. 116–203.

19. *Statistical Abstract of Latin America* 24 (1986): 720, based on IMF figures. When time, savings, and foreign currency deposits are included (M2), the figures for the money supply are: 108 billion in 1973, 1.57 trillion in 1976, and 8.2 trillion in 1980.

20. Bolsa de Comércio de Buenos Aires, *Agricultura e industria en la Argentina* (Buenos Aires: Bolsa de Comércio, 1980), p. 114.

21. Santiago Cuquejo, "Some Fallacies of Protectionist Thinking," *RRP*, 12 July 1965, pp. 25–26.

22. Martínez de Hoz, *Bases*, pp. 150–51, 154.

23. *RRP*, 10 February 1976, p. 158.

24. Fundación de Investigaciones Económicas Latinoamericanas (FIEL), *Por que 100 empresas lideres no cotizan en la Bolsa? Encuesta de opinión* (Buenos Aires: FIEL, 1977), pp. 64–66.

25. UIA, *Memoria y balance*, (Buenos Aires: 1981), p. 11; *RRP*, 11 May 1977, p. 585; *La Prensa*, 16 July 1977, pp. 1, 7.

26. *Mercado*, 6 May 1976, p. 32.

27. The new statutes, published early in 1979, set up a general council of 240 members that elected a governing council of 48 that in turn chose 10 of its members to form an executive committee. At every level, half of the representatives would be chosen on a regional basis and half would reflect sectoral interests. Every region would have equal representation, but sectoral representation would be in proportion to that field's share of the GNP. Neither MIA, MEDI, nor MUI were satisfied with the arrangement, which ended in 1982 with MEDI and MUI first combining to form the Movimiento Industrial Nacional, or MIN, and then splitting off from the UIA altogether to form a rival organization, the Argentine Industrial Council (CAI), with headquarters in Córdoba. See *Confirmado*, 4 January 1979, pp. 10–12; and Adolfo Dorfman, *Cincuenta años de industrialización en la Argentina, 1930–1980: desarrollo y perspectivas* (Buenos Aires: Ediciones Solar, 1983), pp. 380–81.

28. L. Beccaria and R. Carciofi, "The Recent Experience of Stabilizing and Opening Up the Argentine Economy," *Cambridge Journal of Economics*, June 1982, p. 153; Martínez de Hoz, *Bases*, pp. 138–43. Argentina was able to take advantage of the U.S. embargo on grain to the Soviet Union by making large grain sales there despite the Videla regime's strong anticommunist bias.

29. Beccaria and Carciofi, "The Recent Experience," pp. 154–56.

30. Gary W. Wynia, *Argentina in the Postwar Era: Politics and Policymaking in a Divided Society* (Albuquerque: University of New Mexico Press, 1978), p. 230; *RRP*, 20 January 1978, p. 98; and 31 January 1980, pp. 120–21.

31. Beccaria and Carciofi, "The Recent Experience," p. 157.

32. Ibid., pp. 159–62; *RRP*, 27 June 1980, p. 937; 11 July 1980, p. 40; 18 July 1980, pp. 70–72; 10 September 1980, p. 363. On the labor shortage, wages, employment, see Argentine Republic, Ministerio de Economía, *Argentine Economic Development, April 1976–December 1980* (Buenos Aires: Ministry of Economy, 1981), p. 24; *Mercado*, 21 August 1980, p. 16; *The Wall Street Journal*, 16 July 1979, pp. 1, 26; *RRP*, 10 January 1979, pp. 18–19; 8 June 1979, pp. 847–48; 20 September 1980, pp. 436, 442, 447–48; and 30 September 1981, p. 410, based on figures from the Instituto Nacional de Estadística y Censos.

33. Aldo Ferrer, *Puede Argentina pagar su deuda externa?* (Buenos Aires: El Cid Editor, 1982), pp. 64–65.

34. Ibid., pp. 71, 72.

35. Jorge Schvarzer, "Estrategia industrial y grandes empresas: el caso

argentino," *Desarrollo Económico*, October–December 1978, p. 316; *PP*, 11 May 1971, p. 20; *Latin America Weekly Report*, 12 September 1980, p. 4; and 12 February 1982, p. 4; *SOMOS*, 12 February 1982, pp. 46–48.

36. *La Prensa Económica*, December 1981, pp. 12–13; *Quarterly Economic Report, Argentina*, April 6, 1981, pp. 13–14; *RRP*, 11 March 1981, p. 292; *SOMOS*, 13 March 1981, pp. 46–47.

37. *Latin America*, 4 April 1980, pp. 6–7.

38. *RRP*, 10 April 1980, pp. 479–80.

39. Ibid., 31 January 1979, pp. 116, 120; 20 April 1979, p. 546; 23 August 1979, pp. 247–49; 9 November 1979, pp. 747–48; and 30 April 1980, p. 592.

40. Ibid., 31 January 1979, p. 120.

41. Ibid., 10 April 1980, pp. 479–80.

42. *Mercado*, 22 June 1978, pp. 29–33.

43. *SOMOS*, 4 April 1980, pp. 4–9. Trozzo, who was in Mexico at the time of the collapse, became a fugitive. He eventually was arrested by the Mexicans and extradited.

44. *RRP*, 30 April 1980, pp. 593–96; and 14 May 1980, pp. 648, 651; *SOMOS*, 2 May 1980, pp. 52–54.

45. Martínez de Hoz, *Bases*, pp. 80–82, 86, 231; *Mercado*, 19 February 1980, pp. 18–28; *RRP*, 31 July 1980, pp. 122–24.

46. Horacio García Belsunce, *Trece años en la política económica argentina (1966–1978)* (Buenos Aires: Emece Editores, 1978), pp. 241–46; *RRP*, 31 August 1976, pp. 313–15; 30 November 1979, pp. 863–66; 10 October 1980, pp. 528–32. Aldo Ferrer, "The Argentine Economy, 1976–1979," *Journal of Inter-American Affairs*, May 1980, pp. 135–38, 151–52, 155–57.

47. INDEC, *Censo nacional económico, 1985* (Buenos Aires: INDEC, 1986), p. 11; Azpiazu, Basualdo, and Khavisse, *El nuevo poder ecónomico*, pp. 125–39.

48. Azpiazu, Basualdo, and Khavisse, *El nuevo poder económico*, pp. 191–98.

49. INDEC, *Censo nacional económico, 1985*, p. 45; and INDEC, *Censo nacional de población y vivienda, 1980, Serie D, Población: Total del país, por província, departamento y localidad, República Argentina* (Buenos Aires: INDEC, n.d.), p. cxix.

50. INDEC, *Censo nacional económico, 1985*, pp. 11, 45; and INDEC, *Indicadores industriales, 1974–1978*.

51. Azpiazu, Basualdo, and Khavisse, *El nuevo poder económico*, p. 102; Dorfman, *Cincuenta*, p. 113 (based on INDEC figures); and Dorfman, "La crisis estructural de la industria argentina," *Revista de CEPAL*, August 1984, pp. 130–33.

52. Wynia, *Argentina in the Postwar Era*, p. 230; Jorge Raúl Cermesioni, "Cargas sociales: quien benefician?" *Carta política*, March 1978, pp. 58–59.

53. For the full text of this law, see *RRP*, 30 November 1979, pp. 871–75, 895–99.

54. *Latin America*, 28 January 1977, p. 25; and 18 February 1977, p. 52; *RRP*, 17 February 1977, p. 202.

55. Santiago Sénen González, "90 Years of Argentine Trade Union Activi-

ties, 1891–1981," *RRP*, 9 December 1981, pp. 768–70; *RRP*, 31 August 1978, pp. 319–20; 8 September 1978, pp. 385–86; 10 January 1979, pp. 27, 30; 20 April 1979, p. 559; 11 May 1979, pp. 677–78; and 20 September 1979, pp. 436, 442, 448.

56. For 1971 figures, see Rubén Rotondaro, *Realidad y cambio en el sindicalismo* (Buenos Aires: Editorial Pleamar, 1971), pp. 371–72. For 1977 and 1980, see *Mercado*, 25 May 1978, p. 21; and 27 November 1980, p. 26.

## Chapter 19

1. *RRP*, 29 June 1984, p. 570; 10 August 1984, p. 106; and 13 November 1985, p. 393; *SOMOS*, 29 April 1987, pp. 54, 57.

2. *RRP*, 10 April 1981, pp. 440, 448; *SOMOS*, 27 March 1981, pp. 43–44.

3. *RRP*, 10 June 1981, pp. 738–39, 786; and 30 June 1981, pp. 831–32; *SOMOS*, 5 June 1981, pp. 5–6, 8; 26 June 1981, pp. 51–53; and 25 December 1981, p. 4.

4. *Latinamerica Press*, 6 October 1983, p. 7; *RRP*, 30 December 1981, pp. 859–64; and 6 February 1982, pp. 202–4; *SOMOS*, 12 February 1982, pp. 4–8; 21 May 1982, pp. 55–57; 4 June 1982, pp. 56–57; 11 June 1982, pp. 56–59; and 2 July 1982, p. 61.

5. Marcelo Luís Acuña, *De Frondizi a Alfonsín: la tradición política del radicalismo* (Buenos Aires: Centro Editor de América Latina, 1984), 2:146, 174–77, 196–220.

6. Acuña, *De Frondizi*, pp. 222–23, 228.

7. Manuel Mora y Araujó, "La naturaleza de la coalición alfonsinista," in *Todo es Historia* (July 1985), pp. 38–45; and Ignacio Llorente, "El comportamiento electoral en el Gran Buenos Aires," ibid., pp. 58–67.

8. Daniel Azpiazu, Eduardo M. Basualdo, and Miguel Khavisse, *El nuevo poder económico en la Argentina de los años 80* (Buenos Aires: Editorial Legasa, 1986), p. 102; Alvaro Abós, *El posperonismo* (Buenos Aires: Editorial Legasa, 1986), pp. 188–89; Gary W. Wynia, *Argentina: Illusions and Realities* (New York: Holmes & Meier, 1986), pp. 145, 153, 176–78; Mónica Peralta-Ramos, "Toward an Analysis of the Structural Basis of Coercion in Argentina: The Behavior of the Major Factions of the Bourgeoisie, 1976–1983," in *From Military Rule to Liberal Democracy in Argentina*, ed. Mónica Peralta-Ramos and Carlos H. Waisman (Boulder: Westview Press, 1987), p. 61; Carlos H. Waisman, "The Legitimation of Democracy Under Adverse Conditions: The Case of Argentina," in *From Military Rule*, ed. Peralta-Ramos and Waisman, p. 97.

9. Such a course of action was urged, in fact, by Michael Monteon in his essay "Can Argentina's Democracy Survive Economic Disaster?" in *From Military Rule*, ed. Peralta-Ramos and Waisman, pp. 21–38.

10. *RRP*, 30 September 1983, p. 309; 20 December 1984, pp. 577–78; and 21 August 1985, p. 135; *Expreso*, 22 May 1987, p. 53.

11. *RRP*, 12 July 1984, pp. 12–15; 10 August 1984, p. 114; and 11 January 1985, p. 13.

12. Wynia, *Argentina: Illusions and Realities*, p. 181; *RRP*, 19 June 1985, pp. 516–18.

13. Wynia, *Argentina: Illusions and Realities*, p. 182.

14. Hjalmar Schacht, *The Stabilization of the Mark* (London: Allen & Unwin, 1927); Constantino Bresciani-Turroni, *The Economics of Inflation* (London: Allen & Unwin, 1953), chaps. 9 and 10; Karl R. Bopp, "Hjalmar Schacht: Central Banker," *University of Missouri Studies*, 14, no. 1 (January 1, 1939): chaps. 2 and 3; Robert Crozier Long, "Hjalmar Schacht's Reforms: A Letter From Berlin," *Fortnightly Review*, 122 (August 1924): 158–69.

15. *RRP*, 18 April 1986, p. 303.

16. *SOMOS*, 22 July 1987, p. 49; 5 August 1987, p. 53; *La Nación*, 29 July 1987, p. 16.

17. For example, the *RRP*, 29 November 1985, p. 460, noted that Buenos Aires city councilmen are paid 880 australes a month, at a time when the average wage in Argentina is only 200 australes, and even a major general on active duty gets only 550. After serving his four-year term, the councilman is entitled to a lifetime pension of 720 australes a month.

18. *RRP*, 31 August 1983, p. 195; 13 June 1984, pp. 510–11; 13 March 1985, p. 204; and 11 July 1986, pp. 14–15; *Mercado*, 28 February 1985, pp. 18, 22, 24, 26. Since Perón's overthrow in 1955 there have been seven tax "whitewashings" by which, in return for paying a set fee, the government agrees to "forgive" tax evaders. This is to encourage money held overseas or in mattresses to flow back into the legitimate economy. The fee must be low enough to act as an incentive, yet high enough not to insult the law-abiding citizens who paid their taxes on time. The whitewashings were in 1956, 1962, 1967, 1970, 1973, 1977, and 1986. *RRP*, 20 August 1986, p. 128. Most evaders do not take advantage of these offers for fear that their names will go onto a DGI list.

19. *SOMOS*, 8 July 1987, p. 49; and 22 July 1987, p. 52; *Buenos Aires Herald*, 5 July 1987, p. 2.

20. *SOMOS*, 20 May 1987, pp. 56–57; and 5 August 1987, p. 54; *Mercado*, 30 July 1987, pp. 42, 48–49; *Expreso*, 22 May 1987, p. 53; *RRP*, 30 September 1983, p. 309, and 20 August 1987, p. 139; *La Nación*, 3 August 1987, p. 8.

21. 3,647 in YCF; 97,935 on the railroads; 10,446 in Aerolineas; and 4,959 in ELMA. See *Expreso*, 22 May 1987, p. 53.

22. *RRP*, 30 September 1971, p. 521.

23. Ibid.

## Chapter 20

1. Carlos H. Waisman, "The Legitimation of Democracy Under Adverse Conditions: The Case of Argentina," in *From Military Rule to Liberal Democracy in Argentina*, ed. Mónica Peralta-Ramos and Carlos H. Waisman (Boulder: Westview Press, 1987), p. 100.

2. Ricardo del Barco, "Del gobierno militar al régimen peronista (1943–1955)," in *1943–1982, Historia política argentina*, ed. Carlos A. Floria (Buenos Aires: Editorial del Belgrano, 1983), pp. 32–33.

3. Gary W. Wynia, *Argentina: Illusions and Realities* (New York: Holmes & Meier, 1986), p. 114.

# INDEX